Navigating Through the Storm

Reinventing Education for Postmodern Democracies

EDUCATIONAL FUTURES
RETHINKING THEORY AND PRACTICE
Volume 34

Scope
This series maps the emergent field of educational futures. It will
commission books on the futures of education in relation to the
question of globalisation and knowledge economy. It seeks authors
who can demonstrate their understanding of discourses of the
knowledge and learning economies. It aspires to build a consistent
approach to educational futures in terms of traditional methods,
including scenario planning and foresight, as well as imaginative
narratives, and it will examine examples of futures research in
education, pedagogical experiments, new utopian thinking, and
educational policy futures with a strong accent on actual policies and
examples.

Navigating Through the Storm

Reinventing Education for Postmodern Democraies

Aharon Aviram
Ben-Gurion University of the Negev, Beer Sheva, Israel

SENSE PUBLISHERS
ROTTERDAM/BOSTON/TAIPEI

A C.I.P. record for this book is available from the Library of Congress.

ISBN 978-90-8790-977-2 (paperback)
ISBN 978-90-8790-978-9 (hardback)
ISBN 978-90-8790-979-6 (e-book)

Published by: Sense Publishers,
P.O. Box 21858, 3001 AW
Rotterdam, The Netherlands
http://www.sensepublishers.com

Printed on acid-free paper

ACKNOWLEDGEMENTS

The ideas portrayed in this book have been maturing over two decades of work that my colleagues in the Center of Futurism in Education at Ben-Gurion University in Israel and I have been doing in schools and educational systems, both in Israel and abroad. These ideas were first portrayed in papers I published in both English and Hebrew throughout the 1980s and 90s and then in a systematic integrative view on the need to reinvent education in a volume entitled "Navigating in the Storm" published in 1999 in Hebrew. The responses the book generated and further practical and intellectual experiences I have had since led to the extensive contemplation on and elaboration of the vision reflected in the revised and expanded version in this book before you, which I chose to name "Navigating through the Storm."

In our day-to-day work, my colleagues reinforced my belief in the need for and possibility to develop and implement educational processes which are completely different from those currently referred to as "educational"; they provided me with intellectual inspiration to dream of a different kind of education, while serving as a sounding board for me during our work together and throughout the writing process of this work, at times challenging my dreams with "reality checks" and calls to reexamine and refine my thesis, for as we all know, doubts can fertilize intellectual inspiration. I owe them all a debt of gratitude.

My thanks especially to Noga Arbell, who together with me did the meticulous work of editing and reworking the English version of the manuscript needed to adapt it to a non-Israeli audience, and to my colleague Yael Ronen who accompanied and systematically supported all aspects of this very demanding adaptation process and in her diligence, commitment, high professionalism, and wisdom made this version of the book possible.

That said and done, the responsibility for the final version is, of course, mine, and mine alone.

TABLE OF CONTENTS

TABLE OF CONTENTS

INTRODUCTION: EDUCATION IN A STORMY WORLD*

In this initial chapter I make the first steps towards clarifying the essence of the main argument of the first part of the book. This first part of the book is predicated on and provides great detail of the claims that modern education systems are foundering in postmodern democracies, and thus require that education in post-modern democracies be reinvented using a process of mindful, strategic thinking. The book's second and third parts follow the mindful strategic thinking such reinvention requires and outline a detailed, systematically substantiated blueprint of altogether new educational processes and goals designed to optimally realize democracy's most basic Humanistic values in the new postmodern situation.

These critical claims were crystallized during my work with tens of schools and educational systems over the last twenty years, both in Israel and abroad, and within an ongoing "conversation" I have had with the main relevant theoretical and empirical discourses. They are the motivational force behind this book, both in its "deconstructionist" stance in the first part, and in the "constructionist" stance in the other two parts. I will delineate them in this chapter in three rounds: in the first section I will portray them in the most general way through the ship metaphor reflected in the title of this volume; I will then proceed to present the book structure which reflects these claims and their constructionist consequences in a schematic way; then I will continue to the third round that clarify those claims in a much "thicker" and detailed manner. These preliminary descriptions are not aimed to systematically substantiating these claims which will be done in during the first part of the book itself.

A SHIP LOST IN UNCHARTED STORMY WATER

Imagine, if you will, a ship, a large vessel carrying passengers, which all of a sudden finds itself in unknown and uncharted water. The ship's captain and crew are unfamiliar with the rules of navigating through this new ocean, as they did not expect to reach this part of the world nor did they prepare for it. Everything they thought they knew about currents and winds, the instruments they use to determine direction, the ship's helm, even the North Star—none of these apply, function, or respond in any comprehensible way.

Now imagine that this ship, which is drifting aimlessly, as its sailors no longer have any effective way to guide its progression or even define a direction toward which they should be guiding it, is caught in a powerful storm. The ship is thrown in all directions, tsunami-size waves wash over its deck and its hull is broken by the rocks it is thrust against. By this point, the passengers of the ship are panicked.

---

*This title is a paraphrase of Richard Livingstone's *Education for a World Adrift* (Livingstone, 1944).

The captain, wishing to protect his and his staff's professional honor, not to mention prevent demands for refunds, does everything in his power to at least seem as if he is still in control of the battered vessel. He and his crew use their now useless nautical knowledge to feign such control, to pretend to be working hard to navigate the ship and lead it to a known, safe haven.

As the ship drifts aimlessly deeper and deeper into the storm, the sailors' simulated efforts to guide it become more and more feverish and less and less effective. They have no idea where they want the ship to go or how to navigate it there, yet they are too panic-stricken to make any mindful effort to learn even the most basic of the new rules of the uncharted waters and winds around them and to extrapolate from them new navigation guidelines. They are certainly in too much of a frenzy to be able to think rationally about locating a goal they would like to direct themselves towards. Instead, they waste their final and quickly draining resources on not losing face in front of their passengers, and continue to use the same knowledge and skills which have already proven useless in their struggle to weather the storm, completely ignoring the risk they stand of drowning the ship altogether.

The first part of the book you are about to read depicts just such a ship caught in a similar storm roaring in uncharted water. The proverbial storm in uncharted water is the series of postmodern upheavals which demolished every aspects of the human situation known until about twenty or thirty years ago in but a few short decades. The ship so badly damaged by this storm is Western education systems whose captains, officers, and primary decision makers have yet to recognize both the totally new nature of the stormy reality they find themselves in and their inability to clearly and consistently point at any desired and realizable goal within it, let alone mindfully navigate towards it.

The captain, officers, and sailors' desperately feigned rescue and navigation attempts are analogous to the endless, ever repeating, series of superficial changes and reforms Western educational systems are plagued with. These "changes" have become an integral, often ritualistic, part of educational activity in almost all Western educational systems over the last two generations. The "reforms" are often depicted as "holistic," "systemic," and aimed to enhance "paradigmatic change" in one educational system or another. However, as these reforms are irrelevant to the real fundamental causes of the crisis, they are neither systemic nor actual reforms. They certainly deepen the hold of the old paradigm and render the dire situation of education systems ever more hopeless with each failed "attempt."

The goal of this chapter, and, in a more substantiated way, of the first part of the book, is to give citizens, decision makers, and educational communities in postmodern Western democracies a much needed and overdue wakeup call. This wakeup call is essentially different in its nature, suppositions, and goals from the many texts lamenting and deploring the sad situation of education systems/students/ teachers in various Western counties, a lamentation that has become part and parcel of the common ritual of "educational reform."

These texts usually begin with deploring the hopeless situation of the education system from one or a few perspectives (falling grades, expending inequalities, increasing violence, addictions, teachers' burnout, etc.), diagnose *The* root problem(s) (teacher exclusion from school's decision making, school's rigid dependency on an external bureaucracy, school's immunity to "free market forces," formal frontal teaching methods, and so on and so forth) and end with pointing to some *panacea* or combination of panaceas that *if only* practiced would allegedly solve the root problem. Among the most common alleged panaceas of the last generation one can find: "teacher empowerment," "school based management," "parental choice," "constructivist teaching and learning," "teachers' accountability," "school effectiveness," "universal standers," equipping all students with PCs and laptops or connecting them to broadband Internet, or (one of the most recent "battle cries") enhancing "mobile learning." I could dedicate the entire section to this list of educational reforms, which reflect many diverse and often contradictory perspectives and ideologies, focus on numerous aspects of the school or educational systems, and have different resolutions for their plight, and still not come close to exhausting it.

In counterdistinction, the view presented and defended in detail in the first part of this book is too realistic to allow such optimism or belief in quick or even slow fixes, not if those take place within prevailing modern education systems. It is impossible to deduce from it an overall "if only" solution. Rather it calls on the sailors and officers to wake up and, for starters, realize and admit to themselves, to each other, and to their passengers that our education ship is aimlessly drifting in uncharted, stormy, postmodern water which is totally different than the modern water it was designed and built to navigate in.

It also calls for a realization that in order to navigate effectively through this amassing postmodern storm, we need to immediately abandon our current, futile, obsession with mindless changes which are not based on recognition of the radically new nature of reality and do not address the core problems, yet waste endless time and resources.

Finally, it calls for us to (a) design and execute a macro-level, integrative mapping of the stormy water and winds and the powers they exert on the ship; (b) clearly formulate basic goals for education which stem from the Humanistic tradition basic to postmodern democracies; and (c) based on the previous two tasks, form a strategic thinking process to determine how we can optimally reach the desired Humanistic goals in the postmodern situation.

THE BOOK'S STRUCTURE

The main argument delineated in the book's three parts is presented in the following order: The first chapter of the book and of *Part One* shows that the rapid transition from the modern to the postmodern era has rendered the modern definitions of contemporary education systems anachronistic and anomalous. The modern definitions of the five basic parameters that characterize every system: goals, content, organizational structure, conception of and attitude towards target audience and its mobilization, and *modus operandi* or, in this case, didactics, are rapidly and intensively undermined today.

Chapters Two through Five focus on the first four of the five basic parameters, and describe the collapse of their modern definition in more detail. The fifth parameter, didactics, is often discussed throughout this part of the book and therefore no special chapter has been dedicated to it.

Examination of the postmodern reality and the school systems which operate within it reveals an ominous truth: as effects of the postmodern era encroach further into every aspect of Western society, the gap between modern education systems and the reality within which they must operate widens. The significance of the activities, for both students and teachers, within these systems, has virtually vanished, the functionality thereof is seriously impaired, and the products of these crippled systems are becoming an actual threat to liberal democratic values. The first part therefore calls for an overall, mindful, systematic process of redesigning the human educational endeavor in order to adjust it to the needs of postmodern Liberal Democracies.

Part Two of this book is predicated on the assumption that the aforementioned need for strategic, macro-level, educational rethinking and for a reinvention of education to better suit the needs of postmodern democracies is recognized. This part offers a redrawn map of the postmodern storms and one possible new design for the ship of education based on it, as well as desired goals for it in light of the Humanistic values basic to postmodern Liberal Democracies. This design is aimed to harness the new postmodern powers to the implementation of the desired educational goals.

In other words, this part provides a detailed and substantiated path for implementation of the required systematic thought process called for by the first part of this book. It is but one example for such implementation. It is obviously the one I believe must be employed as it offers the most necessary constitutional elements: the definition of the values based on Humanistic tradition as the guiding North Star of education in postmodern democratic societies and the understanding of the postmodern situation within which framework these values must be optimally implemented.

Part Two therefore suggests an alternative educational paradigm which I believe to be both desirable and attainable in the context of a postmodern democracy. Chapters Six through Nine discuss the five basic system parameters: goals, content, organizational structure, target audience, and its mobilization. In these chapters I argue that postmodern education should adopt three core complementary goals derived from, and supportive of, the perpetuation of a liberal democratic worldview: individual autonomy, morality, and dialogical belonging. These chapters also extensively explain how these goals can be implemented in the postmodern era.

In delineating the preferred, still Humanistic yet postmodern oriented, system, I underscore three guidelines necessary in any system which aspires to educate in postmodern democracies, which contemporary modern education systems fail to meet. (a) The system must contribute to the sustainability and vitality of Liberal Democracy. (b) The system's activities must be meaningful to young people and adults within the system. (c) The educational system must be compatible with postmodern processes and capable of functioning well within the social and economic contexts of a postmodern reality.

Part Three of the book emphasizes the urgency of launching this huge, demanding project of educational reinvention and of pointing out the first steps necessary to operationalize this process in a manner compatible with contemporary modern systems. This part contains the final chapters of this volume, and thus the clarion call to address the challenges presented by this book immediately, to put them on top of tomorrow morning's agenda. It underscores the urgency of mindfully implementing Humanistic, postmodern education and charts a course for postmodern Liberal Democracies to take from here on. Following this course should ideally lead new (and to some extent old) educational communities to design and implement the badly needed Humanistic, postmodern education system which I entitled in this book "Autonomy Oriented Education."

In Annex One I describe in further detail the myriad of approaches and discourses with which I have had an ongoing daily dialogue for the past twenty years about the acute problems plaguing the very foundation of contemporary education systems and concepts analyzed in this book. Readers who wish to know "where I come from" can find in that chapter a systematic depiction of these approaches and the way my views emerged out of the long ongoing "conversations" I had with them.

The book can and should be read on two different levels: its first foundational level leads to the above appeal for democratic education systems to respond to the postmodern tsunami-size changes in a macro-level, strategic, fashion. Such a response should consist of a rethinking of all the basic educational questions from scratch which would hopefully result in a reinvention of education. The second level, which stems from the first, consists of a systematic, substantiated, attempt to implement this strategic thought in the direction I find the most adequate both normatively and descriptively. However, the first level's call for a rethinking of education may very well lead to the drawing of different blueprints for a wholly new education system which nonetheless still fits the need of postmodern democracies. Thus even readers who take issue with the second level of my argument, or any of its parts, and reject my particular plan for redesigning education, should still be ethically and socially committed to materializing the thinking process the first level of my argument demands. Such readers are more than welcome to see the second level of my argument or those of its parts they disagree with as a methodological demonstration of the feasibility of the very demanding task of reinventing education.

In contrast to the all-too-familiar "educational lamentations" in existence today, this book does not offer a specific solution to a specific problem or even set of problems. It rather calls on all involved in education to step back and look at the bigger picture and the huge predicament the ship of education is in so they can formulate a better, more useful, solution to it than their futile attempts to reattach the ship's hull boards as the powerful postmodern winds blow them away one by one. To use a Hindu metaphor, it is a call to tear away the Maya Veil that allows educators and decision makers to think that the obsessive re-pinning of the ever-loosening boards is going to solve anything and force them to realize that it is a major cause for the problem's exacerbation. The constant attempt to fix the symptoms is actually preventing us from having a chance to even see the need for much more extensive, macro-level, strategic thinking about the root causes of the postmodern disease and about the effects of its incessant tsunami-sized attacks on the way things used to be.

The second generation of the postmodern era is making its first steps these very days. The speed and intensity of the changes this era brings about are accelerating and intensifying with each passing day as is its revolutionary impact on every aspect of our lives. The early beginning of the postmodern era can be traced back to the 1960s and since then, especially during the last two decades, it has unrecognizably changed almost every dimension of the human condition. Some of the most obvious and powerful of the tsunami-like waves of revolutions which forcefully carry the postmodern changes forward are briefly indicated below (I elaborate on all of them and few other, connected, postmodern revolutions in Chapter One):

- A series of ground-breaking, ICT-based realities (PC-based, multimedia and CD-Rom-based, Internet-based, WWW-based, mobile terminal-based) that have engulfed us one after the other from the early 1980s onward, changing again and again the way we work, communicate, think, buy, and even flirt; and of course rendering the book based culture that dominated the West since Gutenberg fade quickly away.

- Economic and political globalization trends which changed everything we knew about economy several times since the 1980s. These changes have led, among other things, to permanent amplification of the intensity and speed of technological innovation and economic competition. As a consequence, several rounds of organizational upheaval occurred, creating thinner, more dynamic, outsourcing-oriented economic organizations all over the world. Virtually all economic organizations have by now integrated the new organizational order into their daily operations. These series of revolutions practically obliterated all previously accepted structures in the labor market and in career management and created instead a much more fluid, permanently changing, labor market wherein "tenure" or even "career" (in the sense of it being the linear structure of one's professional development) and in some contexts even "work" no longer exist.

- A cultural relativist revolution which led to a breakdown of the belief systems and ideologies which guided human beings throughout history and were more often than not based on objectivistic foundations.

- A disintegration of all "natural," unconditional, social belonging frameworks human beings have ever known: community, the extended family, the nuclear family, the workplace, neighborhoods, and so on.

- Radical erosion of all previously accepted definitions of social roles and conventions: "legitimate family" vs. "living in sin," "men" vs. "women," "old" vs. "young," "children" vs. "adults," "natural sexual tendencies" vs. "unnatural" ones.

- Practically inconceivable (until but a decade or two) technological innovations in the medical and biological spheres. As a result of these advances we are rapidly approaching a period in which medical science can easily "repair,"

change or replace any human organ or part thereof, as well as predetermine
the characteristics of potential human being.

Since we all surf the endless heavens of the digital reality, consume and produce
within the global economy, function as employees or employers in the fluid labor
market, and are citizens of the postmodern relativistic culture and amorphous
societies, the above changes have radically changed all aspects of our lives. They
have already done so a few times over and in many different ways. One possible
way to bring home to the readers the intensity of these upheavals is to point to the
irony of the human situation we find ourselves in.

The sinister irony of the human situation in our time stems from an impossible
(or psychologically unbearable) combination of exponential growth in the range of
freedom and choice available to most individuals in the postmodern world, as a
result of the above and other postmodern revolutions and a complete disintegration
of all ethical and social systems which supported our ancestors who had a much
more limited range of choices.

This new human situation begat a rapid spread of depression and anxiety all
over the Western world, in amounts never before seen, as individuals became less
and less able to shoulder the awful burden of the cruel irony mentioned above.

Each of the aforementioned revolutions affects the very core of human existence, the "laws of nature," so to speak, that our parents and their parents before
them took for granted. Doubtlessly we are in the midst of the most radical, intensive,
and rapid change the human situation ever underwent. In the following chapters I
systematically elaborate the extent and nature of these changes and their effects on
everything we ever knew and were accustomed to.

These tremendous, ongoing and ever accelerating, interconnected revolutions
cannot be summarized by any one clear map. There has been, and may yet be, an
infinite number of partial attempts to create such a map or meta-picture of the
accelerating cultural, economic, technological, social, political, psychological, and
ecological tsunami waves, which change, over and over again, everything we
know. Such attempts referred to the postmodern reality as "the end of history," "the
coming of the last man," the era of "clash of civilizations," "the flat world," "fluid
modernity," "post-Fordist society," "post capitalistic society," "technopoly," and
so on and so forth.

Still, I will venture in a sinful attempt to make such large-scale generalizations
for the sake of making two points:

Most thinkers dealing with the subject believe our time to be a turning point;
many consider it the most significant one in human history, one after which
"nothing will be the same anymore." Furthermore, even when emphasizing different aspects or using difference perspectives, it is easy to see many similarities
between the different descriptions of the postmodern changes. In the following
chapters I shall point out three such basic structures that cut across all levels of the
human condition in postmodernity: a lack of linearity, of stability, and of continuity.

In spite of the widespread agreement among thinkers, representing a variety of
disciplines and perspectives, about the factual aspects of the situation, their normative evaluation thereof could not be more different and therefore is subject to

constant debate: While some thinkers bemoan postmodernity as the era of the last man, lament our enslavement to technology and the economic powers dominating it, the disintegration of our "selves," and the loss of the West's belief in its own credo, others celebrate it as the era of permanent playfulness, full liberation from the heavy social or psychological structures (including that of "the self"). They perceive it as an era of unimaginable breadth of human ingenuity and of the ultimate victory of Western beliefs in Liberal Democracy and liberal economy.

Such thinkers may not deny the heavy toll, mentioned above, this wonderful new world exerts but they argue either that it is to be to shouldered *solely* by us, the "generation of wilderness," while a new brand of human beings can already be spotted growing in our kindergartens, a humans which do not require the stability, linearity, and continuity which were lost to us. Or, that such a price, for whoever pays it, is worth paying given the huge profit Western democracies stand to gain from postmodernity.

POSTMODERNITY AND THE UNAVOIDABLE FAILURE OF MODERN EDUCATION SYSTEMS

Fortunately we do not need to decide between the many intellectual opinions mentioned above. What matters to us is that all involved agree that we have passed a crucial turning point, probably the most significant one in human history.

We can now approach the subject at hand: the essential, inherent, inadequacy of the education systems prevalent in postmodern democracies. Contemporary education systems were designed and formed during the peak of the Second Industrial Revolution, on the basis of traditional Platonic curricular foundations, known throughout history as the "liberal (i.e., purely theoretical) curriculum." This curriculum was originally designed for an individual free of the burden of making a living, and was of course adjusted to suit the emerging needs of industrial societies. There is no way, and in this book I shall provide ample explanation and proof to this claim, for a modern-Platonic education system to successfully function in the postmodern reality. The gap between the structures and conceptions by which Western education systems function and the chaotic and incomprehensible reality in which it must operate is subsequently perpetually widening at an incredible speed.

This gap renders the education system non-functional from both a social and an organizational perspective. Socially speaking, the current education systems no longer serve society or its current economic and cultural needs as it opposes everything presupposed by them. Organizationally, given the above situation, the current systems can no longer operate smoothly or even fake smooth operation. An unbiased "Martian gaze" cannot but see the current systems as a lunatic or surrealistic reality hanging on to what cannot but be described as obsolete, strange, and extremely costly rituals that may or may not have been meaningful in previous eras, for incomprehensible reasons.

Members of the educational community are in fact expected to function in an impossible and intolerable situation characterized, among other things, by:

- Teachers who are charged with an authoritative role and expected to "keep the class in check" although the social culture and school organizational culture within which they operate are not able to provide even the most minimal backing for that authority, in counterdistinction with their modern and traditional predecessors who generously supported it;
- A study of the disciplinary subject-matters which have very little, if any, meaning for either teachers or students, because curricula are often at odds with students' practical or psychological needs and contrary to the dictates of dominant relativistic culture they encounter outside the classroom, wherein utilitarian values do not ascribe any importance to theoretical study for its own sake These curricula are also increasingly irrelevant to a growing portion of the changing labor market;
- A learning environment saturated with incessant change of approaches and methods, wherein teachers and students are constantly required to readjust themselves to accommodate the steady stream of "updated" didactic views and methodologies as the good old stable methods of the modern (and obviously traditional) past have lost any grip they may have had on the system.
- Schools inundated with scores of "projects," "interventions," "processes of change," "reforms," and "restructurings" which in many cases do not relate to each other and are frequently patently contradictory, all of which exact from the schools an enormous toll in wasted energy, attention, time, and money, while the end product often amounts to no more than "much ado about nothing";
- Schools and teachers who must contend with conflicting demands and contradictory, shifting, and confused desires of multiple target audiences: the state, parents, the community, young people, and educational experts—since the "good old" educational goals of the past are no longer able to serve as a compass.

Such impossible circumstances are neither natural to the educational context nor necessary. This was not the circumstance in which education systems of the past, not even the recent past, had to function. These are all symptoms of a profoundly dysfunctional system which seeks to feign meaningful operation despite the growing chasm between it and the reality around it. They create organizational confusion which imposes tremendous mental stress on all those "caught in the system." Administrators, teachers, pupils, and parents all find it hard to comprehend what has transpired, the significance of the chasm, the great speed at which it is widening, or its cognitive and organizational implications.

Many (actually most) postmodern democracies are aware of the rise in disciplinary problems, violence and drug and alcohol abuse among young people. They are also aware of the drop—at best stagnation—of levels of scholastic achievement. Parent and student dissatisfaction is ever growing; teacher burnout is accelerating beyond control, and most importantly the contradicting reforms that keep sweeping the system all start with festive declarations and huge spending and disintegrate into oblivion within but a few short years, leaving the system, at best, unharmed, but at worst even more mangled than it was before.

These are all symptoms of an essentially dysfunctional system, which is completely at odds with the external reality it is supposed to serve and therefore to large extent acts in a vacuum.

In this situation it is our duty, if we care about young people and the future of our societies and ourselves, to mobilize all our intellectual, professional, and financial resources to try to utilize what little influence we may have on the course of history. Instead of allowing our educational systems to drift away in the postmodern storms, we must do our best to navigate through the storm at any moment in time. In order to navigate these stormy waters, we must do our best to understand:

- What kind of impact has postmodernity had on Western education so far?
- Why?
- What kind of future impact can we predict it will still have? (Understand the postmodern storms, winds, and turbulences.)

Most importantly, we must answer the following normative or ideological questions:

- What direction do we want Western societies to take in the (say) next two decades?
- In light of the above direction, what goals should we set for desired education systems (goals that should guide our navigating efforts)?
- How can we best help education systems move in this direction?
- Can we utilize the postmodern storm to navigate in that direction?
- How can we utilize the postmodern storm to navigate in that direction?

INNOVATION FIT ONLY FOR THE PAST

As things are, no Western educational system or international forum has yet to address the above questions systematically. Instead, international organizations (for example the OECD which runs the PISA: Program for International Student Assessment, which surveys scholastic achievement using world applied standardized tests every few years) are busy grading national systems according to students' achievements in the most "respectable" disciplines (math and sciences, of course) as if those few centuries-old standards still have the same validity they did two thousand years ago.

National systems celebrate these and similar[1] findings as ancient tribes used to celebrate the awakening of nature after a long winter sleep (in case they are graded high in the exams), or practice atonement rituals and asking ancestor spirits for forgiveness (in the much more frequent case of low national grades). Every four years when these grades are published (in most nations who perceive themselves as graded "too low") the ritual of accusations, *mea culpa* admissions, calls and plans for "urgent investigations," "reforms," and obviously commitment to huge investments is celebrated again; PISA is a major international education festival, but there are smaller scale international ones[2] as well as national[3] festivals that note various kinds of success according to an irrelevant grading system in a dysfunctional learning process of a curriculum that has long lost its cultural meaning. As a result of such testimonies to the failures of Western education systems, ideas of "change," "reform," and "innovation" have been adopted into the educational discourse over the last four decades. These concepts are actually the core of educational discourse in the last four decades. These rituals are repeated every year (national test results) or every four years (international results) as well as whenever "new" information about falling grades, rising violence, addiction, or teacher burnout is published.

Naturally the superficial changes included in the relevant discourse do not penetrate deep enough; they do not touch the foundation of the modern paradigm which stands at the base of the prevailing educational system and of its unavoidable failure. Many of the "reforms" implemented are inconsistent with one another in a manner that to a large extent cancels them out altogether. The few which manage to "escape" that fate are swept away by the current, all powerful, makeup of the system and the vested interests it relies upon (or at least what many educational stakeholders *believe* to be their vested interests). Often, as in the case of PISA and similar international evaluations, the criteria for judging the system are also sources for determination of its performance as failed. At the end of the day, "the more it changes the more it remains the same" (a school change saying coined by John Goodlad three decades ago) describes this discourse of changes which brings about no change quite well. To paraphrase Shakespeare, it is much *talk* about nothing.

The comparison with tribal rituals, which I made above, seems to be obvious and inescapable. Let me elaborate on it further so the absurdity of the situation is eminently clear to the reader. Think of a tribe which was for some reason left alone in a remote rainforest (that is, if the growing hunger brought on by postmodern economies left any such forests intact). Once the rainforest is demolished, and the inhabitants therein, who were never "tainted by civilization," are forced to integrate within nearby cities, most of what they know and do will be irrelevant to the postmodern urban situation they all of a sudden find themselves in. The only difference between this fable and the standing of education systems in postmodern reality current situation is that while the chasm between the tribesmen and their neighbors was gradually created over thousands of years, the huge gap between Western societies and their educational systems began to form not so long ago at all, in the 1970s.

It is clear, given the urban conditions they face, that the tribespeople's life routine will be irrevocable disturbed. If they try to hunt for deer or pigs on the highway, they will bump against cars, which as a rule are not vulnerable to their arrows. Even if they are lucky enough to hunt a "sleeping" (i.e., parking) one, they will not gain much sustenance from their "kill." They will not be able to dig in the ground, now covered in rock-hard asphalt, for water. There will in fact be very little exposed ground to be found anywhere in the cement jungle wherein they now reside, and what little they may find will probably be polluted and poisonous to them. Their sexual norms and ways of rearing their children will quickly land them in a jail cell for violations of the Western rules about polygamy, child abuse, and pedophilia.

They may struggle for a while, ignoring an external reality they could not possibly conceive in the past (the "denial phase"). Once they realize that something beyond their grasp no longer allows them to carry on their old, familiar ways of life, they will become depressed and apathetic (the mourning phase). Then they will make desperate attempts to adapt. They will try to create new rituals, designed to appeal to the spirit of the "new animals" (cars) to allow themselves to get caught or they will fashion new prayers and dances to convince the spirits of their ancestors to supply them with food and water. (This "acceptance and adaptation phase" is still designed in light of their old paradigm.) Being cultural light years away from any of the civilizations around them and having no way to make sense of what is going on in the postmodern world, their attempts to adjust, which are out of any touch with reality, will fail completely and they will inevitably, gradually, perish.

That is, unless some anthropologically oriented philanthropist donates enough funds to form reservations for them, in which their needs will be catered to and any external influence will be strictly forbidden.

This is what, to large extent, happened to the modern school in the postmodern era. The generous philanthropist in their case is the state and local authorities. Using laws and social arrangements, the higher authorities have been protecting education systems, preempting any interference between them and the incomprehensible menacing reality that appeared unexpectedly at their doorstep. Law and social customs not only guarantee education systems a monopoly (either as public or private institutions, they have been the almost sole legitimate source of supply for "education"), they also make "the consumption of their services" mandatory. They usually also cater to all the systems' financial needs without them ever having to show any real contribution to society (current student grading standards, even in our standards-stricken era, have nothing to do with such a contribution).[4] Protected by an enforced monopoly and fully financed, education systems continue to carry out their old surrealistic rituals regardless of the world around them.

But the borders between schools and external reality are not hermetically sealed and the state-instituted protection afforded to the education system is becoming more and more difficult to maintain. What makes things difficult in the age of schools is the fact that those who have to function within the tribal system ("children," "students," and many of the "teachers") enter the reservation in the morning and return to their homes in the outside civilization every afternoon. Most of the younger members of this tribe, and many of the older ones (or teachers), abandon the "homo modernicus" façade they must put on for the sake of the tribe the minute they leave the school gates and return to their much more adequate to our era "homo postmoderinicus" behavior.

So even if the endless generosity of the millionaire continues to safeguard the sanctity of the surrealistic rituals indefinitely, schools will not be able to remain aloof and ignore their surrounding environment for much longer. As a result of the constant friction between the tribal rituals protected by a state-sanctioned monopoly and the surrounding reality, carried inside in the hearts and minds of many of the young tribe members and teachers, the system is plagued by a host of gradually noisier grating sounds, as its operation is slowly but surely advancing toward a complete halt.

The rising levels of tectonic civilization clashes lead in our case, as was the case with the tribe's people, to immense, chaotic, unmindful, change processes that have yet to have any coherent, sustainable, and transferable impact on the system. The old civilization is losing its grip on the little territory left for it every day and does not stand the slightest chance to hold on in lieu of the engulfing opposed civilization. Despite this inevitability, nothing meaningful seems to be changing. The endless change processes that take place in schools today are pseudo changes. Their main goal seems to alleviate the pain caused by the cognitive dissonances which necessarily arise from this anomalous situation. They make sure that these dissonances and the discomfort they cause *never actually lead* to any meaningful changes and allow schools to continue marketing themselves to society and to their own employees and students as "innovative," "pioneering," and "advanced."

EDUCATIONAL CHANGE: AN EXPENSIVE WAY TO ALLEVIATE THE PAINS OF COGNITIVE DISSONANCES

The mindless processes of "change," mentioned in the previous section, surrounding the system at this time are dangerous for a number of reasons. First, they are dangerous because they are economically and energetically draining. While being mindlessly implemented they are accompanied by colossal, inexcusable squandering of resources.

Secondly, from a social and educational standpoint, the booming industry of "school change" or "reform" is both short-sighted and overly technocratic; short-sighted since these attempts at "innovation" stem from a very partial understanding of the postmodern civilization it is trying to adapt to and the role of education therein; technocratic, since these attempts are nothing more then a passive adaptation of postmodernity's external "symptoms" (which are often automatically equated with "progress" and "advancement" like digital technology, privatization, or decentralization) without passing any ethical judgment on the various characteristics thereof. As such, these adaptations are nowhere near the pro-active changes required in order to tackle the enormity of the problem we now face. They are not consciously formed in light of an ethical or ideological view and do not consider the huge advantages vs. awesome dangers adapting to this new civilization entails given this view. Being short-sighted and technocratic as they are they are doomed to fail.

Thirdly and in addition to the above negative consequences, the poorly-designed products of the useless attempts to "reform the system" have created in the last forty years a dangerously insane system, obsessively addicted to voodoo therapies and catch phrases: "reforms," "restructurings," "interventions"; bottom up, top down, organizational, curricular, didactic, holistic; or focused on specific problems like decreasing level of literacy, increasing levels of violence, and so forth and so on. These change processes just keep repeating and mutually destroying themselves and each other, always promising hope for "salvation." This hope already has its own nickname in educational literature: perennial expectation for a "panacea" that miraculously solves all the problems once and for all.

It has also led to the development of a separate discourse which we can refer to as meta-level lamentation discourse on the "predictable failure of educational reform" (to quote the name of a book by S. Sarason, a leading expert of educational change in recent decades, who has realistically analyzed the end result of his and others' permanent attempts to change the system) which is still "stuck deep" in the old modern paradigm and usually only leads to another suggestion for a new (or often old) panacea.

This reforms-oriented obsession has become another tier of the deeply rooted problem, aggravating the crisis, which is already acute enough, further and further still.

Fourth, since these voodoo remedies do not really better the situation, but rather just add to the mess it is currently in, they create a norm of "double talk" and hypocrisy. This is probably the highest of this long list of prices and costs stemming from the change-oriented obsession. In the last generation, teachers and administrators have learnt to speak the postmodern language of the outside world, but since the school's essentially modern structure prevents them from really implementing postmodern oriented changes, and since they have figured out by now that tomorrow there will be another (often opposite) change, they empty the language of all its meaning by using postmodern "in," "reforms-oriented" language to describe the "good old" modern routines they are all too familiar with.

The damages caused by this reality are enormous. First and foremost, it creates an inherent organizational failing, as it prevents the system from reaching any mode of functioning stability and thus hinders any possibility to actually contribute to society. But the really frightening problems which ensue from this reality are the psychological and social ones. In many Western societies today young people are raised in an absurd, surrealistic environment which is dominated by "double talk" and hypocrisy. They absorb several hidden yet extremely powerful messages from that environment: that life is absurd or devoid of meaning, that language is empty and essentially deluding. This reality massacres both senses (the existential and the semantic) of the inner drive for meaning which is basic to all that is good in human beings.

BACK TOWARDS THE FUTURE

The above argument I made about "double talk" may sound a little abstract. To clarify it, let me briefly analyze one representative example: an advertisement published at the end of the previous century by a leading teacher training college in Israel. This is but one, arbitrarily picked, example out of an enormous array of educational discourses based on unconscious or subconscious "double talk" employed by the involved stakeholders:

The ad title read: "A Guiding Light for Eighty-five Years." Beneath it was a picture of a lovely little boy sitting in class with an open book, eagerly raising his hand. The caption read: "Teaching is one of the most important factors shaping future generation," and then, using conventional advertising logic stated that "Only at College X, with its eighty-five years of experience and advanced and innovative educational approach, will you be able to acquire this profession at the highest level."

The college's future-oriented outlook and the need for change and innovation were cited at least twice within the ad. The college claimed to "shape future generation" using a "progressive and innovative educational approach." But the graphics accompanying the promising text depicted the total opposite. The overall impression is similar to that of a 1908 ad by a 220-year-old horse-drawn-carriage manufacturer (after the advent of the motor vehicle), sporting a driver patting his team of horses claiming to be "tomorrow's vehicle with the speed and comfort of yesteryear."

The methods employed by the current education system to impart knowledge, epitomized by the image of a child with an open textbook and raised hand, are just as antiquated as in the telecommunication and computer age as a horse-drawn-carriage is in the age of Formula One racing cars.

The essential dissonance between the world of education and the "real world" is reflected in the advertisement in several other ways.

First of all, the advertisement equates "education" with "going to school," yet, an ever increasing percentage of young people in the Western world no longer "go" to school at all, but rather study at home as part of a growing home-schooling movement.

Secondly, if we assume for the sake of the argument that school in the modern sense of the term will nevertheless continue to play a major part in Western education, the advertisement assumes that "school" is a specific physical location, a "classroom," situated in a specific edifice: "the school building," removed from "life" outside. But much like other organizational structures, the importance of the school building or location as a whole is challenged today by ICT capabilities whose impact is evident by the emergence of virtual and semi-virtual organizations in all areas of human activity, other than the realm of education, that is. There is no reason to assume that the definition of school ten or twenty years from now will include a specific location.

Cloistering the learning process as an isolated activity within a "school," or in other words in a given location significantly removed from the adult world and real life, is no longer sustainable. It was possible and meaningful when knowledge and patterns of life were relatively static and preserved over time. In such an environment it made sense for the individual to first "prepare for life" and then "embark on life" equipped with the necessary knowledge and skills acquired during the preparatory period. But when living in a world where you must continuously study because yesterday's knowledge is no longer relevant today, a distinction between "learning" and "life," between "getting ready" and "the real thing," between schooling as something independent of one's daily existence and the individual's work, social life, and leisure time, becomes pointless.

Third, the ad presupposes that learning is based on book-learning, while in fact in Western societies books, at least the three-dimensional "autarchic" objects we have called by this name for the last five hundred years, are rapidly losing their dominant stature as the primary medium for transmitting information to alternative media, mainly to ever-changing kaleidoscopic e-texts on the Internet.

Fourth, the ad is predicated on the existence of a hierarchical organizational structure based on rigid dichotomies. In other words, it assumes that there are those who decide and those who act upon decisions, those who ask questions and those who raise their hands and answer, while the identity of questioners and answerers remains constant. This kind of rigid hierarchical structure is practically obsolete in a world where there exist "learning organizations" in almost every realm other than that of education.

Fifth, the ad automatically assigns the role of raising a hand to children, and assumes that the questions will always be answered by adults. In "real life," even if the custom of raising a hand to receive the floor is preserved in some circumstances, one can expect some role reversals, which will increase with time, where adults and children alike both raise the questions and provide answers.

Lastly, the ad title proudly proclaims the college to be "a guiding light," showing the way forward to new generations of educators. Truth be told, I am not at all convinced that teachers, the college educators, or anyone else in the education system for that matter, indeed know "the way." What is much worse: I am afraid that very few people in postmodern education systems have systematically attempted to study the processes that have led postmodern education systems to lose their way or the means by which an alternative may be found.

Up until two or three decades ago there was a way, which was complex yet clear-cut. Its main goal was, as it has been for over the last two and a half millennia of Western culture, to teach students how to lead a Good Life, a life which reflected a transcendental value system that required the individual to relinquish his or her ego in order to serve predefined "sublime values" of one kind or another. Such values could be religious, rationalistic, socialist, national, "universal" liberal values, or a combination of one or more of the above. In modern reality these "sublime values" have for the most part been based on modern ideologies, including Scientism, the belief that modern science could solve all human problems and lead us to progress, its offshoots (socialism and liberalism), or competitors (mainly nationalism), each based on a clear-cut perception of what would help create a desirable human being. The second goal of education, which underlined sublime purposes, was latent but no less important: training or socializing students for work on the production line by copying the factory's rigid hierarchical organizational structure and its basic norms, rigid obedience and precision accompanied by a sense of alienation.

Modern schools achieved the above objectives with remarkable success. In fact, they still do. The problem is that the first category of goals no longer applies to Western culture the way it did for the past two and a half millennia. As for the second category, the norms of the workplace and the labor market have changed to a large extent once manned production lines and rigid organizations designed to control the assembly line workers disappeared. Thus to speak of "the way" as though it is clear to the leaders of the above college is misleading to say the least.

In conclusion, the advertisement is a good indication of the depth of the malady: the ad proclaims the college to be able to "educate future generations" using "innovative methods" based on a clear-cut "way" in light of which college staff will "guide" tomorrow's teachers, while in fact it relies on an anachronistic approach to education and does not show even a hint of consciousness of the immense challenge they must face in order to do so. Sadly, if such confusion reigns in teacher training, what can one honestly expect of teachers once the reality of the classroom hits them at last?

The above advertisement was indeed chosen at random, but it is representative of the mindset prevalent among many of today's teacher training institutions. We can find any number of additional examples, rich with "promising" slogans, saturated with all the right buzz words claiming to be "future oriented," "innovative," "constructivist," "student oriented," and "problem based," slogans which unconsciously cover up old conceptual and practical patterns and mask a growing sense of impotence.

This is of course to be expected when the foundations of core institutions begin to crumble; human beings tend to hold on to the pillars of the old and the familiar as the only visible source of stability. But standing firm on what is fast becoming dysfunctional and immaterial to prevailing reality only increases the danger which threatens not only the sustainability of the education system but also the health of societies who will not be able to remain democratic and enlightened when their core socializing institution fails to function or worse, functions as an effective source for ethically and developmentally negative education.

FORWARD TOWARDS THE FUTURE

While the previous section clarified how most educators and champions of educational change retreat while believing themselves to be moving forward, this section portrays the steps that should be taken in order to make actual progress.

Educators and society at large do not have the luxury of choosing between a meaningful and functional modern system and the postmodern one. Rather, today, they face two very different options: One is to irrationally cling to the current hybrid system, an essentially modern system, hectically busy with "change processes" which contradict each other or themselves and are painted with postmodern and innovation-oriented colors. Such a system will grow more and more absurd, economically wasteful, and psychologically and socially detrimental, as it conveys the unavoidable message that life is absurd and vacuous.

The second option requires that we get to the root of the problem, acknowledge the magnitude of the change necessary to tackle it, and address it in a mindful, macro-strategic, and ethically oriented manner. A new, efficient system must be forged, one which is relevant to the postmodern reality and relies on postmodern processes to educate towards the Good Life as defined in light of basic Humanistic values.

Clearly there is only one relevant option here. This option consists of admitting the need to rethink and redesign education from scratch, to stop taking the two-and-a-half-millennia-old Platonic tradition and structures or the two hundred-year-old modern schooling systems basic to western culture (i.e., the disciplinary curriculum) for granted.

The way things stand at the moment, replacing the well trodden educational path with an entirely new one seems redundant and wasteful to most educators and relevant decision makers. I hope that making all concerned realize the extremely heavy toll paid in pounds, euros, and dollars and much more importantly, in the decreasing chances young people have to develop as psychologically healthy individuals, is an effective way to enhance recognition of the urgent need for a rethinking and reinventing of education. In other words, Western democracies must realize, and do so very soon, the importance of them successfully dealing with the multiplying internal and external threats they face, or the consequences of their ignoring the situation may be very dire indeed. To educe such an understanding one must dedicate a lot of time and resources:

- to analyzing the deep cultural, social, and economical roots of the current education crisis,
- to analyzing the profoundly ingrained processes which ensue from these roots, that have systematically led to the failure of one reform effort after the next during the last fifty years,
- to developing a horizon broad enough to enable us to see as many aspects of the whole picture as possible. Such a perspective should include recognizing that failing scholarly achievements are only one symptom of the same root problem, as are rising levels of violence or addiction among youth, rising levels of teachers' burnout, the systemic addiction to pseudo educational changes, and the spread of "double talk" in the system. The root problem is of course the rising levels of alienation which are caused by the system's absurdity and the rising gap between the modern system and the postmodern world around it.

But in order to develop such wide horizons, profound understanding, and sharp systematic analysis, we must abandon the postmodernistic cynicism, technocratic indifference, and lack of faith in strategic change processes led by reason which characterizes most political decisions makers.

Paradoxically, this total lack of faith in mindful, radical, change exists in a time when human being are affected, more than ever before in human history, by a long series of radical revolutions some of which, mindfully planned and rigorously fought for, radically changed history and human life.

Among these revolutions we can count the "inconceivable" modern ones (scientific, technological, social, medical), implemented throughout the two last centuries. These previously inconceivable revolutions, intentionally and systematically planned and propagated by the founding fathers of the scientific revolution and enlightenment, beginning in the fifteenth century and continuing until at least the eighteenth, erased pre-modern social and psychological structures which dominated human thought since practically the dawn of history such as authoritative societies, slavery, and total subjection of property or disenfranchised individuals, of women, of children, of sexual minorities, of national or ethnical minorities. With the coming of age of postmodernity, once the rate and extent of these revolutions exponentially accelerated, what one day seemed unrealizable fiction became but a trivial fact of life the very next: deciphering the human genome, conquering space, performing complex operations from a distance, distance learning, home-schooling, erasing all the parameters which previously unequivocally separated between genders and age groups, social legitimization of transgenders and hermaphrodites, and so on.

There is no logical reason to assume that while all the above revolutions were possible (some of which based on thorough, systematic, long term analyses, visions, and strategies), rethinking and redesigning education is not.

It is true that today's politicians, decision makers, and most educators may not have the necessary courage, broad enough horizons, and other capabilities needed to implement such an intentional revolution. But the same was the case for those civil servants and politicians who tried to protect the divine rights of kings, the practice of slavery, infringement of the right of people of color, disenfranchisement of women and property-less men, and rejection and inequality of homosexuals and transgender. In all the aforementioned cases the primary claims were that such a step is inconceivable, would be "unnatural," and would shake the foundations of human social existence. If there is anything we can learn from our own history it is that what today's cowardice and narrow-mindedness might present as impossible is what tomorrow shows to be necessary and the day after may turn into a fact of life.

This book is written with both the hope that Western education in postmodernity will enjoy a fate similar to that of the above mentioned changes and the belief in the ability to increase the chances for rethinking and reinventing education to take place by:

- Presenting the reader with a broad analysis of the postmodern cultural crisis. This crisis inevitably creates the profound educational crisis that sustains the aforementioned need for the rethinking and redesigning of education.
- Presenting the reader with an outline for a possible and, I believe, desirable educational system based on three hundred years of Humanistic thought and its adaptation to the new needs and constraints of the postmodern reality.
- Arguing that the default scenario, wherein we passively drift in the postmodern storm, permanently and pointlessly faking "reforms" with no compass to direct those reforms in any productive direction, is too psychologically and socially dangerous for us to allow it to go on any longer.

SUMMARY

The stakes are far greater than education in and of itself. The current diffident efforts not only leave the educational ship drifting without direction but also expose democratic societies to the danger of being shattered to pieces on the rocks of a purely technocratic approach to education, favoring drifting with the current over the more difficult yet imperative navigation through the storm. When allowing captains with tunnel vision to use very partial and erroneous maps, democratic societies run the risk of being beached on the shores of social breakdown by strong currents that they have left themselves no way to foresee.

The justification for the most fundamental structures of the most extensive and expensive public system in postmodern Western democracies is foundering. To mindfully tackle this apocalyptic event, we must critically examine the Holy Grail, the innermost sanctum of the paradigm which exclusively dominated Western education for the past two and a half millennia. That this paradigm survived the trials and tribulations of time for as long as it did cannot in itself be a justification to maintain its dominance in the present. The dominance of practices such as burning "witches" and other "heretics," slavery and the subjugation of people of color, women, Jews, and homosexuals was just as obvious for many centuries; some even date back to the dawn of civilization. However no one today will argue that they are therefore justifiable simply by their past prevalence. These social structures were "unchallenged realities," they had enjoyed an absolute hold on individuals' minds, as strong as that of the laws of nature, until they were subject to thorough examination which inevitably led to their demise. Today almost all of them are just as unquestionably rejected by at least most if not all postmodern-day individuals.

In the same way, we now need to make the first steps in the (probably long) process of freeing our minds from this absolute mental and social grip the modern way of thinking has on our systems of education; we must "de-school society" and our minds, as Ivan Illich called it few decades ago.[5]

In this Introduction, the first chapter of the book, and its third part (Chapters Ten and Eleven), I paint my argument and the practical implications thereof with broad strokes of the proverbial brush and present the reader with a general outline of my thinking. But should the reader wish to understand the substantive validity of my arguments more deeply he or she must delve into the main chapters of this book as well.

Even if some or even most of my arguments are found, upon examination, to be invalid, the simple fact is that there are good *prima facie* reasons to question the desirability of the basic suppositions of the prevailing educational paradigm and the educational structure and *modus operandi* it inevitably creates—structures and *modus operandi* almost all our youngsters are compelled to adhere by during their constitutive years. If only for that reason they should be thoroughly examined and alternatives to them should seriously be considered. We owe it to our children. We owe it to our society. We owe it to ourselves.

PART ONE

A CRITIQUE OF MODERN EDUCATION

THE CRISIS OF MODERN EDUCATION
IN THE POSTMODERN ERA

INTRODUCTION

The postmodern era is rapidly rendering Modern Western education systems obsolete. Although the decline of the modern era[1] and the rise of the postmodern era began a mere three or four decades ago, this amazingly short, yet most dynamic, era in human history has revolutionized every aspect of our lives. The postmodern revolutions, while diverse in their nature, are characterized by common patterns which set the postmodern era radically apart from the modern and traditional periods that preceded it.

This change caused a radical decline in relevance and functionality of modern education systems. The basic organizational and didactic parameters of Western education were formed in the image of the modern era, while more profoundly modeled to abide by a twenty-five-hundred-year-old Platonic curricular structure. These definitions, designed to serve the needs of a modern society, have become meaningless, and hence dysfunctional, in the wake of the postmodern revolutions. The chasm between the systems' basic modern-Platonic parameters and the reality in which they must function, as well as the nature of the society they must serve, has turned the entire system into an absurd, dysfunctional, anomaly.[2]

Current Western education systems are still viewed as a "natural" and exclusive educational choice for an overwhelming majority of citizens in Western societies. As claimed above, these systems are an adaptation of the theoretical curriculum outlined by Plato, customized to fit the needs of an industrial, modern society, predominantly based on modern scientific practices. Plato's Utopian education system was based on theoretical learning of the fundamental scientific disciplines of his time. He perceived knowledge of truths, or the pursuit thereof, as reflected in these disciplines, to be the core of the Good Life. This term was used in his, and later Western, philosophy to denote the best life a human being can and should have, or the life that best reflects and expresses human beings' unique essence, Rationality, and hence guarantees the highest level of (what is today referred to as) well being. Accordingly, Plato perceived education to be a process which allows students to achieve the highest privilege: being introduced to the Good Life. His curriculum was later developed and adapted by generations of classical thinkers and educators, by Christian theologians in the Middle Ages and later by Renaissance educators. The Modern Era gave it its last extensive adaptation, fitting it to the needs of universal public education serving science-based, industrial modern nation-states societies (as discussed in Chapters Two and Three).

3

Postmodernity,[3] characterized by relativistic *weltanschauung* and an unstable and hectic lifestyle, represents a new period, in fact an entire new Western civilization. These changes have pushed the prevailing modern curriculum beyond its expiration date. To address the problems which arise from the anomaly of a *modern-Platonic* system functioning in an *anti-Platonic postmodern* world, we must take into consideration the unprecedented scope of the problem. Educational communities and postmodern liberal[4] democratic societies must recognize that a systematic, extensive quest is in order. *In a nutshell we are called upon to reinvent education from scratch.*

This quest should go far beyond the incessant waves of "reform," "change process," and "reconstruction process" that have been plaguing all Western education systems over the last four decades. All such halfway measures serve only as an alibi which aggravates the problem and prevents the desperately needed complete, fundamental, *reinvention* of the education process.

Plato, the "founding father" of Western education, aspired to supply his fellow Athenian citizens with a rational worldview and an educational process which could provide them with security, harmony, existential meaningfulness, and ethical norms. These attributes could no longer be meaningfully ascertained by Athens' traditional mythical, religious, and tribal social structures, which were in a state of collapse. Plato's curriculum, based on learning theoretical disciplines which (allegedly) reflected the truths about the physical world and desired human life, had a much longer "shelf life" than he could ever have envisioned: its many variants served Western civilization and its education for two and half millennia.

Our lives today are characterized by a cultural and socioeconomic crisis similar to that which weighed down Plato's Athens. Due to the "Death of God" and the "End of Ideology," we can no longer afford to go on assuming that the previous social or cultural structures are sources of stability, meaning or ethical-existential guidance. The underpinning of these values has collapsed. As a result, the foundations of the educational processes connected with it have collapsed as well. Thus we find ourselves needing to recreate Plato's imaginative and courageous endeavor. We must replace the education systems' modern-Platonic model with a totally different alternative tailored to the wholly new circumstances of the postmodern era, whilst, it is important to emphasize, maintaining and serving the basic Humanistic values that comprise the core of Liberal Democracies (for as long as we wish to hold on to these values and sociopolitical structures).

In this chapter, I take the first few steps towards clarifying the above statements. The chapter is comprised of three sections: the first section defines the term "postmodernity" and characterizes the era identified by this name. The discussion in this section depicts the revolutions that have brought about the emergence of postmodernity at all levels of human existence and the elements these levels all have in common. Finally, this section illustrates the abyss separating modern and, certainly, traditional society from the postmodern era.

Following the description of the chasm separating the first two societies from their successor, the second section of the chapter portrays the enormous gap between the essentially modern version of the Platonic conception of education characterizing

Western education systems and the postmodern reality. This reality is already well established just outside the classroom door and renders everything behind those doors meaningless and obsolete.

Finally, the third section outlines the two strategies which can substantiate my claims. I then corroborate these claims using the first, relatively simple, strategy and introduce the methodology that will serve to validate my claims in light of the second, far more demanding, strategy to be discussed in the next four chapters of Part One of this book.

THE RISE OF POSTMODERNITY

What is Postmodernity?

The first harbingers of a third stage in the history of Western civilization, known as both "postmodernity" and "the postmodern era," began appearing during the late 1950s and the 60s. This third stage in human history followed two previous eras: the agricultural-traditional and the industrial-modern. Signs that new times are upon us have been increasing since the 1970s in every possible aspect of the human condition, and in the prevailing socioeconomic, political, cultural, and psychological realities. We are now, in the first decade of the twenty-first century, already deeply immersed in the second generation of this third stage of Western civilization.

Other descriptive terms used to typify contemporary times from various perspectives include "post-capitalist society," "post-Fordist society," "the age of unreason," "the flattening of the world," the "shrinking of space-time," "the end of history," or the era defined by a "clash of civilizations."[5] No matter what perspective is used to analyze postmodernity, whatever term is used to "baptize" it and however it is characterized, many commentators agree that an entirely new reality has emerged in the last forty years, unlike any previous stage in human history.

Among the many concepts that are used to describe this new era in Western culture, I found three early coinages especially influential and successful in expressing the essence of the changes on three main levels: "post-industrial society," "third wave society," and "postmodern society." They differ from one another in their scope, frame of reference, and foci.[6,7]

"*Post-industrial society*" focuses on the economic dimension, particularly on the changes in the production patterns and labor markets of the Western world since the 1950s. Changes in these aspects of human economic life have greatly intensified in the three decades that have passed since the publication, in 1973, of Bell's book in which the term was coined.[8] Daniel Bell, and many others who followed him, use this term to single out the changes that have resulted from the takeover of automation and computerization, as well as the emergence of the services branch as a leading sector and chief employer of labor in today's economy. Just as the Industrial Revolution replaced agriculture as the predominant economic factor, services are now establishing hegemony where Industry once ruled. These changes had dramatic effects on the labor market and the nature of work, as well as on the constellation of socioeconomic power. These are all denoted by the term in question.

The "*third wave*" reflects a wider outlook. For Alvin Toffler, who coined the term, and many others who follow in his footsteps,[9] it relates not only to the realm of economics and employment, but also to modifications in dominant patterns of social and organizational structures deriving from the "Information and Communication Technology (ICT) Revolution" and other technological revolutions affecting our times. One of the dominant features expressed by this concept is the demise of hierarchical, centralist, and synchronic organizations which require that all concerned with their activities be present at the same time and in the same place (I later refer to this requirement as "lococentricrism").

These rigid modern organizations, designed to produce standard products for mass consumption ("mass production"), have been replaced in the last four decades by flexible organizational structures oriented towards specific market segments, or even catering to individual needs and tastes ("mass customization"). This blindingly fast shift has affected all aspects of human existence. Lately, Thomas Friedman has referred to some aspects of these phenomena as "*the flattening of the world.*"[10]

The term "*Postmodern Society,*" as used here, is the widest in scope. Stemming from post-1960s discourse on architecture and art, its meaning was later expanded to encompass all the aforementioned aspects, while emphasizing the worldviews, cultural and conceptual structures of our times.[11] In its common usages it expresses the shift from an objectivistic-monolithic perception of reality and epistemology to a relativistic-pluralistic one. In this volume the term "postmodern" is employed in a more general, less focused, perspective as a "catch-all" phrase that seeks to encapsulate in one concise term the essence of our age. It refers to all the revolutions characterizing it: economic, sociological, psychological, conceptual, and cultural, as well as their combined impact on all aspects of human existence.

Founding Revolutions of Postmodernity

The contemporary thinker Neville Wakefield describes the postmodern human experience in these words:

> "In the place of a world ordered according to monolithic truths, linear grids and representational stability, we are faced with a set of unstable and volatile equations that correspond to a collapsed or imploded representational space. Previously solid references have been replaced by disorientating flux, stable subject positions by schizophrenic wanderings, steadfast relationships by the pragmatism and contingency of coalitions, calculated risks by terror, known dangers by the invisible reign of the unknown."[12]

During the previous century, Nietzsche,[13] who clearly predicted the main epistemic, cultural, and social element of the postmodern condition, described its essence, on these levels, as a world devoid of any set of stable coordinates. In the blunt but eloquent language characteristic of his writings he wrote:

"Where is God gone?" he called out. "I mean to tell you! We have killed him, you and I! We are all his murderers! But how have we done it? How were we able to drink up the sea? Who gave us the sponge to wipe away the whole horizon? What did we do when we loosened this earth from its sun? Whither does it now move? Whither do we move? Away from all suns? Do we not dash on unceasingly? Backwards, sideways, forwards, in all directions? Is there still an above and below? Do we not stray, as through infinite nothingness? Does not empty space breathe upon us?"[14]

The transient, fluid, "*non-stability*" expressed in these two citations reflects a series of momentous revolutions spanning all the core spheres of current human life and activity. For the sake of our presentation here, I shall break down, somewhat artificially, the emergence of the postmodern era in Western civilization into a (partial and somewhat arbitrary) list of revolutions, each of which caused an upheaval (or rather series of upheavals) in an important sphere of human life:

- In the *Technological* sphere, the "*Digital Revolution*" of the last few decades is constantly changing our lives. This revolution consists of a series of accelerated waves of ICT or digital innovations and discoveries which have completely altered the way we communicate, work, buy, sell, create friendships, mate, choose and design our lifestyles. "Digitization" refers in this respect not only to the technological aspects of this revolution but also to its fragmenting-hyperlinking impact on all levels of human life. We can name, among many, upheavals caused by the invention of the fax, the PC, the VCR, the laptop, multimedia and CD ROMs, the Internet, the World Wide Web and hyperlinking, Broad Band Internet and mobile wireless Internet terminals. This long series of changes led us quickly to the biggest of all ICT transformations known so far, "ubiquitous computing," which may have seemed like science fiction yesterday, but is quickly becoming a trivial fact of our lives today.

  In this last wave of change, wired (or rather wireless) connections link together all objects, including human subjects (with the help of wearable and/or micro computers implanted on their person). All objects and human subjects communicate through these links, using every possible media outlet, creating a reality in which any type of information is transmitted from anywhere to anyplace on the globe at anytime. This in turn might very well lead, in five or ten years, to new apexes, still believed to be nothing more than science fiction nowadays, which Kuertzweil refers to as "the age of intelligent machines,"[15] a time in which computers will become smarter them us. According to Kuertzweil, only a short leap separates that point in time from one in which what is now perceived as a purely surrealistic reality becomes very real indeed; an "age of spiritual machines," in which computers might turn quantity to quality and develop an independent consciousness.[16]

- In the sphere of *Medical & Biological Research,* the "*Babylon Tower Revolution*" has taken hold. The name I chose for this revolution reflects the fact that this is the first time in human history (if we believe the story of the

Tower of Babylon to be but a myth) that human audacity, or hubris (I leave it for the reader to chose), allows us to invade what was, up until now, regarded as an exclusively divine domain. Therein God enjoyed an obvious relative advantage over human beings: creation of life. It consists of an almost inconceivable series of developments and discoveries, some of which appeared practically science fictional until the very day they were announced. Among these we can count decoding the human genome, a potential ability to produce various organs from live stem cells (halted for now only by ethical restraint, which will probably be broken quite soon), a new kind of artificial fertilization, and the combination of telemedicine and nano-medicine with biological and digital technologies which allows us to perform complete internal operations using miniscule fibers or swallowable pills.

Thanks to these waves of medical innovations we are quickly approaching a period in which medicine will have no problem "repairing," changing or replacing any part of the human body, including entire organs or parts of them; we will be able to prevent potential problems altogether by dictating specific human characteristics and manipulating the genes of potential or living human beings. It is mind-blowing to imagine the eternal psychological, ethical, and social repercussions of these capabilities on everything we have known about "man" or "the individual," including the most basic definitions of these terms.

This is especially true when we combine recent medical developments with the new developments in chemical psychiatric treatment, which already today enable us to change meaningfully the character of an individual using the extremely effective "new generations" psychiatric drugs developed over the last three decades. Two examples, and not necessarily the most meaningful, of this are: (1) Viagra, which until recently was used solely to treat erectile dysfunction but has now been found to encourage feelings of love and create within its user a need for intimacy; and (2) the significant progress made in the development of a "forgetfulness pill" which will allow individuals to completely erase unwanted memories from their brain (or, in less positive scenarios, this pill can be used by ill-intentioned people to erase the memory of an unaware individual).

Once our internal and external organs can be replaced, repaired and even pre-designed, once our most intimate and personal desires and emotions can be easily regulated by medication, once our memories can be manipulated by a pill and can even be, in the not too distant future, rewritten using Internet based memory loaders ("designer memories" is only one of many possible names for this), what will be left of the relative stability and continuity we now identify as "an individual," a "person," an "agent"?

- In the *Economic sphere*, over the last two generations we have witnessed the "*Flattening of the World Revolution*" (to borrow a term Thomas Friedman recently coined). It stems, first and foremost, from the technological developments and the effects thereof mentioned above. These created a "new economy" in which huge sums of money or information can be digitally transferred from one end of the globe to another, changing the nature of investment and the manner in which stock exchanges function, as well as affecting many kinds of labor that can now be digitally outsourced to any place on the globe. Economic globalization processes, combined with the digital revolution and the global takeover of neo-liberalism and the open markets economy, have also dramatically enhanced the transferability of materials, merchandise, human beings, and physical labor ("immigration"). Likewise, these processes led to a permanent acceleration in the intensity and speed of competition, which in turn created a dramatic change in all possible spheres of the organizational world, the postmodern labor market and hence the postmodern human situation.

- In the *Labor Market* we are facing a *"Loss of Career Revolution."* This consists of the floundering of the original Latin meaning of the term "career"—a track. This stems from the propagation of a fragmentary, "jumpy," and hectic professional life which no longer fits the metaphor of a linear and continuous track. This radical change is a result of the fierce economic competition that has led to a series of transformations in the organizational structures of all economic organizations. From large international conglomerates to small family companies, businesses have been forced to become thinner and more dynamic, to outsource many of their "in house" jobs, and hence rely on a very small core of permanent employees. They have also been forced to replace many of the long term employees whose positions were not outsourced, relevant professionals whose contractual engagements with the company were either short (from a few months to a year) or intermediate term (say two years).

In this reality, the "accepted" structures of the labor market and the professional career could no longer exist. More specifically, these changes include, among others:

- The disappearance of tenure, accompanied by frequent changes in one's location and the nature of employment.
- The creation of permanently dynamic individual "careers" and professional life in which radical changes in one's profession are frequent, or in which the individual is involved in several unrelated occupations at the same time. These last two points are mainly responsible for removing from the term "career" its traditional and literal senses.
- The emergence of "new professions," which rely on practical knowledge and personality characteristics (initiative, charisma, communication skills, flexibility, the capacity to adapt and so forth), are constantly being created. These professions compete against the old "academic" professions, which rely on the acquisition of formal knowledge and a diploma testifying to that effect, for status and respectability.
- An acceleration of the development of all professions (old and new) which requires intensive, life long learning in order to stay in one place.
- Yet another revolution relevant to the sphere of the Labor Market is the "End of Work Revolution." To some extent this is a "sister revolution" to the aforementioned one, but it differs in the immediate extension of its effects

far beyond the labor market. Its origins are twofold: on the one hand, the near doubling of human life expectancy in the last century which accelerated in the last few generations (a dramatic revolution in itself), and on the other the growing efficiency and digitization of production and services. Consequently, the proportion of time dedicated to work in Westerners' lives has dramatically decreased. At the apex of the modern era many individuals started working at the age of six or seven. These individuals worked twelve hours a day, six days a week, and death (at the age of forty-five to sixty) or severe incapacitation were the only causes of retirement. In contrast, in today's Western societies, one does not fully join the work force before the age of twenty-two or twenty-three, and one enjoys twenty to thirty years of high quality life after retirement. The work day is (at least in most mid-level jobs) nine hours long, and the work week is five, or often four, days long. This change inevitably has an enormous impact on all spheres of life. To phrase it concisely: for the first time in human history, around one billion people in Western societies (and soon at least two million more in Asia and Latin America) must adjust to a lifestyle that is not exclusively work oriented, while our religious and ethical systems, as well as our social structures, legislation, and mentality, are still fully harnessed to the enhancement and glorification of work ethics.

- In the spheres of *Gender Definition* and *Social Roles* we see a revolution we can name the "*Collapse of All Social or Biological Distinction.*" This revolution consists of the floundering of "veteran" (i.e., dominant in traditional societies, as well as in modern ones) dividers such as "legitimate family" vs. "living in sin"; "men" vs. "women"; "old" vs. "young"; "children" vs. "adults"; "normal sexual tendencies" vs. "unnatural or abnormal ones." Lately, even "truths" accepted since "God created Adam and Eve," such as simple biological distinctions including the existence of only two dichotomous genders, have been challenged in more then one way. For example a hermaphrodite lifestyle is slowly being legitimized (i.e., people with both sex organs are allowed to live their lives as they are without forcing them to choose a gender and undergo surgery to remove the additional organ). Women who choose "men-like" lifestyles (or rather those which used to be associated with "men" in the good old days), and vice versa, are no longer considered anything but normal and sex change operations are legitimate in a growing number of communities. All these changes combined amount to a disintegration of the dichotomous "biblical" distinction between "man" and "woman" and its replacement by an endless myriad of possible combinations of sexes and genders which cannot be clearly defined. This is only one, if not the most "shocking" (at least for whoever grew up in the "old 'modern' world"), result of the blurring of all social roles and dichotomies.

- In the sphere of *Belonging or Supporting Social Structures,* we have witnessed a revolution which resulted in the "*Transformation of Society into a Mass of Strangers.*" This revolution stems from the disintegration of all unconditional social belonging frameworks that human beings have ever known.

The religious community lost its relevance to most modern individuals already during the modern age. "The death of God," or in other words, the rapid secularization of Western society, led to the floundering of an unconditional commitment to a specific religious community which until a century or two ago almost all Westerners perceived as a rock solid belonging framework. In the last few generations other, mainly modern, pillars of belonging crumbled as well. The "end of ideology" has been rapidly expanding, dismantling, one by one, all the "grand visions" which shaped the modern era such as rationalism, "Scientism," socialism, liberalism, and nationalism. When those fell, all ideology-based social frameworks such as political youth movements, or local party and labor union branches, as well as any cultural clubs attached to them, followed suit. These frameworks were extremely important to societies in ex-communist countries, as well as, until the 1960s and 70s, to countries such as Italy, France, and the UK, which were characterized by strong labor unions and an influential socialistic tradition.

For most Westerners, the local urban neighborhood has also disappeared. In the "far away past" (in many cases two or even four decades ago) urban neighborhoods, in the social sense of the term, were enhanced by urban areas which consisted of two or three story buildings facing each other, with windows that could be opened, open balconies and common courtyards, all of which encouraged communication between neighbors. These urban areas have been giving way, in Western societies, to rows of anonymity-encouraging, "stand alone" skyscrapers, or "condominiums," which have no balconies or windows that one can actually open (which is not a problem now that the buildings are "fully air-conditioned"). It seems that the last nail in the coffin of the "local neighborhood" was hammered by suburban hypermarkets, malls, and Internet based shopping, which replaced the local grocery store which for many functioned as its bastion.

As a consequence of the above processes, Western societies have become masses of strangers, characterized by large numbers of individuals who have no geographical or mental watering hole. They have nowhere to call "home," no stable social framework to which they can identify themselves as belonging. More recently, with the "disappearance of place" and of stable work, or tenure, "the workplace" has ceased to function as the stabilizing social framework it was for so many people in the modern era until but a generation ago.

One by one all belonging, and hence security-enhancing, social structures have been picked off and demolished by the modern, and then, much more brutally, by the postmodern, reality. Following the religious community, the ideological cell, the local neighborhood and the "workplace" we are now coming to the inner most sanctum of modern belonging, the nuclear family.

The nuclear family is in itself but a faded relic of the extended, much more stable, family of pre-modern times. Until recently, the nuclear family functioned as the bastion of socio-psychological support for Western individuals in an otherwise harsh outside world (or so at least it was perceived). However, even this very basic social structure can no longer provide its members with feelings of social stability and security. For many, belonging to a nuclear family is no longer a default scenario, and the number of individuals who live alone or who have an "unofficial relationship" (a term which is quickly losing its meaning given the fact that the "official relationship" is losing its status as the natural default) is steadily growing. Among those who chose to construct a basic belonging unit in the form of a nuclear family, many fail to sustain it as the rate of divorce is rapidly on the rise (50% or even 60% in some Western societies).

As a result of these processes of change, the nuclear family is no longer the island of stability and tranquility it used to be (or was at the very least perceived as being), rather it has been reduced to just another conditional and transitory contractual belonging framework which can easily be replaced by another. This change in the nuclear family's standing in society has been strengthened by the full legitimization of what was perceived until but a generation ago as "alternative families," such as single parent families, single gender families, and so on. The legitimacy of any, or all, of these various choices is increasing, as is the legitimacy of experiencing more than one alternative and changing one's mind as often as one's fashion.

This floundering of the known social frameworks which supplied most individuals in modern Western societies with security certainly has its advantages: it provides the individual with a much larger degree of freedom and range of extended self-expression. However, it also exacts an awesome toll: a loss of the islands of stability, continuity and security in individuals' lives.

- In the sphere of *Belonging to National or Cultural Entities* we have to face a *"Conceptual Globalization Revolution."* This revolution is a continuation of the previous one, and relates to the largest belonging entities: cultures, nations, or ethnic groups. The transformation caused by the above revolution stems from waves of economic and political change, together with the technological, media, and digital revolutions that have globalized more than just the world economy. It has changed everything we knew about time and place, obliterating the role of "place" in even the most basic human interchanges, and altering the meaning of time. Along with these changes, perceptions of the "same time" or "same place," two very basic coordinates of any human activity, have been completely altered. Consequently, growing numbers of individuals no longer perceive themselves as belonging to the national, ethnic, or cultural "entities" in which they physically dwell (to the extent that such still exist) and whose time zone they share. They either lose altogether the concept of "belonging" in this larger sense, or often compensate for its loss with "many small" kaleidoscopic, unstable belongings to various interest-related, professional, or virtual groups.

- In the same above sphere, we also find the *"Glocalization Revolution."* This revolution is a byproduct of the previous one. It is, in fact, a reaction to the globalization which co-exists with it, and involves the attempts of individuals and ethnic or national groups to hold on to their common cultural roots in the face of the menacing, ever-increasing, globalization storms (the tsunami waves of change do not all work in the same direction). Individuals all over the globe are trying to return to old traditions, to revive old extinct languages and old national and ethnic identities. This trend has led to a rise of intra and inter-cultural tensions and conflict which are sometimes exacerbated to the point of all-out war.

- In the sphere of *Public Security*, the revolutionary waves of change which are sweeping away all that is known about the human condition in the Western world are accompanied by the development of what Toffler dubbed the *"Third Wave War."*[17] In other words, a new "genre" of world terror has developed, one which possesses unconventional weapons and mobilizes all the miraculous advancements of the digital communication and media age, as well as chemical and biological developments, for the good of its cause. This in itself is a power that can create radical historical shifts through only one or two relatively small-scale activities.

- In the *Ecological* sphere we cannot avoid the *"Global Warming and Pollution Revolution."* This revolution is a direct result of the intensive, globally accelerating, technological "advancement" of the last few generations. It includes the now well-documented global warming which in turn causes the polar icebergs to melt and increases the frequency and intensity of tsunami waves, typhoons, and many other types of devastating storms (real, not metaphoric, ones) which damage large areas of the globe. If the storms continue to plague us even at the current rate, not to mention an increase of it, these devastating ecological processes will most likely change all our lives and uproot hundreds of millions of people from their home environments all over the globe. This in turn is bound to bring about new waves of geopolitical upheavals.

- In the *Cultural-Conceptual* sphere we must refer to the *"Postmodernistic Revolution."* It consists of a series of epistemic, ethical, and cultural revolutions most identified with the postmodern era. It is important to distinguish (here and throughout the book) between "Postmodernity" as the name of our era, and "Postmodernism," the title usually given to this set of worldviews. The adjective "postmodernistic" stems from Postmodernism and refers to an ideological or conceptual tendency. While the book in its entirety is related to postmodernity, this paragraph is dedicated to the postmodernistic revolution, one of its major characteristics on the cultural level. This revolution may be less clear to the general public (although discussed *ad nauseam* in intellectual circles for almost two generations now) and hence should enjoy a somewhat longer elaboration.

This revolution has largely been based on a shift from an objectivistic worldview in the epistemic, scientific, ethical, and aesthetical spheres to relativistic views. The relativist perspective denies humans the ability to achieve knowledge based on access to objective reality, and even questions the meaningfulness and usefulness of concepts such as "truth" and "objective reality." This viewpoint pervades more then just intellectual and academic discourse. Most of the

13

Western secular middle classes and professional circles today no longer harbor faith in a single "solid" or absolute foundation for human knowledge, or in an "objective set of values" or "aesthetical criteria." Many of them have lost not only the belief in the possibility of such objective foundations, but also their desirability. In place thereof, beliefs in the arbitrary, the transient, and the partial nature of any "knowledge," value, or aesthetical standards have become dominant.[18] In contrast, traditional and modern societies rested their founding philosophy on a firm belief in the possibility and desirability of social harmony and stability in this world, and aspirations for an even more stable and more harmonious world in the "world to come," or in some harmonious ideal future society in the case of modern societies.

There is no denying that the dynamic industrialization and democratization processes characterizing modern society toppled the social order and religious ideals that typify traditional societies, and revolutionized the life of most individuals within rather short spans of time.[19] However, the modern revolution replaced traditional concepts and structures with different, yet still stabilizing, concepts which allowed for the emergence of a new social order and new social structures based, in some places, on Humanistic democratic concepts, and in others on socialistic or nationalistic ideologies, or a combination of all of these.

These new modern structures were based on a belief in the realization of the human potential through science and rationality leading to *progress*. This idea was clearly a modern one. The modern ideal of "progress" was an offspring of the religious belief in the "world to come" and was as vital to modernity as "salvation" was to traditional societies. Both were perceived to reflect the belief in the possibility of a categorical and harmonious solution to all human problems. The modern belief in progress through reason and science was no less strong and no less conceived to be universally valid than the religious belief in salvation through faith, prayers, or religious/mystical purification was in earlier times.[20] The epitome of these modern expectations is expressed in the Marxist utopia, which aspired to bring about a social reality wherein *all contradictions will be resolved*.

In short, like traditional society, modernity was based on a belief in an objective reality, accessible to human knowledge. Like its predecessor, modernity relied on allegedly universal social and psychological coordinates, which reflected this belief, and on ideals of aspiration to reach "*the end of history*," to use Hegel's well known concept, recently re-used by Fukuyama, referring to the utopian future of universal and eternal peace, harmony, and individual self-realization.

The postmodern experience, on the other hand, is the antithesis to all that has preceded it. The relativistic views dominant in it often accept and even relish the loss of harmony and stability in this world, and of any aspirations for harmony in a future world.

A key concept for understanding the postmodern experience is the concept of "game." Some prominent postmodernist thinkers compared all human activity to a series of games, each defining itself and disconnected from the others, as well as from any external "reality," "justification," or "foundation." All of these concepts are believed to be passé and meaningless by thinkers heralding extreme versions of relativistic postmodernist themes and their many followers in the arts, media, advertising industry, and the general public that is (usually) unconsciously influenced by them.

The basic view that this concept conveys is the perception of human life as a series of activities that neither reflect an external reality nor lead to objectives external to the activities themselves. Within this view, no one game can be perceived to be objectively preferable to another, because no objective standards or values exist to allow for a meaningful comparison. The only outcome of involvement in such arbitrary games (i.e., living) perceived to have some meaning (a term which is actually out of place in postmodernistic discourse) in this context is *jouissance*,[21] which stands in dramatic contrast to traditional societies' pursuit of "salvation" and the modern pursuit of "progress."[22]

Relativism, of itself, is not a new phenomenon in Western cultural history. However, in the past, relativism was the sole province of small minority groups who occupied the apex or margins of the social pyramid, insular groupings that lived "beyond" the social limitations applicable to the rest of society. Moreover, even in societies which embraced relativism, the practical expression of egoism and hedonism, natural psychological offsprings of relativism, were limited by the need of most people to struggle to maintain their physical existence.[23]

Our times are the first in human history in which relativism, audio-visually intensified by the media, the Internet, and the powerful "all-pervading" marketing and advertising industries which make our society tick, has penetrated every household. Relativism has become a legitimate and manifest mindset, championed by a growing middle class who, enjoying unprecedented political freedom and economic power, can afford to actualize the values stemming from this worldview. Life patterns and lifestyles that in the past were the privilege of a handful of individuals whose behavior was hidden from view, for example the debauchery of higher echelons of the church during the Renaissance, have today, to one degree or another, become legitimate and even serve as ideals (to the extent that this term still has some meaning) that the majority strives to realize.[24]

With this perspective in mind, the difference between traditional and modern societies can be compared to the change between two dialects of the same language, while the difference between modernity and postmodernity is more akin to a "complete switch" from one language to a totally foreign tongue, not even a member of the same linguistic family.[25]

Moreover, while the European shift from traditional epistemic and cultural patterns to modern ones was a gradual one, which stretched over a period of at least four hundred years between the fifteenth and nineteenth centuries, the shift from modernity to postmodernity in today's Western world happened within a mere three to four decades. Generally, it is agreed that the onset of the postmodern world can be dated to the 1960s and 1970s. Since then, this rapid transformation has dramatically changed our world.[26]

- In the sphere of *Dominant Conceptions of Consumption and the Self* (the relationship between these two seemingly unconnected foci will be clarified in the following paragraphs), we see a revolution which consists of the "*Propagation of Infinitely **Changing** Choice*" in all levels of human life. This is a second level revolution which stems from the combination of most of the above revolutions. It involves the exponential growth in the range of freedom and choice available to most individuals in the post industrialized world. One way to illustrate this point, on quite a trivial level, is by pointing to the radical transitions that the postmodern and economically developed world underwent within but three or four generations. We moved from "drugstores" or grocery shops which offer a variety of fifty to eighty products and a choice of one or two brands at most, to the supermarkets which offer many hundreds of products, several brands for each type of product. These later became hypermarkets which have on display thousands of products and in the last decade or so we find ourselves surfing the infinite "heavens" of the virtual market, which offers practically infinite, or at least a humanly un-exhaustive, number of products of any possible kind, all of which can be found in hundreds or thousands of brands and versions. These changes have eroded everything we knew about the continuity or identity of the self.

These seemingly "naïve" changes, when combined with a few others, each revolutionary in its own right, have led to the erosion of everything we knew about the self. I am referring to the rise in the standard of living which occurred over but one generation, the intensification of competition and the development of "miraculous" technology which created more personal freedom than human beings ever enjoyed before, eroding almost any limiting norm. This state of affairs created a world in which everything is open for choice. However, the nature and level of choice we have one day changes dramatically by the next. In this world everything, including our range of choice, is changeable and in fact changing, in shape, size, and quality.

Here too we can start with quite a trivial example. Every time we visit, either actually or virtually, our super- or hypermarket, or shop online, we are tempted with new logos, packages, and types of, for instance, cheese, on display on the shelves, while old ones disappear from one day to the next. However, we do not have to go far to reach examples which touch the core of the meaning of "being human": permanently renewing existential or "identity changing products," including revolutionary body and face changes ("face lift" will soon become passé, why lift it when we can change it altogether?), as well as sex change operations, and an ever increasing level of legitimization for "alternative" lifestyles (these are, after all, products designed especially for such life choices on the "existential hypermarket").

We are flooded daily with choices which affect the deepest foundations of human life: our most intimate relationships, our profession, our gender, our physiognomy or face, our emotional patterns and character. It is a world in which "everyone can perpetually invent and reinvent themselves" in every possible sense of the word, or so at least we are all promised (and the more affluent among us can certainly realize this).

- In the *Psychiatric* sphere we see an *"Invasion of Meaninglessness Revolution."* This is a third level revolution, which is to large extent enhanced by the previous *"Propagation of Infinitely Changing Choice Revolution."* This revolution consists of "the progress paradox" (to quote the title of a recent book on the subject):[27] the richer, freer, and more powerful we become the more miserable we seem to be. As a result, depression and anxiety have become the most widely spread epidemics in the last two decades, accompanied by ever new psychiatric drugs consumed in exponential quantities. Anxiety and depression necessarily grow out of living in total uncertainty, with no guiding compass in the form of a stable set of values or social or familiar frameworks. It is even more unbearable when the extent of choice we have is infinite and the very nature of this infinity changes on a daily basis. This combination expresses what Hegel called the irony of history. We were not "destined" to carry such an ever growing burden of choice, certainly not while all the ethical or social frameworks, which at their best supported a much more limited extent of choice, crumble underneath our feet

Here ends the list of revolutions and upheavals that have affected us in the last few decades. It is certainly not an exhaustive or exclusive list. Other lists can, and have, "cut" the ontology of the human situation differently. But it suffices, I believe, to convey this main message: each of the above revolutions suffices, in and of itself, to change the practicalities of human life, and the meaning of "being human." The impact is millions of times more awesome when they come together, in great tsunami-like waves, sometimes attacking us from many directions (or on various dimensions of life) at the same time, or following one another as each new wave has more horrendous effects than its predecessor. The chaotic inter-connections between them empower many of them exponentially and their impact on the human situation is immeasurable. Let us remember that all this has sprung to life during but the last three decades (the beginning may have been a little earlier, but most of it could be ignored for the first decade or two). We are, therefore, in the midst of the most radical, insensitive, and rapid change the human situation ever underwent.

Meta-Structures Common to Postmodern Phenomena

Examination of the causal relations between the aforementioned revolutions is an extremely complex, if not impossible, undertaking. There is a tendency among various thinkers to be swayed by a form of professional bias, viewing processes in their own field as the "first cause" of the postmodern revolution. Thus, for example, economists would tend to regard the acceleration of capitalism that has been permanently modifying basic patterns of production as the primary catalyst. Communications scholars cite new communication patterns stemming from the ICT revolution as the wellspring of the postmodern age. Organization and manage-ment professionals see changes in the typical organizational structures as the fountain of change. Philosophers, literary critics, and art critics will argue that the relativistic revolution known as "postmodernism" is at the root of all other changes.

There is no "natural winner" in this debate. The advent of postmodernity engrosses endless series of relationships and dynamic effects in a chaotic system. Luckily, a precise definition of causal relationships is not relevant to the under-standing of the new era, of the ever-widening chasm between it and the old, modern, era, and the impact thereof on the modern Western education systems. All that is important is that we acknowledge the following fundamental facts:

- The postmodern revolutions represent a fundamental, comprehensive change of the most deep-seated patterns of human existence, some of which were thousands of years old, in every possible sphere.
- This comprehensive change consists of several meta-structures recurring on all levels and in all aspects of human existence. These meta-structures consist of:
- Dramatic erosion of the levels of *uniformity, linearity,* and *stability and harmony* as compared to the parallel levels of these attributes characterizing the human situation in the modern, not to speak about the traditional, eras.
- More importantly—the disappearance of the belief in the possibility of such characteristics of human activity; and—
- Most importantly, the disappearance of the ardent aspiration to attain these three attributes (I refer to stability and harmony as two aspects of one attribute).

In the following sections I will refer to the floundering of the three meta-structures. This erosion of pre-modern structures is coupled with a lack of the primarily modern aspiration or belief in our ability to reach a harmonious "steady state."[28] I will also demonstrate and establish the aforementioned points with a brief overview of five different planes of human activity: the labor market, the mindset dominant in Western culture, and the social, psychological, and technological levels.

The Labor Market. When one compares the career structure of the average worker at the peak of the modern age, say during the 1950s, with current occupational structures, the differences are patently clear. Modern careers followed a *uniform* pattern of *linear* progress: studies or professional training, low level commencement of work, and gradual advancement to more complex and responsible tasks, based on experience. This was a *linear* stage-by-stage path in which one progressively accrued experience, status and remuneration within a *stable* career environment in the same profession or line of work, often in the same place of employment, until retirement.

For the postmodern professional, on the other hand, "*non-uniformity,*" "*non-stability,*" and "*non-linearity*" are the rules of the game. *Non-uniformity* means that today's professional faces an array of patterns for "career" (the inverted commas reflect the fact, mentioned already above, that due to the postmodern changes the term has lost its essentially linear original sense) development that co-exist side by side. Parallel to the declining traditional career path that is still possible in a rather large number of organizations, schools for example, other work patterns, differing in their degree of "*non-stability,*" have emerged and gained increasing popularity.

Today's career paths are extremely "jumpy" or "*non-linear.*" Individuals change their fields of endeavor, at times to totally unrelated professions, several times during their lifetime. Others combine intense periods of employment with extended periods of unemployment, during which they pursue other interests, or follow two, three, or four different professional paths with different emphases at the same time. Most of the new postmodern occupational modes are inherently *unstable* in the sense that one cannot expect to stay in the same place or, in many cases, not even in the same occupation, for more than a few years. In many cases experience has ceased to be an asset one can rely on and has become a burden. Nowadays, succumbing to inertia, and hence to past experience and *linearity*, almost necessarily spells occupational and economic suicide.[29]

More than the frameworks "on the ground," it is the effect on the prevalent beliefs and aspirations of individuals that is significant in this respect. Thus it should be emphasized that following this *de facto* hectic structure, most professionals (certainly the youngest among them) lost even the cognition of other possible developmental paths and take the prevailing "jumpy," extremely fragmentary one as the only one possible and desirable, the one at which they must excel in order to "make it." This stands in direct contradiction to the aspirations of their parents and grandparents. For them, stability in one workplace for a long period of time, usually their entire working life, which offered slow linear development, was the natural expectation; in many cases it was also the *de facto* situation. Most individuals in their fifties or forties among us still remember their parents demanding, and their teachers warning, that they should "study so you have a stable position and are able to support your family." Today, none of the assumptions basic to this credo hold anymore, certainly not the one which claims that long periods of study promise stability, or long term economic security.

The Dominant Mindset. The *non-uniformity*, *non-linearity*, and *non-stability* or *harmony*, is rapidly turning into a "holy (and dominant) trinity" of the postmodern *mindset* or the postmodern *conceptual-cultural* sphere. Modernity, much like the earlier traditional society, was characterized by a reign of various ideologies and worldviews which professed to explain all of reality (*uniformity*) with universal and eternal explanations (*stability*), aspiring to encompass, in a unifying and harmonious way, all physical and spiritual phenomena. More important is the promise of a totally *harmonious* future: salvation in the world to come (in traditional societies) or progress in the expected end-of-history (in modern societies), a period characterized by Hegel and Marx, among many others, as one in which "all conflicts will end," and by Kant as a period of "permanent peace" and affluence. Modernism justified these by a systematic, rational approach which developed its arguments methodically stage-by-stage (*linearity*). These attributes clearly characterized modernity, from the views of Bacon, Descartes, and Newton through those of Kant, Hegel, Comte, and Marx, up to the more skeptical, phenomenological, and positivistic approaches of twentieth-century philosophers.

Postmodernity, on the other hand, is typified by an opposite position. It relinquishes any pretension for *stable-harmonious*, *uniform*, *methodical*, or *linear* justifications or explanations, not to speak about expectation or striving for *future stable harmony.* These are pejoratively described in the postmodernist jargon as the meta-narratives. From Nietzsche and Wittgenstein (in his later work), through Heidegger and then Foucault, Lyotrad, Derrida, and Barth, to more recent dominant relativistic philosophy, the postmodernist "conventional wisdom" champions segmented, constantly changing language and conceptual games (*non-uniformity*), lacking any pretensions of access to truth, universality, or eternity ("*non-stability*" or *harmony*) as well as the necessary connection between them (*non-linearity*).[30]

The Social Sphere. A similar analysis of postmodern life also applies to society, wherein one encounters growing legitimacy for a plethora of lifestyles and different definitions of social roles. A woman can now define her role, not only according to the still largely prevailing traditional and modern patterns of "wife," "housewife," and "mother." She also has a choice between defining herself as a "traditional" liberal-feminist, fighting to gain access to the same rights and resources men enjoy, or, alternatively, as a radical feminist, fighting to enforce (what she takes to be) feminine norms of empathy and connectivity, instead of the predominant male control, on her own life circle or on society as a whole. In reaction to these trends, which have been gaining a lot of influence since the sixties, a "reactionary" "back to basics" trend has emerged in the last two decades, consisting of a growing number of "disillusioned" women (e.g., those tired of trying to fight on three juxtaposing fronts at the same time: the professional front, the parental front, and the sexy/attractive spouse front), who prefer the role that conservative non- or anti-feminists believe in, and, sometimes, advocate a return to "more traditional" roles for women.

These patterns, and their corresponding lifestyles, as well as many others and even combinations thereof, are expressed in contemporary literature, cinema, television, and daily life, reflecting the *non-uniformity* allowed and even encouraged by societal norms in the postmodern era. One can also easily detect "*non-stability*" in current prevailing attitudes. For instance, women are no longer expected to remain loyal to any one role or definition throughout their lifetime; it is increasingly acceptable for a woman to change direction, opting for a radical change, without having to justify to herself or others the "logic" of such a move, or show any link between her choice and past modes of behavior. *Non-linearity* is reflected in "arbitrary" explanations for such reinventions of the self as "I needed this," "I followed my heart," or "I felt like it," when opting for new and different patterns.[31]

As exemplified earlier, legitimization for social divergences and pluralistic definitions of the roles of "men," "children," and "the elderly," as well as "the family," are as prevalent as the new latitudes extended by society to determining gender identity and defining interpersonal patterns of life.[32]

The Psychology of the Individual. Another process that expresses the general spirit and structures of postmodernity on the psychological level is the "disintegration of the individual." The traditional perception of the "self" as a *stable* entity, identical to itself, and continuously aspiring to *harmonious linear* expression of its "inner" core (the "true self") is still dominant, even flourishing and enjoying quite a renaissance amongst new age and Humanistic psychology followers. At the same time, a myriad of contradictory perceptions has become equally dominant in contemporary psychological circles, as well as in contemporary films and literature (*non-uniformity*). And so, theories that perceive the "self" as only a (still largely linear and relatively stable) narrative one tells oneself about oneself, that can and should be changed when inappropriate (the "infiltration" of *non-linearity* to the scene),[33] "co-exist" alongside what can be still be branded conventional psychological theory and common-sense views. Opposing theories and views which perceive the term "self" as referring to an illusion stemming from the reification (i.e., turning into an object) of an arbitrary collection of flashes devoid of any *stable* essence and lacking any *linear* developmental continuity flourish side by side. Adherents of this radical postmodernistic view reject any aspiration to harmonious self expression as senseless, illusory, and subjecting the individual to domination by rigid and hence undesirable fiction. These postmodernistic perceptions are not only found in philosophical, psychological, and literary texts or films, but are also becoming the reality of everyday life, side by side with continuingly "resurrected" modern ones.[34]

The Technological Revolution. The advent of computers, multimedia, the Broad Band-based Internet and various mobile gadgets and mobile terminals lead to a par excellence undermining of *linearity*, *uniformity*, and *stability* in our lives.[35] Hypertext is *non-linear* by definition. So is the random collection of televised clips that make up pop programs, talk shows, and news shows.[36] Cable and satellite channels invalidate patterns of *uniform* viewing in a given community or society, as does the Internet. Until two or three decades ago a few national channels exhausted the range of electronic media possibilities available to most citizens of Western societies. Today, due to the Internet, cable television, and the diffusion of third- and fourth-generation mobile "telephones" (which also function, for some years now, as terminals for overall Internet-based connectivity), everyone, everywhere, has access to an infinite number of communication options and entertainment possibilities, devoid of any unifying framework or *uniformity*. Habits such as incessant "zapping" between channels and "surfing" back and forth between electronic "market stalls" or other kinds of web sites, blogs, or forums, as well as the new glorified skill of "multitasking," epitomize the growing "*non-stability*" in postmodern society.[37]

In addition to the five levels mentioned above, all other aspects of our lives operate within the same emerging dominant behavioral patterns: spending leisure time, interpersonal communication, relationships (the postmodern alternative to the modern "love," which side by side with "relationship" still dominates our imagination), consumption, the permanently rising level of divorce, an individual starting a "second" or "third" disconnected "chapter" in their life and accordingly children having two families (in all possible shapes and forms of this term today). All these patterns are painted by the *non-linearity*, *non-uniformity*, and "*non-stability*" brush that resides at the core of the postmodern condition.

The sharp and rapid shift to *non-uniform*, *non-linear*, and "*non-stable*" patterns we are witnessing synchronously in all areas of life are neither anecdotal nor superficial processes. No area remains immune to their impact. No individual can escape their far-reaching effects on all major aspects of one's life. No institution can afford to misread their significance or, even worse, ignore the postmodern upheavals altogether.

Yet all Western education systems seem to have a careless, ostrich-like response to postmodernity. It cannot but be characterized as what psychologists diagnose as total denial, or the loss of any sense or reality. This denial is especially grave due to the vital social and developmental responsibility Western education has in our age of dramatically promising and extremely hazardous changes. Banks, tele-communication companies, or medical institutions (to use three randomly chosen, arbitrary, examples) all went through several waves of radical adaptation to the new human condition. At the same time, the captains of education who should have been the first to reflect, mindfully and rigorously, on the ramifications the new human situation has on the educational endeavor have not even come close to a shred of consciousness of their responsibility.

THE FLOUNDERING OF MODERN EDUCATION SYSTEMS IN POSTMODERNITY

Plus ça change, plus c'est la même chose[38] ("The more it changes, the more it remains the same")

The Obsessive Addiction to Educational Reforms Syndrome

While most researchers of postmodernity, regardless of their professional per-spectives and emphases, will eventually agree with my above characterization of the era, many will disagree with my meta-level typification of postmodernity. The first possible point of disagreement will consist of some observers' classification of the inherent instability of the postmodern condition as a hectic transitory period preceding the stabilization of a new world order. However most "prophets of post-modernity" would agree that postmodernity is a period in its own right that brings to a close the eras of stable paradigms.[39] Another challenge to the classification of postmodernity as essentially different from the preceding Modern era, to which I subscribe, arises from those who see it as accentuation and acceleration of established modern patterns, especially economic ones, and refer to it as "late modernity."[40]

These questions of meta-level characterization, while legitimate and interesting, are immaterial to the crux of the problem as far as this volume is concerned. What *is* important here is to understand the postmodern experience, however it might be defined on the meta-level, and the implications thereof for the educational endeavor and for education systems.

The education system is directly influenced by the postmodern condition, pro-bably more so than any other institution. The simple explanation for that is found in the practical definition of the word "education" as "the shaping of a person in light of a desired model." Society has always defined the meaning of "desired," and subsequently determined the goals of education, as well as its target audience (the students), its content, and its organizational structure. In other words, education systems have traditionally been cast to fit the existing consensual, stable, socio-cultural mold. The "onslaught" of the postmodern storm of our time has destabilized the last version of these molds and has undermined the fundamental parameters of educational endeavors as defined in and by modern society.[41]

As already stated above, education systems should be expected to show the utmost sensitivity to these radical changes, in terms of both their impact on the prevailing (still modern through and through) definitions of their goals, content, methods, and other basic parameters, and hence on their functionality, and of the need to balance off some of their potentially dangerous derivatives. But the Western education systems have yet to show awareness of either the impact of the postmodern revolutions on the functioning ability of the prevailing parameters thereof, or the potential ethical and social dangers postmodernity may pose to them.

Over the past three decades Western education systems' objectives have ceased to be self-evident along side all their other fundamental parameters: education's target audience, content, organizational patterns, and *modus operandi*. Still, during this most intensive and dynamic period in the history of Western civilization, education systems in the developed world have maintained their "business as usual" mode of operation as if nothing fundamental has changed, as if the Western education systems' very *raison d'être* has not been undermined in the least, and as if no new definitions of their social role and mission should be urgently sought after. An endless chain of superficial (and extremely costly in every possible sense) reforms, some recurring every few years, others sharply contradicting earlier or even ongoing reforms in the same systems or schools, are used as band-aids, providing nothing more than escape from the fundamental cognitive dissonance that plagues education systems in the postmodern era, and justification for their lethargic response to the changes in the Western reality. Almost all these reforms have been totally inadequate and failed to meet the needs created by the depth of the crisis.

This need for a radical and holistic fast-paced change is an extraordinary situation, unprecedented in the past "track record" of Western or other education systems and unparalleled by anything to which they previously had to adapt. The closest example would be the rapid adaptation of the diffused modes of education in the traditional agrarian society to the emerging hierarchic and universal public education required by the modern industrial era around the turn of the twentieth century. This was done, as claimed above, by adapting the Platonic curricular model to the mass public education of modernity, whereas in earlier times the model served to educate only the clergy and later the bourgeoisie and sometimes the aristocratic elite. In many countries, the whole transformation took place, at least in terms of laying the foundations (unshaken until today), over two or three decades.[42] Still, in the previous case, core principles of the basic Platonic curricular structures remained unchanged. Today, however, we need to re-invent education from scratch, including the basic educational programs (the term "curricular" might not be appropriate for them anymore since it does not necessarily rely on the *Platonic foundations* of *theoretical studies* with which it has always been equated in the past twenty-five hundred years).

There is also no precedent to the enormity of the change required on all levels in any other present-day system or organization. The private sector, NGOs, and public organizations have all been dramatically changed several times over the last few decades. At the same time, the educational system essentially remained intact. In the last three decades, Western education systems have thus become a natural reserve of the traditional and modern eras that have been pushed aside everywhere else by the postmodern forces. Paraphrasing Kuhn's distinction between "normal" and "anomalous science" of scientific paradigms (the first explaining all known facts, the second incompatible with major "core" facts),[43] Western education systems have become anomalous systems in the sense that they have lost touch with the reality in which they operate.

The anomaly of Western education systems manifests itself in its day-to-day activities. All those involved in education, whether teachers, school principals, parents, students, or scholars and researchers, are keenly aware of the prevailing sense of discontent growing in an overwhelming majority of Western systems, a feeling that educational activities are overshadowed by countless difficulties and that the means to overcome these obstacles have so far eluded everyone.

Difficulties and discontent are reflected in the increase of teachers' "burnout"[44] and the spread of parental and the general public's dissatisfaction. These lead to politicians' repeated promises all over the Western world during at least last three decades to "finally fix" education, ensuring that "no child will be left behind." These in turn lead to huge reforms which require huge investments yet yield no positive results and cause even graver problems, leaving more children further behind in even worse conditions than before the "reform." These difficulties are further reflected in the rising resentment, alienation and the subsequent violence, addictions, substance abuse, and suicide incidents among students.[45] It seems that in North America the students' alienation has recently reached unimaginable expression extremes: a growing number of incidents of one or two students or ex-students who go on a rampage in school and massacre as many of their classmates and teachers as possible, accompanied by a "cult" (which is what it has actually developed into since the well known massacre at Columbine High School)[46] in which thousands of other students celebrate these massacres and admire the perpetrators, regarding them as "heroes," on web sites and in blogs dedicated to these issues.[47]

Over the past few decades, innumerable documents and books, often expressing frustration and ferment, have been written to point out the failures of various countries' education systems and their contexts, and to offer a host of solutions.[48] This body of literature and the deep, chronic dissatisfaction it reflects have generated waves of reforms and change processes and served as catalysts for countless projects thought to herald the "right reform."

These waves of change have often been, and still are, based on either an obtuse definition of the problem or self-contradictory design; on other occasions they simply ran in contradiction to another parallel "change processes" designed to fix the system, thus canceling out each other's effect. Confusion and conflict have many times rocked entire education systems and consumed enormous amounts of resources. Obviously, the miracle cures, or *"panaceas"* as they have often been referred to in education, never fulfilled their promise.

A review of the previous attempts at "salvation" of the education systems will show the configuration of the "structure of the disciplines"-oriented curricula in the 1950s and 60s, then the student-oriented, progressive educational approaches of the 1960s and the early 70s. The mid-1970s and 80s were marked by a variety of equality-oriented reforms, including attempts at creating a large "comprehensive" school, and administrative approaches that emphasized the "accountability" of educators and "effectiveness" of individual schools. By the end of the 1980s and the beginning of the 90s we find programs championing parental choice, decentralization and delegation of authority, "school reconstruction" and "teacher empowerment," which went hand in hand with often contradicting calls to "go back to basics" and establish "universal standards" (I elaborate on this point below).

During the 1980s and 90s, schools all over the Western world were tempted to go through "holistic changes" focusing on "school-based management" and/or "networking" with other schools in various "coalitions" aimed at "restructuring" and enhancing "holistic reforms." As far as didactics are concerned, "constructivist" or "active" methods of teaching-learning and "experiential" methods or approaches based on "authentic problems," "project-based learning," "portfolio-based learning," and "alternative evaluation" methods were ardently preached by academic and professional circles. The above didactic concepts have reflected many similar approaches with different small scale emphases, each of which, like all other educational "gospels" of the last two generations, has had its own "gurus," believers, and circles of followers.

During the very same period, in parallel and quite often together with the above organizational and didactic reforms, all Western education systems were inundated by four tsunami-extent waves of reforms. The expectations accompanying these reforms were even higher than their astronomical costs. I refer here to the four waves of computerization: the first in the early 1980s, the second during the mid- to late-1980s, the third in the mid- to late-1990s, and the fourth, in the last few years, with the widespread advent of the Internet that swept over all education systems in the West. Each wave was more "promising" and more costly than its predecessor. The first focused on the "introduction of computers to schools," usually meaning special computing laboratories into which the pupils were herded once or twice a week in order to be able "to work individually with computers" in a process (allegedly) customized to individual rhythms, which was supposed to solve all learning problems. In the wake of the failure of this wave, the second, the "introduction of computers to the classroom," relied on a rationale directly opposed to that of its predecessor and was expected to address all learning problems by (allegedly) integrating ICT with the daily activities of teaching and learning. The third wave introduced CD-ROMs and multimedia to school computers; this again was expected to solve all learning problems by making learning more interactive and attractive. Later this was extended by the fourth wave, the panacea of "connecting every classroom to the Internet" celebrated by almost all Western leaders and ministers of education since President Clinton.[49]

President Clinton seemed to believe or wanted his electorate to believe, as did all other Western leaders, that the Internet would bring about the progress and "salvation" that education systems had been seeking. He, like almost everybody else in the West, associated computers and the Internet with "progress" and believed progress to be the solution to all human problems, including educational ones, a strong modern atavism in a postmodern era.

After the failure of endless ICT-based projects in the previous two decades, this last wave was expected, like others before it, to remove the obstinate problems "once and for all." Unfortunately, the huge public expenditure to connect every school, classroom, and student to the Internet, yielded nothing more than a trivial default scenario, one which most children and adults in the West reached without any public funding or sanction. In other words, nothing was achieved. Today, the vast majority of students in the West are connected to the Internet, simply because they live in the digital era and speak its language, just as they were connected to electricity and running water in the modern era. This dramatic process has taken place without any relation to formal education and in spite of schools' persistent failure to adapt themselves to the digital era. Furthermore, as has now been revealed, this connection in and of itself is irrelevant to the solution to any educational or learning-oriented problems. In fact, computerization has created some horrendous problems of its own. For example, it is difficult to imagine how the Columbine massacre could have created youth cults in a different state of affairs, one in which not "every child is connected to the Internet."[50]

It seems that baseless, or more accurately although less polite, mindless, optimism does not allow the facts of our reality to have any impact on educational thinking and planning. We are now witnessing what might be a fifth wave, which is nothing more than an improved version of previous attempts. At the basis of this wave lies, for example, the "*panacea*" of a simple one hundred dollar terminal, wirelessly connecting any student on the globe to the Internet, a "revolution" led by the MIT ICT "guru" Nicholas Negroponte. This goes hand in hand with the widespread myth that small-scale wireless terminals, now becoming so prevalent, will bring about salvation.[51] It is just another symptom of the conditioned inclination to perceive any "new generation" ICT gadget on the market as the key to saving education. Based on recurring past failures and the essential inability of the modern system to function in a postmodern reality, I am going to dare to make an extremely well founded prediction that this wave is doomed, like its predecessors before it, to complete failure in addressing the fundamental weakness of education systems as theoretically analyzed generally in this chapter and more specifically in the next four.

While teachers struggled with ever-changing organizational, didactic, and technological panaceas, often contradicting each other and themselves, they also had to somehow manage, or pretend to be managing, another awesome reformist trend. This set of reforms was clearly ideologically oriented. In the 1980s, in the wake of the above failures, a new battle cry to go "back to basics" began echoing in the halls of education ministries and political discourse. It emanated first from dominant conservative quarters in Britain under Prime Minister Thatcher (1979–90) and in the USA under President Reagan (1981–89). They demanded that all educational institutions meet a scale of "universal standards" (based on quantifiable knowledge and achievement-oriented) which contradicted many of the previously mentioned reforms.[52] In many countries these conservative policies are still in force, together with many of contradictory vestiges of the earlier (usually, but not necessarily) more ideologically progressive reforms.

We have enough experience with the "back to basics" conservative gospel and the categorical credo of universal quantifiable standards to argue that there is "nothing new under the sun." Like all the previous reforms, the conservative reforms failed to live up to their promised outcome. They did however add new problems such as large-scale cheating on national exams, a lack of validity of national tests, and so on.[53]

As if the mass of senseless "fusions" of contradictory reforms the school teachers and students had to deal with was not enough, the general or "holistic" reforms of those troubled decades were accompanied by an endless number of less pretentious, more specific, but certainly not more coherent reforms. Such reforms highlighted, among other things, an extremely large array of "small-scale fixes" to more specific prevalent educational problems, ignoring the fact that while the building is crumbling down there is not much sense in redecorating the living room. To give only few examples from the endless list of such "remedies": improving methods of literacy or science teaching; correcting students' "intuitive" understanding of concepts that run counter to scientific ones; integration of female students into math or science courses; inclusion of "ability challenged" pupils into regular classes; development and implementation of an endless series of methods to fight school violence and addiction among young people; introduction of different teacher training methods; the application to schools of evaluation and quality control methods borrowed from general organizational theory and practice (TQM was the most popular for a number of years).[54] The list of such specific reforms goes on enough to fill a whole chapter. But in almost all cases, the endless series of specific reforms attacking schools in most Western societies, together with the more pretentious contradictory ones adopted at great cost to the overall system, did not deliver the goods.[55]

Together with the never ending enthusiasm for new, costlier, reforms that have now become the obvious core of the academic, practical, and political discourse on education, over the past two decades another, higher level, discourse devoted to dissecting the dismal performance of the changes and reforms that swept over the system developed. This meta-level discourse mainly developed in narrow academic circles, attempting to explain away the past failures while throwing cold water on the enthusiasm of the various would-be reformers.[56]

Still the aforementioned failure never bothered the politicians fixing and re-fixing education, or the herds of professionals and administrators following their declarations. All this "hubbub" went on without anyone pausing to reconsider the obsessive addiction Western education systems in the post-1960s period had to "changes," "reforms," "restructuring," "innovation," and "advanced projects." It seems that all these hectic, hysterical, restless, and mindless change-oriented acti-vities mainly reflected (and still reflect) the psychological and social need of the professionals and decision makers involved to deal with their cognitive dissonance and to market themselves and their "endeavors" to society.

This dissonance continues to beset educators, administrators, and decision makers who are aware of the growing functional difficulties and increasing meaninglessness of their work. They are also mostly cognizant of their complete lack of any clear, meaningful, comprehensive alternative, and of the hopelessness of finding a saving grace in the "gospels" of the last two generations that have misleadingly posed as alternative solutions, such as "parental choice," "school based management," "national standards," the forming of "networks" or "coalitions" of schools, "systemic change," "holistic change," "teacher empowerment," "communities of practice," "constructivist teaching," or the use of "alternative evaluation methods." Focusing on "effective schools," "accountability," "quality control," "reflective teaching," "critical teaching," and "teaching for understanding"—to mention a few more of those flawed, conflicting "panaceas" designed to address all possible aspects of the schools' secondary structures and activities yet never deal with the fundamentals that must be radically rethought—has therefore failed to deliver the promised cure. Given the ever more difficult task of having to market an inherently counterproductive system to society as "advanced" and successful, politicians, administrators, and school principals have desperately been "grasping at the straws" of these endless "educational reforms."[57] However, this "reforms addiction" merely exacerbated the problems that the reforms were designed to solve.

Thus, we have reached the totally absurd situation, which almost everyone seems to believe to be a normal state of affairs, in which entire education systems in the West have increasingly succumbed to *the obsessive addiction to educational change* syndrome.

This reforms-oriented obsession has turned into a second level of the deep-rooted problem which aggravates the current crisis, a crisis which was acute enough before this. Since these do not really help correct the system, but rather just mess it up further, these voodoo remedies create a norm of "double talk" and hypocrisy. Teachers and administrators have learnt, in the last generation, to use the postmodern jargon and pretend to implement changes imported from the outside world. However, since the schools' essentially modern structure prevents any actual implementation thereof, and since school workers know that tomorrow there will be another (often opposed) change, they revert to emptying the jargon of any true meaning by using postmodern "in" "reforms-oriented" language to describe the "good old" modern routines with which they are well familiar.

The damages of this reality are enormous. On the organizational level, this behavior prevents the system from reaching any semblance of stable function through which the school can contribute to society. Much more frighteningly, this also has a serious psychological and social impact. Young people are being raised in many Western societies today in surrealistic environments which do not make any sense to them and which are dominated by "double talk" and hypocrisy. They absorb several tacit yet extremely powerful messages (usually the hidden message reflects the constitutional foundation of the system's current educationally significant mode of functioning): that life is absurd or devoid of any meaning or that language is empty and does not have any clear reference (as postmodernistic thinkers have been wrongly claiming for the last several decades now). Many Western systems nowadays are guilty of this massacre of the inner drive for meaning, a drive basic in both its senses (the existential and the semantic) to anything good in human beings.

The Unrecognized Need to Re-invent Education

The dominant mood in "canonical" literature on education and educational change presupposes (usually tacitly so) the prevailing Platonic-modern underlying infrastructure, upon which most educational activity is based, to be relevant and valid in this day-and-age. According to conventional wisdom, the system is "fine," there are just "kinks" to be ironed out, one or a few factors at most require mending for the entire machine to function perfectly. The research and publications in these contexts, as well as all the discourse levels or reforms which bewail the failures of education systems, propose sweeping or partial reforms, and conduct post-mortems on the failed series of reform waves just to propose another one. They are all tainted by the same fundamental flaw: they are conducted within the existing, outdated, modern-Platonic paradigm of educational thought and action. Even when sweeping reform prophets use the now outworn terms "paradigm shift" or "second-order changes" almost all of them do so within the prevailing modern paradigm. Any "paradigm" they purport to change is usually a secondary aspect in the over-riding, all-powerful modern paradigm, based on the twenty-five-hundred-year-old Platonic paradigm which almost all heralds of school change take to be given and obvious.[58]

The malady, however, is much wider and deeper in its scope and, as in any case of obsessive addiction, used to cover an escape from fundamental problem(s), it will be fatal if it is not recognized and soon. We are dealing with a lethal level of growing disparity between the most basic assumptions of the existing education paradigm, a paradigm designed and developed mainly in the modern era built on the Platonic curricular foundations, and the postmodern reality that is engulfing it, quickly rendering it irrelevant, a memorial to times long (or rather recently but rapidly) gone. The various waves of reforms, as well as their post-mortem analyses, are like desperate attempts to improve a horse-drawn carriage after the invention of the automobile by replacing horseshoes with wheels to keep pace with the times.

As things stand, members of the educational community are expected to function in an impossible and intolerable situation characterized, among other things, by:
- Teachers who are entrusted with performing an authoritative role, and are expected to "keep the class in check," while the prevailing social and organizational cultures no longer provide them with even the most minimal backing for that authority, unlike their modern and traditional predecessors who enjoyed very "generous" support from the same structures;
- An ongoing teaching of scientific disciplines-oriented subject matters which no longer have any meaning to either teachers or students. This is the case because curricula are often at odds with students' (and many teachers')

practical or psychological needs, and contrary to the dictates of the dominant relativistic culture which lies "beyond the classroom door," where utilitarian values do not ascribe any importance to theoretical study for its own sake;

- A learning environment saturated, as a result of the above, with incessant changes of the approaches and methods used within it, in which teachers and students are constantly required to adjust and readjust themselves to a steady stream of "updated" didactic views and methodologies;
- Schools inundated with scores of "projects," "interventions," "processes of change," "reforms," and "restructurings" that, in many cases, do not relate to each other, and are frequently contradictory of one another. This exacts a tremendous toll in wasted energy, attention, time, and money, while the end product often amounts to no more than "much ado about nothing";
- Feverish activity bordering on hysteria, in which teachers, administrators, and students are "locked," always dealing with emergency situations and a constant fear of "non-compliance with requirements," "standards," or "non-provision of material";
- Schools and teachers which are expected to comply with conflicting demands; the contradictory, shifting, and confused desires of many different target audiences: the state, parents, the community, young people, and experts;
- A permanent blurring of the meaning of words, as all too often one can find no clear connection between words and deeds. In fact there is almost no expectation anymore for words to have a clear and stable meaning.

Such impossible circumstances are neither natural to the educational context nor are they necessary. They did not characterize education systems in the past, not even in the recent past (at least not until the end of the 1950s). They are symptomatic of a deeply dysfunctional system which seeks to operate despite the growing schism between school life and life realities, leading to organizational confusion that generates tremendous mental stress among all those "caught up within the system." Still, in most cases, administrators, teachers, pupils, and parents alike find it hard to comprehend both the significance of the schism and the great speed at which it is expanding, and its cognitive and organizational implications.

Thus, we must start with a diagnosis which will allow us to locate the real source of the problem, and then determine its scope. Only afterwards can we hope to offer recommendations for appropriate action. The fact is that up until now almost all institutionalized educational communities in the West have been obstinately "looking in the wrong place."

Rectifying the situation requires recognition of two key points:

- The modern Western education systems are fast becoming anomalous due to the rapid erosion of the functionality, and hence the meaningfulness of the dominant modern-Platonic definitions of the basic parameters still characterizing them in the postmodern era.
- Educational communities (including most "school change" professional communities) are not cognizant, or successfully suppress conscious cognition, of the depth and vastness of the anomaly. They behave as if the system is

still normal and secondary adjustments to it will suffice to "fix the problem." Or, to put things in Kuhn's terms again, the majority of those operating at all levels are still functioning as solvers of secondary "riddles" (or small-scale problems) *within the framework of an existing paradigm*. Unfortunately, to date there is no serious research seeking to formulate an *alternative paradigm* in spite of frequent declarations to the contrary.[59]

The Proverbial School as an Anomalous Organization

Let me now elaborate on and clarify the claims made in the two previous sub-sections.[60] School systems, like any organization, can be characterized using six general parameters:

- **Goals.** This parameter defines the achievements to which the organization aspires, or the value(s) it wishes to produce.
- **Content.** This parameter indicates the types of activities the organization carries out for the sake of producing the above value(s).
- **Organizational Structure.** This parameter characterizes the organization in terms of management structure, decision making processes, and patterns of communication.
- **Target audience.** This parameter defines the "customer base" of the organization, or who the organization perceives itself to be serving.
- **Target Audience's Mobilization.** This parameter indicates how the organizations' administrators believe they can recruit consumers for its product(s) or service(s).
- *Modus operandi.* This parameter defines the methods employed by the organization to achieve its goals in the framework of the specific definitions of all other parameters.

The parameters are not of equal importance. Each organization possesses core or *essential parameters*, parameters whose prevailing definitions cannot be conceived of as possible objects of modification by those operating within the organization or those in need of its goods or services. In doing so, the organization would cease to be perceived by them as the "same organization." All others are *secondary parameters*, parameters whose definitions can be modified without the organization consequently losing its essence, or conceived to be "changing altogether." As in many dichotomous distinctions, we are speaking of a continuum in which an organization's objectives usually constitute an essential parameter and the *modus operandi* is usually perceived to be a secondary parameter. The rest of the parameters can be assigned various values along the continuum (the value assigned is mostly a culturally dependent factor).

If we follow the above distinction we can differentiate between the two types of problems with which organizations or institutions contend: first-order problems and problems of the second order. *First-order problems* are those that can successfully be solved by modifying the existing definitions of secondary parameters within the context of unaltered definitions of essential parameters. Usually, altering some aspect of the *modus operandi* or some aspects in the organizational structure will solve first-order problems. *Second-order problems* can only be solved by redefining essential parameters. Here, again, we find a continuum: at one end we have first-order problems par excellence, and at the other, second-order problems par excellence; in between we can find problems in varying degrees of proximity to either category.[61]

A typical first-order problem can be solved within the existing definition of the essential parameters. Take for example the decrease in the number of products a factory produces resulting from the wear and tear of its equipment. The problem will remain first-order as long as it can be addressed simply by repairing the old malfunctioning machinery, changing some productions modes to compensate for the dysfunctioning old machinery or (taking more drastic action but still within prevailing definitions of the essential parameters) completely reorganizing the means of production so as to bypass the old equipment and take advantage of newer lines of production.

A second-order problem requires a second-order solution, or the changing of definitions of the essential parameters of the organization and hence a leap into a new organization, or even a non-organizational context all together. Thus, for example, returning to the factory scenario, a second-order problem will arise if the problem of decreasing production cannot be solved by any first-order solutions along the lines discussed above. Such a state of affairs may be due to declining profitability of its specialized product stemming from external circumstances. In this case, a second-order solution might mean stopping production altogether and importing the end-product instead. If such a move is economically undesirable, then selling the factory and investing the money in the stock market can be considered.

Let us take now a third step and move on to the definitions of "normal" and "anomalous" systems I used above. According to Kuhn's analysis of scientific revolutions, a crisis will develop in a dominant scientific paradigm, or "normal" science, when a major "anomaly in the fit between theory and nature" develops.[62] Such a crisis renders the discipline or paradigm in question "anomalous," eventually leading to the formation of an alternative paradigm.

Kuhn's concept of "anomalous" vs. "normal" can be used outside the scientific context and seems well suited to typifying organizations: an *anomalous organization* would be one exhibiting a deviation in compatibility of one or more of the prevailing definitions of the organization's essential parameters from the reality in which it operates. Such an anomaly leads to situations in which a first-order solution will not suffice. For example, let us say that in the above factory the decrease in production does not stem from defective or antiquated production equipment but from a decrease in demand resulting from much cheaper imports from India or China, or from the fact that the product itself has become obsolete, like typewriters in the era of "word processing."

In this case the firm has become anomalous, or the chasm between it and the rapidly emerging reality has become too large to be bridged by a first-order solution. A redefinition of (at the very least one) essential parameter, the aim of the organization or the nature of its business, is required. Moving from production to the import business (in the case of cheaper products in the market) or reinvesting capital into computer production or, in a more extreme case, in the real estate business (in case of an obsolete product) are three radical second-order changes. These processes radically change everything the firm does, not only the aim of the firm but also the nature or content of its activities, its organizational structure and, in the third case, actually abolish the firm.

By contrast, as long as first-order solutions remain effective, the firm could be termed a normal organization, that is, one still in tune with reality. It does not require second-order solutions but is able to solve its problems using relatively modest first-order changes.

Let us now return to the prevailing education systems. This larger application of Kuhn's definitions enables us to say that present-day education systems are *anomalous organizations* that suffer from a sharp and widening dissonance between them and the reality within which they operate, not unlike the typewriter manufacturing example given above.

An Unrecognized Anomaly

Educational organizations continue to cling to the modern definitions of their six parameters. These definitions, which have lost all functionality, and therefore all meaning, in the postmodern age, create the increasing disharmony in education systems all over the Western world which Kuhn describes as a disharmony stemming from an "anomalous paradigm." Yet, despite mounting difficulties in their performance, the organizations' anomaly goes unrecognized, as it is extremely well hidden by the *obsessive addiction to the ever-recurring-change* syndrome.

This state of affairs in which the education community is oblivious to its true condition is parallel to the stage in the development and demise of scientific paradigms, a stage Kuhn refers to as the "Crisis" stage. Kuhn's crisis is typified by:

- The existence of "pronounced professional insecurity"[63] among scientists, stemming from the continuing "failure of normal science to solve its riddles properly."[64]
- Despite the insecurity, the majority of scientists continue to work within the existing paradigms for lack of a satisfactory alternative: "once it has achieved the status of paradigm, a scientific theory is declared invalid only if an alternate candidate is available to take its place."[65]

The increasing insecurity and discontent among educators and decision makers since the 1970s stems from the functional difficulties at all levels which I already indicated, as well as from the continuing failure of various reforms to make any meaningful improvements. This phenomenon was best articulated by the development of a whole branch of literature bemoaning the systems' inexorable decline as described in the above sections,[66] as well as the well documented phenomenon known as "the predictable failure of educational reform,"[67] "tinkering towards utopia,"[68] or the "myths of school self-renewal."[69] In spite of these signs of impending collapse due to the irrelevance of education systems in the prevailing reality, the majority of those involved with the systems continue to assume that the existing modern definitions of the fundamental parameters of education are still valid and functioning. The aforementioned syndrome of obsessive addiction to recurring and repeating change processes, largely facilitated by the fact that the system's clientele is a captive audience (a point elaborated upon below), is probably the main mechanism which has allowed distorted perceptions of reality to prevail for so long.

In some ways, the present situation in education seems to follow the pattern of East European regimes which failed to adjust their essential parameters to the new realities following the postmodern revolutions. The spread of relativism and the consequent "end of ideology" revolution accompanied by the ICT revolution introduced "the wonders of the Western lifestyle" to most living rooms in Eastern Europe. Since the regimes continued to function in this new postmodern reality as they had functioned in the old modern one, their failure to adapt to changing times resulted in their complete and very sudden demise.

It is not easy to criticize educators for a lack of cognizance of the system's anomaly. First, as Kuhn noted in his examination of how scientific revolutions take place, one does not usually abandon a dominant paradigm as faulty and dysfunctional, as it might be, as long as there is no "safe alternative." While there are many fragmentary signs of a new mindset,[70] a new, integrated, alternative paradigm has yet to crystallize to the point of constituting a viable option to the current one.

Another "attenuating factor" consists of the fact that the current educational paradigm's loss of meaning and function hit the education system with unprecedented, mind-boggling speed. The process of change that separated a nomadic hunter-gatherer's existence from a traditional-agricultural society occurred over many hundreds of thousands of years and the shift from a traditional to a modern society that peaked in the second half of the twentieth century took several hundreds of years to complete. Yet, the revolution that gave birth to the first postmodern generation rampaged onto the scene in only two decades (from the end of the 1960s to somewhere in the 80s), and we are now already deep into the second postmodern generation, much "crazier" (from a modern perspective) than the first one! No wonder, then, that Western education systems find themselves lacking any coherent sense of direction without a compass to help them find their way: their prevailing instruments and other navigation aids were designed for a world whose coordinates have all very suddenly disappeared.

In addition to a lack of awareness of the problem at hand, education systems in all Western societies enjoy an at least practically, and in most cases legally, enforced monopoly on the education market. This fact in turn cannot but considerably reduce their incentive to engage in the extremely demanding revolution, even if their captains were aware of it. Such a revolution may in fact be perceived by many of them as a threat to their jobs and way of life. Many parents, educators, principals, administrators, and academics in the field may very well not be able to cope with the new educational reality, just as many bureaucrats of the ancient Marxist regimes could not cope with free market economy, or coach drivers could not adapt to the world of the "horseless carriage" later known as the "automobile."

In other words, education systems enjoy an exclusiveness, guaranteed and pro-tected by laws and social arrangements, that forces a large part of the population to daily consume its products for twelve or thirteen years.[71] By "forced" I refer not only to the legal enforcement of most of the twelve- or thirteen-year educational process on all individuals belonging to a certain age range, but also to the fact that in many Western countries even the choice of a specific school is still dictated by the public systems. By "monopoly" I refer to the fact that within the above double enforcement in most countries there is practically, and often legally, only one possible model of education, even when I include private schools in the picture. This single model is the Platonic educational process based on the learning of the "truth bearing" scientific disciplines as adapted a century or more ago to the (then) new, modern circumstances.

Thus, on one hand we have this exceptional combination of an enforced mono-poly, while on the other enormous cognitive and emotional obstacles, most importantly the high chances that one may be jeopardizing his or her livelihood, stand in the way of anyone who wishes to update the current system and re-invent education to befit postmodern reality. It is possible to understand why in such a situation policy makers, educators, principals, and academics lack any *real* moti-vation to respond in an appropriate manner to the crisis at hand. Such a situation therefore guarantees obstinate denial of the true reality and obsession with "escape mechanisms" that can mask the cognitive and emotive dissonances the education system inevitably faces today.

Imagine a company that manufactured carriages during the very first years of the twentieth century, enjoying a three layered enforced monopoly similar to that of the education system in today's Western society. Not only would the law of the land prohibit any competition from rival companies offering a similar or different method of transportation (canal navigation, for example), but it would also force any citizen in a certain age range to travel with the protected company a certain distance, in very specific paths, dictated by law, each day (such a law may be justified by arguing that touring in nature or visiting other cities contribute to citizens' health, personality enrichment, and development).

Now imagine that the company's drivers and administrators hear rumors about the development of "horseless carriages." They also hear that in other countries the use of this new means of transportation is spreading quickly. Would they have any real motivation to consider adapting to the new way, knowing that some, probably many, of them will not be able to drive the new "carriages"? Why change, if their enforced monopoly can continue forever? To assume there would be such a motive goes against everything we know about human nature. The same principle holds for most policy makers, teachers, and administrators working in the prevailing anachronistic education system.

Nietzsche envisioned postmodernity in terms of its sudden conceptual and cultural impact:

This tremendous event, is still on the road and is wandering; it has not yet reached the ears of men. Thunder and lightning need time; the light of the stars needs time; deeds, though done, still require time to be seen and heard.[72]

Indeed, due to the above, very peculiar, situation, the postmodern revolution is still beyond the ken of almost all educators, as well as most professionals and academics dealing with education.

One increasingly encounters feelings that "something is wrong," "it's not working," and that "things can't go on like this much longer." But in the quest for a solution, educators concentrate on first level changes in their work methods and the systems' organizational structures, all within the framework of the essential existing parameters.[73] In other words, they seek first-order solutions to second-order problems, rather than daring to "think outside of the box" which is exactly what the prevailing education systems, shocked by this impending second-order calamity, need.

THE ANOMALY HYPOTHESIS AND ITS TWO SUBSTANTIATION STRATEGIES

A hypothetical diagnosis can be substantiated by indirect empirical and/or direct theoretical means. The *indirect empirical substantiation* strategy consists of looking for predictable corroborations (or refutations) of the hypothesis. That is, the rational individual or scientist first predicts concrete signs that would be expected to emerge if the hypothesis is true. He or she then ventures to discover if such signs are indeed to be found and if they are developing as predicted by the hypothesis. As long as these predictions are corroborated by reality, the hypothesis from which they stemmed can be held as true. Once they are refuted, he or she has to start suspecting the validity of the hypothesis.

The *direct theoretical substantiation* strategy consists, on the other hand, of a direct theoretical analysis that shows that the discussed hypothesis is a necessary consequence of a valid argument claimed to rely on true premises or, in other words, a "sound argument."

Going back to the factory example, indirect empirical corroboration of the hypothesis concerning the factory's emerging anomaly will show that while consumption of its product has been gradually decreasing over (say) the last three years, the overall consumption of the kind of product it is producing has (at least) remained steady and the gap between the past and present level of consumption is filled by cheaper imports of the same product (assuming that the factory is the only producer of this product in the local market).

Direct theoretical substantiation will be achieved through a large-scale macro analysis of the major relevant economic trends leading to the conclusion that a meaningful and probably long-term and sustainable gap has been opened up between the relevant cost of labor and raw materials in certain developing countries and similar costs in the firm's location (assuming an open global market).

The theoretical analysis relies on accepted macro-economic theories and is formed from assumptions made about past and future macro-economic trends. Although such an analysis cannot be directly checked, it should not be discarded out of hand, as it does have an enormous explicatory power in showing that the directly observed patterns of market behaviors are not arbitrary, but make sense or stem from a state of affairs that is understandable. Such an understanding can be used for further predictions and mindful, planned, corrective strategic activity. The more detailed and reliable the direct theoretical substantiation and indirect empirical predictions are, and the more we find empirical corroborations for these predictions, the more we have "the right" to stick to the relevant hypothesis, treat it as true, and behave accordingly.

Direct theoretical corroboration of the above "anomaly hypothesis," a hypothesis concerning the growing anomaly of Western education systems, will include:

- Analyzing suppositions basic to the definitions of essential parameters in prevailing education systems.
- Analyzing ongoing revolutions which characterize the postmodern reality.
- Demonstrating, through detailed comparison, that the prevailing definitions are losing their justification, meaning, and functionality in the context defined by the above revolutions.

This theoretical substantiation of the anomaly hypothesis is complex, mediated by relevant theories and assumptions (that must be well grounded) about the past, present, and the future of many aspects of the human situation. However, at the same time the anomaly hypothesis' predictions can be, quite easily, evaluated directly and empirically.

What kind of predictions should one draw from the anomaly hypothesis concerning prevailing education systems? In order to answer this question let us start with two "*Gedanken* experiments."[74] Imagine a Japanese *Noh* Theater performing in front of a Japanese audience who are deeply versed in the culture and tradition of the theater and understand, appreciate, and enjoy any gesture made on the stage. Imagine also that some "evil genius" (a concept formulated by Descartes for other kinds of thinking experiments) plays a trick and, unseen by the actors, gradually replaces the Japanese audience in the dark theater hall with Western spectators who have no knowledge of *Noh*, Japanese culture, or language. What consequences can we predict?

I suppose it is a safe bet to predict that the actors will gradually begin to sense a meaningful change in audience response, from interest and excitement to boredom and alienation. These will be expressed first by the sounds of creaking chairs, yawns, whispering, then rising to the level of insulting yells directed towards the stage. As things grow worse, some spectators might throw soft objects like eggs and tomatoes at the stage, and others will leave.

Now imagine a situation in which the spectators are a captive audience forced to stay in the theater for several hours. It would not take long for higher levels of frustration to develop, resulting in growing levels of violence directed first at the actors and theater. Next, as the levels of frustration and aggression rise, the violent feelings would increase. And finally, if there were no escape from the theater, individuals in the audience might exhibit physical aggression towards the actors and each other; they may even get to a point where they turn the aggression on themselves. Predictably, some *Noh* actors would leave the theater, seeing no point in continuing to entertain under such absurd conditions. However, others, forced to stay because of the salary they are paid by the theater, will eventually feel heightened frustration, alienation, fatigue, and various psychosomatic illnesses that will be characterized by experts as "professional burnout."

Let us now take a third step and imagine that the captive Western audience is compelled to watch not one, but an endless chain of Noh performances during all their working hours for several years. What in the previous example was just a transient phenomenon, has now become a way of life which cannot but create a deeply rooted set of emotional, cognitive, and behavioral patterns. Frustration and aggression become embedded in the spectators' personalities, leading them to display increasing levels of violence which gradually and steadily lead to a hostile atmosphere that eventually becomes the "natural aspect" of the theater environment.

In response to some primary levels of curiosity, some audience members may have initially attempted to make sense of what they perceive as strange, incomprehensible, repetitive singing and the mechanical, monotonous, and minuscule movements performed on stage. However, this curiosity would eventually dissipate, and, if the audience were asked periodically what is taking place, their ability to answer would dramatically decrease with time as the boredom level rises, until the audience's very restricted ability to follow the plot in an unknown language vanishes altogether.

Given all these insurmountable problems, the actors, those who choose to stay despite the circumstances, will constantly find themselves under psychological pressure and physical threat from the alienated audience, and in an aggressive atmosphere. They will suffer from increasing levels of "professional burnout," and will complain, take sick leave, become apathetic, show fatigue, and take solace in criticizing the audience on a permanent basis.

Experts called in to handle this myriad of problems the audience and actors are suffering from are likely to suggest various kinds of small, specific remedies such as, for instance, empowerment workshops, management or accountability methods, and constructive teaching methods, to name but a few of the infinite arsenal of contradicting "wonder drugs" experts like brandishing nowadays.

Tenure-less postmodern academics who can barely hold on to their shaky positions by tediously correcting ten-page papers in well trodden paths (otherwise the papers will not be published) and writing endless proposals for mobilizing "external funding" aimed to please the sources of such funding, necessarily have tunnel vision. They can never see the horizon, and have neither the energy nor the motivation to try to hypothesize about it.

Thus, a youth violence expert will not attempt to deal with addiction (since he or she "lacks the required expertise") or even dropping math grades (since it is "outside her or his scope"). It will never occur to an expert called to deal with dropping math grades to deal with the problematic history grades at the same time, since "she or he knows nothing about history and the methodology of its teaching," not to mention teacher burnout (because "these are all together different subjects") and so on and so forth.

Thus all the remedies suggested by the experts will necessarily be worse than useless. The symptoms will just keep mounting and the damage to the hall, stage, and the even the building itself will require constant and frequent repair. Various programs to fight the alcoholism, drug abuse, and aggression, courtesy of the quickly expanding groups of experts who make their living off "handling" these problems, will have to be constantly established and extended but again, in vain.

As long as the root causes of these syndromes are not attended to, the programs will fail and more "systemic," and therefore more expensive, reforms will be required. These reforms might include restructuring the theater to lessen the space between the stage and the seating in the hope that this will reduce alienation between the actors and the audience. Or alternatively, more "hard-nosed" experts may suggest distancing the stage from the audience in order to defend the actors, or to hire armed guards to search for weapons, drugs, and/or alcohol, or the installation of metal detectors to find weapons that the audience may be carrying. They may also advocate the administration of "productive punishments" to those caught carrying weapons or use "positive reinforcement" devices for those who do not. All such measures will exacerbate the growing budgetary problems, which in turn lead to further deterioration of the theater's physical condition and the mental crisis of those caught in it. And so the cycle of causes and effects is accelerated for ever.

Now we move on to our second thought experiment. Let us imagine a Muslim *madrasa* in a Pakistani provincial town, or an Orthodox Jewish *cheder* in Brooklyn, or an Amish one-room school in Pennsylvania. Imagine also that these schools are "spirited away" by our hyperactive "evil genius" (trying to replicate his *Noh* success) to a secular, upper middle-class community in Santa Monica, California. In order to have "real fun" the evil genius would leave intact the curriculum, didactics, books, and other teaching aids typical of religious schools, as well as the basic behavioral norms, building, and even the religious inscriptions on the walls. However, the teachers and the students would be local.

It is not difficult to predict what would happen. Referring to the first example, the Muslim case, the teachers who have miraculously learned the Islamic texts by heart have no idea what they are saying, or why, and the students have even less of an idea about what they are being taught. When the school Muezzin calls the believers to prayers and they are asked to kneel on the carpets, all the students can do is giggle—at least on the first day. But if this routine went on for weeks, months, and years, and if students were legally held captive and the teachers who stay on did so mainly for their paychecks, we would begin to see the same phenomena as in the *Noh* Theater.

We have finally closed the circle. As far as the indirect empirical substantiation is concerned, I can now draw conclusions from the thought experiments to the prevailing education systems. Human beings, when forced into absurd or meaning-less situations for a long time, will always behave the same: feelings of senselessness or absurdity will lead to frustration, which will in turn develop into various forms of aggression, or feelings of anxiety or apathy. Those feelings will eventually be vented out through any escape mechanisms available.[75] Those who perform in front of such an audience, or teach it, become exhausted. Many of them leave, and many of those who stay suffer from what is characterized as "burnout."

If the anomaly hypothesis is correct, the symptoms charactering the two example audiences captured in a senseless long-term situation will manifest themselves in prevailing education systems all over the postmodern Western world, and they will increase as the anomaly increases. In other words, a Western audience held *ad nauseam* in *Noh* Theater or secular middle class students caught for many years in a religious school will lead to boredom, alienation, frustration, and aggression being built into their personalities. To return to the subject at hand, postmodern young people, trapped for many years in a modern school, will probably display exactly the same symptoms, since they find themselves in exactly the same kind of situation: long-term captivity in a framework whose language, requirements, and basic structures are meaningless to the captive audience. This is the essence of the anomaly hypothesis (I will further elaborate and substantiate its details in the next four chapters).

Is there any doubt that all the relevant symptoms can be found in abundance around us, and are magnified as the anomaly becomes evermore acute? This, I suppose, is a rhetorical question. Almost all Western societies are grappling to one extent or another with all or some of the following educational problems (most of which were already mentioned above), and increasingly so:

- Growing indications of heightened feelings of alienation among students.
- Rising levels of depression and anxiety among young people.
- An exponential increase in violence among youth. This aggression is directed towards the school, teachers, "friends," themselves, and other available targets. Most recently school massacres "inspired" by the "Columbine" incident turned into a cult that is rapidly gaining in popularity and admirers, becoming a model for students all over North America and beyond.
- Growing incidence of alcohol abuse among young people.
- Rising levels of substance abuse.
- Rising levels of suicide and suicide attempts among young people.[76]
- Poor and deteriorating scholastic achievement, as well as levels of literacy and numeracy in many Western countries.[77]
- Abject failure to achieve overall societal objectives such as social integration and equality.
- Repeated failures of reforms, change processes, and other long- and short-term "fixes" to the problems.
- Increasing budgetary problems.
- Rise in teacher burnout and dropout, exceeding in most instances the burnout levels of extremely demanding and stressful professions like law enforcement, medicine, and the like.[78]

The last point requires a moment of reflection. The most reasonable explanation for this claim is very meaningful for corroborating the anomaly hypothesis. While law enforcement officers and medical staff know the value of their work for the individuals they serve or for society at large, the educationalists' hardships are steadily growing, while the meaning or value of the work they do for their students or for society are at best quite vague *in their own eyes*. They do not have the comfort of knowing that they supply other individuals with real values like security, better health or longer life, or anything that comes close to such clarity concerning the "good" they produce. The hardships they endure, as far as their professional self perception is concerned, are meaningless to one extent or other. Furthermore, in most Western societies they are unrewarded economically and socially, perhaps because those societies do not understand their contribution and cannot exactly clarify what it consists of, except for supplying babysitting services for young kids.

What is meaningful for the indirect empirical corroboration of the anomaly hypothesis in this explanation is the claim that many educators do not see much value or meaning in their work. The anomaly hypothesis explains the burnout and dropout processes not by the general cognitive blindness of educators, but rather by the lack of anything that can be seen. In other words, they do not produce much value, and therefore enjoy no job satisfaction that can compensate for the hardships they undergo. Other's in demanding positions, such as police officers, doctors, and nurses, whose job remunirations are (in many cases) relatively low, especially compares with the hadship endured, can at least balance those hardships in their minds with the benefit they perceive themselves as creating (for society and others, not just themselves). This is the case, according to the hypothesis, not because education is no longer a valuable human endeavor, but due to the growing gap between the way it was implemented in the past, and is still implemented today, and the actual needs the sudden new reality has created that the system is unable to contain, let alone respond to, these needs. Given these conditions, teaching cannot maintain the meaning it had for all those involved in it in the past, or produce the good it did throughout most Western history up to the last two generations,[79] a good which is urgently needed today

To return now to the main line of discussion: as far as the direct empirical substantiation strategy of the anomaly hypothesis is concerned, over the past three or four decades of the new postmodern reality, the literature depicting and analyzing its various aspects has provided ample detailed documentation of all phenomena that can emerge from a continuously and increasingly anomalous and hence absurd and dysfunctional system.[80]

The next four chapters of this book are dedicated to corroborating the anomaly hypothesis using the direct theoretical substantiation strategy. Each of these chapters is devoted to one of the basic parameters of any education system—goals, content, organizational structure, and target audience—and theoretically substantiates the claim that the modern definition of the relevant parameters is dysfunctional, anomalous, and meaningless, given the ascendance of the postmodern revolutions.[81] Two other parameters, recruiting the target audience and the *modus operandi*, are treated within the framework of the four chapters. In other words, these four chapters are dedicated to the thorough explication and substantiation of the four key claims that together comprise the arguments at the base of the theoretical corroboration of the anomaly hypothesis:

- *Educational Goals.* Modern definitions of the goals of education have lost their justifications, and hence their meaning and functionality, in the postmodern era as a result of the engulfing, relativistic revolution which characterizes the era. Western education systems have turned, in the last generation, from systems dedicated to the formation of young peoples' character, in light of well respected ultimate values, into aimless organizations. Consequently, these organizations have lost their cultural and social *raison d'être*. These organizations cling to technocratic and instrumental means as a defense mechanism, destructive though it may be, and turn them into "goals" where no real goals exist anymore (Chapter Two).

- *Educational Content.* In our relativistic age, the modern curriculum, which consists of basic scientific disciplines, a carry-over from the classical-liberal curriculum[82] which stemmed from Plato's objectivistic epistemology, has lost its justification and meaning on the cultural level. In this case, as in the previous one, relativism has led to a collapse of the traditional objectivistic philosophical justification of the curriculum and hence to a loss of its meaning and functionality. Given the far-reaching changes in the labor market and the workplace, the modern curriculum has become much less socially and economically justifiable on the practical level as well. Thus, the basis for the school curriculum suppositions, which remained valid on both the philosophical and practical levels of justification over the last twenty-five hundred years, have been dramatically foundering in last three or four postmodern decades (Chapter Three).

- *Organizational Structure.* The modern school's rigid, stable, hierarchical, and lococentric organizational structure stands in opposition to the flexible, dynamic, flat, virtual or semi-virtual, "crazy"[83] organizational structures developing in the postmodern era. Thus, the school is a floundering, anachronistic relic of yesteryear on the organizational level as well. (Chapter Four).

- *Target audience.* One of the major postmodern processes in the social arena consists of the "disappearance of childhood" or, more accurately, the disappearance of clear and stable differences between "children" and the "adult." Consequently, suppositions basic to education concerning the nature of its target audience and its mobilization strategies, which ruled education systems over the past twenty-five hundred years, up to and including the modern age, have broken down. No longer is it self-evident to assume that education is a process aimed at enhancing the development of immature, inexperienced "children" towards maturity by mature, knowledgeable, and experienced "adults." Today, it is not hard to find common situations in which the opposite is just as, if not more, self-evident: young people are initiating adults into a better understating of the world (Chapter Five).

SUMMARY: WHERE AND HOW TO BEGIN

If the education community is to follow the dynamic process that science, and all other developing cultural contexts, follow, an initial stage of generating consciousness of the anomalies is necessary. This stage requires systematic activity of an educational vanguard consisting of groups of thinkers, researchers, and policy makers coming to grips with the root causes of the system's problems: the unprecedented and growing gap between education and the surrounding postmodern environment. These groups should reach the most expansive possible awareness of the immensity of the crisis, as well the deepest possible appreciation of the fact that a solution cannot stop short of a complete and radical reconsideration of the system's most basic paradigm.

In the terms I used above, for a second time in Western history, the present education system must be discarded in its entirety (at least during the initial thinking process) and make way for *tabula rasa*-based thinking in a thorough systematic and strategic manner, designed to reinvent education from scratch. The challenge to the vanguard groups' will be to formulate entirely new concepts of education, leading to entirely new paradigms (different concepts, different paradigms), and to "sell" their solutions to their societies.[84] To enhance such a process, the following four chapters comprising Part One of the book survey and analyze the categorical inadequacy of the modern educational paradigm in the postmodern age.

In order to achieve the positive and ambitious goal of inventing education for postmodern Western democracies, such vanguard groups will require solid starting points. To this end, they will have to go back to basics, to the bedrock of the most fundamental philosophical questions concerning the Good Life and the "nature of man," which tend to be shunned during times of confusion and conceptual earthquakes like ours for fear of the infinite abysses into which they may lead us.[85] They will need courage and perseverance to look these questions "in the eye."[86] They will also need some template for thinking about and dealing with these fundamental philosophical questions, and then all layers of educational function stemming from them. A possible systematic preparation of the ground for a desired educational program adequate for the new postmodern situation and guided by desired Humanistic values is the focus of Part Two of the book.

Part Three substantiates the claim that the present aleatory, sporadic, mindless "changes" dominating the realm of educational reforms, which eventually "evaporate" or cancel each other out, must be replaced by entirely new educational paradigm(s) created within a framework of mindful and strategic thinking along the methodological model this book follows. It also shows that, in spite of the fact that we require the most radical possible paradigmatic change, in some cases the move towards this change can be gradual, as long as it is directed by a clear and operational vision of an entirely new paradigm.

THE DISAPPEARANCE OF EDUCATIONAL GOALS IN THE POSTMODERN ERA

INTRODUCTION

The modern education systems' goals, the most fundamental parameter characterizing any organization, are foundering in the postmodern era, as a result of the relativistic, postmodernist worldview which is rapidly spreading among the contemporary elite and middle class.

Relativism, considered by many to be the core feature of postmodernity, is the source whence spring other ideological characteristics of the postmodern era, such as pluralism, the loss of transcendental value systems, and their replacement (mostly) by many variations on the egoistic-hedonistic worldview. The modern goals of education (not to mention the traditional ones) were all rooted in objectivistic foundations. Over the past generation relativism has eroded these foundations to the point of disintegration and disappearance.

In this chapter, after characterizing the nature and "flavor" of postmodernist relativism, which lies at the root of the disappearance of the prevailing goals of education (Section 1), I describe the acute and radical nature of this disappearance (Section 2). I then proceed to sketch an outline of the nature of the utopian ideated discourse on the desired goals, in light of this disappearance. This discourse would be systematically conducted as it should have been already, had professionals, educators, and decision makers acknowledged the void left where educational goals once existed. For this sake, I carry out a discussion between seven main prototypical voices which "echo" back and forth in the prevailing cultural "wilderness" without provoking any real response.[1] The discussion delineated in this chapter reflects and concretizes the depth and breadth of the bewildering abyss that replaced "the goals of education" and lurks beyond today's educational practice, while in Chapter Six (Part Two) it serves as a foundation, an "Archimedean point" that will allow us to launch a positive argument and suggest amended goals for postmodern democratic societies.

DOMINANT VARIATIONS OF POSTMODERN RELATIVISM

The alliance of relativistic views, the dominant epistemology of the postmodern era, is manifested in Western societies in a myriad of variations ranging from the seemingly sophisticated and intellectual academic relativism through the cynicism of politicians and power brokers to the vulgar relativism of the "man in the street."

The following description of a few of these manifestations is schematic and unavoidably partial.

- The *first* version of postmodern relativism begins with "postmodernism," a term often mistakenly identified with the name of the complex and rapidly changing era we live in: "Postmodernity." Postmodernism is a "highbrow" relativism adopted by various intellectuals and pseudo-intellectuals dominant among Western academics in certain disciplines, mainly the humanities and some of the social sciences. It is usually wrapped up in incomprehensible jargon imported from the post-Second World War, post-structuralist French intellectual elite which in turn were greatly influenced by pre-War German philosophy and social sciences. This jargon mainly expressed the French elite's (former members of the Marxist salons) disappointment with Marxism and its attempt to proceed with the typically French, narcissistic, game of *epater les bourgeois* ("to shock the middle classes"), despite the absence of the "good old" objectivist socialistic or Marxist foundations.

  In Anglophone and other Western countries, the use of this incomprehensible jargon has in many cases lost the original motivation that led to its formation in the cafes, salons, and lecture halls of *la Rive Gauche* in the 1950s, '60s, and '70s. It now mainly typifies those who belong to the left-wing intellectual elite and try to carry on the fight for justice and freedom even in a new world in which these words have largely lost their meaning in the wake of the relativistic attack on the objectivistic foundations which accorded them meaning in modernity. The opacity of the original French narcissistic love-making with one's self using language as a medium helped Western intellectuals hide the impossibility of their quest; once they lost their objectivistic foundations, "freedom" and "justice" also lost their meaning.[2]

  Outside France (and later on in France as well as the general Western influence rebounded), it also became, since the 1970s, a status symbol for the bourgeois professionals and intellectuals who did not necessarily share the basic motivation of the small group who started it all. The influence of these intellectuals and academics of humanities and social sciences, in both European and Anglophone countries, on the universities and on the media constitutes the lion's share of legitimization for relativism from the 1970s onward.

- A *second*, much cruder, version of relativism emanates from market forces and the new liberalism. This version is the language of the people who really turn the wheels of postmodernity. It reduces all the complexity of human life to the financial "bottom line," because "nothing else really matters."

- The *third* version, a byproduct of the logically impossible combination of the above two versions ("impossible" since the first "camp" vehemently attacks the second), is the slick and psychologically sophisticated relativism of the advertising, entertainment, and media industries eager to please their marketing masters and investors by largely borrowing from the linguistic repertoire of the first group.

- The *fourth* version is found in the bored, apathetic, relativistic indifference of the technocrats who oversee the daily activities of governmental, international organizations (the European Union, the United Nations, the World Bank, the OECD, etc.), corporate establishments, and NGOs. These technocrats do not understand the patois of the intellectuals and have no interest in the marketing brand of relativism. They care mostly about submitting their reports or "deliverables" and collecting air miles at the expense of the taxpayers or the corporate account. Their aim is to "neutralize" language to the point where it is as fuzzy and uncontroversial as possible.

- The *fifth* version is the "vulgar" relativism of the masses that are intermittently influenced by the language of the first group and enslaved by the endless flow of new brands and products fabricated by the second group and marketed by the third. They adhere to the basic maxim of our new relativistic world: "I consume therefore I am."

- The *sixth* version is comprised of the cynical relativism of the political class. Politicians are ambitious and aggressive enough to live lives based on lies and distortions, justified by the idiom that "everything depends on one's perspective," Alcibiades' 2,500-year-old dictum that "justice is the interest of the powerful," or Machiavelli's cynical advice to his prince. Thus, they glean snatches from the intellectuals' rhetoric and a partial understanding of the main "truth" of our era, but do not care enough about this "truth" to immerse their intellects in a deeper understanding of what all this vocabulary stands for, beyond the obvious: "I am shown (on television), therefore I am."

Have I left anybody out? Certainly I have. There are endless variations on postmodernism and countless brands of relativism affecting Western life in postmodernity. However they all boil down to the obstinate, dogmatic belief in the sanctity of disbelief, or to a categorical enslavement to the "holy truth" that "there are no truths," that everything is "in the eye of the beholder,"[3] that the world is therefore nothing but an endless series of arbitrary social or language games, or rather very large, ever-changing, groups of such games impacting on and reflected in other games. Alternatively we can sum up postmodernism as dictating that we understand anything that seems to us to be knowledge or justice as nothing more than "disinformation" deliberately disseminated by power structures (as crucially claimed by thinkers in the first "camp" and shamelessly admitted by all others in Alcibiades-like joy).

But once the world is perceived through postmodernist eyes as nothing more than virtual reality nothing matters, not even the true value or meaningfulness of one's own utterances. After all, such utterances are also just a game. As long as one's partners in the game nod approvingly to what one says and as long as the paycheck, royalties, or dividends keep coming in on time and one can afford the designer jeans, the summer house in the "hottest" location, or the latest Porsche or, (for the masses who fantasize through soap operas, telenovelas or, more "actively," through virtual Internet games), Fiat or Mitsubishi model, then everything is fine.

Relativism and its psycho-social offspring—egoism, cynicism, and boundless hedonism—are very far from being new to the Western world. However a strange coalition combined of Plato, the Jewish prophets, Jesus, and St. Paul successfully fought it off; not without cost, though, as Europe and its residents were consequently subject to the rule of Dogmatism for two thousand years. During this long period, relativism and its offspring, though vanquished over and over again, were not obliterated and tacitly persisted, hidden under thick layers of hypocrisy among the aristocracy and Church leaders in the Renaissance, buried in silence among peripheral philosophical sects, or kept behind high castle or prison walls as with individuals like the Marquis de Sade.

In our era, relativism and its offspring are once again raising their heads (many years after its first clear expressions by Alcibiades, his friends, and their teachers, the Sophists). Only this time, they are no longer confined to the "veiled" elite or the periphery of unknown skeptic philosophers, no longer are they hidden in the underworld. Today, for the first time in human and certainly Western history, since Neoplatonism and Christianity overcame the relativism of the Hellenistic period, the relativist lifestyle is becoming the default, accepted by almost any secular individual who is "invigorated and empowered" enough to enjoy a high quality of life, or, in other words, to consume at will. This rampant relativistic mood is rapidly spreading in our "flat world" beyond Western societies, conquering even the most distant corners of the earth.

POSTMODERN RELATIVISM AND THE DISAPPEARANCE OF THE MODERN EDUCATIONAL GOALS

Is there any chance that the crisis-ridden Western education systems can remain unaffected? The answer is obviously negative. In two generations relativism has created a "black hole" of unasked and (seemingly) unanswerable questions about the very foundation of the educational endeavor.

Throughout the history of Western civilization questions referring to the nature of the Good Life and the implication thereof on the goals of education and the right to educate have rarely been asked. This was not because they were hard to answer. The opposite was true. In traditional religious or modern ideological societies, the answers were so obvious that the questions barely ever surfaced. Today too these questions rarely surface, but for very different reasons.

The illuminated mountain on which the answers to these questions once stood (in the faraway modern era now mostly forgotten, which was last celebrated during the self-assured '50s, the utopian '60s, and early '70s) has, in the last two generations, turned into a bleak deserted abyss. This "black hole" is so dark, infinite, and threatening that teachers, principals, parents, decision makers, politicians, and most theoreticians including even the vast majority of philosophers are afraid to look into it. They prefer to look at "small-scale riddles" (to use Kuhn's term) and tech-nocratic questions like how to integrate more female students into the mathematic and scientific fields, how to improve literacy, how to limit violence, and how to use ICT to better teach eighth grade history. Piecemeal problems at least (allegedly) offer the (false) hope for possible solutions. But nobody asks the *basic* question: what is the aim of it all? Without first answering this question, tackling piecemeal problems turns into nothing more then an absurd addiction to enacting reforms as mythical and irrational as ceremonial dancers begging the spirit ancestors to bring their descendants rain or bestow on them good health or affluence.

Sometimes, especially audacious philosophers do stick to their traditional vocation and in one way or another face these questions.[4] Troubled non-philosophical writers may also touch on them from their perspective within the large range of the socio-political spectrum. But they do not speak to each other, and do not form any ongoing systematic rational discourse on the subject.[5] Nor do they have any impact on the general educational discourse or on policy makers, not to mention any daily practice in the education system itself. They do not make real impact even on the philosophical discourse, which is still primarily postmodernistic, focusing to a large extent on issues which interest postmodernistic philosophers alone. For instance, feminists, multiculturalists, and anti-colonialist philosophers concentrate their criticism on unjust power structures in education. Their writings have very little real affect on the general academic discourse, not to mention practitioners' or policy makers' discourses.

More importantly in this context, it simply never occurs to postmodernistic thinkers engaged in this critical "project" (to use a term they like) that for their criticism of the unjust distribution of education and its suppressive nature to have any value there is a need for an educational process, or at least a clear model of such a desired process, which has meaningful goals to postmodern democratic societies. Then, and only then, the question of its just formation and distribution can and should be asked. At present their criticism is directed towards an unjustifiable and meaningless project, which is doomed to inevitably disintegrate. Their criticism is therefore similar to a reexamination of the design of the second floor of a building while its first floor and foundations are not yet on the drawing board. In other words, not addressing this issue renders the very essence of their criticism flawed.

The few voices which do address the above foundational issue are buried under the infinite, all-devouring darkness of the "black hole." Because almost no one among those who control the education systems or the discourse about them is willing to admit there is an essential problem, almost no one is prepared to systematically and analytically respond to the voices of the few who do face it and the answers they propose.

What makes this current crisis unique is not the mere debate over the meaning of key concepts in educational thinking. Throughout history, the meaning of the Good Life, and the right kind of education stemming from it, was debated on both the theological and philosophical levels. However, the present crisis is much more acute, because it features a unique combination of three unprecedented elements:

- Numerous contradictory conceptions of the Good Life and education exist side by side in all Western societies and among most social sectors (except fundamentalists of various sorts). In the past, opposing views primarily existed in different societies or sectors or at most in different classes of the same society. However, today contradictory points of view frequently exist in the same social class or sector, or even within the worldview of a single individual, rendering (in the last case) a large portion of Western parents and educators "educationally confused" or "disoriented" (which are learning, thinking, and acting disabilities that for some reason haven't yet been sanctified in the canonical texts of the discipline of special education).

- As follows from the black hole metaphor, in most cases the "confused" are not "perplexed." In a generation that celebrates the "loss of truth" and vehemently rejects what little is left of (what is believed to be) "the vanity of rationality" and the "tyranny of systematic thought," it is OK to be confused, it is OK to transmit confused values or assumptions to one's children; it is actually unavoidable and "good" because it shows one to be "pluralistic," "tolerant," "open-minded," and "politically correct."

  This phenomenon has no precedent in human or Western history. Even among the last generations of the modern era, individuals were fully immersed in the conception of the Good Life of their society/social sector, be it religious, rationalist, socialist, nationalist, humanist, or liberal (in the "thick" sense of the term[6]) which they mostly took for granted and educated unquestionably in its light.

- Despite the many different perceptions of the Good Life in the past, few thinkers doubted the existence of one true meaning of this concept, truly reflecting what the Good Life *should* stand for. Obviously, all proponents considered their own conception closest of all to the Truth. However, postmodern relativism, at least in its more extreme versions that have per-colated down from intellectual postmodernism to all the other social levels, has laid aside the premise that one conception can *in principle* be more correct or better than another. Similarly, postmodernism has "deconstructed" the view that one can meaningfully aspire to be able to rationally resolve the acute disagreements between different conceptions. In an era that has forsaken any hope of reaching a consensus about "rationality" or any rational decision making criteria for such fundamental debates, resignation to what is known as "immeasurability" seems to be unavoidable.[7]

Therefore, today's postmodern reality is the first in history in which education (and especially public education) is unable to act in light of a transcendental or any other coherent value system and thus cannot strive to inculcate it to the "educatees" as education has always done since the dawn of human culture and history.

Today, for the first time in Western history, education systems are unable to act on the basis of any social agreement, not even one perceived to be merely consensual (as opposed to objectively justified). In order to reach a consensus on views considered by their proponents to be arbitrary or subjective or pure social conventions, all potential discussants need to accept *a priori* "rules of the game" concerning decision criteria. But the dwellers of the epistemological and ethical black hole cannot even reach such a basic, minimal consensus. There is no one, common, fundamental game, no "The Game" anymore. It seems impossible to reach agreement on "the rules." The concept of a "game" clearly defined by its rules was in itself corroded by extreme postmodernist relativism, not to speak of "ultimate rules" which have power beyond specific games.

In the last generation we have lost the naïveté that allowed all our ancestors to believe in the existence of distinguishable rules that precede and direct or allow the formation of "objective" or at least consensually accepted knowledge. In other words, even the "good old" distinction between material statements, statements of factual information about the world, about which there are likely to be endless disagreements, and formal statements or logical or semantic rules that do not contain such information but guide the formation of the previous statements and are universal, was joyfully "found" to be untenable a generation ago.[8] Most postmodernist thinkers boast of, and celebrate this state of affairs as a kind of "total liberation."[9]

Thus, it seems impossible to talk about "public education," that is, state-run education, in Western, secular, relativistic, Liberal Democracies, and still relate to the original meaning of the term "education," to wit, encouraging the development of an individual in light of a model of the Good Life defined as "desirable."

Moreover, it is the first time in history that the influence of relativism is exponentially intensified by the electronic media's penetration of every home, engulfing us with wireless gadgetry networked to the cacophonic World Wide Web during all our waking hours. We are still very far from being able to fully assimilate the significance of this radical revolution whose explicit and tacit advertising and glorification of hedonism and consumerism, in all its shapes and forms, is solidly based on the relativistic-egoistic lifestyle.[10]

The breakdown of the definitions of the goals of modern education is a direct result of the dominant relativistic-egoistic-hedonistic *weltanschauung* on at least two levels. The first has to do with the main goal of education as understood throughout history: "acculturation,"[11] or the initiating youths into their own culture. Throughout Western history, including the modern era, education was perceived as a process designed to aid the individual's upward progress on the (so-called) ladder of human existence to the desired state[12] defined by the individual's culture, a state which was conceived as essentially different and better from the natural human state. In other words, education was perceived as aiming to elevate individuals beyond the level of seeking to fulfill mere natural, material needs to an exalted spiritual level in the light of a transcendental ideal surpassing the natural and egoistic.

This transcendental ideal could be the worship of God in traditional society, knowledge of the Truth or of progress inspiring "scientific knowledge" in traditional and modern rationalistic societies, a commitment to the struggle for social justice in the modern socialist and Marxist societies, a commitment to the cause of national liberation or resurrection in many emerging modern national societies, or a commitment to one version or another of what was perceived as the set of "universal Humanistic values" or the "rights of man," etc., in many modern liberal societies, or some combination of these.

The traditional and modern transcendental goals of education cannot be justified in the relativistic context, certainly not in the naïve way they were justified up to a generation or two ago in almost all Western societies. Paradoxically and tragically, we find ourselves in a period when, after an unprecedented development of the body, the soul which it has nourished and protected has been totally lost. In other, less poetic, words, the education systems in the Western world have expanded in our generation to dimensions undreamt of before, serving a vast range of populations: anyone unfortunate enough to fall between the ages of four and eighteen, compelling them to attend educational institutions for ten to fourteen years. Note that not so long ago a large portion of the population did not receive any formal schooling, and for most of those who did the standard was (only) four gloomy years of "grammar school" from which they graduated to the harsh realities of mines and production lines. Ironically and tragically, *the justification of education's traditional and modern goals and therefore its raison d'être were lost, an unprecedented occurrence in its own right, at exactly this moment of unprecedented expansion of schooling.*

This intense process is rendering the education system's activities totally meaningless for students and teachers alike. This claim explains, at least partially, the many maladies which beset education systems in contemporary Western societies. Over the last few decades there has been an ongoing decrease of literacy levels, a spread of ignorance among students and teachers alike, a decline or obstinate stagnation of scholastic achievement,[13] an increase in violence,[14] a rise in drug and alcohol abuse among students,[15] rising rates of suicide and suicide attempts by young people,[16] and ever-increasing rates of teacher burnout and dropout.[17] Is there a possible psychological or social malaise that is not included in this list of "problems contemporary schools have to face"?

As the disintegration of education's *raison d'être* is the deep-rooted cause leading to the aggravation of these phenomena, we cannot and should not therefore go on ignoring the most fundamental questions:

- Is there a need for an educational process in a reality where the distinction between the mundane and the natural on one side and the exalted and the ideal on the other is being eroded?
- If so, what can it aspire to? What can education's goals be?

In answer to these questions, one can argue that the loss of transcendental values does not necessarily entail a loss of social consensus, and that the aim of education is to serve this consensus even if it does not focus on transcendental values. Moreover, it can be argued that the aim of education today should be the encouragement of the individual's self-realization, the aim that arises from individualism which is the central value in the reality of postmodern society. In a society which no longer perceives "the worship of God," "the quest for Truth," or "the fight for Justice" or for "national liberation," or even for more extensive fulfillment of the "universal rights of man," to be self-evident or absolute exalted values, one may reasonably assume that the "worship of the self" can be considered a main educational ideal.

This argumentation leads us toward the second level of the crisis affecting educational goals in postmodernity, relating to education as contributing to the development of the individual rather than to acculturation. The radical relativism permeating many levels of society in the postmodern era prevents us from accepting even the validity of "individualism" as the leading educational value for two complementary reasons:

- One cannot claim that there is a consensus within Western societies, even on the value of individualism. Thus, for example, both feminists (at least many of them) and communitarians (most of them) are vehemently attacking this value. The former view it as a male value that ignores the basic human need for close intimate relationships with other people, and the latter as a value that dismisses the fundamental human need for social identification and communal commitment. Both view the value of individualism as contrary to human nature, causing personal alienation, social disintegration, and misery.[18]

- Even those who accept the educational and social importance of individualism do not agree on its operative psychological and educational meaning and implications:
- Does "encouragement of personal self-realization" mean helping the individual to achieve academic excellence in order to attain acceptance by a prestigious institute of higher learning, and thereby, according to the conventional approach to education, obtain the guarantee of a high standard of living in adulthood?

  Or

- Should this expression be understood to imply a demand to help individuals to express their own authentic values in life, even though these might not coincide with high scholastic achievements as the disciples of open, progressive, and democratic education contend?

  Or, alternatively,

- Does the operational meaning of "encouraging personal self-realization" perhaps require us to help free the individual of the false, alienating attitudes that modern capitalistic society, and even more so postmodern neo-liberalism and capitalism, have covertly internalized in the individual, attitudes which are a necessary condition for self-realization, as Radicals and neo-Marxists, very dominant in postmodern educational discourse, contend?

At the base of the three educational views mentioned above we find three different and contradictory perceptions of the Good Life, human development, learning, and democratic society: the conventional achievement-oriented view, usually relying on neo-liberalism, the "open" or "progressive" education model, and the radical Marxist concept. Both latter educational approaches are usually critical of the socioeconomic views of neo-liberalism.

These three views naturally lead to contradictory conceptions of "individual self-realization." All three perspectives (and several others not mentioned here to avoid further complexity) are currently accepted by philosophers, parents, students, and professionals, although the first has gained the widest credence among the general population. Similar perplexity and ambiguity exist today regarding every other individualistic concept proposed to characterize a desirable educational goal, such as "autonomy," "rationality," "self regulation," "self direction," "independence," "entrepreneurship," "leadership" (very "in" lately), "authenticity," "self realization," "empowerment," and I could go on and on. Actually, as words stop being carved in stone and become "fluid" (to quote a term coined by Z. Bauman) we witness two complementary processes—each term can (and often does) have an infinite number of meanings (i.e., is rendered meaningless); and there is a linguistic inflation: the fuzzy linguistic territory is flooded with new or renewed terms, as if to cover its extending hollowness with the buzzing noise of the increasingly "sophisticated" discourse based on "the brave new (postmodern) language."

Given the disappearance of the classic transcendental goals of education and the ambiguity and confusion surrounding the definitions of possible alternatives, and what seems to many to be the inability to rely on any solid rational foundation in order to come to terms with these problems, a number of previously, almost untouched, questions, should come to the fore:

- Does the concept of "public education" still convey a viable alternative in postmodern Liberal Democracies? In other words, is there any validity to a systematic, mindful attempt, on behalf of democratic societies, to shape the next generation in the light of a specific desirable model of the Good Life?
- If not, what is the alternative?
- Is it total renunciation of the postmodern democratic public education pretension to educate, leaving education (as many teachers and "educators" in their practice actually do) to "whoever is responsible" and limiting the role of public education to (allegedly) "value-free teaching"? Given the disintegration of the nuclear family, and more largely of any social or communal framework, isn't the only realistic alternative in this vacuous reality education by the unholy alliance between the Internet, console games, and television or, in other words, market forces and advertising?
- Isn't this alternative too dangerous, particularly given the "disintegration of society"?
- If the above is too dangerous, in the light of which values, among the above or other values, can we educate?

The problem is largely aggravated by what most recent liberal thinkers consider to be the "value neutrality" liberal states should be committed to. The state's obligation is not to rely on any "conception of the Good Life" in relating to its citizens, but to supply them with a framework in which they can choose and realize any conception of the Good Life they decide.[19]

It seems that if the liberal state is to remain neutral between different conceptions of what "Good" is, it should stick to a formal policy framework in the distribution of all "goods" that can be considered as pre-conditions for choice and implementation of its citizens world-views, education included. But if there are only social or contextual languages or "games" and no "super game," or formal neutral decision making procedures, there seems to be no foundation for the liberal state to rely on.[20]

At present there are no clear answers to these questions, certainly no answers that enjoy a broad consensus. Furthermore, while there are individual voices that have been trying to come to terms with these questions, there is no *systematic* on-going discussion focused on such issues which relates specifically to education.[21] By "systematic discussion" I mean a discussion in which the individual thinkers are committed to rationally relate to each other's answers, and in which issues solved (even by reaching agreement to the disagree) are not endlessly repeated, and hence there is conceptual development or progress acknowledged by the various participants.

As I have emphasized above, this is an unprecedented situation in the history of Western education. In the place of the foundational, clear, and coherent perceptions of the Good Life that have guided (for better and worse) Western societies throughout history, there is now nothing but a silent "black hole." The confusion accompanying this silence is taken by many to be a normal and even desirable state of affairs. It is also accompanied by an obstinate attempt to look the other way and deal with technical, technocratic, secondary questions concerning educational practice, practice which has lost its very goals and *raison d'être*.

SEVEN RESPONSES TO THE CRISIS IN EDUCATION: OUTLINE OF A UTOPIAN DISCOURSE

In the following pages I will try to, somewhat artificially, reconstruct one version of the lacking discussion out of several meaningful individual voices that have been raised in "the wilderness."22 In light of this reconstruction within the discussion, the attempts to tackle the crisis in the last generation may initially be divided into four main conceptualized "camps":

- Those who accept without reservations postmodern reality, including its characteristic relativism, as desirable and claim that in this day and age the state-governed education system has neither the right nor the ability to educate, and must therefore completely renounce its pretension to do so.
- Those who accept postmodern reality with its characteristic relativism as given and, to some limited extent, also desirable,[23] and claim that the education system must educate towards autonomy so that young people will be able to mindfully choose their own values and implement them in the new, devoid of absolute values, world.
- Those who accept postmodern reality, including relativism, as given and, to some extent, as desirable, and therefore claim that our relativistic starting point prevents resolution of the debate about the aim or goals of education by some generic or universally accepted answer and maintain that it must be left open to ongoing social and political negotiation and debate.
- Those who reject the postmodern condition and sometimes also the relativism therein, characterizing it as a state of human decadence. These thinkers believe that it is mandatory for schools to educate according to a value system that conforms to a socio-cultural standpoint opposed to the attitudes dominant in postmodernity. They usually present themselves as either relating and aspiring to return to an earlier ideal society, a social existence which has been (allegedly) suppressed by opposing postmodernist values that have (allegedly) usurped the students' minds (the "conservatives"), or to a future utopian society in which desired justice and freedom-oriented values will be implemented (the "Radicals").

In the present-day chaotic reality, one would hardly expect the above "camps" to speak with one voice (after all, although they sometimes attack one or more of the other voices, they hardly speak to each other directly). Furthermore, these "camps" are of course fictitious and were "grouped" here purely for the sake of making the discussion below possible. In fact, it is much noisier and more confusing "out there" as each "camp" and sub-camp speaks in many vacillating voices,[24] and each of them shouts its position in an endlessly echoing nothingness.

For the sake of this discussion I will do my best to perform the impossible and present these camps and their sub-camps as coherent in themselves and as participating in a rational discussion in which the borderlines and the common denominators are clear. Awareness of the opposing conceptions' multiplicity and their mutual criticism, while forming some order in and among them (even if as a "noble lie" or as "using a ladder" to be discarded later, as Wittgenstein would have said[25]), is vital for comprehending the depth and severity of the lack of consensus over the goals of public education in a postmodern democratic society and for trying to make sense of it all. Thus, henceforth, I will attempt to map a seemingly clear terrain, ignoring all the fluctuations and fuzziness that would otherwise render such presentation impossible.

In the following presentation, I not only present each view or sub-view, but also immediately follow it up with the main criticisms of opposing views that seek to undermine it. Although lengthening and somewhat "overburdening" the discussion, I do this in order to emphasize the extent and intensity of the conflicts and disagreements.

I would like to make one last general introductory remark of epistemic importance to which I will not be able to refer in detail below: the above description of the four categories of views tacitly relies on a general distinction between the three epistemic starting points that largely impact the response of educational thinkers on the current crisis:

- Radical or postmodernist relativism denies the possibility of commensurability or meaningful discussion among holders of opposing views, or even reliance on reason for the formation of a justified educational view. These views are usually held by thinkers in the first camp.
- Moderate relativism, consisting of either cultural relativism or skepticism, assumes the possibility of a meaningful rational dialogue even between holders of opposed views or reliance on formal (i.e., procedural or "devoid of content") rationality as a supporting pillar of the response to the crisis. Beyond this assumption, epistemologically speaking, there is an oceanic difference between cultural relativists and skeptics.[26]

Still, both these epistemic views allow reliance, to some extent, on rational discussion, analysis, and debate in response to the current educational crisis. This is possible thanks to what the cultural relativists take to be widespread cultural conventions of rationality, and the skeptics perceive as limited universal perception of *formal* reason. Thus, when I describe those belonging to the above two camps as "relativistic *to some extent*," I mean that they are either skeptics or social or cultural relativists.

- Rationalism is the view shared by those who believe in our ability to rely on reason in order to know *material truths*. This epistemic view can serve as the foundation of conservative views on education in the fourth camp of postmodern "rejectionists," although conservatives can also be cultural relativists.[27]

Also, the epistemic situation "out there" is complex and rarely logically tidy. I cannot go into further detail here. Still, I hope I have said enough to enable me to refer to the epistemic issues below *en passant*.

The Technocratic Response, or: Surrender of the Aspiration to Educate

The View. What I refer to here as "the technocratic response" to the disappearance of education's goals is prevalent among teaching staff, parents, and many administrators and policy makers who accept the postmodern situation, as well as the postmodernist relativism dominant in it, as given but do not regard it as a problem. Indeed, the technocrats believe relativism to be desirable and maintain that in this situation, there is no point in pretending to educate. The majority of technocrats actually apply their approach to everyday life, without naming or systematically formulating it.

One can distinguish between two categories of technocrats. Let us call them, for the sake of this discussion, "the pedagogy oriented" and "the functionalists." Those belonging to the first category perceive teaching of the formal, explicit curriculum as the main educational goal of school, while their counterparts do not. According to the functionalists, teaching and learning serve only as cover activities to the true functions of schooling: socializing students to the norms of society by the "tacit curriculum" (see below).

According to the pedagogy-oriented technocrats' view, ideologically mobilized state education is no longer possible and cannot be justified since it is divorced from daily practice and cannot be reconstructed in the relativist and non-ideological reality in which we live. It is *no longer possible*, because the majority of today's students come from a social reality dominated by relativistic, individualistic attitudes and diverting them towards an alternative epistemology or value system is unlikely. Moreover, as many of the teachers live in this reality, it is difficult to assume that they have the pathos required for an alternative value educational process. According to this view, ideologically mobilized state education *cannot be justified*, even if it was possible, because the democratic state is committed to value and ideological neutrality in its activities and decision making, and must avoid giving arbitrary preference to any one worldview over another. Thus, any preferment of a specific concept in education, or in any other sphere in a relativist-democratic society, will be arbitrary and therefore unjustifiable.

The pedagogy-oriented technocrats can be roughly divided into two groups according to the degree of extremism of the conclusions they draw from the arguments above. Most of the technocratic view's supporters hold the relatively moderate claim that the goal of present-day education is to teach, as opposed to "to educate," that is, to pass on to students those (allegedly) ideologically neutral basic skills and fields of knowledge perceived to be essential for "efficient functioning" in the reality in which they will live.

The less moderate adherents add to that the education system's obligation to avoid, as much as possible, imposing on students knowledge any specific subject matter and to present them instead with varied options from which they may be able to choose freely. According to this view, if relying heavily on a specific system of values for the purpose of education cannot be justified in a relativistic democratic society, then by the same token formulating a curriculum based on a specific value system cannot be justified. Another expression of this position is the argument that formulating a curriculum cannot be neutral; it is an intrinsically educational act and, as there is no justification for imposing education, there is also none for imposing the curriculum therein.[28]

The more extreme technocrats of this group went a step further, and came to the conclusion that the education system in its present form cannot be justified. They contend that if education's entire objective is to instill basic skills and enable students to choose between the various fields of interest, ideologies, ways of life, and knowledge, then in many cases in our open, computerized reality, this objective does not justify the degree of imposition on which it is based. Thus, they hold that many students will acquire skills and achieve greater success in their choice without the mediation of an education system. They might maintain that only a greatly diminished format of the education system can be justified: teaching basic skills, enabling and encouraging choice in students whose environmental conditions or level of cognitive development do not allow such choices to be made naturally.[29]

The other main category of the technocratic position, the functionalistic approach, is much less idealistic, and, as will be clarified in a moment, is more likely to protect the system from the preceding conclusion. The functionalists (to borrow this term from larger sociological spheres) see the system as charged with the maintenance of social functions that have no connection with education or teaching (in the sense of enhancing intellectual or cognitive development) and hence with the formal or explicit curriculum. These social functions are "channeling" students towards social roles on the basis of scholastic achievement. Some of them refer to "the tacit curriculum," i.e., school organizational structure reflecting the norms of future occupational roles, through which students internalize school norms which are identical to the norms of society and the economy.[30] Thus, while perhaps acknowledging the epistemic difficulties in justifying any curriculum or pedagogical orientation, they will dismiss this side of the educational endeavor as secondary and immaterial and justify the existing or similar system by its functional contributions to society and economy.

Critiques of Technocracy. The argument against the pedagogy-oriented versions of the technocratic view boils down to one point: even if we wanted to, avoiding education is impossible. The choice of educational view is a forced option.[31] The true distinction is not between ideologically mobilized education and ethically neutral education, but between education that is conscious, active, and directed versus passive or unconscious education. The latter form of education exists when the public system gives up any active attempt to educate toward a set of predefined ideals and thus necessarily allows young people and their "educators" to be influenced by the values reflected in and guided by the "forces in the field" that engulf them.

Today these forces reside almost exclusively in the electronic media and the Internet sponsored by the huge adverting industry, serving, in turn, the market forces dominated by the desire to maximize profit. Thus, the state education system "avoiding education," in any of the above technocratic versions, is tantamount to according sole legitimacy to educate to MTV, television soap operas and talk shows, the Internet and its related "chat and blog culture," and various other forms of advertising surrounding us. "Educational neutrality," so the counterargument goes, is tantamount to turning young people into captive audiences of the two ultimate values dominating all foregoing spheres: making money and having fun. It forces them to be prisoners in the cave of greed and the endless search for bodily pleasures simply by denying them experience with any alternative worldview.[32]

The formal demand for value neutrality in public education is impossible and senseless on purely logical grounds and therefore the state has no choice but to make a conscious decision regarding the desirable educational goals. Only those who wholeheartedly accept the influence of the "forces in the field" as the *sole desirable* source of educational impact can call for avoiding any active or intended education in light of a predefined set of values by the public system.

Critics of the pedagogy-oriented technocratic view will of course reject the latter possibility and argue that it is undesirable to assume that young people will grow into individuals with a chance for well-being if they are exposed solely to the prevailing market-oriented influences and the two ultimate values dominating them, without the correctional intervention of the public education system opening them up to alternative, healthier, worldviews and lifestyles.

The critics can defend their views from three alternative positions. The *first*, although it does not essentially criticize the postmodern social reality, does however argue that the Good Life demands a degree of autonomy and mindfulness within its framework. According to this view, these two attributes are unlikely to develop "naturally" given the exclusive and adverse impact of the media and advertising on most young peoples' lives; therefore, they must be actively and intentionally educated in light of the desired values of their conception of the Good Life.

The *second* possible position would also accept the postmodern reality and argue that young people should be educated towards what is perceived to be the Good Life by relevant public groups in this reality. In contrast to the first position, the second position does not *a priori* define the concept of the Good Life, not even as based on the individual's autonomy and mindful decision making; rather, this view leaves the definition open to constant negotiation among the relevant social groups or parties, namely, the parents, the broader community, and the state or the professionals who represent it.

The *third*, most radical, view perceives postmodern reality, partly or in its entirety, as corrupt. From this standpoint, the role of education is to protect the student from a corrupting reality by critically exposing the said reality's evils and then presenting the student with a desirable alternative. Thus, this radical view presents the desired ideal as originating from the "correct" concept of the Good

Life and the nature of society and culture required for its achievement. This critique calls for young people to be educated under the aegis of the *desired* values. These "desired values" are defined differently by different adherents to this view and will be presented in detail below.

As will become clear later on in this book, the three critiques are the alternative dominant voices "out there." Each of the next three sub-sections is dedicated to clarifying one of them. Until now I have mentioned only the criticism that can be mounted against the pedagogically oriented technocratic view. However, this criticism also refers, indirectly, to the functionalist version of the technocratic view. Dismissing the pedagogical value of formal education, so the counter-argument will go, and focusing only on its socializing functions as described above, would justify education only if and when one adheres to the norms of the postmodern, neo-liberal, market-oriented society completely. Having said that, the criticism made against the first group of technocrats applies here as well.

The Liberal Response, or: Education towards Autonomy

The View. Once we have forsaken the technocratic response, education towards autonomy turns out to be the next favorable alternative.[33] Education towards autonomy ranks high in the current educational discourse, at least on the declarative level in the sense that it "decorates" many official policy papers in Western countries, as far as the many declarations concerning the desirability of "the autonomous" or "the independent" (or "self-regulated," "self-directed," "engaged," "reflective," etc.) "learner" or "individual" are concerned.[34]

Many understandings of the idea of "the autonomous individual" emerged during the history of Western philosophy, some of which contradict one or more of the others.[35] In spite of the popularity of this educational value on the declarative level, there are very few attempts to understand the possible meanings of this term within the postmodern educational context or to adopt the most desirable one, according to a presumed value system. There have been even fewer attempts to actually implement the oh-so-popular goal of "education for autonomy."

Three of these understandings seem to represent central models of "the autonomous individual" and "education towards autonomy" which are appropriate for our era: one which reflects the *rationalistic* perspective of autonomy, a second that displays an *emotivistic* view of autonomy, and a third model represents a combined, *rationalistic-emotivistic* understanding.

The three models share a common assumption: autonomous individuals are those who "determine the laws that guide their lives by themselves," which is the literal meaning of the word "autonomous." The differences between these models are encapsulated in their answers to two basic questions:
- Where does the individual's autonomy "reside"? Or, in other words, what component in the person's personality is reflected by self-determined laws?
- How are these laws determined?[36]

As I show below, the differences between the respective answers create significant contradictions between the three concepts of educating towards autonomy and the educational programs resulting from them.

The *rationalistic model* originates with the Kantian concept. In the educational thinking of the last two generations, it is found in the work of Robert Dearden and Gerald Dworkin among others. In this model autonomy is "a resident" of a person's rationality. A law determined by an autonomous person must therefore be accepted in accordance with rational considerations. "Rationality" is perceived in this context to be procedural, a formal system of rules that do not obligate the individual to adopt any position on descriptive or normative issues. (This view relies on the epistemology I referred to above as the "skeptical" and can be referred to also as "critical rationalism."[37])

The educational program born out of this model focuses on the development of rational thinking. In principle, one can think of many alternative ways of developing rationality,[38] but the philosophers who have dealt with this subject have generally recommended the teaching of the usual scientific disciplines that generally comprise the Western school curriculum. These were considered to be (allegedly) developing human intelligence, or rather, human intelligence and rationality were considered to consist of, or be equal to, the modes of thinking developed by these disciplines.

Rationality-based autonomy has been extremely influential in Western philosophy since Kant, and has dominated educational philosophy up to the last generation.[39] In the last generation an alternative model, more inclined to emotivism, or to giving far more space to the individual's desires and feelings, has replaced rationality to some extent.

The *emotivistic* model perceives emotions to be the "location" of the autonomous agency or individuality. Thus, this model views an autonomous individual as one in whom no internal or external barriers prevent the expression of emotions. Reason in this model is only (to quote Hume) the "slave of the passions,"[40] the faculty in charge of choosing the best plans for achieving goals set by emotions.

A romantic version of this model has developed since the eighteenth century. In this view, emotions are believed to express the aspiration of the self toward the— often elusive—calling. It was "triggered" largely by the impact of Rousseau (mainly due to secondary books like his *Confessions* and *Les rêveries d'un promeneur solitaire*). This is the model of autonomy that could most easily be attributed to the common and extremely influential image of Lord Byron, for example, or to the hero of Schiller's *The Robbers*.[41]

The *rationalistic-emotivistic* model may be divided into two versions, the first represented by John White in the last two generations and the second by Eamonn Callan. White's is the more systematic of the two; in fact, his is the most systematic concept of educating towards autonomy of our time.[42]

In White's view the goal of education has always been to help the individual accomplish the Good Life. But in the current relativistic reality, one concept of "the Good Life" cannot be justified as being better than another. Accordingly, the choice of a concrete meaning for "the Good Life" must be left in the hands of the individual and the term Good Life be defined today as "what each individual, after due consideration, determines is the Good Life for him or her self." In other words, education today cannot inculcate the individual with any one true concept of the Good Life. However, it can and should help one to develop as an autonomous person who is exposed to choices and knowledge of relevant information, so that these factors will help facilitate a definition of what the Good Life is for him or her.

According to White, individuals strive towards maximal fulfillment of their desires; hence, in this model autonomy "resides" in the individual's desires. The "self-determined law" as formed by the autonomous agent is one which aims to bring about maximal fulfillment of desires. Still, the process of determining the law is rational; it rests on reflective recognition of the relevant desires on the one hand, and upon ascertaining the best way to fulfill these desires in a given reality on the other.

This model is to a meaningful extent, although not altogether (as will be clarified in a moment), opposed to the rationalistic one. While in the rationalistic model, rational activity in itself is making the individual autonomous, in this model (and the next) rational activity is only a means to realizing aspirations (the values or "deeper," longer term, desires motivating the individual) while maximizing the fulfillment of these aspirations is what renders the individual autonomous. According to this (and the next) model, individuals will be autonomous only to the extent that they succeed in recognizing their basic aspirations and are free to do their best towards realizing them.

White holds that education is necessary because the majority of people are unlikely to acquire the requisite cognitive abilities, attitudes, and knowledge for making an informed choice about the Good Life by themselves. From White's standpoint this is particularly true with regard to the *knowledge* required for autonomous choice. This knowledge includes consciousness of different ways of life and worldviews, and of various categories of activity central to human life, such as work, social involvement, and fields of interest.

White suggests that every society tends to direct the individual towards the dominant worldviews and occupations within it, while a correct choice, based on mindful consideration, requires the recognition of as many alternatives as possible. Education's role is to provide the needed tools for making an informed, mindful choice, and to supply as broad as possible a range of "outside-the-box" knowledge which will enable life choices. White stresses that therefore educating towards autonomy should amount to a process of desocialization, a process which will free individuals from the absolute, naïve belief in their society's values or accepted ways of life. This goal should be realized by employing a very broad educational program designed to familiarize the educatee with as many alternatives as possible in all the central spheres of human life, extended way beyond the limited alternatives which the current curriculum of theoretical learning is characterized by.

White's thinking is predicated on our current inability to give objective and universal meaning to the concept of the Good Life. Eamonn Callan depicts a different version of the view supporting educating towards autonomy.[43] Callan bases his philosophy on our inability to give meaning to the concept of the "Ultimate

Goal" or "*summum bonum*" (literal translation: "the highest good"). In fact, both concepts commingle, as the Good Life was perceived in the past as leading to the Ultimate Goal of a person's life.

Classic rationalist philosophy perceives a life that has not led to the Ultimate Goal to be absurd and meaningless, as each action in it leads only to the next rung of the ladder with no final purpose. In this classical view, the Ultimate Goal of human life necessarily amounted to a fulfillment of a personality characteristic that is unique and essential to human beings: the attainment of knowledge. The goal of knowledge was perceived as the recognition of the Truth. Therefore, in traditional rationalist philosophy, the Ultimate Goal in life is the quest for, and the knowledge of, the Truth. As the aim of education is to help the individual to achieve the Ultimate Goal (or "supreme good"—"*summum bonum*"), traditional rationalist philosophy viewed the quest for, and knowledge of, the Truth as the goals of education.

Callan is aware that in the present, relativistic, generation we are unable to hold on to the claim that knowledge of the Truth is the Ultimate Goal of human life, and thus the aim of education. However, he accepts the basic argument of the classic rationalist view, to wit, a life lived without a supreme purpose, or purposes, is absurd and meaningless. In other words, Callan claims that if individuals have no activities they want to perform for their own sake and everything they do is only a means for achieving other ends, then they do not live a good life. This requires education to lead individuals towards the Ultimate Goal(s) in life, that is, to those activities that will be preformed for their own sake and that the main reason for engaging in them is the mere performance thereof. As such, they do not serve as a means to enhance other goals or values or "prepare the ground" for other activities. Because today we are unable to support the idea of there being a single universal Ultimate Goal, the closest alternative Callan proposes is educating young people to pursue their *interests*.

In Callan's definition, an interest is an activity a person performs for its own sake. Up to this point, the definition is similar to the definition of the Ultimate Goal. Still, it sharply opposes the traditional concept as Callan claims that *any activity* can be an interest as long as the following conditions are met:

- The individual is involved in it for its own sake.
- The involvement is made out of choice and awareness of the concessions required by that choice.
- The activity must include some kind of development of the individual involved in it.

Thus, Callan defines "an autonomous person" as one capable of seeking, locating, and developing interests. Like White, he claims that this process should be guided by the aspirations of an individual driven forward in search of maximal fulfillment. According to Callan, just as the goal of education in the past was to help the individual identify with the knowledge of the Truth, the Ultimate Goal of life, its present goal should be to help every individual to develop as an autonomous person, a person capable of identifying and developing his or her interests.

It must be stressed that Callan's goal (as opposed to White's) is not to enable individuals to get to know or experience as many fields of interest as possible. Nor is it to enable them, at the end of their education, to know the interest in which they will be involved throughout life. Rather, the goal is to inculcate people with the concept and value of a "commitment to interests," with an understanding of their importance for a satisfying life, and with the knowledge, commitments, and abilities required for seeking, identifying, and developing their interest(s).

From Callan's standpoint, education, intended to maximize the above goal, is vitally important if everyone is to attain the Good Life. Because of the competitive-hedonistic worldview in which young people live today, a view directed towards external and measurable achievements on the one hand and superficial gratification of desires on the other, the chances that many youths will grasp the importance of interests to their lives and develop them on their own are not great. Callan's concept of education aspires to help overcome the impact of the temptations of immediate gratification and the dominant superficial, hedonistic, and materialistic worldview, thus opening up the possibility of achieving well-being based on search for, and long-term realization of, interests.

This process, Callan says, requires educators to help students develop the needed abilities for seeking, identifying, and realizing fields of interest. For the process of the search for interests to progress, educators should instill a sense of reflection, consideration, and the implementation thereof in the educatees. The educational process should therefore include introduction of a meta-process aimed at helping young people understand the vitality of interests to achieving a satisfying life and acquiring the abilities, commitments, and knowledge necessary to achieve this end.

In his 1988 book Callan relied primarily on relevant philosophical literature.[44] It is important to note at this point that later, a rich psychological research focusing on interests and connected concepts (e.g., "intrinsic motivation") and their correlation with well-being and autonomy was developed confirming empirically all of Callan claims.[45]

When comparing these last two versions of the emotivistic-rationalistic model, I find they have much in common. They share the views that:

- The autonomous person independently chooses a personal way in life.
- The aim of education should be to empower and assist individuals to develop their autonomy.
- Autonomy depends first and foremost on the degree to which the processes of choice are directed towards and are successful in fulfilling the person's true basic aspirations.
- Education should concentrate on developing all the abilities and attributes necessary for choosing a course of life optimal for self-fulfillment.
- Education should serve to help the individual achieve the Good Life even in the postmodern reality.

Both models view the Good Life as grounded in consciously choosing one's most desired way of life, and both perceive the desired way of life as that which will most induce fulfillment of basic desires. Furthermore, an assumption common to both models is that most young people will have difficulty choosing their desired way of life without the aid of some educational process, hence their view that education should strive to enhance young peoples' ability to develop as autonomous individuals. Lastly, in both views the aim of educating towards autonomy is perceived as neutral from a value standpoint, that is, it is perceived as not reflecting a preference for any particular conception of the Good by the liberal democratic state, thereby warranting its adoption by any such state.

However, there are also meaningful contradictions between these two educational models, which can be summed up in three central spheres:

- Each model is based on a different concept of "knowing reality." White emphasizes "learning about" while Callan stresses "experiencing."
- Each model reflects a different concept of choice. White's concept originates from the classic rational model of choice from within the largest possible number of weighted alternatives, and thus demands a broad curriculum that encompasses as many alternatives as possible. Callan's concept of choice is modeled on trial and error, wherein one chooses the first option that seems reasonable, tries it out, and only if it fails, moves on to the next possibility. Accordingly, he does not call for a comprehensive program but rather for a process of "experiments in living,"[46] a process of search by elimination which one works through until an interest one is satisfied with is found.
- Each model relates to a different range of choice. In White's view the autonomous person, independently and after due consideration, chooses his or her way in various spheres of life: worldview, lifestyle, work, interpersonal relations, and fields of interest. White seems to suppose that all of these spheres have equal weight in the autonomous "life-plan." In contrast, Callan relates to interests as having a central and preferred place in what makes up the life of the autonomous person.

Critiques of Education towards Autonomy. Each of the three models described above can be criticized in light of the basic assumptions of the others. This "internal" critique will not be dealt with here as the differences between the three models of education for autonomy have been presented extensively enough to enable the reader to get a good picture of what this "criticism within the family" might amount to. Rather, I describe the "external" and "generic" critiques of the general aim of education towards autonomy, namely, a critique that may be raised against all the three models.

The first point of contention with Autonomy Oriented Education (AOE) arises from the previously discussed technocratic perspective. The technocrats would argue that all this talk of "educating for autonomy" is nothing more than "hot air" about an unrealistically high-browed ideal. The role of education, so the technocrats might claim, is to prepare young people for "real" reality. This, in turn, so the technocrats would continue, should be done either by making young people acquire relevant factual knowledge and skills allowing them to successfully compete in the labor market and in organizations they work with (the pedagogy-oriented technocrats), or by "programming" them to internalize the norms necessary for functioning in the postmodern labor market and organizations (the functionalists among the technocrats). Educating them to be autonomous (mainly in the emotivistic and emotivistic-rationalistic senses), so the technocratic argument will conclude, might very well enhance their development as autonomous individuals, but at the same time probably render them unemployable and therefore create nothing more than frustrated individuals.

The second source of probable criticism of the ideal of education for autonomy is the perspective hereinafter referred to as the concept of *conscious social reproduction.*[47] According to this view, the value of personal autonomy is certainly a legitimate value in a postmodern democratic society, but it does not enjoy *a priori* priority over other possible values that might also be considered desirable and legitimate in this context, such as, for instance, the development of a specific national or religious identity. Therefore, favoring this value over others in education in a democratic state is tantamount to giving unfair, un-democratic preference to only one "desired" value over other possible "desirables."

The third area of contention with the ideal of education for autonomy may come from the direction of the category of views I hereinafter refer to as *education towards desirable social values*: a set of views all together opposing the aspiration for neutrality characterizing the previous views. These views perceive the social reality existing in postmodern Western societies as negative and dangerous. According to them, education towards autonomy contents itself with providing tools to help the individual find a way in this reality. It thus conveys to the student a confirmation of said reality, or to put more critically: it prevents the student from aspiring to overcome it. It is certainly not dedicated to exposing its corrupt foundations and introducing students to alternative social realities as more desirable. Thus, according to this generic critique, the autonomy oriented educational process is fundamentally as corrupt as the reality into which it tacitly but necessarily and forcefully initiates the students. Clearly, each of the sub-categories of this last critique portrays the dangers and the desirable alternatives differently. I describe them here briefly and expand on them in the subsection on "Education towards Socially Oriented Values."

The first sub-group of the third category of critiques of the model of education towards autonomy reflects the concept hereafter referred to as *education towards the transcendental*. Education towards autonomy, according to this more specific critique, emphasizes personal choice and self-realization as ultimate values, especially in White's and Callan's versions, which basically stress the fulfillment of desires. Thus, it seems to reinforce the relativistic and hedonistic trends dominant in postmodern society, trends which strip human beings of their essence. This critique relies on the assumption that the essence of humanity is the aspiration for transcendence, that is, the eternal aspiration to go beyond any existing situation and transform it into a better one. This transformation is only possible in light of a clear and absolute set of values that distinguishes between good and bad, inferior and exalted. Relativism does not allow for these distinctions and so is necessarily condemned by this view as divesting human beings of their nature and dignity.

Therefore, so the critics would contend, the view of education towards autonomy reinforces the dangerous trends of postmodernity, contributes to (to use the Nietzschean pathos and terminology) the "*beastialization of man,*" and should therefore be disqualified outright.

The second sub-group of the third category of critiques consists of neo-Marxist thinking and reflects the concept hereinafter referred to as *critical pedagogy*. Though the neo-Marxists would probably acknowledge that education towards autonomy might have positive value, they would hasten to add that, in a post-modern reality built on capitalistic foundations, this education is meaningless because the chances that the autonomous individual can be truly fulfilled under the capitalistic yoke are extremely slim. Thus, the Neo-Marxists believe that the existing reality does not allow for the existence of *true* education towards autonomy. Unless the reality is radically changed along neo-Marxist lines, education towards autonomy is at best meaningless and at worst dangerous, since it tacitly justifies the prevailing reality.

The supporters of this view would maintain that what is needed, first and foremost, is a critical pedagogy that will help expose the mechanisms of economic, social, and cultural cognitive subjugation exerted on the population by the dominant capitalist forces turning the wheels of postmodern reality. Only when individuals are consciously liberated from subjugation by these mechanisms will they have a chance to be able to think and act autonomously. These critics would probably also add that education pretending to reinforce individual autonomy without expounding the dominant power structures and liberating the students' consciousness from suppression by them is in fact serving the mechanism of deceit and suppression the existing power structures put in place.

The third sub-group in the third category of critiques reflects the concept hereafter referred to as *social relativism* based on the belief that education towards autonomy places too much emphasis on individuality, and thus widens the present social schism, weakens the shared platform of society, and endangers society's very existence.

The fourth sub-group in the third category of critiques mirrors the concept of *communitarian relativism*. The critique emanating from this sub-group is predicated on the belief that education towards autonomy is erroneous in its assumptions regarding human life. Supporters of education towards autonomy, so these critics would hold, view the individual as "living in a vacuum," as if his or her identity is exclusively shaped by personal choices.

These critics would continue that the truth is quite the opposite: the individual's identity, in fact, mirrors "social embeddedness" and the individual's choices cannot but reflect values deriving from this embeddedness in a very specific socio-cultural context. Thus, they would conclude, education towards autonomy, which is based solely on alleged "independent personal choice," necessarily misleads individuals with regard to the nature of their personal identities and encourages alienation of individuals from the natural sources of their identity, thus contributing to the misery of individuals and the disintegration of society. Both of these phenomena are characteristics of postmodernity.

Here ends our journey through the most probable critiques which the most influential views that oppose "education for autonomy" view might mount. I do not know to what extent it is possible to have a rational discourse leading to a decision between the view of education towards autonomy and the above-mentioned critiques and the sub-concepts they entail. In any case, there has not been, to date, any attempt to create and lead such a discussion, certainly not in the profound, rational, sense of the term. This sense requires systematic, ongoing, developing discourse in which each view relies on sound argumentation and is treated with respect by substantiated counterarguments. Consequently, the discussion created would have been one in which each voice is either refuted and rejected, or improved or accepted as an important brick in the slow, systematic construction of a body of knowledge.

What we have instead are many opposed and lonely monologues made within an infinite, cacophonous chaos. Often such voices are couched in political demagogy, concealing thin arguments, the response to which by other lonely voices is sporadic at best. It is heard in a different corner of this arbitrary and noisy reality, and is quickly lost in the ongoing cacophony, just as the original voice was, and so on and so forth. What we have "out there" is "eternal repetition of disconnected voices quickly lost in the horribly strident, undefined background noise," sounding like atonal music.

This being the case, individuals involved with the system as educators, decision makers, administrators, and parents simply act intuitively, responding "on the spot" to various pressures on a basis of a "view," reflecting at least some of the opposed positions discussed above and again later below.

The Republican Response, or: Conscious Social Reproduction

The View. Like the two previous views of the desired goals of education (the technocratic view and education towards autonomy), conscious social reproduction is based upon acceptance of the relativism characterizing postmodern reality both as a given and as desirable.[48] Like the education-towards-autonomy view (but in opposition to technocracy), this position also supports the need to educate even in the existing relativistic reality. However, it rejects the possibility of theoretically and universally deciding what should be the aim of education in a relativistic postmodern democratic society. It limits itself to indicating the desired social procedure for setting educational goals for each community. The most prominent proponent of this view is the American philosopher Amy Guttmann, and I will now consider her position.

In contrast to the technocratic position, Guttmann[49] has no doubt that institutionalized public education in a democratic society has the ability and right to strive towards shaping a desirable human being. She claims that the desire to impart values, and to enhance social reproduction in the light of these values, is part and parcel of the concept of the Good Life in every society and cultural group, including democratic society as a whole. However, she recognizes the serious problems the democratic state faces in the present-day relativist reality when a decision about the set of values on which education should be based must be made.

Her solution distinguishes between "substantive value" and "procedural value." The former provides a concrete response to the questions: What is the Good Life? What is the desired society which enables the Good Life? The latter responds to the meta-question: how are the two previous questions to be dealt with in the concrete communities the democratic society is comprised of? According to Guttmann, the democratic state cannot give theoretical priority (i.e., abstractly, prior to a concrete social debate taking place) to one substantive value at the expense of another when determining the aim(s) of education. Were such a preferment to be given, the group supporting that value would also gain *a priori* preferment in the concrete social game. In a relativistic reality such a preferment could not be rationally justified. However, the democratic state can and should implement the procedural value of conscious social reproduction into the discussion concerning the objectives of education.

Guttmann's term "conscious social reproduction" describes the procedure that relativist postmodern democracies, aware of the constraints stemming from the liberal democratic demand for ethical neutrality, should follow in order to reach the unavoidable decisions necessary for laying the foundation for any educational procedure. It refers to the process of preserving society's cultural continuity through a rational debate among the members of local communities (at the lowest level) or of the whole society (at the highest levels) on desirable changes in their common way of life (i.e., culture). The word "conscious" here means a rational debate conducted on the basis of democratic principles of tolerance of all positions and avoidance of discrimination, so as not to prevent any individual or group from participating in the social debate.

To Guttmann's thinking, the ultimate goal of a general democratic society, and thus also the meta-goal of education therein, is conscious social reproduction in which all the relevant respondents to a pending question are invited to participate and to attempt to tip the scales in their own favor, given that everyone observes the rules of democratic rational discourse. This is different from concrete communities, within which conscious social reproduction might strive to achieve specific, material (i.e., not procedural) goals, having more to do with the preservation or enhancement of a specific culture or way of life.

Determining a meta-goal for education is not enough as it is a predominantly abstract goal. More tangible, meaningful goals are created as a result of many public debates in local communities of a larger democratic society, who follow Guttmann's procedure. The outcomes of these debates are determined according to the nature of the participants therein and the balance of powers between them. Thus, for Guttmann the decisive question is: who has the right to participate in the concrete debates, dedicated to determining the operational goals of education, taking place in the many concrete communities which comprise the democratic society? In her answer, Guttmann reviews what she believes to be the three views most essential to the history of Western educational thinking, perceptions to which one can return for answers in the sphere of education. Guttmann names those three thought patterns: the Platonic response, the Lockean response, and the Millian response.

The *Platonic response*, according to Guttmann, is the basis of what I previously termed above "education towards the transcendental." For Guttmann, this means that a hypothetical state, relying on an unequivocal cognition of the Good Life is an ideal state, which therefore has an exclusive right, in light of this cognition, to determine the goals of education. The *Lockean response*, according to Guttmann,[50] transfers the right and responsibility for deciding on education's goals to the parents, meaning that the state leaves education solely in the parents' hands, to be determined according to their own personal values. Guttmann's interpretation of the *Millian response* dictates that the state must leave the determination of educational goals up to the individuals undergoing the educational process, while the state is limited to laying the necessary educational foundation for such a determination and to a neutral presentation of possible lifestyles. This idea comes close to White's concept of education towards autonomy.

However, Guttmann maintains that in a democratic-relativistic society no one of these three possible responses can be adopted to the exclusion of the other two, because it is as impossible to choose one over the others as it is to choose between concrete goals of education. Any one position we would adopt, to the exclusion of the others, will amount to contradicting the democratic commitment to *a priori* non-preferment of any one worldview.

Guttmann believes this is also true of the concept of education for autonomy, perceived by the previous view as having an obvious priority in a Liberal Democracy. As she says, the values of liberty and autonomy are fundamental to a *specific* perception of the Good Life, and as such are *a priori equivalent to values basic to other views*, thus ineligible for *a priori* preferential treatment in the democratic framework.

Guttmann identifies three groups, each representing one of the three concepts, whose participation in concrete democratic debates on the goals of education she considers to be essential. These three groups include: the state, or rather its representatives thereof, who should defend the interests of the general democratic society; second, the parents who reflect their and their community's worldview on the well-being and desired development of their children; and last, experts who represent commitment to professionally defend the interests of those being educated.

Guttmann holds that in every community context, the operational education goals should be the result of rational democratic debate among representatives of these three. Hence, each community's goals will reflect a certain balance between the democratic state's aspiration to socialize educatees into a societal-democratic system of values, the parents' and local community's aspiration to preserve their worldview, and the experts' aspiration to foster in students a critical approach to all views and present them with as many alternatives as possible so as to enable them to choose independently from them. The first aspiration is presented later by Hirsch and Bloom, the second by MacIntyre, and the third was presented above by White.

In conclusion, Guttmann retreats to the meta-level due to what she perceives to be an inability to formulate universally substantive goals for state-governed education in a postmodern democratic society. Instead of directly identifying the nature of the substantive educational values in a democratic-relativistic society, Guttmann bypasses the question by going one level higher. Here she asks what the nature of the debate on the previous question is and who should be represented in it. To the first part of the question, she replies that the debate must be guided by an objective to maintain conscious social reproduction. To address the second part she suggests mandatory participation of the three groups described above. Clearly, once she has determined the nature of the debate, the identity of the participants, and the interests they will protect, she has also determined patterns that will affect the debate's outcome. But as interactions and different power relationships emerging from the three aforementioned points of view differ in various community contexts, it remains true to say that Guttmann avoids determining the substantive goals of education.

In the spirit of the times, Guttmann does not present her view as an indisputable truth or an absolute solution for the current educational dilemma. Rather, she posits it as a reasonable way to deal with the situation, one which takes into account all the components of the problem of education in the relativistic reality and is well-suited to the spirit of democratic society.

Critiques of Conscious Social Reproduction. Guttmann's concept is an interesting attempt to deal with the problematic nature of determining goals for education in a postmodern democratic society. However, from the education towards autonomy perspective described above (which I prefer to a great extent as will be shown in Chapter Six), Guttmann's approach rests on withdrawal from Liberal Democracy's most fundamental or defining commitment to develop its citizens' autonomy. Furthermore, her position sidesteps the debate on the goals of education and substitutes it with one on the meta-question of those who will determine the goals of education. In other words, Guttmann's assertion that the essence of democracy is embodied in the process of conscious social reproduction apparently reflects a "pluralization" of Rousseau's (to some extent) and Dewey's (to larger extent) procedural republican concepts of democracy.[51] In these concepts, democracy is primarily defined as a framework which enables rational and just communal decision making processes, based on the public's active participation and focused on different aspects of the future of the community.

The followers of the education-towards-autonomy view can argue (rightfully so, in my mind) that when Guttmann's concept of democracy is accepted, her educational concept becomes understandable and justified. However, in the setting of the *liberal* concept of democracy, *her claim that individual freedom and development of the individual's autonomy have no special status in a democracy is clearly invalid.* Those who adopt the liberal-democratic model obviously ascribe ultimate importance to these values; therefore, in the framework of the liberal-democratic conception, opting out of a debate about the meta-question constitutes an infringement of the most basic democratic credo.

Adherents of the neo-Marxist and technocratic approaches could criticize Guttmann's concept by arguing that it amounts to nothing more than a *de facto*

71

legitimization for unjustifiably imposing the arbitrary educational concepts of cultural elites who control society, or specific communities therein. The supporters of education towards socially oriented values could additionally argue that Guttmann's approach allows the prevailing corrupt reality and overrides the ideal and the desirable in all matters pertaining to the determination of the goals of education.

Should I repeat here what I emphasized at the end of the previous section? There has never been any attempt made to systematically develop an ongoing, rational discussion about conscious social reproduction and its critiques. It is just another, though academically respected, voice in the cacophonous void in which prevailing Western education systems find themselves.

Let us now proceed to present and examine one final category of views, made up by several voices, *education towards socially oriented values*, and consider the four very different approaches comprising it.

Education towards Socially Oriented Values

The basic characteristics of this category of views, which distinguish it from the previous three positions, are its trenchant criticism and rejection of the postmodern reality. Generally speaking, despite the wide differences and meaningful contradicttions in their views, the common denominator linking the many, varied adherents to this view is what might be called their transcendental aspiration towards a different, better, reality based on values opposed to those dominant in the postmodern era, and hence to educational goals which will replace any set of goals compatible with dominant postmodern values. They largely differ on answers to questions like which of society's values should be changed, and how the alternatives are to be justified.

They also differ in their epistemic starting points or approaches. The *first and second approaches* within this view are objectivistic. The *first* calls for a return to the values of Western rationalist culture as reflected in the basic concepts of eighteenth century American (or any other Enlightenment) society. These values are justified, in this context, as reflecting the exalted truths regarding the Essence or Nature of Man. The *second approach* within this view calls for education towards the values of a desirable, but as yet nonexistent, society stemming from the social criticism found in the desirable society of neo-Marxist theory.[52]

The next two approaches, in contrast to the two above, are relativistic, or more accurately, culturally relativistic. Contrary to their predecessors, both are founded on an acceptance of the argument that a specific value system cannot be objectively justified, but neither are they reconciled to the individualism, pluralism, and value chaos which seems to stem from relativism and characterize society and education today. Still, they are blatantly opposed to each other.

The *third approach* calls for educating towards values which form the basis for today's general democratic society, as opposed to the values of specific communities. This is, according to the supporters of this position, not because these values are "objectively valid" or "exalted," but for instrumental reasons: because this kind of common education is vital for democratic society's continued existence, sustainability, and (mainly) economic prosperity.

In contrast, the *fourth approach* accepts the existing pluralism and calls for educating young people within the parameters of their specific communities. Proponents of this approach do not claim it has greater validity than other possible ones. Rather, the claim is that education towards a clear system of values is vital to the development of human self-identity and that such clear and coherent systems can no longer be found outside specific communities that share, in theory and practice, the same set of values. Hence, adherents of this approach appeal to form ideologically homogenous communities within a pluralistic democratic state and to educate in light of the values that define them.

These four approaches to the view above are now described in more detail below.

The Conservative Response, or: Education towards the Transcendental View

The view I refer to here as "Education towards the transcendental" is in fact an attempt to reconstruct the Platonic project and adapt it to our time. Plato lived in a relativistic society and believed that relativism and its psychological "satellites," extreme egoism, hedonism, opportunism, and cynicism, eradicate the four cardinal virtues—wisdom, courage, moderation, and morality—which he viewed as essential to the Good Life. Plato therefore advocated that a desirable education should be based on these absolute virtues so that young people would internalize and be fortified by them against the prevailing, inevitable, corruption of society.

This view's most prominent herald in the last generation was the late American philosopher Allan Bloom.[53] Bloom believed that the relativistic attitude which rules postmodern society, with all its psycho-sociological side effects, causes the erosion of "human essence" among the young people born into our postmodern age, and that fighting this process is the goal of education.[54]

At the basis of Bloom's view lies the assumption that the essence of humanity is the transcendental aspiration, an aspiration towards a reality that is more exalted than the existing one, and criticism of the existing reality in the light of this aspiration. Bloom maintains that the Humanist curriculum that developed in the Western rationalist tradition nurtured this aspiration. This Humanist tradition was based on a study of "the Great Books," a study designed to present the students with "visions of greatness" or perfect models of desirable human life and thus to evoke in them the transcendental aspiration.

Bloom further claims that nurturing the human aspiration for transcendence must also be the aim of education today. Moreover, he stresses that action leading to this aim is most crucial today, because the powerful forces of the pop/rock-saturated, relativistic-hedonistic reality are working to neutralize the higher virtues in the minds of young people. These undesirable realities are turning them into "unidimensional" (a key term in Herbert Marcuse's philosophy that one is often reminded of when reading Bloom's criticism) creatures in thrall to satisfying their bestial instincts.

73

On the social level, Bloom claims that the values of traditional rationalism shaped the underlying values of America's founding fathers, and that the constitution and other basic political instruments based on these values provide the underpinnings for the subsistence and prosperity of American society. In Bloom's estimation the present disintegration of these values constitutes not only a danger to individuals, but also to the very existence of American (and it is certainly possible to add Western Humanistic) culture.

Just as Plato accused the Sophists of "buttering up" their students and legitimizing all their latest fads instead of trying to educate them in accordance with the desired virtues, Bloom accuses current education systems of largely reflecting, since the 1960s, the relativistic positions basic to postmodern reality. To his thinking, educators tend to prefer curricula that fulfill the educatees' relativistic-hedonistic-practical expectations instead of aspiring to elevate them beyond the unidimensional reality in which they are (allegedly) imprisoned. Thus, education betrays its original etymological definition: "to lead out."

Bloom bases his solution on an appeal for a return to the Great Books, which he believes to be Western culture's inalienable assets that can present students with visions of human greatness and can reestablish the "preeminence of man." In other words, Bloom proposes basing education on the humanistic disciplines of philosophy, history, and literature, and on the classical texts that meet the criteria of what he refers to as "visions of greatness."

Critiques of Education towards the Transcendental. This position's major contribution is its meaningful widening of the horizons of potential discourse about the desired state of postmodern society and education. Its criticism of the postmodern societal and educational realities is enlightening. The alternative it depicts is based on an epistemological view and worldview which, despite having provided the very foundations for Western civilization, are unknown and unimaginable to most individuals today. Such criticism and the alternative position it represents is of great value, even if we do not accept the assumptions and recommendations of the stance out of which it arises, because it provides a perspective that enables us to view the self-evident in a different light.

However, this value is also the source of the view's weakness, for Bloom bases it on assumptions that contradict the epistemic, existential, and educational views of most Western secular individuals to such an extreme extent that the chances it will be seriously considered are virtually nonexistent. Adherents of the technocratic approach or supporters of educating towards autonomy will probably view Bloom's educational recommendation as an attempt to return to the fossilized authoritarian teaching methods of the early days of the modern education system in a best case scenario. In a worst case scenario, Bloom's ideas would be viewed as a suggestion to indoctrinate educatees to accept a specific conservative worldview. Neo-Marxists, supporters of communitarian relativism, and others will argue that it is an essentially suppressive view, serving the interests of certain social elites (white, middle class, male, etc.).

This opposition, in the eyes of those who support the idea of educating towards the transcendental, does not reflect a weakness of the concept itself, but rather reveals again the failings, short-sightedness, and unidimensionality of the critics' views.

The Neo-Marxist Response, or: Critical Pedagogy

The View. Like the view of educating towards the transcendental, critical pedagogy perceives the existing social reality as distorted and thus distorting the nature of the individuals living in it. But supporters of critical pedagogy perceive the distortion of the existing and the desirable alternatives as very different from those defined by supporters of the previous view. Their position, extensively inspired by neo-Marxism, holds that human beings, by their very nature, aspire to achieve a life of liberty, creativity, and self-expression, while in the capitalist reality they become fossilized and alienated, shackled both economically and mentally to the capitalistic race for profit.

This distortion of human nature is made possible by the "superstructure," institutional and cultural mechanisms dominant in capitalist society that portray life as free, its goals as just, and itself as based on objective truths, while in fact these are nothing more than ideological structures justifying the existing oppressive situation. The existing education is therefore merely one of the superstructures, possibly the central one, because it initiates and indoctrinates young people to accept this suppressive reality and as such it is the activator, a *sine qua non* for all other forms of suppression.

In this kind of reality, the ultimate goal of desirable education would be first and foremost to free the individual's consciousness from its enslavement to the suppressive superstructures, including the education system, its curriculum, and any other primary aspect thereof, by exposing their arbitrary and suppressive nature.

Overall, supporters of this view do not propose a detailed alternative curriculum. Rather, they advocate a "liberating didactic methodology" whose principles comprise a dialogical relationship between teacher and students, a curriculum which addresses the students' actual problems and aims to present those problems as resulting from the distorted and suppressive social structure they live in, a genealogical analysis of the central social institutions including the official curriculum, designed to reveal their oppressive roots. In other words, they advocate exposing the narrow suppressive interests these institutions serve and the arbitrariness of their basic assumptions and values.[55] Some of them advocate "teaching as a subversive activity," or, in other words, they call on teachers to ostensibly follow the normal curriculum but to utilize its content to achieve the goals of critical pedagogy.

Critiques of Critical Pedagogy. The criticism that can be raised against this approach is almost identical to that of education towards the transcendental. The advantages and disadvantages of critical pedagogy's agenda are both rooted in the utopist assumptions thereof, which essentially contradict conventional wisdom. Those who argue against the basic assumptions of this view and thus support one or more of the other views presented here will doubtlessly view critical pedagogy as an attempt at Marxist indoctrination. The likelihood that the various echelons of policy makers will accept this approach is virtually non-existent. Adherents of critical pedagogy will understand this reality as a consequence of existing education superstructure, which caters to the needs of the enslaving elite.

It can be argued that the critical position of critical pedagogy projects great power, because such teaching can shed an entirely new and different light on reality for the students, as long as this perspective can be presented to them critically and together with others which oppose it. Yet from the perspective of critical pedagogy at least, this recommendation is flawed. Adherents of critical pedagogy would claim that such an argument expresses yet another aspect of the suppression of consciousness typical of our educational institutions and worldview, one known as "suppressive tolerance." The very fact, in their estimation, that a view proposing a total alternative is described as just "another perspective" that should be presented together with others opposing it in order to enrich the student's world empties it of its revolutionary power and thus contributes to the suppression.[56]

The Social Instrumentalist Response, or: Aspiration to Enhance Cultural Literacy

The View. In contrast to the two previous views, which are basically objectivistic,[57] the view dubbed here "social instrumentalism" emanates from acceptance of the basic relativistic assumptions of postmodern society. But as opposed to the relativistic positions that are mostly individualistic (except for the "conscious social reproduction" view which attempts to balance between individualist and social perspectives), the cultural literacy view infers from its basic cultural, relativistic foundations the need to educate individuals towards a common social language necessary for the social and economic functioning of society. This recommendation derives from the (alleged) need to neutralize the threat to efficient function and continued existence of society (allegedly) arising out of the highly pluralistic and multicultural relativism dominant in postmodernity.

One of this concept's most noted proponents in the last generation is E.D. Hirsch.[58] Hirsch's view is based on the claim that American society's continued existence is endangered by the high degree of pluralism and fragmentariness now dominating it. He argues that pluralism and the cultural splits currently characterizing American society are gradually eroding the common cultural-linguistic network flowing from a uniform cultural-educational tradition that in the past functioned as the foundation of that society. In his opinion, this pluralistic process disrupts society in all spheres and endangers its ability to function and its future existence.

Hirsch believes that society, especially a contemporary democratic society, must ensure a minimal level of efficient communication among its members to enable effective economic, societal, and political function.[59] In order to address this need, Hirsch argues that education must strive to integrate all students into a society which shares a common cultural-linguistic roof. The concrete purport of this recommendation is to provide educatees with broad but superficial knowledge of a few thousand concepts which, according to Hirsch, constitute the basic foundations of Western culture together with those exclusive to the American culture. Hirsch proposes such a list and details didactic and curricular "scaffoldings" that are supposed to help teachers teach in its light.[60]

Critiques of Cultural Literacy. Criticism of Hirsch can be leveled from two directions. From the objectivistic direction, namely, Bloom's view of education towards the transcendental or the doctrine of critical pedagogy, it can be argued that Hirsch accepts the prevailing reality as is and, in fact, he wants education to socialize students into the (alleged) unidimensional or enslaving reality which is quite simply corrupting. Such socialization, according to this critique, betrays the very essence of education. More specific claims of this critique will vary, of course, according to their source: either education for the transcendental or critical pedagogy.

Another obvious critique that can be leveled at Hirsch from both these and other quarters could consist of the claim that even if one accepts Hirsch's concerns and most of his suppositions, the belief in the ability to socialize anyone to Western (or any other) culture just by the teaching of long lists of concepts is ridiculous and faulty. Western culture (as any other) consists of much more than just concepts; it consists of thinking processes, feeling patterns, and certain values guiding human behavior in all basic spheres. These processes, patterns, and values have roots going back thousands of years. One cannot transmit them just by superficially teaching a list of concepts.

Another argument can be leveled against Hirsch from the pluralistic relativistic view or the multi-cultural direction. This would contend that in principle it is impossible to create a single list of conceptions that fairly represents the main streams of American or any other society without it being necessarily biased toward the worldview or tradition of certain social groups. Thus, Hirsch's list of concepts would be considered arbitrarily coercive and biased towards Anglophone Western culture, ignoring the numerous communities living in the framework of other cultures (Spanish, Chinese, etc.). This critique would conclude that the attempt to teach only the Anglophone and European cultures that underpin the American reality is actually cultural imperialism employed by the (still) dominant culture against many important minority cultures which, in the relativistic-pluralistic reality, cannot possibly be conceived as inferior.

The Communitarian Response, or: Back to the Polis

The View. The final criticism of Hirsch's position reflects the basic assumptions of communitarianism. One of the most outspoken proponents of this view in the last generation is Alasdair MacIntyre.[61] In spite of the fact that the analysis and argumentation of these two thinkers take place on different levels (Hirsch on the linguistic, sociological, economic level and MacIntyre's on the ethical, philosophical, historical level), MacIntyre's view, like Hirsch's, stems from acknowledgement of (what he believes to be) the existing cultural-societal split and (in the case of MacIntyre) the impossibility of all-embracing social discourse and co-existence.

Still, MacIntyre's view distinguishes itself from the previous one on three essential points. First, MacIntyre focuses mainly on the breakdown of ethical discourse in Western culture. Second, in this context, the great danger proceeding from the situation, to MacIntyre's way of thinking, is the limits of the individual ability to develop a clear and solid identity. Given that the proper formation of a young person's identity requires the internalization of a clear ethical code, growing up today, in a world of ethical void and chaos, constitutes a real threat to the identity formation of the individual. The third and main difference is comprised of MacIntyre's belief that in the existing relativistic reality there is no way to establish a uniform conceptual and value system relevant to all members of American society (or most other large Western societies). He concludes that the only possible way to overcome the danger is to establish specific community level institutions in which such uniformity can exist.

MacIntyre supports education provided by the community aimed at endowing its young people with the community's values and worldview. Concrete examples of MacIntyre's concept might be education in various religious or culturally based schools, or in the Greek *polis* whose Aristotelian concept constitutes the central model for MacIntyre's desirable reality.[62]

Critiques of Communitarianism. Criticism of this view can stem from all the previous views, but let us begin by noting one counterargument that is common to all: arguing that every community must be allowed to educate towards its own values accords legitimacy to educate towards values clearly contradictory to the Humanistic or rationalist values which constitute the core of Western culture. Thus, legitimizing education of this kind can result in (to give some examples frequently used in this context) granting permission to Hindu groups to cremate widows on the funeral pyres of their dead husbands, or to African groups to practice and educate for female circumcision, or enabling Khomeinistic groups to educate towards blind obedience to an *ayatollah*. Beyond the fact that the critics perceive these values to be undesirable, MacIntyre's position is likely to lead to a paradox: pluralism, which stems from Western values of equality, tolerance, and decency, can lay the groundwork for education towards values that clearly run contrary to these basic values and which can eventually lead to the destruction of the original pluralistic values.

In addition to this common counter-claim, the adherents of the pedagogic branch of the technocratic view and of the education-towards-autonomy view would criticize this view as potentially leading to the suppression of the individual's freedom and autonomy (by legitimizing education in totalitarian communities, for example). Supporters of education towards the transcendental or of the critical pedagogy views would condemn the communitarian view as one which may easily lead to a narrowing of the individual's horizons, because education limited by a framework of (what they would take to be) superstitions prevents realization of the individual's human essence. Meanwhile, disciples of conscious social reproduction and of the technocracy would attack this approach as likely to contribute to chaos and to cultural disintegration of democratic society at large.

Here, too, as in all the previous cases, choosing rationally between communitarianism and the attacks on it, as well as between the various attacks, seems to be an endeavor that might exceed the limits of rationality alone, and may have to do with a "leap in the dark" towards one of the systems of belief from which these views stem. Still, no attempt has ever been made to lead a discussion between these views, even if only to agree on what they disagree on and map relevant possibilities.

SUMMARY

Our long journey through representative thinkers and views that have attempted to respond to the acute crisis stemming from the disappearance of the modern goals of public education in postmodern democracies has now ended. All the views discussed here are products of educational thinking in a postmodern democratic society and they all aspire to remain, in different ways and to various degrees, loyal to democratic ideology. During this journey we have avoided views that consciously and blatantly reject or are not grounded in democracy, such as the various fundamentalist or fascist doctrines that have enjoyed rejuvenation during the past generation, in reaction to the ideological void and confusion which haunt the core of democratic thinking.

I would like to think that this journey through the representative views responding to the educational crisis has created a reasonably ideated map of what could have been the discourse, if one in which various thinkers and writers on the subject would be able to locate themselves when developing their responses had actually taken place, allowing various stake holders the possibility of a (somewhat more) mindful choice.

Although the majority of the views discussed here were developed in academic or intellectual environments, the confusion they display is mirrored in the current disarray which educational decision makers, as well as the public and especially parents who are concerned about their children's education, seen to be in. Thus, I also hope I succeeded in showing the reader the immensity of the problem and the grave differences that democratic postmodern society has to face in its attempt to rationally deal with this profound crisis and define the overall goals of education in our culturally diverse times.

While in the past, even the recent past, educational goals were clear, at least in certain social frameworks, including that of modern democratic societies, in today's postmodern democracy these goals have become extremely blurred. Moreover, it seems obvious to many that there is no way to actually face the problem. As a result, (conscious or unconscious) ignorance of the situation seems to be "the best course of action."

Thus, where once there were clear goals, today the path is lost amid confusion and anxiety and whatever technocratic obsession with detail happens to be in vogue as the expedient escape mechanism. Consider, for example, the fixation on final exams based on "national standards." Once, not so long ago, completing the final exam meant that the student was now a mature person who was considered to be ready for life as it should be lived in accordance with society's values leading to the Good Life. "Maturity" or "graduation" meant ability and commitment to live the Good Life.

The knowledge these tests (allegedly) attest to was perceived as, at the very least, a necessary and sometimes even sufficient condition for maturity. Today, however, all that remains from the original terms' rich and very demanding meaning is an indication that a person has successfully obtained a diploma which attests to knowledge of certain subjects which the educatee attained. Whatever terminology is used, this diploma allows acceptance to higher education which is mistakenly (see the discussion on over-education in the next chapter) perceived as a necessary condition for reaching profitable socioeconomic positions. As opposed to the past, none of the subjects one has to "learn" to get this diploma has any positive *internal* cultural value, certainly not in a society that cherishes only the instrumental aspects of knowledge. The vast majority of these subjects have no bearing on the individual, his or her interests or social needs (as I shall elucidate in the next chapter). These terms, whose literal meaning was still appreciated two or three generations ago, have become vacuous today, an atavistic relic from a chronologically very recent though mentally very distant culture in which knowledge paved the way to the Good Life only through its internal value.

How, then, is it possible to educate in a public system whose foundations have "suddenly" disappeared and whose goals, stemming from a rich cultural heritage, have been replaced by bureaucratic procedures devoid of meaning? In the metaphorical language of this book's title, how can the ship of education navigate in the stormy postmodern sea if its captain and officers woke up one day with amnesia, and had no recollection of the destination set for them in the past or even a memory of the way by which they ought to lay a course?

The answer is, of course, that in such a situation there is no possibility of educating. If we do not steer the vessel in light of clear goals that reflect the basic values of Liberal Democracy, while systematically harnessing postmodern forces to the fulfillment of these values, the ship of education will be helplessly tossed and turned by the storm until it breaks up and finally sinks.

Is there a way out of this maelstrom? I believe that even in postmodernity the ship of public education can and should have clear operational goals and that it has a good chance to be mindfully and strategically steered towards them. In Chapter Six I shall indicate the desired way of regaining our direction in the tempestuous, postmodern confusion, and define the course which will bring the ship of education through the postmodern sea following the stars of liberal democratic values. In Chapters Seven through Nine, I shall indicate the educational, curricular, peda-gogic, and organizational frameworks deriving from educational goals which are valid for the Liberal Democracies of our times and demonstrate how postmodern forces can be mobilized for their implementation.

Before we can find a way out, we must first understand the enormity of the educational catastrophe in which Western culture has found itself. In order to help the reader gain some understanding of what we are actually going through (only "some" due to the immensity and complexity of the problem), beyond the "loss of attainable goals" dimension of the crisis, I will also add, in the chapters to come, an analysis of the disappearance of the meaningfulness of education's content (Chapter Three), the disappearance of the functionality of education's organizational structure (Chapter Four), and the disappearance of education's target audience (Chapter Five).

THE DISAPPEARANCE OF JUSTIFICATION FOR THE THEORETICAL CURRICULUM IN THE POSTMODERN ERA

INTRODUCTION

The second parameter of any organization, *activities* or *contents*, relates to the actions the organization takes in order to achieve its goals. The primary activity of education systems today revolves around teaching a theoretical curriculum, based on the study of fragmentary theoretical subjects that (allegedly) represent the scientific disciplines dominant in today's academic culture.[1] The origins of this curriculum can be dated back to the objectivistic worldview of the ancient Greek. Different versions of this worldview have dominated Western education for the past two and a half millennia. The objectivistic epistemology that has dominated Western culture for most of the last twenty-five hundred years provided the justification for and meaning of this worldview. Within this view, the search for, and procurement of, "pure knowledge" or "Truth" was perceived as the ultimate value or good in human life. Education in such a context meant learning the various disciplines which lead to or help reflect upon the "Truth."

This epistemic foundation, which was deeply rooted in many different Western societies for many centuries, has all of a sudden disappeared in the last two generations. In the skeptical and relativistic postmodern era, the discourse on "Truth" or "pure knowledge" has become meaningless. Human knowledge is no longer viewed as an ultimate good for human life in and of itself but rather as instrumental, as a tool for achieving desired benefits, usually materialist ones. Consequently, the most fundamental and solid structure and basis of Western education, what I call here the *spiritual justification for the theoretical curriculum*, has foundered within but a few short decades. As a result of this fundamental change, the long period of compelled study of this curriculum suddenly became an unjustifiable and hence meaningless endeavor.

Concomitantly with the spiritual justification for the theoretical curriculum, over most of the same, very long, period of time, some prominent *practical justifications* for it also prevailed. This justification was, in a way, a "parasite" on the spiritual justification as it was, first and foremost, a reflection of the fact that "possession" of theoretical knowledge was perceived as having high value in and of itself, as the ultimate Good or *Summum Bonum*. As such, possession of knowledge was perceived as socially "respectable" and those learning it or who seemed to know it were accorded high social status. Thus possession of high-level theoretical knowledge facilitated the achievement of socioeconomic status, for but a chosen few in socially stagnant eras, and for many in eras which enjoyed high levels of upward social mobility.

We should not assume that the practical justification for possession of knowledge meant that the learner could accrue from it any direct or immediate benefit. The theoretical curriculum was seldom useful or even relevant to the tasks the individual needed to carry out in his or her high-level status or job. Theology, basic to the theoretical curriculum in the middle ages, was not relevant to the administrative tasks the graduate of Jesuit colleges (to take one example) very often fulfilled; nor did the study of ancient Greek and Latin in British boarding schools throughout the nineteenth century contribute to the conquest of new colonies and to domination over their "natives," tasks graduates of these school often had to fulfill. Still the possession of theoretical knowledge often correlated with positive social stigma and, when possible, upward social mobility. This correlation between (alleged) possession of theoretical knowledge and chances to achieve high social status became very significant in the modern era, especially from the end of the nineteenth century, an era of enormous upward mobility of the working classes.

The reasons why employers accorded importance to seemingly useless knowledge are subject to many hypotheses in labor market study. Suffice it to say that the working classes (if we restrict ourselves to the modern era for the purpose of this example), in their struggle for upwards social mobility, aspired to acquire that which functioned, for their generation, as a positive stigma of the bourgeoisie: a certificate testifying to graduation from high schools and later on, institutions of higher education. As possession of such certificates increased, employees turned to it as a necessary and often sufficient condition for being hired. Again there are many hypotheses responding to the question why this was the case. It is quite evident though, that the naïve "common sense" view according to which there is a correlation between the number of years one spent learning and one's competence is often far from universally true. Still these two phenomena, the rise in working class's acquisition of graduation certificates and the concomitant rise in employers' tendency to use these certificates as a precondition for hiring, laid the foundation for the modern pattern of social mobility, thereby driving forward the expansion of the education system in the modern era to extremely rapid and unprecedented extents.[2]

However, over the last few decades, this practical justification has also suffered from rapid erosion by several revolutionary phenomena which characterize the postmodern labor market. Over-education is one such phenomenon. As ever-increasing numbers of college graduates compete for the same job openings, the status their graduation certificates bestow on them depreciates. The result is a greater number of unemployed graduates and a devaluation of the wages for those who are lucky enough to have work. We can also see an increase in college graduates working in jobs for which they are overqualified, which inevitably leads to growing professional dissatisfaction. Other relevant phenomena characterizing postmodernity include: the extension of leisure and reduction of time dedicated to work by many individuals in almost all Western countries (even if not at an identical pace), extremely rapid anachronization of academic certificates, and the formation of "new professions" which require practice-based knowledge and personal attributes rather than formal or theoretical knowledge. Thus the power and sustainability of the practical justification for the theoretical curriculum has been worn thin in the last two generations.[3]

To conclude: the spiritual justification for the theoretical curriculum has totally "evaporated" and its practical justification has been radically eroded over the past two generations. This profound change in circumstance has eradicated the individual or social rationale or justification for the extremely demanding, long, and expensive process of enforced leaning of the theoretical curriculum. This radical change in circumstance did not however change to any relevant degree the support and finance society still offers this seemingly redundant yet highly costly activity. To put it in less academic terms, the current education system is good for nothing, meaningless, and absurd for most individuals involved with it, although it is as highly demanding and costly as ever.[4]

This is certainly a very strong claim, a claim most readers may find very difficult to "digest" or even examine open-mindedly. This chapter is therefore devoted to the clarification and substantiation of it, and I hope to encourage the readers to reexamine their deeply rooted prejudices on this issue, the same way other social arrangements, such as the subjugation of women or slavery, which were fully accepted and well established for millennia, were called into question and consequently deemed obsolete by past generations.

I begin with an analysis of the concept of "meaningful human activity" basic to my argument in this chapter. I shall then rely on this analysis in order to outline a framework and detail the criteria with which we can indirectly evaluate the level of meaningfulness learning activities have for the individuals engaged in them. I need to do it indirectly because it is impossible to interview or even speak with the individuals that were forced to learn the theoretical curriculum throughout the two and half millennia of its domination of Western Society.[5] Next I shall use this conceptual framework to demonstrate the high level of meaningfulness the theoretical curriculum, which relied on the above two justifications, enjoyed for the past two and a half millennia.[6] I then proceed to clarify the nature of the three fast-paced processes which are rapidly eroding the meaning of the theoretical curriculum for the postmodern era.[7] Briefly, these processes are: the relativistic revolution, which is undermining the two thousand and five hundred year-old cultural backing the curriculum and its spiritual justification previously enjoyed;[8] the radical postmodern revolutions in the labor market that have eroded the practical justification thereof;[9] and the positivization[10] and fragmentariness of human knowledge which has eroded its unity, thus contributing to the negative effects of the erosion of both its spiritual and practical justifications.[11]

Finally, in the last section I will point out some severe damage caused to contemporary schools' ability to function, brought on by the dissolution of the meaningfulness of the theoretical curriculum. In recent years the system actually conveys a distinct anti-educational message to those who are compelled to stay in the system. This meaningless and absurd education process that all youngsters are compelled to go through for so many years results in grave psychological, cultural, and social damage.[12]

THE HUMAN YEARNING FOR MEANING: AN ANALYSIS

The next two sections are dedicated to the substantiation of the claim that the theoretical curriculum has lost, in the last two postmodern generations, the justification and meaningfulness it enjoyed throughout its long history. In order to form this argument I forge in this section the theory of what I call "the human yearning for meaning" and draw from it criteria for indirectly assessing the level of meaningfulness students can accord their activities with. A more direct approach such as questioning the students is impossible since most of them are no longer available for questions, not to mention answers. These criteria will allow me to compare the availability of sources for meaning to students learning the theoretical curriculum during its long past and more recent history.

I explicitly refer mainly to the meaningfulness of *learning activities* of the theoretical subjects since it is what interests us here. Still, the analysis in this section is generic in principle and relevant to most kinds of human activity.

The view of meaningfulness I present here stems from suppositions which have been basic to Western culture from the times of Plato and Aristotle and are still very dominant in contemporary concepts of planning and quality control, performance analysis and improvement, organizational development, human resources development, organizational culture, and leadership.[13] This view is also supported by prevailing psychological theories, such as attribution theory and its derivatives, cognitive dissonance theory,[14] Victor Frankl's Logotherapy,[15] action theory,[16] SDT theory,[17] and the research of "interests."[18]

This view can be briefly summarized by the following argument: Human beings wish to perceive any activity or set of activities they are engaged in as meaningful. Satisfying this yearning is a primary condition for their well-being. The main source for a sense of meaning, if and when it prevails, stems from conception of an ultimate good(s) or benefit(s) which the individual involved perceives as either identical to the activity they are engaged in or as attainable through this activity. A secondary yet important source for a sense of meaning is a sense of unity or integration of the various elements comprising the above concept(s) of Good. In other words, the more this Good is perceived to be one integrated entity, the higher the chances are that its conception will lead to a sense of meaning.

The above-mentioned concepts of Good can be spiritual or practical (these terms are used here in a special technical sense which will be clarified immediately). A "spiritual Good" is any ultimate life goal perceived as valuable for its own sake. Such a Good is not adopted for the sake of later material or other gains. A "practical Good" refers to any goal whatsoever that does not satisfy the above condition. The concept of unity can refer to either spiritual or practical goals.

On the basis of this conceptual framework, I will delineate below several groups of criteria that can help compare the level of meaningfulness the culture of various Western generations lent to theoretical learning.

Orders of Benefits

The *first* group of criteria for assessing meaningfulness consists of the prevalence of Good(s) or benefit(s) (spiritual or practical) in whose light one can understand her or his activities and justify them. This group of criteria is divided into two categories:

- *Quantitive distance* of the learning activity from the desired goal, i.e., the number of steps that separate the learning activity in question from the desired goal(s).
- *Chronological distance* of the learning activity from the desired goal, i.e., the time span the learner believes to be separating the activity in question and the achievement of the ultimate goal.

These two sub categories are largely independent of each other. The qualitative distance can be graded according to four main orders of benefit which demarcate the distance of the learner from the desired good:

- First-order benefits exist when students are either interested in learning for its own sake or believe that the process of learning involves implementation of a value(s) or goal(s) which they value in of itself, regardless of any higher value or goal the process may be able to help them attain.[19] In this case learning has intrinsic values for the learner and is therefore the ultimate goal and does not function as a means to another external end. This perception of learning as a goal in and of itself denotes that spiritual goals are in play.

In all the rest of the orders, learning is justified by extrinsic goal(s) which vary in their degrees of qualitative distance from the activity at hand.

- *Second-order benefits* exist when young people believe that learning, even if not identical to realizing their goals, directly supplies them with means: cognitive abilities, skills, financial, institutional, or social support or other means necessary to the achievement of these goals, be they spiritual or practical.
- *Third-order benefits* exist when young people believe that the acquisition of knowledge will lead to the attainment of behavioral qualities or other personal attributes they perceive as vital for acceptance into social institutions or social contexts which they perceive as necessary for achieving second order benefits. Here we have three steps: lower-level means leading to higher level means leading to the goal in question.
- *Fourth-order benefits* exist when young people believe that the knowledge they acquire through studying a certain subject is necessary for receiving a diploma which is necessary for acceptance to any of the above social institutes or social contexts. Belonging to such contexts (third-order benefits) is perceived as necessary for receiving second-order benefits. In other words we now have four steps separating the goals from the learning activity in question.

Logically speaking, it is possible to continue this list of orders of benefits *ad infinitum*, but in the actual educational-social situation we refer to, the above-mentioned have been the most relevant orders.

Another subgroup in this group of criteria for assessing meaning consists of the chronological distance (as opposed to the qualitative one referred to above) between *immediate benefit(s)* and *long-term benefit(s)*.

While *first-order qualitative* benefits necessarily require immediate benefits from the activity, such a relation is not necessary between this and the other orders. Students can perceive second-order benefits that are either short term or long term. The same is true for the third and fourth orders. This is why we have to distinguish between qualitative order of benefit (first subgroup) and chronological ones (second subgroup).

Orders of Unity

This second group of criteria refers to the second source for meaning: perceived *unity* in a spiritual or practical goal, *and* the activities serving it. In other words, it refers to the perceived level of integration among the various elements comprising the learning goal (either spiritual or practical) and the perceived coherence among the processes leading to them. This group consists of a hierarchy of criteria pertaining to the extent of unity the learner attributes to the goal and activities of the learning she or he is engaged in.

- The *first, higher, order of unity* exists when solid, clear, and *necessary* connections are believed to exist between all subject matter included in the curriculum and between them and a unifying framework.
- The *second* or *intermediate order of unity* exists when complementary relationships are believed to exist between the subject matter included in the curriculum. This order does not require conception of necessary relations but just that the students can understand how subjects taught in one discipline can relate or add to subjects taught in another.
- The *third* and *lowest* order of unity exists when the learners can understand the curriculum without believing there to be any contradiction between the various contents included in the curriculum.

Cultural Backing

The *third group* of criteria actually includes only one criterion: the *extent of cultural backing* the curriculum enjoys. This concept refers to the degree of support the students' culture or *weltanschauung* accords the basic assumptions and objectives of the curriculum (for more on *weltanschauung*, see Chapter Six). It has a direct impact on the previous two groups of criteria and is directly and positively correlated with them. As such it can be understood as the fundamental root cause for meaning, mediated by the extent of benefit the curriculum offers and the extent of unity it enjoys.

Historically, the more powerfully ingrained the perception of the learning process as leading to a Good (spiritual and or practical) was in a culture, the higher the order of justification in terms of benefit and unity of the curriculum in the minds of the learners was. In other words, as the level of importance society accorded the learning process increased, so did the level of meaning accorded to it by the learners.

Degrees of Meaning

The *fourth group* also comprises only one concept, which reflects a combination of the main variables previous groups have related to. It deals with the *degree of meaning* the curriculums enjoys. In other words, this concept relates to the degree to which students regard the curriculum's content or the activities that take place within it as meaningful. Such perception stems from two general sources:

A. The level of benefit they believe the curriculum may accrue for them. This depends on:
   a. The qualitative order of benefit (spiritual or practical) they believe can be attained from performing it or the number of steps they believe they must make in order to attain the benefit.
   b. The chronological order of benefit or the duration of time they believe to be necessary before the benefit can be attained.

B. The order of unity (spiritual or practical) they perceive the curriculum as having.

The contribution of both these sources to the level of meaningfulness the study of a curriculum enjoys has correlated throughout history with the extent of cultural backing the learners' culture or worldview lent to it.

As already claimed, both the variables indicating meaningfulness and the extent of cultural backing influencing them can reflect either a spiritual view of life wherein one aspires to live according to values he or she perceive as good in and of themselves, rather than means to living up to other values, or one emphasizing primarily practical benefits such as money, status, pleasures, and so on, which by definition cannot but be understood as means to attaining other values. In most cultures throughout history both these views were powerful and important. While high spiritual values were always proclaimed from rooftops, in their shadows often dwelled officially condemned, yet usually quite influential, practical ones.

This duality will be clarified in detail in the next section. For now, suffice it to note that the disappearance of the spiritual source for meaning and the acute erosion of the practical sources thereof which are both taking place in the last postmodern generations, are the results of the profound changes in cultural backing which are responsible for the rapid evaporation of all the pillars supporting the meaning of the curriculum for its students.

In order to concretizes this claim let us take for example an individual living in a culture which accords high status to those who learn or have knowledge of theoretical disciplines and appreciates theoretical and abstract knowledge for their own sake. It this culture, the more abstract knowledge is, the more its beholder is revered (similarly to the ideal Platonic society). It is fair to assume that the level of meaning the learning activity has for our individual is very high since it provides him or her with first-order justifications to do so (or first-order quantitative and chronological benefits). In other words, the learning activity is conceived by the individual as a good in of itself, or even as the ultimate Good. No further steps are necessary; no additional chronological distance separates the learning activity from the good it is perceived as bestowing.

The high order of spiritual justification this individual accords the curriculum does not prevent her or him from also according it the highest level of practical benefit. "Learned individuals" in Germany or gentlemen in Britain were ranked high on the social ladder (among the growing German bourgeoisie and in both the aristocracy and bourgeoisie in Britain). This might sound paradoxical to the reader, since on a purely logical level the spiritual good seems by definition to exclude any practical one. But in the reality of the human psyche these two seemingly contradicting poles "lived well" with one another and at times even enhanced each other.

Our individual will also perceive his or her learning process as being of the highest order of unity since all the disciplines he or she learns are perceived as belonging to the same framework, that of learning which contributes (first and foremost) to the spiritual goal above and are perceived as logically necessitating each other. The Seven Liberal Arts which comprised the curriculum throughout most of its history were perceived in just such a way throughout most of that time.

We now have two very good reasons to believe, merely on the basis of our knowledge about the immediate and very strong cultural backing the curriculum enjoys, that all learning processes in our individual's learning paths (even the dull and boring ones) have the highest level of meaning for him or her, this *without ever having to talk to the person in question directly.*

On the other hand, if we look at an average student of an average school any-where in the USA or Europe or any other Western society today, we can assume, without exchanging one word with her or him, on the basis of knowledge of the general social and cultural circumstances of our times alone that the curriculum the postmodern individual has to "learn" enjoys an extremely low level, if any, of cultural backing. This individual is highly unlikely to perceive all or, at the very least, most of the disciplines taught within it as having any spiritual justification which could lead them to perceive it as being good in and of itself or leading to such good; nor will they find any practical benefits which may lead them to per-ceive it as yielding any social respectability. At most, the postmodern individual will think the curriculum has some fourth-order practical benefit since the standard-ized learning process is (often mistakenly) conceived as leading to a diploma which can assure high socioeconomic status.

Furthermore, chances of our individual perceiving the curriculum as having any level of unity are incredibly slim since unity is necessarily a result of spiritual or practical benefit, which the individual is unlikely to receive from learning a cur-riculum which enjoys only a fourth-order practical benefit. Early modernity, on the other hand, did provide the theoretical curriculum with cultural surroundings that made it possible to perceive it as unified and integrated in light of ultimate justify-ing goals. However the nature of its surroundings in the postmodern era is drama-tically different. This transformation will be discussed in detail below (section 3.3).[20]

Ordinarily, this scenario, together with the disappearance of educational goals discussed in the previous chapter and the problems discussed in the next two, is the root cause for most of the grave problems plaguing education systems all over the world and of their devastating psychological and social effects. Still this eventuality is not without exceptions.

To understand how such exceptions can prevail (a necessary step if we wish to understand the alternative presented in the second part of the book) and how necessarily rare they must be within contemporary education systems, let us look at another theoretical example. Imagine an individual who voluntarily studies history of philosophy, mathematics, and German. There is no necessary logical or cultural connection between these three disciplines. But they can be connected and in fact complement each other in the individual's mind if his or her main interest is the philosophy of mathematics, and he or she perceives history of philosophy and mathematics as the two main supporting pillars of this discipline, and mastery of German a must in order to understand the major works in these disciplines written in the nineteenth and early twentieth centuries.

Learning the aforementioned disciplines is certainly justified for her or him by the highest order of quantitative and chronological benefit since in this example the learning process in and of itself is his or her interest or vocation. Given this justification, the study of these three, now mutually supportive, disciplines, now also enjoys a first-order of unity in her or his view.

Unfortunately, such cases are extremely rare. There is ample direct and indirect evidence of the validity of the argument concerning the evaporation of justifications for the curriculum. Directly such evidence consists of literature on rising alienation which is a mirror image of the level of meaning Western education has for its students.[21] Indirectly such alienation causes a myriad of side effects: The level of violence in schools has reached an unprecedented high as shooting and killing sprees are becoming more frequent occurrences and the execution thereof is considered "in" by a growing number of students in Western countries in recent years (perpetrators enjoy the admiration of a large number of young people who visit websites that document and celebrate such activities).[22] Addiction and alcoholism levels are also on the rise, as are levels of depression and of the consumption of anti-anxiety and anti-depression medications among young people.[23]

Although these phenomena may be the result of more then "just" alienation and a lack of meaning students experience at schools, there are good reasons to believe that the effect of any other cause is augmented and exacerbated by the alienating school experience.

Arguing that schools are plagued by rising levels of alienation and decreasing levels of meaning in the last few postmodern decades, unlike in the long history of Western educational which preceded them, is at this stage no more than a claim which requires substantiation in order to become a fully developed argument. In order to develop this argument I will therefore maintain in the following sections that:

A. The theoretical curriculum enjoyed, in its two and a half millennia history, a high degree of meaning for those following it. Such a meaning was predicated on:

    a. Students' perception of the curriculum as bestowing high benefits of the first and second orders, and

    b. Students' perception of the curriculum as having first- or second-order unity.[24]

B. In the last postmodern decades the degree of spiritual meaning attributed to the curriculum in all the above areas has been drastically reduced. This is the case due to, first and foremost, a dramatic erosion of the cultural backing and resultant level of unity students perceived the study of the curriculum as having and the benefits it imparts.[25]

C. Another source for this erosion is the postmodern labor market which left little room for the practical justifications which have supported this curriculum in modernity and in previous eras.[26] Thus, today learning the curriculum has become meaningless or absurd for almost all students.[27]

D. This loss of meaning has had a devastating effect on many aspects of students' lives, their communities, and society in general.[28]

THE THEORETICAL CURRICULUM IN THE PAST: LEARNING AS A HIGHLY MEANINGFUL ACTIVITY

The modern theoretical curriculum Western societies currently follow is rooted in the millennia-and-a-half-old Seven Liberal Arts Curriculum, which in different and changing variations has dominated Western culture until this very day. This curriculum has been divided into two parts since the Roman era: the *trivium* subjects that included the origins of what was much later called "humanities"—rhetoric, logic, and grammar—and the *quadrivium* subjects which include the various sciences of that time: arithmetic, geometry, astronomy, and the theory of music. The last two were actually derivatives of the first two. These disciplines were taught in Latin for centuries. Only in the second half of the nineteenth century, following the scientific revolution and the development of nationalism, were most of the traditional disciplines in the curriculum replaced by modern sciences, national literature, and history which were all taught in the students' mother tongue.

    Throughout this two-and-a-half-millennia-long period, changes in the contents of the curriculum were extremely significant. This was especially the case in the nineteenth century as in it the contemporary modern scientific-national curriculum was developed, a curriculum in which almost all the curriculum subjects were altered in a long chain of profound changes. Still the curriculum's basic structure (a division between math and the natural sciences on the one hand and the humanities, and later social sciences, on the other), its goal, teaching theoretical knowledge, and its basic *raison d'être*, the view according to which theoretical knowledge and the possession thereof are sanctified as the ultimate good in human life, went unchanged and virtually untouched.[29]

    The liberal curriculum was formed in Rome during the first centuries AD as *humanitas*. It was predicated on the notion that the individual can realize his own humanity through his encounter with exemplary human visions from the past.

Humanitas is an offshoot of the Hellenistic idea of *paideia*, which arises out of the educational approach developed in Athens during the fourth and the fifth centuries BC. In other words, in order to find the source of the theoretical curriculum which dictates the learning process young people are forced to uphold today, one must go back to classical Athens.

During the period in question, Athenian society, formerly dominated by a military aristocracy, adopted a democratic form of government bolstered by commerce. This new system of governing converted Athenian society into a culture which relied heavily on a broad "middle class." New educational patterns developed as a result of this socio-cultural change and, at the same time, the aristocratic-militant education, which instilled youths with the values of Homer's *Iliad* and *Odyssey*, disappeared from Athenian society altogether (though it was preserved in Sparta).

The Sophists, who formed the vanguard of Athens' new educational processes, earned their living by giving private lessons to the children of the elite. Children were handed over to the Sophists' care when they were eleven or twelve years old, after having completed some sort of "elementary education" taught by a specially appointed servant or slave. This elementary level education included reading, writing, arithmetic, music, and Athenian customs and traditions.

Sophistic education was perceived similarly to the way we perceive present-day high school education. This was an essentially utilitarian education designed to provide the upper (slave-owing) classes, who did not have to work for their living, with the training required for success in the social and political life of democratic Athenian society.

The main skill the young Athenian of this era required in order to succeed was eloquence and persuasion as resulting from command of the art of rhetoric. Anyone endowed with such skill had a good chance to persuade the people's assembly to elect him to public office, thus ensuring him prestige, power, and wealth. In addition to rhetoric, young Athenians also needed to learn logic in order to present valid arguments (or at least make arguments look as if they were valid, and adversaries' arguments seem invalid), grammar in order to correctly articulate those arguments, and a conversance in traditional Greek literature and poetry in order to spice speeches with appropriate known and loved quotations.

The Sophists also taught the sciences of the times, which were all based on mathematics including astronomy and musical theory. These sciences were viewed as beneficial to the young "careerist" for practical activities such as military leadership and seamanship, as well as for presenting himself as an authority on the ways of the world before the people's assembly. All the famous Sophists practiced this form of education, but it is particularly associated with Isocrates, the last of the great Sophists.[30]

The Sophist curriculum enjoyed all the aforementioned sources for meaning: since it stemmed directly from and reflected the culture of democratic Athens (which was relativistic, egoistic, hedonistic, and ascribed great importance to values such as success wealth and personal glory), it enjoyed full cultural backing. From the above cultural backing students could conclude that the curriculum had spiritual and practical benefits.

Since the skills and attributes acquired in Sophist education were perceived by Athenian society as vital to the Good Life, or *arete*, the virtue characterizing the Good Life of the Athenian citizen, it was therefore perceived as having spiritual benefit of the first-order.

Since this education relied on contents designed to provide learners with the knowledge needed to succeed in practical and social life in the present and, more particularly, in the foreseeable future, it was most probably perceived as practically beneficial. The benefits therein were probably mainly second order benefits.

The attributes which together comprised *arete* and the learning activities leading to them were conceived as completing each other and creating a unified whole, the ideal Athenian man and citizen. The curriculum could therefore also enjoy unity of the first or second order.

One may reasonably assume, therefore, that students regarded their studies of this curriculum as extremely meaningful and were highly motivated to succeed in the educational process.

The original Sophistic curriculum later generated two variations, both of which decisively influenced the history of Western education. Both versions wholly or partially adopted the content of the original curriculum, though each used its subjects differently and justified their use in different ways.

Plato proposed the first modification on the Sophists' curriculum in his *Politeia*. His curriculum recommended an initial study of mathematics and its various branches of arithmetic, geometry, astronomy, and music and later engaging in dialectics. Dialectics, the Platonic version of rhetoric, included one principal difference from the Sophists'—Plato does not see it as leading to any practical or material benefit of the first or second order. Rather, he sees the study of dialectics as enjoying a spiritual benefit of the first-order, or put another way, as necessary for attaining knowledge of the absolute Truths. Similarly, Platonic justification for the study of mathematics eschews its practical applications and benefits and views it as developing the student's ability for abstraction in preparation for engaging in dialectics.

The structure and justification for the Platonic curriculum emanate from Plato's epistemological view. Plato tried to provide an objectivistic-idealistic alternative to the dominant relativistic-hedonistic conception which was prevalent in ancient day Athens. He perceived this conception as paving the way to social, political, and psychological disintegration and decadence and as a sure way to the maximization of human misery. According to Plato, human beings' purpose in life is not to attain power, wealth, and pleasure as the Sophists maintained and as was reflected in the popular Athenian worldview, but rather to seek knowledge of the Truths and ideas which are the eternal and absolute essences of all beings. The educational process, according to Plato, should aim to train young men and women (he was, for his time and cultural background, surprisingly open to "feminist" values) to lead the Good Life or a life based on (his version of) *arete*, or a life that human beings are worthy of, ergo a life lived in the search of or attainment of knowledge of Truth.

The fundamental principles of Plato's educational program will not be discussed here.[31] These principles were never fully (or even extensively) practiced in any society. The true extent to which Plato realized his program in his own academy is unknown, but without a doubt, if we presuppose for the sake of this analysis the implementation of the Platonic Utopia, in Plato's ideal society, the attributes of his educational plan would have enjoyed the highest possible level of cultural backing since it follows directly the *raison d'être* and ultimate goals of this society. It would have also enjoyed the highest level of meaning in the framework of such an imagined society. That is to say: in a Platonic culture and society, both qualitative and chronological first-order spiritual benefits of such a curriculum are apparent as the curriculum helps the student learn the Truth which is the ultimate Good in such a framework.

As for practical benefits, the Platonic education system was supposed to uproot the need for them in the students (at least in those reaching the higher strata of the educational process). So in an ideal Platonic utopia this concept would have no meaning and no reference group. But even if we imagine for a minute a more realistic deviation from this ideal and the total uprooting of egoistic desires it entailed,[32] I believe students in this "deviated" society could also accord the curriculum with high-order practical benefits since in such a realistic deviation from the pure utopia, the higher one was (or perceived as being) located on the ladder leading to the knowledge of Truths, the higher his social status would be. This "deviation" was actually basic to most Western societies and curricula, throughout history, as will be clarified below.

Due to the cultural backing the curriculum would undoubtedly enjoy, to the exclusion of any other option, it would also enjoy the highest order of unity on the spiritual level and in fact on the practical level as well, at least in the deviated version. In this utopia, the curriculum's various ingredients would be perceived and presented as logically necessitating and supporting each other and together contributing to the achievement of the educational goal in a fully integrated way.

Following the curriculum would have been an extremely difficult and demanding effort for any student living in the Platonic Utopia but at the same time it would have had profound meaning, as every one of its aspects would be perceived as leading the student to fully live the best possible life a human being can have.

While Plato's variation on the Sophist curriculum sprung from his opposition to the Sophists' epistemic-ethical relativistic worldview, the second deviation from the Sophists' educational conception was the result of events that took place in Athens and throughout the "civilized world" late in the fourth and during the third century BC. By these I refer to Alexander the Great's conquest of Greece and of the East and the development of the Hellenistic culture that integrated Greek culture with the cultures of the conquered Eastern territories.

This integration begat crucial changes in the curriculum's scope and justification. The scope of Isocrates' and the Sophists' curricula emphasized a wide range of instrumental learning, while underscoring rhetoric and the mathematical sciences of the time which were believed to be essential to administrative, military, and political success. The Hellenistic curriculum, on the other hand, focused on a study of the Greek language and the great literary works of Greek culture to the exclusion of most other educational fields. What contemporary terminology terms "secondary school" (the first level of education was executed at home by a special servant or slave in Hellenistic society as well) the educators (*grammatikos*) were primarily dedicated to teaching Greek grammar, including also theory of grammar, morphology, and creative (literary) writing. Students also studied the literary masterpieces of Homer, Hesiod, Pindar, Sappho, Euripides, Menander, Demosthenes, and Isocrates. This tradition of teaching the Great Books, which was dominant in Humanistic education until but a generation or two ago and still has an impact on it till this very day, originated from the Hellenistic curriculum. While mathematics and its various branches, which were an integral part of the original Sophist curriculum, were not completely omitted from the Hellenistic curriculum, they were considered minor subjects at best.

The source of meaning for the curriculum also shifted during the Hellenistic period. The Sophists' curriculum was dedicated to helping students improve their practical and political skills and hence their chances to acquire power, influence, glory, and riches. In contrast, the Hellenistic curriculum drew meaning and justification from a more cultural and theoretical oriented program. With the decline of the political strength of Athens and the collapse of its democratic regime, Greek citizens could no longer achieve power and affluence with the skills and knowledge procured during the course of their education. Accordingly the curriculum no longer enjoyed the same first- and second-order benefits justification. In other words, the skills inculcated in the curriculum were no longer conceived both as leading to the achievement of *arete* and as needed for practical success in life; the curriculum was no longer a process of training the young towards their future social, political, military, and commercial leadership roles.

Having lost its original cultural backing, the curriculum gained different support from the Hellenistic culture. This consisted of the belief that an educated individual, in possession of eloquence and social grace, is an individual who makes full use of his humanity and thus has an "entry ticket" to the right social circles. The curriculum therefore enjoyed support on of second- and third-order benefits.

First, it had enjoyed support on a spiritual level, to the extent that the learner took the Hellenistic ideal of the Good Life seriously. Second, it enjoyed support on the practical and social levels, since the acquisition of behavioral qualities requires acceptance into, and assuring the respect of, the influential or "dignified" social strata. Finally, the curriculum also enjoyed second-order-level unity since the disciplines taught within it were perceived as accompanying each other in the formation of the educated person.

It is plausible to say that a curriculum enjoying such justifications would be highly meaningful for the students who followed it, though from a different perspective than that of student of the previous curriculum. The word that best expresses the new justification is *paideia*. This term embodies the idea that a student's soul is shaped during the educational process by values the student internalizes through the study of literary masterpieces that express "human greatness." Put another way, if the Sophists' objective was to train an active citizen, the Hellenistic educators' goal was to develop the spiritual skills of a "man of culture," a member of Hellenistic civilization, as opposed to the barbarian who remained outside Hellenism.[33]

Considerable differences between the objectives, structure, and content separate these two variations which developed out of the Sophist curriculum, the Platonic and the Hellenistic. However, in contradistinction to the Sophists' original, both the newer versions are deeply rooted in the essential characteristics of the theoretical curriculum to this very day. Even more importantly, these versions are responsible for the change in the justification for education to this day, for the shift from the practical benefit the Sophists focused on (with the spiritual benefits merely supporting the practical ones), to focusing on the spiritual benefit as having merit in its own right (with the practical benefit becoming but a byproduct as will be clarified below). These versions are the cause for the conception of theoretical study as valuable in and of itself which is fundamental to and dominant in Western culture, as well as for the necessary ensuing contempt this culture has for any approach which includes even a whiff of utilitarian attitude in it (although, ironically, the same curriculum does accord its students with considerable practical benefits as will be clarified below).

This was a critical turning point in the history and fate of the curriculum since it accorded the curriculum with the spiritual justification and aura which were its only explicit support through the ages. Subsequently, it is also responsible for the malaise stemming from the curriculum today since the collapse of this justification is the root cause for the acute depreciation of the meaning the theoretical curriculum has in the postmodern age and for the ensuing alienation of students and burnout of teachers, with all their devastating effects.

It is possible to argue that while the effects of the Hellenistic curriculum were limited to content and form of study, Plato's version provided the epistemic basis for the cultural backing of his and the Hellenistic conception throughout Western history. Plato laid the cornerstone for the objectivistic worldview that has been dominant in Western culture over the past two and a half millennia in one variation or the other.

This view rests on the assumption that an objective reality, knowable to the human mind, exists. Belief in the existence of such a reality is essential to understanding the theoretical curriculum's source of meaning: Plato's objectivism. This objectivism, in all the many variations it had throughout Western history, was the source for the objectivistic assumptions which enabled the generations up to the most recent decades to believe that a curriculum based on pure theoretical activity is justifiable and accord it with the necessary cultural backing and ensuing meaning.

Although specific details of the justification and subject matter of the curriculum varied extensively throughout the long post-Hellenistic period, the curriculum never lost its core justification on both the spiritual and practical level.

On the spiritual level, the curriculum was believed to accord life with meaning by providing human beings with values and lifestyles believed to be good in and of themselves and hence as constituting the ultimate objectives of human life. Throughout history, this justification was sustained by a belief in the existence of an Ultimate Truth and in the human ability to know that Truth. Based on this belief, the theoretical curriculum was perceived as teaching all truths worthy of knowing or at the very least as paving the way towards knowledge thereof.

Similarly, on the practical level, possession of the knowledge acquired by following the curriculum was regarded as a sign of belonging to higher social strata, or at least to an "employable class" for those who were not fortunate enough to be born to the upper classes in eras which did not enjoy much social mobility. This aspiration was common in young people wishing to cast off the shackles of misery that chained the average European farmer in the Middle Ages to his birth-place and circumstance as a vassal of an aristocrat,[34] and the blue collar worker to the production lines during the Industrial Revolution. During periods which were blessed with social mobility, it was possession of curriculum-based knowledge or of a diploma (allegedly) attesting to possession thereof that guaranteed access to upward social mobility.

As we can easily see by the following, these two justifications blatantly con-tradict each other. While the first, spiritual, justification relies on the assumption that life's ultimate purpose *is* a theoretical search for Truth for its own sake (*arete*, *humanitas*, knowledge of God, or the virtuous life), the second stresses a practical search for a powerful, or at least profitable, social role, which can yield quantifi-able material assets as the ultimate purpose. Despite this apparent contradiction, the flexibility of human consciousness allowed both justifications to coexist for centuries and even reinforce one another.

The underlying assumptions of the first justification, so long as they were meaningful and valid within Western culture, attributed sublime significance to the content of study and made it seem vital it in the eyes of students and enhanced its prestige, which undoubtedly facilitated the function of the second justification. At the same time, the second justification greatly reinforced the students' motivation to take the first justification seriously which for many of them might have been too abstract to one extent or another.

The liberal curriculum was "sanctified" in Rome: first in Cicero's educational writings, then in Quintilian's writings, published in the first century AD. Finally, it became engraved on the collective consciousness of generations of Western society through the writings of Martinus Capella in the fourth century AD.[35] Cicero is responsible for coining the Latin term *humanitas*, which is comparable with the Greek *paideia* and *artes liberales* or "liberal disciplines." The study of these dis-ciplines was only open to the *free* citizen, *released* from the burden of earning a living, which is one (and probably the original) explanation to the term "liberal edu-cation" exclusively denoting theoretical education during most of Western history.

Other, more spiritual, explanations had to do with the dominant assumption that only through theoretical learning while free from the yoke of material necessities can the individual liberate his soul from its animal part and focus only on what is unique and essential to the human being: the spiritual or rational aspect of the soul. As already claimed, during the constitutive periods of this curriculum, this was perceived as a necessary and sufficient condition to the Good Life, the only life which allows a human to be free enough to express their humanness, hence the only life worthy of living.

The liberal subject matters were, as determined by Cicero, literature (parallel to grammar), rhetoric, philosophy (parallel to dialectics or logic), mathematics (arithmetic), geometry, astronomy, and music.

Following Cicero, Capella made two claims essential to understand the history of the curriculum and the meaning it had throughout Western history:

- There are seven liberal disciplines or subject matters (the seven determined by Cicero).
- These subjects are of interest only to "celestial creatures," that is, only subjects that are purely intellectual or spiritual in essence and have no relation to man's drives and practical life may be included in the list of the *arte liberals*.

The liberal curriculum Capella cannoned, which focused on the seven *artes liberales* and was perceived as leading to *Humanitas*, was a direct offshoot of the three earlier version of the theoretical curriculum. As in the curriculum taught by the Sophists, the Hellenistic *grammatikos* and the curriculum formed by Plato, it enjoyed full spiritual and practical justification and unity and hence the highest possible level of meaning.

Up to the beginning of the modern era, the theoretical curriculum underwent three other major transformations (which are actually comprised of hundreds of smaller ones) which created three more primary variations of the curriculum. The first was the Christian version of the Roman liberal curriculum. The formation thereof began in the fifth century AD and was taught in cathedral schools.[36] The second, scholastic, version was developed in the eleventh century AD. This version placed greater emphasis on logic and philosophy than its predecessors, which were more rhetorical-literary orientated.[37] The third version was the Renaissance Humanistic reaction to the scholastic approach which in fact returned the curriculum to its Hellenistic-Roman content roots.[38] Throughout this long period, for reasons identical to those relating to the earlier versions, these three major versions of the liberal curriculum enjoyed the highest level of cultural backing, justification, and unity, spiritual and practical.

The modern versions of the theoretical curriculum shaped in the nineteenth and early twentieth centuries remain dominant throughout the world to this day. *This (in many variations) is the curriculum many millions of young people are compelled to learn throughout their constitutive years.*

Until recently, these modern versions served the relevant prevailing ideal of human life and thus were perceived by the learners as having first- and second-order (short and long term) spiritual benefits. In most cases they were also perceived as having second- to fourth-order practical benefit since students of the curriculum were bestowed with the accreditation necessary to belong to the desired social classes. The conceptual cultural framework assuring the above benefits also guaranteed a high level of unity of the first and second order. In order to illustrate this claim, below I detail the three modern versions of the curriculum.

Three different approaches to education emerged during the nineteenth century, in the three principal European countries. In Britain, the traditional curriculum which reflected a combination of the Humanistic and scholastic models was predominant at the high school and university level; its justification was mainly Platonic and Aristotelian. In post-Revolution France an empiricist-pragmatic conception of the curriculum became dominant and, during the first half of the nineteenth century, the neo-Humanistic approach was predominant in the classic German Humanistic *Gymnasium*.[39] During the second half of the nineteenth century and throughout the twentieth century, reaction against this approach intensified, mainly in the form of the *Realschule*, which represented the empiricist-utilitarian perception.

In all three cases the earlier trend which associated theoretical high school studies with admission to university was strengthened. Universities served as the main providers of liberal professionals who first had to be educated in the liberal arts or their modern counterparts. The rationale was very simple and obvious: young people must be educated to become human beings who fully express their humanity, in the only way known to be relevant according to the culture at hand, before they can become medics, lawyers, engineers, or administrators, potential office holders for the developing bureaucracies of the European societies.

Thus, for example, the *abitur* (matriculation) was introduced into the German *Gymnasium* as early as the late eighteenth century, but only in the early nineteenth century did it become a prerequisite for admission to university. Furthermore, only classical curriculum graduates of the *Humanistische Gymnasium*, and one hundred years later graduates of the *Realschule* as well, were eligible to take the exam. In other words, *Gymnasien* teaching the liberal arts became the exclusive channel through which the middle classes could gain admission to government bureaucracy and upward social mobility. A similar process also took place in Britain and France.[40]

The curriculum the Humanistic German *Gymnasien* primarily followed was a replication of the Greek syllabus with some of the Latin syllabus added to it. The relevance of this curriculum to the study of medicine, law, administration, or to any other practical requirement the future of the majority of students may have had was minimal. Therefore, any practical benefits students could gain from these studies were from the third or fourth order at best. The knowledge *Gymnasium* studies equipped students with distinguished them as members of *die Gebildete*, the German educated middle class. This in itself was a necessary and usually sufficient condition for acceptance to desirable jobs, but no more. This was also true in relation to students from exclusive private schools (called "public") in Britain. In contradistinction, after the empiricist-pragmatic worldview took over in revolutionary and post revolutionary France, students could gain second-order benefits from at least the part of the curriculum that could be perceived as relevant to their future occupation.

Without a doubt, in all three societies, the dominant culture provided solid cultural backing to the curriculum's purposes. The English gentleman, the German "educated man," and the French Cartesian bourgeois-rationalist represented coherent human ideals. Each was a concept deeply rooted in the cultural tradition of the society and the position they each enjoyed was supported by objectivist assumptions and values, which of course differed from case to case. Students of the theoretical curriculum in these societies arrived at school and later at the university after they had already absorbed these basic values and ideals which supported the curriculum and the study thereof and were therefore motivated by the aspiration to realize them. He or to some extent as time went on, she, perceived the subject matter, which was extremely theoretic and somewhat irrelevant to the student's life in the majority of cases, as coherently serving a socially desirable purpose.

For this reason, while the practical benefits of the curriculum were long term and only of the third and fourth orders, the spiritual benefits were probably perceived as high, of the first and second orders, and often immediate, by many students molded in light of the dominant culture. For many, the mere learning of a subject was perceived as "elevating the mind' (an immediate first-order spiritual benefit), for others as "only" leading to the acquisition of objective knowledge and thus to the expected future "elevation of the mind" (longer term second-order benefit).

From the above historical review we have good reasons to conclude that even if over the greater part of its existence the content of the theoretical curriculum was boring, nevertheless it was very meaningful to those who followed it throughout its two--and-a-half-millennia existence.

As shown above, this meaning was based on solid cultural backing and the two sources of meaning it supported: various orders of (practical and spiritual) perceived benefits and various order of perceived (spiritual and practical) unity.

The cultural backing for the curriculum relied, during its long history, on various versions of objectivism. The original Platonic version and all those which ensued from it—Aristotelian, neoplatonic, Christian, scholastic, Humanistic, and empiricist—all supported the fundamental assumptions about the nature of the world and the desirable human life upon which the various versions of the theoretical curriculum rested. These objectivistic conceptions also accorded the curriculum with first and second orders of unity since all its elements were perceived as logically related, complementing and supporting each other, and forming together the "complete knowledge" necessary and sufficient for a Good Life.

The spiritual benefits from following the curriculum stemmed directly from the cultural backing. In all the previous periods, including modernity, Western cultures and the students raised within them perceived the model of life to which the curriculum educated as elevated and respectable. In most cases (perhaps even all with the exception of post-revolutionary France) the *Capella dictum* held true, the curriculum was perceived as uplifting human beings to an almost angel-like level of existence.

As for practical benefits, during the foundational periods of the curriculum (fourth century BC Athens and the Roman Republic of the third and second centuries AD), those were of the first and second order. The subjects included in it were directly relevant to both the students' everyday life during their studies and to their future occupations (which in these periods were actually relatively short term benefits, as the future was but a few years away from the studies time in the majority of cases). Later in history, the practical benefits of the curriculum were downgraded to third and fourth order, as students following it acquired the accreditation and testament they needed to belong to desired social classes and thus pave their way to social and political success. Much later, from the end of the eighteenth century and during the nineteenth, students followed the curriculum to acquire a diploma which functioned in much the same way.

Since the third century BC and during the last two and a half millennia, the theoretical curriculum has typically featured the following basic attributes:

- Knowledge acquired within the curriculum's framework has been theoretical; lack of practicality was an essential condition for subject matter to be included in the curriculum.
- The acquired knowledge was totally unrelated to the students' immediate biological, psychological, or social needs.
- The various subjects were studied fragmentarily with no interrelationship.
- The curriculum was the legacy of society's upper classes—or at least (when the upper classes were illiterate) of the "employable classes."[41]

In all the curriculum's many metamorphoses throughout the centuries, including the twentieth, and within all the cultural contexts in which it prevailed, the theoretical curriculum enjoyed full cultural backing and hence was perceived as bestowing upon learners thereof spiritual and practical benefits in an integrative way and high level of meaning. Contrary to this past background, today the theoretical curriculum has lost almost all its meaning to the people involved in it. This is a result of the breakdown of its cultural backing and unity, and hence the elimination of both practical and spiritual benefits that can be attained by following it.

DISAPPEARANCE OF THE LIBERAL CURRICULUM'S MEANING IN THE POSTMODERN ERA

We have good reason to believe that during the last two generations the meaning of the curriculum for those compelled to follow it has dramatically diminished. This is true both in comparison with the meaning the modern curriculum had for previous generations of students until, say, the 1950s or 60s, and certainly in comparison with the meaning its earlier versions had for many generation of students in the past two and a half millennia. This drastic devaluation is the result of recent blows to the four sources of the curriculum's meaning, namely, the degree of cultural backing it enjoys, the degree of spiritual and practical benefit that it is perceived as offering, and its degree of unity on both spiritual and practical levels in the eyes of the learners.

In the following subsection, I elaborate on and explain the severe damage the lack of cultural backing inflicted on the modern liberal curriculum in the postmodern age and the way the relativistic revolution affected, in fact created, this shortcoming. To this end, I shall point out the traditional arguments and views that have justified the curriculum in the past, explain how the currently dominant relativistic world-view eliminated the validity of these views and thus the relevance of the curriculum relying on them to the postmodern student. Moreover I shall explain the reasons for the total failure of the desperate attempts to put forward alternative arguments designed to provide the old curriculum with new relativistic justifications where such justification can no longer exist.

In the three subsequent subsections, I signify the loss of spiritual benefits and the more fundamental layers for the practical benefit as a direct result of the above process. I then explain the erosion of what was left of the practical benefits as a consequence of the postmodern revolutions that in the last few decades turned the postmodern labor market upside down[42] and elucidate how the foundering of the cultural backing of the curriculum, augmented by the recent dramatic disintegration of science, eroded all that was left of the curriculum's unity (3.3).[43]

The Relativistic Revolution and the Erosion of Cultural Backing and Spiritual Justification for the Liberal Curriculum

As I already showed in Chapter Two, the objectivistic justifications that provided solid foundations for Western education and its transcendental goals for two and a half millennia cannot be accepted in the framework of the relativistic worldview prominent today. As a result, the cultural backing, granted to the theoretical curriculum in earlier periods, was irrevocably lost.

The Platonic version of the theoretical curriculum was based on the suppositions that theoretical study led to the knowledge of Truth, and that knowing Truth purely for its own sake with no other practical benefit (which in this context would mean harnessing the divine "in man" to his bestial parts, an unthinkable notion in Plato's view) was the ultimate goal of human life, a necessary and sufficient condition for living (what Plato called) the Good Life. While this version was never fully, or even extensively, implemented, the numerous objectivistic conceptions of knowledge and of life goals which stem from and rely on it were adopted by all later Western cultures and have supplied the liberal curriculum with sound epistemic-ethical foundation for approximately two and half millennia.

The Hellenistic version of the curriculum and its various later offshoots stemmed from the beliefs that there exists an identifiable universal human essence, that it is possible to correctly know it, and that the authors of the Great Books (Homer, Pindar, Cicero, Virgil, and in later periods and versions of this curriculum, writers on the scale of Shakespeare and Goethe) knew and reflected its essence. Therefore, the study, preferably by heart, of their works was believed to help students know the desired virtues, identify with them, and internalize them. The two meanings of "knowing something"—the narrower cognitive one, "being able to reflect the object of knowledge," and larger biblical existential one, "being unified with the object of knowledge"—were often integrated into this justification central to Western culture.

In this as in many other cases, including Plato's very early one, the basic metaphor for the educational process was that of an artist imprinting the student's soul, which was perceived as similar to soft, amorphous clay, with the desired form. The learning process was equated with sculpting clay or dyeing cloth and in this analogy the fully designed statue or colorful cloth (to refer to the metaphor Plato actually used) was one and the same with the desired human being, a person ready "for use," ready to lead a Good Life.

As far as the first "character molding" stage in the educational process was concerned, Plato, reflecting very deep and sophisticated psychological insight, relied on what we today call "active learning." In Plato's version of the curriculum, rote learning was only one of many instruments of the process. Students also participated in dramatic scenes, played musical pieces, and even improvised based on what their educators considered to be the "great works of art" of the past. However, in many later versions of this process, repetitive rote learning helped students develop the ability to quote the great masterpieces quickly and eloquently, an ability which became in and of itself a prime objective and main part of classical studies.

However large the differences between the various curricular versions may have been, the goals, assumptions, and metaphors basic to them all were always the same. I will now make a big historic leap over the very long period ruled by various versions of the Hellenistic model, to the time where the education process at the core of Western culture adopted the empiricist-pragmatic modern curriculum. This curriculum relied on objectivistic assumptions according to which modern empirical science is what enables the student to know the truths about material reality. Beyond the practical benefits of having this knowledge, an individual in possession of it was perceived as "enlightened" or an "*éclairé*," an individual who sees the light of truth, the most noble and esteemed ideal in modern eyes, as opposed to the *ignoramus*, the religious, the superstitious, and the "*obscurantist*" who are all shrouded in darkness and have no chance of seeing reality clearly enough to allow them to understand the universal truths.[44]

The German neo-Humanistic conception shared this reliance on objectivistic assumptions. In this case, these assumptions determined *inter alia* that there is a personality "nucleus" which constitutes the real nature or "true self" (to use more recent terminology) characterizing each individual, a nucleus one can identify (although never categorically, the Humanists were objectivists *and* skeptics) and should strive to realize. In other words, according to the Humanists, one's vocation in life was to continuously strive to know one's nature and realize his or her potential according to it (within the last two views, women were perceived as equal, at least in principle, for the first time in Western history, if we ignore Plato's declarations concerning the equality of women that never materialized. Several very influential women indeed played an important role in the formation of German Humanism).[45]

During the last two generations, an intensive process of devaluation has eroded the hold objectivism had on Western society, leaving room for the relativism which now rules in its stead. This relativism is none other than the same "good old" view Plato attempted to bury underneath the seemingly solid objectivist foundations. He was successful for two and a half millennia where Western culture is concerned; however now relativism is "back in town," this time aggravated a million times over by the media and advertisement industries which dominate our lives today. Within such a relativistic culture the twenty-five-hundred-year-old foundations of the theoretical curriculum and their later, modern, variations don't stand a chance. They will necessarily crumble, they have in fact already faltered, and with them the cultural backing of the theoretical curriculum will disintegrate to nothingness.

One may argue that while the original traditional objectivist justifications do not function anymore in our skeptical, relativist culture, other justifications can be found to accord the same curriculum new meaning relevant for us or rather for youngsters in our culture today. It is in fact possible to discern two large categories of such attempts to justify the use of the theoretical curriculum in a relativistic cultural setting. I will refer to the first as the "transcendental attempts" and to the second as the "utilitarian attempts." These are the two significant categories of attempts one should examine when wishing to ascertain the feasibility of a justification for the theoretical curriculum in our relativistic culture. If these are found to be totally baseless in our culture, we will be able to argue not only that the traditional justification can no longer function in postmodernity but also that the theoretical curriculum cannot be justified today and hence lacks any relevant cultural backing. This is what I will now attempt to prove.

Both the above categories reflect a move away from objectivism and toward cultural relativism. They stem from the assumption that while one can no longer find an objectivist universalistic justification for the theoretical curriculum, a justification based on some consensual cultural function can indeed be found.

However, beyond the above common denominator, these two categories are very different from one another in their structure, distribution, and appeal. I chose to name the first category "transcendental" based on a term adopted from Kant, who first coined the term, by one of the leading thinkers responsible for this line of argumentation. This term expresses the relevant philosophers' belief that they could deduce justification for the liberal curriculum from a mere use of terms basic to our culture and language in a kind of semantic or logical hocus pocus.

The second category of cultural relativist argument developed in the last two generations intended to safeguard the theoretical curriculum is the instrumental one. It is also the most commonly used one, both in daily and political discourse about education and in theoretical writings. This category consists of the attempt to show that one or another version of the theoretical curriculum or at least some of its parts are necessary for the enhancement and development of desired attributes in young people, which in turn are perceived as instrumental to the achievement of goals believed to be socially desired.

The arguments belonging to both these categories are invalid and absurd and hence cannot supply justification for the theoretical curriculum in the postmodern era. Once we acknowledge this fact we cannot ignore the fact that this once gloriously dressed king is now completely naked, or, in less poetic terms, the fact that the theoretical curriculum lacks any justification or backing in today's cultural context is openly exposed.

The first category of arguments was developed by a group of leading British philosophers of education from the end of 1960s until the early 1980s. It was a reaction to what they took to be the major philosophical problem and hence the experiential domain of (early) postmodern philosophy of education. They called it the "Justification of Education" when by "education" they meant the liberal curriculum that the British (or, more generally, Western) middle and high classes had for generations accepted as the only possible manifestation of education.

During the early 1980s the same group and their followers in philosophical circles became aware of and recognized the impossibility of constructing such a justification and gave it up.

Given that these attempts had no impact on any educational or social context outside the (somewhat dreary) academic ivory tower of Anglophone philosophers of education, there is little reason to waste time regurgitating these ideas, especially when remembering that the original harbingers of these philosophical attempts had the academic integrity and rationale to admit the failure and impossibility of success of their endeavor.[46]

Suffice it to say that these attempts were similar to the scholastic effort to prove the existence of God using just the definition of the concept "God." In other words, these were tautological attempts to show why merely questioning the justification for education requires that we accept the validity and justification of the liberal curriculum. The mind boggles at the thought that serious philosophers labored for years to present and defend arguments of this kind, which were seriously considered to be well-founded by other philosophers of education for almost two decades. This situation can only be explained by the desperate desire of all those involved to justify the existing curricular structures, even after the drastic change and practical disintegration of the dominant epistemic view on which they were originally based and which accorded them justification and meaning.

In contrast, the instrumental view common in today's discourse is not, at first glance, as obviously illogical and absurd as the transcendental one. However upon a slightly deeper examination it is as flawed and senseless as its counterpart. This view has had an infinite number of variations over the last few generations, variations which all had the same universal structure. Due to the structural similarities of the various manifestations of this view, examining and disproving the validity of the basic common structure should be proof positive of the view's impassivity. The common denominator in question can be reduced to the following logical structure:

I. A is a desired social goal in light of which students should develop cognitive or personality attribute(s).

II. B is an educational process that leads to the achievement of A.

III. Ergo: we must realize B in our education system.

A can range from success in final exams, through the acquisition of deep or structural knowledge of certain disciplines and the ability to intelligently relate to problems in these disciplines, to a more "innovative" approach demanding that students acquire the ability to "learn how to learn" and develop problem-solving abilities (almost always concerning and in the context of the prevailing theoretical disciplines).

B may consist of a large, practically infinite number of educational approaches ranging from frontal disciplinary teaching (which is still the dominant way of teaching in spite of the endless declarations to the contrary during the last two generations) through problem- or project-based, active or constructivist teaching, to various modes of collaborative or ICT-based teaching and any one of the infinite number of variations on each or combinations between them.

Prima facie this structure seems to be a simple, valid, and straightforward one. It seems that all one has to show is that A is indeed desirable in a certain socio-educational context and that B can indeed lead to A's realization, in order to justify the implementation of B, which is one of the many versions of teaching of the curriculum. But if we examine this argument closely, something almost all practitioners "relying" on one of the curriculum's versions never really do, the problems we must overcome in order to actually substantiate this argument are revealed in all their insurmountable "glory."

Anyone who has attended the few first classes in any introduction to logic course, or, actually, anyone blessed with some basic common sense will realize that in order for III to be a valid conclusion of the combination of I and II, we must add at least four more steps to the logical process. I will later show that none of these additional steps are either logical or practically possible.

The steps we must substantiate in order for III to be a valid conclusion include:
1.
   1.1. There is a valid way to verify that A is at all realized.
   1.2. There is a valid way to corroborate the claim that A has been realized for all (or most) relevant cases (i.e., in all cases wherein B was implemented, A was indeed achieved).
2. Only after these two claims have been successfully proven in each specific context can we, as indeed we must:
   2.1. Show we have ways to prove that B was indeed the cause of A.
   2.2. Prove that there are no variables which could have led to A regardless of the implementation of B.
   2.3. Corroborated claim 2.1 for all relevant cases and contexts.
3. Once we successfully and fully defended claims 1 and 2, we must also show that:
   3.1. We have a way to verify that B is the best or at least the optimal way to achieve A.
   3.2. We actually corroborated claim 3.1.
4. After successfully corroborating 1, 2, and 3, we still have to show that:
   4.1. It is possible to make sure that when we rely on B to realize A, there is no heavy psychological, social, economic, or ethical price which renders the realization of A through B cost-ineffective or even worthless in the grand scheme of things.
   4.2. We actually corroborated claim 4.1.

The above requirements are the most basic rational requirements that must be met before any rational agent buys so much as a refrigerator or a car. They also stand at the core of various quality assurance methods dominant in the corporate world and in NGOs today. They should guide policy and decision making in any and all meaningful endeavor, especially one with such long term impact on the life of so many citizens and future of society as the educational endeavor.

When these four stages are not carefully followed and found to supply satisfactory justifications for decisions reached and steps taken, decision makers responsible for this shortcoming are publicly reproached, fired, and sometimes even brought up on legal charges for failing to take measures necessary to guarantee the justification for their decisions/actions. In all such cases decision makers are similarly accused of acting irrationally and hence failing to meet their most basic professional or social duties.

The current education system and its compulsory teaching of a predefined curriculum never underwent the scrutiny of corroborating these four basic claims in relation to any of the endless number of instrumental justifications prevailing in it. Should such an attempt be made we will soon find that none of them can be corroborated in the current state of affairs.

Let me briefly substantiate this claim:

Logical step 1 requires a way to show that A is realizable. In almost all cases in which postmodern democracies actually declare what their desired educational goals are, they are very loosely defined. There is no other way to define them in today's relativistic, pluralistic, democratic society. Any definition such a society may reach is a result of political compromise and deliberate blurring since it must satisfy many, very different, stake-holders with diverse, sometimes even contradicting, worldviews. In other words, the postmodern context does not allow for a way to define educational goals clearly enough to allow concrete operationalization thereof. If the goals cannot be clearly defined, it is impossible to verify that they (i.e., A in the schematic argument) are achieved.

Furthermore, even if educational goals are defined clearly enough to be operationalized in a certain society, at a certain moment of time, to allow for an objective empirical examination, it is extremely unlikely that this examination will be relevant in the long term or even consistent over a period longer than, say, three to five years at best. This is the case because democratic societies are prone to changes of regime as well as dominant world and educational views every few years. Thus for example (even if we ignore the basic definitional problem) shifts from liberal or leftist social and educational policies to conservative ones and vice versa, which have taken place in many contemporary democracies over the last two generations and are likely to do so again, leave no room for long term examination of the results of the contradicting educational policies enacted by these countries. Given that most educational goals require much longer periods of time to bear fruit, short term examinations are quite meaningless and have very little to do with rational justifications.

In other words, practically, the type of examination required to substantiate the claim in question, that A is realizable and has been realized, is impossible to perform in prevailing Liberal Democracies.

Step 2 asks that in the highly improbable case that A has been shown to be realized, B can be shown to be the cause for A. In this context it is important to remember that there are many variables that can intervene in the process, such as parental and environmental influences, the impact of the media, economic situation, political circumstances, and so on. We must also consider the side-effects an empirical research process can cause in and of itself, e.g., schools and teachers will most likely use every "trick in the book" to show success, whether or not it exists. In such a reality, it is practically impossible to show, or even have good reasons to believe, that B is indeed the cause of A.

Regardless of the above, it is practically impossible to have a valid long-term control group in this context and no one can claim to have reached any valid empirical result without one. So, even if we assume (the impossible) success meeting the requirements of step 1, we are bound to fail meeting the demands of step 2.

But let us assume, for argument's sake, that we have successfully reached step 3. Step 3 requires that even if we can show a causal link between B and A, we also verify that B is the optimal means to achieving A. Unfortunately, there are, in principle, an infinite number of ways to achieve any educational goal and it is practically impossible to examine and compare all or even most of them with B, the way we actually chose, in order to show that it is indeed optimal.

In contrast, it is very easy to prove for any definition of B that it is NOT optimal by comparing it to but one alternative and proving it can work as well or even better than any method used for theoretical leaning (our current B). This has in fact already been done. Various home schooling or de-schooling methods have been examined and successfully demonstrated that the liberal curriculum is far from being the only way to achieve today's declared educational goals; it has in fact been proven to be less effective and in some cases ineffective in achieving these goals than the alternative methods.[47]

Let's ignore, for the sake of argument, the above and assume that we can actually reach step 4. This step demands that the main side effects stemming from the realization of B be evaluated and proven to be a worthwhile price to pay for achieving A. I am unaware of any serious attempt to balance the benefits of any method of compelled learning of the theoretical curriculum in light of the desired goals against its potential damages. Take for example the huge and ever-increasing *economic* cost of education based on the theoretical curriculum. Has there ever been a serious attempt to examine the cost-effectiveness of this educational framework *against reasonable alternatives* to show this economic burden is justified *in light of desired educational goals*?

Such an examination is actually more possible than any of the steps which preceded it, however it will only be relevant after those steps are fulfilled and validate that teaching of the theoretical curriculum in lieu of any of the endless available methods is at all worthwhile. Since this is impossible, so is formulating a justification for compulsory learning given its economic cost.

The economic cost is only one kind of cost; there are many others, such as hatred of learning that compulsion and the irrelevance of the curriculum seems to breed in many students as well as the many other psychological damages caused by long term compulsion of irrelevant activities as discussed in this book, not to mention the moral damage of this unjustifiable infringement of students' liberty.[48]

The compulsory theoretical curriculum was never justified in light of any of these costs, not to mention the accumulated cost of their combination. Unless proved otherwise it seems that it fails the tests of step 4 as well as all the others.

According to my argument there are only two ways to justify the theoretical curriculum in a relativistic postmodern culture: transcendental and instrumental.

The transcendental justification, although it does little more than perform a kind of scholastic hocus pocus, was taken very seriously by a large group of Anglophone philosophers of education in the first generation of postmodernity. It had no impact whatsoever outside departments of philosophy of education, and was declared, in the eighties, by its own initiators as invalid and leading to a theoretic *cul-de-sac*.

On the other hand, the instrumental argument, in its many guises and variations, was considered to be the main rationalization for the theoretical curriculum in the last two postmodern generations. This justification draws its power from its (misleading) *prima facie* simplicity and obviousness. Thus it may seem to actually justify compulsory teaching of the curriculum.

Still a not too deep examination reveals the inability of this line of argument to actually provide rational justification as it is quite easy to show how both logically and practically it is impossible to corroborate it. This justification is therefore nothing more than a straw-man desperately trying to support what other Herculean like supports can no longer hold together.

Ergo, the theoretical curriculum is necessarily unjustifiable in postmodern Liberal Democracies. Since cultural backing is a necessary precondition for any level of spiritual benefits and unity to exist, the theoretical curriculum has lost these two pillars of support and hence its meaningfulness.

Young people today are not aware of the desperate transcendental claims or of the impotence of the instrumentalist arguments and their inability to justify the theoretical curriculum in postmodernity. Still they intuitively feel what I logically prove in this book: in counterdistinction with their predecessors throughout Western history, they cannot accord the activity they are compelled to perform on a daily basis any justification and it is therefore meaningless for them.

This cultural vacuum at the basis of the theoretical curriculum is no different than the vacuum critics found looming underneath practices such as the subjugation of women, of minorities, of people of color, and so on. In all these cases, subjection was based on what were at the time perceived as universally accepted rational arguments. Once the rationale of the argument was proven flawed and was no longer supported by dominant cultural prejudice, the practices collapsed or were at least exposed as the vacuous rationalizations disguised as valid reasons they were.

In order to concretize this claim further, one need only compare the two versions of the modern cultural backing for the meaning of the curriculum, with the emptiness lurking at its foundations today, as they are epitomized in the French and German students mentioned earlier in this chapter. In both cases benefits were perceived as stemming from an integrated or unified concept of what a successful life is and the curriculum therefore enjoyed another supporting pillar for its meaning.

None of these ways of thinking are relevant in our relativistic age and, more importantly, there is no other way of thinking to replace these modes of thought that can help us perceive theoretical learning as leading to the Truth or even to truths, if only because reaching such truths is no longer perceived as an important social goal.

The Postmodern Labor Market and Its Effect on the Practical Justification
for the Liberal Curriculum

For over one hundred years, college graduates in the United States enjoyed preference in the labor market. They attained interesting and prestigious jobs and a high income, and the rate of unemployment among them was low.

Carnegie Commission on Higher Education Report, 1973

More Americans take jobs for which they are overqualified.

***Wall Street Journal*, January 16, 1976**

What is a college BA worth?

Columbus Dispatch, June 2, 1980

Graduate job prospects slide.

BBC News, 11 November, 2002

The above citations express one of the labor market revolutions that envelope the United States and most industrial, as well as many developing, countries since the mid 1970s. In the state of affairs caused by this revolution, higher education is no longer sufficient to ensure its possessor a satisfying, high-income job. This is but one of a group of revolutions that characterize the postmodern labor market, dramatically reducing the benefits derived from long years of theoretical studies. The decrease in the instrumental meaning the theoretical curriculum has for students quickly follows suit.

When a contemporary high school student asks a teacher or parent, "Why do I have to go to high school and learn things that are mainly uninteresting and do not contribute anything to my life?" their answer will likely be: "Because you know very well that if you don't go to high school and don't graduate, you'll have no future." This is the only answer parents were left with after the disintegration of curriculum's unity[49] and the total loss of its cultural backing and possible material benefits.[50] Honestly, even this very vague argument is quickly losing any grasp it may have previously had on reality.

The over-education revolution has characterized the labor market in many Western societies for a long time now, at least the last four decades. However, nowadays, the automatic connection between higher education and a promising career has been severely impaired and with it the ability of parents, teachers, and students to perceive theoretical studies as a sufficient introduction to a promising career.

Another important phenomenon that complements and increases the impact of the previous development is what I call "the rise of 'new professions.'" This phenomenon is still in its formative stages and it is therefore too immature for me to be able to point to it as the third major transformation in the nature of the "labor market" in the history of industrial and postindustrial era but it may very soon "get there."

In the first such transformation the majority of employees, who were farmers or farm workers up until that point, became industrial workers as a result of the nineteenth- and early-twentieth-century Industrial Revolution. In the second wave of change, which matured in the 1960s and 70s, the majority shifted again, from blue collar production line workers to "free professions" based on formal academic studies.

In the third labor market makeover, the one we are witnessing today, the market is moving away from its exclusive orientation toward formal diplomas and academic knowledge to a more portfolio (or proven recent past achievements) based system, wherein personal attributes and relevant types of charisma are just as important, if not more so, as formal education.[51] This is particularly the case for service providers such as designers of various kinds (graphic designers, web designers, fashion designers, party designers, hair designers, stylists, etc) artists, art-oriented roles (DJs, art consultants), coaches of various kinds (financial, political, image, conjugal, and so on), caterers, chefs, lobbyists of various kinds, and so on.

We should remember that in the global economy, the highly competitive market is becoming rapidly dependent on "immaterial attributes" such as image, ambience, form, packaging, and marketing in counterdistinction from the tangible possessions (land, cattle, merchandise) and formal systematic knowledge which typified the market in the very recent past. In today's reality, the former attributes and services account for a rapidly rising portion of the gross domestic product of nations, much of it at the expense of the latter. It is more than reasonable to assume that with rising affluence and leisure, the percentage of these attributes in the labor market will increase further and further.[52]

A third revolution which contributes in the postmodern era to the loosening of the exclusive hold the academic diploma previously had on the market is the loss of tenure[53] and the rapid fluctuations in the labor market which make a diploma attained but ten or even five years ago valueless in the current market conditions. According to Drucker's[54] statement, which is now already considered conservative, an organization that does not forget everything known by its staff every four years at the most, and is not able to reinvent itself from scratch to fit its changing environment, is doomed to fail. Senge[55] and Cunningham,[56] among others, emphasize the crucial importance for the organization to be a "learning organization" immersed in a constant process of endless change.

Many researchers in the field have noticed a shift in recent years from standard jobs (full time, full year, single employer) to "non-standard" work patterns. An example for such patterns can be found in the rise of part-time, contract, and temporary jobs, as well as in self-employment, all far from being constant or certain. These changes are making the attempt to cling to a diploma as an official stamp which proves its holder as "master" in a certain clearly and rigidly demarcated field of knowledge, and thus secure for him or her steady, long-term employment, seem almost pathetic for many individuals.[57]

Beyond these three labor market revolutions which are highly likely to erode the diploma-oriented fourth-level benefit, lurks a much more radical threat to fourth-level benefits of the curriculum. It springs from a much deeper strata of the human situation and consists of the "end of work" phenomenon.

The term above was coined by Jeremy Rifkin, a notorious American economist, in his book entitled thus, published in the mid 1990s.[58] It was later discussed by other theoreticians.[59]

The phenomenon this term describes consists of the fact that the amount of time human beings dedicate to their work is gradually (even if slowly and not always linearly so) decreasing. In the beginning of the industrial age, young people were employed as early as six to ten years old and worked continuously, sometimes as long as twelve hours a day, six days a week, until they were too sick to work or died, usually no later than at the ages of forty-five to fifty-five. Today, on the other hand, in many (mostly European) countries, young people join the labor market as late as their early twenties, sometimes even later than that, working only five (and in some places even four) days a week, for an average of seven to nine hours a day. Unlike their predecessors, they are entitled to breaks and vacations as well as longer "non-work" periods, either voluntarily or involuntarily as a result of state subsidized unemployment. They retire during their mid-sixties and, thanks to the increase in life expectancy, enjoy at least twenty to thirty more years of life in much better conditions than their earlier counterparts could ever dream of.

It is true that there are two exceptions to the growing number of professionals who enjoy this process (or suffer from it when they lack the autonomy necessary in order to make productive use of it). On the higher echelons we can find a rather small group of high-ranking CEOs, and professionals in various managerial positions who work many more hours a day that often spend much of their time in planes and hotels all over the globe, inseparable from their laptops and mobiles. On the other end of the ladder are many individuals who earn very limited salaries which are barely enough to survive on, and therefore need to work in two or more jobs a day to support their families. Those belonging to the first category earn enough to retire relatively young so the total of their working hours per lifetime are not necessarily increased in the grand scheme of things (unless they choose to stick to this intensive schedule regardless of their financial needs). This certainly is not the case for people in the second category.

It is also the case that there are meaningful differences between societies which operate on the basis of welfare policies of various degrees (Scandinavian and other West European societies mostly) and others who follow more *laissez faire* oriented dictums (the US, the UK, and some Southeast Asian societies to name a few).

Still the basic facts relevant to this issue—the dramatic increase of human life expectancy over the last century and the just-as-dramatic impact of automation and optimization of work efficiency—are too powerful to be marginalized by periodical fluctuation, social status discrepancies, and differences between societies. The overall result of these phenomena is, if not the "end of work," at least a gradual decrease of the weight work has in the course of human life. These phenomena are likely to lead to further depreciation of the fourth-level benefits of following the theoretical curriculum, which are necessarily connected with one's desire to get an academic diploma in order to achieve "good job" in the labor market.

All the processes discussed above are not always mature enough or as obvious as their spiritual benefits counterparts. Nevertheless, even if the impact of each of the above processes is not as evident and straightforward, the pooled influences of them all together is highly likely to lead to a more than significant enough impact. Even if young people and their parents are not yet fully conscious of this impact, they must be seriously considered when we evaluate fourth-level benefits of theoretical studies in the foreseeable future.

Furthermore, the practical benefits of the theoretical curriculum hinge on a fourth-level, extremely long term, insecure, and fragile payoff. Over twenty years of theoretical learning of mostly irrelevant information are on average necessary in order to attain the coveted average diploma. In most cases, another ten or more years of hard, financially unrewarding work is required before the learner can reap the promised economic fruits. Given the dynamism of postmodern labor market it is far from certain that the learner will ever reach this "picking point" at all.

Paradoxically, this process makes the competition between diploma holders even fiercer and creates for many an apparent need for higher, more prestigious diplomas. Thus, the process contributes to the dominant perception of a diploma as an important prerequisite condition for success, much more so than it was a few generations ago. This view is strengthened by statistics showing that in most societies there is clear correlation between level of diplomas (attesting to a level of education) and income levels.

Still, the view is inherently paradoxical for several reasons: first of all, when one dedicates so much time and so many resources to attaining a diploma, even if the desired job is secured as a result, in many cases that job would not yield anything close to a sufficient payoff for the huge investment made in order to attain it, especially not when compared with potential alterative payoffs for a similar investment elsewhere. Secondly the chances to actually find such a safe, high yielding, tenure-based job are dwindling every day. In fact, it is much more likely that the diploma holder will find him- or herself moving from one job to the next, as the level of the job actually decreases as one get older. The chance to find only jobs for which one is overqualified is also rapidly increasing.[60]

The above paradox is a result of employers' tendency to demand higher levels of diplomas from potential employees as the market seems to be flooded with diploma-carrying job candidates. Labor market experts have been debating the causes for this phenomenon (the ever-increasing employer demands) for a long time.[61] It is, however, abundantly clear that higher level diplomas attest to actual higher level ability to excel in a particular line of work only some of the time. In many cases it is therefore irrational of employers to set the bar as high (as far as formal diploma is concerned) as they do. Still today's labor market is dominated by employers' demands which therefore influence and increase the employees' (and their parents') investment in attaining diplomas.

What is even worse is the upward unproductive spiral this irrational behavior seems to cause: the more common a diploma is, the less likely it is to be a sufficient job procurement indicator. The more fierce the demand for higher level diplomas is perceived by young people and their parents, the longer the period of learning they are ready to invest in it will be. And yet the longer the training period is, the smaller the eventual payoff seems to become, and the less cost-effective the investment in a higher diploma seems to be (for the student and for society) and so forth and so on.

Thus while there is a correlation between level of diploma and level of income, it does not mean that the investment in higher diplomas is necessarily justified by the payoff it eventually yields. It might very well be the case for many individuals that while the correlation itself is increased, the actual economic benefit of diplomas decreases.

The above claims are of course not without exception. There are certainly many cases wherein investing in a long period of study had a worthwhile economic payoff. However what we should take into account in our case are the following facts:

- The economic reality "out there" is far from steady or reliable and it is extremely diverse. Where the justification of investment in long years of study is concerned, there are huge differences between the various disciplines and professions and even within the various disciplines between different periods of time,
- In many cases the above description does apply.
- And most importantly,
- Young people have no way of knowing, during their increasingly prolonged race for higher diplomas, what the outcome in their particular instance will be.

It may be the case that most young people are not familiar with all the details of the above analysis, but they must at least be well aware of the volatile nature of the labor market and their ensuing inability to predict their success within it. Thus, whatever the specific nuances of the paradox are, it undoubtedly supplies us with good reasons to believe that the more intense and demanding the unending spiral race becomes, the more it should lead to a decrease in its perceived economic payoff, and an increase in its inherent risks in the eyes of learners.

Given this reality, the fourth practical benefit of theoretical learning, the only (somewhat shaky) meaning the curriculum still hinges on, is dramatically depreciated. Students are left with very little reason to perceive the curriculum as instrumentally meaningful. What is worse, this reality sends an extremely dangerous psychological and social message to young people (as will be shown in the last section of this chapter).

Scientific Professionalization and Its Effect on the Unity of the Liberal Curriculum

Beyond perceived cultural backing and spiritual and practical benefits, the curriculum's meaning to those who follow it also depends on the students' ability to perceive it as unified or integrated. This foundation was traditionally, from Plato's days onward, predicated on the common purpose all the curricular ingredients shared:

the molding and realization of a desirable human being. Each item of content studied was usually perceived as contributing in some way to this end goal.

From its inception, the modern scientific curriculum was perceived as enjoying the highest order of unity. This perception of unity originated from the perception of science as a unified, coherent system which reflects and explains all knowable phenomena. This conception, which the founding fathers of the scientific revolution all adhered to, proved extremely influential among the educated classes and scientists at least until the late nineteenth century. A clear expression of this perception of science can be found in Descartes' description of Philosophy as a system of "complete knowledge." In his description Descartes employs the following metaphor of a tree to reflect "complete knowledge": the tree's roots are metaphysics; the trunk that springs from those roots is physics, and the branches are mechanics, medicine, and ethics.[62]

Descartes laid the foundations for what we may term "the perception of science as a *vocation*." In this view, scientific research (a) expresses the human need to know the Truth; (b) is based entirely on scientific methods that ensure the knowledge of complete Truth; (c) is characterized by the systematic operation of a method which begins with metaphysical foundations and from it gradually covers all spheres of human research which are all mutually dependent on, and derived from, one another; and (d) ultimately brings its follower to a rational answer to the question: how should one live?

This perception of science as a vocation guided the great rationalists of the seventeenth century, the German Humanists (such as Goethe and Wilhelm von Humboldt), and idealistic philosophers from Kant through Hegel in the eighteenth and early nineteenth centuries. Paradoxically, this evolutionary concept of science was also the basis for the views of Auguste Comte, the father of positivism and modern sociology, as well as many of the philosophers and sociologists he influenced. The perception of science as a vocation had a decisive effect on modern science and university and high school education up to at least the 1850s.

That said, we cannot say that the unified Cartesian perception of science is the sole basis of modern science. Approximately one hundred years after Descartes, Hume vehemently attacked and rejected the optimistic assumptions of science as a vocation and as a complete system.[63] In his counterarguments, Hume separated questions of metaphysical from empirical knowledge and both of those from ethics, thus refuting the belief in a single coherent and complete (or final) scientific method by which humanity can know the complete Truth about reality. This ensured, so to speak, the unity of the sciences. In his arguments, Hume laid the foundations for "the conception of science as a *profession*," a notion which had a significant effect on the scientific world from the mid-nineteenth century as the positivistic opposition to the Humanistic and idealistic conceptions of science spread first in Germany and later in other Western countries.

A scientist following this approach has no interest in engaging in metaphysics, nor the ability to do so. A more radical version of this idea, which is very dominant in our time, argues that there is no guarantee that science depicts the world as it really is, and advocates the view that science is at best a tool for improving humanity's material conditions. According to this view, the scientist, but a "gray" professional, defines a limited occupation for her- or himself, within a specific scientific paradigm, and carefully examines connections between the variables in the limited boundaries of the disciplinary context. There is no connection whatsoever between this kind of science and the lofty questions regarding the nature of reality or the purpose of human life. This view certainly rejects any conceptions of a unified world studied and presented by a unified scientific method or system.

The perception of science as a profession gained dominance in the nineteenth century. Acceptance of science as a profession gradually took hold in academic circles and in public opinion during the late nineteenth century and the first decades of the twentieth. This acceptance was largely influenced by the brilliant success of empirical science of that time and the technologies it generated. Increasing demands for technology, driven by economic interests, led scientists to specialize in narrow professional niches and abandon any belief in, or aspiration to, a holistic system of knowledge.[64]

At present, this perception of science enjoys exclusive domination of Western thought. Today, anyone declaring him- or herself a supporter of the conception of science as a unified complete system (the Cartesian, Kantian, Hegelian, or even Comptian) is regarded as eccentric at best, or lunatic in worse cases.

The implications of this situation with respect to the unity of the scientific curriculum are quite straightforward and direct. Most students who followed the modern curriculum in past centuries were doubtlessly unfamiliar with the complexities of Descartes, Kant, and Hegel, but the spirit of the philosophers' thinking penetrated and guided even the minds of laymen. In other words, the predominance of these thinkers' philosophies influenced the way teachers and students in previous centuries perceived physics, chemistry, biology, history, and ethics, even if studied as separate disciplines, as parts of one unified whole, a complete system based on a rock solid meta-scientific foundation and therefore connected to one another and of course to "reality" and to the human situation.

In contrast, the contemporary predominant view of science as a profession does not allow for a unified view of the curriculum to exist. The scientific disciplines are completely distinguished from one another and detached from reality, from common sense, and from the realm of ethical and practical decisions. Furthermore, within each discipline one can discern various research paradigms that rarely converse with or can even understand one another.

This perception drastically affects basic theoretical thinking about the curriculum and contemporary curricular theory, that is, the theory of curriculum development.[65] Of course, students are unfamiliar with these behind-the-scenes theories, but their textbooks and teachers undoubtedly reflect those views which are basic to them. As this is the tacit and explicit message emanating from their teachers and other sources of knowledge, students take them to be self-evident. Consequently, students cannot see the connections between the various disciplines, between the various components of the same discipline, between the disciplines and reality, or between the disciplines and the existential or ethical problems preoccupying them. In short, subject matter has become dramatically compartmentalized and fragmentary.

This total disintegration, and loss of any thread of unity, of the sciences and subject matters give the *coupe de grace*, if one was even necessary at this point, to students' ability to gain any spiritual benefit from the curriculum, as it extensively limits the already constrained and quite meaningless practical benefit therein.

MEANINGLESSNESS AND ITS DEVASTATING COST

It follows from the last section that until the recent past, the theoretical curriculum enjoyed full cultural backing, unity, and meaningful spiritual and practical benefits. Today, in counterdistinction, we have very good reasons to assume that the theoretical curriculum enjoys none of the above and is therefore meaningless to most students compelled to learn it. Students today study the curricular subject almost exclusively for the purpose of attaining a diploma or some fourth-order, extremely long term, practical benefit and even this very fragile foundation has little value in comparison with its value but two or three generation ago.

Still, we can ask: What is wrong with that? Why should we be concerned with the dramatic rise in the meaninglessness of the theoretical curriculum? The answer is that we should be terrified by this current state of affairs for the following two reasons:

- The acute depreciation of the meaning the theoretical curriculum has to its followers is probably one of the primary reasons for most of the functional failures of contemporary education systems.
- This loss of meaning leads Western education systems to base themselves on an educationally and socially destructive hidden curriculum.

To understand the first reason let us return to the story of a religious school transferred with its curriculum and teaching patterns from its natural surroundings to an entirely secular environment mentioned in the third section of Chapter One.[66] It is clear that this imagined curriculum, which was entirely meaningful to it original pious students, will be totally meaningless to its new, secular crowd. It will lose all the cultural backing it previously enjoyed and offer its student very little by way of perceived spiritual benefit as the knowledge it imparts will be useless in a secular society and its unity will not be understood by the secular students.

Imagine that the non-religious students were compelled to attend the religious school and their advancement in life depended on their receiving a diploma testifying to their conversance in this completely incomprehensible and irrelevant content taught in this school for twelve long years. The obvious result would be growing frustration leading to the array of negative phenomena discussed in Chapter One— mounting alienation, depression, aggression among students—all of which would probably lead to a dramatic decline in scholastic achievements. Additionally we can expect to see "escape from reality" (and from the alienation it causes) oriented phenomena such as violence between students and toward faculty members, alcoholism, and various drug addictions. These are likely to induce burnout and performance difficulties among the teachers who are forced to deal with these increasing levels of alienation and all its derivatives, while they themselves are not sure of the value of their teachings, and all this, for relatively low salaries.

The moral is clear. Increasing dissatisfaction with the performance of education systems and talk of the "crisis in education" constitute a chronic condition that inflicts almost every education system in the Western world today. All the above symptoms have been sighted in most of these systems in the course of recent years[67] and have led to an endless series of school reforms, reforms which to a great extent ended in utter (and usually costly) failure, discussed in the previous chapters.[68]

The decrease in the meaning of the curriculum to its followers is a basis for a unified (albeit not exclusive) "root explanation" for the main shortcomings of the current education system.[69]

As for the second aforementioned reason, the subliminal devastating message the "hidden curriculum" conveys to contemporary students is comprised of two concentric circles: the smaller, inner, circle represents the damage to the value of knowledge in and of itself; the larger, outer, circle symbolizes the damage to the development of young people.

I already alluded earlier in this chapter to the smaller circle, namely, the message that the process of acquiring knowledge has no intrinsic value or meaning and knowledge is but an external tool, a necessary condition for the individual which, through the diploma its acquisition begets, attains a desirable job. In most cases the knowledge or the information education imparts are irrelevant to the job in question. This message most probably strengthens the students' already prevailing post-modern contempt for theoretical knowledge and anti-intellectual mindset, both of which clearly stand in opposition to the theoretical curriculum's most basic traditional goal and *raison d'être*. Due to the radically changed circumstance in which it now functions, this curriculum which for centuries instilled in its followers respect for the Truth and theoretical knowledge as the ultimate goals of human life has today become counterproductive in this exact respect.

The hidden curriculum's bigger circle convey to students the clear message, which they can already receive from the media and advertising which engulf them in the postmodern world, that life is absurd, that the goal of the human endeavor is always extrinsic and consists of nothing more than a permanent infinite spiral struggle to increase financial profit and material pleasure. This message is indiscriminately conveyed to all students who are obliged, in their most crucial formative years, to study subjects that are meaningless to them. The sole explanation that can be presented to them today for their learning of these subjects is an extrinsic-utilitarian value: "If you do not study you will not be awarded a diploma, and without one, you will not be admitted to university. If you are not admitted to university you will not be able to secure for yourself a profitable job which will ensure your ability to enjoy the pleasures of this world." This hidden curriculum further enhances the powerful external forces that mold students' souls to fit this narrow, one-dimensional, utilitarian, hedonistic *weltanschauung* without exposing them to or allowing them to seriously consider any meaningful alternative worldviews.

SUMMARY

Over the last few decades, writers on education have identified and noted with growing concern the narrowing of horizons and reduced intellectual curiosity among youth,[70] as well as a long array of indications of a growing educational crisis in Western societies. The solutions they recommended can be divided into three main categories.

The first category of writers advocates reforms and calls for the transformation of schools' didactics to make them fit "the requirements and necessities of the digital/knowledge/Life Long Learning based era," "new cognitive knowledge," or "knowledge stemming from brain research about learning," or just "the new constructivist/active/project-based/problem-based/experiential methods of teaching/learning." These writers advocate change processes aimed at creating more open or learner-oriented didactics that usually go together with other reforms like "introductions of computers into the classroom," the "empowerment of teachers," the restructuring of school," and so on.

These attempts boil down to a terribly wrong assumption that the problems are mainly didactic, and that teaching methods should therefore be changed according to one didactic panacea or another. Once these are fixed the "good old" curriculum (with some cosmetic changes to befit the above "fixes") will function again.

On the other hand, the second, conservative, category of writers advocates the solidification of "good old" rigorous learning of theoretic knowledge, shaking off the previous attempts at change. They further recommend going "back to basics," enhancing "cultural literacy" or keeping up the "national standards," all the while making sure "no child is left behind." This view can be summarized by the assumption that there is nothing wrong with the curriculum and the main problems in today's schooling emerge from too open a didactic approach (the same approach advocated by the first category of thinkers) which is a malignant residue of the spirit of the 1960s and 70s. According to these thinkers, once we "purify" schools of these damaging remains things will go back to what they used to be in "the good old days."

The two above categories often represent two opposed ideologies: conservative and liberal (to use the American vernacular in this context). This does not stop many decision and policy makers all over the Western world from pushing forward a third view which combines the above contradicting ones together. The slogan in this case is: "as long as students learn the knowledge required by the standards we set, we don't care how they get there." This is an obviously hollow and impossible to implement approach. Many of the methods employed by the first category, if validly implemented, cannot guarantee the achievement of a given quantitatively evaluated "quanta" of knowledge the second category demands. This self contradictory discourse is the one dominant in today's practical discourse on education, much to its devastation.

None of the three approaches to education accepted by the educational discourse—the purely liberal, the purely conservative, or a "fusion" of them together—is really relevant or helpful to the understanding of the root cause for the growing crisis in education. They rather make a meaningful contribution to further conceal the root of the problem.

In more positive terms I hope I have succeeded in showing that:

- The root of the problem with teaching the theoretical curriculum lies in its growing meaninglessness or absurdity for the learners thereof.
- The above absurdity stems from the erosion and collapse of the four pillars of meaning that supported the theoretical curriculum for almost two and a half millennia: cultural backing, spiritual benefit, practical benefit, and unity.

This erosion and its subsequent collapse are the result of three ongoing revolutions on three cultural levels:

- The relativist revolution that eroded any and all cultural backing the theoretical curriculum previously enjoyed and with it the spiritual benefits and some fundamental aspects of the practical benefits the curriculum previously offered its followers.
- Upheavals in the labor market which extensively eroded most of the practical benefits the liberal curriculum previously offered.
- The positivization and fragmentization of science which led to the disappearance of curricular unity, both spiritually and practically.

Ironically, the curriculum aimed at enhancing its students' respect for learning and their love of knowledge in order to help them develop as broad-minded individuals is necessarily encouraging, in today's reality, the development of narrow-minded, one-dimensional, cynical hedonists.

THE DISAPPEARANCE OF STRUCTURAL FUNCTIONALITY OF THE MODERN SCHOOL IN THE POSTMODERN ERA

INTRODUCTION

One of the parameters which characterize organizations and systems detailed in Chapter One is organizational structure. The organizational structure of the basic unit of prevailing modern education systems, the school, is modern by nature: linear-hierarchical, fragmentary, standardized, and lococentric.

The term *linearity* denotes a continuum wherein to reach a certain stage all the preceding steps must first be followed. Linearity is a necessary but insufficient condition for a hierarchic structure, that is, for a linear-vertical structure whose purpose is to provide instruction from the top down and information from the bottom up. *Fragmentariness* indicates sharp, rigid distinctions between the various units, functions, and activities within the organization. *Standardization* signifies an organization which manufactures great quantities of a standardized product with no distinction between various consumers' needs.[1] A *lococentric* organization is one which concentrates all those operating within it in one place at one time, or put differently, an organization based on what I have termed elsewhere the "principle of the unity of time and place."[2]

These four characteristics also define the typical factory structure, the prototype of modern organization. This identity between schools' and factories' fundamental structural characteristics is no coincidence; the school is a modern organization fashioned at the height of the modern era. Its primary objective was to socialize young people into the norms and *modus operandi* of the engine of modernity: the assembly-line-based factory.[3]

The organizational structure of societal institutions and organizations regarding all the aforementioned four main characteristics has been radically altered in the postmodern era. This is particularly apparent at the economic level where relentless, permanently accelerating competition makes organizations most sensitive to the changes around them. During the last generation, companies and corporations throughout the world have undergone several rounds of fundamental structural change towards decentralization and *"chaordization."*[4] These dramatic changes include growing flexibility of role definitions and division into autonomous units, thereby replacing linear and vertical chains of command with lateral lines of communication together with a significant flattening of the hierarchic structure.

In a similar vein, automation has led to the conversion of the postmodern organization from production of masses of standardized goods or services ("mass production") to manufacturing products or services "tailored" to the needs of specific market segments, sometimes at the level of the individual consumer ("mass customization"), thus leading to the disappearance of the tight grip of standardization that characterized the modern era. As computerization allows companies to spread rapidly all over the globe in search of cheap labor or markets, organizations are no longer lococentric. And for the same reason, even among the more conservative organizations, the number of people performing distance work from home, a remote office, or anywhere on the globe, really, is permanently increasing, thus exempting the organizations from the grip of the modern principle of unity of time and place.

While fragmentariness is still relatively powerful in postmodernity, given the Internet revolution, the knowledge explosion, the growing complexity of the new postmodern world, and its constantly changing "kaleidoscopic" environment, all professionals are obligated to work within a social network of knowledge support which enables them to cope with the ever-increasing flood of knowledge, changes, and the need to multi-task. Thus, connectivity in all the senses of the term has become a major prerequisite for professional survival and success. This loosens the grip of modern fragmentariness on the professional environment.[5]

While the constantly mounting pressures of postmodernity during the last few decades have led all other organizations in the above directions through a series of several dramatic and traumatic (for many employees) revolutions, schools all over the Western world still preserve all the original four characteristics noted above. Consequently, in its present structure, the school speaks an "organizational language" that is essentially incomprehensible to its pupils and most of its teachers, who are exposed to and speak a much more updated vernacular in the world outside the classroom.

The modern school structure has been subsequently rendered dysfunctional on at least two levels:

On the first level, like any other organization that does not conform to the demands of the present-day reality, the school necessarily suffers from increasing difficulties in its daily routine activities. Henceforth, I will relate to *dysfunctionality* limited to the organizational boundaries of the school as "*dysfunctional* (or its opposite, *functional*) in the organizational sense," or else I will relate to it as "the school's increasing difficulties with *operating functionally*."

On the second, larger, and more essential level, the anachronistic "organizational language" spoken by the school prevents it from reaching its goals as a socializing agent for future socioeconomic function and as an acculturating agent initiating young people into the modes of living, thinking, evaluating, and interacting dominant within their society. Yesterday's organizational structure cannot serve today as a socializing and acculturating mechanism for tomorrow's culture and society. Henceforth, I will relate to this much larger meaning of *dysfunctionality* as "*dysfunctional* (or its opposite, *functional*) in the larger social sense," or else I will relate to it as "the school's increasing inability to *be functional*, to perform the function required by the society and culture it is supposed to serve."

Analytically these are two totally different senses of the term "dysfunctionality," although empirically it is very probable that these two levels will have an impact on each other. Schools suffer acutely from dysfunctionality in both senses, for the same root reason: the cultural gap, which is expanding every day at lightning speed, is separating the school from the external reality in which it has to function.

This being the case, the following question necessarily arises: is there any justification for the assumption, or any chance, that schools will be able to function when they are run according to above mentioned anachronistic organizational principles? In Section 1 of this chapter, I discuss this rhetorical question in general while addressing the two traditional goals of education, socialization and acculturation, and school's four modern organizational characteristics. I argue that given its essentially modern characteristics, the school in postmodern reality is an organization plagued by severe contradictions and so it is inevitably dysfunctional in both the above senses.

A discussion of all four above characteristics is so wide in scope that we necessarily ignore many important details. In order to compensate, at least in part, for this fact, Section 2 focuses on only one of the school's four characteristics, lococentricity, and discusses it in greater detail in light of the basic above question.

GROWING DYSFUNCTIONALITY OF SCHOOL STRUCTURE: A GENERAL PERSPECTIVE

In this section I show that with regard to the two perennial goals of education, acculturation and socialization, and the four basic modern characteristics described above, the modern school has suffered from fatal organizational contradictions in the postmodern reality and has become dysfunctional in both the senses of the word.

Goals of the School and Its Organizational Characteristics

As noted in Chapter Two, education in Western culture (and actually in all cultures) has always had two primary goals:

- Acculturation is the preservation of cultural heritage insuring its continuity by teaching content perceived to be exalted, important, or vital within the cultural contexts of the given society in which it functions. Western societies considered "the Great Books" or "the Seven Liberal Arts" to be such content in the past. In the modern age "the scientific disciplines" took over that role.
- Socialization to function in society comprises the second goal. This meant, in the modern reality, internalization of the norms and patterns of activity required in order to properly function on the assembly line or any other organizational settings imitating it.

The existing school remains essentially a modern institution. Its four basic characteristics, linear-hierarchy, fragmentariness, standardization, and lococentricity, which typify it on all levels, represent not only the prototype of modern organizational thinking and operation, but also much more deeply, they reflect the basic modern culture, epistemology, and ontology. These four characteristics were totally compatible with the modern version of educational goals and enabled the realization of these goals over the past century. But clearly, they are no longer effective in the postmodern era. Let us now discuss each of them in some detail.

1. *Linear-Hierarchy* is certainly a result of modern epistemology in which human knowledge is a stable "staircase" constructed towards achieving the overall goal of conquering nature which will (allegedly) enable the pursuit of human happiness. An outstanding depiction of this concept is Descartes' Tree of Human Knowledge. According to Descartes' image, the foundations of human knowledge consist of metaphysics (the tree's roots), and from there knowledge progresses step by step through mathematics (the base of the trunk) and physics (the trunk itself), continuing upwards to mechanics (the first branch), physiology (the second branch), and finally ethics, a science which enhances the individual's chances for a satisfying and happy life (the uppermost branch).[6]

In parallel to the above epistemic explanation of the spread of linearity (henceforth, "linearity" will often denote the combined term "linear-hierarchy"), communication researchers claim that the dominance of linearity in modernity emanates from the invention and spread of printing and the consequent conversion of the West from an oral culture to a culture based on the written word, in which reading became the principal means of information transfer. The act of reading is linear in nature, joining one letter to the next and one word to the next and so forth. It is also hierarchical, as a complete unit of knowledge—an excerpt, a chapter, a book—has clear priority over its components.[7]

Linearity also became the keystone of modern organizational thinking, which viewed the organization as a well-defined linear hierarchical ladder, whereby all employees have a clearly and rigidly defined role and each occupies a specific rung on the ladder. Thus, instructions "step" down linearly without skipping any of the ladder's rungs, while information about the execution of instructions or organizational needs "climbs" up in the opposite direction.[8]

All of the school's organizational attributes are dominated by this type of linear thinking. On the micro level of the school's administrative structure, which is clearly modeled after the modern "scientific management" concept,[9] the decision making system is hierarchical and flows down a linear scale from the principal to the vice principals to the subject directors to the teachers and finally to the students. On the macro societal level, every school is part of an education system that has a centralized and hierarchical structure (the top of the ladder varies from one Western society to another, as responsibility for it can be located at the federal, state, county, municipal, or local board levels).

The same is true of the activity and "advancement" young people make at school. Children progress from one grade to the next along a linear-hierarchical ladder on which each rung is considered more advanced than its predecessor. The structure of the school's curriculum and didactics has similar linear-hierarchical characteristics as well: the entire curriculum is organized by stages, from easy to difficult and from simple to complex. This is also the case for the "lesson plan," a key term in the linear didactics of the modern school, which is also organized along the same linear-hierarchical lines.

2. *Fragmentariness* in the modern age is derived from sources similar to those of linearity and it in fact complements it. Fragmentariness is fundamental to the modern, positivistic conception of reality and knowledge dating back to the eighteenth century, a conception that divides the world into totally discrete fields each of which constitutes the jurisdiction of a specific discipline.

In this context a distinction must be drawn between the basic rationalistic scientific concept of modernity that developed in the sixteenth and seventeenth centuries, and the empiricist-positivist concept that developed in the eighteenth century and reached its zenith during the nineteenth century. Although the rationalistic conception, reflected in Descartes' above-mentioned metaphor of complete science, among other sources, already included the distinctions between the scientific branches, they still strongly mirrored the holistic paradigm dominant to the premodern religious worldview, which saw the different sciences as branches of the same tree.

Empiricism and the Positivism that followed it were also stages in the secularization process characteristic of modernity. These epistemological approaches completely abandoned the holistic components that could still be found in the epistemology of the rationalistic modern era at its inception. This worldview viewed the natural processes as arbitrary combinations of atoms of "dead" material and each of the scientific disciplines that developed during that period as completely separate from one another, each dedicated to the study of specific processes.[10] This perception is largely responsible for the spread of the fragmentariness in modernity.

On another level, fragmentariness typifies the act of reading which combines separate units of letters, words, and sentences, each having an independent existence. And it is also essential, of course, to modern organizational thinking which was founded on Adam Smith's writings and peaked in Charles Taylor's concept of scientific management at the beginning of the twentieth century.[11] The development of the division of labor and specialization forms the backbone of modern organizational thinking, whose purpose is to maximize profits from mass production performed by individuals along a conveyor belt. This organizational structure dictates that each worker repeatedly performs only one task which, from his or her point of view, is totally disconnected from the activities of other individuals, and from the complete product.[12]

Expression of this fragmentariness is prominent in the school on several different levels. First, there is the curriculum whose various subjects are dissociated not only from one another but also from the outside world and, most gravely, from real science as developed within the scientific disciplines.[13] Second, within the administrative structure, teachers are defined by narrow disciplinary affiliation, and each one basically works independently and separately from all the others; whatever cooperation exists between them is very limited and mostly predicated on disciplinary identity. Third, young people are grouped and separated by age in all significant school routines. Finally, the school's architecture is designed around "classrooms," or learning boxes isolated from one another. They are so isolated that the expression "behind the classroom door," the title of an influential book from the 1970s,[14] became a catchphrase depicting the isolation of teaching activities.

This isolation is also expressed by the more academic term defining school in general as "a loosely coupled system"[15] due to the fragmentariness characterizing its structure.

3. Like the previous modern structural characteristics, *standardization* also stemmed from modern objectivistic (rationalistic or empiricist) epistemology. Modern objectivistic epistemology has been based on the assumptions that for every question there exists only one correct (i.e., standard) answer; that there are those who know the answer (scientists); and that this knowledge should be used for guiding all relevant human activity, and hence lead to its standardization.

Apparently, standardization also reflects the dominance of the book (albeit in this context not necessarily the printed book) in Western culture as the only source of all authority, as the proverbial Scriptures of the monotheistic religions function.[16]

In modern organizational thinking, standardization received conscious expression in the capitalist concept of "efficiency" as systematically developed by Adam Smith and his followers in modern management theory. According to this approach, as long as activity in any sphere is based on uniform standards and can be divided into atomic "pieces" (fragmentariness) it will be much easier for a designated group of employees to specialize in chain-production of these "pieces," hence making tasks simpler and faster to perform, easier to control, compare, and reward, and so to maximize profits.

In the nineteenth and twentieth centuries, standardization spearheaded modern organizational thinking, especially in Charles Taylor's scientific management theory that recommended precise measurements of workers' performance on the production line based on uniform standards of efficiency and output, for the sake of maximizing productivity and hence profits.[17]

In the educational context standardization governs the school's basic values universally and on all levels.[18] At the administrative level all school staff are judged by the same norms, such as the ability to ensure quiet and obedience and to generate scholastic achievement among the student population. At the students' activity level, all students are evaluated in light of the same set of standards relating to the level of theoretical knowledge they manage to acquire. Thereupon, students are "streamed" into standard ability groups like "the completion stream" or "the matriculation group."

Though it gave way to the progressive spirit of the 1970s and early 80s, standardization of cognitive achievements became the battle cry of conservative reformists in many Western societies by the end of the 1980s.[19] "National Standards" were equated with "no child left behind" and similar slogans that still dominate, to a great extent, the official discourse of education.[20] As a result, the curriculum requires all of the school's educatees to develop similar universally standardized skills and measurable knowledge in the subjects that comprise the standard curriculum. They must learn theoretical knowledge defined by the same standard (usually mistaken and misleading[21]) understanding of science, uniformly perceived throughout the world, so much so that a child completing the third grade in Montreal can continue with relatively few difficulties in to the fourth grade in Warsaw, Sydney, or Berlin.

4. *Lococentricity* or the principle of unity of time and place significantly reflects the modern organizational conception that mirrors the factory model that began developing in the nineteenth century.[22] This principle demands that all core organizational activity occurs at predetermined times in predefined groups in a predestinated location, according to a uniform format prescribed for all members of the organization.

Lococentricity necessarily arises out of organizational and management approaches based on the three previous characteristics. A very high degree of control is required to achieve real-time coordination of the various activities in a hierarchical organization which manufactures standardized products by means of a conveyor belt, operated fragmentarily by workers, each performing a specific action. Up to the advent of ICT (information and communication technology), the only possible way to sustain this kind of control was by performing all the activities at the same time and place so that the "foreman" or "inspector" could simultaneously supervise the entire chain of production or activity.

The "supervision-oriented" approach to modern management and the subsequent lococentric organizational structure required appropriate physical structures to enable maximal managerial control by one person. Thus, it extensively influenced the architectural design of all modern organizations, built to ensure as much control and surveillance as possible.[23]

Naturally, lococentricity governs all levels of the school and manifests itself in all aspects of the educational activity. All students follow a predetermined schedule. This timetable applies to the same place, namely, the school building (or site) and the classroom, and takes place at the same temporal intervals ("lessons") for all the school's students. These aspects of the activity structure are mirrored in the teacher's strict schedule, which includes predetermined encounters with student groups ("classes") in specified classrooms, labs, halls, and so forth. These facts obviously influence the school's general organizational structure, which concentrates all those operating within it in one location.

The school building is designed to hold *all* the students and teachers and to facilitate all the school's activities which take place at the same time and within its four walls. All this is achieved by modes which enable control of the youngsters by the adults as much as possible. (I discuss the major role of lococentricity in modernity in general and as a central characteristic of the modern school in more detail in the section on "The Anachronistic Principle of Unity of Time and Place" below.)

School as a Socially Dysfunctional Institution

Having pointed out the school's two aims and its four fundamental modern organizational characteristics, we can proceed to discuss how these two categories of parameters, when combined, create deeply-rooted contradictions which in turn foster organizational obstacles that render today's school totally dysfunctional in both senses of the term.

I begin by relating to the school's dysfunctionality in the general social sense of the term, discussing first those contradictions relating to the school's aim of acculturation, or initiation of the students into the "mysteries" of their society's basic culture. I will then proceed to discuss the school's dysfunctionality as socializing organization whose putative aim is to inculcate in young people the norms and modes of behavior necessary for effective performance in today's and tomorrow's institutional contexts.

As mentioned earlier, the knowledge structures on which the school relies for the sake of acculturation are wrongly[24] considered in "the school world" to be derivations of the scientific disciplines. The problems in this sphere stem from the radical changes in the concepts of "knowledge" and "learning," basic to both science and to Western culture in general, which took place in the last three decades. Hence, the modern meanings of these concepts, on which the school necessarily (due to the four fundamental modern characteristics that still define it) relies, have become obsolete in the postmodern culture. This fact has rendered the school's present-day ways of teaching and learning essentially dysfunctional and counterproductive from the perspective of its role as an acculturating agent.

As far as the concept of "knowledge" is concerned, the postmodern collapse of the objectivistic perception of "knowledge," which was based on the concept of "knowledge" as the true "mirroring of objective reality," has resulted in a drastic decline in the importance of "general knowledge," that is, knowledge learned for its own sake and not for any practical or instrumental external purpose. This conception of "pure knowledge" was in turn the essential spirit of the definition and justification of the liberal curriculum. (See Chapter Three for an expansive discussion of this topic.) This collapse of the concept of "knowledge" necessarily leads to the collapse of both the concepts of "general knowledge" and the "liberal curriculum" and, hence, to the disintegration of their justification as the ultimate educational goal and further—to a disintegration of the justification to use them as primary educational means.

Dealing with this problem calls for the adoption of a new pragmatic view of "knowledge," one that John Dewey and his progressive disciples proposed over one hundred years ago,[25] but no one has ever seriously applied (except in a few peripheral "alternative" schools[26]). This new approach sees human knowledge not as "a mirror of nature" (to use Rorty's term) nor as a mirror of any external reality whose test is the degree of its compatibility with this reality, but rather as a collection of tools designed to enable human beings to cope with the world for practical benefits.

Actualizing this pragmatic concept of knowledge in the school requires turning the focus of the teaching-learning activity on to real problems that learners will face. And indeed, it is not by chance that terms like *authentic problems, experiential learning, inter- and meta-disciplinary curricula, problem-based* or *project-based learning* have become popular in today's education academic jargon and also in many Western education systems, at least on the declarative level. However, given the school's existing organizational structure, these declarations have no significant backing in the actual practice of most schools.

In order for this "new"[27] concept of "knowledge" to be realized, the four essential modern characteristics of the school must be removed. This is the case for the following reasons:

- Authentic problems (problems that reflect real situations the learner has to face or is interested in facing) and the means for facing these problems will necessarily differ from place to place and from learner to learner. An institution based on standardization is unable to accept as legitimate any meaningful inter-school or intra-school variation on the curricular level.
- Dealing with authentic problems means granting a high degree of freedom to schools, teachers, and students in defining problems and the means for handling them. Institutions and systems based on a hierarchical structure cannot afford such levels of freedom.
- Genuinely dealing with problems, authentic or not, is often chaotic and open-ended, leading to unexpected twists and turns during the research process, and surprising results in the best case scenario. An institution whose concept of "learning" rests on rigid linearity, which requires teachers to guide the learning process from the very beginning so that a certain solution, known in advance, will be reached at the end and certain predefined information will be inculcated, is unable to deal with the chaos or at the very least "the unexpected" which accompanies the tackling of real problems.
- Real problem-solving (again not necessarily authentic) is often a meta-disciplinary task which requires integration between several fields of knowledge. It cannot respect the rigid boundaries between curricular subjects taught in the school, between the school and the outside world, and between the school subjects and real scientific disciplines which characterize it. An institution predicated on fragmentariness and lococentricity cannot afford to honestly deal with real problems.

In view of the above, it is clear that in today's postmodern culture the modern school is shaken by two essential contradictions:

- Externally, or as far as the relationships between the school and the world outside its gates are concerned, there is an essential contradiction between the modern definition of "knowledge" still fully dominant in the school, and postmodernity's dominant culture that has led to the rapid spread of very different concepts of knowledge, even in the foundations of the scientific disciplines. These disciplines are still (allegedly) taught in schools, but in accordance with the epistemology of the past.[28]
- Internally, or as far as relationships between different trends within schools are concerned, many partial and hesitant attempts to introduce curricular, didactic, and organizational elements embedded in the postmodern definition of "knowledge" clash with the school's modern organizational characteristics, which still suppress any real chance such a process has to succeed. These modern characteristics guarantee the school's inability to acculturate its students to the concept of "knowledge" dominant in postmodern culture and science.

Following the radical changes in the conception of "knowledge" as redefined by postmodernity, the postmodern condition has also fostered a transition in the meaning of "learning," which is the counterpart of this concept. It is a transition from a rigid objectivist-behaviorist view of learning to a much more flexible, skeptical, or often relativistic, "constructivistic" view (the last being the most frequent term used for this new approach to learning).

While the former, modern, conception regarded the learners' minds as basically passive vessels for "archiving" a given quantity of content, the latter sees students as active agents occupied with solving problems that are of relevance and interest to them, by reconstructing their cognitive structure, and views them as an important source of authority and decision making in the learning process. Learning is no longer perceived as the passive accumulation of bits and pieces of information that the teacher "pours" into an "empty vessel," but as a proactive process of constructing new cognitive structures produced by the learner.[29]

Here too the overriding domination of the four above modern characteristics of the school, which reflect and reinforce the modern perception of "learning," prevent any real implementation of the "new"[30] concept of learning. Thus, for example, the diploma that is designed to attest to knowledge of the scientific disciplines and to the passive learning such knowledge entails, enhanced and supported by the four modern characteristics, is considered the apex of the educational process.

Side by side with the continuing dominance of the modern concept of "learning," many attempts have been made in the last three decades all over the Western world to redefine the learning process in the spirit of constructivism.[31] Thus, we increasingly encounter attempts to encourage *constructivist learning,*[32] *active learning, self-regulated learning,*[33] or *experiential leaning* together with *alternative assessment methods.*[34]

Active learning and alternative evaluation methods are usually presented in the prevailing "school talk" as falling in line with the traditional disciplinary, standardization-oriented approach as well as the lococentric structure of schooling. Changes are often suggested but they are almost always defined within the modern paradigm and based on the four modern characteristics. The students are expected to function within the fragmentary, linear-hierarchic, standardized, and lococentric framework of the prevailing school system and curriculum, and at the same time "act as scientists or researchers" in light of the "new" constructivist conceptions of "learning."

This dominant mode of "school talk" is, like many other modes in this discourse, nothing less than an attempt to square the circle. No scientist would function as a researcher in fields they have not chosen to work in and in which they have no interest. Moreover, no scientist could seriously manage to research more than one or two questions or problems at the same time. True research, at least the ideal of true research, which the school is supposed to enhance, requires emotional commitment, true curiosity, and the investment of time, attention, energy, and other resources that do not allow spreading one's efforts over numerous fragmentary endeavors at the same time.

In the same way, no scientist would be truly interested in researching standard, fake problems. By "standard," I mean problems that are being simultaneously researched by many millions of other scientists repeating the same process over and over again. By "fake," I mean problems whose solutions are known in advance to those who require students to "experiment" with them. Furthermore, true research is far from being linear; it involves unknown, unexpected turns in the process, and almost unavoidable disappointments with the findings.

In other words, educational methods like active learning, self-regulated learning, or constructivist learning mandate choice, interest, focusing, specialization, and many detours and errors, including learning from errors, all of which negate the imposition of lococentric methods of the fragmentary learning of "true knowledge" perceived as stemming from some ten standardized subjects, as dictated by school's structure and curriculum.

To sum up this last point, together with the contradiction discussed earlier, because it acutely separates the two conceptions of "knowledge"—the postmodern one and the one dominant in Western education systems—the school suffers from a complementary contradiction between the conception of "learning" dominant in it, which is still linear, standardized, fragmented, and lococentric, and emerging post-modern conceptions of "learning." Learning in light of constructivism or self-regulated learning requires providing learners with the opportunity to define the various parameters of the learning process in line with their cognitive structure, fields of interest, and learning styles. A standard hierarchical system that measures learning progress using a standardized, compulsory, linear scale which fragments knowledge and compels young people to "learn" specific subjects at specific times and in specific places is clearly unable to provide the required minimal conditions for learning in accordance with the constructivist concept.[35]

In this context, too, schools suffer from contradictions on two levels, parallel to the two discussed in the context of the perception of "knowledge":

- Externally, between perception of learning dominant in postmodern thought, research, and culture and the perception dominant in Western education systems and required by its structure.
- Internally, between the dominant school talk which desperately tries to adapt itself to the postmodern conceptions of "learning," and the modern organizational characteristics dominant in the school that necessarily suffocate these attempts and reduce them to empty declarative shells.

So far I have detailed two complementary sets of contradictions, characterizing the school today as far as the concepts of "knowledge" and "learning" dominant in it are concerned, in light of their relationship to the role of the school as an acculturation organization. Another group of contradictions eroding today school's functionality, in the larger social sense of the term, stems from the growing schism between the school's second central objective, socialization into future roles, on the one hand and its hierarchical-fragmentary-lococentric-standardized-oriented structure on the other.

As I already noted, postmodern organizations are dynamic, constantly changing, and endlessly reinventing themselves. They embody very flexible, flat (less linear and hierarchical) and virtual structures, and rely on relatively flexible role definitions of their employees. An education system that is hierarchical, lococentric, and standardized obviously cannot enhance socialization for future roles in such organizations.

We can identify attempts in all Western education systems to enable and encourage more spatiotemporal and role definition flexibility as well as variety and choice. But these attempts, in the vast majority of Western schools, necessitated by the four modern organizational characteristics.

Spatiotemporal flexibility, should it exist, is limited by extremely rigid restrictions that cannot be breached, namely, the "school day," the physical confines of the school building or site, and the rigid location of the "classroom." In the same way, attempts to annul the school's age uniformity (using chronologically heterogeneous classes), or the modern rigidity of role definitions are very limited and remain, in the many places they do exist, within the realm of "going through the motions."

The bottom line is that none of the waves of the organizational "tsunami" caused by the virtual-digital and globalization earthquake raging for more than three decades outside the schools walls[36] seem to have penetrated into the internal structure of most Western schools.

Thus, here, too, we find contradictions on the two aforementioned levels:

- Externally, between the school's basically modern structure, still fully relying on the four modern characteristics, and the new, radically different in many essential aspects, meaning of "socialization" stemming from the nature of postmodern institutions and organizations.

- Internally, between the four modern characteristics of the school noted above and the persistent attempts to cautiously introduce various ranges of organizational flexibility and openness into it, attempts which are constantly suffocated by the above-mentioned characteristics.

School as an Organizationally Dysfunctional Institution

Up to now, I have referred only to contradictions gravely besetting the school's ability to be functional in and for postmodern society, as either an acculturation or a socialization organization. But the advent of postmodernity leads to another level of dysfunctionality in the school which is now unable to carry out its traditional *modus operandi* without increasing difficulties that lead to growing levels of alienation between students, burnout among teachers and staff, and frustration for everybody.

To give one meaningful example, the lack of compatibility between the system's rigid hierarchical structure and the postmodern reality is manifested, *inter alia*, in the contradiction between the authoritative role the teacher is required by the school's modern structure to perform, and the postmodern reality that has "cruelly" eroded all the modern "pillars" supporting the teacher's authority.

By virtue of the linear-hierarchical structure, teachers must maintain authority, that is, they are naturally expected to "hold the class in check," "control the class," and so on. In the past teachers enjoyed the necessary solid backing of authority that allowed them to successfully (in most cases) function. They drew their authority from a variety of sources: authority could have originated from the religious nature of some communities, in which teachers, functioning in *loco parentis*, completed the spiritual holy chain of God, Pope, king, and father. In more modern times, the teachers' authority in socioeconomically poor, secular societies originated from their being the only holders of the keys to knowledge, knowledge which was perceived to lead to respected positions and socioeconomic success. In the cultural circumstances of the "good old days," the very essence of a teacher represented a kind of knowledge that bestowed on the holder thereof respectability and social status. This stemmed from the modern rationalistic appreciation of the search for truth and of "pure knowledge" (i.e., knowledge untainted by practical concerns) as the most sublime value in human life.

All these sources backed the teacher as *an authority*, respected due to his or her inherent "teacherly" attributes regardless of the institutional power and the ability to reward or to enact sanctions. Beyond these sources of the teacher being *an authority*, up to two or three generations ago, the power of corrective measures backed by harsh physical or psychological punishment administered by teachers, as well as the positive rewards they could bestow on young people, solidly backed them as being *in authority*, that is, they were ostensibly respected or feared due to the powers of punishment or reward invested in them.[37]

However, the past two generations of postmodern influence have eroded and gradually deprived teachers of the underlying sources of both these kinds of authority. The teacher, *per se*, is not *an authority* anymore, since God has died and with his demise the long chain of authority and respectfulness emanating from him (as the first source of the teacher as *an authority*) has collapsed. Theoretical knowledge, knowledge for is own sake (the second source of the teacher as *an authority*), has lost all its appeal in the wake of the postmodern relativistic revolution. And teachers also have long ceased to reflect the model of socioeconomic success cherished in modern times (the third source of the teacher being *an authority*). Now it is only instrumental knowledge, knowledge that contributes to socioeconomic success, that is cherished and this kind of knowledge has never been a major source of authority for teachers.

Even the little instrumental value that was attributed to the knowledge they have been endowed with is gradually vanishing too. In today's world it is personal charisma, daring, inventiveness, creativity, or mere logical ability that paves the way to success in an ever-growing group of *new professions* that rely only on personality rather than formal knowledge (the PR person, the copywriter, the spokesperson, the sales/marketing person, the party designer, the DJ, the caterer, the image consultant, the programmer, the portfolio manager, the bartender, the blogger, the web designer, etc.). The instrumental value of subjects taught in school still partially exists only for the classical formal learning required by the "old" or "modern" professions (physicians, lawyers, engineers, academics, etc.), but its value is certainly decreasing and its exclusive dominance has vanished.

At the same time, we are living in an age characterized by the disappearance of "childhood" wherein children are granted a large range of rights defending them from the "wrath of teachers" (and adults in general). In such an age the powers of punishment and reward that have backed up the teacher's authority as being *in authority* since the very early days of education have largely been taken from teachers, or if these powers still exist, they have become vacuous, because "children" do not attribute any meaning to them anymore.[38]

What is left are incidental means of authority primarily bound up in personality: charisma, humor, a stern countenance, a deep frightening voice, and so on. The majority of teachers who naturally lack these attributes find themselves having to play the role of an authority figure and to "control the class" with little or no cultural backing, organizational capability, or any other means of doing so. Such broad institutions as Western public and private education systems cannot be supported by the incidental personality attributes of those on whom their functionality rests. Thus, a very active source of the ever-increasing functional failures of the system opens up.

This organizational conflict between modern modes of action characterizing prevailing schools and the postmodern reality has also manifested itself in the schools' dominant mode of learning that has become practically unrealizable. The school still functions mainly as a place of book-based learning and of lectures based on books. As such, reading and writing still constitute the main channel for imparting information and learning in the classroom. This characteristic was required by the printed book that flourished since Gutenberg's era as the main means of communication in modern reality but is totally unsuited to the postmodern reality dominated by large plasma screen televisions with hundreds of digital channels to choose from, MP3/4 players, 3-D consoles, Web-based games, and full mobile connectivity to broadband multimedia programming on the ubiquitous, ever-accelerating Internet. In such a reality, the main channels for information and learning transfer are multimedia clips, game formats, email, and blogging, which abound with dynamic graphics and audiovisual stimuli but are extremely poor in information and certainly knowledge in the schooled sense of the term. Information is mainly transmitted through extremely "thin" symbolical modes. In this reality, the printed word, as far as it still exists, has also adopted a "clippy," "thin," "symbolic" feel that is essentially different from the depth it had in the distant days of book-based language and communication.

Young people can no longer speak and understand the book-based language still exclusively dominant in the school.[39] This basic contradiction between the didactic communication mode essential to the modern school and the fundamentally contradicting postmodern communication modes to which young people have been socialized is rapidly becoming more acute as the power of the electronic technologies in our lives exponentially intensifies.

This essential communication gap is comparable to that which would exist between an elite company of Shakespearean actors performing before an audience of non-English speakers, who are foreign to British culture and who have never heard the name Shakespeare. If such performances were to take place, coercively, every day, for a few hours a day, for years, before the same audience with the same Shakespearean repertoire, the captive audience showing no interest in, or knowledge or understanding of what is going on the stage would eventually become bored, then frustrated, and finally violent, while the actors would "get exhausted" and burnout (see the equivalent more detailed example of the Japanese Noh Theater in Chapter One). This is exactly what takes place in our schools, due (also) to the growing gap in language and modes of communication. It necessarily creates and will continue to create an unavoidable increase in the number of problems in the schools' ability to function in any reasonable way, whatever its goals are.

Up to now I have discussed two acute contradictions impeding schools' ability to function or "carry on without too many causalities" and the accelerating difficulties affecting its daily routine (regardless of its social goals or functions). These stem from the disappearance of the foundations of teachers' (alleged) authority and the huge discrepancy between the school's modes of communication and the postmodern communication modes young people have been internalizing, that has "suddenly" (within two or three decades) emerged.

Although certainly acute, these are not the only contradictions "suddenly" and rapidly developing between the postmodern age and the modern modes of functioning dominant in the school. Other contradictions include the school's treatment of children as if they are essentially inferior to adults, and of theoretical knowledge as valuable for its own sake. Both these conceptions, which have lost their validity in the postmodern reality, are relevant here but will be discussed in other contexts throughout this book.

In short, nearly all young people entering the school gates every morning carry with them, as sons and daughters of the postmodern era and its ways of thinking, seeing the world, learning, and communicating a set of cognitive, conceptual, emotional, and behavioral "ticking bombs." As these explode one by one, they will continue to jeopardize the school's ability to function (in the narrow organizational sense of the term) in any reasonable way. As almost any teacher knows, the endless series of explosions he or she has to deal with on an almost hourly basis have reduced the work in most schools to a nothing more then a permanent struggle for survival.

Given this situation, modern schools have only three alternatives: to change and rapidly adapt to postmodernity, to disappear, or to adopt some form of "inflatable air bag" to protect them from a "head-on collision" with the oncoming power of postmodernity. All other public and private organizations had to adopt either the first or the second way. The compulsion and monopoly on which schools rely and by which they seem to be "protected" from antagonistic external pressures (see discussion on this issue in Chapters Seven and Ten) might have been perceived as allowing them to adopt the third alternative.

By "adopting the third way" or using a "protective inflatable air bag," I am referring to the rapid development, expansion, and adoption of the culture of "double talk." This form of self-protection has been created within Western education systems to legitimize the significant gap between declarations of goals and objectives which in most cases sound postmodern, and the still essentially modern measures taken in light of such declared goals. This "double talk" has created an acute second-level functioning problem in today's schools which increases their dysfunctionality in the organizational sense: no organization can function effectively as long as its employees know that the words they use have no real meaning because their real meaning cannot be implemented but are instead being used as a PR exercise designed to merely satisfy the school's internal and external politics.[40]

In light of this "double talk strategy" and in an attempt to be seen to be modifying the traditional modern modes of school activity, increasingly frequent statements about the need to change perceptions of "knowledge," and hence of "teaching" and "learning," have been heard over the past three decades within Western systems. As I have already claimed above, innumerable voices have been calling in the last decades, all over the Western world for a shift in methods to *project-based,*[41] *problem-based,*[42] *self-regulated,*[43] *active,* and *experiential* or *constructivist*[44] learning leading to *reflective assessment* methods instead of exam-based assessment or *alternative modes of assessment* instead of final examinations,[45] and so on.[46] However, when examining the progress in terms of the realization of these goals, we find that generally what has actually been happening is conventional teaching and learning with teachers still largely employing the content, learning patterns, and means of assessment of the "good old days."[47]

A huge gap has been rapidly growing between the acknowledgement that schools have to adapt to the new reality in the ranks of teachers, principals, and various experts involved in the flourishing "school change" industry on one hand, and the enormous "gravity" of the old modes of the school's function, sanctioned by its four dominant organizational characteristics, on the other hand. This gap leads to a "double talk" phenomenon unique to education in our era, or more precisely, the use of postmodern language to describe a reality and activities that are modern through and through.[48]

Analogously, over the past decades, we hear frequent calls for more organizational autonomy to be given either to the teachers through "teacher empowerment" or to the schools through "school-based management." These calls, again made in the postmodern spirit, are frequently articulated as policy statements or demonstrative declarations. It is usually just a lot of talk about a lot of fuss that has very little to do with the reality behind the empty talk, or as I called it above, "double talk."

Here, too, when examining what is actually happening, we find a near total ambiguity regarding the school's freedom of action vis-à-vis the education system's dictated "national standards" or that of the school staff vis-à-vis management's determination to reach these standards. In keeping with these standards, schools are held up against a rigid "grid" that constantly measures their "ratings" in relation to set goals (exactly as factory production line quotas are measured in light of the projected "norms" expected of them). Subsequently, the school's ability to empower or allow teachers to act autonomously is very limited.[49]

In the highly industrialized climate of Manchester or Chicago from the mid-nineteenth to the early twentieth century everything was measured against such rigid grids, and no one dared speak about "production workers empowerment" or "self-management among teams of workers."[50] No attempt was made to alleviate the harsh realities of the production line, and, as a result, a lot of energy is dedicated in schools today to doing exactly that.

Due to the exclusive monopoly they enjoy and the compulsion their function is based on, the Western education systems have managed to survive in this ambivalent and confused milieu for a relatively long time. But the likelihood is that over the next few decades, as postmodernity gains strength, the ambivalence and confusion will intensify. As a result, we will be seeing increases in teacher burnout, student alienation as their feeling that they wasting their time intensifies, parent frustration, and citizens' concern that they are investing huge resources into permanently failing and increasingly (physically and psychologically) dangerous education systems that have no clear attainable goals. It is extremely likely, therefore, that in the foreseeable future we will reach the moment of truth wherein Western education systems will be forced to undergo vital changes, or become the legacy of those who have no other alternative.

THE ANACHRONISTIC PRINCIPLE OF UNITY OF TIME AND PLACE

In the previous section I laid out an overview of the four central characteristics of the school as a modern organization, and of the contradictions and dysfunctionalities these create in a modern school when trying to operate in a rapidly "postmodernizing" reality. In this section, I focus exclusively on one of these characteristics: the lococentric structure of the school or what I have also called "the principle of unity of time and place" or "the unity principle." My primary objective here is to present in greater detail how schools' lococentricity can no longer be justified if effective learning is to be encouraged (functionality in its organizational senses),[51] and schools' two primary goals, acculturation and socialization (functionality in the social sense), are to be achieved.

Let us start with a more detailed definition and characterization of the term. By "lococentricity," I refer to an essential structural characteristic of the modern education system that is related to the primary learning process. Within the school's traditional structure, the *primary learning process* was dedicated to the inculcation of students with new knowledge while the object of the *secondary learning process* was a revision of or preparation for new primary learning. The secondary process consisted largely of homework. As noted above, the unity principle is yet another expression of the educational sphere of epistemic, economic, social, and architectural thinking patterns that dominated modern society. These patterns are the core elements of the modern situation, or of what defines modernity. They are found in any "cell" of any of its main contexts. Thus, the patterns were reflected in contexts as different from each other as:

- Newton's concept of absolute space and time, conceived as an unchanging eternal container of the cosmos.[52]
- The factory/office organizational structure based on centralization and synchronization.[53]

- Modern urban planning and architecture enabling supervision through the agency of visual control by an unseen observer as reflected by Bentham's panopticon.[54]

In modern Western education systems, this principle has had at least the following four different aspects:

- All students undergo the primary learning process in one place, the school building (or site), and in the same time frame ("school day"), from morning until sometime in the afternoon.
- In the framework of school's space and time, the students experience the primary learning process in groups determined by age that maintain their identity over time ("classes" or "grades") and learn the same subjects in the same time units ("lessons"), in the same rooms ("classrooms"), and thus necessarily in the same way and under the same environmental conditions.
- The uniform time frame for primary learning is not only school-specific but also homogeneous throughout entire education systems and in fact throughout the world, with only slight temporal differences. This homogeneity is derived from the generally accepted schedule in which studies take place every working day from morning until sometime in the afternoon. Within this period, an unchanged, universal (with only secondary differences) timetable determines lesson times, usually units of forty-five or ninety minutes, separated by two kinds of breaks: short ones of around fifteen to twenty minutes and longer ones of around thirty minutes.
- Primary learning takes place continuously from the perspective of school days, school months, and school years with the exception of predetermined vacation periods that are the same for all students with some minor differences allowed due to religious tolerance in some countries where students have different holiday periods off from school.

The unity principle is taken for granted in almost all Western education systems to the point that almost no one can imagine a primary learning process that deviates from its requirements.

There are very few exceptions in public education in Scandinavian countries and there is a very small minority of open schools, all over the Western world, usually working outside the public system, or established private systems on the periphery, that offer an open learning environment which allows some deviation from aspects 2 and 3 of the principle. But such deviations function only on a limited scope, while aspects 1 and 4 of the principle remain dominant, even in those exceptionally open schools; that is, the presence of the entire student body in the school is confined to a uniform time frame and to continuous learning processes.[55]

The only full exclusion from the grip of this prevailing principle is found among young people involved in home schooling, where no laws concerning physical presence prevail and the parents guiding this process are at liberty to implement the educational view and regime of their choice and according to their own time frame. But this form of education takes place outside of the school, beyond the bounds of any public or private system. In most countries this educational method must still fight for its legitimacy or is only partly recognized.[56]

Two conclusions follow from the above. First, the unity principle is not an absolute "must" in education, and it is possible and probably also beneficial to depart from it. Thus, for example, children educated in a home schooling environment usually do better in knowledge and cognitive tests, as well as tests for social skills and emotional maturity, and have (at least) the same level of success in higher education.[57] Additionally, the modern dominance of this principle in educational thinking and endeavor is still so strong that attempts to deviate from it exist marginally, if at all, and in a very limited scope.

In spite of the emerging signs of erosion in its periphery, this principle still seems to most of us to be an essential part of education to such an extent that it is imperative to remind the readers that most educational frameworks preceding the modern system did not rely on the unity principle. Thus, for instance, private education enjoyed by the sons and daughters of the nobility and the bourgeoisie in past centuries lacked any dimension of unity of time and place (albeit, it did have a high degree of content unity that is unrelated to our subject). In the village schools in the United States and Europe up to the second half of the nineteenth century, individual students' absences for hours, days, and sometimes even weeks and months, due mainly to their important role in the work force on farms doing seasonal work, was common, a clear contradiction to the strict requirements of the principle of unity.[58] The same is true for the apprenticeship mode of learning common among the "laypeople" in past centuries that took place in private homes or workshops and had nothing to do with the hierarchic, highly bureaucratized organization called "school," which we learned only later to identify with education.

The dominance of the principle is, therefore, exclusively modern. Some readers may claim that the fact the principle has achieved such significance in the modern Western education system demonstrates its functionality in both senses of the term discussed above: the organizational sense referring to school's ability to function smoothly, and the larger social sense referring to the schools' ability to be functional in society.

The relationship between the unity principle and the school's ability to function (or its functionality in the organizational sense) should be judged largely from the perspective of the contribution of this principle to the purpose of the effective implementation of the learning process, the school's purported main activity. The relationship between the unity principle and school's functionality serving society (or the school's functionality in the social sense of the term) should be judged in light of the school's two main social goals, socialization and acculturation, discussed above. In the upcoming subsection,[59] I clearly demonstrate that from the standpoint of the learning process, we have good reasons to displace the absolute dominance of the unity principle in the education system, as it has become dysfunctional and irrational from this perspective. This is due to five theoretical, pedagogic, and practical revolutions that have occurred separately over the past three decades in the fields of *learning styles, multiple intelligences, interests, distance and open learning*, and the rapid evolution of *Information Communication*

Technology (ICT). In the subsequent subsection[60] I argue that in postmodern Western society the dominance of the unity principle cannot be defended on the grounds of the school's functionality in light of its broader goals of socialization or acculturation or other social aims.

Let me stress here that the criticism I raise against the unity principle is not aimed at the principle itself, but rather at its *absolute dominance* in the education system. I have no doubt that the moment its absolute power over the postmodern education system diminishes, there will be room to consider integrating some of its four constitutive elements into the educational process, the methods and scope of their integration to be determined by the demands of various subjects and students and the merits of each case.

The Organizational Dysfunctionality of the Unity Principle

The first reason to dramatically restrict the unity principle's overwhelming dominance is very simple: as applied to a learning institution, it renders the institution inefficient to the point of being unable to function. Individual *learning styles* differ in all possible respects as do the conditions learners require for efficient study. There are reasons to believe that as the learning framework becomes more adapted to the individual's learning styles, the learner's motivation to learn and his or her ability for deep learning will increase. But as long as the unity principle dominates the education system, the possibilities for addressing learning styles remain extremely limited. Hence, the dominance of the unity principle renders the school dysfunctional as a learning institution.

The concept of learning styles and the (basically trivial) acknowledgment of the meaningful differences between individual styles of learning still has no meaningful effect on educational thinking and endeavor. Educational thinking and endeavor has been and generally still is characterized by the attempt to find the universal panacea for the disappointing achievements of Western education systems. Only in the late 1970s, following repeated failures to find a uniform solution and in the wake of a number of preliminary studies, did several researchers conclude that the education systems' continued failures in teaching originated (also) from the inability to acknowledge and cater to individual differences, and that a total turnabout in thinking and research was called for.[61]

This has led to the theoretical-research-practical trend of learning styles, which to date has been implemented by only a small handful of schools and to the acknowledgment of a very limited range of learning styles. The approach has aimed at (a) identifying the core areas wherein students differed from one another in their learning styles; (b) developing tools for identifying the students' different learning styles; (c) implementing studies that examine various learning styles and their effect on the students' motivation to study and on the results of the learning process; (d) training teachers and administrators to identify different learning styles; and (e) encouraging teachers and administrators to adapt the school structure to the students' varied learning styles.[62]

Studies using this approach showed that individuals differed from one another in their learning styles at least on four different levels: cognitive, personality, physiological, and social. At the cognitive level such studies distinguished, among other areas, between inductive and deductive students; between field-dependent and field-independent students; and between visual, auditory, kinesthetic (learners who prefer to physically move when learning), and tactual (learners who prefer touch) learners. At the personality-type level, researchers distinguished between impulsive and reflective learners and between independent learners and those who prefer structured learning.

At the physiological level, they distinguished between individuals who prefer particular hours of activity and learning ranging from the early morning to nighttime, as well as between individuals who prefer various types and intensities of light and background music. This level also included distinction between preferred posture and room temperature for study, and the need to eat and drink, or not, while studying have been mentioned as meaningful. At the social level distinctions were made between those who prefer studying alone, with a friend, or with groups of friends, or from authoritative adults.

This list of distinctions is only partial and arbitrary. According to one count, researchers found at least thirty-two different, albeit often interrelated, modes of learning and desirable learning environments.[63]

These studies also often claim that (a) when the learning framework is adapted to individual learning styles, the motivation to learn significantly increases; and (b) the effectiveness of the learning process is noticeably enhanced when learning environments are taken into account.[64]

Obviously, the exclusive dominance of unity of time and place seriously limits the schools' ability to cater to their students' different learning styles. How is it possible to adjust temperature levels, light quality and intensity, background music preferences and levels, and physical posture and comfort to fit the needs of all thirty pupils studying in one small room? How would it be possible to start the school day (or night for the "night birds" among learners) at different times so that the various needs of learners are met if they are draconically required to learn together in the same small room during the same time? How is it possible to adapt the learning process, its nature and sequence, to both the inductivists and the deductivists among the learners, to field-dependent and field-independent students, when they all learn during the same time and in one place from one teacher? And so on and so forth... One may reasonably conclude that if such adaptation is impossible, or is only marginally achievable, both the students' level of motivation to participate actively in the learning process and the school's effectiveness as a teaching institution is significantly reduced.

The learning styles approach has spread sporadically throughout many places in the last three decades. However, in almost all cases, the learning styles supporters have stepped back from undermining the dominance of the principle of unity. Rather, they have concentrated on encouraging and training teachers to identify the students' learning styles using learning style diagnostic tools, while responding to the different styles as far as possible within the extremely constraining space-time limitations of the school and classroom.

For example, some teachers and schools have created two or three different sitting areas in the classroom relative to the windows or other sources of light and temperature. Elsewhere, different types of classroom seating were provided or cushions were placed next to hard chairs for optional use.[65] Students who wished to do so were encouraged to study by themselves, and those disturbed by classroom background noise were urged to use earplugs or a Walkman to block out the noise.[66] Study material has been presented through various media (auditory/visual/kinesthetic/textual) that "covers" the majority of the class members' styles.[67]

One school applying the learning styles method introduced a curriculum wherein the students of the various classes study the main subjects at different times in rotation, albeit throughout the normal school day, in order to respond to the students' different chrono-biological needs.[68] In the past few years several attempts were made to cater to different styles through ICT-based platforms allowing for personalized learning. But these are still very rudimentary attempts relating to a very limited range of styles and other differences, and what is more important, they too do not dare to break down the rigid walls of the unity principle.[69]

All these attempts, the older ones as well as those based on ICT in the last decade, can be summed up as attempts to slightly vary the uniformity of teaching methods and environmental conditions determined by the dominance of the principle of unity, without even trying to seriously combat the unity principle's underlying dominance. Their levels of success in responding to personal differences are negligible when compared with (a) the real range of differences among the students, and (b) the scope of possibilities that would be opened to students were they allowed to follow at least part of the curriculum outside the school, in their homes or elsewhere, in their own time, and in whatever way suited them.

Can the effectiveness of earplugs or MP3 players be compared with the student's own room, which can be arranged any way he or she prefers in terms of background music or noise, heat, light, working position, times of learning, and so on? It is also clear that as hard as the teachers may try to respond to the various combinations of the students' cognitive learning styles, their ability to do so within the classroom's constraints is extremely limited. For teachers to respond simultaneously to a variety of needs and styles, they must prepare their teaching of each subject to suit the different students' inclinations from the standpoint of their cognitive styles, inductive and deductive learners, field-dependent and field-independent learners, auditory and kinesthetic learners, and so forth. Clearly, teachers cannot even come close to achieving this goal.

The most common application of the learning styles method today has a further limitation derived mainly from the teachers' authoritative mode in this context, namely, their authority to conduct a diagnosis of the students' learning styles. This role completely eclipses the students' ability to experiment and search out their own learning styles.[70] It seems that taking the learning styles approach calls for a serious stand to be taken against the "root of all evil" and not just against the symptoms. But with rare exceptions, the followers of this approach remain shackled to the unity principle.

Instead, they should call for a far more flexible school structure. Such a structure would allow the student a degree of freedom, depending on the subject being studied, the student's needs, and the school's character. Students could choose to study at home or elsewhere at a time suitable to their chrono-biological temperament. Obviously, the moment the element of flexibility is introduced into schooling, the number of possible learning situations and modes will markedly increase. At home, students can adjust the times for study, room temperature, the kind and intensity of light, background music (if any), learning position, food and drink intake (if any), and company (if any), according to their own needs. Moreover, each learner can have a much larger number of learning channels and modes at home than in the rigid classroom space-time framework, especially using Internet-based learning platforms catering to personal differences,[71] provided of course that the school's program and curriculum are properly designed.

From a technological perspective, in the digital era study materials can be presented to the learner in various ways additional to the accepted linear textbook and lecture format. Thus, today, students may choose from a variety of tools and modes of study or combinations thereof to suit their needs. This multiplicity of channels will probably increase exponentially when the still "hesitant" personalized ICT-based learning systems existing today cater to a much larger range of styles and other personal differences. It is just a question of time. But even today, once the child leaves the school and the tight grip of the unity principle dominating it, the number of channels and modes of learning multiplies, practically ad infinitum.

These conclusions about the dysfunctionality of the lococentric structure in educational organization are reinforced tenfold in the face of another theoretical-methodological revolution that took shape more or less during the same period, and which matured enough to reach the awareness of educators during the 1990s. I refer here to the rapid spread of the *multiple intelligences* approach developed by the American psychologist Howard Gardner.[72] Gardner's argument is based on common sense, just like the claims made by adherents of the learning styles approach. Still, like the learning styles approach, it is considered revolutionary due to the school's senseless lococentric structure.

Essentially, Gardner claims that individuals differ from one another in their basic abilities, which he calls "intelligences."[73] According to Gardner, while some people are endowed with superior logical or cognitive intelligence, others excel in artistic or cultural intelligences, or introspective or athletic intelligences, and so forth. The road to desirable personality development, in Gardner's view, resides in developing strong intelligence(s) while also encouraging the development of the weak intelligence(s) to reach at least a certain minimal point. Developing the individuals' stronger intelligence can often lead to progress in his or her other, weaker, intelligences. This view argues against the standardized attempt to develop the same (cognitive) intelligence in the same way in all learners, as is the case in today's education system.

The reader has probably noticed that Gardner's claim is similar in many ways to that proffered by supporters of the learning styles approach. There is one meaningful difference, though: the learning styles approach emphasizes *modes of action*, while Gardner's approach accents basic *capacities* or *abilities*. Both approaches stress the differences between individuals; both recommend encouraging the individual to identify that which is unique in him or her and treat that uniqueness as a basis for desirable education development; both approaches are fundamentally trivial (in the positive sense of the term) and "reveal" what every thinking person has always known: people are different from one another. They are "revolutionary" only in that they reject the dominance of the standardized, lococentric, modern educational paradigm which rests on an exclusive belief in certain universal modes of learning and on a single, cognitive-logical intelligence.

When we combine the learning styles approach with the multiple intelligences approach, it becomes even easier to understand the importance of choice and freedom in learning. But above all, we understand far more deeply that the unity principle excessively limits this vital choice range and hence impedes the develop-ment of the learners' personalities and their chances for a satisfying life endowed with well-being.

There is no chance that most young people will be able to find sufficient expression for their different intelligences while "imprisoned" at the same time in one building, usually in an area of approximately twenty-two square feet per person, in which conditions are necessarily ill-suited to the implementation of human differences and hence to human development.

In the common constrained conditions, students endowed with creative intel-ligence will necessarily lack the means and space for expressing their talent. Those gifted with athletic prowess or "good hands" will lack the space and means for expression of their physical needs. Moreover, what little facility there is for creative or athletic intelligences will necessarily come at the expense of that apportioned to those with cognitive intelligence, and so on and so forth.

Parallel to the rapid dissemination of these two trivial (in light of the common sense perspective) and revolutionary (given the dominance of the unity principle in schools) concepts, the past two decades have seen a third approach, as trivial and revolutionary in the same two senses, that is both complementary and augmentative to the previous two concepts. I refer to the newly developing research on *interests*. An interest is an activity to which one commits him- or herself purely for its own sake and not for any external recompense whatsoever. This does not mean that secondary reasons do not exist in many cases of the realization of interests. It does, however, mean that even if there were no such secondary reasons the individual would continue to pursue the interest with the same zeal.

Any activity can be considered to be an interest if it meets the above definition. This general definition can be complemented by a few important characterizations of the nature of interests and their role in our lives stemming both from recent philosophical literature on the issue and psychological research:

- Human beings' interests are the deepest personality element defining their individuality. As such they are different and there is no point in trying to identify interests common to all or most human beings (as opposed to basic common needs, for example).

- Only the individual can know what his or her interests are, sometimes directly, but often after a long process of exploration using reflective trial and error.

- The process of seeking and actualizing interests is of utmost importance to the individual's well-being. Pursuit of—and commitment to—interests can generate satisfaction which arises solely from the realization thereof and does not rely on any other form of external reward, acknowledgment, or recognition. They are therefore our life goals, the only ones left to us after the "death of God" and "the end of ideology." They should therefore function as ultimate values on one's scale of values, values that all other values are justified as serving, values that "justify themselves."[74]

From the above it necessarily follows that helping young people to productively go through the process of search for—and realization of—interests should be at least one of the central goals of the school.[75] It is clear at this stage, following the discussion on the two previous approaches, that as long as the school is dominated by the unity principle, there is no chance of it allowing any such exploratory process, never mind encouraging it. Thus, interests like gliding, windsurfing, bird-watching, mountaineering, visiting museums or the cinema, involvement in political activity in the community, and so on require equipment the school does not have, and are therefore out of the question as long as the process we now call "education" is imprisoned within the constraints of the unity principle.

The above three approaches are complementary. Each one underscores individuality and the need to encourage it, but while the learning styles approach addresses *modes of activity* and the multiple intelligences approach speaks about *categories of abilities*, the interests approach focuses on individual *ultimate goals of life* or *basic intrinsic motivation*. All three are absolutely necessary for effective learning and productive personal development of young people. But none of the three can be properly and fully implemented as long as education is dominated by lococentric organizations.

At this point we can expect the counterargument that, while the lococentric school can never provide the means and spaces required for successful learning, self-exploration and expression, and maximal development on all three levels noted above, this sacrifice can be seen, or at least so the counterargument would conclude, as vital for allowing learning to take place at all, because "how can you make children learn, if you don't bring them together and make them face the learning material?" Or "children need framework and discipline" since "otherwise they will not learn."

My response to such argumentation is that making this claim twenty or thirty years ago could still have been valid. Today, though, making such a claim leads directly to the refutation thereof. In the Internet age, when fourth-generation mobile telephones and wireless computer connections are as ubiquitous as they are, allowing everyone easy connection to the World Wide Web and therefore to practically all possible sources of knowledge, discourse, or experts on any subject, from anywhere, it is certainly conceivable, and actually very easy, to imagine processes of *distance learning*.

This is reflected also by the enormous boost distance learning, stemming from the digital revolution that characterizes the last two postmodern decades, has had. Distance learning processes in the form of "correspondence courses" have existed in the US, UK, France, and many other countries for at least a century,[76] but they were clearly a peripheral phenomenon. They started to enter the mainstream with the establishment of Great Britain's Open University which had its beginnings in the early 1970s. The then-Labor government launched the Open University to give working-class people, deprived of chances to attend higher education in their youth and compelled to work for a living as adults, an opportunity to train themselves in various subjects, or to complete a course of academic study.

Prior to its startup and during its first years, the Open University's activities fell under a dark cloud of doubt regarding its ability to maintain an appropriate academic standard outside the formal structures which at that time were all dominated by the principle of unity of time and place, including at the higher education and adult education levels. Today those doubts are a thing of the past.[77] Following the success of the Open University in Britain, numerous similar institutions have cropped up throughout the world and comprehensive theoretical and methodological thinking about distance learning and extensive literature designed to guide curriculum planners in the formulation of their programs for different forms of the distance learning model were developed.[78]

Since the mid-1990s, when first the Internet and then the World Wide Web began to take hold, distance learning previously based on the mail, telephone, and television spread. Adult education, higher education, organizational training, and what has since become known as Life Long Learning quickly adapted to the digital era and adopted modes of distance learning that are gaining new recruits every day. In each of these levels, Internet-based distance learning is now a trivial fact of life. Only in formal education, at least in the mainstream of public education and most of the private education (with home schooling and some open schooling as the exceptions), does the organizational structure of the educational institution (the school) make distance learning bump up against the (still) obstinate wall of the unity principle.

Together, the *multiple intelligences, learning styles, interests,* and *distance learning* approaches and methods provide the justification, theoretical basis, practical models, and methodologies for preparation of educational programs which are no longer based exclusively on the principle of unity, and thus enable education to cater, at long last, to the wide-ranging variations in individual characteristics and interests of young people. Moreover, we are exposed to the ICT-triggered developments that have changed our lives over the past two decades and enable the even greater flexibility of the *open learning* model—a parallel term for "distance learning," albeit of a greater scope.[79]

At present, open learning methods are limited mostly to adults; very few such applications are open to school level students.[80] The unavoidable question is therefore: why not apply these methods to Western education systems as a whole and thus significantly increase its responsiveness to young people's personal profiles and needs, while enhancing the quality of the learning process and its results?

The first answer that comes to mind is that it is impossible to project from the field of adult learning to that of young people. The reason presented for this shortcoming would probably be something along the lines of depriving young people of their need for a supportive framework based on the constant supervision of a teacher and constant contact with their classmates, a need (allegedly) far greater than the equivalent need of adults; distance learning methods are therefore, so the argument would go, unsuited to young learners.

I respond to such claims as follows: The assumption that young people have a special need for a supporting educational framework based on the unity principle is not self-evident, certainly not as a categorical generalization. The levels of need for such a supportive teacher- or peer-group-oriented framework derive from personality types and hence learning styles. The needs of individuals, old and young, differ in this regard. The assumption's problematic nature is heightened further still when we remember that we are discussing a wide range of ages (from four or five to eighteen), during which human beings go through their most rapid and engulfing personality development. It would be wrong to conclude that what might be true for a large number of five or eight year olds (but certainly not true for all of them), is also true to the same extent at the ages of twelve, fourteen, or seventeen.

However, even if we accept for the sake of argument that young people need a supportive framework, the idea that distance learning will necessarily deprive them of such frameworks is mistaken. Here again the rapid development of ICT and the Internet come into play, enabling anyone to hook up to anyone else for immediate, real time (or offline) communication from anywhere. Online audiovisual and textual communication with a large number of other individuals (sharing, "Skypeing," conferencing), or correspondence by e-mail or in e-forums or virtual communities over time with any number of people, are all trivial possibilities in today's reality in which young people are much better versed than the older generations.

Thus, postmodern, virtual, flexible, and constantly changing social frameworks of various kinds can and have replaced the once rigid social framework of modern times.[81]

The new ICT-based means of communication, applied for learning purposes, creates a number of possibilities:

- For teachers, to maintain real-time communication from a remote location with each of their students.
- For students, to maintain real-time communication with every other student.
- For a group of students, either with or without a teacher, to maintain real-time communication with each other.
- For a group of students under a teacher's supervision, to discuss over time any subject of their choice allowing all participants to publish messages, arguments, or information they have gathered in a "virtual public place" whenever it is most convenient to them.
- For the individual students to log onto the latest updated website and receive in real time information on any subject of interest to them.[82]

Numerous applications of this kind exist today, even in formal education, although the great majority operate "under the wing" of the principle of unity of time and place.[83] These uses of ICT are still new and their educational implications are even newer. Undoubtedly, the far-reaching ramifications of ICT have not yet penetrated the consciousness of the majority of educators or educational thinkers, so at best they are using ICT tools to reinforce modern patterns, just as the first telephones were used as an advanced telegraph or the first televisions as a radio with pictures.[84]

The truth of the matter is that given the extremely rapid development of the Internet and World Wide Web since the mid-1990s and the amazing development of a variety of terminals (PC, laptop, third and fourth generation mobiles, palm pilots, etc.) connecting anyone from any place to anywhere, enables distance learning methods across the rigid borders of prevailing education systems. Such a high level of connectivity and the methods of distance education based on it enable us today to respond to all levels and aspects of the students' various fields of interest, intelligences, and learning styles, while preserving close contact among students, between students and their teachers, and between all involved in the learning process and the most up-to-date sources of information.

A decade or so ago, learning from a distance and maintaining an educational framework based on close and constant contact (both in real time and over time) among the learners and between them and their teachers was still a contradiction in terms. Now, in the wake of the ICT revolution, the marriage between distance learning, extensively catering to individual differences on all levels, and intra-educational contact has become possible by readily available means.[85]

This is an educational revolution, no less important than the evolution of the writing surface from stone to clay to papyrus and finally paper, or the invention of the printing press. It is probably even much more powerful, because it engulfs all aspects of human life and affects (or will soon affect) all individuals living in this world, not just a small minority of literate, elitist priests or bourgeoisie as the previous revolutions (at least) up to the twentieth century did.

The awesome power ICT can have over the educational processes allows us to combine the four processes of educational thinking and action that have developed in parallel, independently of one another, over the past fifteen years: methodologies of open and distance learning developed primarily for adults, learning styles, multiple intelligences, and interests. The concrete result of the five-point union between ICT and these four theories or methodologies adds up to the total anachronization of the unity principle. It enables instead the formation of an educational organization that supports a flexible social structure which allows compliance with—and encouragement of—the students' learning styles, intelligences, and interests.[86]

The Social Dysfunctionality of the Unity Principle

In the previous section I discussed the dysfunctionality of the unity principle only from the perception of the school as a teaching institution. It may still be argued that I have ignored certain social roles of the school that make the unity principle's dominance vital. In this section I briefly note the most plausible arguments in this context and respond to them even more briefly without any pretensions to exhausting the subject; I have given this subject the space it merits elsewhere.[87]

The most predictable counterargument will rely on the conception of the school serving as society's babysitter. Usually this role is not openly declared, but because of the vital part it plays in serving the economy in general, and many family units more specifically by allowing parents "to go to work," it might have merit. This role, so the argument might go, mandates the concentration of all students in the same place and at the same time, during the morning and early afternoon hours, while their parents are at work. Hence, the unity principle is a requirement for our society and economy to function smoothly.

My response to this claim is fourfold. First, it ignores the wide range of ages under discussion; surely babysitting services are not required to the same extent for five-year-old pupils and eighteen-year-old students, yet today the principle applies across the board to the primary learning process of all the age groups. Second, not all parents have an equal need for babysitting services, yet the service is "provided" for all or, more precisely, imposed upon everyone without exception. Third, over the past two decades the phenomenon of the disappearance of childhood has drastically accelerated. The main thrust of this phenomenon is the rapid blurring of the differences between "children" and "adults" (see Chapter Five); therefore, the need of contemporary children for babysitting services is gradually decreasing as compared to the corresponding need only one or two generations ago.

Fourth, and this is my main argument, with the transition from an industrial to a post-industrial society, the labor market has been dramatically changed by a number of processes that in many cases have rendered the babysitting function of school unnecessary. These include a dramatic shift from blue-collar to white-collar jobs and therewith an obvious independence of the employee and a diminished attachment to one specific workplace; shorter working hours in many Western societies; and an ever-increasing number of people working from home and at "unconventional" hours, to use the terminology of the industrial society.[88]

These processes have two characteristics that affect the functionality of the unity principle vis-à-vis the goal of supplying babysitting services. For one, because a growing number of parents no longer need to be away from home for the purpose of work, their need for babysitting services is therefore reduced. And equally, for those parents who do go out to work, there is a constant reduction in the uniformity of work hours, so demand for babysitting services operating exclusively during so-called "ordinary working hours" (a concept which is becoming rapidly fuzzy in a twenty-four-hour-a-day, seven-day-a-week world) is also decreasing.

The recent accelerated growth of the home schooling movement in the developed Western countries supports these arguments. In the United States over one million (estimates put the number at two million and there are probably many more)[89] children learn exclusively at home (without any school attendance) with their parents acting as educators.[90] This is just the first step of a major new trend in postmodern education. Given this trend, the babysitting function of school becomes obsolete for many parents.

Another possible counterargument in defense of the unity principle arises out of the declared role of the school as a socializing agent. Here orthodox educationalists might claim that the school exists in part to ensure the normal development of the social aspect of the students' personality,[91] and that to this end an active social life within its confines must be ensured. The justification of the unity principal is therefore, among other things, the need to develop such a social life which is (allegedly) impossible to achieve without an encounter between all students at the same time and place.

My reply is twofold. First, even if we accept the social need of all students *belonging to one particular group or class* to meet in a certain spatiotemporal realm, this does not mean that *all the school's students* must meet in one place at one time. Second, it does not follow that the same sub-divisions of students (classes) must always meet at the same time and place, and certainly not day in, day out as is the case today. Even a school relying on a much lower level of lococentricity than required by the unity principle would be able to maintain the social grouping known today as "a class" and ensure that all its members meet at certain times that are not necessarily routine or identical with the meeting times of other groupings and do not necessarily happen in the same place.

Additionally, it is quite unnecessary to presume that only lococentric organizational structures can satisfy the social needs of young people and advance their normal social development. A number of studies that followed the social development of young people educated in the aforementioned home schooling environments by their parents show that these students achieved a better balance of their social skills compared with young people of similar attributes who "went to school." These findings can be interpreted and explained in different ways, but they clearly show that organized group encounters in a central building or site, day in, day out, at exactly the same hours, are not vital for the development of youngsters' social skills, and that the kind of encounter typical in today's schools possibly even retards social development.[92]

Another predictable counterargument refers to the second meaning of the term "socialization": training students to conform to the accepted behavioral and normative patterns of their future workplaces. This counterargument would hold that the student's future workplace, the factory or office, is also structured around the unity principle, as all the workers labor in the workplace during the same or similar set hours. Students should therefore be conditioned to function within this paradigm.[93]

My reply to this argument relies on the claims I made in the first section of this chapter:[94] The transition to a postmodern society manifested, in the last three or four decades, in a dramatic transition to production within a far more flexible space-time format than that of an industrial society. In Western societies, the concept of "going to work" is rapidly becoming obsolete for an increasing number of people who work from home and who communicate with their workplaces via the Internet. Hours of work, too, are gradually becoming more flexible and varied.[95] In such a reality, universal socialization to the rigid patterns of the unity principle means socialization to a reality that has become a thing of the past.

SUMMARY

In the first section of this chapter, I related to the basic goals of the school, socialization and acculturation, and showed how the school's four modern structural characteristics—linear-hierarchy, standardization, fragmentariness, and lococentricity—create irresolvable functional problems for the school in the postmodern era when:

- Considered in light of these goals, or from the perspective of the school's ability to be functional to postmodern societies which it should serve (i.e., from the perspective of its social functionality).
- Considered from the perspective of school's inability to function as an organization, without accelerating costs and difficulties, and its repeated failures on all possible levels (or from the perspective of its organizational functionality).

I showed how the modern school has become inherently anachronistic in the postmodern era and hence dysfunctional in both above senses of the term "dysfunctional."

In the second section of the chapter, I focused and elaborated on lococentricity or the principle of unity, and showed that its continued exclusive domination in schools drastically prevents the present-day school from functioning and being functional in postmodernity.

THE DISAPPEARANCE OF SCHOOLS' TARGET AUDIENCE IN THE POSTMODERN ERA

INTRODUCTION

The fourth parameter defining any organization is its target audience.[1] In this chapter I argue that "children,"[2] in modernity the target audience of schools, no longer befit any previous definition which made them such an appropriate audience for modern schools. This is due, in part at least, to a phenomenon Postman identified back in the 1980s as "the disappearance of childhood."[3] This is one of the most dramatic consequences of the great upheavals of the postmodern era, which profoundly changed the definitions of the most basic social roles.

The far-reaching implications of this phenomenon for schools' target audience are symbolically represented by two verdicts addressing issues of minors' rights and their legal standing handed down by the Florida courts back in 1992. More specifically, these verdicts deal with "children's" right to file lawsuits independent of "adult" representation.

In one case a verdict handed down determined that twelve-year-old Gregory Kingsley should be removed from his birth mother's custody and transferred to the custody of George and Elisabeth Ross, his adoptive parents. The judge determined that in light of his mother's conduct and lack of interest in her son's condition, she was unqualified to function as a mother and her rights to serve as a parent to her son should be terminated.

It may seem that there is nothing new in this verdict. Courts in the US, in fact in most Western countries, usually annul the rights of biological parents when judges are convinced that it is in the best interest of the "child." The innovation in this case is the fact that the child approached the court himself; the court determined that a minor had the right to appear before the court and demand to be legally severed from his birth mother.[4] The judge also ruled that Florida state law recognizes that all human beings are equal before the law and the law does not comment on their age. The court therefore ruled that Gregory Kingsley's legal status and his right to demand the termination of his birth mother's right of parenthood are impossible to deny.[5]

The second case involves the matter of Kimberley Mays, who was switched at birth with another infant in the hospital. The mistake was discovered ten years later when the child with whom she was switched died as a result of surgical complications. In the proceedings in which Kimberley's biological parents sued for custody, the court decided that the minor had the right to independent standing.

When the court reached this decision it interpreted the clause in Florida state law, which grants right of standing to any "person," as applicable to "children."[6]

We cannot overstate the importance of the precedent these two verdicts set. They lay the foundations for "children" to prosecute their parents or other "adults," teachers for instance, on the grounds of illegal conduct such as violence, fraud, and so forth, and created an opening for "children" to "divorce" their parents or select "adults" other than their biological parents to be their legal guardians. In the long term, verdicts such as these may be a first step towards enabling "children" to demand the right to live without parental guardianship and as a result to determine their own, independent lifestyle.[7] The very existence of such possibilities will doubtless bring about additional, crucial changes in parent-child relationships and in minors' status in society. These are likely to trickle down from the legal sphere to a more general erosion of distinctions between "children" and "adults."[8]

This is not a tale for the faraway future. The rulings granting Gregory Kingsley and Kimberly Mays legal standing in court, handed down back in the early 1990s, expressed a seminal change in many aspects of the child's status in today's Western societies. We can also see these changes taken beyond the legal arena, "children" as young as fourteen in the US can now apply for emancipation from their guardians, and similar allowances exist in various other Western countries. If this trend continues in the same way and with the same intensity that has characterized it during the last three decades, modern concepts of "childhood," which are still dominant in our society, will become a thing of the past very soon.

One may reasonably assume that the movement in this direction will continue, because the aforementioned verdicts, which accord more self determination rights to "children," both reflect and contribute to the process of "the disappearance of childhood,"[9] a radical change which developed Western societies have been undergoing for at least the last three decades. This process is a part of one far greater wherein all dominant modern definitions of structural patterns and polarized social roles are eroded in postmodern Western societies. These changes occurred particularly in the basic social unit, the modern nuclear family, and in age and gender roles therein.[10] They all stem from the deep-rooted developments underlying postmodernity (see Chapter One).

The disappearance of "childhood" has involved a number of profoundly powerful processes. These include the ICT revolution, a factor contributing to the practical disappearance of the crucial need for literacy, the lack which has rendered "children" "incomplete," the loss of the naïveté that typified "childhood" in modernity[11] and the relativistic revolution, a corrosive factor in the breakdown of the authoritative relationships between "children" and "adults" maintained in the modern age.[12]

Furthermore, the general speed and intensity of the revolutions we are experiencing also contribute to "the disappearance of childhood." In fast-changing times such as periods of emigration, war, and disaster, akin in their effects on the human condition to the radical transition to postmodernity of recent years, young people tend to cope better than "adults," a fact which doubtless contributes to the erosion of the hierarchical system of power relations which in modernity defined the complementary duo: "children" and "adults." It is highly likely that these, and other processes, will intensify over the coming decades, and the process of the disappearance of "childhood" will therefore gather further momentum.[13]

In this chapter I review various aspects of "the disappearance of childhood." I then argue that the change in the social reality which causes this phenomenon mandates a radical change in educational thinking due to the fact that postmodernity can also be characterized by the disappearance of education systems' target audience, or at the very least the modern definition thereof. At the same time, modern Western education systems are still essentially designed for "children" who, as in modernity, are perceived not only as young, but also as "incomplete" creatures. The systems' goals have (allegedly) been to provide minors with what they need in order to attain the status of maturity. As such, "children" were perceived to be passive subjects of modern education processes.

In light of these facts a rhetorical question arises: How can an education system designed for "children" as defined in modernity and based on the sharp modern distinction between "children" and "adults" function when modern "childhood" and modern distinctions between "childhood" and "adulthood" are disappearing from this world?

In the first section of this chapter,[14] I describe the changing legal status of "children" in Western societies, which is but one manifestation of the more extensive social process wherein "childhood" is disappearing. In the second section,[15] I outline the general postmodern changes in the definition of social roles, and the subsequent "disappearance of childhood," showing this phenomenon to be deeply rooted in postmodern developments. The third section[16] analyses the phenomenon of "the disappearance of childhood" and highlights a number of processes deeply imbedded in postmodernity which are the root causes of this phenomenon. Finally, the fourth section[17] concentrates on the implications of this phenomenon for the modern school.

THE SHIFT FROM PATERNALISTIC PERCEPTIONS OF "CHILDREN" TO THEIR PERCEPTION AS FULL SUBJECTS[18]

Western legal systems' view of "children" and their rights has gradually changed over time as the outlook of society shifted. In pre-modern times, until around the seventeenth or even eighteenth centuries, most countries treated "children" practically, and often legally, as objects (similar in their status to pets or household animals), possessions of their parents. The parents were therefore entitled to do with their offspring as they pleased, even subject them to hard labor, starvation, mutilation, and various other brutalities without any state or other intervention.[19]

Over the years, a gradual change took place in the status of "children" in Western societies, expediently so with the onset of the twentieth century. "Children" were no longer perceived as objects, but rather as "potential subjects."[20] The state increasingly intervened in parent-child relationships, demanding that parents protect their "children" and provide them with some basic necessities and prohibiting child abuse and neglect. What is encompassed by the terms "basic necessities" and "abuse" has widened dramatically in the course of the twentieth century. The universal legal principle this trend generated, consideration of "the best interest of the child" as overriding any other concern when deciding "children's" fate, was dominant through most of the twentieth century, guiding the legal proceedings regarding "children," such as cases of adoption and custody.

This principle stands in opposition to the principle that previously dominated the attitude towards "children" in that it places the "*child's*" *best interest* well above the "adult's" *interests* when deciding "children's" fate. However, the modern perception of "children" is still somewhat aligned with the pre-modern past, as "adults" are still the only legal entities entitled to decide what the "best interests" of the "child" are. The "adults" in question are parents, caretakers, and educators acting *in loco parentis* and judges, social workers, and psychologists appointed by the state to make decisions when the "natural caretakers" are for some reason deemed unable to judge what constitutes the best interest of the "child."

Another major shift in the legal perception of "children," even more dramatic than the aforementioned one, took place over the last two or three decades. Nowadays, "children" are increasingly perceived as "small adults" who deserve not only legal protection as "potential subjects,"[21] but also as possessors of actual rights to decide about, or at the very least be heard in, legal matters pertaining to their own fate. These are the first breaches in the paternalistic modern attitude toward "childhood," and the ethic of the "best interests of the child" that dominated it. For the first time, a legal discourse on "children" as actual possessors of rights, including those regarding their self-determination (as opposed to their welfare rights), or on the "rights of 'children'" began to be aired.[22]

Concepts such as "the rights of the child" or "children rights" first entered social and legal discourse in Western countries as but a reflection of the demands of fringe groups for "child suffrage."[23] However later on, once the public struggle began to bear fruits, they began reflecting major shifts in the attitude of social and legal institutions towards "children."[24]

Earlier parental obligations were perceived as part of parent-state relationship, where "children" had no standing or right be heard. The new approach to the legal protection of "children" views parental obligations as preserving "children's" rights, that is to say that "children" are part of the relationship, a relationship between parent, child, and state.[25] Recognition of the "children" as subjects who enjoy rights, an ongoing revolution, constitutes a substantive change in every aspect of the perception of, and attitude towards, young people.

Since the issue is still in its initial stages, the discourses concerning the "the best interest of the child" and the "rights of the child" are often still intertwined. This new paradigm for the perception of "childhood" and "children" recognizes the "child's" ability to understand the matter under discussion and reach reasonable decisions relating to his or her future, even if the relevant "adults" believe that the "child's" decision does not serve what the "adult" perceives as the "child's" interest.[26] A "child's" ability to make decisions about meaningful personal interests, such as changing her or his religion, culture, or place of residence, is recognized and expanded by the legal systems of a growing number of countries.[27] A good example for such recognition is the Elian Gonzales case, in which the court instructed US immigration officials to ask a six-year-old boy whether he wanted to return to Cuba or remain in the US.[28]

While most Western countries are clearly moving toward emphasizing the "right of the child" and the perception of "children" as having rights similar to those of "adults," unless it is specifically proven that their judgment and understanding is too impaired to make independent choices, there are meaningful differences between these countries concerning the speed of this change. The main difference is the country's understanding of the default scenario. While some countries' default scenario follows the above perception and accords "children" the legal rights and duties of "adults" from quite early age,[29] others' default scenario is still based on a more traditional view of "children."

As the US plays a leading role in the conceptual changes in the Western World, I will now focus on the changes its legal system underwent in regard to the rights of "children." Punishment of "children" in the US is often similar to that of "adults." "Children" as young as twelve years of age can be sentenced to death in some states.[30] There are large differences between the states' attitudes towards "children." However, we can say that this shift in the social and legal status of "children" in the US began during the 1960s[31] and has since made extremely meaningful leaps. There are other countries which are following a similar path, such as the Netherlands and Sweden.[32] In contrast to the rapid progression of "children's" rights in these countries, there are many Western countries wherein this process was notably slower. The default scenario in such countries still leaves the final word in decisions about "children's" interests up to their parents and legal guardians, although exceptions to this rule are slowly yet consistently multiplying.

One such country is the UK.[33] Though the UK default is the more traditional view of "children's" status, this position is constantly and vehemently criticized by many "children's" rights organization, affecting slow yet steady changes in all legal and social systems. For instance, the UK Department for Education and Skills supports CRAE's[34] development of a program promoting the participation of "children" in decision making. This program is based on the assumption that "children's" opinions are as important as those of "adults" and that they should therefore be involved in making decisions about their own rights.[35] The direction in which the Department for Education and Skills is going is quite clear: it aims to expedite the transition from the "interest of the child" to a focus on the "rights of 'children.'"

Another country which is implementing this shift relatively slowly is Israel.[36] Though a transition can clearly be identified, there is still a clear, default distinction between "children" and "adults."[37] In Israel parents must consider their "children's" opinion, but only when "children" are able to articulate a coherent point of view. The Israeli Judicial system allows parents to contradict and disregard their child's decision if they can prove to the court that the decision goes against the "child's" interest. The Justice system in Israel allows minors to sue, but their parents must first agree to such action.[38] Changes in this basic Israeli attitude were the result of US influence. For example, Section 4 of the 1995 Court for Family Affairs Proceedings Law recognizes the right of a child to independent legal standing before the court. This law determines that: "In matters pertaining to family affairs which relate to the minor…the minor may file a claim, either by himself or through a close friend…in any matter wherein his or her right may suffer real harm." Court rulings also recognized the right of "children" to independent legal representation, as opposed to the appointment of a legal guardian whose "adult" opinion speaks for the "child's" interest.[39] Another verdict of this court recognized the right of "children" to file suit against their parents in torts due to neglect and abuse.[40] Although this particular judgment was handed down after the "children" had reached majority, the precedent it set had tremendous affect on the status of minors as well.

"Children's" right to express their opinion in matters concerning themselves prior to their reaching majority (age eighteen) has already been recognized in various Israeli laws. For instance, the law recognizes actions which minors are allowed to perform without their legal guardians consent as legally binding and demands the child's consent for some major changes in his or her life: religious conversion of a child ten years or older requires the child's consent; an adoption order is conditional on the consent of any child older than nine, or a younger child who is able to understand the proceedings; girls are allowed to terminate a pregnancy without their legal guardians consent.[41] However, despite the important changes that took place over the past two decades, the general provision applicable in all cases where no specific provision overrules is that parents have authority over their "children" and that "children" are obliged to be obedient to their parents.[42]

Even amongst countries which implement changes in "child" status slowly there are noticeable changes in pace. The UK is rapidly according "children" the legal status of reliable witnesses, as "children" are legally obliged to testify as witnesses in court (unless the judge rules that they are incapable of giving reasonable testimony). In Israel, the court can decide that a minor should testify in chambers, in less intimidating circumstances, such as the judge and lawyers wearing plain clothes instead of the mandated black robes, in the presence of an escort, or completely outside the regular court building.[43]

Internationally, the 1989 Convention on the Rights of the Child set standards for "children's" status vis-à-vis the law. Although the 1989 Convention preserved the spirit of the Declaration of the Rights of the Child of 1959,[44] viewing the "child" as

By reason of his physical and mental immaturity, [in] need [of] special safeguards and care, including appropriate legal protection, before as well as after birth.

A move towards change is apparent in several of its clauses. Thus, Paragraph 12.1 of the Convention very meaningfully determines that:

States parties shall assure to the child who is capable of forming his or her own views the right to express those views freely in all matters affecting the child, the views of the child being given due weight in accordance with the age and maturity of the child.

The Convention also endows "children" with various legal rights including freedom of expression and thought, freedom of religion and conscience, the right to be heard in legal proceedings, and the right to privacy. Until recently these rights were taken for granted in all matters pertaining to "adults," but granting them to "children" is highly innovative.[45]

We may summarize by saying that although the implementation of the view of "children" as subjects endowed with the right to self-determination has not yet reached its full potential, its presence in and effects on the laws of most Western societies and International Law are intensifying. As (former) Israeli Chief Justice Meir Shamgar said in one of his verdicts relevant to this issue:

> The full implication of the concept of the rights of the "child" has not yet coalesced and the boundaries of these rights have not yet been delineated. The concept has still not become a general and methodic legal theory, and there are still many open questions. We are still at the beginning. Having said this, the extensive legal literature in this sphere over recent decades prevents us from ignoring the steps taken towards recognition of "children's" rights and the legal development of the matter. One must not forget that judicial principles relating to the equal rights of women and minorities also evolved as innovative doctrines, and now there is no one who does not recognize them or opposes them.[46]

CHANGES IN BASIC SOCIAL STRUCTURES

The change in the legal status of "children" is, as was noted earlier, a manifestation of a more profound psycho-sociological upheaval: the "disappearance of childhood." This phenomenon is only one aspect of the social postmodern revolution that has generated radical changes in all basic social categories.

These changes generated a complete re-evaluation of the modern age, social and gender roles, and of the basic social unit still known as the "nuclear family." Let us begin by examining changes in *age roles*, which in modernity relied exclusively on the developmental model. According to this model, human life consists of certain absolute, rigidly defined ages: infancy, childhood, adolescence, "adulthood," and old age. This perception was reflected in the metaphor of climbing a mountain. The first three stages comprised the ascent, the objective of which is to train the individual for "adulthood," perceived to be the "real life." "Adulthood" was equated with having reached the mountain's top, a period of life during which the individual is a mature and productive member of society, endowed with appropriate rights and duties. In old age the individual was perceived as gradually descending from the peak and departing from active life.

There are at least four dimensions in the modern notion of the universality of the aging process: the very need for a metaphor describing it was perceived all-embracing and universal. Its division into the different aforementioned stages was perceived as universal, the characteristics of each stage were seen as universal, as was the delineation of the specific age range of each stage.[47]

This concept of life is far from imperative. Many traditional societies recognized only the stages of infancy (ages of zero to six), "adulthood," and old age. The meaning of these ages was also different: in many medieval societies infants were never pampered; they were far from perceived as the center of family life, not to mention often unloved (due in part to the very high mortality rate of infants).[48] In these times, old age rather then "adulthood" was considered to be the peak of life.

Turning from age roles to *gender roles*, modernity was ruled exclusively by a dominant, clear-cut dichotomy between female and male roles. Men were regarded as possessors of self-control and rational thinking, as having the capacity to postpone gratification and, therefore, as capable of shouldering the burden of economic, political, and military activity. Women, on the other hand, were perceived as similar to "children," lacking rationality, unable to postpone gratification and thus limited to function within the family unit.

This duality is not inevitable. In most of Western societies the rigid division between male and female roles has relaxed during the last centuries, during the eras of economic instability, war, natural disaster, and other threats to security, when women's contribution to communities' survival was just as vital as men's.[49] As far as postmodern societies are concerned, gender roles underwent several upheavals since the great feminist revolution of the 1960s, and again now, in what some may consider the post-feminist era, wherein women have a large array of role definitions to choose from.

Moving on to the third dimension of basic social roles, in modernity the *family unit* was society's basic building block. This unit was obviously understood as the nuclear family, consisting of a husband, wife, and two or three "children." As mentioned above, the husband was the "breadwinner," while the wife ran the household and raised the "children." Though this family structure was deemed necessary in modernity, it was in fact a substantial change from the extended family which was the basic social unit up until modernity.[50]

All modern social thinking and the resultant social legislation rested firmly on the supposition that these structures relating to age and gender differentiation, as well as the family structure and roles, were necessary and universal. Thus, for example, all Western legislation relating to age roles was clearly founded, in all issues concerning the granting of rights and imposing of duties, on the modern divisions between infancy, "childhood" and adolescence, and "adulthood" and old age. Purely chronological criteria defined these periods, and they were perceived in nearly the same way throughout the Western world.

For purposes of taxation, inheritance, home mortgages, and other kinds of financial legislation, lawmakers and the courts relied exclusively on the nuclear, heterosexual family as the only basic social unit. Thus, for example, parents automatically received social security allowances for their "children," and only a spouse of a citizen of the opposite gender was entitled to citizenship, if he or she was an alien, after marriage. This also applied to gender roles: Only the woman as the childbearing sex was entitled to maternity leave, while in relation to taxation laws the husband was automatically labeled "the head of family," that is, the chief provider, unless he died or became permanently incapacitated. Many of these indicators still hold today, though in most Western societies radical changes have occurred over the last two or three decades.

These three concepts are interrelated in various ways. For example, age and gender roles significantly affect the nature of the family and vice versa. Concepts of "childhood" and "childbearing age" that pertain to a long stage in human development meaningfully influence the concept of the nuclear family and the role of females in it. In this context, women and "children" were defined relative to, and in contrast with, "adult" men.

Due to their interlocked connections, we cannot change one perception without changing the others as well. In postmodernity the claim of the above perceptions of three social dimensions to universality and exclusivity has been radically undermined. Age roles are challenged by the process of the disappearance of "childhood."[51] Concomitantly, the understanding of the nature of maturity and old age is changing. The elderly are no longer passive or separated from active life. Proof of this change can found in the radical rise of awareness and legitimacy of this age group's sexuality in the last generation.[52]

Clearly, the reversals of age roles cannot but dramatically affect parent-child relationships, and hence the perception of family and its structure. The radical changes in the perception of the basic social unit to which the term "family" no longer applies are evident, unless we strip the word of its modern meaning and accept it as equal to "basic social unit."[53]

In other words, the notion of family must be expanded to include the changes that have taken place in four different spheres. The first change is the significant increase in the percentage of individuals living without any familial framework[54] or who live in a "non-institutionalized framework," that is, out of wedlock.[55] Second, the single parent family is becoming increasingly common.[56] Third, recognition of homosexual marriage or same-sex families is on the upsurge.[57] Lastly, the number of "conventional" marriages which end in divorces is increasing.[58] In short, not only is the importance of the traditional (heterosexual) nuclear family in social life decreasing but it is also losing its stability.

The four basic characteristics of the modern family: (1) two individuals of (2) opposed genders (3) living together with (4) the blessing of religious or secular authorities, are no longer perceived as prerequisites for a "family unit" to exist.[59] The single-parent family destroyed the first of the above conditions, and same-sex families the second. In an age wherein traveling for leisure or work is a trivial characteristic of life, "living together" has become an abstract or virtual experience for a growing number of couples and the blessing of spiritual or secular authorities now seems secondary, if not redundant, for many couples.

These developments are necessarily accompanied by changes in, in fact a revolution of, women's status in society. Ever since the 1960s, a constant and relatively successful feminist struggle was waged, first to equate women's rights with those of men, and then, over the last two decades, to give feminine worldviews the same standing and influence as the masculine.[60] The gradual success of this two-stage struggle has changed the status of women and the perception of femininity in society enormously. The feminist struggle also led to the development of a phenomenon known as the "new masculinity," which in essence is a redefinition of the masculine image and the male's social role, in accordance with the complementary changes in female role definitions.[61] To complicate the picture, in the last decade or two we have become aware of post-feminist or even anti-feminist trends, and masculine attempts to re-establish and re-legitimize the "macho" concept of men. In some cases, attempts were also made to return to a more conservative perception of the family as consisting of the "warm couple in its marital nest," supplying stability and protection to their "children" against the hardships of a chaotic world.

But these reactive processes do not contradict, just complicate, the previous claims. This is the case because what all these phenomena have in common is not that they replaced the structures dominant and exclusive in modernity with other dominant and exclusive postmodern ones, but rather that they undermined the very *exclusivity* any structure previously enjoyed. They transformed possible structures into a pluralistic inventory of legitimate structures, which coexist with ever-developing alternatives and intermixtures.

Anyone who accepts the above claim that social structures and roles are characterized today by an unprecedented level of plurality cannot but face two explorative processes: The first, theoretical in nature, reflects the desire to understand the process, its roots, and its implications. The second is in essence practical: understanding the currently prevailing and consequent expected changes in legislation, social policies, and educational policies.

In the sections that follow, I relate to both these explorative processes, but focus primarily on the phenomenon directly relevant to our discussion: the "disappearance of childhood."

THE DISAPPEARANCE OF CHILDHOOD

The Phenomenon and Its Manifestations

Neil Postman[62] coined the phrase "the disappearance of childhood" in a book published in the mid 1980s. In Postman's view, this phenomenon is essentially a combination of two complementary processes that have intensified over the last decades: "children" becoming more similar to "adults" and "adults" becoming more similar to "children." In general terms there is a blurring of the distinction between "children" and "adults" that has gained dominance in Western societies in the last two or three modern centuries and remained dominant at least up to the 1970s.

According to Postman, a main feature of the convergence of "childhood" and "adulthood" is a result of the disappearance of naïveté. Up to a generation or two ago, "children" were kept in a state of innocence as a result of their ignorance of the "facts of life": sex, death, and violence. Today, little attempt is made to protect young people from being exposed to these "facts of life." On the contrary, in music and literature specifically designed for "children" and youth we can find a conscious attempt to expose them to sex, death, and violence, all in stark contrast to the recent past.[63]

Postman maintains that the disappearance of this ignorance and naïveté, and hence of "childhood," is manifested in a series of phenomena such as the gradual disappearance of special "children's" clothes (such as the sailor suits that were very popular in early twentieth century), noticeably distinct from those of "adults." Other examples for past child-oriented phenomena which have disappeared over the past few decades include the use of special didactic "sugar coated" language when speaking to "children," as well as special songs and music for "little ones."

A glance at magazines designed for young people or advertisements directed at today's youth shows that sex is in fact a central motif. Furthermore, in current films and television series youngsters are frequently portrayed as those "who understand life" better than their parents, and who sometimes even instruct the "old folks" in the secrets of digital mysteries, latest fashions, or the best ways to start dating again (for divorced or widowed parents).[64] Not surprisingly, the last two decades have witnessed an increase in the use of images of young people as sex objects. At the same time, we also witness a remarkable increase in "children" using what in the past were considered "adult" patterns of behavior. There has been an apparent increase in the levels of crime perpetrated by "children" and in the levels of their drug and alcohol abuse, as well as in the percentage of suicide attempts among them.[65] All these phenomena are different manifestations of one underlying process: a termination of the "child"-likeness of young people, as "children" become more and more "adult"-like.

As previously claimed, at the same time a complementary process whereby "adults" become more similar to "children" is also taking place. It is manifested in the erosion of the central characteristics of modern "maturity": the ability to plan ahead, capacity and motivation for emotional self-control, and capability to postpone gratification. By this I refer mainly to "adult" men because, as has already been established, women in the "not-so-far-off past" were conceived as "child"-like. Expressions such as "act like a man" or "men don't cry" express the quintessence of the type of "adulthood" believed to prevail in the not so distant past among grown men.

In radical contradistinction to the aforementioned past, the dominant psychological approach at present, not to mention overwhelming public opinion and cultural acceptance, is increasingly legitimizing spontaneous behavior and outward expression of emotions by "adult" males. The postmodern male is adopting modes of behavior which, until very recently, were deemed acceptable only for the "weak" or "beautiful" sex (i.e., female): frivolity, coquettishness, and grooming.

It is difficult to question these two complementary shifts towards practical assimilation of "adulthood" and "childhood" in the last generation. What we can debate are the reasons for this process. Below I indicate four postmodern revolutions that can supply separate, yet complementary, explanations to "the disappearance of childhood."

The ICT Revolution and the Disappearance of Childhood

Postman cites television, to which we may now add the effects of the Internet and the World Wide Web, with their various functions and uses (web sites, blogs, chat rooms, and email), and of the revolution brought on by mobile terminals, mainly third- and fourth-generation mobile "phones" (the inverted commas reflect the fact that while these machines may have started out as mobile phones they have for a long time now been mobile multimedia and Internet terminals) as primary causes for the "disappearance of childhood."

In his view, "long childhood," as it was known in modernity, is not a universal human phenomenon. According to Postman, in the Middle Ages up until the invention of printing, long "childhood" was non-existent. Infancy lasted until the age of five or six, thereafter came a swift passage to maturity. For example, "children" fought and killed much like contemporary "adults"; in fact they still do so in Africa to this very day, even though young people obviously differ from "adults" at least in their physical size. During this period "childhood" was at most a physiological phenomenon which had no social or psychological counterparts.

Long "childhood," says Postman, began to slowly develop among the bourgeoisie from the sixteenth century onwards,[66] with the invention of print and the dissemination of books among most members of this class. Printing brought about the creation of "childhood" on three counts:

- It rendered "childhood" functional for the individual and society, because the currency of social communication suddenly became literacy, a skill which cannot be acquired spontaneously but rather requires formal training. Apart from the cognitive process of "learning to read," the act of reading also requires a different kind of upbringing. The written word, in contrast to the oral message, is transferred gradually. Unlike the listener, the reader must possess self-control and the ability to postpone gratification. Hence, print created the need to separate young people from life's natural cycle and provide them with cognitive and psychological training for a life of literacy. In other words, a need for a relatively long process of formal education is what primarily created "childhood." This education, in complete opposition to the naïve popular belief according to which first there was "childhood" and only later was education, developed to cater to the special needs of "children."

- It made "children" possible because it created the ignorance and naïveté that characterized modern "childhood." It is extremely difficult to conceal information when it is transferred orally, because young people can understand the spoken word from a very early age without undergoing any formal training. In contradistinction, written information may be concealed by hiding books or banning their use by "children," or by articulating the written message in a "high language" incomprehensible to "children."

- It facilitated the "dissemination" of "childhood" because it rendered the linear-serial conception of human life and reality dominant. The reader joins one letter to another, then word to word and sentence to sentence in a linear-serial manner. Following the spread of print and reading, linearity and the serial element became the foundations of the Western world's view and facilitated the spread of the linear-developmental conception of human life. The concept of long or extended "childhood" in turn relies heavily on the developmental concept of life and is one of its main expressions.

Postman concludes that television greatly reduces the weight of these three effects of print on our culture which, in turn, erodes the sharp distinction between "childhood" and "adulthood." First, society largely returned to a state of oral and visual rather than written communication. In such a society the importance of literacy diminishes. Doubtless, this process will gather strength in the coming years with the spread of digital tools, like the development of speech recognition and search capabilities on home and mobile computers. Therefore, what Postman claimed about the impact of television has become seven times truer in the digital era due to the decrease in the need to train young people to read from both the cognitive and personality aspects.

Second, Postman claims that television also drastically impairs the hiding of information from "children," because its visual-auditory transfer of content is easily comprehensible to "children" even during their early life. Moreover, television, un-like books, does not allow us to conceal the very attempt to hide certain facts from our "children." When "children" are forbidden to view certain "unsuitable" programs or films they are *ipso facto* being "told" that there is a secret and an attempt is being made to hide it from them. In our information-inundated reality, they are sure to discover the secret. Again, this phenomenon, which one might call "the total transparency of life's secrets," is exponentially enhanced in our Internet-dominated world.

Thirdly, and concomitantly, according to Postman television limits the cause for the creation of a long "childhood" in the first place. As mentioned earlier, tele-vision restores society to its pre-Gutenberg mode of relying on a visual-auditory transfer of information, far less reliant on the linear-serial principle of the printed word. Thus, the weight of linear thinking in our society decreases together with the developmental conception of human life that relies on it, the conception that justifies long "childhood." It is hardly necessary to add here that the chaotic, fragmentary, associative World Wide Web dramatically enhances and exacerbates this phenomenon.[67]

The Collapse of Linearity and the Disappearance of Childhood

As stated earlier, theoreticians who are developing the aforementioned hypothesis usually focus on television and the effect the electronic, and now, digital media have on social processes and institutions. This explanation is in fact an application of McLuhan's[68] general theory on the issue of "the disappearance of childhood." As early as the 1960s McLuhan predicted major changes in the structures and social processes resulting from the dominance of television and other communications media in our lives.

Though the above explanation is credible, we have to regard the disappearance of "childhood" in a larger perspective i.e., as part of the postmodern revolution and as emanating from processes which characterize postmodernity. The intertwining of these factors is much richer and more complex than that which is reflected by just focusing on the digital, media, and communications revolutions. Another plausible explanation, which expresses another important aspect of postmodernity, is the invalidation of the dominant linear-serial perception in Western culture. This phenomenon goes beyond the sphere of influence of the media or digital reality alone and leads to the overwhelming upheaval that has hit the last postmodern generation, encompassing its labor market, individual career structures, ways of life, and in fact this generation's entire worldview.

The classic structure of an individual's professional career at the height of the modern period (from the close of the nineteenth century to the first half of the twentieth) was linear and monolithic. It began with schooling (which lasted from four to twelve years according to the social status of the student), professional training in a specific field (practical or academic, again according to social status), work in that field in one place of work for approximately forty to forty-five years (or until death, whichever came first) usually without any major change, and finally ended with retirement (that is if death, which in that time often took place in the fifth or sixth decade of the individual's life, did not precede it).

The postmodern labor market is gradually eradicating this professional career structure. Postmodern economics are characterized by:

- A constant need to change production models and market new products as a response to fierce competition.
- A constant need to update and learn as a consequence of the above process and the process of "information explosion."

These and other factors bring about the dynamism and instability that characterize the postmodern labor market in stark contradiction to its relatively static, modern predecessor. Of the overall workforce today, the ratio of employees in part-time or temporary jobs or working as sub-contractors is extremely high when compared with the modern era. The need of workers and professionals to frequently and thoroughly update their knowledge or to change their place of work, field of occupation, and the skills on which they rely is constantly growing.[69]

These dynamics take a heavy toll on the force of the monolithic serial perception of human life, which dominated the modern labor market, in three different ways. First, in present-day reality the emerging trends in professional life, alongside the shrinking impact of the linear-serial career, have produced a fragmentary "career,"[70] which consists of an arbitrary and chaotic combination of periods of employment and training with no necessary continuity between them; each is "encapsulated within itself." Second, the monolithic, universally standard nature has disappeared, even in linear careers. In dynamic markets such as stocks, computers, and electronics, we can find today young people in their twenties who hold much more powerful positions than those held by forty or fifty year olds. Thirdly, the postmodern economic dynamics frequently render any prolonged training process towards a specific career ineffective; rather, they reward creativity and adaptability, which are attributes of the young.[71]

These three dynamics join forces to diminish the effect of the linear-monolithic perception, as well as that of long "childhood." Furthermore, at the practical level, they undermine the justification for the still existing extended period of "childhood," which largely separates "children" from "real life," in order to provide them with education that will "prepare" them to face reality. It is extremely difficult to educate young people to contend with a dynamic reality wherein past experience is rapidly becoming less relevant, a reality whose demands are extremely difficult to predict even in the short term, and in which creativity, which is most frequently found in inexperienced young people, is vital for success.

The Relativity of Time and Space and the Disappearance of Childhood

Apart from the two materialistic explanations (i.e., the explanation relying on material processes—the "media and digital revolutions"—and the radical economic changes leading to the chaotization of the labor market and the average career) noted above, it is possible to think of two more causes for "the disappearance of childhood." These relate to the conceptual-cultural aspects of postmodernity (delineated in this and the following subsection[72]), both dealing with the disappearance of "childhood" as part of the relativistic revolution that is central to the postmodern world.

The first explanation addresses the *relativitization of time and space* in the post-modern world. It points to the way that the relativistic revolution leads to a decrease in the weight postmodern culture accords developmental perception, thus ousting the perception of long "childhood" on which it is based.

The objectivization of time and space, whose origins date back to the Renaissance, was one of the essential characteristics of modernity. From the standpoint of the conception of space, this objectivization was manifested in the use of perspective in paintings, that is, removal of the experiential-personal dimensions that typified (for example) maps of the Middle Ages and their "geometricization."

A similar process took place in regard to the conception of time, which was perceived as continuous, unidirectional, and simultaneous since the Renaissance: a constant flow, identical for the entire universe, devoid of any experiential-personal dimension. This conception of time manifested itself in the development of a rich variety of mainly mechanical clocks that rapidly conquered all towers and bour-geois households from the Renaissance onwards.

The clearest expression of the modernistic conception of these two dimensions is, of course, the Newtonian theory of mechanics. Within this framework time and space are perceived as the continuous and unchanging objective dimensions of the "vessel" containing the entire physical reality.

This objectivistic conception enabled an objective measurement of time and space based on a division into absolute coordinates: longitude and latitude in relation to space, and universal time zones set by Greenwich Mean Time. These objec-tive measurements facilitated the presupposition concerning the existence of identical, universal, and simultaneous processes from the point of view of time at different coordinates in space.

Again, the Newtonian theory of mechanics reflects this perception in physics. It clearly expresses the objectivistic nature of modern science, which developed under the aegis of the objectivistic perception of time and space. In this conception science discovers universal laws, whereby all natural objects are located and operate within the objectivistic, unchanging, and neutral vessel consisting of time and space.[73]

From the beginning of the nineteenth century, sociology, as developed by Comte, Marx, and Durkheim, made a conscious and directed attempt to apply the objectivistic-universal-mechanistic perception of science in general, and in physics in particular, to social processes. Psychology, both academic and therapeutic, soon followed, forming the great developmental theories of human life.

These developmental theories would not have been conceivable without the two-layered conceptual foundation consisting of:

• The objectivist conception of time and place; and
• The objectivist-universalistic conception of scientific (or any other rational) explanation or law made possible by it.

The perceived vocation of developmental psychology, both in its descriptive and normative forms, was the discovery of universal laws that describe human growth processes and then guide us in therapy, education, and other relevant activities in light of such laws.

The developmental concept of human life appeared in the eighteenth century in Rousseau's work, as a "cornerstone" in the understanding of human life and education. In his book *Emile*, Rousseau describes the development of the individual from "child" to "adult" as a four-stage process, each stage dependent on successful completion of the previous one. Each level of growth adds new knowledge, ability, and skills over and above those previously possessed by the individual, and each follows a predetermined "schedule" whose end product is the completed human being. Most importantly, Rousseau regards this process as universal (both on the descriptive and normative levels) and as reflecting the "Nature of Man" throughout humankind.

Rousseau's developmental-objectivistic metaphor and all its components, though not necessarily all the specific details of his developmental conception, deeply penetrated modern consciousness. It dominantly manifested itself in Freud's theories on the personality level, in Piaget's theories on the cognitive level, and in the theories of their disciples in recent decades.[74]

This metaphor of development, both in its initial philosophical and later scientific guise, relies on the botanical metaphor, and it provided the setting for the rationalistic justification of extended "childhood." It dictated and justified the removal of "children" from "real life" in order to both protect them and prepare them to face the hardships of life in much the same way that young plants are protected and prepared in greenhouses. Rousseau, the forefather of this approach, went even further and recommended resettling "children" in the natural setting of a removed village, far from the corrupting influences of the city. The idea was to ensure that developmental stages be undisturbed by "noises" and "harmful influences" so abundant in the city and realized in the pattern, order, and schedule of developmental theory, reflecting the way "nature" intended it to happen.

In postmodern culture, the dominance of the objectivistic concept of time and space has been impaired, and our belief in science's ability to identify and objectively describe universal law undermined. An expression of this upheaval concerning the concept of time and space appeared as early as the beginning of this century in Einstein's (particular and general) theories of relativity,[75] and even earlier in Nietzsche's writings at the end of the last century.[76] However, it took several generations for these attitudes to permeate and reach the deeper strata of Western consciousness and culture.

At present, it is difficult to speak about universal, continuous and constant time, flowing according to a forward-directed vector, and about universal "human nature," which develops gradually in objectivistic space and which may be discovered through rationality or scientific research.[77] Hence, the appeal and impact of the (allegedly) universal developmental view, which attempts to depict the growth stages of human beings as universal within a simultaneous and absolute time frame, diminishes. At present it is more reasonable to assess different "childhoods" from an anthropological perspective, as they are characterized by different sociocultural circumstances and different spatiotemporal systems, or to discuss specific normative conceptions of desirable "childhoods" in light of different ethical or ideological systems.[78]

The Relativistic Revolution and the Disappearance of Childhood

The previous explanation depicted the way relativism may have indirectly led to the disappearance of "childhood" by devaluating the status of the basic suppositions concerning time, space, and our ability to offer general, universal, and rational explanations for human nature. In this section I indicate relativism's direct effect on the loss of "childhood." Or put another way, I introduce the second explanation, the phenomenon recognized as the "*crisis of authority.*"

Authoritarianism was the hallmark of parent-child relationships in modernity. In the Humanistic-Liberal society of modernity, parents were held responsible for rearing their "children," thus exercising total authority over them. This paternalistic outlook was predicated on the following argument: (1) There are good and bad (or rational and irrational or healthy and pathological) personal developmental patterns; (2) it is possible to differentiate between these patterns and identify the good (or rational or healthy); (3) in comparison with their "adult" and rational parents, "children" do not have sufficient intelligence or emotional control to differentiate between good and bad (or their above equivalents); (4) parents know what is good for their "children"; (5) *ergo* "children" should be subject to total parental authority (or authority of those acting in *loco parentis*).

This argument originated in the liberal tradition of the seventeenth century, when John Locke expressed it in general philosophical terms,[79] and extended into the twentieth, when it was given a more scientific or psychological and legal expression,[80] and became basic to modernity. The argument leans heavily on objectivistic, epistemic assumptions manifested in the belief that objective truths regarding the right education exist and can be known. These assumptions were supported by both the traditional-religious and modern-rationalistic-scientific worldview. While originally the right education in light of "True Knowledge" was perceived as emanating from the Holy Writ and religious tradition, at the beginning of the modern period it was believed to be an outgrowth of rational thinking or, in the later modern period, of developmental and psychological didactic theories claiming scientific authority.

However, in the postmodern *weltanschauung*, which is essentially relativistic, this kind of support for concepts such as "the right education" is no longer sufficient. The dominant postmodern worldview cannot support arguments based on suppositions concerning objective knowledge of the "right" way to develop and educate. This being the case, the epistemic basis for the authority of parents and teachers (serving *in loco parentis*) collapses in both the eyes of the "children" and of the "adults."

The answer to the question: "Who are you to tell me what to do?" was self-evident in traditional and modern societies, because "adults" (or at least "adults" that were *an authority* or *in authority*)[81] were perceived by themselves and by "children" as knowing the relevant truths, and hence as having the right and obligation to compel "children" to behave in the right way. Today, however, the inability to convincingly answer this question is so clear to many parents that they do not even attempt to exert their authority and instead prefer to develop a friendly relationship or relationship of equality with their "children."[82]

In a situation wherein parents, in their own and as well as in their "children's" eyes, are devoid of authority over their offspring, the traditional-modern, unequal adult-child relationship is undermined, thus in turn undermining the general differentiation between "children" and "adults" which heavily relied upon it.

THE DISAPPEARANCE OF "CHILDHOOD" AND THE EDUCATION SYSTEM

So far we have seen that the legal status of "children" is changing, that this change is a necessary manifestation of the profound and radical social phenomenon of "the disappearance of childhood" and that this disappearance stems from the dramatic change in the definitions of the basic social roles we play, changes which are the result of fundamental postmodern processes. It is, therefore, unlikely that the process of "the disappearance of childhood" will end in the foreseeable future; on the contrary, given that the processes causing it are accelerating and are expected to intensify in the near future, it is quite safe "to bet" on there being an acceleration of this phenomenon.

The ramifications of this process for modern education systems are vast and extreme, threatening at least five of the systems' basic assumptions that stem from the earliest traditions of Western education, dating back to the classical Greek period of two and a half millennia ago:[83]

- School is designed for "children," defined chronologically as the five to eighteen or five to twenty-one age group.
- "Children" can and should be forced to go to school and therein carry out certain activities.
- Only "children" should be students at school; only "adults" can be teachers.
- Only "adults" should determine educational and school policy, while "children," and they alone, should be the object of the educational process at school.
- Within the school's framework, "once a teacher always a teacher, once a student always a student."

All five assumptions are self-evident derivatives of the modern perception of "childhood" and evolve from one another. If "children" are immature, tender beings who must be sheltered from life's hardships and gradually raised and educated for maturity and "adulthood," and if the school partakes in this sheltering and education endeavor, then it is self-evident that only "children" need to go to school in order to acquire an education that will ensure their maturation (first assumption). Since "children" are immature and "do not know what is good for them," we cannot rely on their will but should paternalistically enforce education on them (second assumption). While "children" are at school, they should only perform the role of students, as this is a role for those who need to be sheltered and educated; only "adults" should educate because they are, as human beings who have already matured, the only ones who can know what is good for "children" (third assumption). Consequently, only "adults" are authorized to determine educational policy and apply it to "children" (fourth assumption). It is also clear that as long as "children" remain "children" or "immature," this situation cannot, and should not, change; thus they must function only as students while only "adults" can function as teachers (fifth assumption).

The phenomenon of "the disappearance of childhood" undermines all five assumptions. Let us begin with the last one and gradually ascend to the first, the most essential and well-rooted in the modern (and hence still postmodern) consciousness. Anyone familiar with current school dynamics knows that the fifth assumption does not work at the practical quotidian level. An ever-increasing number of "adults" admit that where acquiring ICT skills is concerned, that is being able to "communicate" with the technology that "runs" our world, "children" are much more advanced than "adults." The same is true for popular music, which for many individuals (not only "children") is the foundation and main characteristic of the postmodern lifestyle: It is not just the knowledge of up-to-date styles of music, but the ability to define oneself and others by the type of music one listens to, which defines the highly important role of music nowadays.

Whereas twenty or thirty years ago individuals would ask each other, "What do you do in life?" referring to one's work, today the first question postmodern individuals ask in order to "identify the other" usually touches on leisure activities, and music is often at the top of the list.[84] In defining oneself and others by one's preferred kind of music, "children" are light years ahead of "adults" and often guide them in this field.

The same is true of fashion. In the last two generations, it has become increasingly important for individuals living in the postmodern era to follow the up-to-date fashion; it has in fact become part of one's self-definition to extents unaffordable to most individuals only a generation or two ago. More generally, with everything that is "in" and "out" as far as leisure activities and lifestyles adopted by the individual are concerned, fashion has become a matter affecting daily life, including dominant modes of speaking, behaving, going out ("tell me which clubs or bars you go out to and I will tell you who you are"), and dating. In all these spheres "children" are much more conversant than "adults" and often provide "adults" with guidance in them.

We can find particular acknowledgment of these facts in daily school life when, for example, "children" help their teachers use various ICT devices or when, in order to be "cool," teachers try to imitate the way their pupils dress, speak, and behave. Furthermore, in many cases individual "children" who use the Internet or other easily available sources of information know much more than their teachers about the subject matter taught in the classroom and teachers cannot but ack-nowledge this fact (the best among them do so happily, but many others do it with a growing sense of professional insecurity).[85] This is a salient expression of *de facto* "adult" recognition of the possibility of role reversal, or of the fact that a teacher is not always a "teacher" in the traditional or modern sense of the term—the one who knows and shows the way—and a student is not always a student—the one who does not know and has to be shown the way.

This undoing of the fifth assumption also applies to the two preceding it. If role reversal in the school is possible at times, why do we automatically assume that only "adults" can teach and only "children" should learn (third assumption)?[86] Similarly, both "adults" and "children" are growing aware of the need to pay more attention to "children" and their wishes when determining educational policy.[87] Examples of phenomena testifying to this can be found in many Western societies over the past few decades: high school students' participation in strikes and demon-strations regarding educational policy making and other issues have become a familiar phenomenon in France, amongst other countries.[88]

If the fifth, fourth, and third assumptions above are gradually undermined by "the disappearance of childhood," it is likely that the second assumption, concerning the justification of the compulsion to go to school and the forcing of school acti-vities on "children," will soon follow suit. The second assumption rests entirely on the notion that "children" have no right to determine their own fate, because they are essentially inferior to "adults" when it comes to the identification and realization of their own interests. But with the blurring of the distinction between "adults" and "children," the automatic justification for coercing "children" "to go to school" "for their own interest" or "benefit" necessarily looses its footing.[89]

All this brings us to the factors undermining the first assumption, the essence of the two-and-a-half-millennia-old Western educational paradigm: education, and certainly institutionalized education, is designed for "children." It is difficult to see how this assumption loses its validity for very young age groups, say until the ages of six to eight (the age of concrete operational development which suffices for practical coping with life and which many "adults" do not advance from, according to Piaget's ultra-conservative evaluation).[90] However, the first assumption appears gradually more problematic regarding older age groups as postmodernity advances. Indeed, from all that we have said, it seems that many of those still defined as "children" are already prepared for life in our dynamic times, sometimes far more so than those we still term "adults." Why then must we assume that these so-called "children" should "go to school" in order to acquire an education that will prepare them for life from "adults," many of whom are likely to be less prepared to meet the challenges of postmodernity than their younger charges?

Moreover, regarding the older age groups among young people, one can imagine a more radical scenario. Here, the shift will turn away from a rigid linear reality of only one "childhood" and one "adulthood" necessarily linked to chronological age, to a new reality of several "childhoods" and "adulthoods," not necessarily related to chronological age (beyond the first "childhood" stretching, say, up to somewhere between six and eight years old). In this scenario "children" will still continue "to go to school" if they so choose—or rather, in the postmodern era when "going" will not necessarily be a part of "schooling," continue to be educated by various kinds of schools and other educational settings. However they chronologically young will not be the only ones educated. Ongoing education may also be the choice of some thirty-, fifty-, or seventy-year-olds, who will define themselves as "children" (probably using a different term), and will likewise feel the need to be educated or reeducated in various kinds of schools (or other kinds of educational environments or organizations of the future).

In fact, the rising popularity of the relatively new term "Life Long Learning," and the many new learning and educational paths, frameworks, theories, and methodologies catering to "adults" is a tangible response to the new needs which postmodernity awoke,[91] and may be a first meaningful step towards the realization of this scenario. This concept reflects recognition of the fact that, in contradistinction to modernity and certainly to traditional societies, postmodern life requires that almost everyone, even individuals who do not go through the radical holistic change described above in the course of their lives, learn all the time. This is the only way that one can adapt to the permanently changing conditions in one's daily life, be able to survive, and thrive professionally or to endow the many newly added days and years of leisure resulting from ever-increasing life expectancy and appreciation of leisure with meaning.[92]

The notion of "childhood" denoted in modernity a period typified by a lack of maturity or readiness for "adult" life. In a reality of non-linear life, extremely dynamic and similar in its intensity to much shorter periods of mass emigration or radical upheaval through war or disaster, it is easy to see how the relatively young and inexperienced are better prepared for life than older, more experienced "adults" bound by past experiences which are no longer relevant.[93]

Meanwhile, one can easily see how a growing number of "adults" are undergoing periods of turmoil in their lives due to changes in their careers, interpersonal relationships, domicile and psychological identity, not to mention gender or other large-scale physiological transitions that dramatically change their appearance (made possible by the "endless heaven of postmodern plastic surgery") or any combination of the above. In short, a rising number of "adults" are going through stages that require them to relearn the foundations of an entirely new lifestyle.[94] From this perspective, they become "children," in need of education. Many such "adults" are presently undergoing "refresher courses" in various forms: psychological therapy; the endless and ever-growing variety of psychological or "folk-psychology," mystical and New Age workshops; a second or third round of academic or vocational studies; traveling to distant "exotic" places; and so on.

If the "disappearance of childhood" becomes ever more pronounced, and if the pace of essential changes in human life markedly speeds up, two highly likely eventualities, the notion that "schools are made for "children" (the first assumption above) will rapidly dissipate. Or, put differently, if the first assumption remains valid, the concept of "children" will probably be redefined as "human beings in a stage of essential passage in their life," in need of a "moratorium"[95] from the ongoing burden of life in order to prepare themselves for their new lives, regardless of their chronological age (except for infancy and very early childhood).

If one accepts this scenario, except for periods of infancy and very early childhood, whose cut-off age is difficult to determine (earlier I relied on Piaget's conservative evaluation of ages six to eight as the critical age[96]), it is still highly likely that "children" will continue to be educated in schools, but:

- The group defined as "children" for this purpose will be comprised of all individuals from the ages of one year to (say) seven as well as many individuals from the ages of seven to ninety (or older, given the permanent lengthening of life expectancy).
- The group known as "adults," namely those who find themselves in a period of relative stability and continuation and are not perceived to be in need of education, will also be more varied from the chronological point of view.
- The duration, content, and objectives of the period of education for the second group of "children" (those older than seven) will vary for different individuals, depending on each individual's level and nature of transition, needs, and goals.
- The definitions of categories of people denoted by designations of "children" and "adults," and hence "teachers" and "students," will be much more flexible: One will be able to seamlessly pass back and forth from one status to the other, or even be considered "adult" (or "teacher") from a certain perspective and "child" (or "student") from another at the same time.

Given the accelerating "disappearance of childhood" and the erosion of the five assumptions that essentially define the modern school from this perspective, there are virtually no good reasons to assume that the school, its student body composed of "children" ranging in age from four or five to between sixteen and eighteen, as we have come to know it in the last modern century, will continue to exist much longer.

SUMMARY

In this chapter I have identified the "disappearance of childhood" as a crucial component of the overall postmodern disappearance of modern definitions of basic social roles and the distinctions derived from them: "men" vs. "women," "adults" vs. "the elderly," "legitimate families" vs. "living in sin," and "children" vs. "adults." I have identified four factors that seem to propel "the disappearance of childhood" forward: the "ICT Revolution"; the breakdown of the linear structure of human life due to radical changes in the labor market; a waning of the objectivistic conception of time and space; and the floundering perception of human life as based on universal developmental structure stemming from that perception and the dissemination of the relativistic worldview leading to the crisis of the authority that was a necessary condition of modern "childhood."

These factors reflect deep postmodern undercurrents, which at present seem to be ingrained into postmodern society and are therefore highly likely to accelerate their influence on it in the future. I therefore inferred from these observations that "the disappearance of childhood" phenomenon will continue and intensify in the foreseeable future. I concluded by describing how the disappearance of "childhood" subverts the basic assumptions underlying the modern school as far as its "target audience" is concerned, such as the notion that schools are essentially designed "to educate " "children" "for life."

I also pointed to the more radical possibility that the ties between school and "childhood" will not be severed; rather the meaning of both terms will radically change. This scenario envisages the possibility that significant ties will cease to exist between the concept of "childhood" and chronological age. Thus, the definition of the category known as "children" will come to denote human beings going through radical periods of change wherein education is required as preparation for a new way of life.

Even readers who do not embrace what at the moment might seem to them as a far-fetched and radical scenario will have no difficulty, I hope, in concluding that the "disappearance of childhood" in the postmodern world renders the modern school anachronistic, especially when viewed from the definition of its target audience.

EDUCATION BEFITTING THE POSTMODERN ERA

EDUCATIONAL GOALS FOR POSTMODERN LIBERAL DEMOCRACIES

INTRODUCTION

Part One of this book (Chapters One through Five) offers an overview of the various postmodern revolutions and their effect on, or more accurately, erosion of the four prevailing modern definitions of the school's basic parameters: its goals, content, organizational structure, and target audience. In this part I also show how this erosion is rendering the modern school dysfunctional (in both meanings of the word as explained in Chapter Four) and its activities meaningless for both students and teachers.

In Part Two (Chapters Six through Nine) I outline an ethical-theoretical framework I termed *Autonomy Oriented Education* (AOE). This I believe is a workable, meaningful, and desirable postmodern alternative to the Humanistic, liberal-democratic, modern perspective. The next four chapters examine the parameters of this alternative in the same order they were discussed in Part One. For every parameter whose modern definition was eroded by postmodernity, I suggest in this part an alternative that will be desirable, meaningful, and adequate for postmodernity.

This chapter presents educational goals, parallel to the failing, prevailing modern definitions of educational goals discussed in Chapter Two, which are desirable and more adequate for a postmodern democracy. Chapter Seven responds to the breakdown of the prevailing school's modern curriculum covered in Chapter Three and describes the desirable curriculum or, more accurately, the desirable educational program, for a postmodern democracy. Similarly, Chapters Eight and Nine respond to the crises analyzed in Chapters Four and Five. In Chapter Eight I discuss desired and workable conceptions of the educational institution's (the word "school" might no longer be relevant) organizational structure; in Chapter Nine I describe the desirable responses to the profound changes wrought on the students, education's target audience, by postmodern culture.

Chapter Two portrays a rather bleak analysis of the intensive and rapid erosion of the modern definitions of educational goals by what could be described as the coming of age of "postmodern civilization." My depiction of the situation may well make the reader feel confused and frustrated. Postmodern reality seems to permit and even encourage any and all definitions, however contradictory, of the educational goals. Technical terms such as "technocratic education," "education towards autonomy," "conscious social reproduction," and "education towards socially oriented values" represent dominant educational views aimed at winning over the hearts and minds of parents, educators, and decision makers as clarified and discussed in

Chapter Two. These educational approaches, as well as their sub-approaches, all affect various audiences in the postmodern era. In this intellectually free-for-all atmosphere, representatives of each position, if and when they refer to each other (which does not happen all that often), "accuse" each other of ignoring or denying human nature, basing their positions on false beliefs, being alien to human beings' and/or education's true nature, and so on.

Seemingly, there is no way out of this conceptual-ethical maze. It seems that the more we harangue each other about the myriad of propositions for the definition of the ultimate goals of state education in postmodern democratic society, the further away we move from the ability to agree on a clear and coherent policy. However, state education systems in Liberal Democracies cannot refrain from taking a clear stand. Any conscious surrender of educational goals or drastic reduction of the scope of educational activities (the two versions of the technocratic option discussed in Chapter Two) necessarily mean adopting the intensive "educational" messages conveyed in the media, advertising, and the Internet that engulf young people today almost hermetically. Thus, any attempt to avoid choosing a side, to avoid committing to one stance in this dispute about ultimate social educational goals, constitutes, in and of itself, taking a stand within the ideological "maze": a stand that, like all the others in this debate, cannot avoid the accusations of being totally mistaken and radically harmful (see Chapter Two, Section 3).[1]

Acknowledgment of the combination of these two seemingly opposed factors, radical conceptual confusion and the unavoidable necessity of adopting a position, is a necessary starting point for any discussion about the profound crisis state education is facing in postmodern democracies.

As noted earlier, modern education first took shape in the second half of the nineteenth century. The educational worldview of that time was based on a belief in Progress and on the need to educate the masses to accept scientific and/or national and/or socialist and/or liberal values in order to achieve Progress. Adherents advocated for the acceptance of each set of these values or combinations thereof as exclusively valid or, in other words, as the exclusive way to achieve Progress.[2] At the beginning of the twenty-first century, many no longer believe in Progress or even understand or know what this term means, and there is no consensus on the exclusiveness, the validity, or even the common meaning of any of the values that were connected with this concept during the modern era. Furthermore, a growing *positive* position has emerged in the last decades, according to which there cannot be a logical way to choose between the contradicting worldviews and conceptions of the Good Life, society, and education which inhabit our world today and (usually unconsciously) guide human beings, activities, and lives.[3]

Given this state of affairs, two basic questions arise: Is there a way out of this maze? And if there is, what is it?

In this chapter I answer the first question positively, and the second with an argument which consists of the following six claims:

1. The modern democratic state has a duty to educate in light of a specific educational view. In other words, it is logically and ethically necessary for the liberal state to adopt a certain educational view and follow it through.

2. Given this duty, education towards autonomy should be the ultimate aim of the liberal democratic state.
3. The most desirable meaning of "autonomy" in postmodern Liberal Democracy is that found in John Stuart Mill's approach.
4. An elaboration of the Millian idea of autonomy, indicating its historical roots in German Humanism, elucidates its importance and relevance for us today.
5. The desirability of the value of autonomy as the main educational goal in postmodern democracies can be defended against potential attacks from all relevant opposing quarters, including the postmodern, feminist, and communitarian views.
6. Two additional values, morality and dialogical belonging (to be defined below), are mandated by and are complementary to autonomy. Together, these values constitute the trio of values that should stand at the foundations of education in a postmodern liberal democratic society.

I shall elucidate and substantiate each of these claims in the following six sections of this chapter.

THE LOGICAL NECESSITY OF ADOPTING A SPECIFIC EDUCATIONAL VIEW

First, the following premise underlying my argument should be substantiated: even in the postmodern reality the liberal democratic state must maintain an intrinsically "loyal" education system, meaning one that strives to achieve defined educational goals or goals designed to support the state as a Liberal Democracy. This argument clearly contradicts the technocratic approach described in Chapter Two.

When the technocrats ask, "Who gave us the right?" clearly the answer should be "Logically speaking, the liberal state has no option other than to educate," whether by action or by *inaction*. Though seemingly neutral, inaction nevertheless does lead to the adoption of a specific educational view, in that legitimacy and exclusivity are granted, either consciously or, more often, unconsciously, to the educational view supported by the "forces in the field." The adoption of this option today automatically means intensive, one-dimensional, education towards consumption-oriented lives necessitated by the market economy, augmented by the global economy, and expressed through all aspects of the media, digital reality, and advertising which engulf all of us during most of our waking hours.

Given that the liberal state must educate, it must do so in light of *its own* conception of the Good Life, *as stemming from the state's basic constitutional foundation* or, in other words, in light of the Humanistic or liberal democratic view that underlies the constitutional structures of all Western Liberal Democracies.

Arguably, there is no logical necessity for a contradiction between the liberal democratic conception of the Good Life and the influences exerted by the "forces in the field." One might even expect that economy-driven "field forces" developing in postmodern Liberal Democracies would, at the very least, be compatible to their "breeding grounds." Yet such an expectation is simply false. In today's world, there is, in fact, a rapidly deepening chasm between the values, assumptions, and worldviews lying at the foundations of Humanism and the Liberal Democracy and the socioeconomic forces prevalent in Western democracies, which paradoxically have developed under the social "umbrella" of these values and assumptions. These "field forces" of postmodern reality exert tremendous pressures, which oppose the most basic values of the Humanistic worldview, on young people. This is indeed the result of a long dialectical process since these forces originated in the values that they now undermine.[4]

But the dialectical nature of the process does not decrease its devastating potential by even one inch. As claimed above, the most significant expressions of the "forces in the field" today are the mutually permeating and reflecting endless-channel television and the forever expanding infinitely inter-linked virtual heavens of the Internet, which are essentially merged into an almost "hermetic" mind-boggling digital reality which engulfs all of us all the time. In spite of its mind-boggling effect or maybe as a result of this "unreal reality" there exists a very consistent system of mutually supporting messages which this reality carries and sustains. Due to its very nature, the digital media transmits a "clippy" (lacking continuity), superficial (or at least severely lacking in depth), one-dimensional "reality," which is present oriented, enhances instant gratification of desires and leaves very little space for long term planning and expectation. On the content level, due to the domination of the advertising industry, television and the Internet communicate an exclusive, one-dimensional, egoistic-hedonistic worldview, which caters mostly if not solely to the needs of this industry.[5] Giving that this is the age of globalization, we are talking about globally engulfing messages; there is no way out, no chance of exposure to alternative understandings of the human situation.

These messages threaten Humanistic values and hence the Liberal Democracy which relies on them, both in the short and long terms. The short-term threat is a result of the messages' tendency to glorify fragmentariness and immediate facile gratification of desires, especially those related to power, money, and sex.[6]

These materialistic hedonistic values come at the expense of values central to the Humanistic view and fundamental to the Liberal Democracy. First among the threatened liberal values are self-realization and its constituents: rationality or long-term planning ability, and reflection or one's ability for critical scrutiny of oneself and one's environment. Second among the threatened Humanistic values are res-pect for the rights of the other to self-realization, or ongoing respect for certain moral duties that are required by the universality of the value of self-realization.[7]

The first long-term threat stems from the intensification of the fragmentary egoistic-hedonistic worldview that postmodern media enhance so well. Such an outlook does not leave room for according life with meaning that transcends striving for physiological pleasure or "jouissances" as they are called in certain post-modernistic writings.[8] It does not support the sometimes difficult and challenging individual search for self-formation or the personal aspiration to accord one's life with intrinsic meaning which are the core goals of Humanism and hence of Liberal Democracy. Furthermore, this outlook threatens the existence of a stable continuous self or "I" which is a *sine qua non* of all other basic Humanistic assumptions.[9]

The second long-term threat pertains to the ethical vacuum created by the forces shaping postmodern consciousness together with the (false) promise of "immediate redemption" touted by postmodern media and advertising. Such a world impels many to turn to various "escape from freedom" mechanisms for "ready-made" answers. Among these are self-forgetfulness, found in various forms of addiction (drugs, alcoholism, workoholism, sex, obsessive-eating, obsessive-dieting, and many more) as well as various absolutist worldviews that promise salvation (fundamentalism, nationalism, or fascism). This process endangered the very existence of the Liberal Democracy as far back as the 1920s and '30s. Today numerous and ominous portents are once again appearing on the horizon.[10]

We can, of course, find many significant actual or potential positive effects that television, the Internet,[11] and the global economy,[12] as well as other processes, have had on today's reality. All the data on this extremely complex subject may not yet (or ever) be in. If it were, it may have pointed to a potential positive as well as negative impact postmodernity has on the development of the self. Yet, at the end of the day, if we truly aim to enhance development in light of Humanistic values, we cannot afford to leave the realm of education exclusively to "the forces in the field." Even the likelihood of there being an enduring threat to the individual's ability to develop in the light of basic Humanistic values should be a major reason for concern. The education system in a liberal democratic society must consciously set itself clear and binding educational targets which stem from the Humanistic view fundamental to such a society.

Setting these goals should be done in a deliberate, mindful way, that is, in a way based on a clear definition and detailed operationalization of the basic Humanistic values on one hand, and on an extensive conscious analysis of the "forces in the field," together with their hypothesized impact and assumed harmful, as well as positive, consequences, on the other hand. This then should lead to a strategically defined attempt to use these forces: harness them, if and when possible, for the benefit of the Humanistic cause and restrain them, if using them proves unattainable, to the extent that it is possible, in light of Humanism's basic values.[13]

THE ULTIMATE GOAL: EDUCATION TOWARDS AUTONOMY

The question that arises out of the above conclusion is: *what educational goals must the liberal democratic society set itself?* To answer this question we need to go back to the four approaches to education that currently dominate educational discourse and practice[14] and examine the desirability of each as a possible infrastructure for sustaining postmodern Liberal Democracies.

Of the four approaches discussed in Chapter Two, two, the *technocratic approach to education* and *education towards desirable social values,* must be immediately disqualified. The first is unsuitable because it makes no pretense to actively set educational goals, and, as shown above, in the postmodern reality there is a high chance that it encourages a worldview and values which undermine and threaten Humanism and the Liberal Democracy.

If the first approach is disqualified for lack of any educational demands that can sustain the Liberal Democracy in today's reality, the second is unfit for the opposite reason: it is over-demanding. All the sub-approaches within the "education towards desirable social values" approach impose on the individual education based on a specific perception of the Good Life. But the essence of the Liberal Democracy, and the variation of Humanism it relies on, rejects the idea of determining a specific, substantive perception of life for the individual, instead allowing the individual to choose from among different perceptions of the Good Life.

The version of liberalism defended here consists of a *conscious acknowledgment of the substantive nature* of "education for autonomy" as the meta-value guiding education. Thus, a more correct way of phrasing this sentence will be: the only value Liberal Democracies should rely on in their educational endeavor is education towards autonomy and its derivatives. This value provides a much larger range of liberty to the individual than the above first level values and it thus allows for many of the first level values that don't radically threaten the dominance of the value of education towards autonomy to exist as well.

Thus, we remain with only two categories of educational approaches: *education towards autonomy* and *conscious social reproduction*. Structurally, both approaches rely on the same strategy. They both perceive liberal democratic societies as committed to neutrality with regard to the conception of the Good Life. Furthermore, both approaches rely on one version or another of skeptical or relativistic epistemology concerning ethics (at least). Their adherents conceive themselves as unable to declare with any certainty that a specific worldview is "more correct" or better than another worldview. Both lead therefore to the conclusion that we cannot choose *a priori* a conception of the Good Life in the light of which the individuals being educated should live. In other words, both approaches rely on the belief that under the above conditions, namely liberalism's commitment to neutrality and the necessary fallibility concerning "ethical knowledge," an *a priori* decision on the *material* goals of public education, goals which reflect a concrete conception of the Good Life, is impossible. This being so and as relinquishing education is a non-starter, both perceptions move towards an allegedly *procedural* and hence *formal* (i.e., not oriented to any specific material conception) understanding of educational goals; that is, towards focusing on a process of determining the way in which a decision about the goals of education is to be made instead of on the goals themselves.

I qualified the understanding of educational goals as "formal" and claimed it to be an "alleged" understanding, because there cannot be, from a logical standpoint, an absolutely "formal" procedure. In other words, an understanding which does not presuppose very specific ontology, epistemology, and often ethics and psychology simply cannot exist. Even when a "neutral" procedure is proclaimed as "just" or "qualitative" in some minimal sense which is claimed to be "formal" or "purely procedural," it too necessarily "hides" an entire range of suppositions about, among others, the *ontology* of individuals' identity, their psychology, the nature of decision making (*epistemology*), the meaning of "just and equal procedure" (i.e., ethics), and so on.

Even if we could have assumed, from a logical perspective, the possibility of following a "fully neutral and formal procedure," from a social or political perspective, proponents of all liberal views "cannot afford" to adhere to such an approach to education. By adopting such a position they will relinquish any power of the state's educational authority to prevent the spread of educational views which are hostile and dangerous to the liberal democratic view. This is not just a theoretical issue; we can find "promising candidates" for such a position in many Western countries nowadays. For example, all liberals, including adherents of both the views discussed above, cannot allow approaches which support anti-rationalism or discrimination against women or any other group to dominate or influence the public discussion on education (or on any other subject). For similar reasons, adherents of the second view cannot allow the individual to relate to autonomy as *only* a springboard allowing him or her to irreversibly jump to any desired direction, even one which will forever inhibit her or him from returning to an autonomous position. I will further elaborate on this point below, concerning the education for autonomy approach which I propose here.

If we return now to the main line of our discussion, this strategy of reverting to a (relatively) formal stance is fundamental to both views. The difference between them boils down to two questions:

• Who decides the goals of education for a certain individual?
• What is the range of freedom the individual is allowed?

The pragmatist or republican position underpinning the conscious social reproduction approach demands that society makes decisions and choices based on a fair debate, accessible to all parties and open to all relevant positions. When following the traditional liberal approach basic to AOE, educated individuals should make such decisions by themselves, in light of their values and interests. The range of freedom the individual is allowed (or the extent of the enforced formal framework) is much wider in the case of the liberal view than in the republican one.

Still, it is impossible to claim that one approach is logically or rationally "more correct" or "valid" than another. The only point that can be made to favor the liberal approach is that the answer to the two fundamental questions stemming from it reflects the constitutional foundations of every Western society. In other words, we are living in a liberal democratic society that chose individual autonomy to be its ultimate value and upholds an overall system of individual rights as well as a system of checks and balances designed to defend these values and guarantee as large a range of individual freedom and defense from interference in individual affairs as possible. The supreme status of the constitution in the majority of Western countries and the fact that it cannot be amended or annulled by a simple majority express the choice of the Liberal Democracy for the "prioritization" of freedom of the individual and of the individual's autonomy and rights over societal discourse, even when rational and fair, as the essential factor in that democracy.

The *raison d'être* for the constitution and its special status in the liberal democratic framework is the protection of individuals, their liberty, and rights against the possible tyranny of social discourse. Tyranny of this kind becomes possible when even a fairly conducted discourse (not to mention worse, yet very probable, cases in which the discourse is not conducted fairly at all) allows a number of participants constituting a majority to legitimately impose their opinion on the minority. In other words, the principles of rationality of discourse and equal and fair access to it, or similar procedural principles, cannot in and of themselves guarantee protection from the tyranny of the majority and to some extent also of powerful non-majority groups.

The only possible way to guarantee the desired result is to protect individual rights from such tyranny by a constitution not easily changed by the majority. This clearly expresses a turning away from "republican democracy," which prioritizes social discourse that can relatively easily turn into what J. Talmon called "totalitarian democracy," preferring instead "Liberal Democracy," prioritizing individuality, autonomy, and the rights aimed at defending them.[15] Hence, prevailing Liberal Democracies should, in the name of coherence, give preference to education towards personal autonomy.

The aim of education in a Liberal Democracy is therefore educating towards an autonomous way of life, which amounts to creating the ability for and the commitment to autonomous choice about (ideally) all aspects and levels of life. To put it another way, autonomy becomes, to a large extent, a "springboard" rather than a final destination. *As long as the individual always reserves the possibility to return to the springboard and re-examine the choice previously made*, autonomy offers a large number of the possible choices. In aiming towards education for autonomy, we help students reach the springboard so that they mindfully and autonomously "dive into" any of the various relevant styles of life.[16] This view can be referred to as a "moderate perception of the springboard conception of education towards personal autonomy." A radical springboard perception of autonomy will consist of "allowing" the individual, once on the springboard, (i.e., once education has succeeded and has enhanced his or her development as an autonomous individual) to make an irreversible autonomous choice to lead an un-autonomous life.

According to this view, which I reject, as will become clear in a moment, such a choice is certainly feasible. Adherents of this view do not see any logical or psychological contradictions whatsoever between education towards autonomy and an autonomous choice by which an individual denies the continuation of his or her autonomy. An example of such a choice can be the decision of an individual to join a religious institution or group which will subject her or him to rigid educational processes which border on (or are identical to) brainwash. It is reasonable to suppose that such a process aims to lead the individual to a "point of no return" beyond which he or she will not be able to resume his or her autonomy or return to the springboard. She or he will be "doomed" to remain in the view he or she jumped into through an altogether autonomous choice. According to the view in question, it is certainly logically and psychologically possible for an autonomous individual, having reached a certain conclusion about the human situation and the dim chances of reaching happiness or self realization in all main alternatives, to join such a process. He or she will know that giving up her or his mere ego or selfhood is a condition for success. She or he will also be well aware of the fact that once given up, a return to the springboard will not be possible.

J. White, probably the most prominent advocate of autonomy as an educational goal in the last two generations, champions this radical view in his relevant books. I on the other hand prefer to adopt a moderate version of autonomy as a springboard and reject the radical interpretation as contradicting the *raison d'être* of liberal education: enhancement of the liberal worldview and its main values. In the light of this view, education should be considered a failure if leading to such irreversible renunciation of autonomy.

As mentioned above, I adhere to a moderate version of autonomy as springboard. This means that autonomy cannot be relinquished unless the abandonment thereof is temporary (even if the period of time in which autonomy is deserted is a long one) and, most importantly, can be reversed. According to my view, the individual reserves the "right" or practical and psychological ability to always return to the autonomy oriented springboard. I believe this moderate view of autonomy as springboard to be the best of all three categories of possibilities from a Humanistic point of view:

- Educating towards a certain (material) worldview, i.e., negating the springboard concept altogether and hence rejecting the Humanistic liberal approach as it was presented here.
- Educating towards autonomy as a springboard that can be irreversibly rejected once used to make "the jump" towards a chosen, not-autonomous, lifestyle. This view, as just shown above, also contradicts the core of the liberal view.
- Education towards autonomy as a springboard which can be tentatively relinquished.

It is true that the last option does acknowledge that the value of education of autonomy has a certain level of materiality, and is not "purely formal." However, as I claimed above, there are no fully formal or procedural values. Any procedure rules out some material options and hence is inherently material to some extent. Moreover, the moderate springboard approach allows for a maximal level of choice and openness within the (moderately material) value of autonomous choice. It thus preserves the Humanistic educational view without allowing it to "go too far" and contradict itself.

WHAT IS AN "AUTONOMOUS PERSONALITY"?[17]

Having made a choice to view enhancing autonomy as a primary educational goal, another question should be raised: what is the meaning of "autonomy"?

1. In the history of modern Western thought, several concepts of the "autonomous personality" have emerged. Elsewhere I have discerned eight such concepts.[18] Still, in a schematic way, it is possible to say that three among these concepts have proven central: the *rationalist, emotivist,* and *emotivist-rationalist.*[19] Common to all three is the assumption that autonomous individuals "hold the reins of their lives" in their own hands, or in other words, they determine for themselves what life's basic values are and aspire to fulfill them. The issues on which the three concepts differ consist of different answers to the question: How does the individual realize self-determination? Or more specifically, which aspects of the individual's personality must take a leading role in one's self-determination?

In the *rationalist* approach the leading factor in determining the autonomous individual's basic values is human reason. Emotions are perceived as subjugated to or fully controlled by reason. At the other end of the spectrum, the *emotivist* approach maintains that emotions are paramount and the individual's values are seen as an expression of the autonomous individual's basic emotions or desires. Reason is perceived in this case as serving the emotions by helping the individual form a plan to achieve the desires dictated by the emotions.

The *emotivist-rationalist* concept of the autonomous individual is a hybrid approach. Like the emotivist approach, it perceives emotions as the source of autonomous individuals' desires and values, yet it also grants reason an extensive and very important role in forming a coherent set of desires and values out of the quite chaotic realm of the emotions; such a role simply does not exist in the purely emotivist approach. The hybrid approach acknowledges the viable role that reason can and should play in:

- "Bringing to consciousness," interpreting and shaping of often unconscious and unclear emotions;
- Distinguishing between "false desires" and "true desires";
- Creating a coherent scale of values out of the confused affective and emotive realm;
- Operationalizing the aforementioned scale.

2. Various versions of the *rationalist* approach, whose foremost proponent was Kant, dominated modern philosophy until two to three decades ago, and still greatly influence the Western, mainly Anglo Saxon, view of autonomy. This approach is severely flawed due to its "schizophrenic" depiction of individuals as beings whose reason is constantly at odds with their emotions in an attempt to "overcome" them. Being responsible for the diffusion of this image of human life into modern rationalism, it has inflicted severe damage on Western rationalism. It is responsible for the common (mistaken) perception of reason and emotions as two "antagonistic" faculties one must chose between. If one strives to be autonomous, this perception categorically demands that preference be given to the first over the second. To use Freudian terms, it requires the individual to live in constant suppression of the emotions (or Id) by reason (or Superego).

Moreover, the rationalist approach in its Kantian form, and in its later derivatives as well, rests on a concept of material reason, that is, a perception of reason as containing within itself information about the world and the Good Life. Such a view is unacceptable in the framework of the skeptical and relativistic epistemological perceptions dominant in postmodernity and in the framework of the ethical neutrality to which Liberal Democracy is committed.[20]

The first proponent of a simplistic, extreme version of the *emotivist* approach was the Scottish philosopher David Hume. Another Romantic and more moderate version was first expressed by Rousseau (so maintains the "dominant history" of philosophy) and later by German and British Romantic thinkers and poets.[21] Extreme emotivism is at least conversely flawed due to its complete disregard to any stable point of the personality (the "ego" or the "self") and its perception of individuals as consisting of unrestrained mass of drives and urges that cannot and should not be ordered or restrained. It also has a simplistic and unrealistic view of emotions as "driving themselves forward" without any necessary cognitive mediation.

Such a perception, as far as it implies the "disintegration of the self," is likely to find favor in some postmodern philosophical circles that celebrate the dismantling of the self. Still it is totally improbable from a psychological standpoint and is also extremely dangerous from the liberal democratic point of view. Apart from anything else, this view rejects the presumption of a stable individual self-exercising (some form) of long-term control of emotions, and it denies the supposition of individual self-direction and hence personal long-term planning. For the same reason, emotivism also does not allow for the assumption of stable interpersonal contractual friendly or intimate relationships predicated on responsibility defined on the basis of the assumption of the identity of those involved in it and in light of a clear system of rights and obligations.

Thus, both the purely rationalistic and emotivistic perceptions of autonomy compromise the very foundation of democratic life.

The *emotivist-rationalist* approach is free of both these categories of flaws. From the psychological standpoint, it forms a balanced and realistic description of the autonomous individual and of the "cooperation" between reason and emotions, fully compatible with prevailing psychological research on motivation and personality,[22] interests,[23] development, and identity formation.[24] This outlook also assumes a procedural perception of reason and is therefore completely compatible with both the postmodern skepticism and moderate relativism epistemological perceptions (even if not with the extreme version of postmodernistic relativism which is, in any case, self contradictory and meaningless) and Liberal Democracies' commitment to ethical neutrality. It also enables the stability and continuity of the personality mandated by the democratic view. I therefore base my view hereinafter on this approach.[25]

In my discussion of this approach to autonomy in Chapter Two, I mentioned two of its contemporary representatives, Eamonn Callan and John White. Yet this viewpoint is rooted in the German Humanism of the early nineteenth century, and its most influential proponent is the nineteenth century English philosopher John Stuart Mill.[26] The Humanist tradition on which Mill founded his ideas and the liberal tradition based on his philosophy presented the most detailed, complete, and acceptable model of the autonomous individual. Therefore, hereinafter, I rely on Mill's perception of autonomy, which continues the previous Humanistic thought from the perspective of the two last generations.[27]

In Mill's philosophy, an autonomous person is self-directed and authentic. *Self-direction* in this context means having the capability and commitment to formulate and realize rational life plans that clearly express defined goals. *Authenticity* means the capability and commitment to strive for self-knowledge and for the translation of one's knowledge of one's personality into an actual "life plan" (another Humanistic term, derived from German Humanism and Mill; the inverted commas reflect the fact than neither the Humanist nor Mill and certainly not myself assume that the individual should rely only on one or exclusive-long-term rigidly formed life plan; it rather refers, in an ideal way, to the general horizon of one's goals and to the aspiration towards them). The term "self-knowledge," if we understand it in contemporary terms, which we must do for it to make sense today, refers to knowledge of one's personal profile, consisting of the three major dimensions of any human action: interest, capacity, and performance style.

Neither Mill nor any of his predecessors or followers related to the above three specific categories comprising the self profile which are hence necessary objects of reflection for the sake of attaining self-knowledge and self expression. Still, I believe these categories to be the most accurate operationalization of the Millian ideal based on prevailing knowledge and research. These three categories respond to the three basic questions one has to answer concerning the direction one's "life plan" should reflect:

- What should be the ultimate goal of my activities (interests)?
- What kind of activities am I capable of successfully performing (capacities)?
- How should I perform my activities in order to maximize my chances for success (performance styles)?

Interests are defined in prevailing philosophical and psychological research as those activities one performs for their own sake (in philosophical terms) or for intrinsic motivation (in psychological terms). In other words they cannot, by definition, serve as instruments to any other activity or goal in one's life. They are therefore life's goals and the source of answers to the first question.

When choosing one's life goals, it is not enough to be conscious of one's interests. Sometimes one might not be able to follow an interest for lack of necessary psychological or physiological attributes or "capacities." For example, a 1.65 m. (five ft. four in.) tall person cannot rationally choose to be a professional basketball player in today's reality (it might have been possible three or four generations ago when individuals used to be much shorter). The same is true of someone lacking high level motor coordination. Or, one may lack the necessary performance "style"; a "night person" cannot rationally aspire to follow a career or an interest that in today's world requires early morning activity.

"Capacities" or "intelligences" (to use H. Gardner's well-known term) are attributes of the individual that contemporary research refers to as reflecting the potential of a certain individual for performing effectively. "Performance styles" or "learning styles" are attributes that contemporary research uses to characterize the mode of actions in which the individual is most at ease and hence most effective. Therefore, capacities and performance styles should serve as a source for the answers to the second and third questions, respectively.[28]

Thus, in my adaptation of the Millian ideal to the terminology of prevailing psychological and pedagogical research, autonomous individuals seek to achieve maximal knowledge of their interests, capacities, and performance styles, as well as of the relationships between these attributes and between them and the context in which the individuals operate. One should attempt to form one's life goals based on optimization of these relationships throughout life.

To this end, autonomous individuals should ask themselves:

- Whether their capacities and performance styles can reasonably support their interest. The answer to this question may depend, in many cases, on the context in which they live. The minimal height required to become a professional basketball player may vary from one era and circumstance (Central African pygmy tribes for example) to the next (USA NBA league in the twenty-first century in contrast). If the answer to this question is positive, one must then ask

- Whether there is some variation on, or sublimation of, the interest that can be supported instead. Thus I may not be an effective basketball player but I might be able to be a sports historian or journalist or a team manager. If that is not the case one must wonder
- Whether it is worth investing in attempts to adjust relevant capacities or performance styles to the original interests. In case no such adjustment seems reasonable, one must ask
- Whether a second-best life goal might be satisfactory. If someone always dreamt of being basketball player, but has also drawn enormous pleasure from the plastic arts, that person can choose to spend long hours painting or just admiring beautiful paintings as a lasting interest or even, if possible, as a foundation for a career. When the first interest or desired life goal seem unrealistic or the investment of time and effort needed to change inadequate natural capacities or inappropriate performance styles is too costly, one can consider turning to another interest of equal value or even somewhat lesser value as the foundation of one's actual life goal.

In the Millian view the development of authenticity and self-direction requires a process of reflective "*experiments in living*" (Mill's words from *On Liberty*). One does not know right away one's personality profile nor is one born with the ability to make rational plans and implement them. Such knowledge and abilities develop gradually and infinitely in the individual through a process of learning about one's self, one's reality, and the relationship between self and reality, as well as by developing rational and emotional abilities necessary for planning and realizing plans through *ex post facto* critical reflection on one's behavior in response to life's various situations. This applies to all aspects of life including leisure, work, social involvement, interpersonal relationships, and the formation or adoption of a worldview.[29]

Nurturing an autonomous person, one who is authentic and self-directed, must be the ultimate goal of education. Encouragement of the reflective developmental process activated by the individual through life experiences must therefore be put forward as the basic operational educational goal of a postmodern democratic society.

THE HUMANIST ROOTS OF THE MILLIAN IDEAL

In the previous section I described the Millian ideal of the autonomous individual as adapted to the terminology of contemporary research. Now I shall add flesh to the bones of this ideal and explain its central position in the Humanist and liberal democratic perceptions for our time, while tracing its historical roots back to German Humanism of the late eighteenth and early nineteenth centuries. I find such a discussion necessary in order to explicate the extremely important role which was almost completely erased from Western consciousness today. This concept plays in Western culture and helps the reader acquire a better understanding thereof. The questions concerning the operational meaning and implementation of the goal of education for autonomy will be discussed in detail in the next chapters.

German Humanism as it is professed in the writings of Wilhelm von Humboldt decisively influenced Mill. Von Humboldt, one of this worldview's most prominent philosophers, founded the first university which was designed to be a modern institution from inception. This university, located in Berlin, was based on his own philosophy, unlike all previously existing universities which functioned as theological institutions for centuries and had to go through long processes of modernization and rationalization. Von Humboldt also contributed greatly to the development of the German Humanistic *gymnasium*. Mill's book *On Liberty* relies heavily on von Humboldt and German Humanism and is doubtlessly one of the central works in the history of Western liberalism, if not *the* central liberal text.

According to *On Liberty* and the German Humanistic tradition, the basic justification for the existence of Liberal Democracy is that it provides the necessary and sufficient conditions for freedom, a "diversity of experience," and the security needed to realize a process of reflective "experiments in living." This process, when productive, is a necessary and (almost) sufficient[30] condition for the development and expression of autonomy. Finally, autonomy of personality is a necessary and (almost) sufficient condition for maximizing human happiness.[31]

To understand the German Humanist's perception of autonomy, we must focus on its three key concepts: *Bildung, Kultur,* and *Berufung*. The term *Bildung*, first adopted in Germany in the 1870s, quickly became popular and acquired numerous meanings. Its original meaning was "a process of self-education wherein individuals gradually discover their own unique personality potential, or vocation (*Berufung*) and shape themselves in order to fulfill this potential." The text which more than any other bears testimony to the meaning of this idea is Goethe's *Bildungsroman*,[32] *Wilhelm Meisters Lehrjahre*,[33] which depicts a young man's struggle to shape and fulfill his personality. The book is characterized by both optimism and skepticism. Its optimism is expressed by assumptions about individuals' ability to realize their unique nature and *Berufung* and achieve (at least for certain periods) internal harmony in terms of reason, emotions, and senses, as well as external harmony with respect to other human beings, society, and nature.

This optimism stems from the assumptions that loosely guided Goethe as well as Herder and von Humboldt and other German Humanists living in this short, yet very intensive and productive, era between the last two decades of the eighteenth century and the first decade of the nineteenth. The assumptions were:

- Reality is an external expression of a single, constantly developing, spiritual essence. The more it is expressed, the more harmony there is in human beings and the more harmonious the relationship between human beings and the world is.
- Each individual is a part of a universal scenario of development of the same spiritual essence, which is sometimes called "God" or "spirit of the world"

(*weltgeist*) or simply "the subject." In this development everyone has a role which is innate to their being. The root meaning of the word *Bildung*, *Bild*, a picture, reflects this belief in the inner picture of the vocation or calling (*Berufung*) of the individual.

- Finally, according to this view, an individual should strive towards the revelation of his or her *Berufung* and fulfillment thereof throughout her or his life.

Skepticism is manifested in the perception of self-realization as a never-ending process. According to the Humanists, as we are finite beings in an infinite reality, we are necessarily fallible. Hence any knowledge one has of one's self, culture, and circumstances of life is necessarily tentative and hypothetical; therefore, no one can achieve an absolute knowledge or categorical resolution of the dilemmas that life places in their way. Examples for such dilemmas, central to human life in Goethe's novel, include: freedom vs. commitment to society and family, the need to make a living vs. the desire for personal expression, and the individual's desire for interpersonal relationships based on love vs. the individual's desire for pragmatic ties based on instrumental considerations of benefit.[34]

According to this view, the process of self-actualization is dynamic and infinite. Thus, self-knowledge and harmonious expression of the individual's vocation and authentic values or, to use contemporary terminology, of a personal profile best suited to the given real-life circumstances, can never be finally realized. They should rather be perceived as regulative ideas or horizons one permanently aspires to and not as goals that can be actually and finally achieved.

In the Humanistic view the necessary conditions for the maximal realization of the ideal of self-development towards harmonious self-expression are:

- *Security*, mainly in the root sense of being protected from harm to one's life, body, and property, but also in the senses of "social acceptance" and stability of social frameworks;
- "*Diversity of experience*" (Mill's term), social and cultural pluralism or prevalence of a variety of modes of living in all major aspects of human life;
- The individual's *Freedom* to choose, change, or form the frameworks required for self-experimentation and self-actualization.

In the Humanistic view, these conditions, once established, can guarantee high chances for the development of self-actualizing, autonomous individuals who enjoy a satisfying life and who contribute to the development of a potent and diversified society and culture (*Kultur*); this culture, in turn, will serve as the cultivating context for the growth and development of other individuals. As mentioned earlier, in Von Humboldt's and Mill's approach, the liberal democratic society is perceived as optimally fulfilling these conditions.

The last sentence leads us towards the complementary concept of the term *Bildung*, namely the concept of *Kultur* or "culture." In its broadest sense, this concept relates to all the facets of human life which are the result of previous human endeavor (as opposed to nature) and modes of life. As such, culture is on the one hand the point of departure for, and the foundation of, the individual's self-actualizing process, while on the other it is the product of individuals' past self-actualization processes.

Culture is a vital basis for self-actualization, because all alternative ways of life one may examine are formed within a certain cultural framework, either in one's own culture or in other cultures. The knowledge of culture is necessary for achieving the individual's self-knowledge and "self-choice."[35] Therefore, one must investigate culture, its basic thinking patterns, and lifestyles in order to understand the self, and also, when so desired, in order to break free of subjugation to these structures in their existing form and become aware of available alternatives. It is only through clear awareness of the cultural framework that has contributed to a person's identity that he or she can become an autonomous agent by choosing to stick to his or her culture, or to some of its aspects, or abandon it, or some of its aspects. Consequently, a study of culture in both its direct experiential sense and its more conceptual or symbolic sense is a prerequisite for any process of self-actualization.[36]

As all individuals live within a cultural framework, their developing ways of life cumulatively result in the constant enrichment and change of that culture. Thus, the self-actualizing individual and culture maintain a constant dialectical relationship of mutual enrichment.

In clarifying the relevance of the Humanistic approach to our times, we must remember that the German Humanists consciously developed this approach and its central ideal of individual self-actualization as an alternative to two other options. These were the rationalist approach of Enlightenment and the French Encyclopedists, and the mainly pious religious, anti-rationalist, reaction that gained great popularity in Germany at the time.

The rationalist conception of Enlightenment brought previously unprecedented scientific and technical achievements to European culture. This explosion of ideas also became an inexhaustible source of hope for drastic improvements or "Progress" in society. The French revolution was perceived by proponents of Enlightenment as the epitome of this dramatic development and proof positive of the great, long-awaited, liberation. Yet as a materialist-determinist approach, the rationalism of the Enlightenment was unable to back up and validate two premises that were per-ceived by many intellectuals of this generation (and other generations) as psycho-logically essential to a good human life: (a) the assumption of individual freedom, and (b) the assumption that human life has meaning which transcends the materialistic level.

As a result of the existential deficiencies characterizing the materialistic-determinist view of the Enlightenment, a religious or mystical reaction spread throughout Germany during the eighteenth century. The main trend thereof was known as "Pietism." This reaction was openly anti-rationalist and fought fiercely against all the Enlightenment-oriented values. Thus in this meaningful moment of history (as in later moments, including, especially, ours) it seemed that one had to choose between two horns of a basic existential dilemma. You could either be a rationalist and lose your faith in human freedom and the transcendental or spiritual meaning inherent in human life, or you could retain those beliefs by giving up rationalism alongside everything Enlightenment stood for and acknowledge the truth of some version of the Christian faith.

For many young educated people of that age this was a destructive dilemma. Relying to one extent or another on the dramatic philosophical breakthrough of Kant's philosophy, and later on Idealism that ensued from it,[37] German Humanism developed as an ambitious conceptual project directed towards providing a third choice for those wishing to base their life on reason without relinquishing the assumptions of individual freedom and life's meaningfulness.

Despite its popularity, the Kantian solution to the same dilemma proved too dualistic and schematic for many of Kant's contemporaries. It was based on a bi-level division of reality, wherein in each division Kant satisfied the demands of one of the two cultural alternatives of his time. The first level was defined by Kant as "the world of phenomena," or the material world, which is governed deterministically by the laws of nature (in their modern materialistic version, as described by Newtonian physics). The second was defined as "the thing in itself," or the spiritual world, which was understood by Kant as governed by the laws of human freedom, spirituality, and morality. Human beings, according to Kant, are citizens of both worlds simultaneously.

Because many German intellectuals of the time found the Kantian solution, despite its huge influence, not to be fully comprehensible and satisfactory, the Humanists of Kant's generation and the generation that followed sought a way to unify the "two worlds," the requests of reason with the requirements of a free and meaningful human life, on one level. They aspired to form an intellectual system that would acknowledge the existence of the material world and obey the demands of reason yet at the same time rely on assumptions concerning the freedom of the individual and life as having transcendental meaning.[38]

The perception of self-actualization, as developed by, among others, Herder, Goethe, and Von Humboldt, meets these requirements. Herein, the individual exists within the givens of reality and culture. However, individuals are free to choose their own way from numerous alternatives that are part of their culture, while at the same time they are liberated from total domination of their culture as a result of their potential for personal reflection and rational criticism and interpretation. Within this view, individuals are perceived as constantly striving towards self-knowledge, knowledge of reality, and understanding of culture in order to strike the right balance between their desires and values as well as between their desires and values on one hand and reality on the other.

This perspective grants full legitimacy to the individual's need for meaning that goes beyond the material, the practical, and the immediate. But in this context, the meaning of life is not derived from any absolute and/or dogmatically understood spiritual reality that is unquestioningly acknowledged as in religion, but from the individual's constant struggle for balanced self-expression and the molding of a harmonious way of life.

The Humanist approach paid a price for this ideal; its proponents had to relinquish the absoluteness promised by both the empiricist objectivism that characterized the French Enlightenment and the transcendental objectivism of religion.

But it was a reasonable price to pay for the creation of a revolutionary human ideal, that is, the ideal of the self-creating, self-actualizing individual.

It is important to note that the Humanist approach lacked a solid metaphysical base or systematic justification, at least in the writings of the three aforementioned philosophers: Herder, Goethe, and von Humboldt. As stated earlier, Humanism was nourished by the assumed existence of a developing spiritual reality, sometimes called "God" or "the spirit of the world," at the basis of the material reality. In this the Humanists were impressed by the pantheistic position of Spinoza, interpreted by them (as opposed to Spinoza) as referring to a dynamic or self-developing reality or divinity. They vaguely and loosely used this dynamic interpretation of Spinoza as support for the optimistic elements in their own thinking. However, none of the three troubled to turn these assumptions into a formulated systematic metaphysical method. Instead, they wrote about these notions only in passing, more as a state of mind than a defined and logically founded metaphysical system. What mattered to them were the existential, psychological, and practical questions, not the formation of a strict metaphysical system.[39]

The current-day need to contend with technocratic or postmodernist trends on the one hand, and fundamentalist or new age religious reactions or nationalist-fascist reactions to the existential vacuum created by these trends on the other, is no less a core problem for contemporary Humanists. Thus, today, we can still utilize the German Humanists' formulation, augmented by Mill and his interpreters (past and present). That is, of course, contingent on its adaptation to the spirit and state-of-the-art scientific knowledge of the times.[40]

CRITIQUES OF THE IDEAL OF THE AUTONOMOUS INDIVIDUAL AND THE RESPONSES TO THEM

Adopting the ideal of the autonomous individual as the ultimate educational goal is likely to evoke at least six critiques.

The first critique will come from *pragmatists* and *disciples of the conscious social reconstruction approach*. They will claim that the development of one's autonomy is not a neutral human ideal devoid of concrete content or a procedural ideal, but rather it is an ideal based on a series of assumptions and values. These include the value of the self-determining individual, assumptions regarding the nature and roles of reason and reflection, and the assumption concerning the existence of the individual's real self. These are all, so the argument will go, possible but not necessary values or assumptions. Therefore, it will conclude, the ideal of the autonomous individual as here described should not be given priority over any other human ideal in a Liberal Democracy committed to neutrality.

My response to this claim is: I admit the facts but deny the charge. The values and assumptions attributed to this ideal do indeed lie at its basis, but a worldview and conception of human life that is not based on any values and assumptions whatsoever is a logical impossibility. Thus claiming that the Humanistic view is based on a set of assumptions and values is making a trivial argument. The question should only be whether these assumptions and values commit us to more than we are already assuming by being Humanists or liberals. The answer is clearly that these values and assumptions are fundamental to the concept of Liberal Democracy, so adopting them does not add anything to the existing underpinnings of the view as it already lies at the basis of our societies and constitutions.

Thus from the perspective of neutrality between worldviews to which Liberal Democracy should be committed, the Humanistic view of autonomy as the ultimate educational value, which I recommend here, does not add to the basic assumptions and values lying at the foundation of Liberal Democracy. Rather, it should be preferred within Liberal Democracies over any other alternative which assumes other and maybe contradicting assumptions or values.

The second critical appraisal will come from various advocates of "*education towards desirable social values.*"[41] This critique will coalesce in the argument that education towards autonomy is, under existing societal circumstances, meaningless at best, or even misleading because it rests on deception. To refer to critiques by two main representative examples of this view, autonomy cannot be maintained in a reality of built-in economic-social discrimination in the neo-Marxists' view, or in a reality of moral and mental corruption and degeneration, as the conservatives see it.

My response to this argument is as follows: Due to their open[42] characteristics, the liberal democratic and education towards autonomy approaches are the only ones within which the veracity of their own principles as well as that of the critiques can be tested and their truth value examined.[43] In contrast, education consistent with each of the criticizing approaches (neo-Marxist or conservative) dramatically diminishes the scope of criticism and freedom, and forestalls any real chance of the seeker identifying the veracity of opposing approaches. From a rational point of view and out of a commitment to preserving ethical neutrality as best we can where knowledge is lacking, education towards autonomy becomes the optimal step, as it allows and encourages criticism and improvement.

The third criticism is likely to emanate from various *conservative cultural and educational views*. According to these views, the ultimate aim of education in Western culture is to inculcate general (or theoretical, disciplinary) knowledge. In their eyes education towards autonomy cannot guarantee the successful inculcation of general knowledge, and therefore it is only worthy of condemnation and abandonment. [44]

My response in this case is: Education towards autonomy and the inculcation of general knowledge are indeed two contradictory educational ideals. But as I showed in Chapter Three, the traditional ideal of educating towards general knowledge has been rendered counterproductive given the deep crisis Western education is experiencing today. In the current state of affairs, following this path does not ensure the inculcation of general knowledge, but the opposite, namely, the dissemination of a contemptuous attitude towards knowledge, rendering the relevant didactic processes meaningless and destructive from an educational and social standpoint (as elaborated in Chapter Three). This fundamental crisis is one of the leading reasons propelling the search for another educational ideal. This view's criticism of the alternative I suggest here cannot be accepted without first refuting the critique I mounted against it in Chapter Three.

The fourth criticism is likely to spring from *conservatives* or *social functionalists* who see the primary function of education as training for future economic-organizational functionality, and as a result will condemn education towards autonomy, in the Humanist sense of the term, as devoid of any socioeconomic value.[45]

My response to such a claim is: While the first part of this critique is correct, the last part is not. Even if we accepted socialization towards future economic-organizational roles as a primary function of education in a postmodern democratic society, and this function of education certainly cannot be ignored, education towards autonomy in the above sense is the optimal way of fulfilling this function while also preserving the basic values of Liberal Democracy. In other words, education towards autonomy is the best way to achieve the two key goals of education: socialization and acculturation, serving the capitalist or post-capitalist economy (although not necessarily in its extreme neo-liberal version)[46] and serving Liberal Democracy. [47]

From the viewpoint of socialization into the post-capitalist economy, the alternative is educating a spineless heteronomous person who, chameleon-like, adapts to the frequently changing postmodern reality, economy, organization, and labor market.[48] It is possible that in the short term, a greater contribution to more efficient industrial-technocratic functionality will be made here, but in the longer term such a "contribution" will deliver a death blow to the existence of the liberal democratic society and, in turn, to the liberal economy.[49]

In contrast, the autonomous individual can adapt to a changing reality and still maintain a constant identity and loyalty to his or her true self and to the basic liberal values, thus contributing, in the final account, both to the economic development of his or her society and to its resilience as a Liberal Democracy.[50]

The fifth criticism is likely to arise from *communitarian* and *feminist* circles currently dominant in certain sectors of academic and intellectual discourse. Communitarians often maintain that the ideal of an autonomous person rests on the erroneous notion of the individual as being self-determining and therefore detached from society and its system of norms and obligations. According to the parallel criticism often made by feminists (though certainly not common to all of them), the ideal of autonomy alienates the individual from the values of caring for and empathy with others which are essential to women (according to one version) or to the "female aspect" of all human beings. The character and identity of the individual, so these critics may argue, are dictated by the social order (communitarians) or by one's relatedness and intimate relationships (feminists); therefore, education that encourages the individual to be detached from society or intimacy is based on a distortion of "human nature," and does an injustice to educatees as well as to society as a whole.

My response to these allegations is: This criticism associates the ideal of autonomy with the rationalist conception which, at its Kantian source, perceived the individual as an empty (i.e., devoid of commitment to any set of values or suppositions) function whose sole aim is decision making, and as such is "un-embedded" in any normative or social context as communitarians like to say. I consider this association of the "autonomous individual" with the Kantian concept of autonomy to be a most notable drawback and therefore I have not adopted it here.

The emotivist-rationalist concept developed by Mill, on which my arguments are based, clearly acknowledges the importance of interpersonal, cultural, and social commitments to the individual's identity and for a satisfying life. But because it is a conception of autonomy, these commitments are not taken to be absolute or irrevocable. Rather, it is conceived within this framework that in a slow and gradual process of reflection on life experiences, autonomous individuals are able to examine their individual commitments even when they themselves are deeply embedded in them. Of course, due to human limitations, individuals must perceive the decisive majority of their commitments at any given moment as self-evident, and can critically examine only one or a few commitments at a time.

Apparently, most communitarians and feminists would not (and cannot) reject such examinations and the changes in commitments that may stem from them. Preventing such critical examination amounts to leveling any kind of radical criti-cism of deeply embedded, yet unjust or erroneous, ways of life which will probably be criticized by feminists and communitarians (individualistic or chauvinist societies to take two relevant examples).[51]

The sixth critique might emerge from *postmodernist quarters*, namely, from those who accept the radical relativism that characterizes certain contemporary intellectual circles, and the connected contempt of rationalism as well as of (what they take to be) essentialism, that is, the assumption that there are permanent objects in reality that can be characterized in a specific and stable way. In this critique, the autonomous person's ideal will be accused of being a typically modern ideal which assumes rationality and an "essentialistic" (constant and ongoing) real self. This ideal will be condemned as vehemently contradicting the postmodern spirit that sanctifies the momentary, the fleeting, and the playful. How then, these critics will likely thunder, can you argue for an educational stance for the post-modern era, and at the same time base it on a modern ideal that is already obsolete?

When responding to this line of argumentation it is important to start by reiterating the distinction between "postmodernity" and "postmodernism" mentioned at the beginning of this book. "Postmodernity" is the name of the age in which we live, an age characterized by a series of revolutions some of which were discussed in the first chapter of the book. "Postmodernism" is a radically relativistic approach or ideology (a term postmodernists themselves will not like, I am sure) which originates in certain understandings of Nietzsche's philosophy,[52] and continued in post-sixties French philosophy as developed by (among others) Derrida, Foucault, Barth (in their case, often combined with some touches of Neo-Marxism), and later by their later American disciples.

In light of this distinction, it is clear that one can be postmodern, that is, live in the present era, and be conscious of the unique nature of this (postmodern) era, arising out of the revolutions characterizing our world, including the relativist trend and its radical marker, postmodernism, without adhering to postmodernism itself.

One can be a self-conscious postmodern and still adhere to a version of objectivism or modernism.

No reader of this book can accuse me of "postmodernism." If I were a post-modernist, I would not have even contemplated the possibility of a systematic analysis of the failures of the modern education system in the postmodern era. Systematic criticisms are taken by the radical postmodernists to stem from meta-narratives which are the arch-evil according to their own meta-narrative (if this sentence seems to be self-contradictory, that is indeed the case; it reflects the contradiction inherent in dominant postmodernistic views' criticisms of the meta-narrative). Moreover, I would certainly have found it difficult to propose a systematic alternative which is nothing but a Humanistic or liberal democratic meta-narrative on the desired education in postmodern era.

Thus, it is clear that as things stand, I am a postmodern because I am living in the here and now, and furthermore I am a self-conscious postmodern, a postmodern individual trying to understand the unique characteristics of his era in as systematic a way as possible. But it is impossible to deduce that I am a postmodernist. Even though I describe the fact that relativistic-mood-inducing postmodernistic thinkers dominate the intellectual sphere, it does not follow that I agree with them.

There is no contradiction whatsoever in being a self-conscious postmodern who rejects postmodernism and yet recognizes the need to propose an alternative education system based on adaptations of modern views, such as German Humanism and Mill's farsighted approach which certainly comprise a core modernistic position.

However, critics may still claim inconsistency between the modern ideal of autonomy and postmodern reality. This inconsistency, so they might claim, is derived from two main sources:

- The rationalist view, basic to the concept of the autonomous individual, which contradicts many of the relativist and skeptical trends which characterize postmodern reality;
- The concept of the constant nucleus of personality ("the true self") fundamental to the perception of the autonomous individual that contradicts the "clippy" character of our times and the "saturated (or disintegrating) self" phenomenon flooded by an endless stream of "clippy" pieces of information, images, video clips, icons, and so on.[53]

My reply in this case is: There is no real contradiction in the first case, because I am referring here to a rationality which is formal or procedural as much as possible and does not assume, again as much as this is possible, information about the world or about the valid value system. Such rationality falls in line with most of the skeptical and relativistic positions that characterize our era, except for the most radical ones that are obviously self-contradicting.[54]

In the second case the inconsistency is far more severe, because our period sanctifies the "clippiness," the lack of constancy and the "anti-essentialism" that prevent any serious treatment of a concept like "the true self." It does it both *de facto*, for example, through the immense impact of the media and the Internet,[55] and at the theoretical and normative levels, through postmodernist theories.[56]

In this case, the inconsistency is, from my standpoint, desirable with respect to both the descriptive and normative contexts. Acceptance of the radical "clippy" and relativistic positions means the abandonment of Western Humanism and liberalism. These last views are based on the conception of individuals who perceive themselves and their fellows as ongoing entities "identical to themselves." Adopting the educational ideal of the autonomous individual is an attempt to consciously fight the relativistic or postmodernist sanctification of the clippy and the elusive.[57]

MORALITY AND DIALOGICAL BELONGING: TWO COMPLEMENTARY ULTIMATE VALUES

In addition to nurturing the individual's autonomy as the ultimate educational value, the liberal democratic society must educate in light of two complementary fundamental values: morality and dialogical belonging. These values are at once direct derivatives of the basic value of nurturing the individual's autonomy and the source of some limitations to the implementation of this value. Democratic education must constantly deal with the dialectical tension created among these three values.

In my use of the term "morality," I refer to the minimalistic connotation fundamental to Western liberalism, to wit:

- One's commitment to the principle requiring every individual "to do as you would be done by," or put differently, simply to avoid causing harm to others;
- One's ability (on the cognitive and emotive levels) to act in light of this principle.

The term "dialogical belonging" (which I coined) refers to:

- One's commitment to the principle requiring one to define one's identity in relation to the human community(ies) or group(s) one identifies with, while at the same time requiring the individual to stand for his or her own values, interests, and rights within the relevant community(ies) or group(s);
- One's ability (on the cognitive and emotive levels) to act in the light of this principle.

Morality derives, simply and directly, from the value of autonomy. The democratic state is obliged to ensure that all young people are given the opportunity to develop as autonomous individuals, and that they can all realize their autonomy. To ensure the autonomy of all, the right of all to develop and realize themselves as autonomous individuals must be ensured. Educating towards morality, which necessarily protects every individual's right to autonomy, is central to achieving this objective. The legal system, backed by efficient law enforcement, aimed at providing individuals with the security and freedom necessary for developing as autonomous individuals and for expressing their autonomy, will only reach its objective in a reality in which the majority would act morally even if no legal system existed.

Educating towards dialogical belonging stems from the ideal of education towards autonomy in at least three ways: The *first, specific, way* consists of the recognition that the ideal of autonomy is one that has developed within Western culture over the last three or four centuries. Its roots go further back to the most fundamental monotheistic layers of Western culture. It draws its meaning and validity for Westerners (and non-Westerners) who were exposed to that historical development. Thus educating towards autonomy is necessarily educating towards belonging, in an important sense, to Western Humanistic culture.[58] Still the two values, education for autonomy and for belonging to Western culture, will be compatible and even mutually supporting if, and only if, the second value is carried out dialogically, in a sense and for reasons that will be made clear immediately.

The *second, generic, way* refers to the social frameworks necessary for a person to develop as an autonomous individual. Being "social animals" it is within a social framework that individuals will identify the experiences by which they will examine themselves, and the cultural content that will serve for their self-definition. In many of these cases, to be able to really express themselves within these social frameworks, they will need to be involved with and committed to them. Hence, they must be educated to belong and be committed to social groups while at the same time develop as autonomous individuals and be able to express their autonomy in the social settings to which they feel committed whether as a matter of biographical fact or by choice.

At the same time, for belonging to support autonomy, individuals must be aware of the fact that belonging to a community or group or culture does not require an enforced belonging to all specific aspects of the community or group or culture, or a dogmatic or blind acceptance of all aspects. They must be aware of the fact that belonging and commitment can, and must, be compatible with the individual's basic right of self-expression and that when necessary they can, and must, strive for a change in the relevant group and its ethos according to their own judgment. They must also be aware of the fact that sometimes when change is deemed by them essential to their self-expression and the probability of such change occurring in the group with which they happen to identify is very low, replacing this group, and sometimes, although relatively rarely, the society or culture as a whole, with an alternative group, society, or culture more favorable to their self-expression is also an option. In both these cases—striving for a change within the group to which they belong and leaving one group for another—it is obviously not only awareness and understanding that are necessary but also the ability to make relevant judgments and act according to them.

The *third way* consists of the recognition that autonomy necessitates dialogical belonging due to the importance of attributes, such as self-confidence, self-efficacy, and positive self-esteem, to the development of self-direction and authenticity, or of autonomy. Belonging to a social and/or cultural framework, which is on the one hand stable and reliable and on the other hand open,[59] during one's childhood years is a necessary condition for the development of these attributes.[60] It is obviously first and foremost the duty of educators, that is, the parents and then whoever assumes responsibility for the child's development, to make sure he or she enjoys this optimal kind of belonging. At the same time, from the age at which children's ability to make judgments concerning their longer term interest starts to develop, educators should start to inculcate them with an awareness of the importance of belonging to a stable and open group for their further development as well as of the importance of expressing their autonomy in the group to which they belong. Furthermore, educators have to do their best to develop commitment and the capability to strive towards the realization of the desired mode of belonging, whenever or wherever it does not exist, in their charges. In other words, it is every educator's obligation to educate the child towards dialogical belonging.

Though these two values and their parallel educational goals derive from the overriding value of educating towards autonomy in a Humanist or liberal democratic society, they may also limit the ideal of autonomy. Morality might limit certain individuals' ability to express their sense of autonomy whenever the desire to perform an immoral act arises, whether as an interest, as serving an interest, or as a whim.[61]

Similarly, dialogical belonging may limit the ability of individuals to express their autonomy at a specific time, because being active in a social or cultural framework might quite naturally require them to act according to a norm that contradicts their authentic will. Endowed with dialogical belonging, the individual might decide to act to change this situation, but even if eventually successful, the change might take some time. During this period, the individual will not be able to express the relevant will and thus his or her autonomy's expression will be limited for this duration.

Another possibility is that the individual is unsuccessful in his or her attempts to change the relevant norm and decides not to leave the group or community in question. This might be the case when the limitation of the expression of the will is judged by the autonomous and dialogically belonging individual not to be important enough, given the energy or other resources that are needed to leave the current framework. Yet another possibility occurs when the relatively large extent of self-expression one experiences in this framework is deemed sufficiently important or satisfying in light of some calculation that takes these factors into consideration. In this case, too, it might make sense in light of the value of dialogical belonging to succumb to limitations on the ability to express one's autonomy.

In order to optimize this dialectical relationship of support and limitation among the three ultimate values in the educational context,[62] we should follow what I term the "principle of reconciliation." This principle advocates education towards morality and dialogical belonging to be accomplished as pluralistically and hermeneutically as possible.

The term "reconciliation" expresses the desire to harmonize these three values as much as possible. The term "pluralistic" indicates the following guidelines that should steer the formation and activity in any liberal educational context:

- In any educational act striving to enhance belonging to a certain culture or group ethos, more than one exegetic alternative to the understanding of the discussed aspect of the culture or ethos will be presented;
- The young person should be encouraged to rationally and reflectively choose between the alternatives, or search for another in their stead.

The term "hermeneutic" requires that all content relating to a culture or a group ethos be presented as a subject open to personal interpretation shaped by the person's current worldview and needs.[63]

If education towards morality and dialogical belonging is to follow the above pedagogic guidelines, the principle of reconciliation will be realized. In other terms, although a certain dialectic tension among the three basic educational goals cannot be avoided, if the two last goals, education towards morality and towards dialogical belonging, will be carried out under the aegis of the above pedagogic guidelines the tension will be minimized.

Adherence to the principle of reconciliation will not only minimize the limitations of the individual's autonomy, as stemming from the two other goals, but is also quite likely to enhance their contribution to the development of autonomy. Thus, educating towards national belonging in the UK context, for example, will necessarily mean reading classic works written by British scholars as opposed to those written by Spanish or French writers. The choice of one set of texts precludes the use of others and thus imposes a limitation. In order to minimize this limitation's damage, teachers should deal with texts pluralistically and hermeneutically, alluding also to sources outside British culture, thus broadening the interpretational possibilities.

Similarly, educating towards basic moral values such as "Thou shalt not steal" and "Thou shalt not kill" certainly limits the individual's expression of autonomy, if such expression "requires" stealing or killing.[64] The presentation of moral dilemmas followed by open-ended discussion, when used as the method for enhancing the development of morality, may still limit one's ability to express one's autonomy in such cases (since as open as such discussion may be, it should, by definition, set some limits to the legitimate behavior). But this method might also support autonomous development by encouraging young people to interpret events, wrestle with questions, extract meaning, and develop their ability for making judgments. Thus, the price that has to be paid for the limitation of autonomy might be recompensed by the development of abilities and attitudes necessary for autonomy.

SUMMARY

In this chapter I have claimed that the liberal democratic state cannot avoid striving towards ultimate educational goals that reflect its basic values. When we do not actively inculcate Humanistic liberal values into the postmodern educational process, we, by default, decide in favor of education towards values dominant in the media and advertising that engulf us all, values which will, over time, erode the very core of the Humanism. It is tantamount to endangering the very existence of liberal democratic society. Given the imperative to educate, the natural choice for the ultimate educational value in a liberal democratic society is educating towards autonomy in the Humanistic-Millian sense of the concept as presented above.

I have further argued that two additional values should complement this fundamental value in any educational process that takes place within a liberal democratic context: educating towards morality and educating towards dialogical belonging.

While necessitated by the value of education towards autonomy, these two additional values might also effect limitations on the realization of autonomy. In desirable educational environments the principle of reconciliation aimed at optimizing the relationship between the three goals should guide the practical educational process.

AN EDUCATIONAL PROGRAM FOR POSTMODERN LIBERAL DEMOCRACIES

INTRODUCTION

In this chapter I outline an autonomy-oriented educational program,[1] designed to help students develop the following key elements:

- Autonomy
- Morality
- Dialogical belonging

The plan herein is but a first step toward the desirable educational program. No attempt will be made to depict a concrete and detailed educational program or to establish hard and fast rules. This chapter's primary objective is to indicate the possibility and feasibility of a viable alternative to the theoretical-disciplinary curriculum which currently exclusively dominates education systems all over the world. In contrast to the prevailing curriculum, the design of this alternative has been guided by:

- The three above ultimate goals of education in Liberal Democracy.
- The desire to enhance the meaningfulness of educational activity for the educatees.

As shown in the first part of this book, the prevailing curriculum is inherently opposed to these three goals and is a major cause of the absurdity (an absolute opposite of meaningfulness) and anomaly of prevailing education systems.

In the first section of the chapter,[2] I present the conceptual foundation of the proposed program. The second section[3] depicts the seven experiential domains stemming from this foundation, domains that should comprise the desired educational program and process. In the third section,[4] I offer a brief outline of the desired educational process and discuss the role of educators to guide and accompany young people through the experiences they encounter in the various experiential domains. In the interest of simplification, most of the discussion concerning the theoretical foundation and the experiential domains relates directly to education towards autonomy. Education towards morality and dialogical belonging is treated briefly in the second section.[5]

THEORETICAL BACKGROUND

Three Preceding Waves of Criticism

Opposition to the existing curriculum, based on claims of its inappropriateness to the sociocultural reality in developed countries, has come to the fore in at least three major waves in the twentieth century. Each wave originated from a different theoretical context and was formed under different circumstances. John Dewey[6] initially raised the issue during the first decades of the twentieth century as part of his broader pragmatic view. His critique was largely adopted in the 1920s and early '30s by supporters of the progressive approach to education. During the 1960s and early 70s, radical critics of education, primarily Ivan Illich,[7] launched a second, overt criticism of the prevailing theoretical curriculum.

Lastly, in the early 1980s, leading educational philosophers in Anglophone countries, headed by R. S. Peters and P. Hirst from the London Institute of Education, rekindled awareness to the unsound foundations of the theoretical-disciplinary curriculum. Consequently, they acknowledged the total failure of their two-decade-long attempt to justify the disciplinary curriculum in our relativist era based on the concept of "liberal education," formed by Plato and Aristotle and upheld thereafter by the long objectivist tradition in the West.[8]

As opposed to the two previous waves, the British philosophers, despite their awareness of the collapse of the Platonic or objectivist foundations of the liberal curriculum, did not deduce from this knowledge the need to abandon the curriculum itself. Rather, this awareness, brought home to them by the Radicals' criticism, sent them in completely the opposite direction. Acknowledging the acute problem besetting the liberal curriculum, they launched a project called "the justification of education."[9] This project consisted of an unsuccessful, as they themselves later acknowledged, attempt to underpin what they believed to be the "good old" tradition of the liberal curriculum, a curriculum they could not begin to consider abandoning, even with new relativistic foundations they did acknowledge.[10] The self-professed "grand failure" of their extremely long, hopeless attempt to supply a relativistic justification to the old liberal tradition created many question marks where naïve certitude once ruled.

Both Dewey's conception of education and the conceptions suggested by radical thinkers (the British philosophers and their followers in the Anglophone world, who did not come up with a suggestion for a new curriculum, but rather attempted to form a new justification for the old curriculum) led to many experimental and alternative educational programs, some of which have endured in various ways to this day. These alternatives have always remained peripheral to the main educational stream. The dominance of the disciplinary curriculum within the mainstream has remained intact in Western countries throughout the last century and the first years of the current one. Supported by inertia, concepts deeply embedded in the Western consciousness and powerful vested interests which stem from its two-thousand-year-old domination, the liberal curriculum has rather easily overcome, on the social level (as opposed to theoretical or rational), the Deweyian and the Progressive's criticism and later the Radicals' blatant attacks. It also remained intact despite the universally acknowledged failure[11] of the two-decade-long attempt by the above British philosophers and their followers to justify it in a relativistic context.

I believe that now, in the first decade of the twenty-first century, in contrast to the decades which preceded it, criticism against the concept, goals, and framework of the theoretical curriculum has a good chance at taking hold. Although both the

Radicals and Dewey already raised valid and sound criticisms of the theoretical curriculum thirty, and even one hundred, years ago, respectively, and although the British philosophers clearly and blatantly acknowledged, more than twenty years ago, their inability to answer similar criticisms, these did not stand a chance of being culturally or socially accepted.

As long as the curriculum was meaningful, at least to some degree, to those learning or teaching within its framework (see Chapter Three), and as long as the education systems function as an initiator into the "production line mentality" was socially accepted and economically necessary (see Chapter Four), that is, until the current generation, the theoretical curriculum stood no chance of being changed. But now, as the first postmodern generation is coming of age, and as the two aforementioned conditions have been undermined (as I argue in chapters Three and Four), the chances of, and the need for, change are rapidly increasing.[12]

The program I am proposing is modeled, to a limited extent, after Dewey's and the Radicals' alternatives, but it goes much beyond those alternatives. My program is also influenced by the failure of the attempts to justify the prevailing curriculum, carried out by the British educational philosophers in the 1960s and '70s. Thus, the suggested program reflects my conviction that the "grand failure" of the past proves, if proof was still needed at this point, the impossibility of justifying the Platonic-based curriculum in our era.

The Basic Humanistic and Liberal Views

While the three historical processes mentioned above remain in the background of the proposed program, it does enjoy the positive influence of the socio-ethical Humanistic worldview and the liberal democratic conception of state and society that stem from it. In these views I include, amongst many others, development of the individual's autonomous personality, and of his or her ability for, and commitment to, dialogical belonging and morality. In effect, these are perceived to be the ultimate values that a Humanistic society, loyal to liberal democratic political principles, should be instilling in its citizens, and hence these are the fundamental goals of education in a Humanistic liberal democratic society. Accordingly, the educational program within these views should be dedicated, first and foremost, to achieving these goals.

At the basis of this alternative educational program lies the conception of *Bildung*, or self-actualization of the individual through a process of exploration and self-formation, developed by the great German Humanists and by Mill.[13] The German Humanists and Mill assumed that three conditions are necessary and broadly sufficient for enabling a productive process of reflective "experiments in living" (again Mill's term): security, freedom, and "plurality of paths" (Mill's term, *On Liberty*). More precisely, these conditions enable a process which can lead to the development, enhancement, and expression of autonomy. The reason why these conditions are only "broadly" sufficient is that Mill also acknowledges the importance of being able to read and write as necessary for the process to be productive.

In Mill's view, the state is obligated to ensure this basic literacy to all its citizens. But he differentiates between the obligation to verify literacy and the obligation to teach reading and writing, emphasizing that his intention is the former. He maintains that teaching literacy is the parents' responsibility, which should be carried out in the child's natural environment. The state should teach children reading and writing only once it ascertains that they have not reached the standard appropriate for their age level, and only when it is unlikely that they will be so taught with their parents' help. Even then, according to Mill, any coercion when fulfilling this commitment should be minimal and should be terminated the moment the child reaches the required standard.[14]

Mill's position stems from his profound aversion to paternalistic coercion in general and, more specifically, to state-enforced coercion in education; an aversion which reflects his liberal hard core.[15] He maintains that coercion of this kind guarantees the shaping of all young people in the same mold, one that may lead to heteronomy and totalitarianism. Within Mill's liberal view, the state's paternalistic coercion is an evil to be shunned, unless, and only to the extent that, it is strictly necessary to avoid a greater evil, such as, in our case, failure to develop autonomous personalities in young people if a certain degree of compulsion is not exerted. Thus, educational coercion that exceeds the minimum required for the development of autonomous individuals is both ethically wrong and practically prone to become counterproductive, as it will contradict the goal education should be serving.[16] Mill's predecessors, the German Humanists, did not address this issue as systematically as he did, but also, more generally, held this position.

Generally speaking, Mill's approach is the only one logically possible from a liberal point of view,[17] and therefore the one that I adopt here. Coercion may be used in education, within a liberal context, only when it is necessary for the enhancement of the development of autonomy. Because of this, educational coercion should be limited to an optimal point at which its dangers to the enhancement of autonomy are minimal and its advantages maximal. Given this perspective, the level of educational coercion dominant in liberal societies from the end of the nineteenth century to this day is unacceptable. It strays a long way from Mill's optimal point, and casts a very long shadow over young people's chances to develop as autonomous individuals. In most cases it has reflected national, military, and industrial interests, which opposed the educational imperatives of a Liberal Democracy.[18]

However, Mill's optimal point was "aimed" too low. In modern, and even more so in postmodern, reality, even if the state ensures the three aforementioned environmental conditions (security, "plurality of paths," and freedom) and leaves young people to their own devices once they have reached the minimal level of literacy, their chances of developing into autonomous (not to speak of dialogically belonging and moral) adults are unlikely. As I noted earlier, the educational default in the postmodern world is anti-autonomous, it enhances heteronomous tendencies, as well as conformism based on loneliness and alienation (as opposed to dialogical belonging),[19] and encourages a kind of narrow egoism which is necessarily opposed to morality.[20] In the following arguments I will refer directly to autonomy alone, although the chances of, and possibilities for, the development of dialogical belonging and morality are under the same sort of threat and to at least the same extent.

We live in a reality controlled by the Internet, vulgar television entertainment, and even more vulgar console games (most of which at least are focused on killing as many of your enemies as possible, be they humans, Martians, or dragons). This overwhelming sanction of hedonism and satisfaction of short-term desires undermines the development of ability for, and commitment to, the long-term planning necessary for autonomy. Likewise, the Internet undermines the individual's chances of developing a stable continuous identity,[21] capitalistic competition throws the individual into a mindless quest for profit and the relativistic-positivistic-technocratic approach inherently sanctifies fragmentariness and aversion to systematic, not to mention deep, thought.

All of the above counteract the ability to create a coalesced identity, a clear and coherent worldview, or the search for life's meaning, a search necessary for the development and maintenance of an autonomous personality. The default in such a world is a deconstructed, extremely neurotic Woody Allen-style[22] "self" living in a Matrix-like "reality" that bears no relation to the desired autonomous individual.[23]

Because the chances that today's young people will develop on their own into authentic, self-directed, autonomous human beings are slim, the liberal state must do its best to ensure the realization of this goal through institutionalized education based on a minimally required degree of coercion. The desired education system should guarantee an environmental framework based on the three above conditions (security, freedom, and "plurality of paths"). The system should also ensure the existence of a process of guided reflection on "experiments in living" designed to mobilize young people's reflection on their experiences, thus enhancing their development as autonomous, as well as dialogically belonging and moral, individuals. I will not deal here with the degree of coercion required, or the desired optimal point. The definition of this point cannot be addressed abstractly, but only in relation to the environmental and population conditions of a given educational organization—perhaps only in relation to specific individuals.

Two Basic Guidelines

While it is not possible to define the optimal "justified coercion point" mentioned above, it is certainly possible, desirable, and necessary to canvass the general Humanistic educational program for information which will allow educators to draw their own individual scheme for such a point. The level of coercion this program should be relying on should change, as already claimed, according to the circumstances of any individual learner. It would never occur to us to hospitalize all individuals suffering from the same health problem for the same period of time. The length of hospitalization is always relative to the severity of each individual's illness. The same should be the case of educational compulsion; the length and intensity of compulsion should be determined individually and include only the amount of time and activity which are considered necessary to guarantee each individual child the best chance to develop as an autonomous person. Still, we certainly recommend the same treatment (or educational program) in the case of similar maladies or educational needs.

Before we can begin to outline the desired educational program, I would first like to present two guidelines that have inspired me, and will hopefully inspire anyone following the program. The first stems from my dual justification for adopting the concept of education towards autonomy: in addition to being the only one that can be justified in a Liberal Democracy, it is the only one the can be meaningful for young people in the postmodern era. Thus, the first guideline stresses the necessity for the designers of the program to be aware of the need to cater to the unique postmodern circumstances, as far as young people's striving for meaning are concerned, and to try to optimize their affect on the education process (i.e., harness the ones which have a positive effect according to this perspective to better the process and the students' experience therein, whilst trying to limit the impact of the harmful ones).

The compass for this optimization effort is not hard to describe: in order to be meaningful, the program should rely, as much as possible, on all three sources of meaning as presented in Chapter Three: cultural backing, coherence, and ability to lead to first- and second-order benefits. A program that cannot rely on these sources, or on at least two of them, in all of its major aspects, has a strong chance of becoming meaningless and absurd, as is the case with the existing program. The desired program should strive to escape this fate and be meaningful to young people by making sure each "educational moment" meets the requirements of at least two of the three sources of meaning.

The second guideline requires the educational program designer to avoid the two dangers that might lurk in a curriculum based on the conceptions of education towards autonomy. These are the subjectivistic and pragmatistic dangers. The first danger might result from overstressing the subjective development of young people, while ignoring the need to define their identity in a sociocultural context. The second danger may ensue from accentuating the practical elements of young people's lives to the exclusion of their need for spiritual meaning.

With regard to the second danger, the traditional liberal curriculum emphasized, at least initially and on the declarative level, satisfaction of spiritual needs, first (in the middle ages and early modernity) religiously and later, under the influence of modern ideologies, rationally, to the exclusion of subjective needs. A converse danger possibly inherent in the proposed program is that it may underscore the immediate subjective and practical needs, while neglecting the spiritual aspects of life. However likely this danger, it may nevertheless be avoidable if the program strives to create a balance between young people's subjective practical and social needs and their spiritual needs.

The Two Basic Questions

Now that the program's justification and the basic guidelines for its design have been clarified, we can turn to drawing its main lines. In order to fill in the main lines of the desirable educational program, we must address two basic questions:

- What types of *meaningful* life experiences are required for encouraging young people's development as autonomous?
- What educational support and guidance do young people need for the process of "experiments" in living to maximize their chances to develop as autonomous individuals? (As I stated above, after dealing largely with autonomy, I will also briefly refer to the other two educational goals.)

In the coming section I address the first question, and, in the final section of the chapter,[24] the second.

THE SEVEN EXPERIENTIAL DOMAINS OF THE DESIRED EDUCATIONAL PROGRAM

Answer to the First Question, or Supporting the Formation of the Foundations, Shell, and Design of Young People's Lives

My answer to the first question is that in order to enhance young people's development towards autonomy in a meaningful environment, the program should evolve first and foremost around experiences in the following seven experiential domains:

1. Acquiring the minimal knowledge required for survival and success in life, and promoting commitment to further the development of necessary knowledge and its use.[25]
2. Developing rational tools for planning, analysis, and criticism. Strengthening the commitment to further develop these tools and to rely on them as much as possible.
3. Developing the ability to cope with organizational and social systems. Strengthening the commitment to further develop this ability and to rely on it as much as possible.
4. Developing the commitment and ability to make and actualize autonomous choices based on interests.
5. Developing the commitment and ability to make and actualize autonomous choices about professional careers.
6. Developing the commitment and ability to make and actualize autonomous choices about social involvement and activities.
7. Developing the ability and commitment of interested individuals to autonomously deal with basic existential questions, and to autonomously form a worldview which will constitute the most meaningful and coherent possible framework for dealing with these questions.

These seven domains of experiences or content fall into three categories:

- The first three domains are designed to ensure the minimal necessary conditions for effective activity in all areas of life.
- The following three domains consist of the (three) categories of activities that together constitute the essence of human life:

    a.   Actualization of interests (activities performed for their own sake, out of intrinsic motivation, which are therefore the source of one's life goals).

    b.   Career development or engagement in activities necessitated by the need to make a living.

    c.   Maintenance of social involvement and interpersonal relationships.

- The seventh domain enables the individual to imbue his or her life experiences with overall coherent meaningfulness. In other words, the seventh domain is designed to ensure sufficient conceptual unity, beyond that of various life experiences, to help develop consistent (or rather, aspiring to be consistent) self-identity.[26]

While all the first six domains are relevant, to one extent or another, to all individuals, the seventh domain refers only to those individuals who feel the need to *consciously and systematically* confront foundational existential questions or to shape a coherent worldview. This is not a universal human need. While all of us must face foundational existential questions during our lives, mainly in times of existential crisis, we do not all feel the need to face these questions consciously and systematically, thus turning the formation of a worldview responding to them into a central focus of our lives.

There are certainly other differences between individuals in the level and extent of this interest. This domain is relevant only to individuals who feel the need to give these questions more directed and conscious day to day attention. Their involvement with it should be proportional to their level of interest in the subjects comprising this domain.

To use an architectural metaphor to clarify the relationships between the three categories of the educational program: the first category establishes solid foundations, the second engineers the frame, walls, and roof of the building, and the third supplies individuals (those who feel the need to control the overall design and redesign of the building) with guidelines for the formation and reformation of the architectural "blueprint" of the building. This can help satisfy their need for an understanding of, and control over, the design principles behind the building.

Despite the above metaphor, the logical order of educational domains should not be interpreted as a required pedagogical order. In other words, in the actual educational process, "laying the foundations" need not necessarily be complete before starting to erect the building itself. In the educational process, activities within the various domains can, and often should, be simultaneous and parallel; the important thing is that pedagogically, and from a holistic perspective, they should support and complement one another.

A desirable program does not necessarily have to be comprised of all the above domains, nor should all the domains be accorded the same degree of importance. Under certain circumstances educators may decide, for example, that the natural environment already "takes care" of certain experiential domains. In some cases, extreme deficiencies may require focusing a program only on the most basic categories; in others, "covering" all the domains will be found to overly restrict young people's freedom and hence is self-defeating. A specific domain may not suit the characteristics of certain groups of young people. For instance, it is clearly the case, as already detailed above, that the seventh domain assumes a specific style of identity-formation: it is not universal.[27] Although *a priori* all the other domains seem universally relevant, we should not exclude the possibility that in some cases any of the first six domains might be found by educators to be irrelevant to a certain individual or group of individuals.

Thus, the above list provides a comprehensive substratum from which diverse educators or young people may choose the experiential domains they deem necessary, and possible, in whatever extent and order, as long as this is done in light of the ultimate goals and basic guidelines of Humanistic education.

The goal of the *first domain* is clear, but begs the question: what minimal knowledge must young people have, and be committed to develop and use, in order to be able to function independently and effectively in reality? Reading, writing, and basic arithmetic should clearly be included and, perhaps, in countries such as Iceland, Israel, or Greece, whose languages are of limited diffusion, also English, or any other relevant *lingua franca* (Chinese might be considered as a candidate in the near future).

Still it is important to emphasize that the goal here need not be the automatic inculcation of basic literacy and numeracy, but rather the verification of an appropriate level of knowledge at a reasonable age. In a world characterized by an explosion of information, "the disappearance of childhood" and early exposure to various kinds of information and knowledge, it is highly likely that many youngsters reach the education system with at least some basic knowledge in these domains, as well as a commitment to their further development and use. Therefore, many young people might presumably skip this domain, or at least have the basic knowledge that will enable them to deal with it in an "offhand" manner, while focusing on other experience domains (which should always be preferred to formal study of literacy or arithmetic).[28]

Accordingly, the system needs to establish three types of procedures. First, an examination verifying that educatees have reached the required minimal standard at a reasonable age must be put into place. The second should support young people who are able to study these subjects in order to reach the minimal required level, in an "offhand" way, while focusing on other experiences. Third, an allowance should be made for systematic teaching of these basic skills to those in need, but only to the extent they are needed as evaluated on an individual basis.

If these procedures are not followed, we will fall into the trap of the undistinguishing, age-based compulsion that is basic to the prevailing system. That is to say, we will be exercising educational compulsion vis-à-vis all young people without distinguishing between specific individual needs and without giving any thought to the degree of compulsion which can be justified given those specific needs, in the same manner and to the same extent it is practiced in the current, obsolete system. Such compulsion is ethically and educationally unjustifiable in exactly the same way that it is ethically and medically unjustified to compel a whole population to be hospitalized over exactly the same period of time, only because a few need urgent life-saving treatment.[29]

The *second domain* reflects the desire to develop rational thinking in young people. Rational thinking consists of the following manifestations of rationality:

- Theoretical rationality: the ability and commitment to seek true answers (or answers that the individual conceives as true using his or her best reasoning powers) to the questions that interest the individual, in the framework of logical thinking.
- Practical rationality: the ability and commitment to identify clear and coherent goals important to the individual, translate them into operational goals, adopt the most appropriate and effective plan to achieve those goals given one's situation, and improve the plan using the feedback received from the implementation thereof.
- Critical rationality: the ability and commitment to critically examine views, habits, policies, and social structures accepted by the subjects or by their community or society.

These three complementary types of rationality are vital for the development of both the individual's:

- Authenticity, based on the reflective processes necessary for self-knowledge. These in turn consist of the individual's rational learning of him or herself through critical examination of the self's responses to actual "experiments in living"
  And
- Self-direction, consisting of rational goal-setting and planning which are essential facets of practical rationality.

Developing these aspects of the individual's personality can be achieved in different ways through the wide variety of methodologies which aim to develop rationality, thinking, and critical thinking which have evolved in recent decades.[30]

The goal of the *third domain* is to enhance young people's ability to cope independently, efficiently, and critically with the systems and organizations that to a large extent comprise the reality in which we live. In postmodernity, as opposed to simpler eras, our lives depend heavily on an intensive network of social systems and organizations. We usually work in or with such organizations: our income is controlled and taxes deducted from it by an organization; we deposit what is left of it in another organization (a bank) and sometimes invest it through other organizations (brokerage firms); our health depends on an organization and our security on other organizations such as the police, the justice system, and sometimes the army.

We are very likely to come across individuals who possess the basic knowledge of the first domain and are endowed with the ability and commitment to rational thinking which stem from the second, but are still unable to function in our reality because they are not able to "break the codes" of the various organizations and social systems that comprise this reality. Therefore, young people, who are unable to deal independently, efficiently, and critically with these systems, or are not committed to acting in such a way, must be encouraged and guided to develop these capabilities and commitments. They have to learn the codes, as well as their genealogy, the various interests they serve, and the range of options available to mindfully work within these codes, or even against them in some cases, in order to best achieve their goals. They also have to acquire the commitments necessary for using this knowledge in the desired manner. In an era that is fully "organizational," the development of such abilities and commitments is as important as learning the Three Rs, or developing ability and commitment for rational thinking.[31]

Let us now turn to the second category of experiential domains. While the first category contains the experiences and content which constitute necessary conditions for functioning independently, the second category contains three domains of experiences and content, which together comprise the core of human life: leisure activities, work, and social life, including interpersonal relationships.

The goal of the first domain in this category is to enhance young people's awareness of the utmost importance of the search for, and realization of, their interests, leading to an increase in their chances of having a Good Life (or "well-being" to use contemporary psychological terminology), as well as enhance their ability for, and their commitment to, the search and its realization. Without a doubt, the search for and realization of one's interests comprises the essence of psychologically and existentially satisfying and productive leisure, that part of human life dedicated to the realization of our life goals or to the activities that we *really* want to do, or live for. More importantly, this explorative search is the core of a satisfying or good human life. We should do our best to design our lives in a way which will enable us to follow our interests as much as possible both in our work (if and when possible) and our leisure time.[32]

In the objectivistic Western tradition of the last two thousand five hundred years, striving for Truth or the search for God, as opposed to practice-oriented learning or activities, were perceived as the ultimate objectives of human life, universal to humankind. As I contended in Chapter Two, this conception is not acceptable anymore in our individualistic, relativist era. Therefore, in this context the concept of "realization of interests" should replace the above objectivistic conceptions of life and educational goals.

Replacing the above traditional conceptions of life goals with the realization of interests as life goals, preserves the deep insight which lies at the foundation of Western rationalist, and also to a great extent religious, traditions. According to these traditions, in order to have a satisfying life, individuals must identify activities that are satisfying of themselves. In other words, in order to have a satisfying or happy life one must shun enslavement to an infinite, existential chain of activities in which every activity is done for the sake of another. Instead, one must locate those activities that can function as the *summum bonum*, the ultimate good, or (to use contemporary psychological terms) life goals. These may be defined as activities concerning which it would be senseless to ask "What is it good for?" since performing them is satisfying in itself. This intuition has been validated philosophically[33] and empirically by emerging research on the subject.[34]

The rationalist, or religious traditions, have respectively considered "the search for Truth" or "knowledge of God" to be an exclusive universal activity which satisfies the condition of human life guided by an ultimate goal which is not justified by a higher goal. In contradistinction, "realization of interests" is based on the assumption that these activities cannot be universally identified. Fields of interest naturally differ from one another and therefore individual exploration and choices are paramount.

In order to better understand the meaning of the concept of interest, let us distinguish between two very different, yet frequently undifferentiated, concepts: "desire" and "interest." This distinction will help the reader understand the core of Humanistic education as described here. A good way to emphasize the meaning of this core is by drawing an important distinction between the approach of open (permissive or "*laissez faire*") education and the program proposed here. Desire can be short-lived or diffused and often does not require a full conscience decision or intentional activity by the individual. In contrast, an interest requires a long-term, conscious, intended, and mindful commitment to a concrete and defined subject (not only theoretical activity of course), and to the preferences and sacrifices this commitment entails. The supporters of open or permissive education are right when they state that the will of the child should be respected as much as possible. They are wrong in not differentiating between short-term desires and long-term commitment to interests.[35] The will or desire of the individual can be a passing whim not to be confused with interest. Passing whims should also be respected, as long as they do not harm others or the young individuals themselves. Still, whenever there is a lasting contradiction between short-term desires on the one hand and ongoing commitments to interests in which the young individual is deeply involved and committed on the other, the educator's role should be to support the latter. In such cases educators should help individuals to overcome short-term temptations that hinder their long-term ability to follow their interests.

The educational process in this domain has four objectives: the technical or logistical (the first two), didactic (the third), and psychological (the fourth):

1. Exposing young people to as much information as possible about possible interests, from nuclear physics to music or art appreciation, poetry reading, mountaineering, building model airplanes, cooking, horseback riding, being a social or political activist, developing an economic venture, performing rock music, playing tennis, raising children, enjoying friendship, and so on *ad infinitum.* Activity of any kind can serve as an interest as long as it satisfies the basic requirement stemming from the definition of the term.
2. Afford young people the opportunity to initially experience activities that potentially appeal to them, and could develop into interests.
3. Help young people to systematically acquire the skills and knowledge required for the development of the interests they wish to experience more profoundly, if, and to the extent that, such skills and knowledge are necessary.
4. Continuously support young people in actualizing the interests (or activities which are "candidates" to become interests) they have chosen.

The fourth, psychological, objective is certainly the most important. In our instant-gratification-oriented culture, the activity of trying out various potential interests, choosing between them and selecting one, or perhaps a few, requires constant educational guidance and support. It is here that the psychological aspect of the fourth domain comes to the fore. Young people should be first and foremost actively supported in the exploration process, which can sometimes be frustrating, confusing, and frightening. Furthermore, they should be encouraged to reflect on the exploration process in order to benefit from the process, gain better self-knowledge, become familiar with their *modus operandi*, capacities, and weaknesses, as well as the compensation tactics they can adopt to tackle those weaknesses. They should be encouraged to infer general self-knowledge from their reflection on specific interest-oriented activities, which will help them in their future choices in all possible experience domains.

This psychological process of supporting the exploration process, reflecting upon it, and learning from it is far from being self-evident. Individuals differ extensively at this level. When presented with the relevant information, some will have no difficulty in selecting their interests, while others will demonstrate various levels of difficulty and anxiety.[36] The educator's extremely subtle role is to help young people who encounter difficulties, to differentiate between desires and interests, and to overcome various kinds of psychological and social obstacles. This assistance must be provided individually, based on the educator's knowledge of each individual's character, interests, performance styles, and abilities, as well as the social context within which they operate.

Furthermore, the educator must differentiate between those productively experimenting with various potential interests and those who prolong the process of exploration because of fear of commitment, lack of self-confidence, or any other social hardship. Individuals in the latter group needs help to overcome the obstacles which prevent them from moving from exploration of interests to the realization thereof.[37]

There is tension between the first sub-objective and the other three. It might be unclear how much emphasis should be placed on exploration during education or informing young people of various possible interests, so that eventually, during a later educational stage or even when they leave the education system altogether, they will find their way by making "mindful choices" based on knowledge about the various alternatives acquired through educational processes. Similarly, the weight accorded to the exploration process vs. the actualization of interests during the educational process may be difficult to define.

Supporters of equipping students with knowledge for later experimentation will recommend a broad educational program, which includes providing information on, or limited experimentation in, *as many* varied interests *as possible*. In contrast, followers of the "exploration now" response will recommend offering *some* general background information, but will prefer encouraging students to dive into the sea of exploration and actualization of interests as early as possible and focus on specific interests as the central element of their educational process.

The argument between supporters of these two opposite approaches is expressed in the literature on the subject.[38] I clearly side with the second approach. Given that the number of interests available is infinite, it is pointless to burden young people with an overload of information about interest options, or to encourage them to have limited experiments with as many domains as possible so that "eventually they can choose for themselves." Such an approach cannot work; they will forget most of those potential interests when the time comes to choose. Moreover, we are living in a reality where accessing information is no problem; on the contrary, young people today can obtain information on any interest they wish. Therefore, in this context educators should not aspire to pass as much information about as large a number of interests as possible, but rather to encourage young people to experience actual exploration and realization of interests or potential interests, and acquire the habits, knowledge, types of awareness, and commitments necessary for these kinds of activity.

The *fifth domain* relates to the socioeconomic reality of our society, and to most of the young people living in it: the need to work for a living. Although it appears that in many countries (especially most European countries) the individual working time is becoming shorter,[39] it seems that in the foreseeable future the majority of people will still be working to earn a livelihood for a significant part of their lives. Moreover, at least in the next decade or two, it seems that work will still be a contributing factor to shaping the individual's identity and will constitute a central axis around which his or her life revolves.

Nevertheless, educational planners should be aware that these characteristics are undergoing significant changes, and that in the next decade or two not only the extent of work during the span of one's life, but also the effect that work will have on the individual's life in the Western world, will probably be dramatically diminished.[40]

The primary goals of the fifth experiential domain fall under five sub-objectives:

1. Providing young people with sound information about the current and expected situation in the labor market and about the advantages and disadvantages of various kinds of professional careers. Achieving this first sub-objective requires an introductory course (either virtual or face-to-face) concerning the labor market, its possibilities and limitations.
2. Providing young people with the opportunity to experience various kinds of work within their choice range. This includes creating opportunities for young people to work for certain periods (weeks or months) in various workplaces of their choice or, should they be unskilled, or lack the necessary, often long, educational process (for example in the case of medicine), to at least reflectively accompany those working at such jobs.
3. Help young people weigh the various considerations involved in choosing work or a career. This sub-objective requires establishing a workshop that can help young people identify and criticize the values that guide them in such a choice from a long list of such possible values, including: maximization of earning level, actualization of a central interest, gaining respect or social power, maximization of comfort, minimization of effort, and so on. Young people should be aided when coping with conflicting values in an attempt to shape a conscious, relatively coherent scale of values in this context.
4. Help with work-related problems. This sub-objective should parallel the practical work periods mentioned in Point 2 above, and consist of workshops that offer guidance when solving all kinds of problems that arise during work.
5. Help acquire the appropriate education required for one's chosen occupation, if one was indeed chosen during the educational period, or at least a "serious

candidate" was indicated. The aim here is to assist those seriously interested in experimenting with a professional career that demands classroom or higher theoretical training.

Here too, as in the previous experiential domain, educational support should consist of both technical and psychological support. The technical support should provide young people with all kinds of practical assistance that might be needed. The psychological backing is needed to help young people through the often frustrating or frightening exploration process. It should also be administered with the intent to encourage reflection on this process and on the interests, performance styles, capacities, and other personality characteristics each individual may unknowingly exhibit during this process, in order to learn the most about the self (during the exploration period) so that the individual will be able to transfer this knowledge to all other relevant areas of life.

The *sixth experiential domain* is comprised of two sub-objectives:
1. Help individuals develop interpersonal relationships in a mature, responsible, and autonomous manner;
2. Encourage social involvement, commitment and relevant abilities in young people in a way that is compatible with the development and expression of their autonomy.

The simplest and most effective way of advancing the first sub-objective is establishing workshops to discuss interpersonal relationships and other subjects proposed by the participants and based on their experiences. Also, it is wise to allow young people to confer individually with their mentors and discuss subjects of their choice.

To achieve the second sub-objective, young people should be encouraged to play an active role in the management of their own educational institutions, as well as get involved in community activities outside these institutions. The first process calls for a high level of democracy within the educational institution. The second requires breaking down barriers between educational institutions and the "external reality," and encouraging young people to participate in some of the main social processes, such as local or national elections (not necessarily as voters but also as journalists, reflecting their observations in a blog, digital journal, or where possible "real" [paper or digital] journal or activists, etc.) or other political processes on various levels.

The rationale underlying this recommendation is the desire to create valuable life experiences that could trigger exploration and reflective examination and discussions and thus, when accompanied by methodologically led reflection, act as leverage for the development of autonomy. Early exposure to "real life" also involves clear dangers for students. It is therefore preferable that such initial exposure be implemented in a mentoring educational framework. This framework will help students productively deal with the main problems and dilemmas raised when they are exposed to social and political experiences.[41]

In many real-life situations, two of the three domains, or even all of them, may converge. A person's career (fourth domain) can be based on interests (third domain), obviously the best scenario from a well-being point of view; another may engage in a deep friendship; yet another's social activity (sixth domain) could be his or her basic interest (third domain). Another case of convergence can occur when a social activity that is the basic interest of an individual becomes a career which exactly matches that activity. Such convergences, whenever possible, certainly contribute to the coherence and harmony in one's life as well as to the level of one's expression of that interest. Education should certainly encourage such convergences, as far as they are possible. Still, since in many cases such convergences are not possible, or are very limited in their extent, the differentiation between the three domains (interests, occupation, and social involvement) should be kept in one form or another, at least until educators have sufficient evidence that actual convergence has occurred in a specific individual case.

At this point we end the discussion of the above three experiential domains, those which cover the three spheres constituting the essence of human life: actualizing interests (or life goals), working for the purpose of earning a living, and developing interpersonal relationships and social engagement.

Some may say that the two groups of experiential domains discussed so far are sufficient to assist the development of young people's autonomy. But one sphere remains, the most important one for some individuals, which is not covered by the two previous: systematic tackling of basic existential questions related to shaping the identity and the worldview of the young person.

Kant[42] formulated the questions that, according to him, all thinking and autonomous people should ask themselves: "What can I know?"; "What ought I to do?"; "What can I hope?" or in other words, not in the Kantian order, "What is the nature of reality? Does it have a purpose?" The most important question of all is: "How should I live, given the answers to the previous two questions?" All people live in light of the answers they give to these questions, albeit they doubtless differ in their need to deal with them consciously and systematically. For some people the need is particularly strong during adolescence, when most people shape their self-identity and worldview,[43] or within a postmodern, often non-linear life reality, when the individual copes for the first time with questions of self-identity and formation of a worldview (in our day and age this process does not necessarily happen during adolescence; the mere concept of adolescence may be the product of the linear modern view of long childhood that is disappearing today).

As shown in Chapter Three, the Platonic and liberal curricula, and the modern era's neo-Humanistic curriculum, were all geared to deal with the above questions, or more precisely, designed to imbue the individual with the rationalistic or theological worldview of educators, which allegedly provided specific categorical answers to these questions. Today, all traces of the original intentions behind these curricula have been lost. Moreover, as I have shown in Chapter Three, the existing curriculum has become meaningless and absurd once the beliefs sustaining its original meanings collapsed. It thus transfers to the students the message that they are doomed to live in an absurd or senseless reality, and that within this absurd situation the only thing that counts is striving for egotistic and material success.

This "sacred" goal is forcefully symbolized within the prevailing educational reality by final exams and certificates. For many, these are the only justification for the prevailing educational endeavor. The certification's only justification is paving the road to an academic degree. This will in turn lead to high level positions in the work force, which mean high earnings, which allow one to "enjoy the good things in life," the (alleged) postmodern *summum bonum*, the ultimate goal of life as portrayed daily by prevailing educational activities.

Now that its original justifying context is lost, this hidden message, transmitted so forcefully through the modern curriculum, is both psychologically and socially destructive. The nihilistic values it conveys can accelerate psychological and social disintegration processes, which are already independently triggered by the dramatic impact of the media, the Internet, the advertisement industry which dominates both and all other aspects of or lives, and the rapid "chaotization" of life in the post-modern reality.[44]

As stated earlier, many young people are preoccupied with basic existential questions. Some search for answers on treks to Latin America and Southeast Asia. Others seek spiritualism in ashrams and workshops which promise redemption and meaning, or in holy books of the established faiths. The one place that does not address these spiritual needs is the school. Education's sole purpose, or the sole purpose that has been left for many after the collapse of the cultural contexts which supported the other more elevated purposes, is "success in the final examinations," a goal which actually delegitimizes the search for meaning to life, or any other spiritual search, for that matter. Thus, the school and the dominant trends of post-modern reality join hands in the intensive de-legitimization of the search for a response to spiritual needs.[45]

The *seventh experiential domain* is there to bolster the rightful place of the basic existential questions *within the Humanistic education system* for those young people interested in consciously and systematically dealing with them. Involvement in this domain should help young people develop a coherent worldview that could constitute a relatively stable source for meaning, supply relatively coherent answers to the basic existential questions and support their personal identity.

The mode of action that can help young people in our individualistic-relativistic culture cope with these questions is divided into two complementary components. The first is a presentation of the main categories of the worldviews that deal with these questions, namely, the various religions and modern ideologies, while at the same time providing rational tools for their analysis, comparison, and criticism—to give a not exhaustive but nonetheless representative list: rationalism, empiricism, relativism, Humanism, existentialism, and nationalism.

The second component combines meta-subjects such as the history of human dealings with these questions, and the broad outlines of possible criteria (coherency, elegance, the degree of solace they afford, the possibilities for their empirical examination, etc.), which can help students make a choice between worldviews.

The concept of *Bildung* (presented in Chapter Six) should serve as the foundation for activity and a source of inspiration. At its core, the original notion of *Bildung* envisaged young people drawing on various existential options from within their own, or other cultures, in order to experiment with various worldviews and in this way shape their own. In return, the "receiving" generation was also perceived as contributing to the renewal and enrichment of their present and future culture through absorbing and reforming cultural modes.[46]

Education towards Morality and Dialogical Belonging

Up to now I have discussed the seven experiential domains that comprise the goal of education towards autonomy. As I said at the outset, I decided to focus mainly on this most basic goal in order to avoid an overly detailed and long discussion. Still, I will dedicate the next few pages to a schematic discussion of the other two goals: education towards morality and dialogical belonging.

As far as the goal of education towards morality is concerned, there is no need to create a special experiential domain for it. The experiences that will inevitably arise out of the above seven domains can provide numerous opportunities for raising questions that will lead to discussions dealing with moral conflicts and dilemmas, thus serving the objective of education towards morality. We only need educators to be especially aware of this goal when they deal with the various experiences arising out of the seven domains, and an ability and commitment to take advantage of relevant experiences.[47]

To a large extent this is also true for the third educational goal: encouraging dialogical belonging. Several central elements of the prevailing experiential domains, if properly treated by educators, can encourage the fulfillment of dialogical belonging, since they require belonging to various groups.

Thus, for example, the fourth domain may require participation in groups focusing on an interest common to all the group members. The fifth may necessitate belonging, if only for a relatively short time, to various workplaces and to professional teams or groups within them. The sixth domain may commit youngsters to belong to various social bodies and community organizations, while the seventh could entail belonging to one's national, and other relevant, cultures. For the majority of young people, belonging to these groups or contexts will be an important aspect of the educational process.

All such experiences of social or cultural belonging could be used by educators accompanying the young people on their explorative journey for the enhancement, through guided refection, of student dialogical belonging. In order to clarify the last sentence and its theoretical foundation, as well as its methodological implication, I would like to introduce at this point two complementary educational perspectives that can be integrated into all the previous domains, and thus help to enhance the development of dialogical belonging in young people. The first perspective relates to the attitude that should be inculcated in young people towards any relevant culture or worldview and the second, towards any relevant group or social entity. These two principles support each other and, in many concrete situations, reliance on both at the same time may also be appropriate.

The first educational perspective, particularly pertinent to the seventh domain, possibly also the sixth, concerns the presentation of culture to young people as a "watering hole" of ideas and modes of living. Individuals should be invited by their tutors and mentors to take an informed stand vis-à-vis the "plurality of paths" that comprise any given culture, express it, defend it, and examine its opposing positions either as a participant in the battle or as mindful voters and contributors to the watering hole of ideas.

This perspective requires that all presentations of culture to young people be done through discussion and open debate about the existential questions which are most important to any individual's life. I believe that there is no reason to assume that a rational, systematic discussion of fundamental, controversial, cultural questions based on mutual respect will necessarily narrow the ideological gap between those who hold different views. However, if the discussion is properly conducted, it can result in strengthening its participants' sense of belonging to the broader culture within which the discussion takes place, while not having to relinquish their autonomy. Participants in the debate may experience feelings in the vein of "if we are arguing about the nature of the same culture, it is an expression of the fact that we all belong to it, and that each of us regards the other as belonging to it." Participation in such discussions can supply young people with awareness of the possibility and legitimacy of belonging to an ideological-cultural context, while expressing within it a voice that may be resisted by many others relating to the same culture or context.

Participation in such discussions also serves the development of autonomy. Given the desired openness, pluralism, and hermeneutical character of the discussion, as well as the high level of self-awareness on behalf of participants within it, the discussion can reinforce the reflective, critical abilities and the autonomy of each of its participants.

While the first perspective relates to the cultural level, the second relates to all kinds of groups young people will belong to during their educational process and is therefore potentially relevant to all seven domains. It entails the concept of the "Open Society."[48] According to this concept, a society, be it on the level of a country, a community, or an educational grouping, is defined at any specific moment by a set of norms to which all members are expected to be loyal. At the same time, in an open society or a group, questioning and criticism any of the society's or group's norms through a procedure of fair, rational debate should be allowed and open to all members. Thus, belonging to any open social group implies both loyalty to its norms and openness of any of them to criticism by any of the group's members, as long as this is done rationally and fairly.[49]

These two perspectives of cultural and social belonging arise from the socio-cultural conception of German Humanism, and are essentially different from both the *melting pot* concept and the *pluralistic* or "*salad bowl*" concept of society which dominate the relevant discourse today,[50] the latter having developed as a reaction to the former over recent decades. The melting pot concept was totally dominant in Western immigrant societies up to the 1960s and 70s, and is still tacitly extremely influential in educational and other social systems. According to this model, society is a monolithic and relatively static entity, or perhaps one going through a gradual and cohesive change, whose worldview and way of life is manifested in a coherent, monolithic, and relatively static culture, expressed in institutionalized, such as political and "cultural," institutions.

The salad bowl concept relies on the basic assumptions of the melting pot, according to which society and culture are monolithic and static entities, but attributes these characteristics to sub-societies such as people of West Indian (Caribbean) or Pakistani origin in the UK, or Puerto Ricans or Native Americans in the USA. It does not support a unified, overall framework, but rather recommends that each sub-society should exist within its own sub-culture and maintain minimal "live and let live" relations with all the others.[51]

The two educational principles suggested here rely on a third concept. In contradistinction to the pluralistic view, it is based on an assumption of existence of an overall integrative society and culture or group, which is viewed as a positive value. Yet, in contradistinction to the monolithic or melting pot view, it does not regard society or culture or the group as static or coherent, but rather as an aggregation of a large number of often conflicting processes, voices, and interests.[52]

Under the proposed concept, belonging to a society and culture or a group means perceiving oneself as an individual whose voice is a significant part of the discourse, or one who is immersed in a continuous conversation (sometimes riddled with conflict) with other voices in the discourse. This concept of belonging, in addition to being loyal to the varied and dynamic social and cultural realities of numerous postmodern societies, is also one that enables the best integration between education towards autonomy and education towards belonging, as required by the principle of reconciliation.[53] This is achieved by emphasizing the open nature of the desired society and the dialogical nature of the individual's desire and commitment to belong to it. This concept of belonging can also serve as a basis for the actualization of the principle of reconciliation.

Within the framework of this attitude to culture and society, the core problems and dilemmas of contemporary Western culture can be identified and presented to young people through their relevant connections to their quotidian life. Young people should then be encouraged to adopt a position in light of the problem or conflict under discussion, substantiate, examine, and express it.

Listed below are a few quite arbitrary examples for such deep sociocultural bifurcations or conflicts that can productively serve as the axis of an ongoing educational discussion in any Western society (of course, other bifurcations, relevant only to specific societies, might be as important to students' lives as the ones mentioned in the list below):

- The deep conflict structured into postmodern culture between the sanctification of acquiring wealth, *ergo* the making of a directed and systematic effort towards this end, and the sanctification of immediate pleasure-seeking or hedonistic, effortless, and "focus-less" *carpe diem* mood and lifestyle.
- The conflict between Western Humanism and rationalism, allegedly basic to the constitutions and management approaches of all Western societies on the one hand, and religious or mystical approaches dominant in either of their classic guises, or in various "new age" forms, in many Western societies, as well as the existentialistic concept of life as an arbitrary set of events that does not lend itself to any rational understanding or analysis, on the other.

- The bewildering conflict between Western rationalism and the "anti-logical" conclusions of quantum mechanics basic to Western science and technology.
- The conflict between rationalism on the one hand and radical postmodern and feminist standpoints which oppose "Western, chauvinistic logocentrism" on the other.
- The hedonism dominant in postmodern societies which on the one hand dictates *jouissance* or enjoyments leading to the worship of food and alcohol, yet on the other idolizes the slim figure, physical fitness, and the ardent fight against cholesterol, high blood pressure and so on.

All of the above conflicting views are dominant in prevailing postmodern Western societies at the same time, and in many cases, for the same people in various contexts of their lives. All these core conflicts of our culture and many other similar ones should, and can be, approached and demonstrated through phenomena and processes relevant to young people's daily lives. Here, too, the open pluralistic and hermeneutic approach should serve to enable maximal actualization of both objectives: education towards autonomy and education towards dialogical belonging.

The last examples relate to the desired attitude towards large-scale cultural or social contexts. Still, the same attitude should prevail to the same degree in all social contexts. More concretely, problems having to do with social life, first and foremost social life in educational groupings or the educational institutions to which young people belong, should be brought to the fore and discussed fairly and rationally. When pertaining to educational frameworks, the decision stemming from these should be implemented, as much as possible, in accordance with the semi-democratic structure of the educational institution recommended in Chapters Eight and Nine.[54]

Following the pluralistic, dialogical approach to culture and the open approach to society and to any social group can help develop the personality characteristic referred to here as "dialogical belonging." Enhancing the development of young people with regards to a pluralistic, hermeneutic, and open approach to belonging or, to put in another way, emphasizing the "dialogical" aspect of dialogical belonging, will serve to prevent a clash between education towards autonomy and education towards belonging. This will be the case especially if the two suggested perspectives towards culture and society are actively followed by reflective discussion designed to enhance the transference of these attitudes, and to connect the relevant acquired knowledge and abilities with all other relevant frameworks.

Guaranteeing Meaning and Avoiding Excess Subjectivism and Pragmatism

Here ends the description of the seven experiential domains basic to the program of Autonomy Oriented Education (AOE). In addition to optimally serving Humanism and Liberal Democracy, a program based on these domains or on some of them will fulfill the demands of the two basic guidelines I have formulated in the first section.

In light of the *first guideline*, AOE will maximize meaningfulness for young people. Such maximization will rest on all three sources of meaning as discussed in Chapter Three:

1. It will have ample cultural backing because its basic assumptions and objectives will be compatible with the individualistic-skeptical worldview dominant in our society. It will elevate young people above their enslavement to vulgar hedonism and consumerism ("elevate" or "bring up" is the original literal Latin meaning of "to educate" or *educere* in Latin), away from the psychologically and epistemologically vacuous and ruinous version of this worldview dominant in postmodernity. It will lead students to the original Humanistic view from which this consumerist view dialectically and destructively emerged.[55]
2. It will be based on a high level of individual unity, created by reflection and the individual search for self-identity and self-expression.
3. It will be structured mainly on activities that can be ostensibly useful in the short or long term, at both the narrow practical level and the spiritual or psychological level. As such, it will be perceived by young people as having first- and second-order benefits, those relevant to their immediate or future problems, interests, or occupations.

The program also meets the requirements of the second guideline, to wit, avoiding *subjectivistic* and *pragmatistic* dangers. Although it stresses the development of the individual's autonomy, it is free of exaggerated subjectivism or pragmatism. The sixth content domain, and the two above perspectives that cut through all content domains, should "neutralize" the subjectivistic danger, and the seventh domain "takes care" of the pragmatistic danger.

An Educational Program, Not a "Learning Program"

When discussing the relation of the suggested educational program to the prevailing disciplinary curriculum, it is important to emphasize that the suggested educational program requires that we cut the ruinous Gordian knot which ties education in the West to the acquisition of disciplinary or theoretical knowledge. As shown in Chapter Three, this is a tie that, in the prevailing postmodern circumstances, necessarily turns education into an inherently counterproductive process.

Still, various disciplines, or "inter-" or "meta-disciplines," may very well be relevant to some experiential domains. Thus, for example, scientific disciplines may constitute a focus of activity in the fourth domain, for those engaging in learning a theoretical discipline as an interest, or in the fifth domain, for those choosing to experience a profession based on theoretical knowledge as an option for a future career. Disciplines such as history, linguistics, sociology, psychology, and philosophy, or an integration of some or all of these, will serve as a basis for discussion in the third domain, which is designed to enhance the development of institutional literacy in young people, including the ability to critically decipher the codes of various institutions. In addition, all the disciplines relevant to the understanding of activities of the main social institutions such as political science, law, medicine, and economics, as well as various interactions between them, will also be involved in discussions relevant to the third domain. Discussions in the seventh domain will probably be based on the history of culture and science, as well as on philosophy, psychology, sociology, and literature, and an infinite number of possible interactions among them.

The role of these disciplines, inter-disciplines, and meta-disciplines in the proposed educational program will be totally different from the role of disciplinary learning in the existing curriculum. The goal will never be to learn them as disciplinary theoretical frameworks, except in cases where they are to serve *voluntarily* as an interest or as the basis for a choice of profession. References to them will be made only for the purpose of dealing with defined problems, probably in a meta-disciplinary way most of the time; particular disciplines cannot cope alone with most of the central problems of the individual's development, and dealing with those very problems is the axis on which the proposed educational program is built.

THE EDUCATIONAL PROCESS

Having discussed the question of content, the time has come to deal with the process. In other words, we have to try and answer the question: "What educational support and guidance do young people need for the process of 'experiments in living' carried out in the above domains, or at least in some of them, to maximize their chances of developing as autonomous, dialogically belonging and moral individuals?" Next I will outline the desired educational process, supplying such support in three steps:

- General characterization of the AOE pedagogical process;[56]
- The three major roles of educators required by the AOE;[57]
- Guiding principles of the AOE pedagogy.[58]

General Characterization of AOE Pedagogy

The main thrust of education based on the concept of *reflective "experiments in living"* consists of *voluntary* and *open-ended experiential processes* followed up by reflective educational *dialogue*, accompanied by an educator *mentoring* young people either individually or in a *basic educational grouping*.

The *openness* that characterizes the proposed educational process does not belittle *the importance of the educator's role* in any way, shape or form. On the contrary, the threats to educatees' chances of developing as *autonomous, moral*, and *dialogically belonging* individuals which stem from narrow hedonistic and egotistic conceptions of life, and from the fundamentalist or mystical conceptions dominant in today's world, are extremely serious. *Nothing in the processes of "experiments in living" within the seven domains, dynamic and intensive as it may be, can counteract, in and of itself, these dangerous influences.* Without *continuous educational guidance*, the chances that the above-mentioned processes will bring about the development of young people's autonomy as well as the other personality characteristics we desire are very small.

The Three Major Roles of Educators Required by AOE

How then can we characterize the desired roles of educators in AOE? There should be three such roles:

1. Traditional *teachers* and teaching will be needed in order to enable the transmission of knowledge required by some of the domains. Thus, for example, arithmetic or literacy required by the first domain should be taught either by direct teaching, when no other way is available, or by indirect teaching, relying on the experiences of young people in other domains, whenever possible (see discussion of first experiential domain above); an introductory course about the labor market may be given in the fifth domain, etc. Loyalty to AOE will require teachers in the proposed program to be equipped not only with knowledge of their field of expertise, but also with commitment to the principles of this educational view and the ability to follow through with them as much as possible (see below for an elaboration of these principles).

2. *Tutors*, like teachers, must also be committed to, and have general knowledge and solid understanding of, the AOE view. Tutors will accompany young people's participation in all experiential or practical activities. For example, tutors will help students develop rationality in the second domain, because one cannot "teach" rationality as one teaches history or any other discipline. The tutors' challenge in this case is to initiate students into the practice of *doing things rationally* (thinking about various subjects is also "doing") and guide their behavior in light of the basic principles of this practice. Tutors should also be assigned to guide young people through the legal or medical systems in the third domain, or to initiate students into all possible fields of interest or occupations in the fourth and fifth domains respectively.

These tutoring roles will require, first and foremost, specific knowledge of *how* to act in various contexts, as opposed to theoretically knowing *that*, basic to teaching today.[59] Tutors will also need experience in the field of counseling and should be *masters* (in the traditional medieval sense relating to masters and their apprentices) of their field of practice, in the same way that the teachers discussed above should master their fields of knowledge.

Initiating the student into any field of practice or sphere of skills and abilities within the framework of AOE should be an entirely different experience than that of initiating students into the same field or sphere within the framework in the prevailing education system. Initiation within the former context necessarily requires attention to the relevant principles of AOE and their implementation. Thus, for example, in all tutoring experiences young people should be allowed as much flexible freedom of choice to engage in various experiences as possible. These experiences, together with their subsequent reflective discussion, should be "used" by the tutor not only to initiate the student further into the relevant field, but also, to some extent, to enhance self-knowledge and self-direction, as well as to develop other personality characteristics required by the three ultimate goals of education.

3. The mentor's role is the core of the desired educational process. While teachers and tutors must, in the course of their other duties, use various specific practical experiences and learning processes for the enhancement of autonomy, dialogical belonging, and morality, whenever possible the mentor's role is purely to enhance students' autonomy, morality, and dialogical belonging. To this end, the mentor will relate to all kinds of experiences and learning processes that young people undergo, both within and beyond the sphere of influence of the educational organization.

The mentor will help young people through an ongoing process of ela-boration, unification, and integration of their various experiences. *This process is the kernel or backbone of AOE.* Its goal is to support and encourage young people to discover their personal profile, defined in terms of interests or life goals, capacities, and performance styles, and develop their self direction abilities through the development of their rationality and emotional intelligence.[60] Self-knowledge and self-direction are the pillars of an autonomous personality. At the same time, the development of young people's morality and dialogical belonging should also be nurtured through, for example, the enhancement of the ability for, and commitment to, empathy and moral reasoning, as well as commitments and abilities relevant to dialogical belonging.[61]

The mentor's role should obviously also include developing and assisting the student in planning his or her tailor-made educational process generally, and in specific domains and sub-domains, when needed.

This role mainly requires:

- True, profound commitment to, and a high-level capacity for, an ongoing aspiration for knowledge and an understanding of human psychology. I refer here to both "knowledge" and "understanding" in several senses including:
  - The scientific sense, including knowledge of personality, motivation, and developmental theories, as well as innovative discourse and research on subjects such as well-being, interests, capacities' learning style and connected concepts, temperaments, personality types, life goals, and positive psychology (or "intelligences") exploration.[62]
  - The larger Humanistic sense, consisting of ongoing aspiration for know-ledge and understanding of human psychology in other areas (such as philosophy, literature, music, and plastic arts).[63]
  - The more affective sense of having and being committed to the develop-ment of the "dialogical" ability or, in other terms, the Buberian ability of "understanding the other from the inside."[64]
- A deep knowledge of, and commitment to, AOE and its guiding principles.
- The ability to conduct a continuous, reflective, methodologically guided (in light of AOE principles) dialogue with one's self, as well as with young people.

I suppose the reader thinks at this point that these requirements will hinder our ability to locate many adequate candidates for such a role. However, while it is indeed an extremely demanding role, the above is the ideal description, to which educational institutions should aspire to come as close as possible. Moreover, candidates for mentoring roles do not necessarily have to possess all of the above attributes, but they should have the ability and motivation to continuously aspire to achieve them. They should be mentored themselves during their educational work in order to enhance such development on the basis of reflection on their ongoing experience (as is often the routine with clinical psychologists, social workers, and alike positions).

Guiding Principles of AOE Pedagogy

As emphasized above, all three of these roles demand profound knowledge and understanding of, as well as commitment to, the overall educational conception of AOE and its guiding principles. We have now reached the point where elaboration is required. The guiding principles fall into two groups: *environmental* and *pedagogic*.

Mill's original three basic principles are included in the first group: "*plurality of paths*," flexible freedom and security. The principle of "*plurality of paths*" requires that educatees will be able to encounter the greatest possible range of relevant experiences in each experiential domain. Emphasis should be given to different types of experiences, rather than to different variations of the same type. Thus, for instance, in the fourth domain, which relates to the development of interests, all the main categories of human interests including, among others, the arts, different kinds of sports, social and political activities, theoretical-intellectual activities, technical activities, economic activities, and so on, should be made available. In the fifth domain, examples of all the main categories of human occupations and endeavors should be presented.

It is important to note here that, in saying that educatees should be "able to encounter the greatest possible range of relevant experiences" in each domain, I did *not* mean that they should *practically* encounter all, or even most of these experiences. I only mean that as many different experiences as possible should be *open* to them for experimentation, if and when *they so choose*. While many students will require long exploration processes and many experience opportunities, it may well be the case that certain young people will experience a "that's it" feeling (or have an "aha!" epiphany, as it is sometime called in various psychology and cognitive fields of research) during their first or second activity in the domain; others may even instantly know what their vocation or interests are before ever experiencing any of the various possibilities. There is no justification whatsoever to compel such students to go through all, or even a small number of other, experiences.[65] All that matters is that:

- Students have the chance, *if they so desire*, to experience as great a range of activities reflecting different categories in the same domain as possible.
- Students know that many different experiences will be open to them for experimentation if they so chose.
- Students receive a general idea of what the various categories are, which can be accomplished through a one-hour introduction or in an hour of reading.

The principle of *flexible freedom* requires giving young people the opportunity to choose voluntarily, as far as possible, from the different experiences in each domain and, to the degree that it is compatible with the program's ultimate goals, from among the different domains.

I am intentionally leaving this issue open, as the answers to questions like "Will all young people have to cope with all domains equally?"; "Can some domains be given preference over others?" or "Will those who want to focus throughout their entire educational process on a single activity in one domain be allowed to do so?" are part of the adaptation of these general principles to a specific program, a process which is beyond the scope of the present discussion.

The word "flexible" in the term "flexible freedom" expresses the presumption that beyond their initial choice of activities, young people should be given the opportunity to change certain parameters or activities, as long as their tutors or mentors consider their choices justifiable *from the educational-developmental standpoint.*

Security refers to three meanings of the term on three levels: physical security, emotional security to be supplied by the stability and continuity of the educational program and educational grouping, and emotional security, stemming from one's acceptance by one's tutors and peer group.[66]

A certain degree of tension exists between the first two "open" principles ("plurality of paths" and flexible freedom) and the demand for emotional security based on system stability, which requires a certain degree of "closeness." There is no way to universally determine the optimal proportion between these two opposing groups of principles. The balance should be managed by educational organizations or educators, in accordance with their specific educational approach, the nature of the student population, and other relevant conditions.

Beyond these three environmental principles, educators should honor three ultimate *pedagogic* principles,[67] ordained by the three central objectives. These pedagogic principles stipulate that educators use the educational experiences, and whatever diverse opportunities that arise or are created, to constantly raise the levels of autonomy, morality, and dialogical belonging in the young people through reflective discussion guided by these principles and based on the concrete methodology stemming from them.

These ultimate principles can be sub-divided according to the basic components of the key concepts comprising the AOE. Thus, as shown above,[68] autonomy is based on authenticity (or self-knowledge) and self-direction. Authenticity is based on self-awareness of one's profile defined by one's interests, capacities, and performance styles. Self-direction is based on practical rationality (i.e., the ability to develop an optimal program in order to actualize these objectives) and on self-control.[69] Educators should, therefore be committed to developing:

- The individual's reflection upon (or self-awareness to) his or her interests, performance styles, and capacities, as well as the interrelations thereof.
- Practical rationality.
- Young people's planning ability, as well as an ability for emotional commitment, self-control, and self direction (an important element of what is

known today as "emotional intelligence")[70] which are needed for the implementation of their plans.

The development of morality, when defined in light of the reconciliation principle, should be based on the development of empathy towards the emotions and pain of others on the one hand, and the development of ethical rationality, or the ability to think and debate ethical issues rationally and critically on the other. Therefore, it follows from the second ultimate pedagogic goal that educators should also be committed to developing:

- Empathy; and
- Ethical rationality.

Developing dialogical belonging requires developing young people's sense of identification with a certain culture, community, or grouping, and the ability to regard this identification as a source from which they may derive meaning. At the same time, it also means developing in young people the ability to define their own voice and defend that voice even in hostile or antagonistic social or cultural circumstances. This in turn means developing:

- Young people's ability and commitment to define their identity by (among other things) identifying with a relevant culture and grouping; and
- Young people's ability to express their own voice/interests/opinions within a culture or grouping and defend their standpoint.

This list of pedagogic principles is neither conclusive nor concrete. My main objective here was to outline an alternative kind of pedagogy, one which enables a meaningful educational process that is desirable and possible in the postmodern democratic and Humanistic milieu. I further elaborated on the pedagogic principles laid down in various places in the book and developed (mainly in terms of the values of autonomy and dialogical belonging) a detailed operational-pedagogical methodology stemming from them and AOE goals, as befitting more concrete educational contexts.[71]

SUMMARY

Taking into account the three ultimate objectives of desirable education in post-modern democracy—encouraging the development of young people as autonomous, moral, and dialogically belonging human beings—this chapter depicted a skeletal outline for an educational program, which has two central components:

- Seven experiential domains which cover a maximal list of experiential spheres required for the young person's development as an autonomous, moral, and dialogically belonging human being.
- An educational process based on the basic maxim of reflective "experiments in living," three basic educational roles and educational principles which fall into two groups: environmental principles for an optimal educational milieu and pedagogic principles that should guide educators' efforts towards bringing out the desired characteristics in young people within this milieu, through guided reflection about their experimentation.

CHAPTER EIGHT

A STRUCTURE FOR EDUCATIONAL ORGANIZATIONS IN POSTMODERN LIBERAL DEMOCRACIES

INTRODUCTION

The description of the seven experiential domains and the basic educational principles in the previous chapter is partial. I intentionally circumvented many practical issues, which will surely arise out of the proposed educational view; I feel these issues should be discussed in later stages, by interested educators and decision makers, as they develop concrete educational programs in concrete contexts that will ensue from the Autonomy Oriented Education (AOE) view.[1]

However, the autonomy oriented educational process does, ineluctably, call for significant structural changes to be made in the basic characteristics of the existing education system and the essential characteristics of the modern school. In fact, they call for a radical shift from the modern school which dominated the educational sphere during all of the last century to an autonomy oriented postmodern organization. There are at least seven essential characteristics, based on presuppositions which lie at the heart of the modern school, that are usually taken for granted by educators and the general public; these presuppositions should be radically changed. Four of these characteristics are internal to the organization of the school, while the other three relate to the relationship between the school on one side and the labor market and the higher education system on the other.

The changes I propose are reviewed in the first section of this chapter.[2] The second section[3] is dedicated to emphasizing the fact that the actualization of these changes creates a postmodern educational organization which is wholly and substantially different from the modern school. The proposed organization will not be marred by the meaninglessness which has become part and parcel of the prevailing school's dysfunctional activity and the many other malaises pursuant of the rapidly widening chasm between the modern school and the reality around it.

REQUIRED ORGANIZATIONAL CHANGES

The *first change* which necessarily stems from the proposed Autonomy Oriented Educational process is an abolition of the educational organization's *lococentricity*, or in other words, we need to override the *principle of unity of time and place* which has been essential to the modern system (see Chapter Four) and still dominates it completely.[4] The need to uproot this principle in order to be able to realize the desired educational program is crystal clear. This change is a necessary condition to open the new educational organization to real life. It is a necessary condition for allowing those young people who choose to pursue interests, professional aspirations, or social activities which are found outside the geographic location of the educational organization (which probably constitutes a majority of young people), to actualize their choice.

This flexibility concerning time and place should be extensive but not total. It should be the general default scenario, further guided in each individual case by considerations of the individual limitations of the students (e.g., the lack of sufficient orientation in the case of the very young and so on) and by other, perhaps conflicting, demands of the educational plan.

The *second change* requires uprooting the prevailing curriculum, which is necessarily disciplinary in content and hierarchical, linear, and fragmentary in structure. This change is designed to provide young people with a far larger reservoir of experiences from which to choose, "supplied by" the infinite, extremely rich, and permanently renewing range of possibilities the postmodern reality offers. This stands in clear contradiction to the rigidly narrow range that exists today in the realm of the conventional, disciplinary curriculum, and will abolish the default need to force students into any special structure (linear or otherwise). To this end, the range of potential experimentation of young people should be freed from any constraint which does not enhance and support the productivity of their exploration process in terms of the ultimate goals of education.

In today's school, young people's range of intellectual and developmental choices is suffocatingly narrow. It is limited by the standard theoretical approach to curriculum design, dominant throughout the world; by the demanding and narrow list of subjects which are relevant mainly to final examinations; by the discipline-oriented specialization of teachers; and by the hierarchic linear and fragmentary logic, basic both to the school organization and to the disciplinary curriculum.

When the default scenario frees young people, either physically or virtually via the Internet, from the confines of the geographic limitations of the educational organization and the confines of the disciplinary curriculum and its underlying hierarchical fragmentary structure, the scope of their freedom to choose experiences relevant to their potential interests, work, or social activities and explore them will expand enormously.

The *third change* constitutes a considerable diminution of another aspect of the educational organization's hierarchical and linear structure, and relates principally to the need for a much greater range of democratic administration in the educational organization. This change grows out of the sixth experiential domain relating to social involvement. It rests on the assumption that true social education is unattainable unless students actually confront real social problems in which they have a personal or existential stake. By this change I am *not* suggesting a total democracy in which students set educational policy, or its fundamental principles, but rather to achieve that measure of democracy needed to educate in accordance with the principles of the proposed approach.[5] If the education is successful, this measure of democracy should increase as the students mature; in other words, the level of democratization will rise as the age of the students does.[6]

The *fourth change* introduces two new educational functions into the education system (in addition to teachers), namely, educators functioning as *tutors* and *mentors*, as discussed in Chapter Seven. Tutors will guide students in a specific domain of experience, and mentors will help them enhance the integration of knowledge attained from the experiences. These mentors will methodologically guide students to productively reflect on their experiences as required for their development as autonomous, dialogically belonging, and moral human beings. Young people's process of exploration should be accompanied both by the ongoing activity of "the basic educational group" and by a personal relationship between the mentor and the student, on varying degrees of involvement as defined by the individual's personal needs.

The educational function of mentors is designed to ensure the integrative and integrating character of the desirable educational process. This function is of the uppermost importance to the proposed educational organization. The mentor's degree of success in methodologically mobilizing guided reflection on the educatees' experiences for the development of their autonomy, morality, and dialogical belonging will largely determine the success of the educational organization in achieving its educational goals. It is certainly the most important and necessary condition for success.

The importance of the mentor's role is a function of both the great openness of the proposed educational organization and the fact that the default result of the educational scenario for young people experiencing today's world runs counter to the values set by the AOE view. It is up to the mentors (and to lesser degree to the tutors and teachers as discussed in Chapter Seven) who rely on the values of AOE and its integral educational methodology to utilize the former in order to prevent the latter. Mentors should trigger in the students the reflection and thinking processes necessary and sufficient for channeling their experiences in a way that enhances the desired aforementioned values.

While the four changes discussed above are internal, or related to the internal structure of the educational organization, the next three are external and relate to the relationship between the educational organization and the outside world. Like the first three internal changes, the fifth and sixth changes also express the desire to ensure as wide a range of experiences for young people as possible, however from an external point of view.

The *fifth change* consists of uprooting what may be termed "the principle of the uninterrupted duration of the education process." This principle is another expression, apart from the hierarchical structure of the disciplinary curriculum and the authoritarian structure of running a school, of the existing education system's linearity. According to this principle every student at a given age range (usually five to eighteen) is expected to stay in the system *continuously* for a certain number of years (usually thirteen).

This principle clearly limits the ability of young people to get involved, during their search for interests, a future career, or relevant social or spiritual activities, with real experimentations in working life and academic studies or any other kind of experimentation whenever these require full and long involvement. Therefore, those young people whose preferred field of interest, occupation, social activity, or spiritual pursuit demands that they break off geographically-based contact with the educational organization for a certain period of time should be allowed to do so, unless there are good educational reasons to prevent, postpone, or limit such disconnection. Students could then suspend their relationships with the educational organization for a while and in its stead work for a year in, for example, an anthropological field of interest, or spend two years intensively studying yoga in a Japanese Zen Buddhist monastery, or work months at a time on a North Sea fishing trawler and so on.

Reasons for preventing, limiting, or postponing such geographical disconnection arise when the mentor believes a certain student is not sufficiently mature to benefit from such a an experience and determines that the student's interests would be better served by waiting another year, or by a shorter period of disconnection instead of a whole year, etc. The mentor's duty here is to be as candid and open as possible with the student when presenting his or her view and to be as open as possible to the student's view, which he or she should seriously consider. The ultimate responsibility and authority should rest with the mentor, although this authority might be gradually reduced as students grow older.

Full involvement with activities taking place far from the geographical proximity of the educational organization for a defined period of time, can, but does not have to, require the student to disconnect his or her ties with the organization. In some cases it might be desirable to maintain contact between the student and the educational organization by simply changing the mode of communication. In such cases, at certain times and for specific subjects, all the activities of the student might take place within the physical domain of other organizations, while he or she remains in constant contact with his or her mentor, basic educational grouping, and friends, reporting on and discussing his or her external activities via the various functions of the Internet.

In order to facilitate such modes of communication, what may be termed "the principle of the autarkic nature of the educational organization" must also be up-rooted and abolished. This principle demands that all activities concerning the educational process take place in the geographic proximity of the educational organization. Abolishing this principle is the *sixth change* required in order to achieve AOE goals. This change requires a switch from the perception of the educational organization as a physical framework necessary to fulfill all the activities of the educational program (as the school is believed to be today) to its perception as a bearer of educational responsibility, whose actualization is enabled through an appropriate educational program, which is not *a priori* bound to a certain geographic location.

There is no *a priori* reason to universally connect all activities, students, and educators to a single, unified, fixed location in order to fulfill the roles of the educational organization. The roles of the educational organization should mainly consist of the following functions:

- Facilitating student engagement in a wide range of experiences required by their educational program, in the geographical location of the educational organization or in other geographic locations, should a specific experience require it, while they still remain under the auspices of their "home" school.

- Accompanying students throughout their experimentation wherever it takes place by mentors (concerning all experiences) and tutors (guiding students in specific experiences), in light of the goals and principles of AOE, either in face-to-face meetings or via virtual meetings and conversations, or any combination of these modes which is found to optimally serve the goals of each student's educational program.

The last two external changes clearly represent a radical change in the relations between the educational organization and the outside world, including academic institutions, workplaces, and social organizations. With regard to academic institutions, the practical expression of the last two changes, particularly the sixth, entails an overlap, partial in most cases, between the final stages of the educational program (known today as "high school") and the first phase of college for those capable of meeting academic requirements and willing to do so.

In today's Western reality, when youngsters go to university at eighteen to twenty years of age, they have little chance for reflective experiments in living.[7] Academic studies today have ceased to be the privilege of the upper and higher middle classes and are now available to all echelons of society. Furthermore, many Western societies have meaningfully decreased the financial support offered to students, support which was, until recent decades, quite generous. Thus, not only are social pressures to complete their studies quickly and start earning a living gradually being exerted on many students at this age, but also, they are quite often forced to contend with objective economic pressures.[8] Moreover, in many cases students have to fully or partly support themselves during their studies. As a result, their academic studies are very often far from being a process of experiments in living, nor are they a moratorium[9] from immediate material or social pressures.[10]

On the other hand, imagine what would happen if the barriers separating the university from the educational organization were toppled. Fourteen- to fifteen-year-old students, or students of even younger age (since "kids" are quickly getting "smarter" at younger and younger ages today), would be able to study at university as auditors or as students working on special research projects or as fully integrated students. Given such an early start, students would gain three or four years of experimentation taking place at a time when they are not yet affected by economic pressure on the one hand, and while they are able to enjoy constant educational support and mentoring under the auspices of the educational organization on the other. The experimentation during this period will likely be immeasurably more open and productive in comparison to the limited "experimentation range" that many students encounter during their academic careers today.

To a certain but very limited extent, this proposal is already being implemented. In some countries an increasing number of outstanding students are allowed to study at university in their last years of high school or at even earlier stages if they are identified as "gifted." Still, it must be stressed that the differences between the existing situation and the proposed structure are fundamental, and are embodied in the following three points:

The aim of involving high school students in academic studies today is to make schools highly attractive to the students and parents by accelerating the students' advancement towards (what is believed by them to be) a profitable career. This aim springs from the technocratic perspective, dominant today in almost all education systems which emphasizes narrow material achievements. My proposed changes, founded in the AOE approach, stem from the desire to enrich the students' variety of authentic experiences and hence their development as autonomous, dialogically belonging, moral individuals.

The second significant difference arises out of the first. While current practice bases itself on the successful conclusion of a number of academic courses in order to gain academic credits, the proposed change will emphasize a widening of the circle of experiences under the guidance of mentors.

An essential change in the experiential scope and its place in the educational process evolves out of the above shift in goals. While early academic studies are currently marginal and reserved mostly for outstanding students, the proposed agenda in the desirable educational organization will be "located" at the heart of the pedagogic process. It will be "located" in the fourth and fifth experiential domains, which relate to experiences in varied areas of potential or actual interests, occupational fields, and social involvement, and will open a far larger range of opportunities to a far greater number of young people.

An additional advantage of these two external changes relates to breaking down the barriers that separate the education system from the labor market and society. Here, too, the intent is to end the current linear-serial relationship which effectively separates the educational process from actual work, social involvement, or engagement in an interest. Furthermore, the idea is to establish conditions which will allow youngsters to devote a long and continuous period of time to work in one or several places, or to experience social activity, or to engage in an actual or potential interest as a key part of their educational process.

With regard to work, the practical aspects of the proposed change are perhaps relatively limited, because many occupations require broad knowledge and long periods of training that high-school age students naturally lack. Yet certain adaptable occupations can help young people experience professions which require many years of higher education at a rather early age. For example, working as hospital auxiliaries will expose students to the entire gamut of medical and paramedical occupations; working as assistants in a court of law can familiarize them with the nature of the legal process. It is important to emphasize that it is not enough to "send" young people out to locate by themselves any kind of activity they wish. It is a vital "logistical" role of the educational organization to make sure that such experimentation is possible and productive, i.e., to set up with the relevant organizations the relevant legal and logistical infrastructure needed for them to host young people and make sure that while staying in the hospital, court of law, or any other organization or context, in whatever capacity, young people will be able to get involved or observe as many roles or aspects of the activity in question as they might be interested in.

This is not an easy logistical goal, certainly not for individuals. That is one important reason why the steady support, in this case logistical organizational support, of the educational organization is vital for a productive process of exploration to take place. Another vital complementary contribution of the educational organization consists of making sure that the experimentation process is accompanied by the necessary mentoring process, one which will closely accompany the students during these experimentation periods, in order to ensure that their work activities serve the general goals of AOE.

In other words, for productive exploration to take place in our discussed context, three necessary conditions must be met:

- The student possesses the knowledge and skills necessary for him or her to take advantage of any process they are exposed to for exploration and self development;
- The student has access to as many supporting "fields of experimentation" as possible;
- The student is accompanied by a mentor that can make sure that the two previous conditions are met according to the needs and circumstances of any individual case and that the experimentations are subject to reflection that will enhance their contribution to the student's self development.

The first and third conditions were mentioned above and extensively discussed in the previous chapter; it is the second condition that was emphasized here.

The *seventh change*, grounded in the goals and content of AOE, calls for the abolition of high school diplomas, at least in their existing form, constituting, with some exceptions, a *sine qua non* for acceptance to university. This change is vital to ensuring the conversion of the high school from a diploma-producing assembly line into a true educational framework, one which enables and encourages reflective experiments in living.

As long as the diploma "sword" hangs over the students' heads, as long as the diploma is perceived as the main or even only goal of high school studies, as long as schools are judged by parents, administrators, and public opinion only or mainly according to the rate of student success in local, national, or international exams and other goals necessary mostly for achieving diplomas, there is no chance that a true educational process can take place. The contradiction between the desirable Humanistic education and "studying" in order to succeed in final exams is too blatant for true education to be compatible with diploma-oriented "studies."

This is even truer in the present state of affairs wherein the sanctification of "standards" has become the gospel of education systems in the West. In many places today, most high school subjects are "learned" and taught purely for the sake of obtaining or surpassing the required grade point average dictated by the prevailing standards, and leading to a diploma. Today's students devote most of their time to "studies" whose only significance is of a fourth-order benefit (to use the terminology I developed in Chapter Three). Meanwhile, they are incapable of devoting time to activities which have first- and second-order benefits, that is, reflective experiments in living relating to their preferred interests, occupations, and modes of social involvement or spirituality.

Similar and complementary arguments against the high school diploma and standards-oriented "learning" have been voiced during the last generation from many quarters in many countries.[11] These voices attack the diploma's and quantitative standards' destructive effect on the educational process in the high school, as well as their anti-egalitarian effects. However, obtaining the "right standard" or the relevant diploma remain the system's main goals in Western societies.

More importantly to our case, this "learning" process distorts the developmental stage, in which young people should be enjoying the necessary moratorium[12] (to use Erikson's most relevant term) and encouragement to be involved in the exploration process needed for the formation of their identity and development of their personality. Furthermore, as shown in Chapter Two, this activity transmits a hidden message to students, one which effectively pulls the rug from under their motivation to seek self-fulfillment or to develop as autonomous individuals.

The high school diploma, in all its guises, as well as the exams students have to pass in order to get it—exams which exclude any chance for true learning—must be abolished. Alternatives to the function the diploma now fulfills in many Western countries, as a selection mechanism on the way to higher education, can be easily found. The options at our disposal are either universal college entrance exams such as the Scholastic Assessment Test (SAT) used in the US, or, preferably, opening the universities' gates to all. Thereafter, first-year grades or the grades of certain first-year courses may be used, as determined by each university or each department, as criteria for ascertaining which students are capable or incapable of undertaking academic studies. The universities can prepare students for studies in those subjects which require prior knowledge, as part of a pre-academic course structure to be established for this purpose.

This course of action would naturally have a cost both in terms of lowered first-year studies standards and the considerable increase in the student population and subsequent increase in demand for budget allocations to fund these changes. But if, in a wider context, we consider the horrendous educational damage caused by the high school diploma and the resultant economic damage, given that financing a harmful process means pure economic loss, then the price to be paid for abolishing the final examinations throughout developed Western countries is negligible.

FROM FACTORY TO EDUCATIONAL LIAISON AND GUIDANCE CENTER

In the previous section I proceeded negatively, pointing out the changes required by AOE in the prevailing school structure. Before concluding this chapter I would like to draw, from a positive perspective, the main lines characterizing the nature of the desired educational organization, and emphasize the essential differences between it and the prevailing school. A desirable educational organization stemming from the above considerations answers three sets of criteria:

- It is designed after the image of the AOE, the view most appropriate to set the goals and procedures of education in postmodern Liberal Democracies. It offers an organizational design optimal to serve such an educational process.
- It is ideally suited to the postmodern reality.

- As a result of the above two characteristics it allows for, and encourages, educational processes which can be meaningful both for students and educators.

An educational organization adopting the proposed AOE program, along with the radical organizational changes that are an integral part of it, will be essentially different from the school as we know it today.

As noted in Chapter Four, at the heart of the fundamental guiding metaphor of the existing school is the production-line based *factory* that serially processes raw material: the students. They are run through the same stages along production lines which are almost universally identical in content, duration, times, and structure. At a uniform age the newly "packaged" graduates leave the factory as identical, semi-finished products complete with high school diplomas and ready to enter the next stage of processing. If this perspective is reminiscent of the well-known scene from Pink Floyd's "The Wall," it is only because this clip accurately and blatantly reflects the most basic guiding metaphor of modern schooling.

In comparison, the educational organization envisioned in the plan proposed here would be entirely devoid of this serial, uniform character. It would function like an educational *liaison and guidance center*, a postmodern organizational structure in its very essence. It would help young people pursue the experiential processes that they need or that interest them, while providing them with the constant support of teachers, tutors, and, most importantly, mentors in their experiments in living.

The first three experiential domains, discussed in the previous chapter, which are designed to ensure the acquisition of basic skills and categories of knowledge necessary for independent function in life (the three Rs and institutional literacy), might become somewhat monotonous for some students, especially those in deep need of acquiring the necessary skills or knowledge. For such students as these, it will not be possible or realistic to always try and combine the process of acquisition of the necessary skills and knowledge with meaningful experiences. Still, an effort should be made to render this stage as short as possible for each individual child and to combine it, as much as possible, with meaningful experimentation and exploration.

Furthermore, except for these three domains, which should also be as flexible and individually customized as possible, the proposed model accords all young people with the chance to develop a personal educational plan. Each plan should be unique and reflect the interests, potential professional pursuits, and social and spiritual activities the individual chooses to follow, as well as his or her capacities and performance styles.

In this context young people should be allowed all the time and opportunities they need to search for meaning or the main goals of their lives and to explore their identity as well as their place in society.

The last five domains in the suggested educational plan, as discussed in the previous chapter, are designed to assist young people to obtain knowledge of the world from perspectives relevant to them and their goals, by involving themselves in actual processes of choice and reflection upon their experience in such a process with the help of their mentors and friends.

Maintaining an even balance between the various experiential domains and the actualization of the pedagogic principles detailed in the previous chapter will provide the necessary optimization of the combination of freedom to experience life with the support, framework, and reflective assistance that young people need.

The contrast between the two metaphors, *the factory* and *the liaison and guidance canter*, stresses the fact that the required change is highly comprehensive and goes much beyond any specific adjustment, as radical as it may be.

Additional reasons for this change are grounded in the need for a transition from a modern organization that is essentially hierarchic-linear, lococentric, fragmentary, and standards-oriented (see Chapter Four) to a postmodern organization whose structure is opposed to all four of these characteristics. This organization is to an extent "chaordic,"[13] virtual, and based on flexibility with regard to time and space, thus enabling and encouraging the holistic experimentation track chosen by each unique individual.

One cannot over-emphasize that the ultimate goal is to actualize the basic educational values of postmodern democracy. The suggested educational program and its postmodern character make it ideal for this purpose, since it fits both the needs of its target audience and the reality in which it is to operate, thus ensuring high functionality, meaningfulness, and a great likelihood of achieving its basic aims.

SUMMARY

Realization of AOE and the educational program which stems from it calls for a series of revolutionary changes in the structure of the educational organization. These radical changes should "rocket" the entire education complex from an organization based on the rigid, closed model of the nineteenth century factory to the flexible, open, liaison and guidance center model of the twenty-first century. As such, the desirable educational organization will enjoy three notable advantages:

- The new school organization will serve the three basic goals of education in a democratic society, namely, encouraging the development of young people as autonomous, moral, and dialogically belonging individuals.
- Educational activities will be meaningful for both educators and educatees.
- The desirable educational organization will operate in organizational harmony with the postmodern reality wherein it exists and which it should serve.

CHAPTER NINE

THE STATUS OF YOUNG PEOPLE IN POSTMODERN LIBERAL DEMOCRACIES

INTRODUCTION

In Chapter Five I described the disappearance of "childhood" and offered four complementary explanations for this phenomenon. The first explanation ties the disappearance of "childhood" to effects of the digital revolution. The second finds roots for this phenomenon in the postmodern economy and labor market. According to the third explanation, the reasons for this upheaval are rooted in dominant relativistic epistemologies and the concomitant crisis of authority which have taken over postmodern Western consciousness. Lastly, the fourth points to the collapse of the modern linear conception of time, place, and human life characterizing the source of the dramatic blurring of the distinctions between young and old we experience in today's postmodern reality.

Since postmodernity is all-encompassing and permeates every aspect of our lives, it is impossible to isolate one of the above as "the true" or "most basic" cause for the disappearance of "childhood." The interrelations of the underlying causes are too complex to allow a reasonable enough distinction between the causes to enable a meaningful discussion of this issue.

Fortunately, it is not necessary to resolve the theoretical questions underpinning the issue in order to discuss the practical questions of the expected and desired legal and social changes in the status of young people and the educational consequences thereof. Suffice it to say, as clarified and substantiated in Chapter Five, that this phenomenon reflects basic ongoing processes which are deeply rooted in the postmodern reality and it is therefore reasonable to assume that it can neither be stopped nor even significantly decelerated in the foreseeable future.[1]

We can extract from the conclusion of Chapter Five two different possible mega-scenarios for the future of "childhood":[2] The first, more moderate version, maintains that "childhood" (immaturity, development, preparation for the future) will continue to exist as the second stage of life, which will begin after the first four to six years of life ("early childhood" or "infancy"). However one of the following will also become part of the common understanding of the upheaval characterizing postmodern reality:

- Passage from this stage to full-blown maturity will gradually become more and more blurred;
- Passage from "childhood" to maturity will occur at different periods for different individuals. In other words, there will be no universal age of passage;
- The duration of "childhood" will become significantly shorter;

- Part or all of the above three possibilities will occur simultaneously.

In the second, more radical, mega-scenario, after the "early childhood" period, the chronological-linear connection between "childhood" (the period of alleged immaturity) and "adulthood" (the period of alleged maturity) will become obscured and lost altogether. In this radical mega-scenario, "children" will be defined as individuals of *different ages* who are undergoing a significant change of identity or a radical change of lifestyle, regardless of any linear, chronological, order.

Thus, for example, it will be possible to say that a forty- or sixty-year-old individual who has undergone a major life-changing experience (e.g., changes of gender, social role, lifestyle, sexual preference, profession, or two or more of these together), is going through a second (or third and so on) "childhood" period. Such an individual would logically be deprived of the same option and participation rights that "children" are not entitled to. But, by the same token, he or she may enjoy the same special rights "children" are entitled to. In this scenario, it will be also possible to say that an eleven-, thirteen-, or fifteen-year-old individual who, having already completed the initial phase of identity formation to a degree that she or he has found a stable identity, social role, occupation, and lifestyle, is mature and accorded all the rights and obligations of an adult. In this mega-scenario, the literal sense of the two complementary terms, "children" and "adults," will not have any necessary chronological connection except for very early "childhood" or infancy.

Even if the more radical mega-scenario was to come to pass (and as surrealistic as it may seem to us today, it is certainly an aspect of a possible future), it is unlikely to be realized within the next decade. Therefore, henceforth I relate only to the first, more moderate mega-scenario. I discuss the implications of the realization of this mega-scenario for the future meanings of "childhood" and "adulthood" and hence for the desired educational process.

I will begin by sketching some probable models for implementing the moderate mega-scenario in very general terms. Each of these models, if, and to whatever extent, it may be implemented, will lead to a different result within the mega-scenario. Then, in the second section,[3] I discuss the impact children's status, as stemming from the above mega-scenario, may have on the education system as well as some of the main scenarios of which it consists. The third section of the chapter[4] will pose the ethical question: to what extent or under which conditions is this mega-scenario, and the probable educational scenarios included in it, desired? This section also offers a general outline for an answer, depicting the desired status of young people in a postmodern democracy vis-à-vis the desired education system described in the previous three chapters.

THE STATUS OF YOUNG PEOPLE IN A POSTMODERN DEMOCRACY

My discussion of the future legal and social status of young people in a postmodern democratic society is initial and tentative. With the limited space I have here, I cannot touch all the possible scenarios and sub-scenarios which fall within the aforementioned moderate mega-scenario. I will therefore briefly discuss the several general scenarios that seem most plausible to me, those which potentially contain the most sub-scenarios. My aim here is not to convince the reader that this will indeed be the case; such a task is too pretentious, if not utterly impossible. Rather I wish to methodologically present the way of thinking that should guide educational planners and policy makers when they consider the future of education in both the predictive (in this and the next section) and prescriptive (third section) phases, and to, very generally, indicate the direction such considerations ought to be taking.

What legally and socially separates "children" from "adults" today is that "children," unlike "adults," enjoy a number of *welfare rights*, while their *right of self-determination*, a basic right in the liberal view, is denied. Consequently, children are denied *option rights* that derive from self-determination, such as the right to sign agreements or to choose their domicile or course of study. They are also denied any *social participation rights*, mainly the many forms of participation in political elections.[5]

Legally, the distinction between "childhood" and "adulthood" is dichotomous and rests on a purely chronological criteria, with most rights being granted at age eighteen or from the age of eighteen, and a few from sixteen and over. Thus for example, in Great Britain (I refer to Great Britain here since it is a good reflection of the general situation in many other Western countries, with some minor discrepancies),[6] almost all rights that have to do with self-determination are accorded to the individual from the age of sixteen and above:

- Sixteen years of age: leave school, buy a lottery ticket, consent to having sex, get married with parental consent, refuse dental or medical treatment, buy cigarettes, get a National Insurance Number, and get a full-time job.
- Seventeen years: learn to drive and buy a car or motorcycle, be sent to prison.
- Eighteen years: get married without parental consent, purchase and drink alcohol (on licensed premises), vote in elections, place a bet, get a tattoo.

While prevalent, with some differences, throughout the Western world, this distinction is not rationally justifiable, mainly because the attributes usually cited as justifying it, namely, the "child's" "relative inability for judgment, rationality, or discretion" can not do the job they are expected to do. However these capabilities are defined, there is no sufficient evidentiary support to the claim that the majority of people over eighteen (or over sixteen, or fourteen, and so on) possess these attributes, or that the majority of people who have not yet reached this chronological barrier do not possess them. Even if such evidence existed in the "far modern past" (which I doubt), the disappearance-of-childhood process taking place within the last twenty years has altogether obliterated any facts that may have been able to sustain such evidence. I have reviewed the attempts made to justify this arbitrary classification elsewhere and have already shown that neither of them can pass the test of rational critique.[7]

Though this dichotomous division between "children" and "adults" cannot be justified, it can be easily understood: it is a symbolic expression of the modern concept of "childhood." Today, however, this perception is clearly changing and the lines between the human stages of life are blurring, as demonstrated, *inter alia*, by the decisions handed down by judges[8] and the confused legal status of "children."[9] An example of change in perception (one of many) is the Elian Gonzales case in the US, in which the court suggested that immigration officials should ask a six-year-old boy whether he wanted to return to Cuba or remain with his Miami relatives.[10] This decision stands in clear contradiction to suppositions which are still accepted as given in dominant social and legal policies, such as compulsory education laws, which usually do not leave room for consulting the "child" in question or ascertaining her or his desires.

Generally speaking, we can see a gradual yet persistent change in the guiding principles of underage custody and guardianship. In the past, only "professionals" were asked to express their "professional" view in such matters and the accepted default on which courts relied in deciding custody disputes was predicated on "objective criteria" such as age, sex, and parent earning capabilities. Today, however, courts in many Western societies seem to solicit the children's opinions and wishes and accord them substantial weight when making their decision. Nevertheless this is an inconsistent process as many courts still follow "the old ways" while others turn to this new one.

The question which therefore arises is: what are the possible and, more importantly, desirable avenues of change in the status of children in postmodern democracies?

As I mentioned, the special status of children today consists of two parts: the first part consists of the *option* and *participation rights* which children do not enjoy and the second are the special *welfare rights*, which they do enjoy. There are many possible models upon which changes in both parts can be designed. It is possible to logically discern three basic models of change in the legal status of "children." The circumstances emerging from the operationalization of each of these models or any possible combinations thereof are all probable future eventuations within the moderate mega-scenario.

The *first model* consists of the preservation of the current distinction between legal "majority" and "minority." It only requires that the chronological line between the two be moved below the sixteen to twenty-one range, at which the present age of majority is usually set, at, say, ten to fifteen or any other acceptable lower range.

The *second model* is more radical. In this model any and all distinction between majority and minority is null and void and everyone is automatically granted all option and participation rights, regardless of age. Its one proviso is that a special authority be created to assist the very young who cannot actualize their rights on their own.[11]

A *third model* also requires the abrogation of the chronological division between majority and minority, but stipulates that a test, irrespective of age, must be completed successfully before each new right is accorded.

These three models are *pure models* in the sense that they are "simple" or "non-complex." Because these models are not mutually exclusive, we may also consider *complex models*, which combine various aspects of the separate pure models into one. Thus, for example, a *fourth model* could combine the current situation with the third model mentioned above. In other words, it can preserve the currently accepted threshold of chronological "adulthood," which grants rights automatically once the individual has reached a certain predetermined age, while also permitting anyone below the threshold who so desires to obtain the relevant rights by passing the appropriate tests.

A *fifth model*, based on the previous one, adds an age restriction so that a relevant test will be administered only on reaching the prescribed age, as is the case today with driving licenses.

A *sixth model* could combine the first and third models. Within it, the chronological threshold of "adulthood" will be substantially lower; however rights will be afforded to people below the prescribed age if they pass the relevant test.

This list does not begin to exhaust all the possibilities; there are many other models which reflect various possible modifications of the legal status of "children" in all matters pertaining to option and participation rights. The list does however provide an indication of the available possibilities and hence possible future scenarios to an extent that suffices for the current preliminary discussion.

Several of the models specified above can, and do, exist side by side. An example for a society that chose to actualize the first model can be found in the 1998 amendment to the British Criminal Justice and Public Order Act of 1994. The amendment lowered the age of consensual homosexual relationships from eighteen to sixteen in order bring the age of consent[12] for homosexual relations into line with that of heterosexual relations.[13] This pushed further the earlier 1994 legislation that lowered the age of consent in homosexual relations from twenty-one to eighteen. Examples for the second model can be found in certain sections of the International Treaty for Children's Rights. The treaty grants children certain adult rights, such as freedom of expression, freedom of thought and conscience, protection of dignity and reputation, as well as many others.

I now move on to the second part of the equation of the special status of children. When considering the above proposed models, I must contend with the consequent question they raise: do the rights granted to children at an earlier age automatically annul the welfare rights which also characterize their special status? The obvious response to this question seems to be "yes." The special welfare rights of children reflect the belief that minors lack the personality aspects necessary for leading an independent life, that they are insufficiently mature in comparison to adults in this regard. If children are this vulnerable, so the argument may go, they should be protected, assisted in a special way. But as granting the right of self-determination and all rights derived from it seems to contradict this assumption, then the special welfare rights, which children are afforded based on the same assumption, should be annulled as well, if and to the same extent that self-determination and all the rights stemming from it are granted.

But there are reasons to qualify this position or even reject it altogether. For instance, one could argue that granting the right of self-determination, together with the resultant option and participation rights, are justified not because all young people are generally more mature than what is now commonly believed, but rather because the independent experiences which stem from the provision of these rights are the best way to assist young people to reach maturity. Proponents of such a view may be aware of the risks of according self-determination and other constituent rights to young people in spite of their acknowledged immaturity, and may therefore argue that:

- The risks should be limited by using some of the models suggested above, that is, setting a minimal threshold for granting such rights, granting them gradually, or granting them only upon successful completion of the relevant tests.
- The benefits of young people developing as autonomous adults so outweigh the risks of according them rights they are not yet mature enough to handle independently that the risks are worthwhile, though it is still prudent and advisable to limit such risks as much as possible.[14]

Those adopting this line of thinking may argue that:

No matter what chronological age is set for according individuals self-determination and participation rights, the maturity of the recipients, a maturity necessary for mindful and meaningful use of such rights, inevitably depends on acquired experience, not chronological age.

Children today have the potential ability for such mindful use at a much younger age than is now acknowledged, but they need to acquire more experience in order to develop this potential into actual ability (as is the case for all individuals, whenever they are granted such rights).

Thus granting children self-determination and option, and participation rights, and initiating the necessary support system of special welfare rights, is the best course of action for a state wishing to create optimal conditions for the independence-enhancing life experiences required for the young people to mature as autonomous individuals.

It is therefore possible to identify four possible "pure" models for the reconstruction of young people's welfare rights, the last two based on the above argument while the first two reject it:

- Complete termination of any and all special welfare rights once young people are granted option and participation rights.
- Selective annulment of special welfare rights based on the level of option and participation rights which a specific young person enjoys.
- Preservation of current welfare rights regardless of the changes in the availability of option and participation rights.
- Enhancement of welfare rights in accordance with the changes in availability of option and participation rights.

As with the discussion about option and participation rights, I do not wish to, nor can I, decide between the models' logical or theoretical foundation or ascertain their chances for prevailing in the future. What matters for the sake of this discussion is the fact that these models (or combinations thereof) can possibly characterize the attitude of future postmodern liberal societies towards "childhood."

The above general outline refers only to possible *expected* definitions of the future status of children; it does not address the question of the *desirable* definitions. Desirability is subject to the more specific developmental and educational considerations that the third section of this chapter deals with.

POSSIBLE IMPACT OF THE FUTURE STATUS OF YOUNG PEOPLE
ON POSTMODERN DEMOCRATIC EDUCATION SYSTEMS

Having presented a general outline of the range of possible anticipated changes in young people's legal and social status, I now move on to examine the possible and anticipated impact these changes may have on the education system.

As underscored in Chapter Five, the disappearance of "childhood" undermines the *five basic premises* underpinning the modern school:

- School is designed for "children," who are defined chronologically, as the five to eighteen or five to twenty-one age group.
- "Children" can and should be forced to go to school and therein carry out certain activities.
- Only "children" should be students at school, only "adults" can be teachers.
- Only "adults" should determine educational and school policy while "children" and they alone should be the object of the educational process at school.
- Within the school's framework: once a teacher always a teacher, once a student always a student.

Even the first, moderate, mega-scenario discussed above subverts all five premises. Within that model there would be no reason to hang on to a long "childhood" period stretching from the age of five to the ages of eighteen to twenty-one, that developed in the second half of the nineteenth century and early decades of the twentieth. It will in fact be impossible to defend the universal dichotomous distinction between adults and children throughout the entire age range. This obviously leads to the collapse of the first premise, which relies on exactly such a universal and long-lasting dichotomous distinction. It also leads to the collapse, or at least to the need to dramatically narrow the effect and importance of, the other four premises, which rely heavily on the first premise—take it for granted, in fact.

Having realized the high probability for the demise of the prevailing school premises due to the disappearance of "childhood" and assuming the moderate mega-scenario of the disappearance of "childhood" prevails, the question arises: what are the possible scenarios for the new status of young people vis-à-vis the education system? We have to distinguish between two contexts for tackling this question here: The first is external to the educational organization and relates to recruiting the "target audience" for "consumption" of educational "services."15 In other words, it addresses the situation stemming from undermining the second of the five basic premises in the mega-scenario by postmodern reality: the notion that the educational process can and should be forced, in its entirety, on young people. The second context is internal and relates to the status of young people within the educational organization, a status which of course changes when the all the basic premises of the school are undermined by the mega-scenario in question.

Changes External to the Education System

Young people today are forced to consume the education system's "services" under compulsory education laws which oblige parents to send their children to school, at times even to a specific school, and often also compels them to follow a certain curriculum (or at least a core curriculum) in the school.

Compulsory education laws were first enacted in most Western countries in the late nineteenth and early twentieth centuries, a time in which there was no question about young people's rights of self-determination; they simply had none to speak of and were perceived as passive objects of the educational process. If awareness of children's rights began developing during this period, it was an awareness of their welfare rights, education being cardinal among those; the idea that children had a right of self-determination or the resultant option and participation rights was, at best, brushed off as ridiculous. Thus, legislators saw no reason to grant young people the right to determine, to one extent or another, the nature of their education, its goals, or the identity of its provider.

The conceptual framework that has supported existing education laws in Western countries is two-tiered. First, the law forcibly determines that children fall under the almost absolute authority of their parents.[16] Second, it compels parents to provide children with education, as it is determined by the state, often in light of a curriculum dictated by the state and usually in a school,[17] generally a specific school, dictated and run by the state.[18]

With the rise in the power, level of education, scope, affluence, and influence of the middle, or rather professional, classes,[19] the second step is clearly losing its effect. Evidence of this significant change is abundant and usually quite dramatic: parents are more involved in school management than ever before,[20] parents' freedom of choice when selecting a school for their children is on the rise ("parental choice" in the jargon of prevailing education systems),[21] and many parents choose to form charter schools, based on non-state-dictated educational concepts and curricula which they view as more appropriate and befitting their children's needs.[22] Finally, and most significant of all, a growing number of parents assume absolute responsibility for the education of their children and home school them.[23]

The first tier on which the law is predicated, the subjection of young people to their parents' absolute authority, is still very strong, but its dominance in society is also beginning to falter. As a result, the practical significance of intensified parental involvement in education also enhances the youths' power and rights in education. Given the disappearance of "childhood" and the diminution of the parent-child authority relationship in the last generation, parents often act as representatives of their children's interests and desires, albeit not always and not necessarily. For instance, many parents consult with their children when choosing a school for them or even decide according to their wishes, particularly with regard to high school education.[24]

Schools that attempt to recruit students in the context of "parental choice" recognize this fact and implement public relations campaigns designed to attract young people just as much as their parents.[25] Far more significantly, many parents who educate their children at home favor alternative individual and pedocentric "unschooling" educational approaches that are predicated on respect for young people's rights.[26] The practical significance of these changes is clear as it gradually renders young people the subject rather than the object of the educational process.[27]

These phenomena are increasingly expressed in the legal sphere as well, particularly in court decisions,[28] which represent a gradual move from the paternalistic view of children, wherein judges believed they had the right and duty to decide what a child's best interest is regardless of his or her wishes, to a perception of children as subjects endowed with the ability to make their own decisions and having the relevant rights which allow them to do so. Within the paternalistic conception of children, the courts decided what the so-called "best interest of the child" was based on external "expert testimonies" given by psychologists, social workers, educators, and other professionals but not on the judgment or expression of the desire of the children themselves. In the newly emerging "child as a subject" view, the courts incorporate into their decisions the will of the children, as expressed by them directly to the court, as six-year-old Elian Gonzales did in the case mentioned earlier, except in cases where the court finds a specific child to be too immature for his or her wishes to be in his or her own best interest. In complete contrast with previously dominant decision making processes, which primarily ignored the child's wishes because children, as a group, were considered "not mature enough to know what their best interest is," the decision making process emerging in the last two or three decades relies, more than ever before, on the child's own desires.

If the disappearance of "childhood" and the reflection thereof in the legal sphere is going to intensify, and all signs do seem to indicate as much, it is extremely likely that the laws of compulsory education will follow suit along one or more of the following lines:

- The period of time in which young people are perceived as "children" or "minors," and thus subject to the laws of compulsory education, will be reduced.
- While young people will be perceived by the law as "children," the legal system will give much more weight to their chosen educational preferences. These will come both at the expense of the state's power over children and at the expense of the practical and legal status their parents have gradually taken over from the state in recent years.
- The legal system will focus on ensuring supervision and that certain minimal standards of young people's knowledge and skills are maintained, while at the same time abandoning the perception of the school as a sole source or framework of learning. On the *formal* yet rarely practiced level, this has already been the case for long time now in the UK, in many American states, and in other Anglophone countries. But only recently, in light of the rapid and massive development of home schooling and flexi-schooling, have authorities *actually* allowed parents to educate their children "otherwise," as the UK law puts it, meaning not in school or not mainly in school.[29]

One result to be expected from these changes could be changing the compulsory education law. Enacting such a law would require that parents of young people (say, up to the age of twelve) be responsible for and make sure that their children achieve a prescribed standard in predetermined subjects, either by sending them to a state or "independent" school or by home schooling or flexi-schooling them.[30] In this scenario, from the age of twelve to the age of (say) fifteen, responsibility would be gradually transferred to the youngsters themselves and the onus to show they have acquired at least the minimal required proficiency of the areas which the state has determined to be essential for a mature and autonomous life would be on them.

According to this scenario, the choice of means by which knowledge and/or skills in the assigned areas are acquired would also be left up to the youngsters' discretion. They would be able to master their desired subjects by any means they deem fit, either by attending a school or a combination of schools to receive special training or study specific courses, or through home schooling or flexi-schooling, thus utilizing a combination of learning alternatives. After the age of (say) fifteen, the default in this scenario would be that the compulsory education laws would no longer apply unless there was an individual reason to uphold it. That is to say that the law may still be applied to specific young people between fifteen and eighteen years of age (or older) who for some reason still require supervision, such as children whose physical or mental disabilities render them unable to define their best interests or to follow up on them. In these cases the law would still oblige them or their legal guardians to establish a specific course of education and/or therapy.

Those who believe this scenario to be implausible should recall that education has undergone momentous changes in recent years; changes which were once considered "unthinkable" have been realized and generally accepted with surprising rapidity and ease. Changes in the compulsory education laws or relevant administrative arrangements over the last two decades in Western countries manifest themselves in the growing tendency to enable parental choice, to allow and even encourage community involvement in school policy and operations, to legalize and establish charter schools managed by parents' associations, and to facilitate home schooling and flexi-schooling.[31]

The above scenario is only one of many, but the trend it descends from is most likely generic enough to continue and to spread. By this I mean:

- Legally and *practically*, society will move away from compulsory *schooling* laws, which make going to school mandatory in most countries, to compulsory *education* laws, laws which set certain minimal educational requirements and the means to verify their attainment, but do not define any organizational means for their acquisition.
- Transferring the responsibility for implementing the law, at a predefined chronological point, from the parents to the educatees.
- Reducing the period of time in a person's life in which compulsory education laws are applicable.

Changes within the Education System

I now move on to the second of the abovementioned contexts: changes we can anticipate in the status of young people within the educational process as long as, and to the extent that, the educational process is managed, controlled, or supported by the state. Here we can expect the erosion of three of the five basic premises mentioned earlier:

- Only "children" should be students at school, only "adults" can be teachers.
- Only "adults" should determine educational and school policy while "children" and they alone should be the object of the educational process at school.
- Within the school's framework: once a teacher always a teacher, once a student always a student.

I begin with the current erosion of the second of the above assumptions. Relevant changes, gnawing away at this assumption's grasp on the system can already be discerned *inter alia*, in the broad involvement of educatees in the running of their own educational process, such as can be observed in open and democratic schools.[32] In such schools, the school council and its elected committees are in charge of making all administrative and pedagogic decisions including the appointment of teachers, budget allocations, and so forth. Students of all ages, together with parents and school staff, participate in the council activities in some form in a "one person, one vote" based system. Similar processes are also taking place, albeit less clearly and formally, in other schools which are not defined as democratic per se[33] and in the gradually growing unschooling branch of home schooling.[34] There are, of course, many other examples of young people's rising voice other then these "institutionalized" ones. Given the steady acceleration of the disappearance-of-childhood process, it is reasonable to suppose that these changes are but the first signs of a much more significant process of corrosion and disintegration of the grasp the second assumption has on the field of education.

I now move on to the current *de facto* erosion of the first and third of the above premises, which are inter-connected, if not analytically, then at least in practice. Many adults (parents and teachers) readily admit that the knowledge of, and familiarity with, the emerging digital civilization which the younger generations have acquired far exceed their own. In many schools, students' superior knowledge and conversance in the new digital reality accord them a higher *de facto* and sometimes even *de jure* status; often these young experts end up instructing their teachers (that is, if the teachers are willing to learn) guiding them through the complexities of the digital revolution.[35]

This is also true, albeit less conspicuously so, in other domains of knowledge and activity. In the reality in which we live, knowledge is rapidly changing and available to everyone who has access to an Internet terminal and possesses basic Internet skills, regardless of their age. In fact, the earlier you acquire these, the better off you seem to be. It is a reality in which, as in all periods of drastic change and immigration, young people are extremely independent and more up-to-date and well-versed in the roles and norms of the important spheres of life than the adults around them.[36] Additionally, we are all perpetual immigrants nowadays for even if we do not change our place of residence, the culture around us is permanently changing at an accelerating rate. The spheres affected by such changes include: fashion, music (which has become today a major self definition factor for today's youth),[37] accepted lifestyles, and what the vernacular refers to as "cool" or "in." It is hard to imagine educational organizations, wherein the adult is always perceived as the teacher, and the minor as the student, operating for much longer in a reality where the youngster's life skills surpass those of their teachers.

In the aforementioned world it is more likely that roles within educational processes will be determined *ad hoc* by the individual's expertise in a specific domain. Age can no longer be a decisive factor in defining one as a teacher or a student. [38]

THE DESIRED STATUS OF YOUNG PEOPLE VIS-À-VIS THE EDUCATION SYSTEM IN A POSTMODERN DEMOCRACY

So far I have discussed changes we may *anticipate* in the way pupils of the education process are recruited and treated within it. The next question I must address is whether and to what extent these changes are *desirable* in light of AOE goals and processes, as described in the previous three chapters.

Let me begin with the positive side: these changes seem favorable in that they will ensure greater independence and freedom for young people. Freedom is an important, necessary condition for reflective experiments in living. This process is a necessary condition for the development of autonomy, morality, and dialogical belonging, the three primary objectives of education in liberal democratic societies. But this independence students will be afforded may be a purely formal one, which does not necessarily guarantee the development of young people in keeping with the above desirable basic values. In fact,[39] this independence could, and is much more likely to, have quite the opposite effect as the economic, marketing, and advertisement pressures, the powerful pillars of postmodern society, inculcate young people with very different values indeed, values of egoism, hedonism, and narrow careerism.

In other words, greater independence is a necessary, but far from sufficient, condition for achieving the desired goals of education. As I explained in Chapters Seven and Eight, in order to ensure the desired personality development, the following educational goals and methods should be rigorously followed:

- Acquisition of skills and basic areas of knowledge necessary for autonomous function in a postmodern society, accompanied by methodological, guided, reflection systematically executed by professional educators, i.e., AOE-trained teachers, tutors, and mentors.
- Active experiments in living in the three central areas of life, or at least one or two of them—fields of interest, work, and social activity (the fourth, fifth, and sixth experiential domains)—accompanied by methodological, guided, reflection, systematically executed by professional educators.
- Active experiments in living focused on fundamental existential questions concerning the human situation and the seventh experiential domain,

accompanied by methodological, guided reflection for those young people who have the motivation or need to do so.

- Productive and autonomous involvement in social and cultural contexts, accompanied by methodological, guided reflection, necessary for young people's development as morally and dialogically belonging individuals, cutting across all or most of the above areas.

The accompaniment and guidance of systematic reflection by mentors and tutors required in all the aforementioned points conveys the basic assumption that in order to have a reasonable chance to be educationally productive, each category of experience must be accompanied by a methodological reflection process, guided by tutors (specific to a certain experiential area) and mentors (guiding the young person throughout all experiential areas). This process is the core and *raison d'être* of the educational process and the main instrument of achieving the basic goals of education.

I believe that the modified or narrowed compulsory education law, mentioned above[40] as a plausible and desired scenario, can provide sufficient guarantee, through the tests incorporated into it, that young people have indeed absorbed the necessary knowledge and skills as per the demands of the first three domains of the educational program as described in Chapter Seven (and the first of the above bullets). Technically, it could also assure participation in some workshops, thus reflecting a few of the requirements of some of the other experiential domains (all the other bullets). But these technical means don't even scratch the surface of the demands the complex and continuous reflective teaching, tutoring, and mentoring processes AOE requires.

Moreover, as it is developmental in nature, the requisite educational process cannot be evaluated by standardized technical means alone. Evaluation criteria should be largely qualitative, adapted to each young individual's personal profile and subject in and of itself to the reflective process central to the educator-educatee dialogue. Similarly, the duration of the educational process cannot be defined by universally standardized "school years," "school days," or "hours." It is entirely possible that different young people will require different durations of exposure to the same educational process. It is also very probable that during the educational process some will develop in the desirable direction with very minimal educational intervention, while others will require prolonged guidance.

Thus there is no way to guarantee a plausible or even minimal satisfaction of the educational requirements stemming from the basic Humanistic educational goals just by drafting a compulsory education law based on standardized criteria and formal procedures. Such procedures, consisting of either passing certain universally required tests based on universally defined standards of knowledge or ability, or of completing a universally defined number of years of education, or of some combination of the two, would not be enough, and would in fact be counterproductive. We must therefore find a way to integrate the positive aspects of the postmodern default scenario, which offers a much wider range of freedom and independence for young people, with the requirements the education system must meet in order to maximize the chances for achieving its goals (education towards autonomy, dialogical belonging, and morality):

- Guaranteeing productive experiences within at least some of the experiential domains. The extent and content of the experiences should be determined by educators for each individual separately.
- Constructing a thorough, ongoing, AOE mentorship program, together with AOE tutorage and teaching process, with the experiential educational process at their core. Such a program should guarantee that the various experiences of young people would be accompanied by:
- AOE-based mentorship accompanying young people throughout all their experiences, for an individualized number of years, in order to help them integrate their reflections on these experiments in a way conducive to the development of the desired values.
- AOE-based tutorage specific to each subject in each of the experiential domains.
- AOE-based teaching, when such teaching is deemed necessary for a specific domain.

The optimal way, for achieving the correct balance between freedom and the compulsion is a balance needed to ensure the above educational requirements are met, should lie *within* the educational framework. Only educators who are highly trained in the suggested Humanistic educational framework and who are endowed with comprehensive knowledge and loyalty to AOE principles have a reasonable chance of actually ensuring that each child is supplied with the level of freedom and independence appropriate according to his or her individual profile, while still guaranteeing the minimally required level of appropriate experimentation and reflective mentoring, tutoring, and teaching in the relevant domains.

Thus, an optimal resolution of the tension between freedom and compulsion in the desired educational process consists of:

- Subjecting all young people in a certain age range to the suggested developmental-educational Humanistic processes, initiated or at the very least controlled by the liberal democratic state. This is, to some extent, similar to the prevailing law of compulsory education but with some essential differences:
- The default universal legal compulsion should be much shorter.
- Universal legal compulsion should only be a framework which allows each young individual to go through an educational process of a length and nature optimal for him or her.
- The desired system to which the suggested law relates should not maintain any of the currently prevalent organizational structure, curriculum, or didactics of the modern school.
- Allowing educators the latitude to give their young charges varying degrees of freedom in accordance with their individual needs and developmental stages. Thus, certain students may be exempted from various commitments if their educators believe these are superfluous or, alternatively, the period in

which students remain under the educational aegis may be shortened, again, if the exemption is considered beneficial to that particular student.

To conclude, expansion of the independence and freedom of young people vis-à-vis the educational organization does have clear advantages as long as: (a) the overall educational authority remains mainly in the hands of the liberal states' confirmed educational experts and (b) any decisions made by these experts is guided solely by considerations related to the basic Humanistic educational goals, i.e., of autonomy, morality, and dialogical belonging, and pedagogic principles derived from these goals.

Given these conditions, the degree of the practical operation of the educators' authority can and should change from one student to another; the basic recommendation being that any form of compulsion be reduced to the absolute minimum required to guarantee the student reasonable (not maximal![41]) chances to develop as an autonomous, moral, and dialogically belonging individual.

It is plausible to suppose that the level of compulsion will gradually be reduced as young people mature. Maturity should also include the possibility to exempt certain youngsters from their obligation to the educational framework altogether, if and when the educators responsible conclude they no longer need it.[42]

At this point I wish to address some probable criticism of the above line of thinking. According to such a line of criticism, the argument above is purely theoretic and ignores the following basic facts of life:

- Every social system will eventually stagnate and serve the interests of those managing it, rather than the social objectives it was designed to serve ("the iron law of oligarchy" coined by sociologist Robert Michels).
- Guidance and mentoring, such as those outlined herein as prerequisite to the educational processes, call for a high degree of self-awareness, commitment to the basic educational goals, wisdom, and empathy, without which the functions of guidance and mentoring will deteriorate to nothing more than arbitrary control over young people by adults. Unfortunately, so the counterclaim may continue, only few individuals possess the required attributes and capacities on a sufficiently high level to perform this crucial role.
- The above two facts of life combined practically guarantee, or at least create a very high probability that, stagnation, and all the ills accompanying it, will become a reality.

Therefore, the criticism can continue, even if in theory the proposed education system is preferable to a one-sided augmentation of youthful freedom and independence through solely employing standardized criteria and tests verifying that students have indeed attained the necessary minimum (the expected default scenario), in practice such a system will not work and will quickly become counterproductive. Taking into account the small likelihood that the much more complex and professionally demanding system will be able to operate productively and actualize the desired educational values, a simple, not at all demanding default system is preferable.

Admittedly, the above noted dangers are real. But they are also very real in other prevailing social systems such as legal, welfare, and health, as well as most policing endeavours. Yet abuses of these systems, many of which are very grave indeed, which often do occur, do not cause us to abandon them. Rather, liberal democratic societies have been relying on a complex system of direct controls, checks, and balances which Sisyphically work to prevent or at least limit these abuses to a tolerable degree.

That said, it is very important to be aware of these "guaranteed" abuses when designing an alternative education system. In the case at hand at least two major preventative steps should be taken:

- The level of unnecessary coercion and other kinds of control over young people must be reduced to an absolute minimum in order to prevent, as much as possible, any temptation educators may have to abuse their charges.
- Control mechanisms designed to minimize these dangers, such as state supervision and enabling young people or their parents to initiate any change they desire in the educational process (change the mentor or tutor, change a specific program within the educational framework, change a specific educational framework all together, etc.) should be embedded in the system.

SUMMARY

It is impossible, and, in this context, unnecessary, to envision the precise nature of future social arrangements regarding the status of young people in society and vis-à-vis the education system. What is important to stress at this point in time is that the present situation, in which young people are denied the right to choose the educational services they "consume" or affect the management thereof and are necessarily seen as passive objects of the system, will not remain in place much longer given the following postmodern processes: the disappearance of "childhood"; the collapse of authority; the new perception of "the child as a subject," contrary to the more traditional, paternalistic conception of so-called "childhood"; and the dramatic consequent change in the legal and social status of young people

The basically modern state of affairs has little chance of surviving the post-modern storm. It is reasonable to suppose that within the next two decades, the level of freedom and independence young people enjoy vis-à-vis the education system will significantly increase.

The expected change in the status of young people in society and vis-à-vis the education system is positive as long as (a) it does not lead to a surrender of educational responsibility by the liberal democratic state, (b) it is channelled through a desirable education system, and (c) the desired education system is one which enhances the desired educational process and leads to autonomy, morality, and dialogical belonging, the ultimate Humanistic aims of education.

PART THREE

THE POSTMODERN REVOLUTION IN EDUCATION: ALEATORY OR STRATEGICALLY DIRECTED?

THE IMPORTANCE OF NAVIGATING THROUGH THE POSTMODERN STORM

INTRODUCTION

The outline of the desirable educational organization described in the previous four chapters optimally reflects three groups of considerations:

- The desire to design an education system guided solely by a coherent and exhaustive list of the *ultimate Humanistic educational values*, a list that when properly implemented will best serve Liberal Democracy (the political system that stems from Humanism) and protect it from the dangers it is exposed to in the postmodern era.
- The desire to adapt the education system to the prevailing reality and make it a *functional postmodern system*; or in other terms, a system that mindfully and optimally takes advantage of the prevailing opportunities while overcoming threats in order to best serve the above Humanistic values in the postmodern era.
- The desire to develop an educational program that will be *meaningful* to the young people of our time and their educators.
- The call for the development of such an education system is clearly utopian; its realization requires a change in what, to many, might seem to be the educational "laws of nature." But "utopian" does not mean unfeasible or unrealistic. These "laws of nature" are in many cases nothing but one-hundred-year-old modern conventions, some of which are, admittedly, extensions of far older conventions. More importantly, these conventions, both the wholly modern ones and those having longer roots, are being intensively threatened by the rapidly rising postmodern "tide." Some of them have already been washed away by the incoming waves.

One must bury one's head deep in the sand (if the mounting tide has left any) in order not to see that most of these conventions are no longer viable because of:

- The rapidly increasing incompatibility between the existing modern school and the rising postmodern civilization.
- The decline in the meaningfulness of the curriculum and school activities as a result of the aforementioned schism between the school and the reality in which it functions.
- The increased dysfunctionality and counterproductiveness of the modern school in the postmodern era.

One must also remember that almost no convention that has ruled human life in the West ever managed to escape radical changes in either the modern or the postmodern era. Modern times have witnessed political transition from monarchies to democracies, cultural transition from religion-based societies to secular ones, and economic transition from an agrarian to an industrialized way of life. The establishment of universal suffrage granted women equal rights, the abolishment of slavery freed the black people, and the extended family gave way to the creation of the nuclear family. These are but some of the deeply rooted traditional social conventions swept away by modernity. As for postmodernity, it is quite impossible to think of any sphere in human life based on conventions that the postmodern world has not radically revolutionized. All modern social roles have melted away, including any distinction of roles between men and women, young and old, children and adults. The "traditional" modern nuclear family crumbled to be replaced by legitimization of every imaginable alternative social framework, all sexual orientations and racial minorities have acquired equal rights before the law, and almost all manner of lifestyle are accepted, including voluntary sadomasochism. The only exception, for now, relates to lifestyle choices rooted in voluntary cannibalism.

With the advent of the postmodern age, we are confronted with the replacement of face-to-face relationships with digital encounters. The medical revolution, coupled with the stamp of social legitimacy, has given rise to the alteration of all and any aspects of human physical, and even many psychological, characteristics. Even what would have seemed impossible a decade or two ago, the (allegedly) "eternal" and "necessary" dichotomous distinction between male and female, has all but broken down with the legitimization of an infinite range of intermediate sexes or herma-phroditic genders.[1]

Wherever we look today, the radical trends changing everything we knew about human life cannot be ignored: Chronic suspicion of all meta-narratives including, in fact especially, those that led to modernity; Modern, wholly hierarchic, control-oriented, institutions are being replaced by postmodern, loosely defined, virtual or semi-virtual postmodern organizations; Traditional literacy gives way to "audiovisual literacy;" Radical reconstruction of the "workplace" beyond all recognition: the "disappearance of place," radical change in work security as modern "tenure" is largely replaced by contract-based or freelance work arrangements, often for several organizations at the same time, an ongoing "disappearance of work," while leisure is gradually but obstinately spreading beyond all previously known proportion. This list can, of course, go on and on.

In short, over last twenty or thirty years the "laws of nature," or rather, the basic characteristics of the modern "human situation," have been breaking down and/or undergoing radical revolutionization. Many, if not all, of these revolutions have a direct impact on possible and desirable education. In light of these processes, the education system has no alternative but to also undergo radical change that will transform it into a postmodern system. The existing education system can no longer afford to continue to prepare its graduates for the previous, now almost defunct, modern reality. Just as rural and home- or apprenticeship-based education "systems" of agrarian society had to radically and rapidly adapt, at the end of the nineteenth and beginning of the twentieth centuries, to the needs and demands of the developing industrial society,[2] so too must modern systems cater to the totally different requirements of the postmodern society.

"So why bother?" one may ask. If change is an inevitable consequence of the many revolutions characteristic of the postmodern reality, why should we parents, educationalists, decision makers, parliamentarians, politicians, researchers, and professionals in relevant areas make any conscious or strategic changes? Why not let the erratic changes that have become a chronic part of education over the last generation go on with the hope they will produce another system, better adapted to postmodernity? To use our central metaphor, the ship will land wherever the wind and tide carry it. We can and should patch the sails, replace the broken masts, and do other maintenance to stay afloat. But, why bother to navigate the ship when we have no control over the stormy conditions?

To answer this fundamental question, I will continue with our maritime allegory. The ship's crew (like ourselves) is sailing into new, unknown, and stormy seas. They realize that very little of their knowledge of known winds and currents applies to this ocean. They also realize their compass and charts are mostly useless, and that all sense of destination has been lost. Given this situation, they have two options:

- To be passively swept along and hope that chance will bring them to a safe haven before the vessel founders on rocky shores or hits an iceberg.
- To make haste and do the best they can to help the captain and navigator learn everything they can about the new sea, winds, and currents under the changing conditions, and to set a new course even if such a course and its possible destinations are based on strong hypotheses. As they move on, these hypotheses can certainly be refuted, corrected, and improved. Meanwhile, everyone must struggle to keep the ship afloat through the storm, to set the most sensible course they can, given the limited new knowledge they have succeeded in gathering, and to do their utmost to navigate the ship towards the best destination possible under difficult conditions.

If the ship's crew are rational, and have some common sense and a desire to survive, they will choose the second, mindful option. This option cannot guarantee a safe landing, but it does guarantee that the best means available to human beings, suddenly thrown into unknown conditions, will be applied in order to increase the chances of survival.

As I explained in the introduction to this book, the winds and tides of the postmodern storm have changed human existence at an unprecedented speed and intensity. The modern schooling vessel was designed for totally different and far calmer climatic conditions. At the same time, the ultimate goal of education, to educate towards the sublime values of society, has been forgotten, together with those sublime highest values. As our metaphor illustrates, two courses of action are open to us today in education:

- Either we remain passive and unconcerned with acquiring a systematic and updated general understanding and evaluation of the new human situation and with redefining our educational goals, and thus let ourselves be swept away to wherever the stormy postmodern sea may carry us. We will trust our luck, and busy ourselves only with a growing number of face-saving "reforms" and "restructuring projects," which are nothing but a hopeless series of desperate attempts to "patch up" aggravating maintenance problems stemming from a deep-rooted, untreated problem which is, at the moment, tearing our ship apart limb from limb.

Or,

- We do our very best to face the new, tempestuous situation and its impact on our schools head on, proactively adapt to the new reality, redefine a coherent list of goals, and enact the best navigating strategies we can formulate to not only save our pedagogical vessel, and ourselves, from utter disaster but also to optimize our chances to achieve these goals.

This second strategy should be based on the most adequate knowledge we can acquire given the nature of the turmoil that surrounds us and the new situation it throws us into. It should rely on this knowledge and be inspired by our desired destination, while permanently encouraging the search for empirical feedback which will help corroborate or refute and correct the knowledge we have already attained.

As rational people and possessors of common sense, we must of course take the second course; we must choose mindful and strategic action. Although such action requires, in the short term, much more theoretical, empirical, economic, and physical effort than remaining passive (except for necessary maintenance work), this is, in the long term, the best policy we can adopt. As mindful human beings, we are bound to choose navigating through the storm, however difficult, over allowing ourselves to be passively swept out to sea to be forever lost in its depth.

In this chapter I defend my stance concerning the need for immediate, mindful, and strategic overhauling of all education systems, given the utterly new nature of the postmodern environment in light of Humanistic or liberal democratic values.

My basic argument is as follows:

- The shift of the Western education systems from modern to postmodern footing is inevitable. The only question is whether this transformation is to be based on relevant understanding of the new situation, guided mindfully and strategically by desirable values; or is it to be allowed to take place in an aleatory careless fashion.
- The aleatory way is a default scenario which operates at the moment in all Western societies.[3]
- The aleatory way exacts a horrendous toll from us on three levels:
  - On the practical level, tremendous economic and functional damage stems from making fundamental decisions in "light of" (or rather, in the darkness and ignorance characterizing) tunnel vision and a non-mindful, non-strategic outlook.[4]
  - Far worse than the damage on the practical level, on the psychological level, an aleatory, non-mindful transformation of the education system leads to the effective and permanent transmission of anti-Humanistic values; it thus transforms schools into anti-educational (from a Humanistic or liberal democratic perspective) institutions.[5]

- The same is true on the social level. A horribly high social toll weighs heavily on us as the aleatory process now reinforces undesirable cultural trends that jeopardize the Humanistic and liberal democratic value system. [6]
- Accordingly, developed Western societies must quickly come to their senses and effectuate a mindful, strategically structured, educational transformation guided by desirable values. Or, in the language I used in Chapter One, we must move away from the unconscious anomaly to one of a conscious anomaly, and we must stop passively drifting with the postmodern current and start proactively navigating our educational ship in a predefined, desired direction.7
- If we choose to undergo strategic and mindful transformation, the values in whose light the educational revolution should be guided in liberal democratic societies are the three discussed in this book—autonomy, morality, and dialogical belonging; the ensuing educational process should generally move in the direction which stems from these values as depicted in Part Two.

THE REVOLUTION IS UNAVOIDABLE AND IS ALREADY UNDERWAY

The ship's hull is already strained and cracking. The sailors and officers are aware of the need to do something. They want to appear "professional" to the passengers but actually do not know what must be done, why, or how. For public relations purposes, and to save their rapidly diminishing professional honor, they must do something. So they keep replacing old and not so old planking with new, they swab the decks, paint and repaint everything in sight, and stay hectically busy with many other small-scale repairs. At the same time there is a lot of boastful talk and shouting designed to make their activity as noticeable as possible to the passengers, who are becoming frightened and confused as they look at the stormy seas and hear the increased creaks and groans of the ship.

As can be expected, without a systematic understanding of the powers threatening the ship and ignorant of a clear destination, the crew's actions are "much ado about nothing." All this hectic activity merely placates everyone's psychological and social concerns temporarily, and even that, mostly among the more naïve passengers. Those passengers not taken in by appearances are starting to think, however hesitantly, about taking some action, either seizing complete or partial control of the vessel, or taking to the lifeboats, in effect, creating their own vessel. In fact, the boldest among them have already done just that.

Or in the language of a moral lesson, as the revolutionary currents of postmodernity rapidly render the school meaningless and dysfunctional and as the problems stemming from this situation increase relentlessly, two meaningful categories of change have taken place in education in the last generation. The first, mirroring the crew's loud, hectic maintenance activity, are those feverish "change processes" that sporadically appear within Western education systems and are mainly virtual or "operate" mostly on the discourse and declarations level. The second originates from the concerns of passengers (i.e., parents and communities) seeking to control their destiny, and is the result of very real pressures, exerted by external factors (e.g., parents, communities, etc.). However, these changes still occur mainly in a *de facto* manner and are not fully acknowledged by most public education systems or, if acknowledged, they do not lead to fundamental changes in patterns of thought and action within the established public education systems. For the time being, these systems prefer to stick to the first "much a do about nothing" strategy of coping with the stormy postmodern conditions.

As for the first response to the storm, one cannot avoid noticing, over the past generation, the hectic activity or, rather, talk, focused on "change," "transformation," "innovation," "restructuring," "reforms," and "paradigm shifts" or "second-order changes" that goes on in schools all over the Western world. It is impossible to imagine educational discourse today without the theme of "school change" taking a central role. Still these changes are arbitrary; they fail to reflect a systematic general understanding and mapping of the entirely new situation we suddenly find ourselves in. Additionally, on the macro level, these changes are not grounded in a coherent change strategy guided by clear ultimate ethical goals.[8]

Still, even if only on the declarative, short-term, or local levels, and even if schools are increasingly swirling in a maelstrom of repeated or mutually canceling, short-lived, changes, the emerging change in language is interesting and cannot be ignored. While very far from being effective practically, one can certainly detect plenty of talk about changes, some of which might even constitute a violation of the aforementioned "laws of nature." In all this heated, tumultuous, and mainly self-defeating activity, a new and still extremely chaotic discourse is permeating the system and causing tension between words and deeds, declarations and actions. This tension is gradually growing, becoming less tolerable, and may, in the end, rock the educational "ship."

On the *didactic* level, standardization and hierarchism still dominate the modern school and, over the last two decades, their power has even increased in many Western countries. Still a longer term perspective will show us that these characteristics are being threatened in the last generation by an opposing discourse. It has infiltrated Western education systems on the level of declarations and policy papers, in conceptions of learning and teaching that certainly contradict school's modern structure. I refer to the "obstinate" calls for "active," "constructivist,"[9] or "problem-based learning,"[10] and other variations of more flexible, open-ended learning: "experiential learning," "authentic learning," "in situ learning," "cooperative learning,"[11] and so on. The educational goal underlying these ideas is "the development of an independent autonomous learner." The more open-ended teaching methodology they rely on as well as the move towards "alternative evaluation methods"[12] required by these ideas go beyond and contradict the given hierarchic structure of school and the fragmented, rigid, and closed structure of the curriculum. This deep contradiction is mostly ignored by the captains of education systems, but is clearly there nevertheless.

These catchphrases are frequently heard in connection with the massive computerization process education systems undergo all over the Western world. In contrast to what was accepted in the early days of computerization, it is patently clear to everyone these days that the computer and the Internet should be an integral part of the learning process and encourage the student's "autonomous" "research-oriented" learning either individually or within the framework of "collaborative learning."[13]

At the same time and not totally unrelated, teaching and educational methods emphasizing each student's uniqueness are filtering into the system, though these too primarily remain on the declaratory level ("personalization" of learning is the catchphrase here[14]). There is much discourse about the need to take into account each student's different learning styles,[15] specific intelligence, or fields of interest,[16] as well as to focus on the development of each individual's emotional aspects and personality, and the development of personal and social skills.[17] This discourse certainly contradicts the basic assumption supporting the prevailing standardized and scholastic nature of modern schooling.

On the *organizational* level the system's hierarchical structure is further threatened by the *bon ton* demand of current educational discourse for "autonomy to the schools,"[18] and the development of "school self management"[19] or "experimental schools,"[20] as well as "teachers' empowerment."[21] All these buzzwords contradict the basic linear, centralistic assumptions which still lie at the heart of the prevailing rigid, highly standardized, bureaucratic and technocratic system.

Beyond the changes which take place mainly on the declaratory level, there are some radical changes that do not depend only on schools but stem mainly from very real external influences. For example, the modern school's classic linearity has been increasingly threatened by the lateral hyper-textual structure of the new digital culture which surrounds it and is already infiltrating it. Modern curricular fragmentariness is threatened by many experimental frameworks that encourage inter- or supra-disciplinary learning which have become prevalent in the system.[22] The system's hierarchism is threatened when the laws stipulating every young person must go to (a specific) school allow for "parental choice" or at least an increasing level of choice between schools,[23] though still to a limited extent, and sometimes also permit other educational options such as charter schools and home schooling.[24]

On the *target audience* level, Western systems have undergone a profound change, a change which went, over the past two decades, beyond the purely declarative stage. In earlier decades, schools in most Western societies (Anglophone countries being somewhat exceptional) had only one target audience: the state (or, in some countries, the local authorities). Today, the school has several target audiences whose satisfaction it must enlist besides that of the state:

- The parents, as individual or organized pressure groups;
- Local and national media;
- Industrialists and other socioeconomic power centers who have a vested interest in impacting the nature of the "product" of the educational process;
- Small and large foundations involved in education relying on specific educational agendas;
- Various academic institutions involved in education in light of specific research agenda;

- The local authorities[25] whose power is constantly increasing in many countries and for whom the care for and (mainly) investment in "the future of out children," has become one of the main items in the political agenda or at least in election campaigns; and
- Young people who have recently begun to appear as an organized political force in some education systems.[26]

In many countries, each group has its own, separate, set of demands and expectations without there being a clear definition of each entity's "legitimate territory."

Another radical revolution occurred on the *target audience recruitment*. Ten or twenty years ago recruitment was mandatory and *going to school* was the only practical option for complying with the compulsory education law. However, today's home schooling, flexi-schooling, un-schooling, and charter school movements, where parents take responsibility for their children's education in a myriad of ways, are gaining popularity by leaps and bounds.

Those most closely involved in one area of the change, real or virtual, or in one of the transformation processes, are usually unaware of their relationship with the other processes on other levels. Nor are they cognizant of the common origins of the new discourse or of some of the real external changes and attempts to come to terms with the crisis of the modern school in the postmodern reality. Still I hope that, for the readers of this book, the common source, as well as the insufficiency of the partial and fragmented nature of any of these attempts to overcome the common crisis, is clear.

Education systems in almost all Western societies, despite the meaningful differences between them, are still essentially based on multi-layered compulsion and monopoly. The universal compulsion to go to school still exists; so does the monopoly of one school model, the modern one, which even private schools in most countries rely on. Many states still employ extensive compulsion on parents to register their children to a specific school within the public education system, and even within the school, in most Western states (with the exception of some of the Scandinavian countries) only a limited and rather peripheral range of choice is available to the students.

These multi-layered levels of compulsion and monopoly, typifying the "recruitment" methods of the modern education system, explain the partial, fragmented, hesitant, and mainly declarative response to the postmodern education crisis at this stage. Such a system, which in many countries and for most citizens (still) does not have to face real competition and whose standardized products are compulsorily consumed by a captive audience, has no real motivation to succumb to change and undergo the often painful and very difficult process connected with such change on both the individual and organizational levels. At present, changes are mainly dictated by either policy makers or well-meaning "school change" professionals and most of them never venture beyond declaration or short-lived activities without any real chance for the sustainability or transferability which characterize true reform. Often these are celebrated and "exported" to the internal circles of the system and to external society as great triumphs. And generally, a year or two after the hullabaloo has been forgotten, no one bothers to check what is left of the once triumphantly celebrated changes.

This slow, partial, and unmindful "change," together with its aforementioned resultant declarations-actions gap and the associated "double talk" phenomenon, as well as the atmosphere of no-confidence, will probably go on and on in the foreseeable future. At the same time, increased pressure necessarily arises from outside the system, stemming from impatient parents and educators, independent schooling, home schooling, or un-schooling movements developing today. As a result of this reality changes in the modern school will probably accelerate, but as long as the political will at the higher echelons of decision making is nowhere to be found, the internal changes to education systems will take place only in reckless, non-strategic, and thus unsustainable ways. Meaningful and mindful changes, to the extent that those will take place at all, will prevail mainly in the periphery of established systems and be carried out by frustrated, independent parents and educators.

THE DREADFUL TOLL EXACTED BY THE ALEATORY REVOLUTION

If the above aleatory forces at work are allowed to proceed on their current course, it is very probable that in a decade or two we will have a totally different education system, one that may very well be suited to our time. However, the aleatory or arbitrary "solutions" of this crisis will inevitably be bundled in tremendous cost to the functional, psychological, and socio-ethical levels.

Functional-Economic Damage

In terms of functional-economic damage, the aleatory revolution in the last generation has led to an exorbitant waste of energy, time, and financial resources. It is also responsible for the permanent erosion of the goodwill and trust of teachers, students, and parents. I describe below two significant, and to some extent, connected examples of this horrible wastage:

- The "introduction of computers to the classroom."
- The introduction of active or constructivist learning methods to schools.

The introduction of computers constitutes one of the major, if not the major, change processes, that entire education systems have (mainly declaratively) undergone in several waves in the last generation. These change waves are characterized by:

- Acknowledgement that the global computerization revolution had "changed the world" and that the way things were being done "out there" could not be ignored by the education system.
- A blind belief that technological development equals "advancement" in learning modes and methods and that this revolution can, at the very least, heal all the school's ailments, if not act as a panacea that will miraculously cure everything.

- This is a manifestation of an older phenomenon typical to the ailing Western education systems. This phenomenon can be called "expectation of a *deus ex machina* solution," or, as it has already been dubbed by some writers, the "panacea syndrome," the hope that some magical external factor will suddenly solve all educational problems.
- A deep and "systematic" lack of understanding of the organizational and didactic meaning of "computerization" and hence of the possible way to integrate ICT and the school.
- A lack of understanding of the relationship between the ICT revolution and the other postmodern revolutions, and the deep, inevitable conflict between school culture and the postmodern culture.

The initiatives which are weighed down by these characteristics rely mainly on absent-minded and non-strategic technocratic approaches wherein the mere introduction of computers to the school and (later) to the classroom was considered the epitome of change. The result has been, unsurprisingly, horrendously costly failures!

The goal of the first and second rounds of computerization of education systems, in the early and mid-1980s, was to equip schools with PC laboratories. At the time, the PC was celebrated as an ideal learning machine, which functioned along Skinnerian lines and could lead to individuation of the learning process, adjusting it to the pace and needs of each student using immediate, specific, performance feedback which in turn would contribute (so it was hoped) to higher achievement. The result did not, to put it mildly, live up to the "promise of the PC."

The third wave came in the late 1980s and early 90s and relied heavily on Multimedia and CD-ROMs. This wave was celebrated as encouraging a more "hands-on," active, and constructive approach to learning. This time, the computers went into the classrooms, the idea being to integrate them into current curricular teaching. States and central authorities became the main players of that era, leading education systems through sweeping and very costly "change processes." The results, again, fell short of the promise. Most teachers could not really "get their heads around" the computer phenomenon or see how they could take advantage of it; some of them did not believe that there were any advantages to be had at all. To put it mildly, yet again no real improvements to the ways or levels of teaching or learning had occurred.

The fourth wave in the late 1990s consisted of connecting all schools to the Internet, which was considered by many (again) to be a "panacea" to all educational problems and a major enhancement to the desired constructivist, personalized, collaborative approaches to learning. However, as we could by now predict, this too had a disappointing impact. No real sustainable and transferable educational change accompanied the huge investment and the promising discourse.

During these highly expensive rounds of change, very few people seemed to question whether the schools were ready to go through the designated processes. Nor was any thought given to the notion of delaying the relentless computerizing campaign, at least for a few years, until the foundations for radical school transformation necessitated by the "clash of civilizations" (modern, book-based school civilization vs. the postmodern digital civilization) were put in place.

Had computerization been implemented with a more prescient understanding of the postmodern digital revolution, its far-reaching effects on every aspect of life, and its close connection with other postmodern revolutions, decision makers would probably have steered clear of the four costly, large-scale "injections" of ICT into modern book-based education systems, which was, at the time, very far from being ready for comprehensive internalization of ICT. Or, if mindfully deciding to "go for it, they should have accompanied the computerization process with a large-scale redefinition of all school parameters.

Had educational strategists acted mindfully (or if there had been any such strategists) they would have tackled the dilemma (at least from the second wave onward) with determination and forethought. They would have either radically restructured education systems in order to render them postmodern and compatible with ICT culture, or they would have, at the very least, refrained from permanent and costly injections of non-relevant ICT equipment and inappropriate training until "postmodernization" of the systems had taken place one way or another.

Support for the second possibility might have come about had mindful planners (unfortunately not an existing species) recognized three other groups of facts that have been obvious for at least a decade and probably more:

In the last twenty-five years, the digital revolution consisted of several stages: from the PC revolution to the Internet revolution, and now to the revolution also referred to as "ubiquitous computing" which contains a rapid spread of palm pilots, third- and fourth-generation mobile telephones equipped with cameras and GPS, notebooks, digital imaging, and various wearable devices. In this last revolution, knowledge is everywhere, and one can connect to the Internet from everywhere and at anytime using a multitude of small handy gadgets. In this reality of ubiquitous computing, "PC laboratories" or "PCs in the classroom" quickly became obsolete, often before they could be put to any effective, meaningful use due to teachers' rejection of them out of fear, antagonism, and the PCs' lack of technological maturity.

Without meaningful "additional budgets" dedicated to the permanent upgrading of PCs as well as to PC repairs and maintenance (budgets that in most cases were not allocated or not sufficiently allocated), the extremely large budgets expended in the first place for purchasing PCs quickly became wasteful in the extreme.

The array of computerized equipment young people have in their homes or on their persons has necessarily been, and will always be, more advanced and sophisticated than that which slow-reacting, cash-strapped bureaucracies can provide to schools. There was never even the slightest chance that schools could compete in this area with most students' homes or wearables. The question that should have been, but was never, asked is: Why should we invest enormous resources in school computerization? Can we not rely instead on privately owned students' "computerization power" and restrict public expenditure to subsidizing those who cannot afford to purchase this "power" themselves?

The facts basic to the previous points have all been obvious, at least in the last decade. They should have alerted (non-existing) mindful planners to abstain from the huge, wasteful, and primarily futile injections of computer hardware into the otherwise financially confined education systems, or at least to think twice before doing so. However, if a decision was made to "go for it," in spite of all the predictable hardships, appropriate steps for overcoming these hardships should have been taken.

The ideal, mindful, and strategic planner should have also compared the added value of such technological injections and all the unavoidable hardships that must be systematically overcome with that of the added value of investing in and dealing with different, perhaps more urgent, system adjustments, such as raises in teachers' salaries (which reside at the bottom of salary ladder in many Western countries, an obvious obstacle to any meaningful improvement of, or change in, education) or a reduction of pupil populations in the classroom (still far too large in many Western countries). Our ideal planners would probably have concluded that given the multitude of needs mentioned above, investing in one or more of the alternatives would probably have returned much higher remunerations.

They could have also reached, relying on different assumptions or different interpretations or responses to the last set of facts, the absolute opposite conclusion. They could have made the huge investments in computing, but those would have been accompanied by a radical top-down transformation of the education system and only if findings showed that relying on students' privately owned "computing power" would not be possible or effective in the new postmodern education system. Such a step would also have made sense.

But reckless and unmindful as they were, they took (I cannot say "chose," because in almost all cases alternatives were not really considered) the easy way, which was also the "worst of all possible worlds" way: they followed the "introduction of computers into the classroom" without any attempt to revolutionize the school accordingly or to incorporate students' private computing power and without guaranteeing the meaningful sums necessary for maintenance and upgrading. And so we see, yet again, the unavoidable failures.[27]

The other related example of wasted resources and effort is the attempt to transition the education systems into *active* or *constructivist learning*. Many associate this form of learning with computerization but it has also had an intensive life of its own. The term "active learning" reflects an approach according to which learning stems from the student, either as an individual or as a group member, coping with a "real problem" (also referred to as an "authentic problem") which originates in the individual's or the group's interest or situation. In this approach the student actively determines, or is at least involved in determining, the parameters for dealing with the given problem.

This learning trend is not postmodern. It has philosophical roots in common understandings of Rousseau[28] and was systematically developed by Dewey and his progressive followers in the 1920s. After its 1920s and 30s heyday, it flourished again in the 1960s and 70s when many radical critics of the prevailing schools supported it. In its postmodern version it is largely supported by cognitive and brain research as well as analysis carried out by postmodern organizational theorists. According to widely accepted research, active learning is precisely the kind of practice students need in order to function later in their lives, as employees, entrepreneurs, and citizens of a changing postmodern world.[29]

Since at least the early 1980s, a wide range of variations of the discourse about active learning has been in vogue, at least on the declarative level, in academic circles and in education systems. In the latter part of this era, the idea got a meaningful boost from the popular view that it (allegedly) fit in well with ICT. As a result, during the past generation, significant efforts to advance active learning in schools throughout the Western world were made using different methods and in different contexts. However, active learning has clearly not pervaded the education system in any meaningful way, with or without the connection to computing.

Had decision makers given more incisive thought to the matter, they would have concluded that active, research-oriented learning contradicts the prevailing Platonic curriculum, the modern hierarchic, lococentric, and rigid organizational structure, and the practical technocratic goals of the modern school; as such the notion had no chance to begin with of being truly integrated into the prevailing modern education systems. As noted in Chapter Four, no researcher is able to seriously study some ten or twelve subjects simultaneously, or seriously study one subject when he or she has to deal with ten others at the same time in a predetermined timetable of approximately forty-five minutes per subject with twenty to forty other random people. No teacher can seriously instruct hundreds of people in research-oriented learning in one day or even in one week, especially when what she or he is actually made to care for are the quantifiable achievements of students, a goal which stands in direct contradiction with that of the enhancement of active learning.

As long as the theoretical curriculum and its inherent disciplinary structure continue to dominate the system and as long as the rigid, hierarchical organizational structure of the school remains in place and the technocratic goals of schooling consist solely of achieving higher grades in light of quantifiable universal standards, there is no likelihood of true research-oriented or active learning taking root.[30]

Had decision makers in Western education systems considered and comprehended these facts, they would have either supported more radical changes in the curriculum, structure, goals, and other basic parameters of education or avoided the vain attempts to introduce active learning altogether. Either way, they would have saved the taxpayers a king's ransom that was, and is still being, wasted on hundreds of thousands of training programs designed to advance the various types of research-oriented learning all over the world. They could have spared teachers the terrible sense of frustration created by the gap between what is expected of them and what they are capable of doing under existing conditions and constraints. They could also have spared feelings of confusion and lack of trust among students and parents which resulted from the huge differences between declaratory intentions and their failure to be fulfilled.

Instead, they tried to eat the cake—enhance constructivist learning—and have it, too, avoiding any meaningful change of the school, leading to all the aforementioned consequences.

These are not the only examples of harbingers of postmodern changes at mainly the discourse and declaratory levels, and the inevitable costly and work-intensive failures that ensue on the practical level. Gaps between declaration and reality included, among others, announcement of autonomous or self-managing schools, whose execution was engulfed in very thick fog around the limits and nature of their autonomy and freedom and the vogue of celebrating various kinds of "innovative" processes which amounted to nothing more than a thick layer of declarations about "experiential schools," "innovative learning methods," "the encouragement of change," the "restructuring" or "transformation of the school," "the empowering of teachers," etc., which have decorated the "good (or bad) old" school culture, which has remained essentially unchanged. These lacunae are the result of attempts "to square the circle" or to realize (a fake realization at that) postmodern modes of actions in systems that are still modern through and through.

The result of these discrepancies is phenomena chronic to education in the post-modern era described such as "the myths of school self–renewal," "the predictable failure of school reform," "tinkering towards utopia," and "a Century of failed school reforms."[31]

Beyond all the enormous, ongoing waste of time and money, the most precious resource we lose because of these exercises in futility are the teachers', students', and parents' belief and trust in the positive effects of new "initiatives," "projects," or "reforms." The consequence of the long string of failed projects, reforms, and "change enterprises" accompanied by an increasing lack of enthusiasm, was the development of a language of "double talk" in the education system, one which did not exist in the past and has no equal (certainly not to the extent manifested in the education system) in other public systems today.

The language used when speaking about education has already become, to a large extent, a postmodern language, one which expresses the reality outside the system and the demands such a reality imposes on the system. But the reality within the education system remains essentially modern, and therefore behind the times, in fact even backward-looking. In order to cope with this ever-growing divergence, teachers, school administrators, and policy makers have adopted "double talk." On the one hand, they speak using postmodern jargon about "research-oriented learning," "authentic learning programs," "encouraging students' interest," "advanced applications in computerization," "portfolio-based learning," "alternative evaluation," "empowering school teams," "encouraging initiatives," "advancing creativity," "encouraging autonomous learning," "developing emotional intelligence," "taking different learning styles and intelligences into account," "developing a school vision," "self-management of the school," "enhancing educational leadership," "supporting experimental schools," or "learning for understanding" or "critical thinking," that should all lead to "striding optimistically towards the year 2000 (in the recent past), 2010, 2020," and on and on.

But at the same time, these experts, decision makers, and educationalists also talk about an institution in which even their great-grandfathers would feel at home; while, in contrast to the school, if they were to wander into a contemporary hi-tech company or hospital, they would be completely lost.

The results of this dissonance are "double talk, a glitch between language and reality in school discourse; the disappearance of the naïve view that declarations and objectives demand adequate application and action; and the introduction of an atmosphere of suspicion and cynicism regarding the language of change or any high level declaration about educational goals.[32]

Clearly, an organization in which these characteristics exist is an ailing one at that. As we can see, up until now the heavy organizational damage caused by "double talk" consists "only" of growing dysfunctionality but has not necessarily led to the organization's destruction. But can anyone imagine what educational damage is caused to generations of young people who grow up in a reality where, in order to survive, they must learn that words are empty of meaning (at least their allegedly lateral meaning), and whose goals are demagogic declaratory statements that cannot stand up to the test of realization?

Probable Psychological Damage

The previous point leads us straight into the second type of damage caused by the aleatory changes in today's education systems: the psychological damage to the students. This damage is the result of the compelled teaching of a theoretical curriculum, which was justifiable and meaningful in the past but has lost its meaning for the students (and teachers) in the postmodern age, as shown in Chapter Three. Today, the only reason for the students to persevere through twelve years of theoretical learning is to "graduate," to conquer what is perceived as a mandatory stepping stone to achieving an academic degree which still represents to many a means to securing socioeconomic success (whether such hopes are justifiable is no longer clear).

As shown in Chapter Three, the message systematically conveyed in the current reality, wherein young people are compelled to study content that has no meaning for them, except (allegedly) as a long-term tool for socioeconomic success, is that life is absurd. In such an absurd reality nothing has intrinsic meaning and every action is justified only by its service to some remote objective. If anything does have long-term meaning, it is the race for money and social power and the pleasures these can (allegedly) provide (after all, isn't that what "climbing the socioeconomic ladder" euphemistically stands for?). The search for the meaning of life or a guiding worldview is necessarily conceived as a waste of time, because such fanciful ideas divert the student's attention from studying for final exams, matriculation, or the SATs, which are the ultimate, overriding goal.

This message, which the school consistently conveys, reinforces the nihilist messages systematically transmitted to young people through television, the Internet, and the relativistic-positivistic-nihilistic worldview currently dominant among the scientific, economic, and political elites.[33] Moreover, it intensifies the anxiety, panic, and often despair felt by young people in the face of the infinite range of choices and intensity of dynamism and chaos that characterize the postmodern reality. These emotions contribute, in turn, to the escape mechanisms young people are bound to develop in the face of postmodern turmoil: violence, student-instigated shooting and massacre incidents in schools, suicide, drug addiction, and alcohol abuse, all of which are on the rise among youth in recent decades. These emotions also directly contribute to the currently "popular" syndromes of depression and anxiety, whose spread has reached epidemic proportions in the postmodern era among adults and even moreso among youngsters.[34]

To fully comprehend the severity of the school's "contribution" to the psychological degeneration characterizing our day and age, we have to understand the nature of what may be termed "the postmodern panic,"[35] its roots, the distress it radiates, and the psychological dangers it embraces. To this end we will digress from our main argument and "open parentheses" within which we will examine the nature of this period and the panic characterizing it. Our digression here is essential to understanding the enormity of the psychological and social dangers stemming from the loss of meaningfulness of the theoretical curriculum.

We live in a period characterized by an unprecedented combination of three processes:
- A dramatic increase in the freedom and range of choice available to individuals in Western societies.
- The collapse of firm value systems that, until recent past, guided individuals through a much more limited set of choices.
- The disappearance or destabilization of all the social institutions from which individuals, until the recent past, drew the security, mental strength, and resilience that enabled them to deal with the dilemmas and troubles of human existence.

In the next few pages I shall elaborate on these three processes.

1. In every aspect of our lives today, we contend with a range of choices that our grandparents, parents, and in many cases, we ourselves up to twenty years ago, never dreamed possible. This is true in everything pertaining to where we live, our professional occupation, our interpersonal and family relationships as well as cultural affiliation, not to mention our choice of clothes, gadgetry, physical appearance, and even the central characteristics of our psychic structure, sexual orientation, and identity.

Previous generations had not even dreamt of such possibilities of choice in the majority of the aforementioned spheres. First, there was no technological wherewithal to perform a rhinoplasty, hair implants, or sex changes and therapeutic or drug treatment for behavioral change or mitigating anxiety were not available; if there existed earlier versions of these procedures, they were primitive, non-effective, or very expensive. Second, there was an absolute social taboo on "illegitimate" sexual tendencies or sex change operations. The limited range of choice available from the technological and normative standpoints in areas like choice of clothes, housing, or occupation was mostly in name only as the vast majority of Western populations lacked the means to take advantage of such choices, even when those were formally available.

In contrast, today's technology, the increased economic and political power and rise in standard of living of the middle class, the massive growth of this class, and the relativistic and pluralistic approaches dominant in Western culture, have turned what was unthinkable two or three decades ago into something taken for granted by many millions of human beings today.

Just take the massive increase in available products from which we may choose in everyday life. The average late-nineteenth/early-twentieth-century "general store" displayed a few dozen products and usually had only one version of each. Now, huge shopping centers open to citizens of the prevailing postmodern societies offer a variety of hundreds of thousands of products, each represented by dozens of brand names. Moreover, the whole world is now becoming an infinitely huge marketplace "thanks" to the Internet, with almost unlimited numbers and types of products available to millions of customers wherever they live.[36]

This vast range of possibilities and choices open to the majority of individuals in Western societies cannot but create severe distress and mental pressures in the individual. This is why postmodernity is described as "the era of panic," panic resulting from the unbounded variety, from the fear one is always "missing something," from the inevitability that for every choice one makes, another "better one" lies waiting around the corner, whether it is computer software, a business association, or the choice of a life partner.[37]

2. This panic is intensified by another significant factor. At precisely the same time that our range of freedom and choices widened beyond all known proportions, the value systems that guided people in the past in the relatively few choices and decisions they had to make were severely undermined.

While individuals in traditional societies were guided by religious values, individuals in modern societies, following the "death of God," were guided by a small number of ideologies and combinations thereof: Scientism, Humanism, Socialism, Nationalism, and "thick liberalism." By the term "thick liberalism," I refer to the liberal view which flourished in nineteenth-century Britain and went much beyond and against the "laissez-faire" economic approach now identified with liberalism, often referred to as "neo-liberalism." Thick liberalism embraces the belief in the self-realizing individual and the welfare, *solidaire*, society which supports this self-realization. In the second generation of the era characterized by "the end of ideology," these ideologies have been badly shaken or crumbled altogether.

Let us start with Scientism, one of the two foundational credos of the Enlightenment and modernity (the second, Humanism, is discussed below). The inherent belief of the ideology is that reason alone as expressed in rational and scientific methodology can solve all human problems. Scientism's control of Western minds and attitudes has greatly declined to become just another one of the various approaches guiding decision making today. Thus, for example, a sick or injured person (say) thirty years ago went to a "conventional" doctor (a term that in those far-off days was hardly known or used, because then there were relatively few "non-conventional" doctors or therapists or "alternative" medicines available to the public and those few were too expensive for most people's standard of living). Today however, the patient, faced with the ongoing erosion of the dominant scientific paradigm, must decide whether to see a conventional doctor or an "alternative doctor." Once the patient opts for the latter, he or she must choose a type of alternative medicine: Chinese, Tibetan, Native American, homeopathic, naturopathic, herbal therapy, Bach flower therapy, reflexology, and so forth and so on.

The defining point here is not that people today have so many more choices than their parents had thirty years ago (this was the previous point), but that they have no guiding paradigm (rational-scientific paradigm or any other) they can employ as an "ultimate paradigm" to guide them through the endless options they face. Each of these (therapeutic) methods is embedded in its own paradigm and is therefore frequently incommensurate with the paradigms of other methods, and even if they were comparable, far too much data is involved in the comparison process for the lay consumer to make an informed decision.[38]

Someone suffering from a psychological, family, or economic problem, or even confronted with an architectural decision will face a similar quandary. In these contexts too, "the man (or woman) on the street" in Western culture might just as legitimately approach a rabbi, a "saintly" man, a fortune teller, or a feng-shui master instead of, or together with, approaching an accepted "expert" operating within the scientific-rationalist paradigm, namely, a psychologist, marriage counselor, economist, or architect.

Here, too, beyond the multiplicity of approaches, the central problem is that no system of "scientific" or rational criteria can help the individual to choose one of them, because each method (including the Western ones) is "contained" in and defended by its own paradigm and there is no ultimate paradigm to help one choose between such vastly differing options. The rational scientific paradigm functioned as such an ultimate paradigm in the modern era. This privileged status it enjoyed to the exclusion of any rival paradigm was one of modernity's main characteristics. In less than a generation it has lost the privileged status, leaving us with no solid ground, no unquestionable foundation to rely on when choosing among competing claims concerning any aspect of our life and well-being.[39]

Let us turn now to Humanism, the second foundational credo of the Enlightenment and modernity, espousing the belief in the universal dignity of all human beings. It is certainly still very much the constitutional pillar of Western democracies and has (often unconscious) meaningful impact on most of their citizens' worldviews, but at the same time it is being severely attacked and eroded in our relativistic era. On the one hand, various multi-culturalists demand (and often get) legitimization and support for non- or anti-Humanist views, and on the other, ethical relativism breeds vulgar cynicism à la *Clockwork Orange* of the previous generation, expressed in this generation by any of Tarantino's films that actually sanctify "casual murder" or "murder for fun." In an age which believes that "everything goes" or that "it all depends on your perspective," the sanctity of the "rights of man" that were meant to defend the basic values of human dignity has been gravely eroded.

Variations of Scientism and Humanism were the supporting pillars of Modernity. Once the first crumbled and the second became severely threatened, the foundations of their offspring—Socialism, Nationalism, and thick liberalism—were shaken too.

I do not think much has to be said about the foundering of Socialism and Communism in the last generation, the dramatic weakening of Nationalism on both sides of the Atlantic, and the metamorphosis of thick liberalism into thin or neo-liberalism. Thin liberalism represents the one-dimensional conception of the individual as either a consuming or producing agent. As opposed to thick liberalism, this extremely thin belief system cannot and does not pretend to support the individual in his or her existential or other meaningful decisions.

Thus, the irony of history has placed us at a crossroads where the exponential increase in human choice and consumption alternatives intersects with the crumbling of worldviews and values which in the past served as a solid foundation for our decision making processes from inestimably fewer choices within far more limited ranges. From this standpoint, we may liken ourselves to people who have to build the tallest skyscraper in history on what retrospectively turns out to be sandy ground that has suddenly begun shifting (if the metaphor of the "Tower of Babel" comes to mind here, it does indeed seem to be appropriate).

3. This ironic and dangerous combination is exacerbated by a third factor: the collapse of almost all the social institutions that were, in one way or another, responsible for education and socialization, and which could have given young people and adults alike the psychological resilience to face postmodern hardships. I refer here to four main institutions.

- Religious communities stopped functioning as educating/socializing institutions for the majority of the population in Western societies back in the modern age.
- Neighborhood communities were extremely meaningful for young people and adults in rural or urban settings during the modern era. Take, for example, the phenomenon of "the neighborhood crowd" which many of us (at least those forty-something and above) can still remember. This reality is disappearing with the move of increasing segments of the population into high-rise buildings in urban areas or to suburbs outside these areas. Either way, in addition to the impersonal elevators or high garden fences, people are shutting themselves off at home with their television sets and Internet-connected computers, where most of their acquaintances are to "be found." Many of them are also permanently traveling and changing working and living locations, and hence do not really belong to any local community or neighborhood. These phenomena, all "normal" aspects of the postmodern era, have led to the disappearance of the "neighborhood crowd" as a viable source of support for most individuals in postmodernity.
- The modern nuclear family that used to be the individual's bastion of power, stability, and education is now undergoing a process of deconstruction in a reality in which both parents (when there are two parents) aspire to succeed in their individual, external to the home, careers, an aspiration which demands long hours at work and frequent travel in support of a career that is immanently insecure and requires living in constant tension. Additionally, we live in a reality of high divorce rates (at least in many Western counties), where approximately twenty-five percent of children are raised in single-parent families, and only a little less than half the young people grow up in families where both parents are also their birth parents.[40]
- Furthermore, the process of the disappearance of childhood, that is, the blurring of differences between children and adults as defined in the height

of modernity, has created a situation where children are "raised" by parents who undergo identity crises and processes of "searching for themselves" which in the recent past were only legitimate longings (if at all) for young people. In many cases today, children are doing the parenting; instead of getting support and security from their parents and family, they often feel in times of personal, family, or economic crises that they have to play the role of "adults" for one or both of their parents. In such a reality, it is becoming increasingly unrealistic, especially for many young people, to rely on the family as a source of stability, continuity, and self-confidence.[41]

- In the modern era, the workplace functioned for many as a source for social support and stable identity. Today, as tenure is quickly becoming the province of but a fortunate few, as individuals change careers several times in their lifetimes, and as most employees work on the basis of either individual short- or long-term contracts or freelancing, often with several organizations at the same time, as many work from home and seldom if at all meet their "colleagues," and as the proportion of time spent working in our lives is gradually but steadily reduced, the "workplace" has ceased to be a meaningful concept for many people. It certainly cannot function as the stable source of social support, belonging, and identity for individuals anymore.[42]

I have reviewed three concomitant processes here: the exponential leap in range of available choices on all levels of the individual's life, the loss of any solid value systems to guide human choice, and the ongoing disappearance of social institutions that previously provided stability and security for young people and adults. Each of these processes suffices to create, for both young people and adults, an unprecedented, amorphous, and chaotic situation transmitting existential *ennui* and social anomie. When combined, these processes threaten the individual's identity and "oneness," a phenomenon known as the deconstruction, disappearance, or saturation of the self.[43] These largely decrease the chances for a sustainable experience of well-being, and bring about the aforementioned stress, panic, and depression.

Here ends the description, characterization, and analysis of what I earlier called "postmodern panic," an extraordinary and unprecedented situation in the annals of humankind which endangers the chances of any individual living in postmodern society to conduct a satisfying life. As a result, it also endangers the continued existence of Western democracies as I will show in the following section. Now that we have considered the severity of the human condition in the postmodern era, we can "close the parentheses" we opened a few pages ago and return to our primary discussion on the psychological damage caused by the loss of meaningful education and by the lack of any mindful strategic response to this phenomenon by Western education systems.

In a reality characterized by postmodern panic, we might have expected the education system to assume responsibility and help young people cope with this panic, its causes, and its resultant psychological pressures and distress. *This educational role is a more important function than any other function education systems were ever entrusted with fulfilling in the past.* In the past, the educational message conveyed by education organizations only reinforced messages, which had in any case been conveyed by other socialization agents: the church, the local community, the extended or (later) nuclear family, and the workplace. Today, on the other hand, the educational message must overcome the opposing messages conveyed by the environment, and repair, as much as possible, the damage these are causing. *There is no other stable socialization organization available that is able to systematically take this mission on.*

In short, this means taking responsibility for overthrowing the modern curriculum that has become, in postmodernity, absurd and educationally counterproductive, and forming an educational program aimed at humanistic education along the lines of the program described in Chapter Seven and other chapters of Part Two.[44] This program should aim to help individuals to coherently shape their identities as autonomous, moral, and dialogically belonging people and accord their lives with meaning so that they have a chance for a meaningful, satisfactory life, even in postmodernity.

But as we have seen, *education systems all over the Western world are abandoning their duty to educate particularly in this reality.* They then add insult to injury: not only are they not helping young people understand and cope with the postmodern chaotic and panic-evoking existential environment, but through their nihilistic, narrowly materialistic and egoism-enhancing messages they are systematically ignoring, frustrating, and delegitimizing young people's craving for a meaningful life and self-realization. Hence, they are greatly exacerbating the situation.

Social Damage

The above discussion leads us into the third type of damage resulting from the growing absurdity of Western education systems and their unmindful and hesitant attempts to respond to the challenges of postmodernity: the grave social danger. The postmodern processes I have described bring about the "saturated self" phenomenon.[45] Here, the self is faced on the one hand by the absence of clear value systems and stable socialization agents, and on the other by an unprecedented abundance of information, contradictory points of view, and overwhelming choices. The self thus becomes Woody Allen's "person-chameleon" (*Selig*) or the deconstructed person (*Deconstructing Harry*), or Robert Musil's *The Man without Qualities*, or Nietzsche's "last man"[46]—the psychological type that was predicted by Musil and Nietzsche to emerge as (what we might call today) the "postmodern human species."

A liberal democratic society needs to rely on its citizens' personal autonomy and morality, both requiring the important characteristic of responsibility: citizens' responsibility for themselves (basic to autonomy) and their responsibility for their fellows (basic to morality). The liberal democratic society cannot prevail for long as a socio-psychological reality if it continuously erodes personal continuity and stability, thus rendering the existence of individuals' responsibility towards themselves or their fellow citizens an unsustainable phenomenon. The erosion of the self and hence of responsibility leads directly to the weakening of the main sustaining fabric of Liberal Democracy and Humanistic society.

In the longer term, it is likely that if this process continues, democracy will become, as Plato predicted for every democratic society, anarchic in the negative sense of the concept, that is, stricken by social *anomie* and lawlessness. Such a society is likely to be eroded from within or to be relatively easily overpowered by external anti-democratic forces.[47] Or in the even longer term the second part of Plato's prophecy—anarchy becoming a tyranny or dictatorship—will likely come to pass.

In more up-to-date terms, in two similar, though much less radical, processes in the last century, the (relatively) high degree of freedom and the erosion of guiding social values created "escape from freedom" mechanisms, which in turn encouraged the rise of nationalistic and fascist trends in Western societies. In other words, the escapist majority created the climate for the nationalist or fascist minority to establish totalitarian regimes rooted in their ideologies. This process led to two horrible world wars, even though the degree of freedom and the undermining of social value-frameworks were at a far lower level at that time than today.[48] In recent years we are again witnessing significant buds of anti-democratic social trends in Western countries, and their conversion into significant political forces.[49] At the same time we are also being confronted with a meaningful increase in external Moslem fundamentalist, anti-democratic pressures. These extremist elements, which are thriving in many Moslem and Western societies, (rightly) take the above processes in Western democracies to be signs of moral decadence and social weakness which will allow them eventually to overcome the corrupt West.[50] The high likelihood of these tendencies increasing in influence and force constitutes a great internal and external danger to the very existence of liberal democratic society in the coming decades.

WHAT ARE THE DESIRED ALTERNATIVES?

If we accept this analysis of the expected consequences of the aleatory process of change in the education system, the question arises: What other possibilities are open to us? Which of them are desirable? To answer these questions, we can describe the education system's expected future from two complementary points of view:

• Worldviews which are likely to be dominant in future postmodern education.
• Future ownership of educational organizations.

From the *first standpoint*, out of the ashes of the modern ideologies that have directed education over recent generations, four categories of alternatives arise: the technocratic, religious, fascist, and Humanist approaches. The technocratic approach totally renounces striving for the meaning or purpose of life (at least as being an important public concern in Liberal Democracies) and, at least practically, encourages the view that life is built on arbitrary, meaningless processes and that the best way for the individual to live in such a reality is by aspiring to maximize material pleasures. In this setup education is conceived as a process designed to help the individual climb up the socioeconomic ladder as high as possible in order to maximize the options available for fulfilling one's desires and cravings.

The religious, Humanistic, and fascist alternatives come out against the nihilism arising from the technocratic approach and preach belief in a meaningful life which takes precedence over momentary fulfillment of individual cravings and desires. The various religious approaches derive this meaning from a transcendental source, that is, a spiritual entity beyond this world (God in the monotheistic religions) perceived as being responsible for the existence and direction of material reality, and from Scriptures that lay out the true way to closeness to this entity through following its commandments.

In contrast to the religious approaches, the Humanistic perspective derives meaning from immanent decisions. These decisions can reflect the desire to follow one's interest or vocation as recommended by the Humanistic approach I rely on in the second part of this book, or by deciding to follow some ultimate moral maxim or any existential principle (as Sartre's protagonists do). The fascist approach may rely on either religious or secular (e.g., pseudo-scientific) foundations, or on an opportunistic combination of both. They have consisted in the past and probably will consist in the future of the attempt to fill in the vacuum created by the technocratic approach with the sanctification and glorification of a certain national or ethnical collectivism depicting the individual life as subordinate to the collective.

In these three frameworks, arising today out of a reaction to the void of technocracy, education is perceived as a process designed to help the individual understand the meaning of life and to develop the abilities and commitments necessary for following and realizing this understanding.

Clearly, among the religious approaches to education, there are infinite divisions between and within the monotheistic religions depending on the ways they define the spiritual entity and its dictates. Beside the monotheistic religions Western reality also witnesses anthroposophy and the increasingly popular Buddhist, Hindu, and mystical approaches that have entered or remerged within it. All these worldviews can serve and have in the past served as educational foundations. The same is true of fascist approaches that can and have referred to many national and ethnic groups and can have socialist, religious, or scientific nuances or sometimes even a kind of liberal nuance.

The Humanist outlooks are also divided, particularly in their answers to the question: What is the source of the human decisions about the meaning of life? And, therefore, where in the educational process does the focus lie? Does it lie in the individual (Humanistic education emphasizes self-expression as I have sought to develop in previous chapters), in the local community (communitarian education), the nation (national education), or in all humankind (education towards commitment to ecological values and values of equality between the world's rich and poor societies)? Or maybe it should refer to a combination of all or some of the above levels?[51]

As things are, all four of these worldviews and their spin-offs and combinations are candidates to function as leading education systems or organizations in prevailing postmodern Liberal Democracies, especially the three approaches that in one way or another threaten Liberal Democracy: the technocrat, the religious, and the fascist (explicated below).

287

From the *second standpoint*, it appears that in the near future the ownership of educational organizations and processes will gradually move from the state or local authorities to the community, parents,[52] industry, and ideological and religious organizations.[53]

The default or dominant educational view in the majority of these frameworks, except those administered by religious or ideological organizations, seems to be the technocratic approach. But in reaction to technocracy and in the wake of its value-existential vacuum, the resultant frustration of the human need for meaning in life will gradually lend religious and fascist education strength and influence in the longer term. Humanistic education has the least chance of developing naturally because, in comparison to the immediate gratification arising from the various religious and fascist views, its promise of meaning is less immediate, less accessible, and harder to digest for most individuals seeking quick, simple answers.

As I have claimed above, this educational approach is the only one that can preserve the existence and durability of Liberal Democracy, *therefore the liberal democratic state must invest heavily and unrelentingly in the realization and fostering of Humanistic education.* Liberal democratic societies must fight the default scenarios: educational views that are clearly anti-Humanistic and the transfer of control of education to non-governmental, non-nationally elected forces that should act as the defenders of Humanistic education.

The last point does not translate into a ban on home schooling, charter schools, or private schools. I believe that a liberal state should not limit the rights of its citizens to educate their children by themselves (either through home schooling, flexi-schooling, or charter schools) as long as those who do so do not deviate from morality or endanger their children's development or cause realistic danger to the state or to any segment of its citizens. Thus, at its heart my recommendation is positive rather than negative. It is not to ban education that is not state controlled, but rather to encourage state-controlled Humanistic public education and a strategic, systematic attempt to render it more attractive than its rivals.

The Humanistic approach recommended in Part Two of the book, Autonomy Oriented Education (AOE), strives to preserve the core values of Humanism in postmodernity, through AOE's three basic goals: developing the individual's auto-nomy, morality, and dialogical belonging. I believe that AOE, through the trio of values at its core, provides an optimal balance between one's self-interests and one's concern for the well-being of others: one's family, community, nation, and all humankind and its environment. I also believe that this version of the Humanistic educational view also optimally combines Liberal Democracy's basic principles, the main patterns of postmodernity, and the desire to develop a meaningful edu-cational program in the current climate. I have dedicated the second part of the book to substantiating these claims. Still, it is certainly the case that others might prefer different balances among the basic commitments of the individual within the Humanistic framework, or would opt for a different version of the basic Humanistic view. The discourse about the best expression of Humanist values and their optimal and meaningful operationalization in postmodern democratic societies should be an ongoing discussion at the foundation of education in these societies. This chapter endeavors to emphasize that the liberal democratic state must strive consciously and systematically towards the realization of these or similar views by identifying the postmodern forces which are working to effect fundamental changes in the education system and try to harness these trends to achieve education's Humanistic goals.

SUMMARY

Increasingly powerful postmodern forces are threatening and undermining all the foundational characteristics of the existing modern education system in Western societies. As a result education systems are undergoing what seems to be an endless series of changes and reforms. Certainly, these are the most intensive changes since the establishment of the modern system at the turn of the twentieth century. "Educational change," "educational innovation," "school restructuring," and "school reforms" have become part and parcel of the educational discourse and practice throughout the last two generations, seemingly in sheer contradiction to the static nature of education in traditional and, to large extent, modern societies.

This phenomenon, "the obsessive addiction to educational changes," stems from desperate attempts of education systems in Western societies to render themselves, yet again, relevant and adequate in the postmodern reality. These changes are potentially no less powerful and far-reaching than those that characterized the transition from the rural and home systems dominant through the nineteenth century to the modern public systems.

Still, as opposed to the rapid and extremely effective processes that led to the transition from traditional to modern education, the postmodern changes are also to large extent "desperate," that is, in many cases either fictitious, residing only in the realm of words, or contradictory, dysfunctional, and counterproductive, or two or more of the above altogether.

In contradistinction to the processes that led to the establishment of the modern system, these "changes" are carried out in an absent-minded and non-strategic manner. The change dynamics seem to serve the socio-psychological needs of (internally and externally) marketing schools and education systems that do not really work as "advanced" or "innovative" institutions, instead of performing the necessary, radical transformations in a conscious, mindful, and strategic way, either in a revolutionary or evolutionary manner (the subject of the final chapter).

This fast-moving, aleatory, and hectic "change processes" exact an enormous toll on three levels of Western systems and societies: the functional and economic, the psychological, and the socio-ethical. In the given social situation, characterized by exceedingly powerful anti-Humanistic pressures, Western societies are paying a heavy price for these aleatory dynamics, one that they cannot afford to bear for many more years. These "changes" seem to lead to the throwing away, on a steady basis, of billions of dollars and euros and to jeopardizing citizens' chances of enjoying well-being. Much more dangerously, this process threatens the social fabric of these societies, and the foundational Humanistic values these societies hold dear.

In order to prevent further deterioration, liberal democratic states must navigate this wild whirlwind of change in a conscious, intentional, mindful, and strategic way, which requires:

- Basing all thought and change processes on the basic values of education in a Liberal Democracy—autonomy, morality, and dialogical belonging (or on variations on these values if found to be more appropriate)—and aspiring to maximize their realization in every set of circumstances.
- Thoroughly and methodically investigating and analyzing the immense post-modern forces that are changing our lives and render the existing system meaningless, dysfunctional, and counterproductive.
- Strategically harnessing the postmodern forces into the systemic and systematic effort for the reinforcement of the desirable educational values.

Should Western democracies choose not do so, a disintegration of public education in Western societies and the conquest of the fragmented systems that will emerge by purely technocratic views on the one hand, or by religious or fascist reactions to the existential void at the core of the technocratic view on the other, will be the unavoidable result. Both these categories of ideologies threaten the very existence of Liberal Democracy.

CHAPTER ELEVEN

IMPLEMENTING AUTONOMY ORIENTED EDUCATION TODAY

INTRODUCTION

I begin this final chapter by pointing to the bold, paradigmatic, cognitive and emotional leaps necessary in order to move away from the dysfunctional, meaningless, modern systems and on to meaningful education systems which serve the ultimate values of Liberal Democracy effectively in the postmodern era.[1] I then propose three basic change strategies for the implementation of these quantum leaps.[2] Finally, I emphasize the fact that even though the necessary educational revolution cannot take place without taking bold paradigmatic leaps, its implementation can be achieved gradually as long as it is guided by mindful, far-sighted, strategic thinking.[3]

THE NEED FOR BOLD, PARADIGMATIC LEAPS

The revolutions necessary for the realization of AOE can be achieved only by overcoming huge obstacles at the conceptual and emotional levels. These obstacles are, epistemologically speaking, conceptual; however the minds of most educators are emotionally deeply attached, enslaved even, to them. Overcoming them will cause in many of them an emotional reaction not dissimilar to that caused to many otherwise "good democrats" by the abolishment of slavery, the liberation of women, or the empowerment of people of color and other minorities.

Two major obstacles must be overcome at the deepest stratum of conceptual thinking and emotional attachment, the first negatively, the second positively.

The first, negative, revolution or "radical conversion" requires that we turn the unconscious anomaly which dominates today's education systems into a conscious one, as described in Chapter One. Educationalists and decision makers must acknowledge that today's educational crisis is unprecedented. They have to become aware of, and deeply understand, the fact that the basic structures of the existing education system, most of which are at least a century old, some dating back two and half millennia, have ceased to function or lost their meaning entirely, becoming dysfunctional and counterproductive in the process.

This underlying conceptual-emotional revolution should lead to a series of "smaller" conceptual transformations, each radical in its own right. Educators and decision makers must disengage:

- From the twenty-five-hundred-year-old view according to which education necessarily equals theoretical learning;

- From the even more ancient perception of education as a process which necessarily involves knowledgeable adults and ignorant young people whom the adults must inculcate with the "right knowledge";
- From the hundred-year-old assumption that education is necessarily equated with "a place called 'school'" (to paraphrase the title of a well-known book, one of many taking this assumption for granted);
- From the four-hundred-year-old assumption that education is necessarily book-based;

And so on.

These and similar disengagements do not mean a shift from the blind automatic belief in the old outdated "truths" to a blind automatic belief in their polar opposites. Rather they require a move from blind automatic belief in the pre-modern and modern "truths" to an ability to consider, in all levels of educational planning, a much larger range of options.

The second necessary conceptual-emotional evolutional conversion is of a positive nature. Educationalists and educational decision makers have to come to terms with the facts that:

- The aim of education is to educate! Even, or rather, especially, in our day and age, education should be first and foremost a process aiming to enhance the development of young peoples' personalities in the desired direction.
- Therefore, educators need to face the questions basic to any educational process: What is the "desired direction"? In the light of which values or goals should we educate?
- It is logically impossible to avoid these questions. Avoiding conscious decision making about the ultimate goals of education necessarily means making them subconsciously, or half-consciously. A lack of intentional action translates to passively handing over the steering of education from the liberal democratic state and its foundation values to the intensive "educational" impact of the social environment we live in today: the media, the entertainment business, the consumerist powers dominant in our societies, and the one-dimensional economic values they serve.
- Making such an unconscious decision necessarily reduces education to a process detrimental to Liberal Democracy and to the students' chances of having reasonably satisfying lives within the framework of the postmodern democracy.
- Western democracies have a clear worldview and set of values that can guide them in the educational project: the Humanistic values and worldview that provide a constitutional foundation to the postmodern Western democracies and (though usually unconsciously, unsystematically, and hence often erroneously) guide most of their citizens' lives. In other words, Liberal Democracy can find in Humanism and in the very rich tradition of the great books that comprise its canon[4] the same kind of support that Christianity takes from the Old and New Testaments and later theological writings, and that Judaism takes from the Torah, Talmud, and later Jewish philosophy.

There is "only" one difference between secular citizens of Western Democracies who "believe" in Humanism and believers of the various monotheistic faiths. Religious people are aware, almost by definition, of their canon and its sacred status, and many of them know its content or at least parts thereof very well and even by heart. However, most "Westerners," even educators, who relate to themselves as "Humanists," do not have a similar awareness of their rich tradition and certainly lack any systematic knowledge of its texts. For them Humanism and Western Liberalism are very vague and aloof values that have little chance of resisting harsh external attacks or attempts to gnaw away at their core. In order to reinvent Western education, educators and other proponents of Humanism and liberalism should rediscover their rich tradition.

- The formation of a postmodern Humanistic education that will serve post-modern Liberal Democracies should be based on, and extract its guiding values from, a thorough exegesis of the rich Humanistic tradition.
- Such an exegesis, as formulated in this book, shows that liberal democratic values boil down to the three basic values of personal autonomy, morality, and dialogical belonging, or some sort of variation on them.[5] These values should therefore become the ultimate goals of education in present day Liberal Democracies.

Following these meaningful conceptual-emotional paradigmatic leaps, educators should commit themselves, consciously, intentionally, and mindfully, to basic Humanistic values; educate in their light; and design and implement postmodern frameworks best suited to serve them. There are many more smaller breakthroughs to be made before educators can act as AOE tutors, mentors, and teachers as previously described in this volume.[6]

Overcoming the obstacles on the conceptual-emotional level leads directly into the practical level. This stage will involve undergoing another series of radical revolutions, because all basic operational patterns of the educational process will need to be reinvented, redefined, and reestablished.

THREE POSSIBLE CHANGE STRATEGIES

In principle, there are three ways to introduce such operational revolutions to any education system: radically, from the top down; gradually, from the bottom up; or a combination of the two approaches. It is impossible to universally foresee or state which of these three ways will best facilitate the needed changes. These obviously depend on the conditions of specific contexts.

Revolutionizing the education system from the top down by the use of decrees and laws is certainly a possibility. Historically, compulsory education laws inaugurated the modern system. As has been noted, in many countries, although not all, not only did these laws determine that every child must be educated, but also that education would be performed in schools, often dictating the specific school as well. They also determined the exact *modus operandi* of education along a single standard, and a compulsory common curriculum. These were, at the turn of the twentieth century, revolutionary laws, accompanied by a series of national and local decrees as well as the establishment of supporting institutions such as schools of education in colleges and universities, national ministries, and local departments or boards of education. History shows that in almost all modern Western states, within two or three decades of the laws' enactment, an altogether new modern educational reality, totally different from the diffused "systems" that previously prevailed, arose and gradually developed into the modern "one best system."[7]

There is no reason to rule out using a similar strategy for the establishment of the desired postmodern system. Actually for such radical systemic revolution this seems to be the most adequate strategy. This might be more difficult, though, because the modern system replaced a weak conglomeration of assorted educational institutions or arrangements reflecting different traditions and conceptions. The postmodern system, however, will have to replace a very strong, well-organized system that has played a critically important role in all Western societies in the last century and is relying on a network of many well rooted vested interests.

But one should not underestimate the public's ability and readiness to accept dramatic revolutions by decree, even when the decree raises strong opposition. For instance, Britain witnessed the formation of a "national curriculum" at the end of the 1980s, the imposition thereof, and the many other centralistic reforms that followed it, on the previously decentralized education system. This has been accompanied by fierce opposition from teacher organizations, academics in schools of education and so on, which did not prevent their quick, vast, and successful (as far as the mere implementation of the reforms is concerned) enforcement. The British experience is just one of the many examples within Western societies.[8] This transformation or at least some of its main offshoots, e.g., imposition of strict, quantitatively defined, national standards on the entire education system, have radically spread over many parts of the Western world. Though I vehemently disagree with the Thatcherite educational policy responsible for the National Curriculum and its offspring, it is certainly a very successful example of the fact that entire education systems can be compelled to drastically change old and well-established behavioral and educational patterns in spite of fierce criticism, protest, and antagonism.[9]

In other contexts, one can point to the ban on smoking in public places and the criminalization of sexual abuse against women and children, abuse that probably went on unimpeded for many thousands of years. Both were implemented in the course of a decade or two at most simply using tough legislation, again in spite of (at least in the first case) intensive protests. These and many other reforms testify to the ability to radically and abruptly change social structures, institutions, and patterns by legislative top-down decrees which can be accepted, if well-defined and coordinated properly, by the majority of the population.

A gradual bottom-up (grassroots) transformation is also possible as long as it is not totally open-ended and it is consciously and mindfully directed by the relevant values and goals. This will certainly require some level of top-down direction and legislation; however the necessary laws can be formulated in a way that will allow a wide range of freedoms and room for creativity to independent teams of educators. In other words, educational institutions may be required by appropriate legislation to make gradual but meaningful changes, in the generally defined desired directions, over a certain number of years, while leaving the choice of changes and approaches up to the individual institutions.

Obviously, endless variations combining modes of change and relationships between the top-down decrees and "moderate" bottom-up grassroots initiatives of "educators in the field" can emerge. What is important to emphasize in this context is the less easily understood fact that however radical and ambitious the goals of AOE (or any other suggested plausible view of postmodern Humanistic education) may seem, the actual process of change can be achieved gradually. This would in fact be a sensible strategy to adopt when modifying *existing schools'* basic patterns, as opposed to *entirely new educational institutions* designed in light of the entirely new AOE model. This recommendation appears workable if, as a counterweight to the negative aleatory processes currently in advanced progress, the proposed evolutionary procedures are based on a broad, systematic, and far-reaching conception of the changes' objectives and if certain additional conditions for sustaining the transformation are met.[10]

The possible gradual nature of such a process for existing schools may seem counterintuitive given the radical and utopian nature of its final goals. To settle this visual contradiction, I shall depict, in the following section, the relatively limited stages that can be implemented gradually, some of which as soon as "tomorrow morning" in various contexts of the educational process, in order to slowly bridge the gap between the existing situation and AOE.

GRADUAL IMPLEMENTATION OF AOE

Herein, I point to several steps for implementation of AOE that can be applied in the short term within any educational organization's two central parameters: its program of educational activity known today as the "curriculum"[11] and its organizational structure.

With regard to the organizations' educational program, re-planning the existing curriculum can be boosted so that its disciplinary structure will gradually lean towards a non-disciplinary, authentic, experiential, and reflection-oriented AOE program. Hence, I propose four partly overlapping and mutually supportive groups of measures that can be taken immediately to achieve this end.

The *first* group consists of a gradual, mindful transformation of the current, dominant, disciplinary-theoretical curriculum into an inter- or supra-disciplinary curriculum. While we have seen many attempts to form an interdisciplinary or project-based program over the last generation, and this experience can certainly be used to help our cause, it is important to note that the our aim is not "interdisciplinary" for its own sake, as has so far usually been the case, but for the sake of approximating the educational program derived from the AOE which they should serve.

For example, the humanities and social science programs can be changed into a non-disciplinary program based on the objectives of the second set of experiential domains as described in Chapter Seven. The main thrust of this transformation will be the development of students' ability to critique the dominant conceptual and social structures and institutions.[12] Similarly, another transformation of the curriculum could be aimed at encouraging students to question the nature of and the possibility or realization of the Good Life as dealt with in the seventh experiential domain.[13] The assumption is that this kind of change will render the educatees' studies more meaningful without an immediate modification of all the other characteristics of the existing school setup.

The main thrust of the *second* group of possible measures for adjusting the educational program is designed to enhance experiences in non-theoretical subjects and spheres which currently exist in the periphery of modern curriculum, and adapt these to an AOE program. This could be done, provided they can be adjusted to experiences that stem from the third, fourth, fifth, and sixth experiential domains, as discussed in Chapter Seven, which, respectively, relate to knowledge of the bureaucracies dominant in society and experiences in fields of interests, occupations, and social activities.

Rough approximations of what I have in mind include, among others, programs such as "Career education," Vocational education," "Industry-oriented education," "Lifelong learning," and "Family life education," which already exist in many places,[14] as well as programs dedicated to simulation of financial investment and business management. Still it is vital to understand that our ability to think of rough approximations to some of the AOE oriented programs which already exist does not in any way mean that the prevailing programs can be "copied" and applied in their current shape. While partially similar to AOE programs, in many cases their format contradicts the essence of AOE.

For example, in order to adjust programs, such as the last two examples mentioned above, to the framework of the AOE educational process, two complementary steps should be taken: First, their importance or weight in the overall educational process should be *prudently* examined, because they may, in part, reflect interests of narrow social sectors (the industrialists in connection with industry-oriented education or banking and brokerage firms in connection with the plan for simulating investment) which may contradict basic sub-values stemming from the main educational values: autonomy, morality, and dialogical belonging. Second, for the same reason, if such programs are implemented, it is essential that the external systems or institutions participating in them are subject to critical educational examination within the framework of the second experiential domain. In other words, one should apply to the above cases the critical approaches already in use for many years in programs relating to mindful use of the media. These programs expose the media's often manipulative aspects and equip young people with tools necessary to defend themselves from such manipulations. These programs, which enhance critical approaches to the media, do not prevent young people from being exposed to the media, and the same is true in our case. Once "equipped" with tools which allow and encourage a contextual, reflective, and critical approach to the experience process, the range of their exposure to the economic domains can and should be extended.

Taking these two precautionary measures might, I hope, contribute to achieving a healthy balance between two contradictory considerations: opening up as many aspects as possible of the "external world" to the students' active experimentation, and enhancing students' ability to detect powerful external interests that may work against their individual autonomous development and protect themselves against them.

Whatever these programs may be, their character should be modified. For example, existing programs designed to encourage the realization of interests still tend to be largely theoretical. The students' work is mostly research on, or writing about, their interests, rather than actually participating in the interest-oriented activities.

In most countries (except for a small number of the schools in some of the Scandinavian countries) educators find it difficult to allow students to be active in their fields of interest outside the school walls. Furthermore, the current educational framework lacks a "mechanism" that can guarantee systematic development of a reservoir of interest fields which represent all categories of activities that may appeal to the students.

In a like manner, existing educational programs do not offer a process of continual, reflective, institutionalized, and systematic tutorial accompaniment, designed to encourage the development of autonomous, moral, and dialogically belonging young people, based on their reflection upon their interest-based experiences. Without such accompaniment, the education system will fail to ensure that young people's experiences are productive in the sense of assisting them to develop according to the ultimate Humanistic educational goals. The current education systems lack at least the two versions of such a reflective process recommended in Chapter Seven:[15] the educational accompaniment in a specific field of interest as expressed in the role of a tutor, and the integrative accompaniment of all experiences as expressed in the role of a mentor.[16]

To recap, we should strive to expand and modify the existing realization of voluntary learning programs in all the abovementioned aspects:

- Actively encourage young people to actually experiment and practice their interests rather than limit their involvement to mere theoretical thinking about it.
- Add as many of the various experiential domains and categories of activities into "the optional experiences reservoir" offered by the school and then help students "browse through" the myriad of experiences at various levels of involvement relevant to the individual students.
- Implement tutorial accompaniment based on the principles of AOE throughout the students' experimentation with, and involvement in, interests, in order to elicit their reflection and to productively guide them as they seek out their selected interests and engage in them.[17] "Productively" in this context means harnessing the process in a way that would trigger and support reflective processes which serve ultimate goals of enhancing young people's development as autonomous, moral, and dialogically belonging individuals.

Similar changes can be implemented in the curriculum ingredients corresponding to other experiential domains of the desirable educational program, that is, in the other non-theoretical programs that currently exist in education systems and are relevant to young people's experimentation with important life domains. These possibilities also include experimenting with careers, various frameworks and modes of social involvement, interpersonal relationships, various worldviews, and their extension.

The *third* group of measures that can bring about some level of immediate change consists of integrating programs originally designed in light of AOE into the existing curriculum. These may include, for example, study programs that familiarize students with the main bureaucracies and institutions in society (the legal, health, taxation, political, banking systems, etc.), the services they provide, citizens' rights in relation to them, and the dangers they may pose to individual freedoms and rights.[18]

The *fourth* group of measures, the most challenging to implement within the existing curriculum, consists of moving programs that can most effectively serve AOE goals from the remote periphery of educational activity, where they are "located" now, to the center of the educational programs' stage. This is a demanding challenge, because it calls for changes (even if gradual) of (at least) two external conditions which prevent, at present, its actualization:

- Annulment of the existing disciplinary, universal-standards-oriented, form of final examinations or, at the very least, a gradual shift towards intra-school evaluation patterns which rely on AOE content and processes.[19]
- A change (which may also be gradual) of the teacher certification patterns, a move away from the present day disciplinary approach to certification towards approaches which enable educators to specialize in a group of subjects or content domains or experiences which exceed any one specific discipline, in accordance with AOE content and principles as discussed in Chapter Seven.

Another large category of measures can be implemented on the organizational level, in order to encourage gradual development of an AOE system. Below I point to three groups of such measures.

The *first* group of measures within the organizational category consists of steps designed to create structural changes in the relationship between education systems and the outside world. As mentioned in Chapters Seven and Eight, programs already up and running, albeit partially and patchily, enable some high school students to participate in university courses, whereupon the university commits itself to acknowledging their successful participation in these courses, if they should become relevant to their future studies.[20] Such programs could be enlarged and extended in the experimental open-ended spirit of an AOE program.

A *second* group of parallel steps would consists of enabling high school students to devote most of their time during a specific period to actualizing a certain interest, worldview, social activity, or professional assignment of their choice, accompanied by appropriate AOE educational support and within a framework geared to ensure maximal educational advantage from the experience.

A *third* group of steps that can be adopted at the organizational level is the democratization of schools. "Democratic schools" based on democratic principles exist all over the world today. Students of such schools participate in determining the school's educational policy.[21] This trend can be encouraged and developed as part of the gradual transformation towards an AOE oriented system as long as it is compatible with the general goals of Humanistic education.[22]

I could continue to give other and more detailed examples along these lines, but I think that those mentioned suffice to concretize the argument that the desired changes can be attained using a step-by-step policy beginning with the adaptation of programs that exist today in many places. Each of the abovementioned measures enables advancement, from a different direction, towards attaining the desired AOE oriented change objectives. There is no doubt that the more comprehensive the measures are, the more schools that take such measures on, and the more far-reaching the changes are, the sooner and more efficiently we will achieve the goal of Humanistic education. Achievement of such a goal will increase the chances of students growing up as autonomous, moral, and dialogically belonging individuals, having a far better chance of enjoying personal well-being and of contributing to the strengthening of the social fabric of postmodern democracies.

SUMMARY

The response to the postmodern revolution's challenges demands that the educational thinker and planner make huge cognitive and emotional paradigmatic leaps. However, one should remember that what is at stake justifies such leaps, and even though the boldness of these leaps cannot be over-estimated, the practical measures applied in order to initiate and implement such a brave move can be gradual. The proviso is that the forward thrust must target the long-range goals of Humanistic education and it must be strategically executed so that in the end the cumulative changes will serve Humanism and allow it to flourish even in postmodernity.

ANNEX 1: MY INTELLECTUAL JOURNEY

The arguments I present throughout the book are laced with either explicit or tacit interactions with a wide range of ideological, theoretical, methodological, empirical, and practice-oriented discourses. Henceforth I will often use "perspectives" to refer to all five kinds of discourses. In some cases my "conversation" with a specific perspective is systematically explained in the relevant section. However in many others the interaction has a more "behind-the-scenes" nature, and is at most mentioned very briefly, as I feel going into too much detail in the body of the book is redundant, especially in light of the scope the book aims to cover. In order to compensate for this shortcoming, the following annex offers an overview of the perspectives I have conversed with during the last twenty years, especially those which served as important sources of inspiration for the arguments laid out in this book.

I believe such an overview could first and foremost allow me to "put my cards on the table" and outline my basic assumptions and values as transparently as my "reflective faculty" allows. This can certainly help the readers understand "what made my stomach ache" (to use a Nietzschean metaphor), the fears and hopes that have motivated me, and thus understand my arguments more profoundly. This level of understanding will facilitate the readers' independent analyses and evaluations of the view I present to them and enable them to transcend the model suggested here and form their own view of the core issues at hand. It also can, I hope, trigger and vitalize prolific debates on these issues. Debates are usually fiercer but also more rigorous and productive when the relevant hidden agendas and motives are exposed.

Most importantly, I hope this survey will give the reader at least a glimpse of the enormity of the issues at hand, the complexity of the questions and problems one has to address when rethinking education, and the large range of ideologies, disciplines, theories, research fields, and methodologies one must examine and address for this sake. I use the word "glimpse" since I am, as is any human being, necessarily limited in my ability to gain systematic knowledge in more than one or two disciplines. When dealing with and utilizing disciplines and discourses beyond those limits, I have had to rely on various levels of more superficial knowledge than I would have liked. In the future, I hope such thinking processes will be developed by interdisciplinary teams that are able to canvass disciplines, sub-disciplines, and other relevant perspectives, as well as the relationships between them, in a much better way so as to reach a more comprehensive and integrative road map for the future.

When using the term "inspiration" I refer to both the simple straightforward or "positive" sense of this term and to the "negative" sense thereof. In the latter case I am referring to a critical response or all-out rejection of a view or at least some aspect of it. Following Nietzsche's claim that if one wants to truly understand a certain view, one must ascertain "what makes the thinker's stomach ache"; the negative sense of inspiration is at least as important as the positive one. Negative sources of inspiration have made my stomach ache and led to the fears and concerns that were often primary motivational forces in the thinking process delineated in this book. The positive sources supported my belief that these aches are curable or that the fears and concerns can, at the very least, be attenuated and that feasible ways for dealing with their sources can be found.

I shall discuss two levels of literature in the following pages: "discourses" and "mega-discourses." "Discourses" are, at least to some extent, ongoing, integrated discussions. Such discussions usually enjoy some common core, concepts, and methodologies and relate to common concerns or issues all thinkers involved in the relevant discussion consciously and intentionally address. "Mega-discourses," on the other hand, are ones I have glued together from many seemingly unrelated discourses. The writers in such "mega-discourses" do not necessarily explicitly relate to one another, nor do they consciously or intentionally address the same core questions. However, when read together, they can be analyzed as sharing a meaningful common denominator which is addressed from different perspectives. I glued these discourses together into "mega-discourses" whenever I found that they all related, at least post facto, to a common "grand issue" in a way which is deeper or at least more comprehensive than any one of them on its own.

Let us now turn to the body of this annex and delineate the scope of my conversations with discourses and mega-discourses which lie at the forefront or in the background of the main arguments of this book. This presentation is divided into three sections relating to the arguments at the core of each of the book's three parts. Each section is then subdivided according to the major propositions the arguments central to it consist of and the discourses or "mega-discourses" relevant to each of them.

PERSPECTIVES BASIC TO THE FIRST PART OF THE BOOK

The first part of this book is designed to delineate the following propositions:
A. Postmodernity is a new civilization which has radically, rapidly and extensively changed every aspect of the human condition.
B. The growing abyss separating modernity from postmodernity has rendered the Western, essentially modern, education systems dysfunctional and counterproductive on the economic, social and psychological levels and devastating for postmodern Liberal Democracies.
C. This growing abyss is the root of the crisis plaguing education systems in postmodern Liberal Democracies.
D. Nothing less than mindful, macro-level, strategic re-invention of education, based on a re-consideration of all its basic parameters from scratch, will be viable, meaningful or desired for postmodern democracies.

Perspectives Basic to Proposition A

The Mega-Discourse on Postmodernity

I rely on the rich, reconstructed, mega-discourse on postmodernity in order to substantiate the first of the above propositions. This mega-discourse presents and analyzes the new civilization which emerged in the West out of the many postmodern revolutions. It emphasizes the growing gap separating the postmodern reality, on all levels of human existence, from the dominant modern and traditional civilizations which preceded it.

I will not go into the details of this particular mega-discourse here since I dedicated the first section of Chapter One[1] to its systematic reconstruction and presentation. Still it is important to relate to this mega-discourse, from a meta-level perspective which is not addressed in the abovementioned chapter.

I said "reconstruction" above since the mega-discourse does not tangibly exist, certainly not in the academic sphere. Most of the publications on this matter have been written within specific discourses which at most relate to but a few of the many dimensions of postmodernity and quite often ignore the other aspects thereof, as well as the interactions between them.

There are indeed publications which from their outset aim at grasping the essence of the main dimensions and aspects of postmodernity.[2] However, at the end of the day, with the exception of a handful of seminal works, they too, though larger in scope, focus on but a single group of radical changes that only relate to few of the possible dimensions of the human situation in postmodernity.[3]

Among the many spheres relevant to this reconstructed mega-discourse we can count discourses about globalization of major aspect of the political spheres as well as the communications and economic spheres; about the ensuing spread of "glocalisation";[4] about the radical changes in the labor market, which to a large extent follow from a combination of globalization and neo-liberal approaches to the economy; about the revolution the common career structure is undergoing; as well as about the profound change in the nature of the nuclear family, of "childhood," and of other basic social roles typical of the modern era. We must also include in our discussion the infinite debates about the digital revolution, and the ensuing digital generations, which can already be chronologically divided into several powerful waves, each changing all aspects of our life, including our modes of thinking, speaking, communicating, and working as well as our leisure activities and consumption patterns.

This mega-discourse also relates to the rise of radical relativism, individualism and hedonism in all spheres of human life and activity. Relativism has long roots in the history of Western culture but has been dramatically enhanced in the last two generations by the communication, digital, and globalization revolutions. In these mega-discourses we must also include phenomena such as the disintegration of the self and of all known modes of social belonging whose ongoing influence on the digital revolutions and the rise of relativism is vital to the understanding thereof.

The aforementioned mega-discourse includes discussions about the possible implications a series of radical bio-medical revolutions can have on known social frameworks. These revolutions gave us access to technologies which potentially allow us to change almost everything about ourselves physiologically, mentally, and cognitively, and this undermines any stable foundation for a continuous identity we may previously have had. The same technologies also allow us to "reengineer" human beings, to clone them, and at least potentially, give us the ability to create "chimeras," creatures combined of human and animals, which until recently belonged solely to the sphere of myth and gothic fantasies. The implication of these abilities is a blurring of what we used to consider our most categorical demarcation lines. In other words, this is another most meaningful contribution to the disintegration of the prevailing, most fundamental, conceptions, norms, social frameworks, and psychological identities.

This mega-discourse certainly relates to the constant exponential extension of the range of human freedoms and choices which stems from many of the above revolutions and has dramatically changed and continues to change conceptions of "human life," its constraints and horizons; it also relates to the rise of fundamentalism both within and outside Western societies, a phenomenon which can be understood as a reaction to the anxiety invoked by this unprecedented range of freedoms which serves, in its turn, as one of the main causes of the clash of civilizations the twenty-first century is witnessing.[5]

As mentioned above, the first section of Chapter One[6] is dedicated to the presentation of the above and other postmodern revolutions, usually discussed in very different literatures that almost never "meet." In addition to studying the impact of postmodernity on all major dimensions of human life in this chapter, Chapter One also depicts my attempts to transcend the specific dimensions and locate the deep postmodern structures that are common to the "earthquakes" shaking them and hence define the postmodern era.

Doing so in a book whose main focus is the impact postmodernity has on education certainly forces me to use a lower resolution than I would have liked. I do believe, however, that this is a worthwhile price to pay, or rather that it is vital that I pay this price in order to paint a macro-level, holistic picture of the radical postmodern upheaval we are going through and express the profoundness of the changes Western civilization and its deep structures are now subject to. This is a necessary condition for true understanding of the need to reinvent education.

The Postmodernistic Discourse

While I touch, albeit very generally, on many specific discourses and perspectives relating to postmodernity, there is one specific discourse which transcends them all in its importance to the examination of postmodernity and the enhancement of understanding of its unique spirit and deep structures: the postmodernistic (a term that should be sharply discerned from "postmodern" as will be claimed below) discourse.

My conversation with this discourse has been very intensive in the last three decades. This is due first and foremost to the extensive impact it has on the academic understanding of postmodernity in humanities and in the social sciences. In many cases it serves as the main perspective through which postmodernity is conceived and analyzed in these contexts. The same is also true for the media and hence the general public and political discourse heavily influenced by these academic contexts.[7]

Since I do not give this discourse or the way it inspired me the place it "deserves" in the book itself,[8] I will portray it and my response to it here. This response consists of a "love-hate relationship." That is to say that while I learnt extensively from postmodernity, I am also critical of it and reject some of its most basic presuppositions and recommendations.

This is not the place to go into a detailed description of Postmodernism. Suffice it to say that this ideology/view/cultural "mood" has had several sources, the most vocal of which is probably the fusion of poststructuralist thinking in France of the sixties and seventies with neo-Marxist trends, and the strong impact of Nietzschean "perspectivist" or relativist philosophy—either directly or indirectly through the impact of Heidegger.[9] Other somewhat later sources are trends such as "multiculturalism,"[10] anti-colonialism[11] and radical feminism.[12]

I will not be distinguishing between the above and other versions of Postmodernism in the future and will refer to them all as "Postmodernism," using the term in its most general sense. The elements of Postmodernism relevant to my understanding of postmodernity are first and foremost its ardent and radical relativism and anti-rationalism, and its vehement attack on views adhering to the search of truth in any absolutist, objectivist, critical, or even cultural sense of the term. This is the basis for the postmodern attack on the possibility and the desirability of systematic thought as well as on the yearning for meta-narratives which lie at the core of Western rationalisms and hence modernity.[13]

Another consequence of its anti-rationalism is the objection of Postmodernism to what is often termed "essentialism," a conception according to which objects and subjects can be defined by some unchanging "essence." This is the source for the postmodern disdain for "the essentialist concepts of 'the self' and the 'mind,'" central to Western rationalism and individualism. In this vein, Postmodernism also rejects the modern concept of the "individual" which relies on the essentialist concepts of the unchanging mind or self and hence also the Humanistic and liberal views based on these concepts. On all of these levels, Postmodernism reflects and enhances fragmentariness, piecemeal thought and activity, and "Heraclitean" or "kaleidoscopic" approaches to human life and activity.[14]

My "love" for this literature is the result of the many ways in which it expresses, consciously, clearly, sharply, and systematically the "essence"[15] of our era and conveys its spirit on the epistemic and larger cultural levels. Any of the main texts of the postmodernistic creed bring home to the reader the (alleged) impossibility to continue holding on to any belief in solid epistemic or social foundations for human life, or to any universalistic or even culturally binding foundation to our judgments, assumptions, or activities.[16] In doing so it very vividly and powerfully reflects the disappearance of linearity, stability, and continuity as stemming from all postmodern revolutions. These three phenomena are the deep structures Chapter One points to as cutting across all postmodern revolutions.

Dominant versions of Postmodernism vehemently criticize what was believed in modernity to be "objective knowledge," claiming that it is ideologically biased superstructures serving the interests of hegemonic elites. Instead, Postmodernism prescribes a kind of free-floating life which reflects the desire for "emancipation" from and "deconstruction" of these very structures.[17]

In its relativistic, Heraclitean, and critical stance Postmodernism is not only reflecting our era, it is also influencing it extensively. This is especially true concerning its impact on the last two generations of Western intellectuals, academics, and students in the humanities and social science departments. These were the proverbial greenhouses wherein most power-brokers occupying prominent positions in the media, digital and more traditional entertainment businesses, advertisement industry, journalism, and other public opinion-shaping spheres were raised and hence the breeding grounds of the "postmodernist mind."

Either reflecting or influencing, Postmodernism does express what is unique in the spirit of our *zeitgeist*. While most individuals today know little of Post-modernism, many of them, certainly of the young digital generation, are fluent in the "postmodernist lingo." This is certainly the case as far as the neglect of any aspiration for attaining a meaningful understanding of reality or reaching any coherent con-ception of a worldview, of life's goals, or even of self-conception or identity. For many, the terms themselves would appear to be "dead terms," incomprehensible and irrelevant. These concepts are simply not included in their cognitive or intellectual "bag."[18]

Thus far we covered my "love" for Postmodernism and the way it positively inspired me. It is possible to say that this inspiration remains positive as long as Postmodernism adopts a descriptive stance, describing the spirit of our time, reve-aling its deep structures and engaging in ad-hoc criticism of its meta-narratives, without attempting to supply us with any binding, all-engulfing critical methodology or recommend an alternative worldview or meta-narrative.[19]

My disagreement with this view begins once it abandons its purely descriptive ad-hoc criticism, and presumes to provide us with a gospel, with the only desirable view, the one meta-narrative that can and should guide us through life.[20]

My basic criticism of Postmodernism, when its proponents adopt a normative prescriptive or view it as a binding meta-narrative, boils down to the claim that this stance, if taken seriously, is both logically impossible and ethically dangerous. As for the logical impossibility, it is already reflected in the above two paragraphs. One cannot criticize the mere existence and use of meta-narratives and be engaged in active deconstruction of them and at the same time rely on a meta-narrative in order to do so. Postmodernistic critics necessarily rely on such meta-narratives (even if they do not acknowledge them) since the critical stance they recommend can only exist if we assume that criticism is possible and desirable and hence also assume *mutatis mutandis*, the possibility of the method of criticism, the epistemology basic to this methodology, the logic basic to the epistemology and the ontology basic to this logic.[21] In short, the systematic criticism of meta-narratives, presented as a binding stance, requires, in and of itself, a meta-narrative to rely on and is hence self-contradicting.[22]

It is important to note that some of the founding fathers of Postmodernism, (Derrida would be the best example[23]) were very reluctant to make any explicit claim concerning the need to adopt the postmodernist deconstructive or critical approach as a systematic and binding method and opposed to turning it into a cornerstone of any ongoing epistemic strategy. They were well aware that recommending such a strategy would lead to the above self-contradiction. Yet they were often interpreted in just such an impossible way by many of their followers. Their specific or anecdotal critical moves were used by followers to create a comprehensive system of criticism, which combined Postmodernism with the Marxian-objectivist appeal in an attempt to deconstruct hegemonic superstructures in order to (allegedly) lead to emancipation.[24] Foucault's writings have often served as foundation for such interpretations (again while he himself refrained from recommending such a move, at least not explicitly). Most importantly it has been this impossible interpretation, alongside the impossible combination of radical deconstructionism and objectivist neo-Marxism, which swept over many faculties of humanities and social sciences[25] in the West in the last two generations. As a result of this interpretation many Western intellectuals, elites, and public opinions were converted to one version or another of the postmodernistic creed.

Internal criticism regarding the above contradiction has recently emerged within the postmodernistic camp, led by (what can be called) neo-postmodernistic, "diasporic,"[26] and (some of the) radical anti-colonialist thinkers.[27] These critics try to expose the above basic contradiction or paradox by suggesting a permanent, ongoing, critical activity that never halts into a stable "self-satisfied" posture. According to these critics, once a knowledge structure is "frozen" it "begins to lie" and becomes a citadel of power structures.

But this neo-postmodernistic criticism suffers from the same problem it criticizes in more "traditional" postmodernistic views. The desire to remain "unfrozen" or "free-floating" should also be deconstructed if one is to remain loyal to its spirit of emancipation and deconstruction. This criticism also relies on a rich array of assumptions, relating to all levels of human life and activity, and therefore, if we follow the line of the critics themselves, can and does serve as the citadel of vested interests. Put in other terms, once it is treated like a stable recommendation for ongoing criticism, it loses its (alleged) edge over all other "frozen" meta-narratives.

There is simply no way for postmodernists to pull themselves up by their bootstraps.[28] Most of them commit themselves to a very rich and demanding array of assumptions and values. The only way to avoid making this commitment is to stay silent, or to use language paradoxically, to demonstrate its impossibility, as Zen masters, for instance, have been doing for years. On the other hand, Postmodernists and neo-postmodernists seem reluctant to adopt this epistemologically and ethically ascetic stance.

Up until now I referred to my logical and epistemological criticism of Postmodernism. My second criticism is of an ethical or normative nature. I believe the postmodernist view to be undesirable since it is socially and psychologically dangerous. By not allowing for essentialism, Postmodernism denies Humanism its most basic psychological, conceptual network which includes concepts such as the "individual," the "self," and the process of "self discovery" and "self-formation" through "reflection." By the same token, Postmodernism denies liberalism its practical, political, and legal core: an acknowledged system of human rights. This is the case since if we cannot talk about "selves" and "individuals" enjoying some level of continuity or stability, we cannot assume that there are, or can be, carriers of rights and thus the concept of "right" loses its meaning. Thus Postmodernism hammers especially long and powerful nails into the gradually deconstructed coffin of Humanism and Liberal Democracy. This process is celebrated by postmodernist groups that, ironically, enjoy, and even need the political and social protection of Liberal Democracy.

From the above two lines of criticism (logical-epistemic and normative) stems another, semantic, one, directed against many postmodernists' lack of distinction between "being postmodern" (which refers to "living in our era") and "adopting the postmodernistic meta-narrative." Quite often, the adoption of postmodernist attitudes or ideologies is presented by writers of this "camp" as necessarily stemming from life in our era.[29] Such thinking is logically invalid because it makes an invalid leap from an "is" description to an "ought" argument thus committing what the philosophic discourse terms, ever since David Hume, "the naturalistic fallacy."[30] It also contradicts the thinkers' own basic assumptions since in order to make this naturalistic leap in the first place they depend on knowledge about our era and must assume that this knowledge objectively describes the era in which we live. The mere concept of the possibility of objective knowledge contradicts the core of their view.

One can be postmodern (i.e., live today and be aware of the peculiar nature of our time) yet choose to be either modernist (i.e., a rationalist adhering to one of the many versions of rationalism including skeptical and critical ones, believing in the need for and possibility of systematic thinking) or postmodernist. I am one example of the possibility of being a modernist in the postmodern era. There are many others.[31]

The fact that we do live in a culturally and epistemologically chaotic and fragmented world, probably the most fragmented and chaotic in human history so far, is not in and of itself a reason for us to accept this state of affairs as the only possible reality or view, and certainly not as the best of all possible worlds (the given may be, and has often been, undesirable to many: the Nazi or Stalinist societies are the most obvious examples) or as a blueprint for a desired epistemology or ethics.

On a parallel level, the ability to construct a stable, permanent, individual "self" is threatened today by the incessant floods of information, and short-term *ad-hoc* acquaintances that bombard the individual and saturate his or her self.[32] But it is impossible and undesirable to deduce from this fact that we have to rejoice in this process or avoid trying to resist it or to limit its impact (this book indeed makes attempts and operative suggestions for such resistance).

As claimed above, in opposition to many of the postmodernistic writers, my view can be described as "postmodern modernism": I live now, I am well aware of the fact that these are turbulent and chaotic times that necessarily cause us to sharply break away from the world we[33] knew (to paraphrase Stefan Zweig's book), but I am not prepared to accept the processes of change taking place in our world as a sheer blessing. I think that they can lead to either social and psychological heaven or hell and that unfortunately, given human nature and the lessons history teaches us about it, if we leave it to chance, we are more likely to default towards the latter than the former. Given this grim predicament, we need a well-organized, strategic, systematic human effort, based on clear and coherent meta-narratives (there certainly can and should be a plurality of meta-narratives) aimed to (socially, economically, and educationally) harness the extremely energetic postmodern process to optimize the chances for human prosperity and well-being.

Still, I am very grateful to several postmodernistic and neo-postmodernistic thinkers who allowed me to crystallize my view through both their understanding of postmodernity and my ongoing debate with them.[34]

The Ecological and Feminist Meta-narratives

For the sake of my more skeptical readers, those who question the feasibility of a project designed to enhance a neo-modernistic view in postmodernity, allow me to point not only to its feasibility but also to the striking success of two structurally similar projects which are in place today. Both are modernistic socio-political struggles taking place in the postmodern era, harnessing all possible postmodern means to their end cause. I refer here to the ecological or "green" endeavor and to the (non-radical) feminist struggle. Both have managed to escape the paralyzing grip of Postmodernism35 and bring about radical positive changes in our lives.

Both are steadily guided by concepts and ideals such as "desired individual development," "well-being," "equal rights" (in the case of the feminists), and "sustainable development" and "rational and optimizing decision making based on scientific findings" (in the case of the ecological movement). As such, they have relied, over the last decades, on defined ideological, theoretical, empirical, and operational values, as well as on assumptions, theories, and research findings integrated into a clear systematic and modernistic meta-narrative. As strange as it may sound to readers influenced epistemologically and psychologically by Postmodernism, this is not too difficult a task even in our age of radical pluralism and relativism,[36] as was also, I hope, made evident in this book.

Both of the abovementioned ventures have been unbelievably successful in the last four decades. The ecological movement developed from a suppressed, somewhat esoteric struggle on the fringe of political discourse to being one of the main foci therein all over the world.[37] The same is true for the longer (non-radical) feminist struggle[38] that adopted the basic modernistic concepts of universal equality, fairness, and human rights and fought to apply them to women all over the world with steadily growing success.

Both have largely and positively inspired me throughout in my struggle with the basic problems of postmodern education, especially once I reached the conclusion that nothing less than "grand narratives," calling for a wholly new understanding of the state of affairs similarly to these grand narratives of the ecologists and the feminists, are necessary for education as well.

Perspectives Basic to Propositions B–D

Now that I have reviewed the discourses and mega-discourses with which I have conversed while forming my view on the dramatic change we have been undergoing in the last few decades, let us move on to the various discourses with which I conversed when forming and defining my views leading to the last three propositions of the argument on which the first part of the book is based. These consist of the claim that a growing gap has developed as a result of the encounter between the new postmodern civilization and contemporary schools, institutions which still decisively reflect modern civilization in all their major aspects (second proposition); this gap leads to an unprecedented educational crisis (third proposition), one which cannot be resolved by the current half-hearted and partial attempts at school change but only through a systematic, grand narrative, re-inventing and re-designing it from scratch (fourth proposition).

I conversed with three different categories of literature during the long process which eventually led to the formation of these three propositions. The first category includes the historical and sociological discourses about the development of education in general and the modern school more particularly. These discourses have led to the formation of the claims basic to my second proposition concerning the Platonic *and* modern nature of prevailing schools.[39] The second is the boundless mega-discourse of school change fundamental to the claims that lie at the basis of all three propositions in several ways to be presented below.[40] The third literary category contains the four discourses that lie at the basis of the now inflationary use of "paradigmatic" or "second-level change." It has helped me form, more specifically, the last proposition concerning the need "to reinvent education" or "re-design it from scratch".[41]

Contemporary Schools as Modern Versions of Platonic Education

The claim that the school as we know it today is a paradigmatic example of a modern institution, aiming to socialize young people to work at the production line, is basic to my view of the prevailing crisis in education. It is not at all farfetched to say that any student of the history, of the sociology, or of the aforementioned postmodernistic criticism of education cannot escape this claim. It has been forcing itself on any thinking process about prevailing educational structures for several decades now.

This claim stems from several discourses. The first deals with the history of the formation of modern education systems in the West starting with the last decades of the nineteenth century.[42] The second is sociological in nature and consists of two main discourses: functionalist sociology[43] and neo-Marxist or radical sociology.[44] Both of these discourses validate the abovementioned claim although the first does so approvingly while the second, neo-Marxist one does so critically. The third discourse, closely connected and even partly overlapping with the previously delineated literature, is the postmodernistic analysis or criticism of the "panopticon" or prototypical modern total organizational structures enabling efficient control which Foucault constructed and many other postmodern thinkers followed.[45] Modern schools together with similar "prison-oriented" total organizations like the factory and the hospital are all indicated in this discourse as paradigmatic examples of such organizations.

While the previous discourses emphasize the radically new nature of the modern school, there is another discourse which brought me to the conclusion that while the modern school is a relatively new organization, it is also the perpetuation of a two-and-a-half-millennia-old curricular and didactic tradition. This is the Platonic tradition of the liberal curriculum. It is the still almost exclusively dominant tradition which is based on the view that the highest echelons of education should consist of learning of Truth for its own sake or, on learning purely theoretical disciplines. These disciplines allegedly reflect Truth and neither have nor should have anything to do with practice.[46]

This view stems from twenty-five-hundred-year-old Platonic, epistemic, and ethical-psychological assumptions which were adopted by Western civilization: Only the search for theoretical Truth can expose the real humane aspects of human beings. Learning the Truth is hence the one and only way to the *Good Life*. The Platonic nature of the curriculum is easy to forget when one is immersed in the previous categories of discourses. Still, this important aspect is revealed by any book on the history of Western curricula in the last two and a half millennia,[47] and can be traced back not only to Plato's *Republic* and many philosophy and education texts and practices since, but also to the obstinate attempts of philosophers belonging to the most influential sub-discourse in modern philosophy of education to resurrect this tradition.[48]

All these discourses brought me to the conclusion that modern schools may be organizationally modern however their curricular core and didactic frameworks are basically Platonic, or at least a modernized version of Platonic education. This conclusion is largely explained and substantiated in Chapters Three (which relates to the curriculum) and Four (which deals with the organizational structure of the prevailing school), and so the above mention of them will do in this context.

The Mega-Discourse on School Change

The mega-discourse on "school change," "educational reform," or "restructuring" is the metaphoric bridge between the above claim and the conclusion that education must be re-invented in postmodern democracy. It is not easy to discern any clearly demarcated discourses or categories of literature in this context, which continuously and systematically revolves around ever-changing fashions of political correctness (in light of changing political views), basic concepts, concerns, and questions. As a matter of fact, the situation "out there" is extremely chaotic.[49] In some issues one can sometimes, for a brief while, indentify what can be argued to be a discourse, but generally speaking this mega-discourse is made of a practically infinite variety of categories of experts, professionals, academics, educators, and administrators involved in the very busy hectic and kaleidoscopic mixture of school change projects and the production of texts relating to them. The differences and often contradictions between the activities and writings of theses experts taint virtually every aspects of their endeavor save their common "worship" of the cause of "school reform" or "school change."

I have elaborated on and substantiated this claim in another book of mine.[50] In that book I also analyzed the acute, multi-layered damage the contemporary obsession with fragmentary school changes causes to the chances for real radical change or the reinvention of education. The issue is further developed in the first chapter of this book so I will not go into it here, except to outline the way by which it has inspired me.

My view on school change has been inspired and supported by the relevant mega-discourse in three complementary ways. To start with, this infinite literature documents all the grave problems Western education systems are plagued with. As I claim in the book, many of these problems, the gravest and most persistent amongst them, are nothing but the symptoms of the chronic sicknesses which plague these systems.[51] Five decades of literature about "reforms" designed to address these symptoms supplied me with ample evidences of their prevalence. Secondly, many of the reformers emphasize the gap between the prevailing education system and the postmodern society it is supposed to serve as well as the need to adapt education to the new era.[52] The problem is that these reformers fail to follow their own recommendation through. They rely on short-sighted tunnel vision, and see only a very partial aspect of the inadequacy of modern education systems. Both their basic claim concerning the need for change and their narrow and insufficient implementation thereof led to the basic claim I am making in this context.

Third, the sheer volume of this literature as well as its hectic and chaotic character are in themselves evidence of the acuteness of the prevailing educational crisis as well as the extent of panic and irrationality characterizing the current attempt to "deal with it." It thus brings home to any open-eyed observer the fervent need for radical rethinking of both the crisis and the infinite number of contradicting remedies suggested in this literature for dealing with it.

Imagine that frantically changing shifts of doctors, each made up of a few dozen physicians, are permanently panicking around a sick man's bed, each worryingly whispering unclear Latin diagnoses and prognoses just to be refuted by the angry whispers of the nearby doctor. Imagine further that each of them prescribes increasing amounts of all possible sorts of "conventional" medicine as well as exotic ointments and concoctions, powdered lizard tails and phlebotomy, insisting that the half-conscious patient take his "miraculous, newly developed cure." The poor patient, desperately trying to hold on to some hope and lacking the energy to resist or re-think the situation, not to mention changing it, takes all of the so-called cures. Unsurprisingly, during all this endless medical frenzy, his illness is aggravated and his symptoms are exacerbated, increasing further the medical frenzy around him and the ridiculous medical menu the poor man is force-fed.

If and when we encounter such a situation, we will surely conclude that something must be very wrong, not only with the sick person but also, and much more importantly, with the "treatment" he is getting. A rational physician in such a situation would chase all the "doctors" out of the room, throw away their pre-scriptions and putrid smoking bottles, and begin a rational process of systematic, thorough set of examinations, comparing and analyzing results and forming a reasonable, single hypothetical prognosis. Then he or she would commence a carefully designed, tentative, treatment, which can be modified, improved or changed according to results (as will any rational expert or professional in any context).

This is exactly the kind of process I am trying to trigger for the treatment of our ailing education systems in this book.

Salvaging "Paradigmatic Change"
In the current state of affairs, of inflationary and vacuous use of terms such as "educational change" or "reform" which are often characterized as "paradigmatic," "second order," or "holistic" changes, even language has been deprived of its ability to sustain real change. Educational-change literature describes practically every teacher who changes his or her methods of teaching first grade reading, and any school that introduces ICT-based learning, as undergoing paradigmatic change. If "paradigmatic" and similar terms are a true depiction of the partial, inept "change" processes which take place in the modern system today, there are no contemporary relevant terms left to describe the required change of the very foundations of this system.[53] This is why I coined the still unused, not-yet-abused terms "re-inventing education," or "re-thinking or re-considering education from scratch" to convey the concept reflected by "paradigm" and "second-level change" before it was rendered meaningless by inflationary use.

In my efforts to salvage what is left of the original meaning of the basic concepts depicting a radical, all-encompassing systematic change, and define the above new terms for referring to it, I have conversed with four discourses:
• Philosophy of science
• Cognitive research
• Organizational theories
• Psychological theories
I was most inspired by the ideas and discussions pertinent to philosophy of science, especially the debate about the development of science that emerged within it since the 1960s. According to this understanding, the development of science sometimes consists of major leaps or "paradigmatic changes" which lead to both radical redefinition and mapping of the object of discourse (i.e., the world as conceived by relevant researchers) and to the ways of approaching it. The examination of the emergence of Einstein's two theories of relativity served in this context as the main trigger for this understanding. The seminal work that encouraged this re-under-standing of the development of science is Kuhn's book *The Structure of Scientific Revolutions*.[54]

The use of "paradigmatic change" in the philosophy of science (and given my understanding of this term) was also inspired by a series of well known cognitive experiments which show that the same figurative structure can be perceived for one moment as being one object (e.g., a vase in one of the experiments) and then all of a sudden perceived as being altogether something else (two profiles facing each other in the above experiments). This has since remained a common way to bring home to students the meaning and possibility of a sudden cognitive leap or "paradigm change."

More or less at the same time Kuhn published his book, the concept of "second order" change has developed both in psychology and organizational thinking to relate to the total reshuffling of the cards and redefinition of the universe of discourse either in the human mind (in the first case) or concerning the goals and way of functioning of an organization (in the second case). Over the last thirty years, as talk about "crazy organizations"[55] and their need to define and redefine themselves every few years gained influence and weight, the term's popularity in organizational theory increased.

As a consequence of these discourses, the conception of the development of almost all other basic cultural domains went through paradigmatic change itself. It was radically changed from gradual accumulation and development to a series of total leaps changing all the rules of the game at once.

These four discourses and the understanding that science, the human cognition, human psyche, organizational function, and all other important cultural domains go through such leaps and total reshuffling have strengthened my conviction that modern education systems cannot be an exception and, given the prevailing acute crisis, must and can go through a similar leap.[56]

The History of Educational Processes' Parameters
Pointing out the need to re-invent education or for paradigmatic (in the original sense of the term) changes in education is only the starting point of my thinking on this issue. The ongoing conversation I have had with another mega-discourse, which consists of several very different discourses, helped me clarify and elaborate on the claim about the need for paradigmatic change in education. I refer here to the mega-discourse which relates to the history of the definitions of the main parameters of Western education systems. Like all other systems and organizations these systems have (both on the system and the single-unit, or school, levels), five main defining parameters: goals, structure, content, methods of activity, and way of approaching, and relating to, the target audience.[57] Each of these parameters underwent many changes in the course of Western education history. Learning about these changes and analyzing them helped me understand the nature of the change needed in the educational organizations of the future. I use "mega-discourse" above since the discourses referring to each of the parameters are totally disconnected from each other. I am not aware of any context which brought them together under the same conceptual roof as I have been doing for the last twenty years.

As far as the first and second parameters (goals and content of education) are concerned, it was the abovementioned history of the formation and re-formation of the liberal (or theoretical) curriculum since Plato (presented in Chapter Three) that helped me understand how irrelevant both the Platonic curriculum and the goals of education still inspired by it really are in our era.

Learning this history crystallized for me the acute need to radically redefine "educational goals" and the "educational program" (see Chapters Two and Three). My re-thinking the desired goals of education and the educational program had ample assistance from the discourse relating to the project of "justifying education" that was central to philosophy of education in the 1970s and early 1980s. This discourse was a reaction to the acute crisis, which seemed to encompass both the justification for the Platonic-modernistic goals of education and the educational program that ensued from it in postmodernist societies. This crisis brought home for many thinkers the need to rethink educational goals and programs and design them to better fit postmodern liberal societies (Chapter Two). However the discourse was flawed as the arguments used by the participants therein were all lacking in logic (as they themselves later admitted).

Most thinkers were desperately trying to find new justification for the traditional goals and curriculum which would apply to relativistic societies as well. The attempt itself was a source of positive inspiration for me, while its desperate and clearly flawed nature was a source of negative inspiration.

In addition to the valuable lessons I learnt from this discourse, I also had enormous help from the combination of three different discourses into one "mega-discourse" about "meaningful human activity." This concept helped me analyze the relevance of the curriculum to Western cultures during various eras from Plato to this very day and to hypothesize about the level of meaningfulness it has for students in those different times, a level which undoubtedly affected their motivation to study it (the discussion of this topic appears in Chapter Three).

The first and most foundational of these discourses was the long tradition that stems from Aristotle's view of practical (i.e., activity-oriented) argument.[58] The understanding I got from this tradition was later sustained and further developed by relevant psychological and organizational theories relating to goal-oriented human activity. These various discourses helped me to form a theory of meaningful activity relevant to the evaluation of educational activities. Relying on this theory I could better understand and "locate" the "disappearance" of the meaning of the prevailing curriculum for its learners (and probably many of its teachers) and the need to resurrect this meaning on the basis of altogether new foundations.

As for the third parameter of school, its organizational structure, learning the history of the modern school's organizational structure and its development throughout the last two modern centuries (elaborated in Chapter Four) helped me understand the way it was designed along the organizational lines of the modern factory in the last decades of the nineteenth and early decades of the twenties centuries.[59] This discourse was essential to my understanding of the need to radically redesign this structure in order to adapt it to postmodern organizational structures.

Finally my conversation with two discourses relating to "children" helped me understand the need to radically change their status in the desired educational organization (reflected in the discussion in Chapter Five). These are "the history of childhood" throughout the centuries, especially since Gutenberg,[60] and the more recent history of the legal change in the status of children.[61]

I will not go further into the above categories of mega-discourses and the discourses of which they consist since I relate to them at length in chapters dedicated to each of them in the first part of the book. Here ends our journey through the discourses that inspired and supported me in forming the propositions comprising the critical or deconstructive argument at the core of the book's first part. Since the book's second part is the positive complement of the radical criticism developed in the first, these discourses often relate to major aspects of that part as well. Let us move now to the discourses which are unique to the second part, discourses from which I learnt much about the relevant issues and which inspired me to develop the constructive argument at its core.

PERSPECTIVES BASIC TO THE SECOND PART OF THE BOOK

In the second part of this book I outline a radically new perception of Humanistic education, appropriate for and meaningful within postmodern Liberal Democracies. Launching such a wide-ranging project in a systematic, mindful, and top-down manner requires that I first delineate to the reader the discourses that helped me define the desired goals of education in a postmodern democracy. Only once this challenge is met (the first mission of the second part) and the nature of the era is fully grasped (a task accomplished in the first part of the book), can one redefine and characterize the various parameters of the desired educational program/ organization (the second mission of the second part).

Perspectives Basic to the Second Part's First Mission, or: Redefining the Goals of Education

The task of formulating desired goals for education in postmodern Liberal Democracies calls for two separate steps to be taken:
- Present and substantiate educational goals desired for and in postmodern democracies;
- Show why the default tendency in our era to remain agnostic or neutral rather than define clear general educational goals should and can be overcome.

Below I will present the discourses I have conversed with for the sake of meeting these two requirements.

The Humanistic Discourses
My understanding of the desired goals for education in Liberal Democracies (described in Chapter Six) stems from my understanding of Humanism, which is the ideological source of Liberal Democracy and as such the North Star that has guided me in my attempt to set educational goals for postmodern democracies. Within Humanism I relied heavily on Humanistic tradition as it was formed in the last few centuries and on current psychological bodies of knowledge, theories, and empirical research that express and substantiate the basic Humanistic suppositions and values today.[62]

Personal Development and the Humanistic Tradition

Humanism relies heavily on the ideals of *paideia* and *humanitas* which were originally developed in ancient Greece and Rome, resurrected and adapted during the Renaissance, and reached an apex (until this very day) in a much more open-ended version in Germany of the end of the eighteenth century and beginning of the nineteenth century. German Humanism, mainly as reflected in the thought of Wilhelm von Humboldt, heavily influenced J.S. Mill's liberal view as expressed mainly in *On Liberty*. Since Mill, Humanism became the most powerful pillar of liberal thought over the past one hundred and fifty years, and (consciously or unconsciously) influenced dominant liberal philosophers of education today as well as the dominant commonsense worldview of the academic, professional, and political classes in the West.

At the core of the tradition stemming from Humboldt lies the concept of "*Bildung*" which in its original sense meant a process of self-discovery and self-creation by a young person through reflective critical journey throughout culture. "Culture" or "*Kultur*" was used in this tradition in the largest possible sense of the term relating to the framework of modes of living and acting dominant in a certain human group or community. German Humanists also developed a literary genre called "*Bildungsroman,*" which served many Humanists as a framework for the experimentation with and operationalization of the concept of "*Bildung*." This genre in general and especially one of the first *Bildungsroman, Wilhelm Meisters Lehrjahre* have had an enormous impact on me as a rich, psychologically appealing laboratory for experimentation with conceptions of human development that is culturally vital for us today.

I was also obviously inspired by secondary sources which offer contemporary interpretation of this tradition and the Millian thinking which stems from it directly.[63] I was further inspired by the writings of John White and Eamon Callan, two philosophers of education whose perception of the goals of education clearly follows the Humanistic and Millian traditions.[64]

Humanistic Research on Personal Development

Philosophical and literary thinking and intellectual experimenting alone is not a sound enough foundation for a vision of postmodern education, not in an era wherein various branches of psychological research have denied the traditional humanistic disciplines (philosophy, literature, and history) the status of the main sources for the understanding of the Good Life (or "well-being" or "satisfying life" in today's psychological language) and human development. That is why I turned to psychological theory and research to find out whether the Humanistic developmental view I found to be so rich, valid, and relevant for our era can be sustained today. This quest has led me on an exciting journey of discovery through many psychological discourses that consciously or (mostly) unconsciously follow the Humanist tradition and translate it to terms of prevailing psychological research and ensuing developmental conceptions and methodologies

Here I can only scratch the surface of the prevailing psychological, Humanistic mega-discourse made up of a very long list of psychological discourses I have conversed with through the years and which offer substantial support for the feasibility of my call to adapt Humanistic goals of education to the postmodern reality. Some of these discourses also helped me operationalize these goals and develop an appropriate operational educational methodology for their implementation. My first steps in this journey led me to the obvious three-generation-old discourses of Humanistic psychology as developed by Maslow and Rogers,[65] to Existential psychology as developed by, among others, Rollo May,[66] to Logotherapy as developed by Viktor Frankl[67] and to Erich Fromm's attempt to combine the Humanistic perspective into one integrated theory about human development and prosperity in a Godless era.[68] All four of these well known discourses emphasize the same developmental elements central to the Humanistic tradition: the aspiration of the individual to discover or create meaning for her or his life through experimentation with various existential modes and reflection on them.

These discourses are the foundations of my search into more recent and more empirically substantiated psychological discourses. I found ample approaches and research lines that (often unconsciously) continue the Humboldtian-Millian Humanist way of thinking in this context as well. Among these I can name: Self Determination Theory,[69] recent research on interests,[70] positive psychology,[71] self-regulation,[72] happiness theory,[73] research on life goals,[74] research on identity formation, and career development through exploration.[75]

Here From another perspective, I also drew inspiration from research on learning, cognitive and performance styles,[76] as well as temperaments and personality types,[77] and from Gardner's research on multiple intelligences.[78]

Contemporary research also supports the claim that autonomy develops through reflective "experiments in living." In contemporary psychological terms, this process is termed "exploration" of various existential and activity modes open to the individual. An individual in such an exploration process is perceived as aspiring to find her or his "inner powers," as Mill would put it, in an ongoing search for his or her "vocation" (*Berufung*) in German Humanist terms, his or her "identity," "career," "life goal," "interests," "self profile," "personal styles," or "intelligences," to use some of the many present-day psychological terminologies.[79]

These categories of research were developed separately from one another and usually do not relate to each other, despite the fact that they were all developed in the last two or three decades along empirical lines mostly in psychological departments. As I already claimed, they rarely rely on Humboldt's or Mill's Humanist and liberal views consciously, however when integrated, and appropriately operationalized, they form a mega-discourse that posits the foundation for a holistic and systematic methodology that can help young people answer the four questions essential to the formation of any "life plan"[80] and hence to any developmental process:

- What are my goals in life? (relevant research: interests, life goals, identity formation)
- What capacities am I endowed with and to what extent are they relevant to the implementation of these goals? (research: intelligences, capacities, self-regulation)

- What are the modes of actions most adequate and effective for me and how can I use them to best achieve my goals in the context wherein I operate? (research: learning and performance styles, temperaments, personality types, and cognitive styles)
- How am I to act in order to find answers to the previous questions? (theories and research of exploration and reflection).

All the above bodies of knowledge, which comprise what can also be called "the mega-discourse on personal autonomy," complement each other and enhance the ability to re-appropriate, update, substantiate, and operationalize traditional Humanistic concepts of the autonomous individual engaged in the *Bildung* process or in the process of reflective "experiments in living" as Mill and Wilhelm von Humboldt called them. They all supplied me with very good reasons to accept autonomy, based on the concept and process of *Bildung* (discussed in Chapters Two and Six), as a necessary condition for well-being and human prosperity.

I take autonomy to be a necessary yet unsatisfactory condition for a satisfying life and, hence, only one educational goal. In Chapter Six I delineate two more such goals: dialogical belonging and morality. The first refers to the need to educate young people to feel themselves as belonging to some cultural or social context (the most relevant to them obviously); but at the same time as committed to a critical proactive and hermeneutical approach towards the relevant society or culture (and hence the qualification of "belonging" by "dialogical"). Such a concept of belonging certainly does not contradict the value of personal autonomy; it is in fact necessitated by it. The process of *Bildung* or exploration described above necessarily requires embeddedness (to use a term often mentioned in this context) in socio-cultural contexts. Here too I was inspired by the German Humanistic tradition and by Mill. This tradition emphasized the relationship between *Bildung* and *Kultur* or between personal journeys of self-revelation, self-expression, and culture. I have found ample support for this view in more contemporary liberal philosophies as well. I refer to several prominent liberal philosophers who acknowledge the need to incorporate some aspects of Communitarianism in the liberal conception of personal development.[81] This view is also supported by empirical research relating to intrinsic motivation (e.g., Self Determination Theory) and exploration. These discourses have inspired my thinking about the mutual support characterizing the relationship between the values of enhancement of autonomy and dialogical belonging.

As for morality, in this book I did not go into detail on this important educational goal for two reasons: First of all, the justification for it is obvious. As emphasized by von Humboldt and Mill, morality is a necessary condition to guaranteeing the universality of any concept of experimenting in living and hence for the development of autonomy. A Hobbesian society of constant struggle and insecurity does not allow for such a process. Secondly, there is extensive literature relating to several methods of education for morality which are compatible with education for autonomy and dialogical belonging.[82] At this stage I feel that I can rely on them.

The Possibility of Setting Compelling Educational Goals

The various branches of Humanism mentioned above have inspired me and functioned as my North Star, so to speak. However, inspiration in and of itself was not enough. While I was travelling through the "Humanistic landscape" I was aware of several influential objections raised in the twentieth century to the very idea of outlining general goals for education, and to any project designed to form a systematic meta-narrative for a desired educational process. The discourses conveying these objections were an important source for negative inspiration for me.

These objections stem from two main groups of discourses: from recent modernist and postmodernist nominalistic stances as well as from prominent conceptions of liberalism. Below I delineate the main claims made in the literature and my justifications for rejecting them.

The Wittgensteinian and Postmodern Discourses

The first discourse I considered consists of late modernistic trends in the philosophy of language. These trends were influenced by the late Wittgenstein's understanding of the function of language. According to this view, the meaning of terms used in language is purely performative, that is to say that it consists solely of the practical uses of the terms in specific social contexts or language games (as they are referred to in this view).

According to criticism raised against projects such as mine in this view, positing general values or goals that cut across various liberal societies, contexts, and eras (from the end of the eighteenth century until our days) takes place outside specific practices or language games and hence lacks any concrete operationalization or meaning.[83]

A variation of this argument developed later within the postmodernistic literature discussed above. This objection opposes any and all meta-narratives on principle. A move such as the one I am proposing is perceived in this context not only as meaningless but also as an attempt to entrench power structures in service of certain hegemonic elites.[84]

My response to the Wittgensteinian allegations of impossibility or meaninglessness of setting general goals is twofold:

- These allegations are self-contradicting since the argument against generalization is itself based on a general and universalistic theory on the nature and function of language and the conceptions of logic, epistemology, and ontology this theory requires (Wittgenstein was obviously aware of this contradiction which affected his tormented way of writing).
- Even if we accept the critics' claims for argument's sake, the Humanistic discourse my argument is located in is sufficiently defined and operational to allow for the meaningfulness of generalizations made with it. It is indeed presented as transcending specific liberal states or societies, but there is nothing to prevent us from assuming that all of these societies are based on the same "language game" as far as their basic ethical and constitutional foundations are concerned. This is the case since the discourses basic to them all stem from the same larger liberal discourse which developed over

the past three hundred years based on a defined, not very long, list of Great Books.

My response to the postmodernistic version of this criticism is to some extent structurally similar. I already elaborated on the postmodernistic view above[85] and showed it to be self contradicting for similar reasons. Furthermore, it was clear to me from the outset that by objecting to any meta-narrative, postmodernists are effectively sanctioning the general educational goals that are now accepted de facto throughout the world—pursuit of power, fun, and money—if only as a default result of their condemnation of any attempt to set and operationalize any alternative, premeditated, goals.[86] Thus the choice we face today is not between adopting universalistic goals and refraining from doing so, but rather between setting general Humanistic goals and accepting the default neo-liberal technocratic goals which are already in place by default. I have also been convinced that setting such goals is actually the best-case scenario available to us as a society. Further justification for it can be found when considering the realistic context of today liberal societies (as opposed to "surfing the clouds" of purely scholastic debates). We cannot ignore the need to face prevailing fundamentalist or fascist alternatives to Humanism and liberalism which are taking hold of Western society in recent decades. The influence these perspectives have is enhanced by escape-from–freedom mechanisms, neo-liberalism triggers, and postmodernist attitudes which provide them with practical, if not always ideological, support.

For those of my readers who wish to preserve the status of neo-liberal hedonistic values as exclusive goals of education, or take the risk of their deterioration to anti-democratic values, I have nothing more to add, at least on the normative level. We simply stand on two totally opposed or even incommensurable starting points. But for those who fear reliance on these values may create a fragmented society and vacuous, identity-less, disintegrated, and miserable individuals, I think I present a sound argument in favor of consciously guiding education in light of autonomy, dialogical belonging, and morality instead of surrendering to the above default scenarios.

Twentieth-Century Discourses on Liberalism

The objections that stem from the above worldviews (Wittgenstein's philosophy of language and Postmodernism) are easy to detect. The discourses supporting them are openly and internationally hostile to the main goal of this book. However in addition to dealing with the "enemy" I also struggled with "friendly fire" from the liberal camp. This has been a much more difficult and demanding battle.

The above objection to the formulation of general values, goals, and systematic meta-narratives has already penetrated (what may be referred to as) the collective late-modern and postmodern subconscious. As such, it is expressed by the main late-modern and postmodern versions of liberalism. In my eyes, most of these versions express the "shrinking" or the "impoverishment" of liberalism. I relate here to the following three very different yet dominant liberal discourses:

- *Neo-Liberalism*, which consists of a belief in a small state and in a market economy as the two defining attributes of liberalism.[87]

- *Distributive Justice-Oriented Liberalism.* This discourse opposes the first and calls for a liberal welfare State relying on an (alleged) ethically neutral process of just distribution of what this tradition also calls "basic goods." These goods (defined differently by different thinkers in this discourse) are those thought to be necessary for any individual to develop or live in light of her or his perception of the Good Life or goals.[88]
- *Liberal-Republican Views.*[89] These views emphasize the "public forum,"[90] or "conscious social reconstruction"[91] as the core of the democratic state. In other words, they consider collective decision making about the future of society, constrained by some liberal conditions (e.g., equality and fair access to the public discussion) to be the heart of democracy.

All three versions of liberalism (although they oppose each other in some of their basic assumptions, values, "temperaments," and recommendations) reflect a desire to remain "neutral" as far as the definition of the Good Life by the state is concerned. This is categorically the case for the first two views, and is true concerning the third view to the extent that it too objects to *a priori* definitions of Good (i.e., definitions set prior to decisions on the Good by the will of the public). In counterdistinction to the two other views, it does support *a posteriori* definition, which can change according to the "will of the public."

In all three cases the objection to the definition of the Good Life by the state stems from skeptical or relativistic foundations; according to all these views, since there is no way to reach an objective or universal understanding of the *Good Life*, it is undesirable for the state to dictate any such conception to its citizens.

All three views have a strong hold on different segments of the postmodern consciousness. All three contribute to the disconnection of liberalism and prevailing liberal democratic societies from their Humanistic roots. All three therefore enhance the "sterilization" of education within prevailing Liberal Democracies.

The third, Republican, view, is simply not based on a commitment to the Humanistic concept of autonomy, at least not as a foundational social principle. As for the first two, while relying on the Humanistic supposition concerning a free-to-choose, autonomous individual, they refrain from according this concept any real substance or concrete meaning beyond the most abstract definition of the term. They do so intentionally, in an attempt to refrain from choosing any one concrete understanding of the concept on citizens of their desired liberal society and thus infringing on the neutrality they see themselves committed to.

Following this commitment to neutrality they take the existence of an autonomous individual as given and focus on guaranteeing the necessary conditions for the *expression of autonomy* in the social framework. They ignore the need of any liberal society to actively enhance *the development of autonomy*. Remaining in the ethereal spheres of abstract philosophical discussion, they ignore the liberal's duty to deal with most trivial psychological, historical, and social facts relevant to her or his view. Autonomy goes directly against very basic human needs—acceptance and security—and hence against the default human tendency for conformity. This is partly why it has never served as a guiding principle for social regimes until the last few generations.

Today's liberal societies are just the latest link in a very old chain of totalitarian regimes. Liberalism is hence but a thin veneer on most of their social fabrics. Almost all frameworks in liberal societies are still based on a simple exchange of social acceptance for conformity. Most individuals still do not enjoy the cognitive, psychological, motivational, and social conditions necessary for autonomous development. Thus autonomy goes against our nature, history, and social frameworks. If one takes autonomy seriously one must harness all social processes to a single educational (in the largest sense of the term, relating to all aspect of social life and to all age groups) goal: enhancing the development of autonomy in spite of human psychology, history, and the makeup of almost all social frameworks. Making sure one enjoys fair access to the free market (as required by the first view) or also to basic goods (as required by the second) is very far from enough to deal with the above obstacles to actual realization of autonomy in liberal societies.

This is where Mill's liberal view has an enormous advantage over the above views. For him, the first and foremost mission of a liberal society is education in the larger sense of the term: doing everything possible to ensure that the social framework and processes enhance the development and expression of individual autonomy.[92] For this sake one should define autonomy in a concrete way which details the personal attributes one must have in order to develop as an autonomous individual aware of his or her preferences and able to carry them out. This requires limiting the range of neutrality or social tolerance in society; however, given that some very probable alternatives are turning liberalism into a vacuous or inapplicable concept and leading to the collapse of liberal societies, it is by far the best deal in town.

Thus, these three discourses were an important source of negative inspiration and helped me clarify and sharpen my own position. The conversations I had with these views were especially fruitful since I share some major presuppositions with each of them yet reject their conclusions, especially those relevant to the present discussion. In counterdistinction to the above "thin" or formal (i.e., "devoid of decision about the Good Life") liberalism, this book relies on a "substantive" or "material" view of liberalism. Furthermore, following von Humboldt and Mill,[93] it is my view that the only *raison d'être* for Liberal Democracies is the optimal implementation of the Humanistic ideal of personal self-realization and hence the values of personal autonomy and its supporting and complementing values: dialogical belonging and morality. Thus I am not "afraid" to set universal educational goals for all liberal societies on the basis of the above desired developmental perception.[94]

As I see it, given the existential vacuum most citizens of prevailing liberal societies live in, the third view is poised to replace human rights with the "general will" (to use the term coined by Rousseau, the founding father of the Republican approach to democracy, or what Talmon called Totalitarian Democracy[95]) or the will of the public as defined by a majority perceived to be the core of the democratic state. It is not that all views pertaining to this category intentionally forsake human rights or will necessarily lead to their rejection but that they can easily slide down the very slippery slope to an erosion of the hold human rights have on Western democratic societies and to a destruction of the core of liberalism. This was indeed the case in the first three decades of the previous century in the Soviet Union, Italy, and Germany. Regimes in all these countries began, at one time or another, with Republican ideas as to the importance of the will of the people and quickly deteriorated to an entirely totalitarian rule.[96]

As for the first two views, they too encouraged, although indirectly, the development of fascism in France, Spain, Italy, and Germany.[97] Ironically, many thinkers in the post-World War II era actually adopted the first two views as means to defend the West and prevent the horrors that ensue from the extremes the third view can deteriorate into from reoccurring. They bent over backwards to ensure that their liberalism was untarnished by a bias toward any one view of the Good Life whether that view stemmed from "the will of the people" as expressed in elections or was decided by a despot or totalitarian elite which claimed their decision reflected what the people *should* want. Defenders of the first two views believed any sort of pre-inclination or bias of this sort was likely to result in history repeating itself once more.[98] Thus they did their best to remain neutral and abstain from defending any substantive view of the autonomous individual. This abstention aggravated the acute existential vacuum at the core of today's liberal societies to a very great extent. Given the fragile nature of the ideal of autonomy and the aforementioned human need for security and conformity, this void is highly likely to be filled by dogmatic or totalitarian views which can originate either within or outside the liberal societies. Ironically these are the same views that post-World War II thinkers were trying to safeguard liberalism against.[99]

All three views endanger Liberal Democracies by refusing to let the state enhance the Humanistic view which is the cradle of Liberal Democracy through its educational and other systems. The dangers to individuals' self-determination and self-expression stemming from this refusal is enhanced in postmodernity by the total legitimation of the default human tendency to indulge in egoism and hedonism, leading to practices that enhance the disintegration of the individual and his or her capacity to constructively lead a satisfying life based on self-expression as well as to social anomie. These phenomena in turn are likely to create a craving for "law and order" and hence for a strong, dictator-esque leader.

We have no right to ignore the meaningful aforementioned lessons history taught us. "Decadence" and "fin de siecle" during the nineteenth century and then during "the Merry Twenties" of the twentieth reflected the two previous eras wherein human life was deprived of its meaning due to the anorectic nature of liberalism practiced during those times. This led to the abovementioned social malaise which begat the two world wars.

Another fact we have no right to ignore is that the above argument reflects more then just an arbitrary analysis of history. This process was foretold by prominent thinkers in the above eras, including Nietzsche, Dostoevsky, and Durkheim, who foresaw much of the decadence and disintegration brought on by the gaping existential vacuum liberalism created at the core of Western culture. These horrors triggered the philosophical, literary, and sociological projects of each of the above thinkers.[100] All three forewarned their disciples of the emergence of "the last man"

(Nietzsche), the legitimization of immorality and murderous crimes (Dostoevsky), and the rise in the level of social anomie, suicide, and other symptoms of deep human malaise (Durkheim). All three believed this dangerous process to be a direct result of the existential vacuum in the heart of the modern, liberal, capitalist state and society.[101] Unfortunately, their worst fears were realized in the processes that led to the First and Second World Wars. My long conversations with these three thinkers, their almost identical, well substantiated fears, expressed in altogether different ways with almost no mutual influence, and the fact that it took but a few short decades for those fears to be realized have had a very strong impact on me and my above substantive perception of liberalism.

Returning now to our postmodern era, another mega-discourse which had significant impact on me in this context consists of various discourses on the impact of the media, the advertisement industry, and of course the Internet, the effects of which are multiplied time and again by the powers of globalization. More specifically I refer to discourses about the disintegration of social solidarity[102] and the "saturation of the self,"[103] as we "amuse ourselves to death."[104] I am afraid that with the manure provided by these phenomena, the ground is a thousand times more fertile today for the horrors that stem from the vacuous core of thin, formal liberalism than it was in the second half of the nineteenth or first half of the twentieth century.

The fact that the Humanistic view I adopted in this book is the most appropriate for helping prevailing Liberal Democracies to fight the above danger is not coincidental. It was deliberately developed by the German intellectuals of the end of the eighteenth and beginning of the nineteenth centuries to prevent young German intellectuals from falling into pietistic fundamentalism in response to the existential vacuum created already then by the materialistic deterministic enlightenment views imported from France.[105] Enlightenment (at least its more influential versions), being materialistic, deterministic, utilitarian, and based on laissez-faire economics (a forefather of today's neo-liberalism) did not allow for any interpretation of human life other than maximization of the basic biological desires.[106] As such, it did not leave any room for suppositions concerning the possibility for a meaning of life which transcends material and human freedom. The Humanistic view was consciously and mindfully forged to supply a third way, which is more substantive than the enlightenment ethos of the time and relies on the assumptions concerning human freedom and a meaningful life based on the aspiration for authenticity and self expression. At the same time, it was, like the enlightenment view, secular and rationalist.

In addition to the menacing internal threat mentioned above, Western Liberal Democracies must now face growing external threats to their long-and medium-term survival from Muslim fundamentalism and the new versions of state-run totalitarian capitalism.[107] This threat requires, even more so than the "cultural contradictions of capitalism" (to quote the title of Bell's book describing the self-destructive mechanism built into thin liberalism),[108] a re-adaptation of the substantive Humanistic concepts of liberalism. Young people today must know and understand what the stakes in this cultural battle are so that they can enjoy and appreciate liberalism and be motivated to defend and fight for human rights and Liberal Democracy.

Formal liberalism was a stance Western democracies may have been able to afford, or at least some thinkers had reasons to believe they did, in the optimistic golden age of post-World War II and even more so after the collapse of the Communist block. They most certainly cannot afford it anymore. Clinging onto this form of liberalism may very well mean throwing the baby (the belief in individual self determination, human rights, and social justice) out with the bathwater (the belief in a substantive definition of the Good Life based on Humanist tradition).

I hope I have clarified the various discourses that inspired me both positively and negatively in my choice of Humanism and the universal values stemming from it as a starting point for the rethinking of education (for any society wishing to be liberal). I further hope I managed to clarify the discourses which led to and enhanced my fierce objection, based on logical, ideological, and ethical grounds, to the attempt to castrate liberalism or deprive it and the educational endeavor in it of their Humanistic foundations.

Perspectives Basic to the Operationalization of Humanistic Goals of Education

It is clear to me that outlining the need and possibility for setting and defining universal educational goals, and pointing to the nature of these goals, is far from sufficient support for an entirely new educational approach. I am well aware of the fact that in order for contemporary educators and decision makers to perceive the project of redefining education as feasible, these goals must also be operationalized and translated to concrete methodologies and educational processes. Furthermore, the operationalization must be based on theories, research, and methodologies accepted by the relevant contemporary scientific and theoretical circles.

It was not difficult to identify a large array of perspectives that easily "lend themselves" as foundations for such a project. I have already pointed many of them out above when dealing with the meaning of the Humanistic educational goals. The discourses mentioned above[109] largely assist in the operationalization of the educational goals as far as the desired educational and pedagogic programs are concerned. In order to rethink other parameters of the desired educational process I have also been conversing with literatures relevant to the organizational structure of the desired educational organization and the status of young people in it.

In my deliberation of the first of these two parameters, the appropriate organizational structure for desired education systems, I "talked with" and relied on dominant organizational theories and research referring to the "learning," "virtual," "crazy," "flat," "chaordic," "outsourcing," "downsized," and "diffuse" organizations which characterize the postmodern era.[110] These organizational discourses and research fields inspired my thinking about and my design of a structure for a postmodern educational organization. It is only natural to assume that as the model of the modern factory-like organization inspired the modern school, models of postmodern organizations should inspire the postmodern educational organization.

When relating to the second of the above parameters, the status young people should have in a desired postmodern organization, I was obviously inspired by social, ethical, and legal discourses which document and recommend the changing of attitude towards "children" from the modern paternalistic one to the postmodern one conceiving young people as subjects.[111]

PERSPECTIVES BASIC TO THE THIRD PART OF THE BOOK

In the third part of the book I call for an *intentional* long-term, macro-level, *strategic* process wherein education will be *mindfully* adapted to the needs and possibilities of postmodern Liberal Democracies instead of *unmindfully drifting with* the changing currents and fluxes of the postmodern storms. I then point to some primary activities that can be undertaken for this sake. My understanding of this strategic process is based on intensive conversations and "confrontations" with four categories of discourses: the technocratic discourse, my arch-nemesis so to speak, and the discourses on piecemeal social reform and strategic thinking which have served me as sources of mostly positive inspiration. A fourth discourse, pertaining to "step by step social engineering," functioned as a source of both negative and positive influence on me.

The Technocratic Discourse

Technocrats do not deal with questions about ultimate goals or desirability. Most of them willingly (or without considering any alternative whatsoever) and naturally succumb to immediate pressures and "cannot afford," for fear of too strong a dissonance, to think on the macro level or in light of long-term ethical perspectives. In the best of cases, their thinking does not reach beyond the number of years which determine the length of their term in office. It has long been clear to me that as a result of this tunnel-like, short-term thinking, technocrats cannot develop the new education Western Liberal Democracies so badly need. The more I understand how extremely deep and extensively spread-out the roots of the technocratic discourse are in education, the more I realize the powerful hold it has over postmodern decision makers' minds and the more convinced I become that there is little chance that the urgently required re-thinking of education will occur spontaneously in the high echelons of decision making in many contemporary Liberal Democracies. As long as the adaptation of education to the new era depends on technocrats and technocratic thinking, we are doomed to continue to suffer from a disintegrating public education system while decision makers, administrators, and educators are mindlessly engaged with useless, obsessive "educational reforms." Western democracies are paying and will continue to pay too high a price in the foreseeable future, in economic, social, and psychological terms, for this default (in both senses of the term) scenario (see relevant analyses above and in Chapter One).[112]

This technocratic view can be easily detected as basic to almost all educational decision making processes in today's Western societies. Still technocracy is not a declared worldview. There is no defined discourse or mega-discourse dealing with it. The use of the term "discourse" in this context is very different from its use elsewhere in this annex. It is impossible to point to literature which directly and explicitly defends it, yet a quick glance over almost all texts on schooling, educational management, planning, computerization of education, the curricula, and teaching of various disciplines, or the infinite literature on "school change," "reform," and "restructuring," is all the reader would need to easily identify it. Being ubiquitous, dominant yet undeclared, and usually disguised behind vacuous slogans and clichés, it is extremely dangerous to the future of our education systems and societies and to the well-being of the next generation.

Take for example the efforts to computerize education. Most projects in this context have focused on questions of quantity: What is the desired ratio of students to computer? How long will it take to connect all schools to the Internet? How broad can or should the relevant transmitting bands be? How much money should be invested? What kind of training should teachers have? To what extent and how should it be incorporated in prevailing curricula? And so on. An essential part of the answer to these questions is usually "the more the merrier," since politicians and high-level civil servants are best served when they have "evidence" of how much they care for education, which in the language of the common political discourse translates to "how much of the budget was allocated to education." But very few ask the "what for" question. Instead everyone presupposes an answer which equates computerization with the extremely vague concepts of "progress," "advancement," and "economic competitiveness."[113]

In the best of cases, when policy makers feel they must refer to some defined "Technology Enhanced Learning" (also known as TEL) goals, they tend to equate it with "new," "innovative," "constructivist," "active," "self regulated," or "personalized" learning processes, which are perceived as a necessary condition for individual or national competitiveness in the global market. This connection between the "new" learning methods and competitiveness is seldom justified, beyond the occasional vague claim concerning "the need for creativity and entrepreneurship" which are "necessary for success in the knowledge society." Furthermore, almost nobody asks the crucial question: is computerization really necessary for the "new" methods to succeed?

In almost all cases these declarations function as nothing more than slogans: there is no evidence that computerization is necessary for or even enhances constructivist learning.[114] Moreover, this mode of learning is actually very far from being "new" or "innovative." It was fervently advocated by Dewey and his many progressive followers as early as the beginning of the twentieth century, when the progressive spirit dominated Western societies or other social contexts (for example in Israeli kibbutzim in the early decades of the twentieth century[115] or in Jenaplan schools founded in Germany during the same period[116]). As for the contribution of these methods or of the computerization of education to economic competitiveness, again there is no evidence that this extremely expensive process gives students or countries a more competitive "edge" than they acquire thanks to the computerization and digitation young people are exposed to in their natural environment outside the school, an environment which is light-years ahead of the extremely (physically, practically, and cognitively) limited process of computerizing education. There is certainly no evidence that this process, even if it provides such an "edge," justifies the enormous resources all societies continuously invest in it, given possible, and usually acutely needed, alternative investments (raising teachers' salaries would be an obvious one for most Western countries).

Most importantly, it is characteristic of technocratic "thinking" to "economize" education and take the enhancement of competitiveness on the social and individual levels as the only or at the very least the main educational goal. But from a rationalistic perspective, before computerization is justified as enhancing competitiveness, competitiveness (i.e., the ability to maintain and enlarge permanent growth in GNP) should, in and of itself, be justified as an educational goal, as should its preference over other desired goals (e.g., autonomy, dialogical belonging, and morality).

Another cliché often used in this context has to do with the need to use the computerization of education to bridge the "digital divide" between those who have access to ICT and those who are not as fortunate. But again this is nothing but a politically correct slogan. Young people from all social strata have access to ICT from mobile phones (as ubiquitous today as wristwatches) or Internet cafés which are not only common but also offer their services at extremely affordable rates. Again there is no evidence that the digital skills of young people from low socioeconomic echelons are inferior to those of the more fortunate of their peers. There are even reasons to believe the opposite is true, since for better or worse high- and middle-class young people are much more exposed to the modern "book-based" culture and hence might have to overcome many more obstacles in their mastery of digital skills.

It is important to emphasize that my last argument was not intended to categorically reject the aforementioned assumptions. I only argue that in almost all cases, they have been adopted thoughtlessly, without any attempt to respond to any opposing argument or potentially refuting facts.[117] It is this thoughtlessness which characterizes technocracy in all other processes common in education systems over the past few decades: building new schools or restoring existing buildings, new curricula design, determining new modes for teacher training, and so on.

Having studied many of these processes I realized that efforts to realize them have been executed, on the most part, on quantitative, instrumental levels alone while the basic questions were never asked. Where new school buildings are concerned, relevant questions would be: Do we need school buildings today to the same extent we that needed them during the modern age? In other words, should postmodern education processes be executed within a twentieth-century lococentric organizational structure?

Where designing new curricula is concerned, fundamental yet disregarded questions include: What kind of educational programs do we want? Why? In light of which values and goals? Which subjects should be included in them?[118] Have we systematically compared the kind of curriculum we want with relevant alternatives and found that it fares better in light of the guiding values? Again, with time I have learnt that these questions are seldom asked, certainly not systematically, and if some political speech or policy paper requires some reference to them nothing but accepted clichés are used to answer them. These clichés have no chance of withstanding rational criticism, but who, in this technocratic world, is interested in facing, or is even aware of the possibility of, such criticism?

While technocracy is pervasive but tacit, its criticism has been explicit and quite loud over the last century. It has actually been a major source for worry in many intellectual discourses, as it was for me.[119] However technocrats themselves have never heeded the criticism of their practices. Furthermore, an overwhelming majority of them, graduating from business, economic, technological department, or programs that focus on administrative, organizational, or technological theories, have never heard about it and are not even conscious of its possibility, let alone existence.

In many universities such criticism is elaborated in room 234, where (say) sociology, history, or philosophy of education or technology are taught, yet completely ignored in room 232, where future economists, engineers, business administrators, or industrial managers are educated. This is a tragic example of the gap between the "two cultures" that characterizes modernity and postmodernity. Coming from the humanities and the social sciences myself, the discourse on this cultural gap[120] has helped me understand both the "other side," with its total ignorance of the possibility and desirability of a critical approach and rational systematic thinking, and the dangers this ignorant approach poses for the future of our society.

The Discourse on Piecemeal Social Reform

An important reservation should be made here. There is one discourse that can be interpreted maybe not as explicitly supporting technocracy, but certainly as lending it support. I refer here to the view known as "step by step social engineering" which traditionally posits itself as a reformist, *laissez-faire* alternative to the more pretentious continental approach of supporting revolutions and ambitious long-term "macro planning."[121] This approach generally lends itself easily to inter-pretations as support for economically conservative policy. As such it heavily influenced the Thatcheristic policy in the UK (among many others),[122] a policy which was largely continued by the "new labor" and has had a huge impact on the entire Western world.

This discourse, although certainly not intended to support technocratic approaches, can be interpreted as *post-facto* supporting a short-term, piecemeal, micro-level approach to policy making, usually characteristic of technocracy. I have hence had a long "conversation" with it, attempting to understand to what extent it does indeed support technocracy; and regardless of this point, what weight should be given to its recommendations. This discourse was especially important to me since I have adopted the Popperian epistemic view which is perceived by many (including Popper himself) as the basis for step by step social engineering. My current response to the abovementioned questions is twofold:

When one *truly* understands its requirements, one cannot use a step by step social engineering approach to support technocracy. While the view does indeed oppose revolutionary steps and long-term macro-level planning, it requires permanent criticism on both the ethical and practical levels. Technocracy, on the other hand, tends to suffocate any criticism.

I found however that I disagree, at least to a significant extent, with the piecemeal view regardless of its relation to the technocratic approach. Step by step, undirected change cannot be the only or even the dominant approach to policy making today, especially not where education systems are concerned. It may have been appropriate in eras of relative stability or gradual development, or for systems that befit their external reality. It can also function as a guiding policy in between radical changes. But if companies—small, medium, and multinational—had adopted it over the last three decades as the only or primary guideline to their policy making and therefore refrained from undergoing the several critical organizational revolutions that they did, many of them would be out of business by now.[123] Ironically it is often business-oriented elites that support the application of this damaging reformist policy in education systems in its most extreme and mistaken technocratic interpretation.

The critical dialogue I have had with this perspective, which stems from epistemic and social views to which I largely adhere,[124] has helped me define my approach to the model of educational policy making necessary today. An outline of this approach appears immediately below.

The Discourse on Strategic Thinking

The underling methodology of this book is a careful combination of revolutionary and reformist approaches. After struggling with the very long, ongoing confrontation (it is almost four hundred years old) between these two approaches to policy making, I have reached the conclusion that a choice between them simply does not exhaust the relevant possibilities; that there is a range of options between, and various combinations of, these two extreme poles. The policy making strategy relevant for re-thinking and re-designing education in the postmodern era should indeed consist of such a combination.

In order to clarify the above statements further, I must transcend, for a moment, the specific Humanist view I am defending in this book as well as my specific criticism of prevailing education systems, and address a higher meta-methodological question about the nature of the optimal method for re-defining education today, an issue which exceeds the subject of this book, and with which I have dealt in other places.[125] Still, it is worthwhile to address it briefly here when dealing with the foundational methodological issues.

The optimal methodological approach to re-defining education should best be entitled "radical evolutionism." This approach requires one to be *radical* and *revolutionary* when establishing the primary *foundational paradigm* for both educational thought and practice. At the same time the later, much longer, *process of development* of the new paradigm and its careful *implementation, examination,* and *improvement* requires an evolutionist, piecemeal, feedback-based approach. In this combined policy making strategy, the primary, radical move demands a mental eradication of previously prevailing assumptions about education, some of which are two and a half millennia old, and then of creating anew a systematic way of thinking about the desired education for postmodern Liberal Democracies. This thinking should be deductive and begin with systematic and coherent answers to the most fundamental questions about the Good Life and the desired society supporting it, which have been ignored for far too long a time in postmodern Western societies. The process should then continue with an analysis of the prevailing social-cultural-economic situation which should lead to the re-designing of the best (in the eyes of the thinkers) model for implementing the desired processes in the given reality. This process should of course end with a model of the desired educational process/organization for postmodern Liberal Democracies.

This is certainly a radical, macro-strategic, deductive thinking process, on the largest possible scale. Still, once the foundational negative leap and the positive re-design of the basic desired model and process of education are accomplished, the desired model should be further developed and examined through an infinite spiral of realization-evaluation-criticism-feedback-realization and so on. At this point, the top-down revolutionary thinking can and should be complemented by a piecemeal bottom-up evolutionary process.

My understanding of the nature of this balanced optimizing approach was largely supported by literature concerning strategic policy making.[126] I am well aware of the fact that no one person can formulate such future-oriented strategic thinking by him- or herself, nor can it be achieved in the framework of any one discipline. It should rather be characterized by strong interdisciplinarity.[127] Furthermore, it should be implemented by at least several interdisciplinary think tanks, working simultaneously for at least ten years, each developing an independent educational paradigm and the educational process stemming from it and then implementing it using the aforementioned realization-examination-improvement cycle. Furthermore, the various paradigms, models, and processes established by these groups should all be made available in every public forum and their survival should be tested in the court of democratic public opinion.

I refer above to "at least several" think-tanks. Actually, as far as I am concerned, there should be as many of them as reasonable for each society, given its size and resources. My reasons for adopting such a pluralistic stance (which is another element of a reformist cautious approach in my radical-evolutionary one) stems from the inherent nature of strategic thinking. Strategic thinking relies on scenarios reflecting different basic assumptions concerning prevailing and future reality and on different hierarchies of values. This should certainly be the case when one speaks about designing new educational models for education in the hectic, always changing reality of postmodern Liberal Democracies. The picture of postmodernity lends itself to many (actually an infinite number of) mappings; the perspective through which one refers to this reality (or questions one asks concerning it) can be very different; and the values in whose light one responds to each of the understandings of postmodernity can certainly vary. The model I present in the second half of the book relies on my reading of postmodernity and on Humanistic and liberal values as I presently understand them. Different readings of postmodernity, understanding it through different perspectives and evaluating it in light of different understandings of Humanistic and any other values, will undoubtedly lead to other models.

The demand for forming a mechanism capable of supplying constant feedback, which could support the democratic and professional discourse and will most probably lead to changes in policy, is inherent to both strategic thinking and theory of policy making in democratic societies formed within and for democratic societies. This mechanism cannot be created in a vacuum but should rather be transparent to the public and respect democratic decisions as long as they fall within the liberal red lines.

Thus beyond the level of the specific model presented and defended in this book, on the methodological meta-level of future-oriented thinking on desired education in postmodern democracies, I support:

- Plurality of desired educational policies and views, each formed by inter-disciplinary think tanks in a top-down manner and in light of macro-level, strategic thinking; these views will reflect, in their different models and processes, their designers' basic social values, educational goals, reading of the postmodern map, and the conclusions they draw from the combination of these foci of their thought.
- Subjecting these models to a permanent process of professional evaluation.
- Subjecting these models to the judgment of democratic public opinion both on the level of the public debate and the relevant democratic institutions.[128]

But this subject far exceeds the scope of this book, which is limited to the presentation of one view, a view that is still itself "on the springboard." So I will not pursue the larger meta-methodological perspective any further at this point. As I have already said, I elaborated on the practical meaning of this approach in other texts.[129]

SUMMARY

The above overview could not possibly have covered all of the theoretical and practical perspectives with which I have conversed during the last two decades and through which the thoughts presented in this book were developed. It also ignored other sources of inspiration, which were just as important and influential on my theory, such as my daily work in schools and education systems, not to mention my constant dialogue with educators, students, decision makers, and parents. Still I hope I have managed to depict the most influential of theoretical and scientific sources for my inspiration. I hope that this overview will help the reader better understand the deeper "stomach aches," anxieties, aspirations, and hopes that motivated me as well as conceptual, ideological, and theoretical aspects of the arguments presented in the following chapters. Even more importantly, I hope that I have outlined to the interested reader the scope of questions, issues, fields, and disciplines one must contend with when rethinking education and the variety of perspectives that have to be "consulted" or addressed during this process and thus the complexity of the issue at hand and the need for an interdisciplinary yet systematic approach in this endeavor.

Awareness of this complexity should not deter the reader from supporting or even being actively engaged in the required processes. A society that successfully deciphered the human genome and is building and manning space stations is certainly able to support productive processes of rethinking its education and future. It is purely a question of social and political will.

NOTES

Introduction: Education in a Stormy World

1 TIMSS (Trends in International Mathematics and Science Study); PIRLS (Progress in International Reading Literacy Study).
2 For instance, SITES (Second Information on Technology in Education Study); LES (Language Education Study).
3 For instance the NAEP (National Assessment of Educational Progress) in the US in the areas of mathematics, reading, science, writing, the arts, civics, economics, geography, and US history.
4 Kohn, 2000, 2004. This is also explained by the institutional theory of education; see Meyer & Rowan, 1992; Morphew & Huisman, 2002.
5 Illich, 1971.

Chapter One: The Crisis of Modern Education in the Postmodern Era

1 The term "modern" is used here and throughout the book as a reference to a historical period and is not synonymous with "contemporary."
2 This term is fully defined and explained in the section titled "The Obsessive Addiction to Educational Reforms Syndrome."
3 The essential difference between two pairs of concepts basic to this book must be clarified at this juncture. It is the distinction between "modernism" and "postmodernism" on the one hand, and "modernity" and "postmodernity" on the other. The latter pair is chronological or historical and denotes the last historical era which ended around 40 years ago, as opposed to the present era. The former pair denotes a group of objectivist ideologies stemming from, or "dialoguing with," the spirit of enlightenment that had a meaningful impact in the previous era, as opposed to relativist ideologies or frames of mind influenced by Nietzschean or Heideggerean relativism as well as various versions of Neo-Marxism which are dominant nowadays in certain intellectual circles. Henceforth, I will consistently use "postmodernity" to refer generally to the era in which we live and not to the "postmodernist" ideologies. The same applies of course to "modernity" and "modernism." It is important to note that although it is true that modernistic ideologies had the upper hand in modernity, they certainly did not exclusively dominate it. The same it true for postmodernistic ideologies and postmodernity.
4 The term "liberal" is used throughout this book in two totally different meanings: As denoting the socio-political ideology basic to modern and postmodern Liberal Democracies. As denoting the theoretical curriculum stemming from Plato's philosophy, known since the fourth century, consisting of the "seven liberal arts" (the root of this use is explained in detail in Chapter Three). The reader should be able to clearly differentiate between these meanings from the context. Here it clearly refers to the socio-political ideology.
5 Friedman, 2005; Fukuyama, 1993; Handy, 1989; Harvey, 1989; Huntington, 1996; Amin, 1994; Drucker, 1993; Kumar, 1995.
6 Several other terms have been used by contemporary scholars to designate various characteristics of the human condition in the present age. In the labor and economic spheres, distinctions are made between the "industrial" and "post-industrial society" (Bell, 1973), between the "Fordist" and "post-Fordist society" (Harvey, 1989), between a "capitalist" and "post-capitalist society" (Drucker, 1993) or the "curved" vs. "flat" world (Friedman, 2005). In the technological and organizational spheres,

we can note distinctions between the "second" and "third wave society" (Toffler, 1980, 1991) and between "rational" and "irrational society" (Handy, 1989). In the cultural-value sphere, we encounter "modern" and "postmodern society" (Foster, 1983; Wakefield, 1990) and "materialist" and "post-materialist society" (Inglehart, 1990). In the psychological sphere, Gergen (1991) presents the emergence of a split between the emerging "saturated self" and the "continuous self" that typified modern existence. In the macro socio-political sphere two opposed characterizations have been suggested to describe the new reality: the first "the end of history," contrasting postmodernity with "history," which characterized previous periods (Fukuyama, 1993), and the second the "clash of civilizations" characterizing postmodernity, consisting of a clash between cultures/religions rather than the clash between modern ideologies that characterized modernity (Huntington, 1996). For numerous other distinctions see Beniger, 1986, pp. 3–6; Bhagwati, 2004; Sachs, 2005. Despite the fact that each of the distinctions focuses on a specific realm of human activity, all interact to one degree or another, and concepts originating in one sphere impact on other major spheres as well.

7 Bell, 1973; Toffler, 1980; Foster, 1983.
8 Bell, 1973; Kumar, 1995; Robison & Crenshaw, 2001.
9 Toffler, 1980; Dunlop & Kling, 1991; Hamelink, 1997; Kling, 1991; Moss & Townsend, 2000; Sampler, 1998; Tuomi, 2001.
10 Friedman, 2005.
11 Harvey, 1989; Connor, 1989; Foster, 1983; Lyotard, 1984; Wakefield, 1990.
12 Wakefield, 1990, p. 132.
13 In this regard, see Aviram, 1993. See also Aviram, 1989, 1991.
14 Nietzsche, 1974, section 125 (The Madman).
15 Kurzweil, 1990.
16 Kurzweil, 1999.
17 Toffler, 1980.
18 Lyotard, 1984; MacIntyre, 1985; Rorty, 1982, 1998.
19 Markusen, 1996; Smith, 1996; Storper & Scott, 1992; Williamson, 1988.
20 Berger et al., 1973; Bowden, 2004; Calinescu, 1987.
21 A French term adopted by postmodernists which refers to extreme enjoyment and pleasure.
22 Foster, 1983; Harvey, 1989; Wakefield, 1990.
23 Ariel et al., 1998; Hankinson, 1995; Popkin, 1979.
24 Bernstein, 1983; Goldscheider, 1991; Inglehart, 1990; Rosen, 1991.
25 Connor, 1989; Foster, 1983; Harvey, 1989; Rorty, 1982.
26 The emphasis on the relativistic revolution in this work reflects my appraisal that this revolution in philosophical thinking represents the postmodern temper in general. It should not, however, be inferred that relativism underlies all the revolutions taking place in other spheres, or that one cannot find important expressions of non–relativistic, or objectivistic epistemological, ethical and aesthetical views in postmodernity.
27 Easterbrook, 2003.
28 Harvey, 1989.
29 Handy, 1989; Bridges, 1995; Rifkin, 1994.
30 Lyotard, 1984; MacIntyre, 1985; Bernstein, 1983; Norris, 1991; Rajchman, 1985.
31 McRobbie, 1994; Moseley & Jacinda, 2002.
32 Inglehart, 1990, pp. 335–370; Goldscheider, 1991; Simon, 1996.
33 Dunn, 1998; Gergen, 1991; Giddens, 1991.
34 Lacan, 1977, 1981; Loewenstein, 1994; Sedikides & Brewer, 2001.
35 The large variety of different electronic tools that handle different forms of information will eventually lead to the development of an "all-in-one" electronic entity encompassing all three functions.
36 Meyrowitz, 1985.
37 BBC News, 2002; Borgmann, 1994; Elias, 2004.

38 Seymour Sarason, one of the most respected, internationally renowned scholars of educational change, used this expression in his book published at the beginning of the 1970s to depict the education systems' "success" in "containing" and annulling any significant change process (Sarason, 1971).

39 This, for example, is the disagreement on the macro-sociopolitical level that took place in the early and mid 1990s between Huntington's The clash of civilizations" (1996) and Fukuyama's The end of history and the last man (1993).

40 Chouliaraki & Fairclough, 1999; Giddens, 1991; Reed, 1996; Young, 1999.

41 Several of these definitions were formulated during modern times. However, the heyday of Greek philosophy in the fifth and fourth centuries BC, epitomized by Plato's theory of the Good Life and education leading to it, gave birth to the first methodical theory of education which all later ones either continued or to which they responded. The Greek, and first and foremost the Platonic contribution, are the cornerstone of education in Western civilization and have remained so up to the present day (see Chapter Three for a detailed discussion of this legacy).

42 Cremin, 1961, 1988; Pulliam & Van Patten, 1999; Tyack, 1974.

43 Kuhn, 1970.

44 Abel & Sewell, 1999; Dworkin, 1987; Friedman & Farber, 1992; Kyriacou, 1987; LeCompte & Dworkin, 1991.

45 On the phenomenon of substance abuse among youths, see Harrison & Luxenberg, 1995; Hawkins et al., 1992. On the relation between stress and drug abuse see Sinha, 2001; Wills, 1986; Wills & Hirky, 1996. On increasing violence among youth, see Bennett et al., 1996; Cook & Laub, 1998; Elliott et al., 1998; Flannery et al., 2004; US Department of Health and Human Services, 2001. On the deteriorating state of mental health and the rise of suicide rates among youth, see Prosser & McArdle, 1996; Roberts et al., 1995; Pfeffer, 1992; Harrington et al., 1994. On the increase in depression and suicides among youth worldwide, see Elitzur, 1995; Donnelly, 1995; Ivarsson & Gillberg, 1997; Joyce et al., 1990.

46 Jefferson County Sheriff's Office, 2008.

47 Kristen, 1999.

48 Abbott, 1994; Angus, & Mirel, 1999; Hirsch, 1996; Meighan, 1997; Perelman, 1992; Powell et al., 1985.

49 White House, 2000. For more examples of ICT projects in the US and other western countries see Culp et al., 2003; Office of Technology Assessment, 1995; CoCN, 2002.

50 Aviram & Richardson, 2004.

51 The "One laptop per child" (OLPC) project (http://laptop.org).

52 Chubb and Moe, 1990; Chubb, Moe & Peterson, 1985; Perelman, 1992; Sarason, 1990; Silverman, 1971.

53 Goodnough, 1999; Smithers, 2002; Wigoren, 2001. On various problems of validity of national tests, see Kane & Staiger, 2002.

54 Downey et al., 1994; Sallis, 1993; West-Burnham, 1997.

55 Cuban, 1990; Fullan & Miles, 1992; Zeichner & Liston, 1990.

56 Gordon, 1984; Ravitch, 2000; Sarason, 1990; Tyack and Cuban, 1995.

57 Cuban, 1990, 1998; Fullan & Miles, 1992; Fullan, 1993; Ogawa, 1994.

58 Aviram, forthcoming a.

59 Aviram, forthcoming b.

60 "The Obsessive Addiction to Educational Reforms Syndrome" and "The Unrecognized Need to Re-invent Education." The following system of concepts is based on a synthesis of theoretical conceptions from various spheres: the sociology and philosophy of science, clinical psychology, Gestalt psychology, and organizational theory. The most basic one is of course Kuhn's philosophy of science (1970). I was also greatly influenced by Watzlawick, 1974; Dember, 1964; Christenden, 1985; Weber, 1984; Thompson and Tuden, 1959; Katz and Kahn, 1966.

61 The distinction between first- and second-order changes is quite common and accepted in current organizational and psychological thinking. It is, however, from a logical standpoint, extremely problematic. For a discussion of these problems see Aviram (forthcoming a). Here, for the sake of brevity, I will use the accepted meaning of this distinction.

62 Kuhn, 1970, p. 81.

63 Ibid., p. 83.

64 Ibid., p. 61.

65 Ibid., p. 77.

66 "The Obsessive Addiction to Educational Reforms Syndrome" and "The Unrecognized Need to Re-invent Education."

67 Sarason, 1990.

68 Tyack & Cuban, 1995.

69 Gordon, 1984.

70 As I have clarified and detailed in several places (Aviram, 1993b, 1998), one can discern the harbingers of an alternative paradigm developing over the last two decades. I refer here to new educational perceptions and approaches such as "learning styles" and "multiple intelligences," "fields of interest," "distance learning," "e-learning," "experiential learning," and "emotional intelligence." The common denominator which binds most of these approaches together is self-empowerment and the transfer of decision making and educational parameters definition to the learner, hence allotting far more room for personal variances. Approaches such as these "open the door" for educational processes that are neither exclusively cognitive nor theoretical. See also my discussion in Chapter Four in which I briefly address most of these approaches.

71 The fact that in most countries parents can choose between public and private schools, and in many countries even select a specific school for their children to attent, does not change the exclusive nature of the system as a whole. This is the case since all mainstream schools, both private and public, "sell the same merchandise," the Platonic-mediaeval, liberal arts curriculum, as adapted at the end of the nineteenth century to the modern era's needs and to the requests of the then flourishing scientific ideologies.

72 Nietzsche, 1882 (eng. trans. 1974), section 125.

73 Of all the educational paradigm parameters, Western education systems have chosen to focus mostly on the problems inherent in the sixth, modus operandi. This resulted in the implementations of school change processes designed to change teaching modes all over the world. Similarly, attention was devoted to certain aspects of the fifth parameter, organizational structure, with attempts in recent decades to introduce a degree of structural flexibility, mainly on the system level, not the school level. At the same time, in many countries, the imposition of universal scholastic standards and the many draconian steps connected with them have increased rigidity. The choice to address these two, of all the problematic issues, indicates that they are "located" in secondary parameters, thus are easier to deal with on a cognitive, emotional, and organizational level. Nevertheless, even here, Western systems have yet to face either issue using a systematic approach or method. Even within these two realms of change, attempts to introduce structural flexibility have been extremely marginal. For example, many Western systems have delegated authority to the school, e.g., engaged in reforms focusing on "school-based management," or of the delegation of some authority to parents, e.g., reforms focused on "parental choice," or on marinating a dialogue and forming coali-tions between various communities outside the school's educators (Hargreaves & Fullan, 1996; Hargreaves et al., 2001; Hargreaves, 2003). Still, even in these cases, the rigid lococentric and hierarchical structure of the school and its domination by the scholastic liberal curriculum, or by the conception of "children" as objects of the educational process to be recruited under law's compulsion, have not changed. Furthermore, at the same time as these limited changes took place, so did opposing changes that were much more dominant. I refer here mainly to changes consisting of the compulsion of an entire system to follow a "national curriculum" or to stick to a set of rigid

quantifiable standards supposedly indicating levels of knowledge or skill that have been in vogue over the last two decades (see Kohn, 1999b).

74 A translation of the German Gedankenexperimenten, related to the well known "Thought experiments" that helped Einstein to create his theory of relativity.

75 Berkowitz, 1989; Fox & Spector, 1999; Kyriacou, 1987.

76 For these points see note 45.

77 Peterson, 2003a; Bennett et al., 1998; National Commission on Excellence in Education, 1983.

78 Abel & Sewell, 1999; Dworkin, 1987; Dunham, 1992; Hargreaves, 1994; Kyriacou, 1987; LeCompte & Dworkin, 1991.

79 Hargreaves, 1994; Fullan & Steigelbauer, 1991; Mohr, 1998.

80 Coombs, 1968, 1985; Jumilhac, 1984; and Ravitch, 2000 represent literature which relates to different countries and periods. See also Kohn, 1999b; Fiske, 1996; Hartley, 1997.

81 Of course, not all the parameters discussed in these chapters are equally essential to the system. It appears here, too, that the modus operandi and possibly some aspects of the organizational structure are relatively secondary. However the scope of discussion in this book is not broad enough to determine which of the education system's parameters are essential and which are secondary. To do so would require empirical research into widespread conceptions of the prevailing education system in Western societies, thus distinguishing between what is taken to be essential and secondary parameters within these conceptions. I was unable to undertake such thorough research and neither have I located any. Consequently, this work relates to the six parameters "as if they were all essential."

82 In this book I consider the terms "disciplinary curriculum," "theoretical curriculum," and "liberal curriculum" to have one and the same meaning.

83 Handy, 1989.

84 See Aviram (forthcoming a) for an elaboration on this point.

85 See Kuhn, 1970.

86 Over the last decade I have engaged, with my team at the Center for Futurism in Education at Ben-Gurion University, in such systematic and methodical thinking and planning in our efforts to develop alternative educational paradigms (see Aviram, forthcoming a; Aviram, Bar-On & Attias, forthcoming).

Chapter Two: The Disappearance of Educational Goals in the Postmodern Era

1 See the section titled "Seven Responses to the Crisis in Education: Outline of a Utopian Discourse."

2 Gur-Ze'ev, 1998, 2001, 2003.

3 If this statement seems to the reader to be absurd or a contradiction in terms, it is because it is just that.

4 Bramall & White, 2000; White, 1982, 1999, 2003, 2006.

5 Aviram, 1996; Bloom, 1987; Meighan, 1997; Perelman, 1992; White, 1997.

6 For a definition of the term "thick Liberalism," see Chapter Ten, section titled "Probable Psychological Damage," p. 279.

7 Bloom, 1987; Davidson, 1973; MacIntyre, 1985.

8 Quine, 1953.

9 Derrida, 1978; Lyotard, 1984; Rorty, 1989.

10 Postman, 1986, 1993.

11 In Chapter Four I will discuss this objective in detail and also the second objective of education, socialization, which may be defined as the training of the individual for future functional patterns. See Harpaz, 2004.

12 This is one of the meanings of the Latin verb educare.

13 Peterson, 2003b; Bennett et al., 1998; National Commission on Excellence in Education, 1983.

14 Elliott, Hamburg & Williams, 1998; Newman, 1999; Lawrence, 1997; Devine, 1996. Since the beginning-mid 1990s there has been a slight decline in youth violence in the US and some other Western countries (see for example CDC, 2004). Though I did not find a clear empirical explanation for this decline it is reasonable to believe that its roots are similar to the reasons for the temporary decline in suicide rates in the second half of the 1990s (see note 15), as well as prevention measures such as metal detectors in schools and various behavioral programs.

15 Smyth & O'Brien, 2004; Haasen et al., 2004.

16 Until the early 1990s there has been a steady increase in suicide rates (see Hendin, 1996; Prosser & McArdle, 1996; Cantor, Neulinger and De Leo, 1999; Dudley, Waters, Kelk & Howard, 1992). The late 1990s and early 2000s saw decreased suicide rates in the US which have been attributed to increased awareness of suicide risk as well as an increase in antidepressants prescribed to adolescents (see Gould et al., 2003), followed by a sharp increase in the last years, after the use of antidepressants decreased due to various concerns (Gibbons et al., 2007; CDC, 2007).

17 Kyriacou, 1987; Abel & Sewell, 1999; Dworkin, 1987; Dunham, 1992; Hargreaves, 1994; LeCompte & Dworkin, 1991.

18 Callan, 1994; Cuypers, 1992; Bonnett & Cuypers, 2003; Stone, 1990.

19 Dworkin, 1982; Rawls, 1971.

20 Rawls, 1993.

21 Aviram, 1994c.

22 I related to views that comprise meaningful options in this utopian discourse that I could not represent by a certain clear prototypical writer or text. In other cases I ignored certain aspects in a writer's views which hinder its presentation as a clear ideal example of a certain view. My first priority was the formation of this ideal, or a well structured, logically clear and "pure" discourse in which the various views are together exhaustive and to a large extent exclusive. This has required me to give up full accuracy in the description of each view.

23 The meaning of this reservation here and in the next category will be clarified immediately below.

24 See note 23.

25 See the closing line of Wittgenstein's Tractatus (1961).

26 The cultural relativists are relativists for all intents and purposes. They make the empirical assumption that individuals in a certain culture share enough basic suppositions, which they take to be self-evident, to allow meaningful discourse either on the possibility of a modus vivendi or even on common ways of life in spite of the secondary differences among them. See for example Rorty, 1980 or MacIntyre, 1985. The skeptics, on the other hand, are rationalists or rather critical rationalists. See Popper, 1963. They believe in certain universal rational laws of thinking which already to some extent guide us all and certainly (as they believe) should do so in improved ways; however, they believe them to be only formal and not material, that is, only principles that guide thought or discussion without supplying any information about the physical world or ethics.

27 In some ironic ways rationalism also represents the "militant temperament" and ethical certainty of the Radicals in the fourth camp and perhaps reflects the tacit or even denied epistemic assumptions of many of them, despite the fact most of them declare themselves to be postmodernist relativists.

28 Epstein, 2007; Gatto, 1992; Holt, 1976; Rickenbacker, 1974.

29 Many elements of the most radical version of this concept are expressed in the positions of the radical critics of the education system in the 1960s and '70s, such as Illich, 1971; Bereiter, 1969; Holt, 1965, 1967, 1976, 1981; and later Perelman, 1992; Bereiter, 2002; Bereiter et al., 1997, 2002.

30 Hurn, 1978; Dearden, 1972, 1975.

31 James, 1977.

32 The reference to the cave alludes to Plato's allegory of the cave in The Republic, which makes a similar claim concerning the society and education of his time.

33 This is the alternative which at the end of the day I will defend in Part Two of the book, but only after presenting the whole range of primary options and refuting the alternatives.

34 See for example, The European Union Lisbon Objective of 2000; Department for Education and Employment, 2001; UNESCO Institute for Statistics, 2003.

35 Aviram, 1986b.

36 Aviram, 1986b; Lindley, 1986.

37 Dearden, 1972, 1975; Dworkin, 1981.

38 Harpaz, 2007.

39 See Friedman, 2002; Richardson, 2002.

40 In Hume's 1969 (original work 1739, 1740), A Treatise of Human Nature.

41 Berlin, 1999.

42 White, 1982, 1997, 1999, 2003, 2006.

43 Callan, 1988, 1994, 1997, 2001, 2002.

44 Callan, 1988.

45 Assor & Kaplan, 2001; Katz & Assor, 2003, 2006; Katz et al., 2006.

46 The assumption that autonomous human beings develop through reflective "experiments in living" is basic to the theory of John Stuart Mill (Gray, 1983). It also constitutes the basis of my own educational perception that will be detailed in Chapters Six and Seven.

47 Gutmann, 1987.

48 Probably in its moderate versions; see the section on "Dominant Variations of Postmodern Relativism," p. 45.

49 I refer to Gutmann's 1987 book—in spite of the fact that she later expressed her view on the subject in other publications (see Gutmann, 1996, 2004) containing very interesting nuances on her original view—since I consider it to be the best prototypical presentation of this view.

50 As far as I understand it, Gutmann's presentation of Locke's and Mill's positions distortedly emphasizes only one aspect at the expense all others, probably in order to remodel their positions within the scheme she seeks to highlight.

51 That is, by applying Rousseau's concept at the level of the local community instead of the general society and replacing the objectivistic "general will" with an ongoing, open-ended rational debate representing at each moment a certain balance of power, and by emphasizing pluralistic elements already found in Dewey.

52 Marx himself was an objectivist. Today, many neo-Marxists and followers of critical pedagogy present themselves as relativists; in my opinion this presentation pulls the rug from under their criticism (Aviram, 1992b; Gur-Ze'ev, 1998, 2003).

53 Bloom, 1987. Bloom only addressed the university curriculum, but his classic conservative argument can be adapted to high school education.

54 A position similar to that held by Bloom was expressed in the preceding generation by Livingstone (Livingstone, 1943). For a discussion of Livingstone's book, see Chapter Three.

55 Freire, 1973; Giroux, 1983; Shor & Freire, 1987.

56 Gur-Ze'ev, 2004; Banks & Banks, 1995.

57 Many postmodern neo-Marxists assert their belief in relativist positions, but relativism and Marxism or neo-Marxism contradict each other (see note 53). I have therefore chosen to address these positions as objectivistic.

58 Hirsch, 1987, 1996, 2006.

59 Hirsch strictly observes the use of seemingly neutral technocratic language from a value standpoint. He therefore refrains from directly addressing values and relates only to conceptions, but there can be no doubt that the whole list of conceptions presented as being fundamental to culture expresses value preferment. Thus, Hirsch actually recommends the inculcation of a system of value positions in the guise of neutrality relating to conceptions.

60 For a few examples, see, Hirsch, 1991a, 1991b, 1991c.

61 MacIntyre, 1980. As stated earlier, MacIntyre bases his communitarian position on the theoretical-empirical assessment by which there is no chance of reaching a large-scale societal consensus.

However, numerous other contemporary communitarians base their positions on a normative point of departure by which it is immoral to impose one group's worldview on another.

62 For more operational versions of MacIntyre view see MacIntyre, 1990, 1995, 1999.

Chapter Three: The Disappearance of Justification for the Theoretical Curriculum in the Postmodern Era

1   For but a few of the major classic writings describing the disciplinary nature of the curriculum see: Harvard University Committee on the Objectives of a General Education in a Free Society, 1945; Schwab, 1962; White, 1977; Hirst, 1974; Adler, 1982; Kliebard, 1987; Schubert, 1996. For some of the many more critical analyses of the theoretical/liberal curriculum from different perspectives, see: Bernstein, 1971; Illich, 1971, 1973; Whitty, 1985; Beyer & Apple, 1988; Papert, 1993; Apple, 1990, 2001; Barmall & White, 2000; Ross, 2000; Posner, 2004; Carmon, 2007.

2   Hurn, 1985.

3   Although not as thin as the power of the previous justification.

4   Aviram, 1990.

5   In the first section, titled "The Human Yearning for Meaning: An Analysis."

6   In the second section, "The Theoretical Curriculum in the Past: Learning as a Highly Meaningful Activity."

7   In the following section, "Disappearance of the Liberal Curriculum's Meaning in the Postmodern Era."

8   See the subsection titled "The Relativistic Revolution and the Erosion of Cultural Backing and Spiritual Justification for the Liberal Curriculum."

9   See the subsection on "The Postmodern Labor Market and Its Effect on the Practical Justification for the Liberal Curriculum."

10 "Positivism" is a modern concept, denoting a perception according to which (a) science bases itself on sensory data that reflects reality, and (b) because science relates to various spheres of reality and to different groups of sensory data that stem from this data, one must make a sharp differentiation between different scientific disciplines. This concept stems from a fierce attack on the mystical understanding of knowledge as well as the modern rationalistic and intellectualistic one. See Comte, 1856; Giddens, 1974. The dominance of the positivistic perception of science strengthened in the postmodern age, but the meaning of the concept changed and the sharp distinction between scientific disciplines is even more powerful. This distinction is no longer perceived as reflecting differences between sensory data reflecting an objective reality, but as stemming from various scientific-social discourses, or "language games." Accordingly, relying on sensory data is no longer justified as stemming from loyalty to objective reality but as reflecting loyalty to the scientific paradigms that established this data.

11 See the subsection on "Scientific Professionalization and Its Effect on the Unity of the Liberal Curriculum."

12 In the final section of the chapter, "Meaninglessness and Its Devastating Cost."

13 For a general overview see Swanson, 2007. For an outline of organizational development as a strategy intended to change beliefs, attitudes, and values of organizations see Gallos (ed.), 2006. For an overview of the field of organizational culture see Schein, 1979, 2004, and Senge, 1990. For an overview of the field of human resource see Tyson & York, 1994.

14 See Festinger, Riecken & Schachter, 1956; Festinger, 1957; Harmon-Jones, 1999; Cottle, 2006; and Cooper, 2007.

15 Frankl, 1959, 1988.

16 Talcot Parsons' "action theory" is based on the assumption that human action is "voluntary, intentional and symbolic." See Parsons, 1937.

17 Self Determination Theory (SDT) shows a connection between higher motivation and a person's sense of autonomy. "According to SDT, people feel autonomous when they feel and/or understand

the value or relevance of the task in which they are engaged, and therefore can identify with it. Feelings of autonomy are particularly strong when the task is perceived as being closely connected to the value, interests, and goals that constitute the core of one's authentic self and identity" (Katz and Assor, 2006, p. 431). See also Ryan 1993; Ryan & Deci, 2000.

18 See Hidi, Renninger & Krapp, 2004; Alexander, 1997; Alexander & Murphy, 1998; Schiefele, 1999; Renninger, Ewan & Lasher, 2002; Reninger & Hidi, 2002; Katz et al., 2006; Ullmann-Margalit & Morgenbesser, 1977.

19 I define the concept of "interest" in the same way as in the previous chapter. It is in this sense the basic literature mentioned in note 17 above understands it as well. Consistent with this definition, a person has an interest in a certain subject when that individual is willing to devote time and resources in the long term (i.e., the interest is not a one-time exercise) and when the interest is also intrinsic and not simply for one's external benefit, and thus the pursuit of the interest constitutes self-development. This is a modification of concepts such as "the supreme good" or "the supreme purpose of life" through the performance of "worthwhile activities." All these concepts express an assumption, dominant in Western rationalistic thought, one which originated in Plato's and Aristotle's philosophies, wherein there exist activities which enable human beings to realize their unique essence. Such an activity was considered the supreme purpose of life and all other human activities and was deemed as performed for its sake. See Callan, 1988.

20 In the section on "Scientific Professionalization and Its Effect on the Unity of the Liberal Curriculum."

21 See, for example, Darling-Hammond, 1997; Kohn, 1999.

22 The most well known of those massacres was the one in Columbine high school in 1999, wherein two students, Eric Harris and Dylan Klebold, embarked on a shooting spree, killing twelve students and a teacher and wounding twenty-four others before committing suicide.

23 Although there is some prima facie evidence that youth violence and drug abuse has decreased in the USA over the last few years (see: NIDA InfoFacts: High School and Youth Trends, 2007), it is still a prevailing phenomenon, and a major cause of deaths and injuries. The aforementioned decrease can be attributed to harsher enforcement which may have led to a decrease in the number of reports, and most probably also to the dramatic increase in the consumption of antidepressants (Gunnell & Ashby, 2004; Reselands, 2006). Similarly, the decrease in suicides and suicide attempts among young people in the last fifteen years is clearly connected to the use of antidepressants, which points to the fact that suicide, beyond any specific cause in a specific case, can be attributed to the general malaise of our time: depression. According to the Centers for Disease Control and Prevention, "Since 1991, the prevalence of many health-risk behaviors among high school students nationwide has decreased. However, many high school students continue to engage in behaviors that place them at risk from the leading causes of mortality and morbidity" (Eaton et al., 2007). The United States Department of Health and Human Services argues that news of a reduction of youth violence is but a myth. "Although key indicators of violence such as arrest and victimization data clearly show significant reductions in violence since the peak of the epidemic in 1993, an equally important indicator warns against concluding that the root of the problem is solved. Self-reports by youths reveal that involvement in some violent behaviors remains at 1993 levels" (United States Department of Health and Human Services [DHHS], Youth violence: a report of the Surgeon General [on-line], 2001). See also the Department of Health and Human Services, Centers for Disease Control and Prevention, Youth Violence: Fact Sheet, and its Web-based Injury Statistics Query and Reporting System (WISQARS); Wynne, 1978; Albas, 1978; Blumstein, 1995; Anderson et al., 2001; Mercy et al., 2002; Nansel et al., 2001; FitzGerald, Stevens & Hale, 2004; OECD, International Network on School Bullying and Violence, 2007.

24 See the second section of this chapter, "The Theoretical Curriculum in the Past: Learning as Highly Meaningful Activity."

25 See the third section of this chapter, "Disappearance of the Liberal Curriculum's Meaning in the Postmodern Era."

26 See the third section of this chapter, "Disappearance of the Liberal Curriculum's Meaning in the Postmodern Era."
27 The "almost" stands for rare individual exceptions such as open schools which allow students to learn only or mostly subjects that interest them.
28 See the final section of this chapter, "Meaninglessness and Its Devastating Cost."
29 An excellent example of an ongoing change in content while maintaining the basic concept and framework of a curriculum in the American curriculum/education system can be found in Burns, 1988. Descriptions of parallel processes in Germany can be found in Albisetti, 1983; Kraul, 1984.
30 Butts, 1973, pp. 110–112.
31 For a discussion of these issues see Koyré, 1994; Lodge, 2000.
32 Actually Plato himself foresaw such deviance and deterioration as he believed was extremely plausible in the implausible scenario wherein his utopia was realized.
33 Butts, 1973, pp. 107–114.
34 For centuries even the aristocrats or the upper classes were illiterate while the educated clergymen performed all functions of civil service.
35 Butts, 1973, pp. 121–134.
36 Ibid, pp. 146–151.
37 Ibid, pp. 168–177.
38 Ibid, pp. 155–182.
39 Ibid, pp. 362–364; See also: Bruford, 1962; Lilge, 1975, pp. 1–36; Swales, 1978, pp. 9–37, 57–73; Albisetti, 1983, pp. 16–35; Schnandelbach, 1984, pp. 12–32.
40 Butts, 1973, pp. 348–364; Albisetti, 1983, pp. 16–56, 171–192; Holmes, 1989, pp. 25–101, 292–314. Regarding the USA see Popkewitz, 1987; Burns, 1988.
41 Even today the situation is not really different; theoretical curriculum learning is still very much in the hands of the middle and upper classes.
42 In the subsection on "The Postmodern Labor Market and Its Effect on the Practical Justification for the Liberal Curriculum."
43 In the subsection on "Scientific Professionalization and Its Effect on the Unity of the Liberal Curriculum."
44 The word "light" is the source of the European parallels of the term "enlightenment."
45 See Bruford, 1975; Cooper, 1983; Taylor, 1992. Beyond the original German humanistic perception and its later derivatives mentioned above, there are many prevailing theories reflecting the same basic view that self-realization is a key element in one's professional development (see Schon, 1983), good and just society (see Callan, 1997), healthy personality, and a sense of "wellbeing" (see Nix et al., 1999; Deci & Ryan, 1995, 2000; Schmuck & Sheldon, 2001; Ryan & Deci, 2000, 2001; Peterson & Seligman, 2004).
46 See Peters, 1983. Also see Portelli, 1987.
47 Rudner, 1999; Neuman & Aviram, 2003; Ray, 2004, 2006b.
48 See Aviram, 1986, 1991a. For other attacks on the curriculum, usually relying on much narrower perspectives, see: Bourdieu & Passeron, 1990; Rogers, 1969; Kohn, 1996, 2004; Popkewitz, 1997, 2004; Franklin, Popkewitz & Bloch, 2003.
49 See the section on "Scientific Professionalization and Its Effect on the Unity of the Liberal Curriculum" below.
50 As shown in the section on "The Relativistic Revolution and the Erosion of Cultural Backing and Spiritual Justification for the Liberal Curriculum" above.
51 See for example Kuijpers & Scheerens, 2006.
52 Many economical theoreticians have pointed to the rising importance of human capital, or "labor factor" in the overall production and productivity growth, using ever more complex tools of measurement, such as the Multifactor productivity (MFP).
53 See, for instance, United States Department of Labor, Bureau of Labor Statistics News, 2006. Although the European job market is more stable than the one across the Atlantic, according to the

labor force survey of 2003, 8.2% of the EU's total employed labor force had moved to another job after one year. Interestingly enough, the vision of united Europe encourages the EU to support this trend, and has declared 2006 as "European Year of Workers' Mobility." See European Commission, European Year of Workers' Mobility, 2006.

54 Drucker, 1993.

55 Senge, 1990.

56 Cunningham, 1999.

57 See for instance O'Reilly, 2001; Handy, 1998, 2001.

58 Rifkin, 1994. See also Rifkin, 2004.

59 White, 1997; Herzenberg, Alic and Wial, 1998; Beck, 2000; Gini, 2001.

60 The idea that university education is directly relevant for employment was formally developed within Human Capital Theory during the 1960s (see Becker, 1975) but it was rooted in practical-empiricist conceptions of knowledge that have become dominant in the industrialized world already in the late eighteenth century. During the 1970s, however, new theories that disagree with Human Capital Theory were developed, which claimed that the link between university education and successful careers do not stem from the curriculum, but rather that such education serves employers with an indicator for candidates' intelligence or class background (Bowles & Gintis, 1976, pp. 81, 112–3, 129–30; Rumberger, 1981, pp. 25–7).

61 Freeman, 1976; Hincliffe, 1987; Levin, 1987.

62 This famous metaphor was delineated in a letter sent by Descartes to the French translator of his book "Principia Philosophiae," and later added as a preface to its French edition. See Descartes, 1991.

63 See Hume, 1978.

64 A clear expression of science perceived as a profession can be found in Weber, 1922. On the contention between the two perceptions in nineteenth-century Germany, see Lilge, 1975; Schandelbach, 1984. See also Aviram 1991a, pp. 143–144.

65 This perception has been dominant over the last decades in the philosophy, sociology, and history of science. Its most prominent expression can be found in Thomas Kohn (1970). It became dominant in the philosophy of education and in fact guided the thinking of Peters, 1973; White, 1973; and Hirst, 1974. In addition it has been dominant in curriculum theory. See for example Schwab, 1962.

66 "The Anomaly Hypothesis and Its Two Substantiation Strategies."

67 For a description of the educational crisis in the world, see for example, Abbott & Ryan, 2001; Bernbaum, 1979; Coombs, 1985; Jumilhac, 1984; Sarason, 1990; Hargreaves, 1994, 1995; Postman, 1996; Meighan, 1997; Hargreaves & Fullan, 1998; Tyack & Cuban, 1995, 2001; Perelman, 1992; Hall & Handley, 2004; Meighan & Siraj-Blatchford, 2005; Benbenishty, 2005; and Neal, 2006. The books by Perelman, Postman, Benbenishty, Hargreaves, Meighan, Hargreaves & Fullan, and Coombs relate to the worldwide educational crisis. Jumilhac's book relates to the educational crisis in France and Bernbaum's book to the educational crisis in Britain. The books by Tyack & Cuban, Neal, Hall, and Handley, and Sarason relate mainly to the situation in the USA. Regarding the intensification of indications of the crisis in the education system in Israel see Elitzur, 1995; Weiss, 1996; Iancu et al., 1997.

68 There is actually a separate branch in the literature which documents these failures, analyzes them, and attempts to explain them. See Gordon, 1984; Rosenholtz, 1985; Sarason, 1990; Perelman, 1992; Tyack and Cuban, 1995, 2001; Cuban, 1990, 2003; Sergiovanni, 2000; Ravitch, 2000.

69 My argument at this point is a hypothesis which derives from the overall theory I presented in the section "The Human Yearning for Meaning: An Analysis," which is supported by circumstantial evidence: the functional and educational failures of the education system. In addition it is supported by the conclusions of a long list of empirical studies, which reinforce the assumption that there exists a connection between various elements in the school and the degree of alienation of its students (see Grabe, 1981; Calabarese & Seldin, 1986; Rafalides & Hoy, 1971; Huling, 1980; Darling-Hammond, 1997; Kohn, 1999). Alienation among students is also a crucial factor in

bringing about phenomena such as frustration, anger, despair, depression, suicide, unwanted teenage pregnancies, vandalism, and drug and alcohol abuse (see above, note 23). Furthermore, for the connection between teachers' alienation and their high levels of tension and burnout see also, among many others, Vandenberghe & Huberman, 1999; Brock & Grady, 2000; O'Reilley, 2005. Despite the fact that some of the above-mentioned articles relate to specific aspects of the hypothesis, I have offered them as reinforcement for there is no source that addresses this hypothesis directly and fully. It may be examined more carefully by following the line of correlations it predicts, for example, correlations between measures which weigh the strength of all three curriculum significance providers for students and phenomena such as drunkenness, drug addiction, and violence among students, or a drop in the level of scholastic studies and achievements. I intend to initiate such studies in the future.

70 See: Hirsch, Kett & Trefil, 2002.

Chapter Four: The Disappearance of Structural Functionality of the Modern School in the Postmodern Era

1   The meaning of the term "standardized" as I use it here is influenced by the identical meaning ascribed to it by Toffler (1980).
2   The term "lococentric" was coined by me in Aviram, 1992.
3   Rogoff et al., 2003; Stedman, 1997; Callahan, 1962; Dreeben, 1968; Hurn, 1978; Tyack, 1974.
4   Regarding "chaordic organizations," see Eijnatten & Fitzgerald, 1998, Eijnatten, 2003; Fitzgerald & Eijnatten, 2002; Hock, 1995.
5   Friedman, 2005; Cartelli, 2006; Davenport, & Prusak, 1998; Nonaka & Takeuchi, 1995.
6   Descartes, 1984 (1644), preface.
7   McLuhan, 1962; Postman, 1982.
8   Mintzberg, 1973; Smith, 1976; Taylor, 1947; Alvesson, 1996; Shenhav, 1999.
9   Taylor, 1911.
10 A notable expression of this shift can be found in Max Weber's well-known 1922 paper.
11 Smith, 1976; Taylor, 1911.
12 This is the source of Marx's theory of alienation used to characterize the nature of modern work; see Marx, 1959.
13 Karmon, 2006; Mervis, 2006.
14 Goodlad & Klein, 1970.
15 Based on Weick's (1976) term.
16 Popper, 1972, pp. 33–65.
17 Taylor, 1911. An amusing cynical and critical expression of the three above-mentioned aspects on the modern worldview and organization, while comparing them with concepts from the Middle Ages, can be found in Mark Twain's brilliant book A Connecticut Yankee in King Arthur's Court (1949).
18 Sarason, 1995.
19 Although the expression "conservative reformists" might appear to be an oxymoron, it is not. In education all sides, when they can, are permanently making reforms working in opposite directions. Through these opposing reforms each side does its best to obliterate all signs of the policies of its rivals. This is the well known "pendulum movement" of educational reform.
20 Kohn, 2000.
21 Kohn, 2000; McNeil, 2000; Sacks, 2000.
22 This model replaced the manufacturing model that existed during the pre-industrial era and at the beginning of the industrial era, wherein production was non-centralized and built around the work of sub-contractors working mainly in private homes. In the nineteenth century, rational management concepts came into being (as expressed in the works of Adam Smith and later in those of Charles Taylor), which made the factory organization model dominant. This model brought all the producers

together at the same time under one roof. The assembly line required that each worker specialize in only one link of a coordinated and controlled process in order to manufacture the complete product. This production model, which was based on the principle of unity of place and time, also became dominant in other organizational contexts central to modern life such as hospitals, old-age homes, prisons, and so was naturally applied in the school (Mintzberg, 1973; Smith, 1976; Taylor, 1947; Alvesson, 1996; Shenhav, 1999).

23 See also Foucault's discussion of Bentham's panopticon concept; Dreyfus & Rabinow, 1982, pp. 220–225.

24 See note 13.

25 Dewey, 1966.

26 For example, in Freinet schools around the world (http://www.freinet.org); Jenaplan schools in Germany (http://www.jenaplan.de) and Holland (http://www.jenaplan.nl); and learning in kibbutzim in Israel until a couple of decades ago, which resembled project-based learning.

27 The quotation marks express the fact that it is very far from being new in the realm of thought and research; it is only radically new for the practice of education.

28 See note 13.

29 Papert, 1980, 1993; Glaserfeld, 1995.

30 Again, as in relation to "knowledge," this concept is far from being new in the realm of thought and experimentation; see note 27.

31 Brooks & Brooks, 1993; Fosnot, 1996; Jonassen, 1994; Jonassen et al., 1999.

32 Jonassen & Land, 2000.

33 Pintrich, 2000; Azevedo, 2005; Paris & Paris, 2001.

34 Olson et al., 2003; Toth et al., 2002.

35 Abbott, 1994; Perelman, 1992.

36 Drucker, 1993; Friedman, 2005.

37 Sennett, 1980.

38 Giroux, 1996; Arum, 2003.

39 Hirsch, 1987; Tapscott, 1999; Marsh & Millard, 2000; Gordon & Alexander, 2005.

40 Hanson, 2001; Meyer, 1977; Meyer & Rowan, 1977; Zucker, 1987.

41 Diffily & Sassman, 2002.

42 Savery & Duffy, 1996.

43 Pintrich, 2000; Azevedo, 2005; Paris & Paris, 2001.

44 Jonassen & Land, 2000.

45 Olson et al., 2003; Toth et al., 2002.

46 Aviram & Richardson, 2004; Hernandez & Goodson, 2004.

47 Pelgrum & Plomp, 2002.

48 Hanson, 2001; Meyer, 1977; Meyer & Rowan, 1977; Zucker, 1987.

49 Kohn, 2000.

50 Toward the mid-twentieth century such language was developed and in most cases was as hypocritical as the school talk.

51 In this section, I shall ignore my criticism in Chapter Three and the previous section of the concept of basic theoretical learning in the modern school, and accept for the sake of discussion that theoretical-disciplinary learning is a central process in the school. This is to show that even if we accept this goal of learning, it is impossible to justify the school's lococentric structure, and all the more so if it is not accepted.

52 Harvey, 1989, pp. 240–323.

53 Toffler, 1980, pp. 58–75.

54 As analyzed by Foucault, see Dreyfus and Raibnow, 1982, pp. 220–225.

55 See note 26.

56 Thomas, 1998; Webb, 1990.

57 Rudner, 1999; Hill, 2000; Webb, 1999.

58 Tyack, 1974, pp. 13–27.
59 "The Organizational Dysfunctionality of the Unity Principle."
60 "The Social Dysfunctionality of the Unity Principle."
61 Dunn and Grigg, 1988, p. 104; Keefe, 1987, p. 1.
62 Dunn and Debello, 1981, pp. 372–377; Dunn and Dunn, 1987, pp. 55–63; Dunn, 2003; Keefe, 1979, pp. 1–18.
63 Keefe, 1987, pp. 7–29.
64 See for example Dunn and Dunn, 1987. The learning style approach has been recently subjected to a blatant (justified) criticism for its lack of scientific rigor (see for instance Coffield et al., 2004). I adhere to this criticism, yet I take it to reflect the situation that the field of research has now reached after its first generation of development and implementation, rather than as a threat to the meaning and justification of this line of research. It might indeed be the case that most research carried out by educationalists has not been very rigorous, but nevertheless such research reflects and acknowledges an undeniable fact (i.e., the differences between our preferred ways of acting and learning), and hence should not be neglected. On the contrary, more rigorous scientific effort is needed to explore this obvious state of affairs and its pedagogical implications.
65 Dunn and Grigg, 1988, pp. 7, 13, 19, 38, 54.
66 Ibid., pp. 8, 23, 38.
67 Ibid., pp. 7, 12, 14, 20, 37, 38, 45, 54, 58.
68 Ibid., p. 20.
69 See for instance Leidig, 2001; Del Corso et al., 2001.
70 iClass, a learning platform developed by the European Commission FP6 funded iClass project (see http://www.iclass.info), made an attempt to face this limitation.
71 See Aviram and Ronen et al., 2007.
72 Gardner, 1993.
73 In his early writings Gardner noted only seven intelligences, but later increased their number. Their precise number and the detailed description of each of them are unimportant for our purposes.
74 Callan, 1988; Boekaerts & Boscolo, 2002; Hidi, Renninger & Krapp, 2004.
75 Callan, 1988. See the discussion on Callan's concept in Chapter Two.
76 Keegan, 1996; Simonson et al., 2000.
77 Harris, 1986.
78 Lewis and Spencer, 1986. This book is one of a series of eight published by The Council for Educational Technology: The Open Learning Guide. They discuss the various theoretical and practical aspects of the subject. Also, Bashir, 1998; Hopkins, 1996; King, 2001; Lewis, 1990, 1997.
79 Lewis and Spencer, 1986. pp. 1–20.
80 For exceptions, see Waterhouse, 1983; Harding, 1985; Harris, 1986; Lockwood, 1995.
81 Harasim, 1993; Harasim et al., 1995; Rheingold, 1993.
82 See Aviram, Bar-On and Attias, forthcoming.
83 Jones, Scanlon and O'Shea, 1987; Aviram, 1997; Palloff & Pratt, 1999.
84 Aviram, 2001; Pelgrum & Plomp, 2002.
85 Aviram, 1997.
86 Aviram, Bar-On and Attias, forthcoming.
87 Aviram, 1992b.
88 Bell, 1973; Harvey, 1989, pp, 165–265; Zuboff, 1988; Toffler, 1980, pp. 223–261, 282–286; White, 1999.
89 Bauman, 2005; Ray, 2006a.
90 Meighan, 1997; Thomas, 1998; Webb, 1990.
91 This is one meaning of "socialization" relevant for functionality in the social sense not discussed in the previous section.
92 Meighan, 1997; Hill, 2000; Webb, 1999.
93 Dreeben, 1968; Parsons, 1955.

94 "Growing Dysfunctionality of School Structure: A General Perspective."
95 Toffler, 1980; Zuboff, 1988; Handy, 1984, 1989; MacKenzie & Wajcman, 1985; Bailyn, 1989.

Chapter Five: The Disappearance of School's Target Audience in the Postmodern Era

1 Referring to children as the school's target audience may be misleading on two counts. First, young people in modernity were perceived more as raw material for the education system than a target audience. Referring to them as a target audience is in itself a result of postmodern attitudes. Second, their being a target audience, that is, a factor or population group whose desires and needs the system is obliged to fulfill, does not mean that children are the only target audience. In the postmodern reality, the following groups and institutions compete for this title: parents, the local community, industry, and the state. In truth, the multiplicity of target audiences, each with its own desires, interests, and expectations, is one of the markers of the perplexity and loss of clear direction characterizing postmodern education systems. I have chosen for purposes of simplicity to ignore these problems in this chapter and refer to young people as the systems' target audience.

2 In this chapter I have placed the terms children and adults in quotation marks. These are two complementary sides of the same coin, a coin whose nature is constantly changing. The quotation marks around them form a shorthand sign designed to indicate that these are modern perceptions that have been losing meaning and validity as categories in the postmodern era.

3 Postman, 1984.

4 Gregory Kingsley's mother later appealed to a higher court, claiming that her son, due to his age, should not have been allowed to bring a case in his own name before a court of law. The appellate court accepted her claim and determined that minors do not have independent standing in the court, thus overturning the lower court's decision. The grounds given for the annulment of the judgment, however, left an opening for future recognition of minors' standing, citing that the current status is only procedural, that is a flaw that can be overcome with technical means, rather than a critical legal flaw, which would constitute an insurmountable obstacle (Russ, 1994).

5 Booth, 1992.

6 Cannon, 1994; Booth, 1994.

7 Booth, 1992, 1994; see also Fortin, 2003; Mesch, 2006.

8 Corsaro, 2005.

9 Postman, 1986; Mayerowich, 1985, pp. 228–231; Medved & Medved, 1999.

10 Corsaro, 2005; Qvortrup, 1996, 2005; Stacey, 1990.

11 Montgomery, 2007; Buckingham & Willett, 2006; Tapscot, 1997.

12 Sennett, 1980.

13 Mead, 1978.

14 "The Shift from Paternalistic Perceptions of 'Children' to their Perception as Full Subjects."

15 "Changes in Basic Social Structures."

16 "The Disappearance of Childhood."

17 "The Disappearance of 'Childhood' and the Education System."

18 A subject enjoys full self determination rights and must be respected as such. This is the source of his dignity, the basic assumption concerning subjects in liberalism which prevents infringement of this right for self determination. Only those who lack the right of self determination and hence cannot be defined as full subjects can be treated paternalistically, with no regard for their wishes or consent.

19 Aries, 1965; Heywood, 2001.

20 The term "potential subject" in moral philosophy means somebody who will develop into a subject or full agent, a human being endowed with all the characteristics required for acting autonomously. As such the "potential subject" has to be respected but is not yet "there" and so has to be educated to

become a "full subject." Meanwhile potential subjects are subject to the custody of full subjects, usually parents in the case of children.

21 See note 20.

22 Dwyer, 2006; Hickey, 2007; Fortin, 2003.

23 See for example Farson, 1974.

24 Archard, 2004; Brooks, Walker & Wrightsman, 1998.

25 See for example the discussion in Crutchfield, 1981; Pardeck, 2006.

26 Archard, 2004, pp. 53–4.

27 See for instance the United Nations Convention on the Rights of the Child, articles 13, 14, and 15.

28 Glaberson, 2000. The weight of the boy's assertion in the final decision was not clarified by the court.

29 In the US, the minimum age at which a minor can be transferred to a criminal court and be prosecuted as an "adult" varies between zero to fifteen years among the different states, including in cases of some non-violent crimes (National Center for Juvenile Justice, 2007). For more on the changing legal status of children see for example Mnookin & Weisberg, 2005; Feld, 1999; Fagan & Zimring, 2000.

30 According to Human Rights Watch (2007), 2,225 current prisoners in the US have been sentenced to life terms for crimes they committed as children.

31 Archard, 2004, pp. 70–71.

32 Beijerse & Swaaningen, 2006; Bradley, 1990.

33 For instance, the UK has a strong punitive system for minors, which emphasizes training, supervision, and support after release (Directgov, 2008).

34 Children's Rights Alliance for England, an alliance of organizations working for the implementation of the Convention on the Rights of the Child.

35 CARE, 2007.

36 For instance, the Israeli legal system designates specially trained plain-clothes police personnel to investigate minors who are suspects or victims of criminal activity; minors cannot be legally responsible for decision making in medical matters; publicizing the identity and other information of minors is subject to strict limitations; and many more such laws (National Council for the Child, 2008).

37 Almog, 1997.

38 Every legal act of minors requires parental consent; see National Council for the Child, 2008.

39 Family case 23860/96 John Doe vs. Jane Doe and others, Takdin-Family vol. 97(2), 19.

40 Case 1916/88 John Doe vs. John Doe, Takdin-Regional Vol. 97(2) 330.

41 Shifman, 1989, pp. 236–238.

42 The Legal Capacity and Guardianship Law, 1962, Chapter Two.

43 (Israeli) Legal proceedings Law (witness interrogation) (amendment number 2) (Special consideration for minor's testimony).

44 The Convention on the Rights of the Child (1989) and the Declaration of the Rights of the Child (1959), UN Office of the High Commissioner for Human Rights.

45 Archard, 2004.

46 Civil Appeal 2266/93 John Doe and others vs. John Doe, Israeli Court Records 49(1)221, 251.

47 A consummate expression of this concept can be found in Erikson's approach, which is an expansion of the Freudian developmental concept (Erikson, 1960).

48 Tuchman, 1978. Elisabeth Badinter's history of the myth of motherly love portrays pre-Rousseauvian France motherhood as a technical role that could (and should) be delegated to a nurse (see Badinter, 1981).

49 Milkman, 1987.

50 Toffler, 1984, pp. 20, 221; Zaretsky, 1976.

51 See the section on "The Disappearance of Childhood" below.

52 Gott, 2005.

53 Silva, 1999.

54 In the US, for example, the number of households consisting of one person living alone increased from 17% in 1970 to 26% in 2005 (US. Census Bureau, 2007a). Family households went down from 81% of US households in 1970 to 68% in 2005 (US Census Bureau, 2007b). In the UK, the number of people living alone went up from 3 million in 1971 to 7 million in 2005 (Office of National Statistics, 2007).

55 The number of unmarried couples living together in the US went up from 3.2 million in 1990 to 5.5 million in the year 2000 (US. Census Bureau, 2007c). In the UK, the percentage of unmarried couples doubled from 1986 to 2005—from 11% to 24% for men, and from 13% to 24% for women (Office of National Statistics, 2007).

56 In the US, the number of children under 18 who live with a single parent was about 20.7 million in 2005 (US. Census Bureau, 2007a). In the UK the percentage of children living with a single parent went up from 7% in 1972 to 24% in 2006 (Office of National Statistics, 2007).

57 For information on the constantly increasing number of European countries that recognize same-sex marriages or unions, see ILGA Europe, 2008; for information on legislation in the various states in the US see Clifford, Curry & Hertz, 2004, pp. 29–44.

58 In the US, the number of divorces per year went up from 393,000 in 1960 to 1,163,000 in 1997 (no complete data is available after 1997; US Census Bureau, 2008). The number of divorces per year in the UK went up from 24,400 in 1958 to 180,000 in 1993. It fell to below 155,000 in 2000 (probably due to the concurrent decrease in marriages) and rose up again to 167,000 in 2004 (Office of National Statistics, 2007).

59 In the UK, the percentage of people living in "'traditional" "family households of married couples with dependent children" went down from 52% in 1971 to 37% in 2005 (Office of National Statistics, 2007). See also Sullivan, 1999; Toffler, 1979, pp. 198–218; Toffler, 1984, pp. 240–261.

60 Friedan, 1963; Gilligan, 1993; Hooks, 2000.

61 Hooks, 2004; Whitehead, 2002. Although it is difficult to argue about the dominance of these phenomena in our society, an ethical debate related to them has developed. The thinkers mentioned above perceive the process as positive, while Paglia (1991) firmly negates them.

62 Postman, 1984. See also Mayerowich, 1985.

63 Beckett, 1997; Thompson & Yokota, 2004.

64 Tapscott, 1999; Strasburger & Wilson, 2002; Buckingham, 2000.

65 See Chapter Two, section on "Postmodern Relativism and the Disappearance of the Modern Educational Goals," p. 48.

66 In this context Postman reinforces Aries' (1962) well-known position that extended "childhood" did not exist in the Middle Ages.

67 Postman, 1984; Medved & Medved, 1999; Nelsen, 1985.

68 McLuhan, 1965.

69 For a discussion of lifelong learning policy and research see Field, 2006.

70 The quotation marks around the term "career" reflect the inadequacy of the terminology, if "career" is meant in its literal sense, i.e., a (linear) way or road. In other words, the modern term "career" is unsuited to describing the postmodern professional lifestyle.

71 Margaret Mead (1970) differentiated three types of societies: traditional societies in which young people learn from "adults," societies in the process of slow change in which individuals learn from their peer groups, and societies in the process of rapid change in which "adults" learn from young people. Doubtless, we live in a society of the third type.

72 "The Relativistic Revolution and the Disappearance of Childhood."

73 Lyotard, 1984; Harvey, 1989, pp. 202–283.

74 Prominent examples of such disciples can be found in Erikson on the personal-social level (Erikson, 1968) and Kohlberg on the cognitive-ethical level (Kohlberg, 1981).

75 Bechler, 1991.

76 Nietzsche, 2001.

77 Rorty, 1989; Lyotard, 1984; Krausz and Meiland, 1982; Harvey, 1989.
78 For a complementary critique of the developmental conception, see Sampson, 1981.
79 Leites, 1979; Pfeffer, 2001.
80 See, for example, the words of Anna Freud on the belief prevalent at the beginning of the twentieth century concerning the ability to prevent pathologies in "adulthood" through correct education in "childhood" (Freud, 1978).
81 For the distinction between these two terms, see Sennett, 1980; see also the discussion of these two terms in Chapter Four, subsection on "School as an Organizationally Dysfunctional Institution," p. 134.
82 Rosenow, 1993; Senett, 1980.
83 These assumptions are tightly connected to the prevalence of a long "childhood" which in turn is connected, as Postman points out, to the dominance of literacy. This was the cause of the assumptions that prevailed in the milieu of the aristocracy of classical Greece, a highly literate social strata, that gained predominance again for the rising Western bourgeoisie in modernity, who were also characterized by high levels of literacy.
84 In the faraway modern past, people identified themselves first and foremost by their profession and then by their family status (married, bachelor, widowed) and sometimes, in intellectual circles, by the novels they read, the philosophers they admired, and their ideologue; in traditional societies it was the inherited social roles that hermetically denied individuals choice. Nowadays, when rigid social roles are no longer inherited (or rather, are defined outside the ceremonial context is some countries), profession and family status have become rapidly changing frameworks and reading materials and ideologies have practically disappeared, the music one hears (hard rock, techno, ethnic, jazz) has become the main characteristic of identification: "I am what I hear," or as a young man wrote in his blog "I am my playlist" (see Bloom on the closing of the American mind).
85 Tapscott, 1999; Aviram & Eshet, 2006.
86 See for example the phenomenon of "Indigo children," a new intelligent "breed" of children who, among other defining factors, prefer systems that require creative thought and see better ways of doing things (Carroll & Tober, 1999).
87 For example, in Israel during the second half of the 1990s student council members participated in discussions held at the national level with the Minister of Education and other Ministry officials who deal with the number, type, and scope of the matriculation (graduation) examinations.
88 For the French high school student strike against government educational reform see Lerougetel, 2005. A common avenue for students to exert their influence on educational policy is democratic schools, which give pupils the possibility to participate in determining education policy. Decisions in these kinds of schools are taken in a democratic process. These schools give their pupils a high degree of influence and participation in all decision making for example: which subjects enter the curriculum or which teachers are suitable to teachs in the school. Also here we find differences between the schools regarding the extent of children's participation; for instance some schools do not allow the pupils' involvement in the recruitment of teachers. Democratic schools can be found in many countries—see Alternative Education Resource Organization, 2007. Democratic schools' policy gives pupils the opportunity not only to make an impact on decision, but to be part ofthe decision making. These processes occur through pupils who are members in the committees that manage the school.
89 Aviram, 1986, 1990, 1991.
90 Piaget, 1960.
91 Field, 2006.
92 Rifkin, 2004; White, 1997; Beck, 2000.
93 Mead, 1970; Tapscott, 1999.
94 Aslanian & Brickell, 1980.
95 Marcia, 1966.

96 It is important to emphasize that criticism against this point of view has been raised for a long time, even by Piaget's followers, and the present tendency is to assume that children are capable of complex, relatively abstract thinking at far younger ages; see Bjorklund, 2004; Siegler and Alibali, 2004.

Chapter Six: Educational Goals for Postmodern Liberal Democracies

1 See Chapter Two, section on "Seven Responses to the Crisis in Education: Outline of a Utopian Discourse."
2 As Progress enjoys God-like status in the eyes of modernists, it is only appropriate that we capitalize the word in this context.
3 See, for example, Lyotard, 1984; Gutmann, 1999; MacIntyre, 1980.
4 In his "The cultural contradictions of capitalism," D. Bell (1976) poignantly catches a part of this devastating dialectical process; other aspects of it are described in R. Bellah's studies, Bellah, 1970, 1971, 1991; Bellah et al., 1985; as well as in Putnam, 2000 and Easterbrook, 2003.
5 McLuhan, 1965; Postman, 1986; Tapscott, 1999; Gordon & Alexander, 2005.
6 Postman, 1986, 1993.
7 Dworkin, 1978; Rawls, 1971; Gauthier, 1986; Nozick, 1974.
8 Postman, 1996, 1993; Bloom, 1987.
9 Gordon & Alexander, 2005.
10 Fromm, 1941; Sternhell, 1994, 1996, 2000.
11 Turkle, 1995; Negroponte, 1995; Amichai-Hamburger, 2002; Amichai-Hamburger & Ben-Artzi, 2002, 2003.
12 Robertson, 1992; Waters, 1995.
13 Aviram & Richardson, 2004; Aviram, 1992c, 1999, 2002b.
14 See discussion in Chapter Two, section on "Seven Responses to the Crisis in Education: Outline of a Utopian Discourse."
15 Popper, 1945; Talmon, 1960; Berlin, 1969.
16 See Aviram, 1993b, 1995; Aviram & Yona, 2003.
17 The term "autonomy" has two basic meanings. (a) The organizational meaning relates to an organizational or political reality in which a person, group, or body is granted permission from those authorized to grant it to act as he, she, or the assembly deems fit. (b) The psychological meaning relates to a specific personality structure or set of personality characteristics. The term "personal autonomy" or "autonomous personality" that I will use henceforth is intended to remind the reader that here I am relating solely to the second meaning.
18 Aviram, 1986b.
19 Lindley, 1986.
20 Kaufman, 2000a, 2000b.
21 Berlin, 1999.
22 Deci & Ryan, 1987; Assor & Kaplan, 2001.
23 Deci, 1992; Hidi, 2000; Krapp Hidi & Renninger, 1992.
24 Flum & Lavi-Yudelevitch, 2002; Erikson, 1968.
25 Aviram, 1995, 1993; Aviram and Assor, forthcoming; Aviram and Yona, 2003; Lindley, 1986.
26 Mill, 1956.
27 See for example Gray, 1983; Løvlie, Mortensen and Nordenbo, 2002; Aviram and Assor, forthcoming.
28 Aviram, 2001.
29 In the present-day period and in the context of the discourse on professional development, Schon developed a perception of learning while reflecting on practical experience (Schon, 1983). A similar concept of exploration based on reflection is also basic to Eriksonian and post-Eriksonian conceptions of identity formation in adolescence and to present concepts and methodologies of

consultancy (Flum & Lavi-Yudelevitch, 2002). In Callan's (1988) perception of autonomy today and Mill's and the German Humanists' perception in the past, such a process is perceived as basic to personality development in general. See also Aviram, 1995, 1998; Aviram & Yona, 2003.

30 The expression "almost sufficient" here and in the next points stands for "sufficient as far as human efforts are concerned" or "except for the intervention of powers beyond human control."

31 Mill, von Humboldt, and other philosophers (with the exception of Kant) who subscribe to the tradition of German Humanism, hardly used the term "autonomy." However, their concept of the "desirable individual" is reflected by the term "autonomy" as it is described above. See Lindley, 1986; Gray, 1983; Aviram, 1995.

32 A literary genre developed by the Humanists as a conceptual laboratory for the study of self-actualization.

33 Goethe, 1997.

34 Eicher, 1966; Swales, 1978, pp. 57–73.

35 By the term "self-choice" I mean the constant struggle of the individual to form an ordered scale of values of different and often contradicting desires and impulses, as well as the constant need to choose a certain way of implementing the chosen values out of the various possibilities prevailing in reality.

36 Bruford, 1962, pp. 184–292.

37 Beiser, 2002.

38 A very clear analysis of the problem that faced the German Humanists and idealists during the period under discussion can be found in Taylor, 1975, pp. 3–50.

39 Albisetti, 1983, pp. 16–36; Bruford, 1962, pp. 428–425; Pinkard, 2002.

40 One of the needed changes is the replacement of the weak metaphysical basis the Humanists gave to their approach with a systematic basis that will be more acceptable in our times. Contemporary psychology, which has been greatly influenced (usually unconsciously) by German Humanism, can provide this basis. See, for example, Assor, 1987; Assor et al., 2001, 2002; Deci & Flaste, 1995; Flum, 1994; Flum & Lavi-Yudelevitch, 2002.

41 See Chapter Two, subsection on "Critiques of Education towards Autonomy."

42 The term "open" is used here in the sense that Popper accords it in The open society and its enemies (1945). In this sense an "open discussion" is a discussion in which no claim is immune from criticism including the norms of the open discussion itself.

43 It is true that the examination of the truth values of assumptions lying at the foundation might be psychologically and epistemologically more difficult to the adherents of this view, but its openness renders such examination possible, which cannot be said concerning the critical views.

44 A similar criticism was made by Ravitch (2000) on all versions of progressive approaches to education in her Left back: A century of failed school reforms.

45 This is the view basic to Hirsch in his "Cultural literacy" and later writings (1987, 2002) and is without doubt the view guiding most decision makers today.

46 Drucker, 1993.

47 White, 1997.

48 Gergen, 1991.

49 This is the case because in the long term a liberal economy requires a liberal democratic society. Liberal Democracy, in its turn, demands citizens who are able to maintain a conceptual consistency and to defend a certain set of beliefs. Therefore, Liberal Democracy cannot align itself with citizens who have no personal backbone.

50 White, 1997.

51 Aviram, 1995; Aviram & Yona, 2003.

52 By "a certain understanding" of Nietzsche's philosophy I mean the perception of Nietzsche as a radical relativist. In my opinion, this perception is fundamentally erroneous and is based on a partial and truncated reading of Nietzsche's fragmentary texts. A systematic reading of these texts will teach us that Nietzsche presents, in accordance with the best traditions of Western rationalist

critique, a critical argument on postmodern society whose development he predicts, and the alternative utopia to it. See Aviram, 1989, 1993a.

53 Gergen, 1991.

54 However, if the relativist critics oppose the mere logical rules of procedural rationalism, then they exclude any possibility of discussion, including the presentation of their own view and the one presented here.

55 Gergen, 1991.

56 Deleuze & Guattari, 1983; Gurevitz, 1997, pp. 103–130.

57 Another, more interesting attempt from this direction can be found in Hillman, 1996.

58 Gray, 1997.

59 "Open" is here in Popper's sense. See note 42, above.

60 See Assor, forthcoming.

61 In the Millean definition of autonomy, on which I rely here, as opposed to the Kantian definition, there is nothing to prevent the autonomous individual from acting immorally.

62 Such dialectical relationships can exist also between morality and dialogical belonging, but I will not go into this subject here.

63 My use of the term "hermeneutic" in this context does not bind me to the relativistic assumptions that are basic to the numerous contexts in which the term is employed today. The relativist position, according to which there is no point in adhering to truth or to the study of "the way things are," does not derive from the argument that every text can have numerous interpretations.

64 Again, in the Millean sense of "autonomy" nothing prevents the individual from being immoral. See note 61, above.

Chapter Seven: An Educational Program for Postmodern Liberal Democracies

1 I use the term "educational program," because the term "curriculum," might suggest basing educational activity on theoretical learning, while my approach stems from outright rejection of this view. I have called the program "autonomy-oriented education" in order not to use the term "humanistic program," which could have been suitable were it not historically "taken" by some reference to the existing theoretical program.

2 "Theoretical Background."

3 "The Seven Experiential Domains of the Desired Educational Program."

4 "The Educational Process."

5 Subsection on "Education towards Morality and Dialogical Belonging," page 253.

6 Dewey, 1966.

7 Illich, 1971.

8 Portelli, 1993; Aviram, 1986a, 1990a, 1992a.

9 Peters, 1973.

10 I refer here to the conception that theoreticians primarily expressed in four books published in the last generation. Two of these books were discussed in Chapter Two: White's The aims of education restated (1982) and Education and the end of work (1997), Cooper's Authenticity and learning (1983), and Callan's Autonomy and schooling (1988). All four acknowledge the need to rethink the aims of education and its curricula, as the title of the first book in this list implies. This acknowledgment is particularly significant for White, who remained among those defending the current curriculum throughout 1970s, and then gradually moved away from this position. The three authors, Cooper, White, and Callan, were influenced by Nietzsche (Cooper) or (probably not fully consciously) the Millean liberal tradition (White and Callan).

11 See Chapter Three for more on this issue.

12 Aviram, 1993.

13 Mill, 1977, Chapter Three.

14 Mill, 1977, Chapter Five.

15 Dworkin, 1978.

16 Mill, 1977.

17 Aviram, 1991; Dworkin, 1978.

18 Aviram, 1986, 1990b, 1991, 1993.

19 Putnam, 2000.

20 Bellah et al., 1985; Kohlberg, 1980; MacIntyre, 1980.

21 Gordon & Alexander, 2005; Gergen, 1991, 2000; Mazalin & Moore, 2004.

22 During the last generation, most of Woody Allen's films portrayed this kind of self. The title of his film Deconstructing Harry (1997) explicitly reflected it.

23 In this matter I identify with Bloom's critique of postmodern reality (Bloom, 1987). It seems to me entirely likely that during Mill's time the default was not education for autonomy, albeit for different reasons.

24 "The Educational Process."

25 In this and the other six domains, I choose a mode of speaking not often used in similar contexts. It refers also to the development of "commitment" and not only the development of "knowledge," "skills," or "ability." I have done so in all experiential domains. The awareness, knowledge, or skills developed should rely on the inculcation of the values one is required to realize when appropriate. The mere acquisition of knowledge or ability without the commitment to use them is worth very little. The opposite, on the other hand, is not true: the mere development of the appropriate commitment can lead to the development of the necessary knowledge, ability, or skills when these become relevant to the realization of the value to which one is committed.

26 Flum, 1994.

27 Ibid.

28 Brown et al., 1989; Brown, 1997; Herrington & Oliver, 2000; Petraglia, 1998; Roth, 1992.

29 Aviram, 1986, 1991.

30 Barell, 1991; Beyer, 1987a, 1987b; De Bono, 1992; Fisher, 1990, 1998; Halpern, 1996; Harpaz & Lefstein, 2000; Harpaz & Lefstein, 2005.

31 Perkins, 1993; Harpaz, 2007.

32 Callan, 1988; White, 1997; Deci, 1992; Deci & Ryan, 2000; Emmons, 1991, 1999; Schmuck & Sheldon, 2001; Sheldon, Ryan, Deci & Kasser. 2004; Hidi, Renninger & Krapp, 2004; Boekaerts & Boscolo, 2002.

33 Callan, 1988.

34 Schmuck & Sheldon, 2001; Sheldon, Ryan, Deci & Kasser, 2004; Deci, 1992; Hidi, Renninger & Krapp, 2004.

35 Callan, 1988.

36 Marcia, 1966, 1980.

37 Callan, 1988, pp. 56–88; Erikson, 1968; Flum, 1994.

38 White (1982) supports the maximalistic approach, while Callan (1988) supports the approach I have adopted here.

39 Beck, 2000; Rifkin, 1994.

40 In this matter see Beck, 2000; White, 1997.

41 This concept is based on Kohlberg, 1980.

42 Kant, 1999.

43 See Erikson, 1950; Flum, 1996.

44 Bloom, 1987; Postman, 1995.

45 See, for example, the Monty Python film The Meaning of Life or the slogan: "Coca Cola: The Taste of Life." The message conveyed by these two phrases, which are but a sample of the infinite number of similar others dominant in our culture, is that all there is to human life is the maximal, endless realization of hedonism (Postman, 1986).

46 The Center for Futurism in Education at Ben-Gurion University is developing an educational program called "A new humanistic educational program" designed to actualize the basic objectives of this experiential domain (Aviram, forthcoming a [Chapter 12]).

47 Kohlberg, 1964, 1971; Kohlberg et al., 1983; Kohlberg & Turiel, 1971.

48 The term was coined by Popper (1945) in his The open society and its enemies. The concept was also basic to Mill (1977) in On liberty and to the German Humanistic tradition that influenced him.

49 Popper, 1945.

50 Yona, 1991, 2005 (Hebrew).

51 Yona, 1991 (Hebrew).

52 Aviram, forthcoming a (Chapter 9); Yona, 1991, 2005 (Hebrew).

53 See Chapter Six, section on "Morality and Dialogical Belonging: Two Complementary Ultimate Values." At the Center for Futurism in Education at Ben-Gurion University a model of a futuristic school, "The Dialogical School," has been developed based on these principles. See Gordon, Keinan & Aviram, 1994, and also Aviram, forthcoming a (Chapter 9).

54 Kohlberg, 1980.

55 Bell, 1976; Bloom, 1987.

56 "General Characterization of AOE Pedagogy."

57 "The Three Major Roles of Educators Required by AOE."

58 "Guiding Principles of AOE Pedagogy."

59 Ryle, 1949.

60 See my discussion of the personal profile in Chapter Six, section on "What is an 'Autonomous Personality'?"

61 See Chapter Six, section titled "Morality and Dialogical Belonging: Two Complementary Ultimate Values."

62 Deci & Ryan, 1987; Gardner, 2000; Keirsey & Bates, 1984; Keyes & Haidt, 2003; Schmuck & Sheldon, 2001.

63 Cooper, 1983.

64 Buber, 1958.

65 Aviram, 1986.

66 For a broader clarification of the significance of these three principles, see Aviram, Bar-On & Attias, forthcoming.

67 The concept "pedagogic" in this context may be misleading because it is associated, in the accepted educational discourse, with "transferring material" or "teaching." This is certainly not the meaning of the concept in this discussion. When I use the term "pedagogic principles" here I mean the principles used to guide educators in relation to the personality attributes that should be nurtured in young people. This is also the reason I do not use "didactics" or "didactical" in connection with my view, because nowadays they are associated with teaching and learning even more than "pedagogy.".

68 In the subsection titled "Answer to the First Question, or Supporting the Formation of the Foundations, Shell, and Design of Young People's Lives."

69 In relation to the concept of self-control, see Aviram, 1995, 2001; Aviram and Yona, 2003.

70 Goleman, 1997.

71 Aviram, Bar-On & Attias, forthcoming; Aviram, 2001a, 2003, 2004b; Aviram & Yona, 2003; Aviram et al., forthcoming a, forthcoming b; Aviram, Ronen, Somekh, Winer & Sarid, 2008.

Chapter Eight: A Structure for Educational Organizations for Postmodern Liberal Democracies

1 A number of examples of such developments can be found in Aviram, Attias, & Bar-On, 1995.

2 "Required Organizational Changes."

3 "From Factory to Educational Liaison and Guidance Center."

4   See also Aviram, 1992, 1994c; Aviram & Yonna, 2003.

5   See Callan, 1988.

6   Callan, 1988. School democracy is implemented in varying ways and to various degrees in approximately twenty-five schools in Israel who follow, in one way or another, the pioneering model of the democratic school in Hadera. This model also influenced schools in many other countries (for a list of democratic schools around the world see http://www.educationrevolution.org/lisofdemscho.html). Many democratic schools practice democracy to the fullest possible extent, which (among others) extends to include the ultimate goals of education. This book, on the other hand, does not leave the ultimate goals of education up to a democratic election among the students, since, as argued several times, from several perspectives in the book's first and third part, those should stem from the basic values of a liberal society and therefore cannot and should not be subject to negotiation. However, everything and anything that can be operated democratically within the framework these goals set should indeed be, and students' participation in the management of their educational institution should increase in accordance with their maturity.

7   A term coined by Mill (1977).

8   The situation in Israel and in some European countries is different from that of the USA. In the USA the tradition of undergoing undergraduate studies as a part of one's "general" or "liberal education" and to some extent as an experiential period, is still strong, while in Israel and France for example, college and university studies are usually career-oriented from the very beginning. However, even in the US, the influence of the "liberal education" tradition is has been radically eroded in recent years by the instrumentalist "performative" approach (to borrow the term Lyotard [1984] uses to describe the radical changes in the understanding of knowledge and higher education under the pressures of postmodernity).

9   The term "moratorium" is used here in the sense accorded to it in Erikson's developmental psychology. See Erikson, 1956, 1968.

10 Statistics, information and reports regarding the financial hardships of students in the UK can be found at the National Union of Students (NUS) Press Pack 2005–2006: Higher Education Student Finance. On-line: http://resource.nusonline.co.uk/media/resource/Press%20Pack%202005.pdf

Regarding the US, an article taken from "USA today" (22.2.2006): "Students suffocate under tens of thousands in loans." On-line: http://www.usatoday.com/money/perfi/general/2006-02-22-student-loans-usat_x.htm

11 Abbott & Ryan, 1999a, 1999b, 2001; Kohn, 1993, 1999b, 2005.

12 See note 9.

13 See Eijnatten, 1998, 2003; Fitzgerald, 2002; Hock, 1996.

Chapter Nine: The Status of Young People in Postmodern Liberal Democracies

1   This is, for example, Postman's opinion. He opposes the disappearance of "childhood" on the normative-developmental level, but sadly admits that there is no institutionalized social way to prevent its development. See: Postman, 1982, pp. 143–153. On this subject see also Medved & Medved, 1999.

2   The term "mega-scenario" refers to a very general predictive conceptual framework comprised of many different concrete scenarios which satisfy the overall general scenario's conditions.

3   "Possible Impact of the Future Status of Young People on Postmodern Democratic Education Systems."

4   "The Desired Status of Young People vis-à-vis the Education System in a Postmodern Democracy."

5   Wringe, 1981; Archard, 2004.

6   The National Youth Agency, 2007.

7   Aviram, 1990, 1991.

8 See for example Houlgate, 1980. The punishment of children is often no different than that of adults. According to Human Rights Watch (2007), 2,225 prisoners currently incarcerated in the USA have been sentenced to life in prison for crimes they committed as children.

9 See Chapter Five, section on "The Shift from Paternalistic Perceptions of 'Children' to their Perception as Full Subjects." There are meaningful variations in the legal distinction between "children" and "adults" among various counties, but the process of eroding this distinction is happening in many places. For instance in the USA, the minimum age for adult prosecution varies between seven and fifteen years among the different states (National Center for Juvenile Justice, 2007). For more on the changing legal status of children see for example Mnookin & Weisberg, 2005; Feld, 1999; Fagan & Zimring, 2000.

10 Glaberson, 2000.

11 Although at first glance this model seems impossible to actualize, thinkers such as Cohen (1981) and Farson (1974) proposed it in a serious, detailed, and well-reasoned way. For a more recent thinker who has taken few steps in this direction see Alaimo, 2002.

12 The age of consent is the age that determines whether or not an act performed with a minor under this age (even if he or she consented) constitutes a felony. The law determines that consent to engage in sexual interaction given under this age is invalid, and therefore the act is legally considered as if it was performed without consent.

13 In the UK, the age of sexual consent between homosexuals was equalized to that of heterosexuals on November 30, 2000 (Changing Attitude, 2007).

14 Another reason might be expressed in the claim that some of the aforementioned models comprise the possibility of the young being granted only a specific option or participation right, for example, after passing a relevant test, thus leaving them unfit to enjoy other option and participation rights. This being the case, the assumption relating to the immaturity of children should not be entirely negated and, therefore, neither should their welfare rights automatically be revoked.

15 The quotation marks used in this sentence imply that although all these terms are often used in this context, I:

Do not necessarily identify with the values that might underpin their use;

Do not think that these terms are fully appropriate;

Make use of them only for brevity's sake.

16 For example, in Chapter Two of the Israeli Legal Capacity and Guardianship Law, 1962.

17 See for example the Israeli Compulsory Education Law 1949, Chapter Two; the British Education Act 1996, Chapter I.

18 See for example the Israeli state Education Law, 1953, Article 20. Numerous European countries have begun to move toward allowing school choice, but in some choice is still limited or nonexistent (see Wolf, Macedo, Ferrero & Venegoni, 2004).

19 Drucker, 1993.

20 Grolnick & Slowiaczek, 1994; Lareau, 2000; Ravn, 1998.

21 Marschall, Schneider & Teske, 2002; Peterson, 2003a.

22 Buckley & Schneilder, 2007; Rooney and Yoder, 2007.

23 Cooper, 2005, p. 395; Ray, 2005.

24 Bosetti, 2004.

25 Mintrom, 2000.

26 Griffith, 1998; Holt, 1981.

27 Meighan, 1997.

28 See Chapter Five, section titled "The Shift from Paternalistic Perceptions of 'Children' to their Perception as Full Subjects."

29 The British Education Act 1996, Chapter I, Section 7. For more information about "education otherwise" than in school in the UK see the website of Education Otherwise (http://www.education-otherwise.org). For general information about home schooling see for example Ray, 2005.

30 This is the formal meaning of the compulsory education laws in many English-speaking countries today, albeit this meaning has been translated into the practical context in a considerably widened scope only in the last decade following the spread of the home schooling movement.
31 Meighan, 1997; Ramsey, 1992.
32 At the beginning of the 1990s, the democratic school in Hadera was unique in Israel. At present, approximately twenty-five schools defined as democratic (though the degree and nature of the democracy they practice is likely to differ from school to school) are operating in Israel. Throughout the world as well, the number of democratic schools, influenced by this model, has increased considerably, although no accurate statistics are known to exist describing this data, according to information provided by Mr. Ya'akov Hecht, head of the democratic institute in Hadera. For a list of democratic schools worldwide see http://www.educationrevolution.org/lisofdemscho.html.
33 See for instance the Jenaplan schools in Germany (http://www.jenaplan.de) and Holland (http://www.jenaplan.nl) and Freinet schools around the world (http://www.freinet.org).
34 Griffith, 1998; Holt, 1981.
35 Tapscott, 1999; Holloway & Valentine, 2001, 2003; Selwyn, 2004.
36 Mead, 1970.
37 A young man's Internet profile I recently read defined him as follows: "I am my playlist."
38 Aviram et al., forthcoming b.
39 As I have already contended in Chapter Six, section on "The Logical Necessity of Adopting a Specific Educational View," and a few other places.
40 In the earlier section on "Possible Impact of the Future Status of Young People on Postmodern Democratic Education Systems."
41 There are good reasons to believe that striving to achieve maximal chances for development through extensive educational compulsion will be counterproductive. In this context, the "minimal" or to the most "reasonable" should have the upper hand over "maximal." This maxim stands in direct contradiction to the prevailing discourse which advocates that young people should have maximal chances to develop and relies therefore on maximal compulsion which renders the implementation of the previous requirement counterproductive
42 This conception is reflected in various ways in two models of the futuristic school developed at the Center for Futurism in Education and Ben-Gurion University. See Aviram et al., forthcoming b; Aviram, Bar-On & Attias, forthcoming.

Chapter Ten: The Importance of Navigation through the Postmodern Storm

1 Butler, 1993; Fausto-Sterling, 1993, 2000; Halberstam, 2005; Prosser, 1998.
2 Tyack, 1974.
3 First section, titled "The Revolution Is Unavoidable and Is Already Underway."
4 Subsection on "Functional-Economic Damage."
5 Subsection on "Probable Psychological Damage."
6 Subsection on "Social Damage."
7 Section titled "What Are the Desired Alternatives?"
8 Ravitch, 2000; Tyack & Cuban, 1995.
9 Salomon et al., 1991.
10 Schmidt, 1983.
11 Sharan, 1994; Slavin, 1990; Johnson & Johnson, 1987.
12 Hanson & Schutz, 1986; Worthen, 1993; Fetterman, Wandersman & Kaftarian, 1996; Cousins & Earl, 1992.
13 Aviram & Richardson, 2004; Aviram, 2000a; Hartley & Collins-Brown, 1999.
14 Dean, 2006.
15 Presseisen, 1990; Milgram, Dunn & Price, 1993; Tobias, 1991; Felder, 1993.
16 Hidi, Renninger & Krapp, 2004; Boekaerts & Boscolo, 2002.

17 Hess & Copeland, 2001; Goleman, 1997.

18 Haymann, Golan & Shapira, 1997; Popkewitz & Lindblad, 2004; Gabbard, 2000; Tanner, 1997; Charter Schools, School Choice Student Achievement, 2004.

19 Hargreaves, 1995; Middlewood & Lumby, 2004; Sharpe, 1996.

20 Greenberg, 1987; Borman, Hewes, Overman & Brown, 2003.

21 Blase & Blase, 2001.

22 Sizer, 1993; Petrie, 1992; Grossman & Stodolsky, 1994; Doll, 1993.

23 Haymann, Golan & Shapira, 1997.

24 Meighan, 1999.

25 Dempster, Freakley & Parry, 2001; Mok, 2005; Hill, 2003.

26 Cervone, 2002; Youniss et al., 2002; Brenes, 2005.

27 Aviram, 2000b.

28 Rosenow, 1980.

29 Abbott & Ryan, 2001; Bransford et al., 1999; Diamond & Hopson, 1998; Hargreaves, 2003; Aviram & Talmi, 2005.

30 See the discussion of this subject in Chapter Four.

31 Aviram, forthcoming a; Gordon, 1984; Popkewitz et al., 1982; Sarason, 1993, 1998; Ravitch, 2000; Tyack & Cuban, 1995; Maxcy, 1995; Hill, 1999.

32 DiMaggio, 1988; Zucker, 1987.

33 Postman, 1986.

34 Wittchen & Jacobi, 2005.

35 A paraphrase of a term used to characterize postmodernity. See Kroker, Kroker & Cook, 1989.

36 www.eBay.com is just one example of how everyone can not only be involved as buyer, but also as seller—of anything. See also Drucker, 1993.

37 Kroker, Kroker & Cook, 1989.

38 Feyerabend, 1978.

39 For a fundamental analysis of this situation from an ethical standpoint, see MacIntyre, 1980. See also Lyotard, 1984; Baudrillard, 1981; Giroux, 1996.

40 Bumpass, 1990; Bumpass & Lu, 2000; Ellwood & Jencks, 2004; Schoen & Standish, 2001.

41 Goos, 1996; Demo, 1992.

42 Mitchell, 1999; Fukuyama, 1999.

43 Aviram, 2001; Gergen, 1991, 2000.

44 See also Aviram, 1999.

45 Gergen, 1991.

46 Aviram, 1993b; Fukuyama, 1993.

47 Huntington, 1996.

48 McLaughlin, 1996; Fromm, 1941.

49 Lubbers, Gijsberts, Scheepers, 2002.

50 Huntington, 1996.

51 Aviram & Richardson, 2004.

52 Both these processes are currently gaining momentum in Western countries.

53 Hargraves, 1997.

Chapter Eleven: Implementing Autonomy Oriented Education Today

1 The first section, "The Need for Bold, Paradigmatic Leaps."

2 The second section, "Three Possible Change Strategies."

3 The final section, "Gradual Implementation of AOE ."

4 Among others, I especially cite the following books: Giovanni Pico della Mirandola's Oration on the dignity of man, Kant's Critique Of practical reason and his What is enlightenment, Goethe's Wilhelm Meister's apprenticeship (Wilhelm Meister's lehrjahre), Schiller's Letters upon the aesthetic

education of man and his The robbers (Die räuber), John Stewart Mill's On liberty, his autobiography, and his The principles of political economy, and Nietzsche's Schopenhauer as educator. I would also add some of the writings of Herder, Wilhelm von Humboldt, Lord Byron, Jefferson, Thomas Paine, Henry David Thoreau, and later liberal thinkers following and interpreting J. S. Mill's On liberty, such as John Gray's Mill on liberty: A defence, as well as the founding fathers of Humanist psychology, viz., Karl Rogers, Abraham Maslow, Erich Fromm, and their followers today, such as Edward Deci and Richard Ryan among others. This is the rich tradition on which I have relied and which has inspired me in the conception and formation of AOE, although necessarily I have not referred to all its trends and all the books that influenced me in my steps towards the formation of this Humanistic educational view.

5　My aim in this chapter is to argue for the urgent necessity of a mindful, strategic approach towards educational change guided by the ultimate Humanistic values. I have no doubt that my understanding of these values and the educational view and methodology stemming from them can and should be criticized by other Humanists and liberal democrats. I hope they will, and as a result a real ongoing critical discourse with practical implications will arise. I hope that this book will contribute to the emergence of such a discourse. Still in the context of this book when referring to "Humanistic education," I cannot but refer to my best and most recent analysis of the meaning of this term as done here. Making such references does not mean that I am not conscious that other versions of these core values exist and might (hopefully) influence the educational discourse, or that other educational views might stem from these ultimate values or other versions of them.

6　Before educators can commit themselves to similar roles stemming from other Humanistic educational views, what matters is not the full acceptance of AOE but educators' readiness to make these leaps and the commitment to a systematic and systemic Humanistic education program geared to postmodernity.

7　Tyack, 1974; Boli et al., 1985.

8　Cuban, 1990; Elmore, 2000; Ginsburg et al., 1990; La Belle & Ward, 1990; Levin, 2001; McLaughlin & Shepherd, 1995.

9　Levin, 2001; Moon, 1995; Tomlinson, 2001.

10　Aviram, forthcoming a.

11　I have chosen not to use this term when referring to the desired development process, because "curriculum" is closely connected in our minds with scholarly leaning activities, while the range of educational activities in the AOE program can and should be much wider.

12　See Chapter Seven, subsection on "Answer to the First Question, or Supporting the Formation of the Foundations, Shell, and Design of Young People's Lives."

13　Ibid. The two latter options were developed as concrete programs in the framework of the Center for Futurism in Education at Ben-Gurion University; the former, in the framework of a program called "A New Humanistic Study Program," and the latter in the framework of a futuristic school model called "The Dialogical School." See: Aviram, forthcoming a.

14　Guichard, 2001; Super, 1976; Stevenson, 2003; Kantor & Tyack, 1982; Cullen et al., 2002; Arcus, 1987; Thomas & Arcus, 1992; Elliott, 1999.

15　Specifically in the second and third sections of the chapter, "The Seven Experiential Domains of the Desired Educational Program" and "The Educational Process."

16　See the discussion of the guiding principles of AOE in Chapter Seven, subsection on "Guiding Principles of AOE Pedagogy," p. 262.

17　The concept "field of interest," under this or other names, served as the basis of at least two models of futuristic schools developed at the Center for Futurism in Education at Ben-Gurion University. A more detailed discussion of the concept in the educational and practical context can be found in Assor, forthcoming, and in Aviram, forthcoming a.

18　See the discussion of these programs in the context of the discussion of the third experiential domain, Chapter Seven, section on "The Seven Experiential Domains of the Desired Educational Program," p. 243.

19 Armstrong, 1994; Birenbaum, 1996 (Hebrew); Gardner 1983, 1993; Herman et al., 1992.

20 A few representative examples of such programs are the "High School Dual Enrollment" in The University of Michigan Dearborn, "Dual Enrollment for High School Students" in DeSales University in Pennsylvania, and "Special Student Enrollment for High School Students" in The University of Wisconsin System.

21 See Chapter Five, note 88.

22 See Chapter Eight, note 6.

Annex One: My Intellectual Journey

1 "The Rise of Postmodernity."

2 Harvey, 1989; Malpas, 2005.

3 Toffler, 1980, 1995; Beck, 1991; Bauman, 2000; Kroker, 1989.

4 Localism-globalism; see Robertson, 1992.

5 See Chapter One, section on "The Rise of Postmodernity"; Ahmed, 2004; Connor, 2004.

6 "The Rise of Postmodernity"; see specifically the subsection on "Founding Revolutions of Postmodernity."

7 Both the left and the conservative wings use it—the former often approvingly and the latter mostly opposing it.

8 The most systematic portrayal of this discourse is in Chapter Three, section on "Scientific Professionalization and Its Effect on the Unity of the Liberal Curriculum."

9 Derrida, 1978; Docherty, 1993; Sim, 2005.

10 Banks, 1995; Shohat & Stam, 2003; Haddock, 2003; Bhabha, 1994; Peters & Lankshear, 1996.

11 Spivak, 1990; Stoler, 1996.

12 Zalewski, 2000; Marchand & Parpart, 1995; Rubin, 1975.

13 Mosteller, 2006; Derrida, 1997; Lyotard, 1984; Foucault, 1989.

14 Fuchs, 2001; Smith, 2004; Sedikides & Brewer, 2001; Deleuze & Guattari, 1983.

15 I use the terms "systemically" and "essence" intentionally and ironically.

16 Peters & Besley, 2007.

17 Fletcher, 2000; Usher & Edwards, 1994.

18 Postman, 1986, 1996; Dunn, 1998; Sarup & Raja 1996; Bukatman, 1993; Smith, 2004; Holstein, 2000.

19 Cagney-Watts, 1991; Eagleton, 1996; Norris, 2002.

20 Paradoxical use of the meta-narrative was of course intended.

21 The logical structure here is interactive and iterative rather than linear. Each of the mentioned levels sustained the others and is sustained by them. I ignored it for the sake of simplicity.

22 Gur-Ze'ev, 2007; Foucault, 1980; Freire, 1973; Aronowitz & Giroux, 1991.

23 See for example Derrida, 1976.

24 Norris, 2002.

25 Bloom, 1987; Zimmerman, 2002; Graff, 1992; Lauter, 1991.

26 Gur-Ze'ev, 2004.

27 Said, 2003; Bhabha, 1994.

28 Aviram & Dotan, 2009.

29 See for example Lyotard, 1984.

30 Hume, 1969. I suppose postmodernist thinkers will naturally attempt to deconstruct the above distinction in response to such criticism, together with the modernistic criticism on which it relies. My answer to this reaction is that if one is to remain loyal to the postmodernist spirit, the criticism should be "deconstructed" as well. In other words, as I already argued earlier, the concept of deconstruction is self-contradictory and hence senseless (as long as it transcends the more traditional concept of criticism). This predicted criticism is therefore vacuous and devoid of substance.

31 Rawls, 1999a, 1999b, 2005; Rawls & Herman, 2000; Rorty, 1989; Kymlicka, 1991; Habermas, 2001; Levinas, 1985; Davidson, 2005—to name a few well known thinkers who are different from each other in many important aspects.

32 Gergen, 1991, 2000; Reid, 1998.

33 Including myself forty years ago.

34 Through their books or sometimes in person (I am especially grateful to Michael Peters and Ilan Gur-Ze'ev who have been an ongoing source of inspiration for me; see for example Aviram & Dotan, 2009).

35 Although many postmodernists coherently or incoherently identify themselves with these views.

36 Aviram & Dotan, 2009.

37 For instance, the battle against global warming, which reflects ecological principles and interests, is not only shared by the administrations of all countries, it is also a popular theme around the world.

38 Gilligan, 1993; Hooks, 2000.

39 Subsection on "Contemporary Schools as Modern Versions of Platonic Education" below.

40 Subsection on "The Mega-Discourse on School Change."

41 Subsection on "Salvaging 'Paradigmatic Change.'"

42 Tyack, 1974; Rury, 2002.

43 Farson, 1974; Dreeben, 1980; Parsons, 1959.

44 Bowles & Gintis, 1976; Bourdieu & Passeron, 1990.

45 Foucault, 1995.

46 Lawton & Gordon, 2002; Marrou, 1982.

47 Brickman, 2007; Power, 1991.

48 Bloom, 1987; Livingstone, 1943; Hirst, 1974; Peters, 1970.

49 In this sense, Tyack and Cuban's (1995) statement about school reform, that "Americans celebrate innovation" (p. 4), is true to many other Western nations. See also Bascia & Hargreaves, 2000; Conley, 1993; Cuban, 1990; Ravitch, 2000; Sarason, 1990.

50 Aviram, forthcoming a.

51 See Chapter One, section on "The Floundering of Modern Education Systems in Postmodernity," and Chapter Two, section on "Postmodern Relativism and the Disappearance of the Modern Educational Goals," for a discussion of this issue.

52 I am talking about "second order" or "paradigmatic" change in relation to mindful response to postmodernity and the various revolutions it consists of: the knowledge society, digital society, information society, post-Fordist society; globalization, global economy, etc.; see Aviram, forthcoming a.

53 Aviram, forthcoming a; see for example Kinsler & Gamble, 2001.

54 Kuhn, 1962.

55 Harvey, 1989; Senge, 2006; Drucker, 2003.

56 Aviram, forthcoming a.

57 Handy, 1998; Senge, 2006; Gallos, 2006; Schein, 2004.

58 Knight, 2007.

59 Tyack, 1974.

60 Aries, 1965; Badinter, 1981; Beckett, 1997; Burquiere, 2004; Heywood, 2001; Montgomery, 2007; Qvortrup, 1996.

61 Archard, 2004; Dwyer, 2006; Farson, 1974; Fortin, 2003; John, 2003; Pardeck, 2006.

62 The adoption of Humanism for our era is a mission that has mostly been ignored by recent philosophy; its "torch" was passed on to psychology.

63 White, 1982, 1997, 1999, 2003, 2006; Callan, 1988, 1994, 1997, 2001, 2002; Valls, 1999; Scott, 1991; Berlin, 1999; Taylor, 1975.

64 Although to the best of my knowledge they do not emphasize this fact; see White, 1973, 1982, 1999, 2003; Callan, 1988.

65 Rogers, 1969, 1980; Maslow, 1968, 1970.

66 May, 1969.

67 Frankl, 1962.

68 Fromm, 1941, 1962.

69 Ryan & Deci, 2000, 2001, 2003, 2004; Deci & Ryan, 1985, 1991, 1995; Ryan, Deci & Grolnick, 1995; Grolnick, Deci & Ryan, 1997; Reeve, Deci & Ryan, 2004; Katz & Assor, 2006; Vallerand, 1997.

70 Boekaerts & Boscolo, 2002; Hidi, Renninger & Krapp, 2004; Hidi, 1990; Katz, et al., 2006; Krapp, 2002b.

71 Seligman, 2002; Seligman & Csikszentmihalyi, 2000; Kahneman, 1999.

72 Paris & Paris, 2001; Zimmerman, 2002; Pintrich, 2000; Butler, 2002; Azevedo, 2005; Boekaerts, 1997; Butler & Winne, 1995.

73 Diener, Suh, Lucas & Smith, 1999; Frey & Stutzer, 2002; Lane, 2000; Bartolini, 2007; Offer, 2006; Easterbrook, 2003.

74 Schmuck & Sheldon, 2001; Sheldon, Ryan, Deci & Kasser, 2004; Sheldon & Kasser, 2001; Kasser & Ryan, 1996; Riediger & Freund, 2004; Wilding & Andrews, 2006.

75 Erikson, 1968; Marcia, 1993; Flum & Kaplan, 2006; Schwartz, 2006; Waterman, 1982.

76 Dunn & Dunn, 1993; Dunn et al., 1995; Coffield et al., 2004; Allinson, Chell & Hayes, 2000; Vermunt, 1992.

77 Rothbart & Derryberry, 1981; Strelau, 2001; Rothbart, Evans & Ahadi 2000; Buss & Plomin, 1975; Putnam, Ellis & Rothbart, 2001.

78 Gardner, 1983, 1993, 2000.

79 Aviram, 2001 (I do not point here to relevant references since they exist in the relevant places).

80 Used here in a very broad sense that does not require long-term or rigid planning and allows easy change of the flexible plan.

81 Kymlicka, 1991.

82 Kohlberg, 1981; Power, Higgins & Kohlberg, 1989.

83 For the discussion on this issue see Peters, 1995; Klein, 1995.

84 Lyotard, 1984; Haraway, 1991.

85 Subsection on "The Postmodernistic Discourse."

86 Aviram & Dotan, 2009.

87 Nozick, 1974; Hayek, 1976, 1949; Boaz, 1997; Machan, 2006; Otsuka, 2003; Mele, 2006; Friedman, 1962.

88 Dworkin, 1977, 2006a, 2006b; Rawls, 1999; Rawls & Freeman, 2007.

89 The main Republican view is originally anti-liberal (Talmon, 1952). Still there are liberals who have adopted some important republican elements without giving up the liberal creed, at least not intentionally.

90 Arendt & Hill, 1979.

91 Gutmann, 1987.

92 Garforth, 1979.

93 Ibid.

94 Hallowell, 1998; Gaylin, 2003.

95 Talmon, 1952.

96 Talmon, 1952; Popper, 1952.

97 Sternhell, 1994.

98 Berlin, 1981.

99 Sternhell, 1994, 1996; Fromm, 1941.

100 Aviram, 1991a.

101 Kroeker & Ward, 2001; Alexander & Smith, 2005; Koelb, 1990.

102 Bloom, 1987; Banathy, 1996; Fromm, 1941.

103 Gergen, 1991.

104 To quote Postman (1986; see also Postman, 1993).

NOTES

105 Taylor, 1975; Lilge, 1948.

106 Bruford, 1975; Berlin, 1989; Taylor, 1975.

107 Huntington, 1996; Blankley, 2005.

108 Bell, 1996.

109 See the subsection on " Humanistic Research on Personal Development."

110 Drucker, 2003; Senge, 2006; Chawla & Renesch, 1995; Lynch & Cruise, 2006; Durand, 2006; Peters, 1987; Hock, 1999.

111 See Chapters 5 and 9.

112 See the subsection on "The Postmodernistic Discourse" above and Chapter One, Section 2.1.

113 Aviram & Talmi, 2004, 2005; Aviram & Matan, 2004a, 2004b.

114 Aviram & Richardson, 2004; Richardson, 2004; Kastis, 2004; Bibeau, 2004; Newhouse, 2004; Pelgrum & Plomp, 2004; Salomon, Perkins & Globerson, 1991; Salomon & Rosen, 2007.

115 Learning in kibbutzim in Israel until a couple of decades ago resembled constructivist learning.

116 Jenaplan schools in Germany (see http://www.jenaplan.de) and Holland (http://www.jenaplan.nl).

117 Aviram & Richardson, 2004; Aviram & Talmi, 2004, 2005; Aviram & Matan, 2004a, 2004b.

118 See for instance White & Bramall, 2000.

119 Marcuse, 2002; MacIntyre, 1980; Postman, 1993, 1996; Whyte, 1956; Ellul, 1964; Horkheimer, 2004.

120 Snow, 1969.

121 Popper, 1952; Hayek, 1976.

122 Hayek (1978) had a big influence on Thatcher (Ranelagh, 1991; Shearmur, 2006).

123 Peters, 1987; Handy, 1994; Drucker, 2003.

124 Popper, 1952.

125 Aviram, 2004a, 2005.

126 Dror, 1988, 2001; Fischer, Miller & Sidney, 2007; Moran, Rein & Goodin, 2006.

127 "Strong" refers to the fact that the relationship between the various disciplines and the internal discourse among them should lead to integrative ideological, theoretical, and pedagogical models that can provide a foundation for new educational practices (see for example the pedagogical model of the innovative iClass platform, whose development I headed; Aviram & Ronen et al., 2008).

128 Aviram, forthcoming a, 2004a, 2005.

129 Aviram, 2005.

BIBLIOGRAPHY

77th Congress *2nd Session* Senate Document No. 159. (1942). Attack upon Pearl Harbor by Japanese Armed Forces: Report of the Commission Appointed by the President of the United States to Investigate and Report the Facts Relating to the Attack Made by Japanese Armed Forces upon Pearl Harbor in the Territory of Hawaii on December 7, 1941. Retrieved from http://www.ibiblio.org/pha/pha/roberts/roberts.html

Abbott, J., & Ryan, T. (2001). *The unfinished revolution: Learning, human behaviour, Community and political paradox*. Stafford, UK: Network Educational Press.

Abbott, J., & Ryan, T. (1999a). Learning to go with the grain of the brain. *Education Canada, 39*(1), 8–11.

Abbot, J., & Ryan, T. (1999b). Constructing knowledge, reconstructing schooling. *Educational Leadership, 57*(3), 66–69.

Abbot, J. (2006). *The 21st century learning initiative* [On-line]. Retrieved from http://www.21learn.org

Abbott, J. (1994). *Learning makes sense: Recreating education for a changing future*. Letchworth, UK: Education 2000. Retrieved from http://www.21learn.org

Abel, M., & Sewell, J. (1999). Stress and burnout in rural and urban secondary school teachers. *Journal of Educational Research, 92*, 287–293.

Adler, M. (1982). *The paidea proposal*. New York: Macmillan.

Ahmed, A. S. (2004). *Postmodernism and Islam: Predicament and promise* (Rev. ed.). London and New York: Routledge.

Aiyagari, S. R., Greenwood, J., & Guner, N. (2000). On the state of the union. *Journal of Political Economy, 108*(2), 213–244.

Alaimo, K. (2002). *Children as equals: Exploring the rights of the child*. Lanham, MD: University Press of America.

Albas, C., & McCluskey, W. (1978). Anomie, social class and drinking behavior of high school students. *Journal of Studies on Alcohol, 39*(5), 910–913.

Albisetti, J. C. (1983). *Secondary school reform in imperial Germany*. Princeton, NJ: Princeton University Press.

Alderson, P. (2000). *Young children's rights: Exploring beliefs, principles and practice*. London and Philadelphia: Jessica Kingsley.

Alexander, J. C., & Smith, P. (Eds.). (2005). *The Cambridge companion to durkheim*. New York: Cambridge University Press.

Alexander, P. A., & Murphy, P. K. (1998). Profiling the differences in students' knowledge, interest, and strategic processing. *Journal of Educational Psychology, 90*, 435–447.

Alexander, P. A. (1997). Mapping the multidimensional nature of domain learning: The interplay of cognitive, motivational, and strategic forces. In M. L. Maehr & P. R. Pintrich (Eds.), *Advances in motivation and achievement* (Vol. 10, pp. 213–250). Greenwich, CT: JAI Press Inc.

Allinson, C. W., Chell, E., & Hayes, J. (2000). Intuition and entrepreneurial performance. *European Journal of Work and Organizational Psychology, 9*(1), 31–43.

Almog, S. (1997). *Children's rights*. Shoken, Tel Aviv. [Hebrew].

Alternative Education Resource Organization (AERO). (2007). *List of democratic schools*. Retrieved from http://www.educationrevolution.org/lisofdemscho.html

Alvesson, M., & Willmott, H. (1996). *Making sense of management: A critical introduction*. London: Sage.

Amichai-Hamburger, Y., & Ben-Artzi, E. (2003). Loneliness and internet use. *Computers in Human Behavior, 19*(1), 71–80.

Amichai-Hamburger, Y., & Ben-Artzi, E. (2002). The relationship between extraversion and neuroticism and the different uses of the internet. *Computers in Human Behavior, 16*, 441–449.

Amichai-Hamburger, Y. (2002). Internet and personality. *Computers in Human Behavior, 18*, 1–10.

Amin, A. (1994). *Post-fordism: A reader*. Oxford, UK: Blackwell.

Anderson, M. A., Kaufman, J., Simon, T. R., Barrios, L., Paulozzi, L., & Ryan, G., et al. (2001). School-associated violent deaths in the United States, 1994–1999. *Journal of the American Medical Association, 286,* 2695–2702.

Angus, D., & Mirel, J. (1999). *The failed promise of the American high school: 1890–1995.* New York: Teachers College Press.

Apple, M. W. (2001). *Educating the "Right" way: Markets, standards, god, and inequality.* New York: RoutledgeFalmer.

Apple, M. W. (1990). *Ideology and the curriculum* (2nd ed.). London: Routledge & Paul Kegan.

Archard, D. (2004). *Children: Rights and childhood* (2nd ed.). New York: Routledge.

Arcus, M. (1987). A framework for life-span family life education. *Family Relations, 36,* 5–10.

Arendt, H., & Hill, M. A. (1979). *Hannah Arendt, the recovery of the public world.* New York: St. Martin's Press.

Ariel, Y., Biderman, S., & Rotem, O. (1998). *Relativism and beyond.* Leiden, Netherlands: Koninklijke Brill NV.

Aries, P. (1965). *Centuries of childhood: A social history of family life.* Vintage.

Armstrong, T. (1994). *Multiple intelligences in the classroom.* Alexandria, VA: Association for Supervision and Curriculum Development.

Aronowitz, S. (2008). *Against schooling: Toward an education that matters.* Boulder, CO: Paradigm Publishers.

Aronowitz, S., & Giroux, H. A. (1991). *Postmodern education: Politics, culture, and social criticism.* Minneapolis, MN: University of Minnesota Press.

Arum, R. (2003). *Judging school discipline: The crisis of moral authority.* Cambridge, MA: Harvard University Press.

Aslanian, C. B., & Brickell, H. M. (1980). *Americans in transition: Life changes as reasons for adult learning.* New York: College Entrance Examination Board.

Assor, A., & Kaplan, H. (2001). Mapping the domain of autonomy support: Five important ways to enhance or undermine students' experience of autonomy in learning. In A. Efklides, J. Kuhl, & R. M. Sorrentino (Eds.), *Trends and prospects in motivation research* (pp. 101–120). Boston: Kluwer Academic Publishers.

Assor, A., Kaplan, H., & Roth, G. (2002). Choice is good, but relevance is excellent: Autonomy-enhancing and suppressing teacher behaviors in predicting students' engagement in school work. *British Journal of Educational Psychology, 72,* 261–278.

Assor, A. (forthcoming). Growth-promoting school: A school that satisfies psychological needs and promotes listening to the self and to others. In A. Aviram (Ed.), *The futuristic school.* Rotterdam, The Netherlands: Sense Publishers.

Assor, A. (1987). Psychological motives and defensive person perception: A brief historical account and revised model. *Social Behavior and Personality, 15*(2), 119–132.

Aviram, A., et al. (forthcoming a). The dialogical school. In A. Aviram (Ed.), *The futuristic school.* Rotterdam, The Netherlands: Sense Publishers.

Aviram, A., et al. (forthcoming b). School as a community of inquiry. In A. Aviram (Ed.), *The futuristic school.* Rotterdam, The Netherlands: Sense Publishers.

Aviram, A., et al. (forthcoming c). School for developing autonomy. In A. Aviram (Ed.), *The futuristic school.* Rotterdam, The Netherlands: Sense Publishers.

Aviram, A., & Assor, A. (forthcoming). In defense of personal autonomy as a fundamental educational aim in liberal democracies. *Oxford Review of Education.*

Aviram, A., Attias, M., & Bar-On, N. (1995). School as a communication center, or: Distance learning as the foundation of education for autonomy. In A. Bruce (Ed.), *Proceedings of the open classroom,* a European Conference on Distance Learning and New Technology, Oslo, September 1995.

Aviram, A., Bar-On, N., & Attias, M. (forthcoming). *School as communication center.* Haifa: Pardes. [Hebrew]

Aviram, A., & Dotan, I. (2009). The absurdity of postmodern educational thought. *Megamot, 46,* 297–317. [Hebrew]

Aviram, A., & Eshet, Y. (2006). Towards a theory of digital literacy: 3 scenarios for the next steps. *European Journal of Open, Distance and E-Learning, 2006*/1 (January-June). http://www.eurodl.org.

Aviram, A., & Matan, N. (2004a). The need for strategic thinking on ICT and education. In *Designing the school of tomorrow: Advanced technologies in education, Proceedings of a conference held in Athens, November 2004.*

Aviram, A., & Matan, N. (2004b). ICT: Does it enhance learning, or jeopardize it? In *Proceedings of international symposium on advanced technologies in education: Designing the science laboratory for the school of tomorrow, Kefalonia, Greece* (pp. 51–56). Athens: Ellinogermaniki Agogi.

Aviram, A., & Richardson, J. (Eds.). (2004). *Upon what does the turtle stand? Rethinking education for the digital era.* Dordrecht, Netherlands: Kluwer Academic Publishers.

Aviram, A., Ronen, Y., Somekh, S., Schellas, Y., Dotan, I., & Winer A. (2007). *iClass pedagogical model and guidelines. Deliverable 3.1 of iClass project*, supported by the European Commission FP6.

Aviram, A., Ronen, Y., Somekh, S., Winer, A., & Sarid, A. (2008). Self-regulated personalized learning (SRPL): Developing iClass's pedagogical model. *eLearning Papers, 9*, http://www. elearningpapers.eu/index.php?page=doc&doc_id=11941&doclng=6

Aviram, A., & Talmi, D. (2005). The impact of information and communication technology on education: The missing discourse between three different paradigms. *E–Learning, 2*(2), 169–191.

Aviram, A., & Talmi, D. (2004). The merger of ICT and education: Should it necessarily be an exercise in the eternal recurrence of the reinvention of the wheel? In F. Hernandez & I. F. Goodson (Eds.), *Social geographies of educational change* (pp. 123–142). London: Kluwer.

Aviram, A., & Yona, Y. (2003). Flexible control: Toward a conception of personal autonomy for post-modern education. *Educational Philosophy and Theory, 36*, 3–17.

Aviram, A. (forthcoming a). *The futuristic school.* Rotterdam, The Netherlands: Sense Publishers.

Aviram, A. (forthcoming b). What is a "Futuristic school"? In A. Aviram (Ed.), *The futuristic school.* Rotterdam, The Netherlands: Sense Publishers.

Aviram, A. (2005). The subordination of education to economy. *Kivumin Hadashim, 12*, 20–37. [Hebrew]

Aviram, A. (2004a). The Dovrat commission report: Recommendations for reorganizing the absurdity. *Eretz Aheret, 25*, 62–66. [Hebrew]

Aviram, A. (2004b). Educational consultancy: Present, expected, and desirable scenarios. In R. Erhard & A. Klingman (Eds.), *Counseling in school in a changing society* (pp. 35–66). Tel Aviv: Ramot. [Hebrew]

Aviram, A. (2004c). The need for strategic thinking on ICT and education. In *Designing the school of tomorrow: Advanced technologies in education. Proceedings of a conference held in Athens, November 2004.*

Aviram, A. (2003). *Theoretical approach and methodology. Deliverable 1.1 of EDCOMNET Project, supported by the European Commission FP5* (Contract IST-2000-2603).

Aviram, A. (2002a). On the need to prefer education to teaching. *Megamot, 42*, 130–140.

Aviram, A. (2002b). Will education succeed in taming ICT? A key-note presentation. In J. Sancho (Ed.), *Proceedings of the II European conference on information technologies in education and citizenship: A critical insight, June 2005, Barcelona.*

Aviram, A. (2001). Towards united fields theory of education for autonomy. In M. Granot (Ed.), *Perot Josef: A collection of papers on education and teaching.* Even Yehuda: Reches. [Hebrew]

Aviram, A. (2000a). Beyond constructivism: Autonomy-oriented education. *Studies in philosophy and education, 19*(5/6), 465–489.

Aviram, A. (2000b). ICT and education: From "Computers in the classroom" to critical adaptation of educational systems to the emerging cyber culture. *Journal of Educational Change, 1*(4), 331–352.

Aviram, A. (1999). New humanistic curriculum. In H. Marantz (Ed.), *Judaism and education: Essays in honor of walter I. Akerman.* Beer Sheva: Ben Gurion University Press.

Aviram, A. (1998). Towards a united fields theory of education for autonomy, or: A suggestion for a new educational paradigm for postmodern democracies (unpublished).

Aviram, A. (1997). Three views concerning IT and education (Unbuplished).

Aviram, A. (1996). The decline of the modern paradigm in education. *International Review of Education, 45*(5), 421–443.

Aviram, A. (1995). Autonomy and commitment: Compatible ideals. *Journal of Philosophy of Education, 29*(1), 61–73.

Aviram, A. (1994a). The anachronistic nature of the principle of unity of time and place. *Iyunim Behinuh, 59/60,* 25–40. [Hebrew].

Aviram, A. (1994b). From curriculum to educational program. *Halacha Lemaasse, 9,* 45–64. [Hebrew]

Aviram, A. (1994c). *Self-direction vs. Socialization as educational aims in the postmodern era.* Center for Education in Technological Society, B.G.U., commissioned by the Pedagogical Department, Ministry of Education. [Hebrew].

Aviram, A. (1993a). Nietzsche's criticism of modernity. In A. Sagi & D. Statman (Eds.), *Between religion and ethics* (pp. 75–94). Ramat Gan: Bar Ilan University Press. [Hebrew]

Aviram, A. (1993b). Personal autonomy and the flexible school. *International Review of Education, 39*(5), 419–433.

Aviram, A. (1992a). Can liberal education be justified in our era? *Iyunim Bachinuch, 57/58,* 15–45. [Hebrew]

Aviram, A. (1992b). Non-lococentric education. *Educational Review, 44*(1), 3–17.

Aviram, A. (1992c). The humanistic conception of the university — A framework for post-modern higher education. *European Journal of Education, 27*(4), 397–414.

Aviram, A. (1991a). Nietzsche as educator? *Journal of Philosophy of Education, 25*(2), 219–234.

Aviram, A. (1991b). The paternalistic attitude toward children. *Educational Theory, 41*(2), 199–211.

Aviram, A. (1990a). *The anachronistic nature of the liberal curriculum in post-industrial society.* Commissioned by the Pedagogical Department, Ministry of Education. [Hebrew]

Aviram, A. (1990b). The subjection of children. *Journal of Philosophy of Education, 24*(2), 213–233.

Aviram, A. (1989). Is the overman a possible human ideal? *Iyun, 38*(3–4), 228–264. [Hebrew]

Aviram, A. (1986a). The justification of compulsory education: The still neglected moral duty. *Journal of Philosophy of Education, 20*(1), 51–58.

Aviram, A. (1986b). The paradoxes of education for democracy, or: The tragic dilemmas of the modern liberal educator. *Journal of Philosophy of Education, 20*(2), 187–199.

Azevedo, R. (2005). Using hypermedia as a metacognitive tool for enhancing student learning? The role of self-regulated learning. *Educational Psychologist, 40*(4), 199–209.

Badinter, A. (1981). *The myth of motherhood: An historical view of the maternal instinct* (R. DeGaris, Trans.). London: Souvenir Press (E & A).

Bailyn, L. (1989). Toward the perfect workplace? *Communications of the ACM, 32*(4), 460–447.

Banathy, B. H. (1996). *Designing social systems in a changing world.* New York; London: Plenum Press.

Banks, J. A., & Banks, C. A. (1995). *Handbook of research on multicultural education.* New York: Macmillan Press.

Barell, J. (1991). *Teaching for thoughtfulness: Classroom strategies to enhance intellectual development.* New York: Longman.

Barmall, S., & White, J. (2000). *Why learn maths?* London: Institute of Education, University of London.

Bartolini, S. (2007). Why are people so unhappy? Why do they strive so hard for money? Competing explanations of the broken promises of economic growth. In L. Bruni & P. L. Porta (Eds.), *Handbook on the economics of happiness* (pp. 337–364). Glos, UK: Edward Elgar Publishing.

Bascia, N., & Hargreaves, A. (Eds.). (2000). *The sharp edge of educational change.* London: RoutledgeFalmer.

Bashir, T. (1998). *Supporting learning through IT and the internet.* London: Open Learning Foundation.

Baudrillard, J. (1981). *Simulacra and simulation.* Paris: Galilee.

Bauman, K. J. (2005). One million homeschooled students. *The teachers college record,* February 2005. Retrieved March 30, 2009, from http://www.tcrecord.org ID Number: 11756.

Bauman, Z. (2000). *Liquid modernity.* Cambridge: Polity Press; Malden, MA: Blackwell.

Bauman, Z. (1995). *Life in fragments: Essays in postmodern morality.* Oxford, UK: Blackwell.

Bauman, Z. (1993). *Postmodern ethics.* Cambridge, UK: Blackwell.

BBC News. (2002). *Turning into digital goldfish*, Friday, February 22, 2002. Retrieved from http://news.bbc.co.uk/2/ hi/science/nature/1834682.stm

Bechler, Z. (1991). *Newton's physics and the conceptual structure of the scientific revolution.* Dordrecht, Netherlands: Kluwer Academic Publishers.

Beck, U. (2000). *The brave new world of work.* Cambridge, UK: Cambridge University Press.

Beck, U. (1991). *Risk society: Towards a new modernity.* London: Sage.

Becker, G. S. (1975). *Human capital.* New York: National Bureau of Economic Research.

Beckett, L. S. (1997). *Reflections of change: Children's literature since 1945.* Westport, CT: Greenwood Press.

Beijerse, J. V., & Swaaningen, R. V. (2006). The Netherlands: Penal welfarism and risk management. In J. Muncie & B. Goldson (Eds.), *Comparative youth justice: Critical issues* (pp. 65–78). London: Sage.

Beiser, F. (2002). *German idealism: The struggle against subjectivism 1781–1801.* Cambridge, MA: Harvard University Press.

Bell, D. (1996). *The cultural contradictions of capitalism* (20th Anniversary ed.). New York: Basic Books.

Bell, D. (1976). *The cultural contradictions of capitalism.* New York: Basic Books.

Bell, D. (1973). *The coming of post-industrial society: A venture in social forecasting.* New York: Basic Books.

Bell, M., Martin, G., & Clarke, T. (2004). Engaging in the future of E-learning: A scenario-based approach. *Education & Training, 46*(6/7), 296–307.

Bellah, R., Madsen, R., Sullivan, W. M., Swidler, A., & Tipton, S. M. (1985). *Habits of the heart: Individualism and commitment in American life.* Berkeley, CA: University of California Press.

Bellah, R. (1991). *The good society.* New York: Knopf.

Bellah, R. (1971). Evil and the American ethos. In N. Sanford & C. Comstock (Eds.), *Sanctions for evil* (pp. 177–191). San Francisco: Jossey-Bass.

Bellah, R. (1970). *Beyond belief: Essays on religion in a post-traditional world.* New York: Harper & Row.

Benbenishty, R. (2005). *School violence in context: Culture, neighborhood, family, school, and gender.* Oxford, UK: Oxford University Press.

Beniger, J. (1986). *The control revolution.* Cambridge, MA: Harvard University Press.

Bennett, W. J., et al. (1998). A nation still at risk. *Policy Review, 90*, 23–29.

Bennett, W. J., Dilulio, J. J. Jr., & Walters, J. P. (1996). *Body count.* New York: Simon and Schuster.

Bereiter, C. (1969). The future of individual differences. *Harvard Educational Review, 39*(2), 310–318.

Berger, P. L., Berger, B., & Kellner, H. (1973). *The homeless mind: Modernization and consciousness.* New York: Random House.

Berkowitz, L. (1989). Frustration-aggression hypothesis: Examination and reformulation. *Psychological Bulletin, 106*, 59–73.

Berlin, I. (2002). *Liberty: Incorporating four essays on liberty.* Oxford, UK: Oxford University Press.

Berlin, I. (1999). *The roots of romanticism.* London: Chatto & Windus.

Berlin, I. (1989). *Against the current: Essays in the history of ideas.* Oxford, UK: Clarendon.

Berlin, I. (1981). *Two concepts of liberty.* Kyoto, Kyoto Prefecture: Appollon-sha.

Berlin, I. (1969). *Four essays on liberty.* Oxford, UK: Oxford University Press.

Bernbaum, G. (1979). *Schooling in decline.* London: MacMillan.

Bernstein, R. (1983). *Beyond objectivism and relativism: Science, hermeneutics and praxis.* Philadelphia: University of Pennsylvania Press.

Bernstein, B. (1971). *The structuring of pedagogic discourse.* London: Routledge.

Beyer, B. (1987a). *Practical strategies for the teaching of thinking.* Boston: Allyn and Bacon.

Beyer, B. (1987b). *Developing a thinking skills program.* Boston: Allyn and Bacon.

Beyer, L. E., & Apple, M. W. (Eds.). (1988). *The curriculum: Problems, politics, and possibilities.* Albany, NY: State University of New York Press.

Bhabha, H. K. (1994). *The location of culture.* London; New York: Routledge.

Bhagwati, J. (2004). *In defense of globalization.* Oxford: Oxford University Press.

Bibeau, R. (2004). Thus Spake Venitia. In A. Aviram & J. Richardson (Eds.), *Upon what does the turtle stand? Rethinking education for the digital age* (pp. 93–120). Dordrecht, Netherlands: Kluwer Academic Publishers.

Bignell, P. (2007). Children & alcohol: Britain's deadly cocktail. *The Independent*, November 4, 2007.

Birenbaum, M. (1997). *Alternatives in assessment*. Tel Aviv: Ramot Tel Aviv University Press. [Hebrew]

Birenbaum, M. (1996). Assessment 2000: Towards a pluralistic approach to assessment. In M. Birenbaum & F. J. R. C. Dochy (Eds.), *Alternatives in assessment of achievements, learning processes and prior knowledge* (pp. 3–29). Boston: Kluwer Academic Publishers.

Bjorklund, D. F. (2004). *Children's thinking: Cognitive development and individual differences* (4th ed.). Belmont, Califorina: Thomson/Wadsworth.

Blankley, T. (2005). *The west's last chance: Will we win the clash of civilizations?* Washington, DC: Regnery Publishing.

Blase, J., & Blase, J. (2001). *Empowering teachers: What successful principals do*. Thousand Oaks, CA: Corwin Press.

Bloom, A. (1987). *The closing of the American mind*. New York: Simon and Schuster.

Blumstein, A. (1995). Youth violence, guns and the illicit-drug industry. *Journal of Criminal Law and Criminology, 86*, 10–36.

Boaz, D. (1997). *Libertarianism: A primer*. New York; London: Free Press.

Boekaerts, M., & Boscolo, P. (2002). Interest in learning, learning to be interested. *Learning and Instruction, 12*, 375–382.

Boekaerts, M. (1997). Self-regulated learning: A new concept embraced by researchers, policy makers, educators, teachers, and students. *Learning and Instruction, 7*(2), 161–186.

Boli, J., Ramirez, F., & Meyer, J. (1985). Explaining the origins and expansion of mass education. *Comparative Education Review, 29*(2), 145–170.

Bolter, J. D. (1984). *Turing's man*. Chapel Hill: The University of North Carolina Press.

Bonnett, M., & Cuypers, S. (2003). Autonomy and authenticity in education. In N. Blake, P. Smeyers, R. Smith, & P. Standish (Eds.), *The blackwell guide to the philosophy of education* (pp. 326–340). Oxford, UK: Blackwell.

Booth, W. (1994). Tangled family ties and children's rights. *The Washington Post*, a3, November 3, 1994.

Booth, W. (1992). Boy wins parental 'Divorce': 12–year-old's case first of its kind. *The Washington Post*, a1, September 25, 1992.

Borgmann, A. (1999). *Holding onto reality*. Chicago: University of Chicago Press.

Borgmann, A. (1994). *Crossing the postmodern divide*. Chicago: University of Chicago Press.

Borman, G. D., Hewes, G. M., Overman, L. T., & Brown, S. (2003). Comprehensive school reform and achievement: A meta-analysis. *Review of Educational Research, 73*(2), 125–230.

Bosetti, L. (2004). Determinants of school choice: Understanding how parents choose elementary schools in Alberta. *Journal of Education Policy, 19*(4), 387–405.

Bourdieu, P., & Passeron, J. C. (1990). *Reproduction in education, society and culture* (N. Rice, Trans.). Thousand Oaks, CA: Sage.

Bowden, B. (2004). In the name of progress and peace: The 'Standard of civilization' and the universalizing project. *Alternatives: Global, Local, Political, 29*(1), 43–68.

Bowles, S., & Gintis, S. (1976). *Schooling in capitalist America: Educational reform and the contradictions of economic life*. London: Routledge & Kegan Paul.

Bracken, P., & Thomas, P. (2005). *Postpsychiatry: Mental health in a postmodern world*. Oxford, UK: Oxford University Press.

Bradley, D. (1990). Children, family, and the state in Sweden. *Journal of Law and Society, 17*(44), 427–444.

Bramall, S., & White, J. (2000). *Will the new national curriculum live up to its aims?* (Impact Policy Discussion Document No.6). Ringwood, NJ: Philosophy of Education Society of Great Britain.

Bransford, J., Brown, A. L., & Cocking, R. R. (1999). *How people learn: Brain, mind, experience, and school*. Washington, DC: National Academy Press.

Brenes, M. (2005). East Los Angeles youth movement for educational justice. *ZMagazine*, September 2005. Retrieved from http://www.zcommunications.org/zmag/viewArticle/13657

Brennen, J. (1996). *Children in families: Research and policy*. London: The Falmer Press.

Brickman, W.W. (2007). *Guide to research in educational history*. Read Books.

Bridges, W. (1995). *Jobshift: How to prosper in a workplace without jobs*. London: Allen & Unwin.

Brock, B. L., & Grady, M. L. (2000). *Rekindling the flame: Principals combating teacher burnout*. Thousand Oaks, CA: Corwin Press.

Brooks, C., Walker, N., & Wrightsman, L. (1998). *Children's rights in the United States: In search of a national policy*. Thousand Oaks, CA: Sage.

Brooks, J. G., & Brooks, M. G. (1993). *The case for constructivist classrooms*. Alexandria, VA: ASCD.

Brown, A. L. (1997). Transforming schools into communities of thinking and learning about serious matters. *American Psychologist, 52*(4), 399–413.

Brown, J. S., Collins, A., & Duguid, P. (1989). Situated cognition and the culture of learning. *Educational Researcher, 18*(1), 32–41.

Bruford, W. (1975). *The German tradition of self-cultivation*. Cambridge, UK: Cambridge University Press.

Bruford, W. (1962). *Culture and society in classical weimar*. Cambridge, UK: Cambridge University Press.

Buber, M. (1958). *I and thou*. New York: Scribner's.

Buckingham, D., & Willett, R. (Eds.). (2006). *Digital generations: Children, young people, and the new media*. Mahwah, NJ: Lawrence Erlbaum Associate.

Buckingham, D. (2000). *After the death of childhood: Growing up in the age of electronic media*. Cambridge, UK: Polity Press.

Buckley, J., & Schneider, M. (2007). *Charter schools: Hope or hype?* Princeton, NJ: Princeton University Press.

Bukatman, S. (1993). *Terminal identity: The virtual subject in postmodern science fiction*. Durham, NC: Duke University Press.

Bumpass, L., & Lu, H. H. (2000). Trends in cohabitation and implications for children's family contexts in the United States. *Population Studies, 54*(1), 29–41.

Bumpass, L. (1990). What's happening to the family? Interactions between demographic and institutional change. *Demography, 27*, 483–497.

Burns, G. (1998). Tradition and revolution in the American curriculum. *Curriculum Studies, 20*(2), 99–118.

Burquiere, A. (2004). *History of family: Impact of modernity*. Cambridge, UK: Polity Press.

Butts, R. F. (1973). *The education of the west*. New York: McGrew-Hill.

Buss, A. H., & Plomin, R. (1975). *A temperament theory of personality development*. New York: Wiley.

Butler, D. L., & Winne, P. H. (1995). Feedback and self-regulated learning: A theoretical synthesis. *Review of Educational Research, 65*(3), 245–281.

Butler, D. L. (2002). Individualizing instruction in self-regulated learning. *Theory into Practice, 41*(2), 81–92.

Butler, J. (1993). *Bodies that matter*. New York: Routledge.

Cagney-Watts, H. (1991). *The contradictions of postmodernism: A feminist critique of postmodernism*. PhD Dissertation, University of Hull.

Calabrese, R., & Seldin, C. (1986). Adolescent alienation: An analysis of the family response to the secondary school environment. *High School Journal*.

Calabrese, R., & Seldin, C. (1987). A contextual analysis of alienation among school constituencies. *Urban Education, 22*(2), 227–237.

Calinescu, M. (1987). *Five faces of modernity: Modernism Avant-Garde decadence kitsch postmodernism*. Durham, NC: Duke University Press.

Callahan, R. E. (1962). *Education and the cult of efficiency*. Chicago: University of Chicago Press.

Callan, E. (2002). Autonomy, child-rearing and good lives. In D. Archard & C. Macleod (Eds.), *The political and moral status of children* (pp. 118–141). Oxford, UK: Oxford University Press.

Callan, E. (2001). Between hope and fear: The future of democratic education. In J. Oelkers (Ed.), *Futures of education: Essays from an interdisciplinary seminar* (pp. 119–131). Berlin: Peter Lang.

Callan, E. (1997). *Creating citizens.* New York: Oxford University Press.

Callan, E. (1994). Autonomy and alienation. *Journal of Philosophy of Education, 28*(1), 35–53.

Callan, E. (1988). *Autonomy and schooling.* Kingston and Montreal: McGill-Queen's University Press.

Cantor, C. H., Neulinger, K., & De Leo, D. (1999). Australian Suicide Trends 1964–1997: Youth and Beyond? *The Medical Journal of Australia, 171,* 137–141.

Cannon, S. (1994). Finding their own "Place to be": What gregory kingsley and kimberly mays' "Divorces" from their parents have done for children's rights. *Loyola Law Review, 39,* 837.

CARE (Children's Rights Alliance for England) — Ready Steady Change. (2007). *An introduction to ready steady change.* Retrieved from http://www.crae.org.uk/cms/index.php?option=com_content & task=view&id=202&Itemid=146

Carmon, A. (2007). *The organization of educational knowledge.* Phd Dissertation. Jerusalem: The Hebrew University of Jerusalem. [Hebrew]

Carroll, L., & Tober, J. (1999). *The Indigo children: The new kids have arrived.* Carlsbad, CA: Hay House.

Carson, T. L. (2000). *Value and the good life.* Notre Dame, IN: University of Notre Dame Press.

Cartelli, A. (2006). *Teaching in the knowledge society: New skills and instruments for teachers.* Hershey, PA: Idea Group Inc.

CDC. (2007). Suicide trends among youths and young adults aged 10–24 Years — United States, 1990–2004. *Morbidity and Mortality Weekly Report, 56*(35), 905–908.

CDC. (2004). Violence-related behaviors among high school students — United States, 1991–2003. *Morbidity and Mortality Weekly Report, 53,* 651–655.

Cervone, B. (2002). *Taking democracy in hand: Youth action for educational change in the San Francisco bay area.* Occasional paper prepared by What Kids Can Do with The Forum for Youth Investment.

Changing Attitude, UK Secular New, Age of Consent.
Retrieved from http://www.archive. changingattitude.org/news_u_s_age_consent.html

Charter Schools, School Choice Student Achievement. (2004). A discussion co-hosted by California State University Institute for Education Reform — California Education Policy Seminar, CSU, Institute for Education Reform, March 2004.
Retrieved from http://www.calstate.edu/ier/reports/Choice Report2004.pdf

Chawla, S., & Renesch, J. (1995). *Learning organizations: Developing cultures for tomorrow's workplace.* Portland, OR: Productivity Press. Retrieved from http://library.georgetown.edu/search/ i?=1563271109

Chevalier, A. (2000). *Graduate over-education in the UK.* Centre for the Economics of Education, London School of Economics Discussion Paper No. 7.

Chomsky, N. (1957). *Syntactic structures.* Gravenhage, Netherlands: Mouton.

Chouliaraki, L., & Fairclough, N. (1999). *Discourse in late modernity: Rethinking critical discourse analysis.* Edinburgh, UK: Edinburgh University Press.

Christenden, S. (1985). Coping with uncertainty in planning. *Journal of the American Planning Association, 51*(1), 63–73.

Chubb, J., & Moe, T. (1990). *Politics, markets and America's schools.* Washington, DC: The Brookings Institute.

Chubb, J., Moe, T., & Peterson, P. (1985). *The new direction in American politics.* Washington, DC: The Brookings Institute.

Clifford, D., Curry, H., & Hertz, F. (2004). *A legal guide for Lesbian and Gay Couples* (12th ed.). Berkeley, CA: Nolo.

Coates, J., Jarratt, J., & Mahaffie, J. (1990). *Future work.* San-Francisco: Jossey-Bass.

CoCN (The Consortium for School Networking). (2002). *US delegation to Europe, 2002: Internet technology and schools.* Retrieved from http://www.cosn.org/resources/international/2002_trip/ government.cfm

Coffield, F., Moseley, D., et al. (2004). *Learning styles and pedagogy in post-16 learning. A critical and comprehensive review of learning style research, highlighting 13 core learning styles.* London: Learning and Skills Research Centre.

Cohen, H. (1981). *Equal rights for children.* Totowa, NY: Littlefield, Adams & Co.

Common, T., & Nietzsche, F. (2006). *The gay science.* New York: Dover Publication.

Comte, A. (1856). *A general view of positivism.* Whitefish, MT: Kessinger Publishing, (2007).

Conley, D. T. (2007). *Toward a more comprehensive conception of college readiness.* Eugene, OR: Educational Policy Improvement Center.

Conley, D. T. (1997). *Roadmap to restructuring: Charting the course of change in American education* (2nd ed.). Eugene, OR: Eric Clearing House on Educational Management.

Connor, S. (2004). *The Cambridge companion to postmodernism.* Cambridge, UK and New York: Cambridge University Press.

Connor, S. (1989). *Postmodernist culture.* Cambridge, MA: Blackwell.

Cook, P. J., & Laub, J. H. (1998). The unprecedented epidemic in youth violence. In M. Tonry & M. H. Moore (Eds.), *Youth violence. Crime and justice: A review of research* (Vol. 24, pp. 27–64). Chicago: University of Chicago Press.

Coombs, P. (1985). *The world crisis in education.* Oxford, UK: Oxford University Press.

Coombs, P. (1968). *The world educational crisis: A system analysis.* Oxford, UK: Oxford University Press.

Cooper, B. C. (2005). *Homeschooling in full view: A reader.* Greenwich, CT: Information Age Publishing.

Cooper, D. (1983). *Authenticity and learning.* London: Routledge & Kegan Paul.

Cooper, J. (2007). *Cognitive dissonance: 50 years of a classic theory.* Thousand Oaks, CA: Sage Publications.

Corsaro, W. A. (2005). Social change families and children. In W. A. Corsaro (Ed.), *The sociology of childhood.* Thousand Oaks, CA: Pine Forge Press.

Cottle, T. J. (2006). *A sense of self: The work of affirmation.* Amherst, MA: University of Massachusetts Press.

Cousins, J. B., & Earl, L. M. (1992). The case for participatory evaluation. *Educational Evaluation and Policy Analysis, 14*(4), 397–418.

Cremin, L. (1988). *American education: The metropolitan experience 1876–1980.* New York: Harper and Row.

Cremin, L. (1961). *The transformation of the school: Progressivism in American education, 1876–1957.* New York: Vintage Books.

Crutchfield, C. F. (1981). Medical treatment for minor children: The roles of parents, the state, the child, and the supreme court of the United States. *Family Relations, 30*(2), 165–177.

Cuban, L. (2003). *Why is it so hard to get good schools?* New York: Teachers College Press.

Cuban, L. (1998). How schools change reforms: Redefining reform success and failure. *Teachers College Record, 99,* 453–477.

Cuban, L. (1990). Reforming again, again, and again. *Educational Researcher, 19*(1), 3–13.

Cullen, J., Hadjivassiliou, K., Hamilton, E., Kelleher, J., Sommerlad, E., & Stern, E. (2002). *Review of current pedagogic research and practice in the fields of post-compulsory education and lifelong learning.* London: Tavistock Institute.

Culp, K., Honey, M., & Mandinach, E. (2003). *A retrospective on twenty years of education technology policy.* Washington, DC: U.S. Department of Education, Office of the Educational Technology.

Cunningham, I. (1999). *The wisdom of strategic learning: The self managed learning solution.* Hampshire, UK: Gower Publishing.

Cuypers, S. E. (1992). Is personal autonomy the first principle of education? *Journal of Philosophy of Education, 26*(1), 5–17.

Damon, W., & Gregory, A. (2002). Bringing in a new era in the field of youth development. In R. Lerner, F. Jacobs, & D. Wertlieb (Eds.), *Handbook of applied developmental science* (Vol. 1, pp. 407–420). New York: John Wiley.

Darling-Hammond, L. (1997). *The right to learn: A blueprint for creating schools that work.* San Francisco: Jossey-Bass.

Davenport, T., & Prusak, L. (1998). *Working knowledge: How organizations manage what they know.* Boston: Harvard Business School Press.

Davidson, D. (2005). *Truth and predication.* Cambridge, MA: Harvard University Press.

Davidson, D. (1973). On the very idea of a conceptual scheme. *Proceedings of the American Philosophical Association, 68,* 5–20.

De Bono, E. (1992). *Teach your child how to think.* Middlesex, UK: Viking, Penguin Books Ltd.

Dean, J. (2006). *Meeting the learning needs of all children: Personalised learning in the primary school.* London: Routledge.

Dear, M. (2000). *The postmodern urban condition.* New York: Blackwell.

Dearden, R. F. (1975). Autonomy as an educational ideal. In S. Brown (Ed.), *Philosophers discuss education* (pp. 3–18). London: MacMillan.

Dearden, R. F. (1972). Autonomy and education. In R. F. Dearden, R. Peters, & P. Hirst (Eds.), *Education and reason, Part 3 of education and the development of reason* (pp. 58–75). London: Routledge & Keagan Paul.

Deci, E. L., Eghrari, H., Patrick, B. C., & Leone, D. R. (1994). Facilitating internalization: The self-determination theory perspective. *Journal of Personality, 62,* 119–142.

Deci, E. L., & Flaste, R. (1995). *Why we do what we do: The dynamics of personal autonomy.* New York: Putnam's.

Deci, E. L., & Ryan, R. M. (2000). The 'what' and 'why' of goal pursuits: Human needs and the self-determination of behavior. *Psychological Inquiry, 11,* 227–268.

Deci, E. L., & Ryan, R. M. (1995). Human autonomy: The basis for true self-esteem. In M. Kemis (Ed.), *Efficacy, agency, and self-esteem* (pp. 31–49). New York: Plenum.

Deci, E. L., & Ryan, R. M. (1991). A motivational approach to self: Integration in personality. In R. Dienstbier (Ed.), *Nebraska symposium on motivation, 38. Perspectives on motivation* (pp. 237–288). Lincoln: University of Nebraska Press.

Deci, E. L., & Ryan, R. M. (1987). The support of autonomy and the control of behavior. *Journal of Personality and Social Psychology, 55,* 1024–1037.

Deci, E. L., & Ryan, R. M. (1985). The general causality orientations scale: Self-determination in personality. *Journal of Research in Personality, 19,* 109–134.

Deci, E. L. (1992). The relation of interest to the motivation of behavior: A self determination theory perspective. In S. Renninger, S. Hidi, & A. Krapp (Eds.), *The role of interest in learning and development* (pp. 43–71). Hillsdale, NJ: Erlbaum.

Del Corso, D., Ovcin, E., Morrone, G., Gianesini, D., Salojarvi, S., & Kvist, T. (2001). 3DE: An environment for the development of learner-centered custom educational packages. *31st ASEE/IEEE Frontiers in Education Conference,* 21–26.

Deleuze, G., & Guattari, F. (1983). *Anti oedipus.* Minneapolis, MN: University of Minnesota Press.

Deleuze, G. (1976). *Rhizomé: Introduction.* Paris: Editions De Minuit.

Dember, D. W. (1964). *Psychology of perception.* New York: Holt, Rinehart and Winston.

Demo, D. (1992). Parent-child relations: Assessing recent changes. *Journal of Marriage and the Family, 54*(1), 104–117.

Dempster, N., Freakley, M., & Parry, L. (2001). The ethical climate of public schooling under new public management. *International Journal of Leadership in Education, 4*(1), 1–12.

Department for Education and Employment. (2001). *Schools building on success: Raising standards, promoting diversity, achieving results.* London: The Stationary Office Limited.

Department of Health and Human Services (DHHS). (2001). *Youth violence: A report of the surgeon general.* Retrieved from www.surgeongeneral.gov/library/youthviolence/toc.html

Department of Health and Human Services, Center for Disease Control and Prevention. (2007). *Youth violence: Fact sheet.* Retrieved from http://www.cdc.gov/ncipc/factsheets/yvfacts.htm

Department of Health and Human Services, Center for Disease Control and Prevention, National Center for Injury Prevention and Control (2007). *Web-based Injury Statistics Query and Reporting System (WISQARS).* Retrieved from www.cdc.gov/ncipc/wisqars

Derrida, J. (1997). *Deconstruction in a nutshell: A conversation with Jacques Derrida.* New York: Fordham University Press.

Derrida, J. (1978). *Writing and difference.* London: Routledge & Kegan Paul.

Derrida, J. (1976). Of grammatology (G. Chakravorty Spivak, Trans.). Baltimore and London: Johns Hopkins University Press.

Descartes, R. (1991). *The principles of philosophy.* The Netherlands: Kluwer.

Descartes, R. (1984). *Principles of philosophy.* In J. Cottingham, R. Stoothoff, & D. Murdoch (Eds. and Trans.), *The philosophical writings of descartes* (Vol. 1, pp. 193–291). Cambridge, UK: Cambridge University Press. (Originally published 1644)

Devine, J. (1996). *Maximum security: The culture of violence in inner-city schools.* Chicago: The University of Chicago Press.

Dewey, J. (1966). *Democracy and education: An introduction to the philosophy of education.* New York: Free Press.

Diamond, M., & Hopson, J. (1998). *Magic trees of the mind: How to nurture your child's intelligence, creativity, and healthy emotions from birth through adolescence.* New York: Dutton.

Diener, E., Suh, E. M., Lucas, R. E., & Smith, H. L. (1999). Subjective well-being: Three decades of progress. *Psychological Bulletin, 125,* 276–301.

Diffily, D., & Sassman, C. (2002). *Project-based learning with young children.* Portsmouth, NH: Heinemann.

DiMaggio, P. J., Hargittai, E., Neuman, W. R., & Robinson, J. P. (2001). Social implications of the internet. *Annual Review of Sociology, 27,* 307–336.

DiMaggio, P. J. (1988). Interest and agency in institutional theory. In L. Zucker (Ed.), *Institutional patterns and organizations: Culture and environment* (pp. 3–21). Cambridge, MA: Ballinger.

Directgov (2008). *Young people and custody.* Retrieved from http://www.direct.gov.uk/en/Young People/CrimeAndJustice/CrimeAndTheLaw/DG_10027708

Docherty, J. (Ed.). (1993). *Postmodernism: A reader.* New York: Harvester Wheatsheaf.

Doll, W. (1993). *A post-modern perspective on curriculum.* New York: Teachers College Press.

Donnelly, M. (1995). Depression among adolescents in Northern Ireland. *Adolescence, 30*(118), 339–350.

Dorn, S. (1996). *Creating the dropout: An institutional and social history of school failure.* Westport, CT: Praeger.

Downey, C. J., Frase, E. L., & Peters, J. J. (1994). *The quality education challenge.* California: Corwin Press.

Dreeben, R. (1980). *The analysis of educational productivity.* Ann Arbor, MI: University of Michigan.

Dreeben, R. (1968). *On what is learned in school.* Reading, MA: Addison Wesley.

Dreyfus, H. L., & Rabinow, P. (1982). *Michel Foucault: Beyond structuralism and hermeneutics.* Brighton: Harvester Press.

Dror, Y., & Club of Rome. (2001). *The capacity to govern: A report to the club of rome.* London: Cass.

Dror, Y. (1988). *Policymaking under adversity.* New Brunswick, NJ: Transaction Publishers.

Drucker, P. (2003). *Peter Drucker on the profession of management.* Boston: Harvard Business School; London: McGraw-Hill.

Drucker, P. (1993). *Post capitalist society.* New York: Harper Business.

Dubson, B. (1995). *The demand for highly educated labor in the Israeli job market over the 1972–1992 period.* A position paper written in the Center for Futurism in Education, Ben-Gurion University, Beer-Sheva. [Hebrew]

Dudley, M., Waters, B., Kelk, N., & Howard, J. (1992). Youth suicide in New South wales: Urban-Rural trends. *Medical Journal of Australia, 156*(2), 83–88.

Dunham, J. (1992). *Stress in teaching.* London: Routledge.

Dunlop, C., & Kling, R. (Eds.). (1991). *Computerization and controversy: Value conflicts and social choices.* Boston: Academic Press.

Dunn, K., & Dunn, R. (1987). Dispelling outmoded beliefs about student learning. *Educational Leadership, 44*(6), 55–63.

Dunn, R., et al. (1995). A meta-analytic validation of the Dunn and Dunn model of learning-style preferences. *The Journal of Educational Research, 88*(6), 353–362.

Dunn, R., & DeBello, T. (1981). Learning style researches defined differences differently. *Educational Leadership, February, 38*(5), 372–377.

Dunn, R., & Dunn, K. (1993). *Teaching secondary students through their individual learning styles: Practical approaches for grades 7–12.* Needham Heights, MA: Allyn and Bacon.

Dunn, R., & Grigg, S. (1988). *Learning styles: Quiet revolution in American secondary schools.* Reston: Virginia.

Dunn, R. (2003). The Dunn and Dunn learning style model and its theoretical cornerstone. In R. Dunn & S. Griggs (Eds.), *Synthesis of the Dunn and Dunn learning styles model research: Who, what, when, where and so what — The Dunn and Dunn learning styles model and its theoretical cornerstone* (pp. 1–6). New York: St John's University.

Dunn, R. G. (1998). *Identity crisis. A social critique of postmodernity.* Minneapolis, MN: University of Minnesota Press.

Durand, R. (2006). *Organizational evolution and strategic management.* London: SAGE.

Dworkin, A. G. (1987). *Teacher burnout in the public schools: Structural causes and consequences for children.* Albany, NY: State University of New York Press.

Dworkin, A. G. (1981). The concept of autonomy. In J. Christman (Ed.), (1989), *The inner \citadel, essays on individual autonomy* (pp. 54–76). Oxford, UK: Oxford University Press.

Dworkin, R. (2006a). *Is democracy possible here? Principles for a new political debate.* Princeton, NJ and Woodstock: Princeton University Press.

Dworkin, R. (2006b). *Justice in robes.* Cambridge, MA and London: Belknap Press.

Dworkin, R. (1982). Liberalism. In M. Sandel (Ed.), *Liberalism and its critics.* Oxford, UK: Blackwell.

Dworkin, R. (1978). Liberalism. In S. Hampshire (Ed.), *Public and private morality* (pp. 113–143). Cambridge, UK: Cambridge University Press.

Dworkin, R. (1977). *Taking rights seriously.* London: Duckworth.

Dwyer, G. J. (2006). *The relationship rights of children.* Cambridge, UK: Cambridge University Press.

Eagleton, T. (1996). *The illusions of postmodernism.* Oxford, UK: Blackwell Publishers.

Easterbrook, G. (2003). *The progress paradox: How life gets better while people feel worse.* New York: Random House.

Eaton, D. K., et al. (2007). On behalf of the centers for disease control and prevention, department of health and human services, United States Government (2006). Youth Risk Behavior Surveillance—United States, 2005. *MMWR- Morbidity and Mortality Weekly Report, 55*(SS05) (pp. 1–108). Retrieved from http://www.cdc.gov/mmwr/preview/mmwrhtml/ss5505a1.htm.

Eijnatten, F. M. van, & Fitzgerald, L. A. (1998). *Designing the chaordic enterprise: 21 century organizational architectures that drive systemic self-transcendence.* Paper presented at the 14th EGOS colloquium "Stretching the Boundaries of Organization Studies into the Next Millennium" Sub theme 3: New Organization Forms, Maastricht, July 10, 2008.

Eijnatten, F. M. van. (2003). Chaordic systems thinking: Chaos and complexity to explain human performance management. In G. P. Putnik & A. Gunasekaran (Eds.), *Business excellence 1: Performance measures, benchmarking and best practices in new economy* (pp. 3–18). Braga: Portugal School of Engineering; Guimarães: University of Minho Press.

Elias, M. (2004, May 4). Short attention span linked to TV. *USA Today.* Retrieved from http://www.usatoday.com/news/nation/2004-04-05-tv-bottomstrip_x.htm

Elitzur, A. (1995). Defense to life: On the mental health professions in failure to confront the suicide epidemic. *Omega: Journal of Death and Dying, 31*(4), 305–310.

Ellin, N. (1996). *Post modern urbanism.* Oxford, UK: Blackwell.

Elliott, D., Hamburg, B., & Williams, K. (1998). *Violence in American schools.* Cambridge, UK: Cambridge University Press.

Elliott, M. (1999). Classifying family life education on the world wide web. *Family Relations, 48*, 7–13.

Ellul, J. (1964). *The technological society* (J. Wilkinson, Trans.). New York: Knopf.

Ellwood, D. T., & Jencks, C. (2004). *The spread of single-parent families in the United States since 1960.* KSG Working Paper no. RWP04–008.

Elmore, R. F. (2000). *Building a new structure for school leadership.* Washington, DC: Albert Shanker Institute.

Emmons, R. A. (1999). *The psychology of ultimate concerns.* New York: Guilford.

Emmons, R. A. (1991). Personal strivings, daily life events, and psychological and physical well-being. *Journal of Personality, 59,* 453–472.

Epstein, R. (2007). *The case against adolescence.* Sanger, CA: Quill Driver Books.

Erickson, H. L. (2001). *Stirring the head, heart, and soul: Redefining curriculum and instruction.* London: Corwin Press.

Erikson, E. H. (1968). *Identity: Youth and crisis.* New York: Norton.

Erikson, E. H. (1956). Ego identity and the psychosocial moratorium. In H. L. Witmer & R. Rosinsky (Eds.), *New perspectives for research in Juvenile Delinquency* (pp. 1–23). U.S. Children's Bureau: Publication #356.

Erikson, E. H. (1950). *Childhood and society.* New York: Norton.

European Commission. (2006). European year of workers' mobility. (2006). *Facts and figures.* Retrieved from http://ec.europa.eu/employment_social/workersmobility_2006/index.cfm?id_page_category= FF

Fagan, J., & Zimring, F. E. (Eds.). (2000). *The changing borders of Juvenile justice: Transfer of adolescents to the criminal court.* Chicago: University of Chicago Press.

Farson, R. (1974). *Birthrights.* New York: Macmillan.

Fausto-Sterling, A. (2000). *Sexing the body: Gender politics and the construction of sexuality.* New York: Basic Books.

Fausto-Sterling, A. (1993). The five sexes: Why male and female are not enough. *The Sciences,* March/April, 20–24.

Fee, D. (2000). *Pathology and the postmodern: Mental illness as discourse and experience.* London: Sage.

Feld, B. C. (1999). *Bad kids: Race and the transformation of the Juvenile court.* Oxford, UK: Oxford University Press.

Felder, R. (1993). Reaching the second tier: Learning and teaching styles in college science education. *Journal of College Science Teaching, 23*(5), 286–290.

Festinger, L., Riecken, H. W., & Schachter, S. (1956). *When prophecy fails: A social and psychological study of a modern group that predicted the end of the world.* Minneapolis, MN: University of Minnesota Press.

Festinger, L. (1957). *A theory of cognitive dissonance.* San Francisco: Stanford University Press.

Fetterman, D. M., Wandersman, S. J., & Kaftarian, A. (Eds.). (1996). *Empowerment evaluation: Knowledge and tools for self-assessment & accountability.* Thousand Oaks, CA: Sage.

Feyerabend, P. (1978). *Against method.* London: Verso.

Eichner, H. (1966). Zur Deutung von 'Wilhelm Meisters Lehrjahren'. *Jahrbuch des Freien Deutschen Hochstifts,* 165–196. [German]

Field, J. (2006). *Lifelong learning and the new educational order.* Staffordshire: Trentham Books.

Fischer, F., Miller, G., & Sidney, M. S. (2007). *Handbook of public policy analysis: Theory, politics, and methods.* Boca Raton, FL: CRC/Taylor & Francis. Retrieved from http://www.loc.gov/catdir/toc/ecip071/2006031906.html; http://www.loc.gov/catdir/enhancements/fy0701/2006031906–d.html

Fisher, R. (1998). *Teaching thinking.* London: Cassel.

Fisher, R. (1990). *Teaching children to think.* UK: Stanley Thornes.

Fiske, E. B. (1996). *Decentralization of education: Politics and consensus.* Washington, DC: World Bank.

Fitzgerald, L. A., & Eijnatten, F. M. van (2002). Chaos speak, a glossary of chaordic terms and phrases. *Journal of Organizational Change Management (JOCM), 15*(4), 412–423. Special Issue: "Chaos: Applications in Organizational Change".

FitzGerald, M., Stevens, A., & Hale, C. (2004). *Review of knowledge on Juvenile violence: Trends, policies and responses in Europe.* EU Contract number JAI/B/1/2003/01 Final report. Retrieved from http://www.kent.ac.uk/eiss/documents/final%20youth%20violence%20report.pdf

Flannery, D. J., Wester, K. L., & Singer, M. I. (2004). Impact of exposure to violence in school on child and adolescent mental health and behavior. *Journal of Community Psychology, 32*, 559–573.

Fletcher, S. (2000). *Education and emancipation: Theory and practice in a new constellation.* New York: Teachers College Press.

Flum, H., & Kaplan, A. (2006). Exploratory orientation as an educational goal. *Educational Psychologist, 41*(2), 99–110.

Flum, H., & Lavi-Yudelevitch, M. (2002). Adolescents' relatedness and identity formation: A narrative study. *Journal of Social and Personal Relationships, 19*(4), 527–548.

Flum, H. (1994). The evolutive style of identity formation. *Journal of Youth & Adolescence, 23*(4), 489–497.

Foucault, M. (1995). *Discipline and punish: The birth of the prison* (2nd ed.). New York: Vintage Books.

Foucault, M. (1989). *Archaeology of knowledge.* London: Routledge.

Foucault, M. (1980). *Power/knowledge: Selected interviews and other writings, 1972–1977.* Pantheon Books.

Fortin, J. (2003). *Children's rights and the developing law.* Cambridge, UK: Cambridge University Press.

Fosnot, C. (1996). *Constructivism: Theory, perspectives, and practice.* New York: Teachers College Press.

Foster, H. (1983). *Postmodern culture.* Worchester: Billing and Sons.

Fox, S., & Spector, P. E. (1999). The model of work frustration-aggression. *Journal of Organizational Behavior, 20*(6), 915–931.

Frankl, V. E. (1988). *The will to meaning: Foundations and applications of logotherapy.* New York: Meridian.

Frankl, V. E. (1962). *Man's search for meaning.* Beacon Press.

Frankl, V. E. (1959). *Man's search for meaning: An introduction to logotherapy.* Boston: Beacon Press.

Franklin, B. (2005). *The new handbook of children's rights: Comparative policy and practice.* London: Routledge.

Franklin, B. M. B., Popkewitz, T., & Bloch, M. N. (Eds.). (2003). *Educational partnerships and the state: The paradoxes of governing schools, children, and families.* New York: Palgrave Macmillan.

Freeman, R. (1976). *The over-educated American.* New York: Academic Press.

Freire, P. (1973). *Pedagogy of the oppressed.* New York: Seabury Press.

Freud, A. (1965). *Normality and pathology in childhood.* Ann Arbor: University of Michigan Press.

Frey, B. S., & Stutzer, A. (2002). *Happiness and economics: How the economy and institutions affect well-being.* Princeton, NJ and Oxford, UK: Princeton University Press.

Friedan, B. (1963). *The feminine mystique.* New York: Dell.

Friedman, I. A., & Farber, B. A. (1992). Professional self-concept as a predictor of teacher burnout. *Journal of Educational Research, 86*(1), 28–35.

Friedman, M. (2002). Kant, Kuhn, and the rationality of science. *Philosophy of Science, 69*, 171–190.

Friedman, M. (1962). *Capitalism and freedom.* Chicago: University of Chicago Press.

Friedman, T. L. (2005). *The world is flat: A brief history of the twenty-first century.* New York: Farrar Straus and Giroux.

Fromm, E. (1962). *The art of loving.* London: Unwin Books.

Fromm, E. (1941). *Escape from freedom.* New York: Holt, Rinehart & Winston.

Fruqiuele, G. M. (1990). From the discovery to the disappearance of childhood. *Studi di Sociologia, 28*(3), 387–398.

Fuchs, S. (2001). *Against essentialism: A theory of culture and society.* Cambridge, MA and London: Harvard University Press.

Fukuyama, F. (1999). *The great disruption: Human nature and the reconstitution of social order.* London: Profile Books.

Fukuyama, F. (1993). *The end of history and the last man.* New York: Aron Books.

Fullan, M. G., & Miles, M. B. (1992). Getting reform right: What works and what doesn't. *Phi Delta Kappan, 73*(10), 744–752.

Fullan, M. G., & Steigelbauer, S. (1991). *The new meaning of educational change.* New York: Teachers College Press.

Fullan, M. G. (1993). *Change forces: Probing the depths of educational reform.* London: Falmer.

Gabbard, D. A. (Ed.). (2000). *Knowledge and power in the global economy: Politics and the rhetoric of school reform.* Mahwah, NJ: Lawrence Erlbaum Associates.

Gallos, J. V. (Ed.). (2006). *Organization development: A Jossey-Bass reader.* San Francisco: Jossey-Bass.

Grabe, M. (1981). School size and the importance of school activities. *Adolescence, 16*(61), 21–31.

Gardner, H. (2006). *Multiple intelligences: New horizons* (Rev. and Updated ed.). New York and London: Basic Books.

Gardner, H. (2000). *Intelligence reframed: Multiple intelligences for the 21st century.* New York: Basic Books.

Gardner, H. (1993). *Multiple intelligences: The theory in practice.* New York: Basic Books.

Gardner, H. (1983). *Frames of mind: The theory of multiple intelligences.* New York: Basic Books.

Garforth, F. W. (1979). *John Stuart mill's theory of education.* New York: Barnes and Noble.

Gatto, J. (2003). Against school: How public education cripples our kids and why. *Harper's Magazine,* 33–40.

Gatto, J. (1992). *Dumbing us down: The hidden curriculum of compulsory schooling.* Philadelphia: New Society Publishers.

Gauthier, D. (1986). *Morals by agreement.* Oxford, UK: Clarendon Press.

Gaylin, W., & Jennings, B. (Ed.). (2003). *The perversion of autonomy: Coercion and constraints in a liberal society* (Rev. ed.). Washington, DC: Georgetown University Press.

Koocher, G. P., & Keith-Spiegel, P. (1990). *Children, ethics & the law: Professional issue and cases.* Lincoln, Nebraska: University of Nebraska Press.

Gergen, K. (2000). The self in the age of information. *Washington Quarterly, 23*(1), 201–214.

Gergen, K. (1999). *An invitation to social construction.* London: Sage.

Gergen, K. (1997). The place of psyche in a constructed world. *Theory & Psychology, 7,* 723–746.

Gergen, K. (1991). *The saturated self: Dilemmas of identity in contemporary life.* New York: Basic Books.

Gibbons, R. D., et al. (2007). Early evidence on the effects of regulators' suicidality warnings on SSRI prescriptions and suicide in children and adolescents. *American Journal of Psychiatry, 164*(9), 1304–1306.

Giddens, A. (1991). *Modernity and self-identity: Self and society in the late modern age.* Stanford, CA: Stanford University Press.

Giddens, A. (1974). *Positivism and sociology.* London: Heinemann.

Gilligan, C. (1993). *In a different voice: Psychological theory and women's development.* Boston: Harvard University Press.

Gini, A. (2001). *My job, my self: Work and creation of the modern individual.* New York: Routledge.

Ginsburg, M. B., Cooper, S., Raghu, R., & Zegarra, H. (1990). National and world-systems explanations of educational reform. *Comparative Education Review, 34*(4), 464–499.

Giroux, H. (1996). Slacking off: Border youth and postmodern education. In H. Giroux, C. Lankshear, P. McLaren, & M. Peters (Eds.), *Counter narratives: Cultural studies and critical pedagogies in postmodern spaces* (pp. 59–80). New York: Routledge.

Giroux, H. (1996). *Counter narratives: Cultural studies and critical pedagogies in postmodern spaces.* London: Routledge.

Giroux, H. (1983). *Theory and resistance in education.* South Hadley, MA: Bergin and Garvey.

Glaberson, W. (2000). The Elian Gonzalez case: The legal questions; Court's ruling is giving experts pause about right of children to be heard. *The New York Times,* April 22, 2000.

Glaserfeld, V.-E. (1995). *Radical constructivism.* London: The Palmer Press.

Goethe, J. W. (1997). *Wilhelm Meisters Lehrjahre.* Stuttgart: Reclam. [German]

Goldscheider, F. C., & Waite, L. J. (1991). *New families, no families?* Berkley, CA: University of California Press.

Goleman, D. (1997). *Emotional intelligence: Why it can matter more than IQ.* New York: Bantam Books.

Goodlad, J., & Klein, M. F. (1970). *Behind the classroom door.* Worthington, OH: Charles A. Jones.

Goodnough, A. (1999). Answers allegedly supplied in effort to raise test scores. *New York Times,* December 8, 1999. Retrieved from http://partners.nytimes.com/library/national/regional/120899ny-cheat-edu.html

Goos, F. (1996). The redefining of the American family through divorce, single-parenting and remarriage and the conflict of values in contemporary American popular culture. *Dissertation Abstracts International, A: The Humanities and Social Sciences, 57*(6), 2688–A.

Gordon, D., & Alexander, G. (2005). The education of story lovers: Do computers undermine narrative sensibility? *Curriculum Inquiry, 35*(2), 133–160.

Gordon, D., Aviram, A., Gorodezki, M., Flum, H., Keinan, A., & Shemesh, Z. (1994). The character of educational initiatives. In J. Danilov (Ed.), *Planning of educational policy* (pp. 97–168). Jerusalem: The Pedagogical Department, The Ministry of Education (a version of a position paper submitted to the Ministry of Education in 1989). [Hebrew]

Gordon, D. (1984). *The myths of school self-renewal.* New York: Teachers College Press.

Gott, M. (2005). *Sexuality, sexual health and ageing.* New York: Open University Press.

Gottlieb, R. (1993). *Forcing the spring: The transformation of the American environmental movement.* Washington, DC: Island Press.

Gould, M. S., et al. (2003). Youth suicide risk and preventive interventions: A review of the past 10 years. *Journal of the American Academy of Child & Adolescent Psychiatry, 2*(4), 386–405.

Gould, M. S., Greenberg, T., Velting, D., & Shaffer, D. (2003). Youth suicide risk and preventive interventions: A review of the past 10 years. *Journal of the American Academy of Child & Adolescent Psychiatry, 42*(4), 386–405.

Government of Israel, Winograd Committee. (2007). *Partial report.* Retrieved from http://www.vaadatwino.org.il/reports.html#null. [Hebrew]

Graff, G. (1992). *Beyond the culture wars: How teaching the conflicts can revitalize American education.* New York and London: Norton.

Graham, G. (2004). E-learning: A philosophical enquiry. *Education & Training, 46*(6/7), 308.

Gray, J. (1997). *Endgames.* Cambridge, UK: Polity Press.

Gray, J. (1983). *Mill on liberty: A defense.* London: Routledge and Kegan Paul.

Greenberg, D. (1987). *Free at last: The Sudbury valley school.* Framingham, MA: Sudbury Valley School Press.

Gregg, M., & Iran-Nejad, A. (2001). The brain-mind cycle of reflection. *Teachers College Record, 103*(5), 868–895.

Griffith, M. (1998). *The unschooling handbook: How to use the whole world as your child's classroom.* Roseville, CA: Prima Publishing.

Grolnick, W. S., Deci, E. L., & Ryan, R. M. (1997). Internalization within the Family. In J. E. Grusec & L. Kuczynski (Eds.), *Parenting and children's internalization of values: A handbook of contemporary theory* (pp. 135–161). New York: Wiley.

Grolnick, W. S., & Slowiaczek, M. L. (1994). Parents' involvement in children's schooling: A multidimensional conceptualization and motivational model. *Child Development, 65,* 237–252.

Grossman, P., & Stodolsky, S. (1994). Considerations of content and the circumstances of secondary school teaching. *Review of Research in Education, 20,* 179–221.

Guichard, J. (2001). A century of career education: Review and perspectives. *International Journal of Educational and Vocational Guidance, 1*(3), 155–176.

Gunnell, D., & Ashby, D. (2004). Antidepressants and suicide: What is the balance of benefit and harm? *British Medical Journal, 329,* 34–38. Retrieved from http://www.bmj.com/cgi/content/full/329/7456/34?ijkey=b6d853a068797f575d21f9dee905f60df5b2071c&keytype2=tf_ipsecsha

Gurevitz, D. (1997). *Postmodernism — culture and literature at the end of the 20th century*. Tel Aviv: Dvir. [Hebrew]

Gur-Ze'ev, I. (2007). *Beyond the modern-postmodern struggle in education: Toward counter-education and eternal improvisation*. Rotterdam, The Netherlands: Sense.

Gur-Ze'ev, I. (2004). *Toward a diaspora education: Multi-culturalism, post-colonialism and counter-education in a post-modern era*. Tel Aviv: Resling. [Hebrew]

Gur-Ze'ev, I. (2003). Critical theory, critical pedagogy and the possibility of counter-education. In M. Peters, C. Lankshear, & M. Olssen (Eds.), *Critical theory and the human condition: Founders and praxis* (pp. 17–35). New York: Peter Lang.

Gur-Ze'ev, I. (2001). Challenging the deception of leftist emancipatory education. *Pedagogy, Culture and Society, 9*(2), 279–288.

Gur-Ze'ev, I. (1998). Toward a nonrepressive critical pedagogy. *Educational Theory, 48*(4), 463–486.

Gur-Ze'ev, I. (1997). *Education in the era of the postmodern discourse*. Jerusalem: Hebrew University of Jerusalem, Magnes. [Hebrew]

Gur-Ze'ev, I. (1995). Henry giroux: Critical pedagogy? *Iyyun, 44*(4), 419–442.

Gutmann, A. (2004). *Why deliberative democracy?* Princeton, NJ: Princeton University Press.

Gutmann, A. (2003). *Identity in democracy: A humanist view*. Princeton, NJ: Princeton University Press.

Gutmann, A. (1999). *Democratic education*. Princeton, NJ: Princeton University Press.

Gutmann, A. (1996). *Democracy and disagreement*. Cambridge, MA: Harvard University Press.

Gutmann, A. (1988). *Democracy and the welfare state*. Princeton, NJ: Princeton University Press.

Gutmann, A. (1987). *Democratic education*. Princeton, NJ: Princeton University Press.

Haasen, C., et al. (2004). Cocaine use in Europe — A multi-centre study. *European Addiction Research, 10*(4), 139–146.

Habermas, J. (2001). *The postnational constellation*. Boston: MIT Press.

Haddock, B. A., & Sutch, P. (2003). *Multiculturalism, identity, and rights*. London and New York: Routledge.

Halberstam, J. (2005). *In a queer time and place*. New York: New York University Press.

Haldane, J. (Ed.). (2004). *Values, education and the human world*. Exeter, Devon: Imprint Academic.

Hall, E., & Handley, R. (2004). *High schools in crisis: What every parent should know*. Westport, CT: Praeger.

Hallowell, J. H. (1998). *The decline of liberalism as an ideology: With particular reference to German politico-legal thought*. London: Routledge.

Halpern, D. F. (1996). *Thought and knowledge: Introduction to critical thinking*. Mahwah, NJ: Lawrence Erlbaum.

Hamelink, C. J. (1997). *New information and communication technologies, social development and cultural change*. Geneva: United Nations Research Institute for Social Development.

Handy, C. (2001). *The elephant and the flea*. London: Hutchinson.

Handy, C. (1998). *Beyond certainty: The changing worlds of organizations*. Cambridge, MA: Harvard Business School Press.

Handy, C. (1994). *The empty raincoat*. London: Hutchinson.

Handy, C. (1989). *The age of unreason*. London: Business Books.

Handy, C. (1984). *The future of work*. Oxford: Blackwell.

Hankinson, R. J. (1995). *The sceptics*. London: Routledge.

Hanson, M. (2001). Institutional theory and educational change. *Educational Administration Quarterly, 37*(5), 637–661.

Hanson, R. A., & Schutz, R. E. (1986). A comparison of methods for measuring achievement in basic skills program evaluation. *Educational Evaluation and Policy Analysis, 8*(1), 101–113.

Harasim, L., Hiitz, S. R., Teles, L., & Turoff, M. (1995). *Learning networks: A field guide to teaching and learning online*. Cambridge, MA: The MIT Press.

Harasim, L. (1993). *Global networks: Computers and international communication*. Cambridge, MA: The MIT Press.

Haraway, D. J. (1991). A cyborg manifesto: Science, technology, and socialist-feminism in the late twentieth century. In D. J. Haraway (Ed.), *Simians, cyborgs and women: The reinvention of nature* (pp. 149–181). New York: Routledge.

Harding, P. (1985). *Flexible learning in small fifth and sixth forms*. Cambridge, UK: National Extension College, Cambridge.

Hargreaves, A., Earl, L., & Moore, S. (2001). *Learning to change: Teaching beyond subjects and standards*. San Francisco: Jossey-Bass.

Hargreaves, A., & Fullan, M. (1998). *What's worth fighting for in your school?* New York: Teachers College Press.

Hargreaves, A. (2003). *Teaching in the knowledge society*. New York: Teachers College Press.

Hargreaves, A. (1995). Renewal in the age of paradox. *Educational Leadership, 52*(7).

Hargreaves, A. (1994). *Changing teachers, changing times: Teachers' work and culture in the postmodern age*. London: Cassell.

Hargreaves, D. H. (1997). A road to the learning society. *School Leadership and Management, 17*(1), 9–21.

Hargreaves, D. H. (1995). Self-managing schools and development planning — chaos or control? *School Organization, 15*(3), 215–227.

Harmon-Jones, E., & Mills, J. (Eds.). (1999). *Cognitive dissonance: Progress on a pivotal theory in social psychology*. Washington, DC: American Psychological Association.

Harpaz, Y., & Lefstein, A. (2005). Teaching and learning in a community of thinking. *Journal of Curriculum and Supervision, 20*(2), 136–157.

Harpaz, Y., & Lefstein, A. (2000). Communities of thinking. *Educational Leadership, 58*(3), 54–57.

Harpaz, Y. (2007). Approaches to teaching thinking: Toward a conceptual mapping of the field. *Teachers College Record, 109*(8), 1845–1874.

Harpaz, Y. (2004). *Conflicting logics in education to critical thinking*. Mandel school. Retrieved from www.learningtolearn.sa.edu.au/colleagues/files/links/conflicting_logics_in_Educ.rtf

Harrington, R., Bredenkamp, D., Groothues, C., Rutter, M., Fudge, H., & Pickles, A. (1994). Adult outcomes of childhood and adolescent depression. III links with suicidal behaviors. *Journal of Child Psychology and Psychiatry, 35*(7), 1309–1319.

Harris, B. W. (1986). Open learning in schools. *Open Learning: The Journal of Open and Distance Learning, 1*(2), 26–27.

Harris, K. (1982). *Teachers and classes*. London: Routledge and Kegan Paul.

Harrison, P. A., & Luxenberg, M. G. (1995). Comparisons of alcohol and other drug problems among minnesota adolescents in 1989 and 1992. *Archives of Pediatrics and Adolescent Medicine, 149*, 137–144.

Harter, S., Bresnick, S., Bouchey, H. A., & Whitesell, N. R. (1997). The development of multiple role-related selves during adolescence. *Development and Psychopathology, 9*, 835–853.

Harter, S. (1999). *The construction of the self: A developmental perspective*. New York: Guilford Press.

Hartley, D. (1997). *Re-schooling society*. London: FalmerPress.

Hartley, J. R., & Collins-Brown, E. (1999). *Effective pedagogies for managing collaborative learning in on-line learning environments*. Pre-discussion paper, *Educational Technology & Society, 2*(2).

Harvard University. Committee on the Objectives of a General Education in a Free Society. (1945). *General education in a free society: Report of the harvard committee*. Cambridge, MA: Harvard University Press.

Harvey, D. (1989). *The condition of postmodernity*. London: Blackwell.

Hawkins, J. D., Catalano, R. F., & Miller, J. Y. (1992). Risk and protective factors for alcohol and other drug problems in adolescence and early adulthood: Implications for substance abuse prevention. *Psychological Bulletin, 112*(1), 64–105.

Hayek, F. A. (1978). *The constitution of liberty*. Chicago: University Of Chicago Press.

Hayek, F. A. (1976). *The road to serfdom*. London: Routledge.

Hayek, F. A. (1949). *Individualism and economic order*. London: Routledge.

Haymann, F., Golan, H., & Shapira, R. (1997). School autonomy and parental choice: Steps in local educational planning. In R. Shapira & P. Cookson (Eds.), *Autonomy and choice in context: An international perspective* (pp. 77–108). Oxford, UK: Pergamon Press.

Heilbrun, J., & Gray, C. M. (1993). *The economics of art and culture — an American perspective.* Cambridge, UK: Cambridge University Press.

Hendin, H. (1996). *Suicide in America* (Expanded ed.). New York: W. W. Norton & Company.

Herman, J. L., Aschbacher, P. R., & Winters, L. (1992). *A practical guide to alternative assessment.* Alexandria, VA: Association for Supervision and Curriculum Development.

Hernandez, J., & Goodson, I. (2004). *Geographics of educational change.* London: Kluwer.

Herrington, J., & Oliver, R. (2000). An instructional design framework for authentic learning environments. *Educational Technology, Research and Development, 48*(3), 23–48.

Herzenberg, S. A., Alic, J. A., & Wial, H. (1998). *New rules for a new economy: Employment and opportunity in postindustrial America.* Ithaka, NY: Cornell University Press.

Hess, R. S., & Copeland, E. P. (2001). Students' stress, coping strategies, and school completion: A longitudinal perspective. *School Psychology Quarterly, 16*(4), 389–405.

Heywood, C. (2001). *A history of childhood: Children and childhood in the west from medieval to modern times (Themes in history).* Cambridge, UK: Polity Press.

Hickey, K. (2007). Minors' rights in medical decision making, JONA's Healthcare Law. *Ethics & Regulation, 9*(3), 100–104.

Hidi, S., Renninger, K. A., & Krapp, A. (2004). Interest, a motivational variable that combines affective and cognitive functioning. In D. Y. Dai & R. J. Sternberg (Eds.), *Motivation, emotion and cognition: Integrative perspectives on intellectual functioning and Development* (pp. 89–115). Mahwah, NJ: Lawrence Erlbaum.

Hidi, S. (2000). An interest researcher's perspective: The effects of extrinsic and intrinsic factors on motivation. In I. C. Sansone & J. M. Harackiewicz (Eds.), *Intrinsic and extrinsic motivation: The search for optimal motivation and performance* (pp. 311–333). New York: Academic Press.

Hidi, S. (1990). Interest and its contribution as a mental resource for learning. *Review of Educational Research, 60*(4), 549–571.

Higgs, E., Light, A., & Strong, D. (2000). *Technology and the good life?* Chicago: University of Chicago Press.

Hill, A. (2000). Children taught at home learn more. *The Observer*, August 13, 2000.

Hill, D. (Ed.). (1999). *Postmodernism in educational theory: Education and the politics of human resistance.* London: Tufnell Press.

Hill, P. T. (2003). *School boards focus on school performance, not money and patronage.* Published in the Progressive Policy Institute 21st Century Schools Project. Retrieved from http://www.ppionline. org/documents/School_Boards_0103.pdf

Hillman, L. (1996). *The soul's code.* New York: Random House.

Hincliffe, K. (1987). Education and the labour market. In G. Psacharopoulus (Ed.), *Economics of education research and studies* (pp. 315–323). Oxford, UK: Pergamon Press.

Hirsch, E. D., Kett J. F., & Trefil, J. (2002). *The new dictionary of cultural literacy: What every American needs to know* (3rd ed.). New York: Houghton Mifflin.

Hirsch, E. D. (2006). *The knowledge deficit: Closing the shocking education gap for American children.* Boston: Houghton Mifflin.

Hirsch, E. D. (1996). *The school we need and why we don't have them.* New York: Doubleday Publishing.

Hirsch, E. D. (1996). *The schools we need and why we don't have them.* New York: Doubleday.

Hirsch, E. D. (1991a). *What your first grader needs to know.* New York: Doubleday Publishing.

Hirsch, E. D. (1991b). *What your second grader needs to know.* New York: Doubleday Publishing.

Hirsch, E. D. (1991c). *What your third grader needs to know.* New York: Doubleday Publishing.

Hirsch, E. D. (1987). *Cultural literacy.* Boston: Houghton Mifflin.

Hirschhorn, L. (1986). *Beyond mechanisation.* Cambridge, MA: The MIT Press.

Hirst, P. H. (1974). *Knowledge and the curriculum.* London: Routledge & Kegan Paul.

Hock, D. W. (1999). *Birth of the chaordic age*. San Francisco, CA; Great Britain: Berrett-Koehler.

Hock, D. W. (1996). *The chaordic organization: Out of control and into order*. 21st Century Learning Initiative.[On-line]. Retrieved from http://www.cyberspace.com/building/ofc_21clidhock.html

Hock, D. W. (1995). The chaordic organization. *World Business Academy Perspectives, 9*(1), 5–18.

Holloway, S., & Valentine, V. (2003). *Cyberkids: Children in the information age*. London: Routledge.

Holloway, S., & Valentine, V. (2001). "It's only as stupid as you are": Children's and adults' negotiation of ICT competence at home and at school. *Social and Cultural Geography, 2*(1), 25–42.

Holmes, B. M. (1989). *The curriculum, a comparative perspective*. London: Unwin Hyman.

Holstein, J. A., & Gubrium, J. F. (Eds.). (2000). *The self we live by: Narrative identity in a postmodern world*. New York and Oxford: Oxford University Press.

Holt, J. (1981). *Teach your own: A hopeful path for education*. New York: Delta/Seymour Lawrence.

Holt, J. (1976). *Freedom and beyond*. New York: Penguin Books.

Holt, J. (1967). *How children learn*. New York: Pitman Publishing Corp.

Holt, J. (1965). *How children fail*. New York: Pitman Publishing Corp.

hooks, b. (2004). *The will to change: Men, masculinity, and love*. New York: Atria Books.

hooks, b. (2000). *Feminist theory: From margin to center* (2nd ed.). London: Pluto Press.

Hopkins, T. (1996). *Using open learning in social work: An implementation handbook*. London: Open Learning Foundation.

Horkheimer, M. (2004). *Eclipse of reason*. London and New York: Continuum International Publishing Group.

Houlgate, L. (1980). *The child and the state: A normative theory of Juvenile rights*. Baltimore: The Johns Hopkins UP.

Huling, L. (1980). How schools size affects students' participation, alienation. *Nassp Bull, 64*, 13–18.

Human Rights Watch. *The rest of their lives: Life without parole for child offenders in the US*. Retrieved from http://hrw.org/campaigns/lwop/summary.htm

Hume, D. (1978). *A treatise of human nature* (2nd ed.). Oxford, UK: Oxford University Press.

Hume, D. (1969). *A treatise of human nature*. London: Penguin. (Originally published 1739–40).

Huntington, S. P. (1996). *The clash of civilizations and the remaking of world order*. New York: Simon & Schuster.

Hurn, C. J. (1985). *The limits and possibilities of schooling: An introduction to the sociology of education*. Boston: Allyn & Bacon.

Hurn, C. (1978). *The limits and possibilities of schooling*. Boston: Allyn and Bacon.

Iancu, I., Laufer, N., Dannon, P., Zohar-Kadouch, R., Apter, A., & Zohar, J. (1997). A general hospital study of attempted suicide in adolescence: Age and methos of attempt. *Israel Journal of Psychiatry and Related Sciences, 34*(3), 228–234.

Idan, A., & Gavron, A. (2000). *The 21st century guide book*. Tel Aviv: Dyonon. [Hebrew]

ILGA Europe. (2008). Same-sex marriage and partnership: Country-by-country. Retrieved from http://www.ilga-europe.org/europe/issues/marriage_and_partnership/same_sex_marriage_ and_ partnership_country_by_country

Illich, I. (1973). *After deschooling, what?* New York: Harper & Row.

Illich, I. (1971). *Deschooling society*. New York: Harper & Row.

Inglehart, R. (1990). *Culture shift in advanced industrial society*. Princeton, NJ: Princeton University Press.

Ivarsson, T., & Gillberg, C. (1997). Depressive symptoms in Swedish adolescents: Normative data using the Birleson depression self-rating scale (DSRS). *Journal of Affective Disorders, 42*, 59–68.

James, W. (1977). The will to believe. In J. J. McDermott (Ed.), *The writings of William James: A comprehensive edition* (pp. 717–735). Chicago: University of Chicago Press.

Jefferson County Sheriff's Office. (2008). *The columbine report*. Retrieved form http://www.boulderdailycamera.com/shooting/report.html

John, M. (2003). *Children's rights and power: Charging up for a new century*. London: Jessica Kingsley Publishers.

Johnson, D., & Johnson, R. (1987). *Learning together and alone*. Englewood, CO: Prentice Hall.

Johnson, D., Johnson, R., & Stanne, M. B. (2000). *Cooperative learning methods: A meta-analysis.* Minneapolis, MN: University of Minnesota. Retrieved from http://www.co-operation.org/pages/cl-methods.html

Johnston, H. (1998). Introduction: Collective behavior and social movements in the postmodern age: Looking backward to look forward. *Sociological Perspectives, 41*(3), 453–472.

Jonassen, D. H., & Land, S. (2000). *The theoretical foundations of learning environments.* Mahwah, NJ: Erlbaum.

Jonassen, D. H., Peck, K. L., & Wilson, B. G. (1999). *Learning with technology: A constructivist perspective.* Upper Saddle, NJ: Merrill, Prentice Hall.

Jonassen, D. H. (1994). Thinking technology: Toward a constructivist design model. *Educational Technology, 34*(3), 34–37.

Jones, A., Scanlon, E., & O'shes, V. (Eds.). (1987). *The computer revolution in education.* Sussex: The Harvester Press.

Joyce, P. R., Oakley-Browne, M. A., Wells, J. F., Bushnell, J. A., & Hornblow, A. R. (1990). Birth cohort trends in major depression: Increasing rates and earlier onset in New Zealand. *Journal of Affective Disorders, 18*, 83–89.

Jumilhac, M. (1984). *Les Massacre des Innocents.* Paris: Plon. [French]

Kahneman, D. (1999). Objective happiness. In D. Kahneman, E. Diener, & N. Schwarz (Eds.), *Well being: The foundations of hedonic psychology* (pp. 3–25). New York: Russell Sage Foundation.

Kaku, M. (1998). *Visions — how science will revolutionize the 21st century.* New York: Anchor Books.

Kane, T. J., & Staiger, D. O. (2002). The promise and pitfalls of using imprecise school accountabilty measures. *Journal of Economic Perspectives, 16*(4), 91–114.

Kant, I. (1999). *Critique of pure reason* (P. Guyer & A. W. Wood, Trans. and Eds.). Cambridge, UK: Cambridge University Press. (Originally published 1787)

Kantor, H., & Tyack, D. (1982). *Work, youth, and schooling: Historical perspectives on vocationalism in American education.* Stanford, CA: Stanford University Press.

Karmon, A. (2006). The organization of knowledge in the school: From a school profession to a pedagogical discipline. In D. Gordon (Ed.), *Subject matters under examination: An alternative to conventional school teaching* (pp. 54–118). Jerusalem: Van Leer Institute. [Hebrew]

Kasser, T., & Ryan, R. M. (1996). Further examining the American dream: Differential correlates of intrinsic and extrinsic goals. *Personality and Social Psychology Bulletin, 22*, 80–87.

Kastis, N. (2004). Professional development for teachers and quality in school education. In A. Aviram & J. Richardson (Eds.), *Upon what does the turtle stand? Rethinking education for the digital age* (pp. 121–134). Dordrecht, Netherlands: Kluwer Academic Publishers.

Katz, D., & Kahn, R. (1966). *The social psychology of organizations.* New York: Wiley.

Katz, I., et al. (2006). Interest as a motivational resource: Feedback and gender matter, but interest makes the difference. *Social Psychology of Education, 9*, 27–42.

Katz, I., & Assor, A. (2006). When choice motivates and when it does not. *Educational Psychology Review, 19*(4), 429–442.

Katz, I., & Assor, A. (2003). *The effect of autonomy support on intrinsic motivation in Jewish and Bedouin children: The meaning of autonomy in different cultures.* Presented at the annual meeting of the Society for Research on Child Development (SRCD) (Tampa, Florida).

Katz, I., Assor, A., Kanat-Maymon, Y., & Bereby-Meyer, Y. (2006). Interest as a motivational resource: Feedback and gender matter, but interest makes the difference. *Social Psychology of Education, 9*, 27–42.

Kaufman, R. (2000a). Everybody hates Kant: Blakean formalism and the symmetries of Laura Moriarty. *Modern Language Quarterly, 61*(1), 131–155.

Kaufman, R. (2000b). Red Kant; Or, the persistence of the third critique in Adorno and Jameson. *Critical Inquiry, 26*(4), 682–724.

Keefe, J. W. (1987). *Learning style theory and practice.* Nassp, Reston: Virginia.Keegan, D. (1996). *Foundations of distance education.* London: Routledge.

Keinan, A., & Aviram, A. (1994). Cultural dialogue as a way for the absorption of new immigrants. *Education, 114*(3), 401–410.

Keirsey, D., & Bates, M. (1984). *Please understand me: Character and temperament types* (3rd ed.). Del Mar, CA: Prometheus Nemesis Book Company.

Keyes, C. L. M., & Haidt, J. (2003). *Flourishing: Positive psychology and the life well-lived.* Washington, DC: American Psychological Association.

King, B. (2001). Managing the changing nature of distance and open education at institutional level. *Open Learning, 16*(1), 47–60.

Kinsler, K., & Gamble, M. (2001). *Reforming schools.* New York: Continuum International Publishing Group.

Klamer, A. (1996). *The value of culture — On the relationship between economics and arts.* Amsterdam: Amsterdam University Press.

Klein, K. L. (1995). In search of narrative mastery: Postmodernism and the peoples without history. *History and Theory, 34,* 275–298.

Kliebard, H. M. (1987). *The struggle for the American curriculum 1893–1958.* New York: Routledge.

Kling, R. (1991). Computerization and social transformations. *Science, Technology and Human Values, 16,* 342–367.

Knight, K. (2007). *Aristotelian philosophy: Ethics and politics from Aristotle to MacIntyre.* Cambridge, UK: Polity.

Knox, P. L. (1991). The restless urban landscape: Economic and sociocultural change and the transformation of metropolitan Washington DC. *Annals of the Association of American Geographers, 81*(2), 181–209.

Koelb, C. (1990). *Nietzsche as postmodernist: Essays pro and contra.* New York: SUNY Press.

Kohlberg, L., Levine, C., & Hewer, A. (1983). *Moral stages: A current formulation and a response to critics.* Basel: Karger.

Kohlberg, L., & Turiel, E. (1971). Moral development and moral education. In G. S. Lesser (Ed.), *Psychology and educational practice* (pp. 410–465). Glenview, IL: Scott Foresman and Company.

Kohlberg, L. (1981). *The philosophy of moral development: Moral stages and the idea of justice.* London: Harper & Row.

Kohlberg, L. (1980). Educating for a just society. In B. Munsey (Ed.), *Moral development, moral education, and kohlberg* (pp. 455–471). Birmingham, AL: Religious Education Press.

Kohlberg, L. (1971). Stages of moral development as a basis for moral education. In C. M. Beck, B. S. Crittenden, & E. V. Sullivan (Eds.), *Moral education: Interdisciplinary approaches* (pp. 23–92). Toronto, ON: University of Toronto Press.

Kohlberg, L. (1964). Development of moral character and moral ideology. In M. L. Hoffman & L. W. Hoffman (Eds.), *Review of child development research* (Vol. I, pp. 381–431). New York: Russel Sage Foundation.

Kohn, A. (2005). Unconditional teaching. *Educational Leadership,* September, 2005.

Kohn, A. (2004). *What does it mean to be well educated? And more essays on standards, grading, and other follies.* Boston: Beacon Press.

Kohn, A. (2000). *The case against standardized testing: Raising the scores, ruining the schools.* Portsmouth, NH: Heinemann.

Kohn, A. (1999a). Constant frustration and occasional violence: The legacy of American high schools. *American School Board Journal.* Retrieved from http://www.alfiekohn.org/articles.htm#null

Kohn, A. (1999b). *The schools our children deserve: Moving beyond traditional classrooms and "Tougher standards".* Boston: Houghton Mifflin.

Kohn, A. (1996). *Beyond discipline: From compliance to community.* Alexandria, VA: Association for Supervision and Curriculum Development.

Kohn, A. (1993). *Punished by reward: The trouble with gold stars, incentive plans, A's, praise, and other bribes.* Boston: Houghton Mifflin.

Koyré, A. (1994). *Introduction à la Lecture de Platon.* Paris: Gallimard. [French]

Kozma, R. (2005). National policies that connect ICT-based education reform to economic and social development. *Human Technology, 1*(2), 117–156.

Krapp, A., Hidi, S., & Renninger, K. A. (1992). Interest, learning and development. In K. A. Renninger, S. Hidi, & A. Krapp (Eds.), *The role of interest in learning and development* (pp. 3–26). Hillsdale, NJ: Lawrence Erlbaum Associates.

Krapp, A. (2002a). An educational–psychological theory of interest and its relation to self-determination theory. In E. Deci & R. Ryan (Eds.), *The handbook of self-determination research* (pp. 405–427). Rochester, NY: University of Rochester Press.

Krapp, A. (2002b). Structural and dynamic aspects of interest development: Theoretical considerations from an ontogenetic perspective. *Learning and Instruction, 12*, 383–409.

Krausz, M., & Meiland, J. (1982). *Relativism cognitive and moral.* Notre Dame, IN: University of Notre Dame Press.

Kristen, G. (1999). Web sites worship Teen Killers. *Denver Post*, December 14, 1999. The Rick A. Ross Institute of New Jersey.
Retrieved from http://www.rickross.com/ reference/shootings/shootings18. html

Kroeker, P. T., & Ward, B. K. (2001). *Remembering the end: Dostoevsky as prophet to modernity.* Boulder, CO: Westview Press.

Kroker, A., Kroker, M., & Cook, D. (1989). *Panic encyclopedia, the definitive guide to the postmodern scene.* New York: St. Martin Press.

Kuhn, T. (1970). *The structure of scientific revolutions* (2nd ed.). Chicago: University of Chicago Press.

Kuhn, T. S. (1962). *The structure of scientific revolutions.* Chicago: University of Chicago Press.

Kuijpers, M. A. C. T., & Scheerens, J. (2006). Career competencies for the modern career. *Journal of Career Development, 32*(4), 303–319.

Kumar, K. (1995). *From post-industrial to post-modern society: New theories of the contemporary world.* Oxford, UK: Blackwell.

Kurzweil, R. (2005). *The singularity is near: When humans transcend biology.* New York: Viking.

Kurzweil, R. (1999). *The age of spiritual machines.* New York: Penguin Books.

Kurzweil, R. (1990). *The age of intelligent machines.* Cambridge, MA: The MIT Press.

Kymlicka, W. (2007). *Multicultural odysseys: Navigating the new international politics of diversity.* Oxford and New York: Oxford University Press.

Kymlicka, W. (1991). *Liberalism, community, and culture.* Oxford University Press.

Kyriacou, C. (1987). Teacher stress and burnout: An international review. *Educational Research, 29*(2), 146–187.

La Belle, T., & Ward, C. R. (1990). Education reform when nations undergo radical political and social transformation. *Comparative Education, 26*(1), 95–106.

Lacan, J. (1981). *The four fundamental concepts of psychoanalysis.* New York: Norton.

Lacan, J. (1977). *Ecrits: A selection.* New York: Norton.

Lamb, R., & Friends of the Earth. (1996). *Promising the earth.* London; New York: Routledge.

Lampert, K. (2003). *Compassionate education: A prolegomena for radical schooling.* Lanham, MD: University press of America.

Lane, R. (2000). *The loss of happiness in market democracies.* New Haven and London: Yale University Press.

Lareau, A. (2000). *Home advantage: Social class and parental intervention in elementary education* (2nd ed.). Lanham, MD: Rowman & Littlefield Publishers, Inc.

Lash, S., & Urry, J. (1987). *The end of organised capitalism.* Oxford, UK: Oxford University Press.

Lauter, P. (1991). *Canons and contexts.* New York; Oxford: Oxford University Press.

Lawrence, R. (1997). *School crime and Juvenile justice.* Oxford: Oxford University Press.

Lawton, D., & Gordon, P. (2002). *A history of western educational ideas.* Routledge.

LeCompte, M. D., & Dworkin, A. G. (1991). *Giving up on school: Student dropouts and teacher burnouts.* Newbury Park, CA: Corwin.

Leidig, T. (2001). L^3 — Towards an open learning environment. *Journal of Educational Resources in Computing (JERIC), 1*(1).

Leites, V. (1979). Locke's liberal theory of parenthood. In O. Oniel & W. Ruddick (Eds.), *Having children*. Oxford, UK: Oxford University Press.

Lerougetel, A. (2005). *French high school students continue their struggle*. Retrieved from http://www.wsws.org/articles/2005/apr2005/lyce-al1.shtml

Levin, B. (2001). *Reforming education: From origins to outcomes*. New York: Routledge.

Levin, H. M. (1987). Work and education. In G. Psacharopoulos (Ed.), *Economics of education: Research and studies* (pp. 146–157). Oxford, UK: Pergamon Press.

Levinas, E. (1985). *Ethics and infinity: Conversations with Philippe Nemo* (R. A. Cohen, Trans.). Pittsburgh, PA: Duquesne University Press.

Lewis, R., & Spencer, D. (1986). *What is open learning?* London: Council for Educational Technology.

Lewis, R. (1997). Open learning in higher education. *Open Learning, 12*(3), 3–13.

Lewis, R. (1990). Open learning and the misuse of language: A response to Greville rumble. *Open Learning, 5*(1), 3–8.

Ley, D. (1996). *The new middle class and the remaking of the central city*. Oxford, UK: Oxford University Press.

Lilge, F. (1975). *The abuse of learning*. New York: Octagon Books.

Lilge, F. (1948). *The abuse of learning: The failure of the German university*. New York: Macmillan Co.

Lindley, R. (1986). *Autonomy*. London: Macmillan.

Livingstone, R. W. (1943). *Education for a world adrift*. Cambridge, UK: Cambridge University Press.

Lockwood, F. (1995). *Open and distance learning today*. London: Routledge.

Lodge, R. C. (2000). *Plato on education*. New Delhi, India: Indian Publishers Distributors.

Loewenstein, E. A. (1994). Dissolving the myth of the unified self: The fate of the subject in Freudian analysis. *Psychoanalytic Quarterly, LXIII*, 715–732.

Lombardo, T. (2006). *Contemporary futurist thought: Science fiction, future studies, and theories and visions of the future in the last century*. Bloomington, IN: AuthorHouse.

Long, G. M., & Toppino, T. C. (2004). Enduring interest in perceptual ambiguity: Alternating views of reversible figures. *Psychological Bulletin, 130*(5), 748–768.

Løvlie, L., Mortensen, K., & Nordenbo, S. E. (Eds.). (2002). Educating humanity: Bildung in postmodernity. *Special Issue of Journal of Philosophy of Education, 36*(3).

Lowe, R. (2000). *History of education: Major themes*. London and New York: Routledge.

Lubbers, M., Gijsberts, M., & Scheepers, M. P. (2002). Extreme right-wing voting in Western Europe. *European Journal of Political Research, 41*, 345.

Lynch, T. D., & Cruise, P. L. (2006). *Handbook of organization theory and management: The philosophical approach* (2nd ed.). Boca Raton, FL: Taylor & Francis. Retrieved from http://www.loc.gov/catdir/toc/fy0602/2005043996.html

Lyotard, J. (1984). *The postmodern condition: A report on knowledge*. Minneapolis, MN: University of Minnesota Press.

Macarov, D. (1996). The employment of new ends: Planning for permanent unemployment. In A. Shostak (special Ed.), *Impacts of changing employment: If the good jobs go away* (pp. 191–202). Thousand Oaks, CA: Sage.

Macarov, D. (1988). *Quitting time: The end of work. Special issue of the International Journal of Sociology and Social Policy, 8*(2/3/4).

Machan, T. R. (2006). *Libertarianism defended*. Aldershot, Hampshire: Ashgate.

MacIntyre, A. (1999). *Dependent rational animals. Why human beings need the virtues*. London: Duckworth.

MacIntyre, A. (1995). Is patriotism a virtue? In R. Beiner (Ed.), *Theorizing citizenship*. Albany, NY: State University of New York Press.

MacIntyre, A. (1990). *Three rival versions of moral enquiry*. Notre Dame, IN: University of Notre Dame Press.

MacIntyre, A. (1980). *After virtue*. Notre Dame, IN.: University of Notre Dame Press.

MacKenzie, D., & Wajcman, J. (1985). *The social shaping of technology*. Milton Keynes, Buckinghamshire: Open University Press.

Malpas, S. (2005). *The postmodern*. London: Routledge.

Mangham, I. (1967). Education for autonomy: Some comments on the educational thought of David Riesman. *British Journal of Educational Studies, 15*(1), 40–50.

Marchand, M. H., & Parpart, J. L. (1995). *Feminism postmodernism development*. London; New York: Routledge.

Marcia, J. (1993). The ego identity status approach to ego identity. In J. Marcia, A. S. Waterman, D. R. Matteson, S. L. Archer, & J. L. Orlofsky (Eds.), *Ego identity: A handbook for psychosocial research* (pp. 3–41). New York: Springer-Verlag.

Marcia, J. (1980). Identity in adolescence. In J. Adelson (Ed.), *Handbook of adolescent psychology*. New York: Wiley.

Marcia, J. (1966). Development and validation of ego identity status. *Journal of Personality and Social Psychology, 3*(5), 551–558.

Marcuse, H. (2002). *One-dimensional man: Studies in the ideology of advanced industrial society* (New ed.). London: Routledge.

Markusen, A. (1996). Interaction between regional and industrial policies: Evidence from four countries. *International Regional Science Review, 19*(1–2), 49–77.

Marrou, H. I. (1982). *A history of education in antiquity*. University of Wisconsin Press.

Marschall, M., Schneider, M., & Teske, P. (2002). *Choosing schools: Consumer choice and the quality of American schools* (New ed.). Princeton, NJ: Princeton University Press.

Marsh, J., & Millard, E. (2000). *Literacy and popular culture: Using children's culture in the classroom*. London: Paul Chapman Publishing.

Marx, K. (1959). *Economic and philosophic manuscripts of 1844*. London: Foreign Languages Publishing House. (Originally published 1844)

Maslow, A. H. (1970). *New knowledge in human values*. Chicago: Regnery.

Maslow, A. H. (1968). *Toward a psychology of being* (2nd ed.). Princeton, NJ: D. Van Nostrand Co.

Maslow, A. H. (1943). A theory of human motivation. *Psychological Review, 50*(4), 370–396.

Mauch, C., Stoltzfus, N., & Weiner, D. R. (2006). *Shades of green: Environmental activism around the globe*. Lanham, MD: Rowman & Littlefield Publishers.

Maxcy, S. J. (1995). *Democracy, chaos, and the new school order*. Thousand Oaks, CA: Corwin Press.

May, R. (Ed.). (1969). *Existential psychology* (2nd ed.). New York: Random House.

Mazalin, D., & Moore, S. (2004). Internet use, identity development and social anxiety among young adults. *Behavior Change, 21*(2), 90–102.

McLaughlin, M., & Shepard, L. (1995). *Improving education through standards-based reform*. Washington, DC: National Academy of Education.

McLaughlin, N. (1996). Nazism, nationalism, and the sociology of emotions. Escape from freedom revisited. *Sociological Theory, 14*(3), 241–261.

McLuhan, M. (1965). *Understanding media: The extensions of man*. New York: McGraw-Hill.

McLuhan, M. (1962). *Gutenberg galaxy*. London: Routledge and Kegan Paul.

McNeil, L. M. (2000). *Contradictions of school reform: Educational costs of standardized testing*. New York: Routledge.

McRobbie, A. (1994). *Feminism, postmodernism and the 'Real me', postmodernism and popular culture*. London: Routledge.

Mead, M. (1978). *Culture and commitment: The new relationships between the generations in the 1970s*. New York: Columbia university Press.

Mead, M. (1970). *Culture and commitment*. New York: Garden City.

Medved, M., & Medved, D. (1999). *Saving childhood: Protecting our children from the national assault on innocence*. New York: Harper Paperbacks.

Meighan, R., & Siraj-Blatchford, I. (2005). *A sociology of educating* (4th ed.). London: Continuum.

Meighan, R. (1999). *Sociology of education* (4th ed.). London: Cassell & Co.

Meighan, R. (1997). *The next learning system: And why home-schoolers are trailblazers.* Nottingham: Educational Heretics Press.

Mele, A. R. (2006). *Free will and luck.* New York and Oxford, UK: Oxford University Press.

Mercy, J., Butchart, A., Farrington, D., & Cerdá M. (2002). Youth violence. In E. Krug, L. L. Dahlberg, J. A. Mercy, et al. (Eds.), *The world report on violence and health* (pp. 25–56). Geneva, Switzerland: World Health Organization.

Mervis, J. (2006). Doing more with less. *Science, 314*(5804), 1374–1376.

Mesch, G. S. (2006). Family characteristics and intergenerational conflicts over the internet. *Information, Communication & Society, 9*(4), 473–495.

Meyer, J. W., & Rowan, B. (1992). The structure of educational organisations. In J. W. Meyer & W. R. Scott (Eds.), *Organisational environments: Ritual and rationality* (pp. 179–197). Newbury Park: Sage.

Meyer, J. W., & Rowan, B. (1977). Institutionalized organizations: Formal structure as myth and ceremony. *American Journal of Sociology, 83*, 340–363.

Meyer, J. W. (1977). The effects of education as an institution. *American Journal of Sociology, 83*, 55–77.

Meyrowitz, J. (1985). *No sense of place: The impact of electronic media on social behavior.* New York: Oxford University Press.

Middlewood, D., & Lumby, J. (2004). *Strategic management in schools and colleges.* London: Sage.

Milburn, C. (2002). Nanotechnology in the age of post-human engineering: science fiction as science. *Configurations, 10*, 261–295.

Milgram, R. M., Dunn, R., & Price, G. E. (1993). *Teaching gifted and talented learners for learning style: An international perspective.* New York: Praeger.

Milkman, R. (1987). *Gender at work: The dynamics of job segregation by sex during world war II.* Champaign, Ill: University of Illinois Press.

Mill, J. S., & Cahn, S. M. (2005). *On liberty.* Lanham, MD: Rowman & Littlefield Publishers. Retrieved from http://www.loc.gov/catdir/toc/ecip0420/2004015989.html

Mill, J. S. (1977). *On liberty. Edited with an introduction by Elizabeth Rapaport.* Indianapolis: Hackett Pub.

Mill, J. S. (1956). *On liberty.* Indianapolis: Bobbs-Merrill. (Originally published 1859)

Mills, R. (2000). *Childhood studies: A reader in perspective of childhood.* London: Routledge.

Mintrom, M. (2000). Policy entrepreneurs and school choice (American Governance and Public Policy). Washington, DC: Georgetown University Press.

Mintzberg, H. (1973). *The nature of managerial work.* New York: Harper and Row.

Mitchell, W. J. (1999). *E-Topia: Urban life, Jim — But not as we know it.* Cambridge, MA: MIT Press.

Mnookin, R. H., & Weisberg, D. K. (2005). *Child, family, and state: Problems and materials on children and the law.* New York: Aspen Publishers.

Mohanty, S. P. (2001). Can our values be objective? On ethics, aesthetics, and progressive politics. *New Literary History, 32*, 803–833.

Mohr, J. (1998). Measuring meaning structures. *Annual Review of Sociology, 24*, 345–370.

Mok, K. (2005). Globalization and governance: Educational policy instruments and regulatory arrangements. *Review of Education, 51*, 289–311. Retrieved from http://www.springerlink.com/content/70032k7151341732/fulltext.pdf

Montgomery, K. C. (2007). *Generation digital: Politics, commerce, and childhood in the age of the internet.* Cambridge, MA: MIT Press.

Moon, J. (1995). Innovative leadership and policy change. Lessons from thatcher. *Governance, 8*, 1–25.

Moran, M., Rein, M., & Goodin, R. E. (2006). *The Oxford handbook of public policy.* Oxford and New York: Oxford University Press. Retrieved from http://www.loc.gov/catdir/toc/ecip066/2006000589.html; http://www.loc.gov/catdir/enhancements/fy0635/2006000589-d.html

Morphew, C. C., & Huisman, J. (2002). Using institutional theory to reframe research on academic drift. *Higher Education in Europe, 27*(4), 491–506.

Moseley, R., & Jacinda, R. (2002). Having it all: Popular television (Post-) feminism. *Feminist Media Studies, 2*(2), 231–249.

Mosteller, T. (2006). *Relativism in contemporary American philosophy*. London and New York: Continuum. Retrieved from http://magik.gmu.edu/cgi-bin/Pwebrecon.cgi?DB=local&FT=%22% 28 OCoLC%29ocm63108326%22&CNT=25+records+per+page

Moss, M. L., & Townsend, A. (2000). The internet backbone and the American metropolis. *The Information Society, 16*, 35–47.

Mundy, P., & Compton, J. L. (1991). Indigenous communication and indigenous knowledge. *Development Communication Report, 74*(3), 1–3.

Nansel, T. R., Overpeck, M., Pilla, R. S., Ruan, W. J., Simons-Morton, B., & Scheidt, P. (2001). Bullying behaviors among US youth: Prevalence and association with psychosocial adjustment. *Journal of the American Medical Association, 285*(16), 2094–2100.

National Center for Juvenile Justice. State Juvenile Justice Profiles. Retrieved from http://www.ncjj.org/stateprofiles

National Commission on Excellence in Education. (1983). *A nation at risk: The imperative for educational reform*. Washington, DC: U.S. Government Printing Office.

National Council for the Child. (2008). Questions and answers. Retrieved from http://www.children.org.il/view_cat.asp?cat_id=41&cat_id_to_look=41

Neal, R. G. (2006). *The deserved collapse of public schools: How we have been Hornswoggled and Bamboozled — Even Flummoxed and Hoodwinked — by Entrenched Educrats, Tyrannical Teacher Unions and Pandering Politicians*. Bloomington, IN: Author House.

Negroponte, N. (1995). *Being digital*. New York: RandomHouse.

Nelsen, R. (1985). The disappearance of childhood. *Canadian Review of Sociology and Anthropology, 22*(2), 303–310.

Neuman, A., & Aviram, A. (2003). Homeschooling as a fundamental change in lifestyle. *Evaluation and Research in Education, 17*, 132–143.

Newhouse, C. P. (2004). Portable computing challenges schooling. In A. Aviram & J. Richardson (Eds.), *Upon what does the turtle stand? Rethinking education for the digital age* (pp. 69–92). Dordrecht, Netherlands: Kluwer Academic Publishers.

Newman, G. (Ed.). (1999). *Global report on crime and justice*. Oxford, UK: Oxford University Press (published for the United Nations Office for Drug Control and Crime Prevention, Centre for International Crime Prevention).

NIDA InfoFacts. *High school and youth trends*. Retrieved from http://www.nida.nih.gov/Infofacts/HSYouthtrends.html

Nietzsche, F. (2001). *The gay science: With a prelude in German rhymes and an appendix of songs* (B. Williams, Ed.). Cambridge, UK: Cambridge University Press.

Nietzsche, F. (1974). *The gay science* (Kaufman, Trans.). New York: W. Vintage Books. (Originally published 1882)

Nix, G., Ryan, R. M., Manly, J. B., & Deci, E. L. (1999). Revitalization through self-regulation: The effects of autonomous and controlled motivation on happiness and vitality. *Journal of Experimental Social Psychology, 35*, 266–284.

Noddings, N. (2003). *Happiness and education*. Cambridge and New York: Cambridge University Press.

Nolen, J. L. (2003). Multiple intelligences in the classroom. *Education — Indianaplois The Chula Vista, 124*, 115–119.

Nonaka, I., & Takeuchi, H. (1995). *The knowledge creating company: How Japanese companies create the dynamics of innovation*. Oxford, UK: Oxford University Press.

Norris, C. (2002). *Deconstruction: Theory and practice* (3rd ed.). London: Routledge.

Norris, C. (1991). *Deconstruction: Theory and practice*. London: Routledge.

Nozick, R. (1974). *Anarchy, state and Utopia*. New York: Basic Books.

OECD, International Network on School Bullying and Violence. (2007). *Bullying among pupils at primary and secondary schools*. Retrieved from http://oecd-sbv.net/Templates/Article.aspx?id=440

Offer, A. (2006). *The challenge of affluence: Self-control and well-being in the United States and Britain since 1950*. Oxford University Press.

Office of National Statistics. (2007). *Social trends No. 37*. Basingstoke, Hampshire: Palgrave Macmillan.

Office of Technology Assessment. (1995). *Education and technology: Future visions* (OTA-BPHER-169). Washington, DC: U.S. Government Printing Office. Retrieved from http://www.wws. princeton.edu/cgi-bin/byteserv.prl/~ota/disk1/1995/9522/9522.PDF

Ogawa, R. (1994). The institutional sources of educational reform: The case of school-based management. *American Educational Research Journal, 31*(3), 519–548.

Olson, L., Schieve, D., Ruit, K. G., & Vari, R. C. (2003). Measuring inter-rater reliability of the sequenced performance inventory and reflective assessment of learning (SPIRAL). *Academic Medicine, 78*, 844–850.

O'Reilley, M. R. (2005). *The garden at night: Burnout and breakdown in the teaching life*. Portsmouth, NH: Heinemann.

O'Reilly, E. (2001). *Making career sense of labour market information* (2nd ed.). Ottawa, Ontario: Canadian Career Development Foundation. Retrieved from http://makingcareersense.org/ default.htm

Otsuka, M. (2003). *Libertarianism without inequality*. Oxford, UK: Clarendon.

Palloff, R. M., & Pratt, K. (1999). *Building learning communities in cyberspace*. San Francisco: Jossey-Bass Publishers.

Papert, S. (1993). *The children's machine: Rethinking school in the age of the computer*. New York: Basic Books.

Papert, S. (1980). *Mindstorms: Children computers and powerful ideas*. New York: Basic Books.

Pardeck, J. (2006). *Children's rights: Policy and practice* (2nd ed.). Binghamton, NT: Haworth Press.

Paglia, C. (1991). *Sexual personae*. New York: Vintage Books.

Paris, S. G., & Paris, A. H. (2001). Classroom applications of research on self-regulated learning. *Educational Psychologist, 36*(2), 89–101.

Parsons, T., & Bales, R. F. (1955). *Family, socialization, and interaction processes*. San Diego, CA: Academic Press.

Parsons, T. (1959). The school class as a social system: Some of its functions in American society. *Harvard Educational Review, 29*(4), 297–318.

Parsons, T. (1937). *Structure of social action*. New York: Free Press, 1967.

Passig, D., & Hasgal, A. (2004). Decentralization and integration: Two contrasting vectors which promise efficient knowledge management. *Complex Organizations. General Systems Bulletin, 33*, 15–20.

Paul, E. F., Miller, F. D., & Paul, J. (1992). *The good life and the human good*. Cambridge and New York: Cambridge University Press.

Pelgrum, W. J., & Plomp, T. J. (2004). The turtle stands on the basis of an emerging educational paradigm. In A. Aviram & J. Richardson (Eds.), *Upon what does the turtle stand? Rethinking education for the digital age* (pp. 53–68). Dordrecht, Netherlands: Kluwer Academic Publishers.

Perelman, L. (1992). *School's out: Hyperlearning, the new technology, and the end of education*. New York: William Morrow.

Perkins, D. (1993). Teaching and learning for understanding. *NJEA Review, 67*(2), 10–18.

Peters, M., & Lankshear, C. (1996). Postmodern counternarratives. In H. A. Giroux, P. McLaren, C. Lankshear, M. A. Peters (Eds.), *Counternarratives: Cultural studies and critical pedagogies in postmodern spaces* (pp. 1–40). New York: Routledge.

Peters, M., & Besley, T. (2007). *Why foucault? New directions in educational research*. New York: Peter Lang.

Peters, M., & Burbules, N. C. (2004). *Poststructuralism and educational research*. Lanham, MD: Rowman & Littlefield Publishers.

Peters, M., Marshall, J., & Smeyers, P. (2001). *Nietzsche's legacy for education past and present values*. Westport, CT: Bergun & Garvey.

Peters, M. (2002). *Heidegger, education, and modernity*. Lanham, MD: Rowman & Littlefield.

Peters, M. (1995). Philosophy and education: "After" Wittgenstein. *Journal Studies in Philosophy and Education, 14*(2–3), 189–204.

Peters, R. S. (1983). Philosophy of education. In P. H. Hirst (Ed.), *Educational theory and its foundation discipline* (pp. 30–61). London: Routledge & Kegan Paul.

Peters, R. S. (1973). The justification of education. In R. S. Peters (Ed.), *The philosophy of education.* Oxford, UK: Oxford University Press.

Peters, R. S. (1970). *Ethics and education.* London: George Allen and Unwin.

Peters, T. (1994). *The Tom Peters seminar.* New York: Vintage Books.

Peters, T. (1987). *Thriving on chaos: Handbook for a management revolution.* London: Guild Publishing.

Peterson, C., & Seligman, M. (2004). *Character strength and virtues: A handbook and classification.* Oxford, UK: Oxford University Press.

Peterson, P. E. (2003a). *Our schools & our future: Are we still at risk?* Hoover Institution Press.

Peterson, P. E. (2003b). *The future of school choice.* Stanford, CA: Hoover Institution Press.

Petraglia, J. (1998). *Reality by design: The rhetoric and technology of authenticity in education.* Mahwah, NJ: Lawrence Erlbaum Associates.

Petrie, J. (1992). Interdisciplinary education: Are we faced with insurmountable opportunities? *Review of Research in Education, 18,* 299–333.

Pfeffer, C. R. (1992). Relationship between depression and suicidal behavior. In M. Shaffi & S. L. Shaffi (Eds.), *Clinical guide to depression in children and adolescents* (pp. 115–126). Washington, DC: American Psychiatric Press.

Pfeffer, J. L. (2001). The family in John Locke's political thought. *Polity, 33*(4), 593–618.

Pfeiffer, C. (1998). Juvenile crime and violence in Europe. *Crime and Justice, 23,* 255–328.

Phelps, R. P. (2005). *Defending standardized testing.* Mahwah, NJ: L. Erlbaum Associates.

Piaget, J. (1960). *The child's conception of the world.* Totowa, NJ: Rowman & Littlefield.

Pinkard, T. (2002). *German philosophy 1760–1860: The legacy of idealism.* Cambridge, UK: Cambridge University Press.

Pintrich, P. R. (2000). The role of goal orientation in self-regulated learning. In M. Boekaerts, P. Pintrich, & M. Zeidner (Eds.), *Handbook of self-regulation* (pp. 451–502). San Diego, CA: Academic.

Poole, M. (2005). *Family: Changing families, changing times.* Crows Nest, Australia: Allen & Unwin.

Popkewitz, T. S., & Lindblad, S. (2004). Historicizing the future: Educational reform, systems of reason, and the making of children who are the future citizens. *Journal of Educational Change, 5*(3), 229–247.

Popkewitz, T. S. (2004). The alchemy of the mathematics curriculum: Inscriptions and the fabrication of the child. *American Educational Research Journal, 41*(1), 3–34. Retrieved from http://aer.sagepub.com/cgi/content/abstract/41/1/3

Popkewitz, T. S. (1997). The production of reason and power: Curriculum history and intellectual traditions. *Journal of Curriculum Studies, 29*(2), 131–164.

Popkewitz, T. S. (1987). *The formation of the school subjects.* New York: The Palmer Press.

Popkewitz, T. S., Tabachnick, R., & Wehlage, G. (1982). *The myth of educational reform: A study of school responses to a program of change.* Madison, WI: University of Wisconsin Press.

Popkin, R. H. (1979). *The history of scepticism from Erasmus to Spinoza.* Berkeley, CA: Berkeley University Press.

Popper, K. R. (1972). On the source of knowledge and ignorance. In K. Popper (Ed.), *Conjectures and refutations.* London: Routledge and Kegan Paul.

Popper, K. R. (1963). *Conjectures and refutations.* London: Routledge and Kegan Paul.

Popper, K. R. (1952). *The open society and its enemies* (Vol. 2., Rev. 2nd ed.). London: Routledge & Kegan Paul.

Popper, K. (1945). *The open society and its enemies.* London: Routledge and Kegan Paul.

Portelli, J. P. (1993). Exposing the hidden curriculum. *Journal of Curriculum Studies, 25*(4), 343–358.

Portelli, J. P. (1987). Analytic philosophy of education: Development and misconceptions. *Journal of Educational Thought, 21*(1), 20–32.

Posner, G. J. (2004). *Analyzing the curriculum.* New York: McGraw-Hill.

Postman, N. (1996). *The end of education: Redefining the value of school*. New York: Vintage.

Postman, N. (1992). *Technopoly: The surrender of culture to technology*. New York: Vintage.

Postman, N. (1986). *Amusing ourselves to death: Public discourse in the age of show business*. New York: Penguin Books.

Postman, N. (1982). *The disappearance of childhood*. New York: Laurel.

Postrel, V. (2003). *The substance of style: How the rise of aesthetic value is remaking commerce, culture and consciousness*. New York: Harper Collins Publishers.

Powell, A. G., Farrar, E., & Cohen, D. K. (1985). *The shopping mall high school*. Boston: Houghton Mifflin.

Power, E. J. (1991). *A legacy of learning: A history of western education*. New York: SUNY Press.

Power, F. C., Higgins, A., & Kohlberg, L. (1989). *Lawrence Kohlberg's approach to moral education*. New York: Columbia University Press.

Presseisen, B. Z. (1990). *Learning and thinking styles: Classroom interaction. In NEA school restructuring series*. West Haven, CT: NEA Professional Library.

Prosser, J., & McArdle, P. (1996). The changing mental health of children and adolescents: Evidence for a deterioration? *Psychological Medicine, 26*, 715–725.

Prosser, J. (1998). *Second skins: The body narratives of transsexuality*. New York: Columbia University Press.

Pulliam, J. D., & Van Patten, J. J. (1999). *History of education in America* (7th ed.). Upper Saddle River, NJ: Prentice-Hall.

Putnam, R. D. (2000). *Bowling alone: The collapse and revival of American community*. New York: Simon & Schuster.

Putnam, S. P., Ellis, L. K., & Rothbart, M. K. (2001). The structure of temperament, from infancy through adolescence. In A. Eliasz & A. Angleitner (Eds.), *Advances in research on temperament* (pp. 165–182). Germany: Pabst Science.

Quine, W. V. O. (1953). Two dogmas of empiricism. In W. V. O. Quine (Ed.), *From a logical point of view* (pp. 20–46). Cambridge, MA: Harvard University Press.

Qvortrup, J. (Ed.). (2005). *Studies in modern childhood: Society, agency, culture*. Basingstoke, Hampshire and New York: Palgrave Macmilan.

Qvortrup, J. (1996). Childhood in a post-industrial world. *Development, 1*, 64–67.

Railton, P. (2003). *Facts, values, and norms*. Cambridge, UK: Cambridge University Press.

Railton, P. (1998). Aesthetic value, moral value, and the ambitions of naturalism. In J. Levinson (Ed.), *Aesthetics and ethics: Essays at the intersection* (pp. 59–105). Cambridge, UK: Cambridge University Press.

Rajchman, J., & Cornel, W. (1985). *Post-analytic philosophy*. New York: Columbia University Press.

Ramsey, K. (1992). Home is where school is. *School Administrator, 49*(1), 20–25.

Ranelagh, J. (1991). *Thatcher's people: An insider's account of the politics, the power, and the personalities*. London: Harper Collins.

Rao, A. R., & Monroe, K. B. (1989). The effect of price, brand name, and store name on buyers' perceptions of product quality: An integrative review. *Journal of Marketing Research, 26*, 351–357.

Rafalides, M., & Hoy, M. (1971). Students' sense of alienation and pupil control orientation of high school. *High School Journal, 55*, 101–111.

Ravitch, D. (2000). *Left back: A century of failed school reforms*. New York: Simon and Schuster.

Ravn, B. (1998). Formal and informal parental involvement in school decision-making in Denmark. *Childhood Education, 74*(6).

Rawls, J., & Herman, B. (2000). *Lectures on the history of moral philosophy*. Cambridge, MA: Harvard University Press.

Rawls, J., & Freeman, S. R. (2007). *Lectures on the history of political philosophy*. Cambridge, MA; London: Belknap Press of Harvard University Press.

Rawls, J. (2005). *Political liberalism* (Expanded ed.). New York and Chichester: Columbia University Press.

Rawls, J. (1999a). *The law of peoples: With "the idea of public reason revisited"*. Cambridge, MA; London: Harvard University Press.

Rawls, J. (1999b). *A theory of justice* (Rev. ed.). Cambridge, MA; London: Belknap.

Rawls, J. (1993). *Political liberalism*. New York: Columbia University Press.

Rawls, J. (1971). *A theory of justice*. Cambridge, MA: Harvard University Press.

Ray, B. D. (2006a). *Research facts on homeschooling. General facts and trends*. Salem, OR: National Home Education Research Institute.

Ray, B. D. (2006b). *Worldwide guide to homeschooling: Facts and stats on the benefits of home school*. Nashville, TN: Broadman & Holman Publishers.

Ray, B. D. (2005). *Worldwide guide to homeschooling 2005–2006: Facts and stats on the benefits of home school*. Nashville, TN: Broadman & Holman.

Ray, B. D. (2004). *Home educated and now adults*. Salem, OR: National Home Education Research Institute.

Reed, M. I. (1996). Expert power and control in late modernity: An empirical review and theoretical synthesis. *Organization Studies, 17*(4), 573–597.

Reeve, J., Deci, E. L., & Ryan, R. M. (2004). Self-determination theory: A dialectical framework for understanding socio-cultural influences on student motivation. In S. Van Etten & M. Pressley (Eds.), *Big theories revisited* (pp. 31–60). Greenwich, CT: Information Age Press.

Reid, E. (1998). The self and the internet: Variations on the "Illusion" of one self. In J. Gackenbach (Ed.), *Psychology and the internet: Intrapersonal, interpersonal, and transpersonal implications* (pp. 29–41). San Diego, CA: Academic Press.

Renninger, K. A., Ewan, L., & Lasher, A. K. (2002). Individual interest as context in exploratory text and mathematical word problems. *Learning and Instruction, 12*, 467–491.

Renninger, K. A., & Hidi, S. (2002). Student interest and achievement: Developmental issues raised by a case study. In A. Wigfield & J. S. Eccles (Eds.), *Development of achievement motivation* (pp. 173–195). New York: Academic Press.

Renninger, K. A., Hoffmann, L., & Krapp, A. (1998). Interest and gender: Issues of development and learning. In L. Hoffman, A. Krapp, K. A. Renninger, & L. Baumert (Eds.), *Interest and learning: Proceeding of the seeon conference on interest and gender* (pp. 105–125). Kiel, Germany: IPN.

Reselands S. (2006). Relationship between antidepressant sales and secular trends in suicide rates in the Nordic countries. *The British Journal of Psychiatry, 188*, 354–358. Retrieved from http://bjp.rcpsych.org/cgi/content/full/188/4/354

Rheingold, H. (1993). *The virtual community: Homesteading on the electronic frontier*. New York: Addison-Wesley.

Richardson, A. W. (2002). Narrating the history of reason itself: Friedman, Kuhn, and a constitutive A priori for the twenty-first century. *Perspectives on Science, 10*(3), 253–274.

Richardson, J. (2004). Literacy, or the art of integration. In A. Aviram & J. Richardson (Eds.), *Upon what does the turtle stand? Rethinking education for the digital age* (pp. 135–151). Dordrecht, Netherlands: Kluwer Academic Publishers.

Rickenbacker, W. F. (1974). *The twelve-year sentence*. LaSalle, Ill: Open Court.

Riediger, M., & Freund, A. M. (2004). Interference and facilitation among personal goals: Differential associations with subjective well-being and persistent goal pursuit. *Personality and Social Psychology Bulletin, 30*(12), 1511–1523.

Rifkin, J. (2004a). *The end of work* (Updated ed.). New York: Jeremy P. Tarcher.

Rifkin, J. (2004b). *The European dream: How Europe's vision of the future is quietly eclipsing the American dream*. Cambridge, UK: Polity Press.

Rifkin, J. (1994). *The end of work: The decline of the global labor force and the dawn of the post-market era*. New York: Jeremy P. Tarcher/Putman.

Roberts, R. E., Lewinsohn, P. M., & Seeley, J. R. (1995). Symptoms of DSM-III-R major depression in adolescence: Evidence from an epidemiological survey. *Journal of American Academy of Child & Adolescent Psychiatry, 34*(12), 1608–1617.

Robertson, R. (1992). *Globalization: Social theory and global culture*. London: Sage.

Robison, K. K., & Crenshaw, E. M. (2001). *Post-industrial transformations and cyber-space: A cross-national analysis of internet development*. Working Paper, Ohio State University Dept. of Sociology.

Rogers, C. R. (1980). *A way of being*. Boston: Houghton Mifflin.

Rogers, C. R. (1969). *Freedom to learn: A view of what education might become*. Columbus, OH: Charles Merrill.

Rogoff, B., Paradise, R., Mejía Arauz, R., Correa-Chávez, M., & Angelillo, C. (2003). Firsthand learning by intent participation. *Annual Review of Psychology, 54*, 175–203.

Rooney, J., & Yoder, D. (2007). *Charter schools: Moving to the next level*. Bloomington, IN: Author House.

Rorty, R. (1998). *Truth and progress: Philosophical papers* (Vol. 3). Cambridge, UK: Cambridge University Press.

Rorty, R. (1989). *Contingency, irony and solidarity*. Cambridge, UK: Cambridge University Press.

Rorty, R. (1982). *Consequences of pragmatism*. Minneapolis, MN: University of Minnesota Press.

Rorty, R. (1980). *Philosophy and the mirror of nature*. Oxford, UK: Blackwell.

Rosen, J. (1991). *The capricious cosmos*. New York: Macmillan.

Rosenholtz, S. J. (1985). Political myths about education reform: Lessons from research on teaching. *Phi Delta Kappan, 66*, 349–355.

Rosenow, E. (1980). Rousseau's. "Emile". An Anti-Utopia. *British Journal of Educational Studies, 28*(3), 212–224.

Ross, A. (2000). *Curriculum: Construction and critique*. London: Falmer Press.

Roth, W. M. (1992). Bridging the gap between school and real life. *Social Science and Mathematics, 92*(6), 307–317.

Rothbart, M. K., & Derryberry, D. (1981). Development of individual differences in temperament. In M. E. Lamb & A. L. Brown (Eds.), *Advances in developmental psychology 1* (pp. 37–86). Hillsdale, NJ: Erlbaum.

Rothbart, M. K., Evans, D. E., & Ahadi, S. A. (2000). Temperament and personality: Origins and outcomes. *Journal of Personality and Social Psychology, 78*(1), 122–135.

Rubin, G. (1975). The traffic in women: Notes on the "Political economy" of sex. In R. Reiter (Ed.), *Toward an anthropology of women* (pp. 157–210). New York: Monthly Review Press.

Rudner, L. M. (1999). Scholastic achievement and demographic characteristics of home school students in 1998. *Education Policy Analysis Archives, 7*(8). Retrieved from http://epaa.asu.edu/epaa/v7n8

Rumberger, W. (1981). *Over education in the U.S. labor market*. New York: Praeger.

Rury, J. L. (2002). *Education and social change: Themes in the history of American schooling*. Mahwah, NJ: Lawrence Erlbaum Associates.

Russell, D. R. (1991). *Writing in the academic disciplines, 1870–1990: A curricular history*. Carbondale. IL: Southern Illinois University Press.

Ryan, E. S. (1996). Futuristic metaphysics. *Education, 117*(1), 70.

Ryan, R. M., & Deci, E. L. (2004). Autonomy is no illusion: Self-determination theory and the empirical study of authenticity, awareness, and will. In J. Greenberg, S. L. Koole, & T. Pyszczynski (Eds), *Handbook of experimental existential psychology* (pp. 449–479). New York: Guilford Press.

Ryan, R. M., & Deci, E. L. (2003). On assimilating identities to the self: A self-determination theory perspective on internalization and integrity within cultures. In M. R. Leary & J. P. Tangney (Eds.), *Handbook on self & identity* (pp. 253–274). New York: The Guillford Press.

Ryan, R. M., & Deci, E. L. (2001). On happiness and human potentials: A Review of research on hedonic and eudaimonic well-being. In S. Fiske (Ed.), *Annual review of psychology, 52* (pp. 141–166). Palo Alto, CA: Annual Reviews.

Ryan, R. M., & Deci, E. L. (2000). Self determination theory and the facilitation of intrinsic motivation, social development and well-being. *American Psychologist, 55*(1), 68–78.

Ryan, R. M., Deci, E. L., & Grolnick, W. S. (1995). Autonomy, relatedness, and the self: Their relation to development and psychopathology. In D. Cicchetti & D. J. Cohen (Eds.), *Developmental psychopathology: theory and methods* (pp. 618–655). New York: Wiley.

Ryan, R. M., & Lynch, M. F. (2003). Philosophies of motivation and classroom management. In R. Curren (Ed.), *Blackwell companions to philosophy: A companion to the philosophy of education* (pp. 260–271). New York: Blackwell.

Ryan, R. M. (1993). Agency and organization: Intrinsic motivation, autonomy, and the self in psychological development. In J. E. Jacobs (Ed.), *Nebraska symposium on motivation, Vol. 40: Developmental perspectives on motivation* (pp. 1–56). Lincoln, Nebraska: University of Nebraska Press.

Ryle, G. (1949). *The concept of mind*. London: Hutchinson.

Sachs, J. D. (2005). *The end of poverty: Economic possibilities for our time*. New York: Penguin Press.

Sacks, P. (2000). *Standardized minds: The high price of america's testing culture and what we can do to change it*. Cambridge, MA: Perseus Publishing.

Said, E. W. (2003). *Orientalism*. London: Penguin.

Sallis, E. (1993). *Total quality management in education*. London: Kogan Page Educational Management Series.

Salomon, G., Perkins, D. N., & Globerson, T. (1991). Partners in cognition: Extending human intelligence with intelligent technologies. *Educational Researcher, 20*(3), 2–9.

Salomon, G., & Rosen, Y. (2007). The differential learning achievements of constructivist technology-intensive learning environments as compared with traditional ones: A meta-analysis. *Journal of Educational Computing Research, 36*(1), 1–14.

Sampler, J. (1998). Redefining industry structure for the information age. *Strategic Management Journal, 19*, 343–355.

Sampson, E. E. (1981). Cognitive psychology as ideology. *American Psychologist, 36*(7), 730–743.

Sarason, S. B. (1998). Some features of a flawed educational system. *Daedalus, 127*.

Sarason, S. B. (1995). *Parental involvement and the political principle*. San Francisco: Jossey-Bass Publishers.

Sarason, S. B. (1993). *The predictable failure of school reform*. San Francisco: Jossey-Bass Publishers.

Sarason, S. B. (1990). *The predictable failure of educational reform: Can we change course before it's too late?* San Francisco: Jossey-Bass Publishers.

Sarason, S. B. (1971). *The cultures of the school and the problem of change*. Boston: Allyn & Bacon.

Sarup, M., & Raja, T. (1996). *Identity, culture and the postmodern world*. Edinburgh, UK: Edinburgh University Press.

Savery, J., & Duffy, T. (1996). Problem based learning: An instructional model and its constructivist framework. In B. Wilson (Ed.), *Constructivist learning environments: Case studies in instructional design* (pp. 135–148). Englewood Cliffs, NJ: Educational Technology Publications.

Schein, E. H. (2004). *Organizational culture and leadership* (3rd ed.). San Francisco: Jossey-Bass.

Schein, E. H. (1979). *Organizational psychology* (3rd ed.). NJ: Prentice Hall.

Schiefele, U. (1999). Topic interest, text representation, and quality of experience. *Contemporary Educational Psychology, 21*(1), 3–18.

Schnadelbach, H. (1984). *Philosophy in Germany 1831–1933*. Cambridge, UK: Cambridge University Press.

Schmidt, H. G. (1983). Problem-based learning: Rationale and description. *Medical Education, 17*, 11–16.

Schmitt, B., & Simonson, A. (1997). *Marketing aesthetics: The strategic management of brands, identity and image*. New York: The Free Press.

Schmuck, P., & Sheldon, K. (Eds.). (2001). *Life goals and well-being: Towards a positive psychology of human striving*. Seattle, WA: Hogrefe & Huber.

Schoen, R., & Standish, N. (2001). The retrenchment of marriage: Results From marital status life tables for the United States, 1995. *Population and Development Review, 27*(3), 553–563.

Schon, D. A. (1983). *The reflective practitioner: How professionals think in action*. New York: Basic Books.

Schubert, W. H. (1996). Perspectives on four curriculum traditions. *Educational Horizons, 74*(4), 169–176.

Schwab, J. J. (1962, July). The concept of the structure of the discipline. *The Educational Record*, 197–205.

Schwartz, S. J. (2006). Predicting identity consolidation from self-construction, eudaimonistic self-discovery, and agentic personality. *Journal of Adolescence, 29*, 777–793.

Scott, G. F. (1991). Romantic history. *Essays in Criticism, XLI*(3), 261–269.

Sedikides, C., & Brewer, M. B. (2001). *Individual self, relational self, collective self.* Philadelphia: Psychology Press.

Seligman, M., & Csikszentmihalyi, M. (2000). Positive psychology: An introduction. *American Psychology, 55*(1), 5–14.

Seligman, M. (2002). *Authentic happiness: Using the new positive psychology to realize your potential for lasting fulfillment.* New York: Free Press.

Selwyn, N. (2004). Exploring the role of children in adults' adoption and use of computers. *Information Technology and People, 17*(1), 53–70.

Senge, P. M. (2006). *The fifth discipline: The art and practice of the learning organization* (Revised ed.). New York: Doubleday.

Senge, P. M. (1990). *The fifth discipline: The art and practice of the learning organization.* London: Random House.

Senge, P. M. (1990). *The fifth discipline.* New York: Doubleday.

Sennett, R. (1980). *Authority.* New York: Norton.

Sergiovanni, T. J. (2000). Changing change: Toward a design science and art. *Journal of Educational Change, 1*, 57–75.

Shanks, P. (2005). *Human genetic engineering: A guide for activists, skeptics, and the very perplexed.* New York: Nation Books.

Sharan, S. (1994). *Handbook of cooperative learning methods.* Westport, CT: Greenwood Press.

Sharpe, F. G. (1996). Towards a research paradigm on devolution. *Journal of Educational Administration, 34*(1), 4.

Shearmur, J. (2006). Hayek, the road to Serfdom, and the British conservatives. *Journal of the History of Economic Thought, 28*(3), 309–314.

Sheldon, K. M., & Kasser, T. (2001). Goals, congruence, and positive well-being: New empirical support for humanistic theories. *Journal of Humanistic Psychology, 41*(1), 30–50.

Sheldon, K. M., Ryan, R. M., Deci, E. L., & Kasser, T. (2004). The independent effects of goal contents and motives on well-being: It's both what you pursue and why you pursue it. *Personality and Social Psychology Bulletin, 30*, 475–486.

Shenhav, Y. (1999). *Manufacturing rationality: The engineering foundations of the managerial revolution.* Oxford, UK: Oxford University Press.

Shifman, P. (1989). *Family law in Israel* (Vol. 2). Jerusalem: The Harry and Michael Sacher Institute for Legislative Research and Comparative Law. [Hebrew]

Shohat, E., & Stam, R. (2003). *Multiculturalism, postcoloniality, and transnational media.* New Brunswick, NJ: Rutgers University Press. Retrieved from http://www.loc.gov/catdir/toc/fy037/2002012494.html

Shor, I., & Freire, P. (1987). *A pedagogy for liberation.* Westport, CT: Bergin and Garvey.

Siegler, R. S., & Alibali, M. W. (2004). *Children's thinking* (4th ed.). Upper Saddle River, NJ: Prentice Hall.

Silva, C. S. (1999). *The new family?* London: Sage.

Silver, L. M. (1998). *Remaking eden: How genetic engineering and cloning will transform the American family.* New York: Avon Books.

Silverman, C. (1971). *Crisis in the classroom.* New York: Vintage Books.

Sim, S. (Ed.). (2005). *The routledge companion to postmodernism.* London: Routledge.

Simon, W. (1996). *Postmodern sexualities.* London: Routledge.

Simonson, M., Smaldino, S., Albright, M., & Zvacek, S. (2000). *Teaching and learning at a distance: Foundations of distance education.* Upper Saddle River, NJ: Merrill.

Sinha, R. (2001). How does stress increase risk of drug abuse and relapse? *Psychopharmacology, 158*, 343–359.

Sizer, T. (1993). *Horace's School: Redesigning the American high school*. Boston: Houghton Mifflin.

Slattery, P., & Rapp, D. (2003). *Ethics and the foundations of education: Teaching convictions in a postmodern world*. Boston: A and B.

Slavin R. E. (1990). *Cooperative learning: Theory, research, and practice*. Englewood, NJ: Prentice Hall.

Smith, A. (1976). *An inquiry into the nature and causes of the wealth of nations* (republished Eds. R. H. Campbell & A. S. Skinner). Oxford, UK: Clarendon Press. (Originally published 1776)

Smith, N. (1996). *The new urban frontier*. New York: Routledge.

Smith, O. B. (2004). *Myths of the self: Narrative identity and postmodern metaphysics*. Lanham, MD: Lexington Books.

Smithers, R. (2002). Schools cheat to boost exam results. *The Guardian*, June 5, 2002. Retrieved from http://education.guardian.co.uk/schools/story/0,,727569,00.html

Smyth, B. P., & O'Brien, M. (2004). Children attending addiction treatment services in Dublin, 1990–1999. *European Addiction Research, 10*(2), 68–74.

Snow, C. P. (1969). *The two cultures: And a second look: An expanded version of the two cultures and the scientific revolution*. Cambridge, UK: Cambridge University Press.

Spivak, G. C. (1990). *The post-colonial critic: Interviews, strategies, dialogues*. In S. Harasym (Ed.). New York: Routledge.

Stacey, J. (1990). *Brave new families: Stories of domestic upheaval in late twentieth century America*. New York: Basic Books.

Stedman, L. C. (1997). International achievement differences: An assessment of a new perspective. *Educational Research, 26*(3), 4–15.

Sternhell, Z. (2000). Fascism: Reflections on the fate of ideas in twentieth century history. *Journal of Political Ideologies, 5*(2), 139–162.

Sternhell, Z. (1996). *Neither right nor left: Fascist ideology in France*. Princeton, NJ: Princeton University Press.

Sternhell, Z. (1994). The birth of fascist ideology: From cultural rebellion to political revolution. In M. Sznajder & M. Asheri (Eds.). Princeton, NJ: Princeton University Press.

Stevenson, J. (2003). *Developing vocational expertise: Principles and issues in vocational education*. Crows Nest, Australia: Allen & Unwin.

Stewart, A., & Malcolm, H. (Eds.). (1994). *Justice for children*. Dordrecht, The Netherlands: Martinus Nijhoff Publisher.

Stoler, A. L. (1996). *Race and the education of desire: Foucault's "History of Sexuality" and the colonial order of things*. Durham, NC: Duke University Press.

Stone, C. (1990). Autonomy, emotions and desires. *Journal of Philosophy of Education, 24*(2), 271–284.

Storper, M., & Scott, A. (1992). *Pathways to industrialization and regional development*. London: Routledge.

Strasburger, C. V., & Wilson, J. B. (2002). *Children, adolescents, and the media*. Thousand Oaks, CA: Sage.

Strelau, J. (2001). The concept and status of trait in research on temperament. *European Journal of Personality, 15*, 311–325.

Sullivan, T. R. (1999). *Queer families, common agendas: Gay people, lesbians, and family values*. Binghamton, NY: Harrington Park Press.

Super, D. E. (1976). *Career education and the meanings of work*. Washington DC: U.S. Government Printing Office.

Swales, M. (1978). *The german bildungsroman from Wieland to Hesse*. Princeton, NJ: Princeton University Press.

Swanson, R. A. (2007). *Analysis for improving performance: Tools for diagnosing organizations and documenting workplace expertise* (2nd ed.). San Francisco: Berrett-Koehler Publishers.

Talmon, J. L. (1960). *The origins of totalitarian democracy*. New York: Praeger.

Talmon, J. L. (1952). *The origins of totalitarian democracy*. University of Michigan.

Tanner, L. N. (1997). *Dewey's laboratory School: Lessons for today*. New York: Teachers College Press.

Tapscott, D. (1999). *Growing up digital: The rise of the net generation*. New York: Mcgraw-Hill.

Taylor, C. (1992). *The ethics of authenticity*. Cambridge, MA: Harvard University Press.

Taylor, C. (1975). *Hegel*. Cambridge, UK: Cambridge University Press.

Taylor, F. W. (1947). *Scientific management*. New York: Harper Bros.

Taylor, F. W. (1911). *The principles of scientific management*. New York: Harper Bros.

The National Youth Agency [of England and Wales]. At what age can I ...? Retrieved from http://www.youthinformation.com/Templates/Internal.asp?NodeID=90845

Thomas, A. (1998). *Educating children at home*. London: Continuum.

Thomas, J., & Arcus, M. (1992). Family life education: An analysis of the concept. *Family Relations, 41*, 3–8.

Thompson, J., & Tuden, A. (1959). Strategies, structure and processes of organizational decisions. In J. Thompson (Ed.), *Comparative studies in administration*. Pittsburg, CA: University of Pittsburg Press.

Thompson, K. M., & Yokota, F. (2004). Violence, sex, and profanity in films: Correlation of movie ratings with content. *Medscape General Medicine, 6*(3), 3.

Throsby, D. (2001). *Economics and culture*. Melbourne, VIC: Cambridge University Press.

Throsby, D. (1999). Cultural capital. *Journal of Cultural Economics, 23*, 3–12.

Tobias, S., & Herbert, L. (1991). They're not dumb, They're different: Stalking the second tier. *American Journal of Physics, 59*(12), 1155–1157. Retrieved from http://adsabs.harvard.edu/abs/1991AmJPh..59.1155T

Toffler, A. (1995). *Creating a new civilization: The politics of the third wave*. Atlanta, GA: Turner.

Toffler, A. (1991). *Powershift*. New York: Bantam Books.

Toffler, A. (1980). *The third wave*. New York: Morrow.

Toffler, A. (1970). *Future shock*. New York: Bantam Books.

Tomlinson, S. (2001). *Education in a post-welfare society*. Buckingham, UK: Open University Press.

Toth, E. E., Suthers, D. D., & Lesgold, A. M. (2002). "Mapping to know": The effects of representational guidance and reflective assessment on scientific inquiry. *Science Education, 86*(2), 264–286.

Tuchman, B. W. (1985). *The March of folly: From Troy to Vietnam*. New York: Ballantine Books.

Tuchman, B. W. (1978). *A distant mirror: The calamitous 14th century*. New York: Ballantine Books.

Tuomi, I. (2001). *From periphery to center: Emerging research topics on knowledge society*. Helsinki, FN: TEKES.

Turkle, S. (1995).*Life on the screen. Identity in the age of the internet*. New York: Simon and Schuster.

Twain, M. (1994). *A Connecticut Yankee in King Arthur's court*. New York: Bantam Books, 1982.

Tyack, D., & Cuban, L. (2001). Progress or regress? In *The Jossey-Bass reader on school reform*. San Francicsco: Jossey Bass.

Tyack, D. B., & Cuban, L. (1995). *Tinkering toward utopia: A century of public school reform*. Cambridge, MA: Harvard University Press.

Tyack, D. B. (1974). *The one best system: A history of American Urban education*. Cambridge, MA: Harvard University Press.

Tyson, S., & York, A. (1994). *Human resource management (made simple)* (3rd ed.). Oxford, UK: Heinemann Educational Publishers.

U.S. Census Bureau. (2008). *Live births, deaths, marriages, and divorces: 1960 to 2006*. Retrieved from http://www.census.gov/compendia/statab/tables/08s0077.pdf

U.S. Census Bureau. (2007a). *Americans marrying older, living alone more, see households shrinking*. Census Bureau Reports. Retrieved from http://www.census.gov/Press-Release/www/releases/archives/families_households/006840.html

U.S. Census Bureau. (2007b). *Families and living arrangements in 2005*. Retrieved from http://www. census.gov/population/pop-profile/dynamic/FamiliesLA.pdf

U.S. Census Bureau. (2007c). *Married-couple and unmarried-partner households: 2000*. Retrieved from http://www.census.gov/prod/2003pubs/censr-5.pdf

U.S. Department of Health and Human Services. (2001). *Youth violence: A report of the surgeon general-executive summary*. Rockville, MD: U.S. Department of Health and Human Services, Centers for Disease Control and Prevention, National Center for Injury Prevention and Control; Substance Abuse and Mental Health Services, Center for Mental Health Service, and National Institutes of Health, National Institute of Mental Health.

U.S. Department of Labor, Bureau of Labor Statistics News. (2006). *Employee tenure in 2006*. Retrieved from http://www.bls.gov/news.release/tenure.toc.htm

Ullmann-Margalit, E., & Morgenbesser, S. (1977). Picking and choosing. *Social Research, 44*, 757–83.

UNESCO Institute for Statistics. (2003). *Literacy skills for the world of tomorrow — Further results from PISA 2000*. Paris: UNESCO Publishing.

Usher, R., & Edwards, R. (Eds.). (1994). *Postmodernism and education*. London: Routledge.

Vallerand, R. J. (1997). Toward a hierarchical model of intrinsic and extrinsic motivation. In M. P. Zanna (Ed.), *Advances in experimental social psychology* (Vol. 29, pp. 271–360). San Diego, CA: Academic Press.

Valls, A. (1999). Self-development and the liberal state: The cases of John Stuart Mill and Wilhelm von Humboldt. *The Review of Politics, 61*(2), 251–274.

Vandenberghe, R., & Huberman, A. M. (Eds.). (1999). *Understanding and preventing teacher Burnout: A sourcebook of international research and practice*. Cambridge, UK: Cambridge University Press.

Vermunt, J. D. (1992). *Learning styles and directed learning processes in higher education: Towards a process-oriented instruction in independent thinking*. Lisse, The Netherlands: Swets and Zeitlinger.

Wakefield, N. (1990). *Postmodernism, the twilight of the real*. London: Pluto Press.

Waterhouse, P. (1983). *Supported self study in secondary education*. London: Council for Educational Technology.

Waterman, A. (1982). Identity development from adolescence to adulthood: An extension of theory and a review of research. *Developmental Psychology, 18*, 341–358.

Waters, M. (1995). *Globalization*. London: Routledge.

Watzlawick, P., Wealand, J. H., & Fisch, R. (1974). *Change: Principles of problem formation and problem resolution*. New York: Norton.

Webb, J. (1999). *Those unschooled minds: Home-educated children grow up*. Nottingham, UK: Educational Heretic Press.

Webb, J. (1990). *Children learning at home*. London: The Falmer Press.

Weber, C. (1984). Strategic thinking — Dealing with uncertainty. *Long Range Planning, 17*(5), 60–70.

Weber, M. (1922). Wissenschaft als Beruf. In M. Weber (Ed.), *Gesammelte Aufsatze zur Wissenschaftslehre* (pp. 582–613). Tübingen: J.C.B. Mohr (Paul Siebeck) Verlag. [German]

Weick, K. E. (1976). Educational organizations as loosely coupled systems. *Administrative Science Quarterly, 21*, 1–16.

Weiss, S. (1996). The alcohol sense in Israel. *The Globe, 4*, 14–15.

Wellmer, A. (1991). *The persistence of modernity: Essays on aesthetics, ethics, and postmodernism*. Cambridge, MA: MIT Press.

Werner, A. (1989). Television and age-related differences: A contribution to the debate about the "disappearance of childhood". *European Journal of Communication, 4*(1), 33–50.

West-Burnham, J. (1997). *Managing quality in Schools: A TQM approach*. London: Pitman.

White House. (2000). *The Clinton-Gore administration record to help close the digital divide*. Retrieved from http://clinton4.nara.gov/WH/new/html/Tue_Oct_3_134626_2000.html

White, J., & Bramall, S. (Eds.). (2000). *Why learn Maths?* London: London University Institute of Education.

White, J. P. (2006). *Intelligence, destiny and education: The ideological origins of intelligence testing*. London: Routledge.

White, J. P. (2003). *Rethinking the School curriculum: Values, aims and purposes*. London: Routledge.

White, J. P. (1999). In defence of liberal aims in education. In R. Marples (Ed.), *The aims of education* (pp. 185–200). London: Routledge.

White, J. P. (1997). *Education and the end of work: A new philosophy of work and learning*. New York: Continuum.

White, J. P. (1982). *The aims of education restated*. London: Routledge and Keagan Paul.

White, J. P. (1977). *Towards compulsory curriculum*. London: Routledge & Kegan Paul.

White, J. (1973). *Towards compulsory curriculum*. London: Routledge & Kegan Paul.

Whitehead, S. (2002). *Men and masculinities: Key themes and new directions*. Cambridge, UK: Polity Press.

Whitty, G. (1985). *Sociology and school knowledge: Curriculum theory, research, and politics*. New York: Routledge.

Whyte, W. (1956). *The organization man*. New York: Simon and Schuster.

Wigoren, J. (2001). Possible Cheating Scandal is Investigated in Michigan. *New York Times*, June 9, 2001. Retrieved from
http://query.nytimes.com/gst/fullpage.html?res=9902EFDE143EF93AA35755C0A9679C8B63.

Wilding, J., & Andrews, B. (2006). Life goals, approaches to study and performance in an undergraduate cohort. *British Journal of Educational Psychology, 76*, 171–182.

Williamson, J. G. (1988). Migration and urbanization. In H. Chenery & T. N. Srinivasan (Eds.), *Handbook of development economics* (Vol. 1, pp. 425–465). Amsterdam: North Holland.

Wills, T., & Hirky, E. (1996). Coping and substance abuse: A theoretical model and review of the evidence. In M. Zeidner & N. S. Endle (Eds.), *Handbook of coping* (pp. 279–302). New York: Wiley.

Wills, T. (1986). Stress and coping in early adolescence: Relationships to substance use in urban school samples. *Health Psychology, 5*, 503–529.

Wilson, H. T. (2002). *Capitalism after postmodernism: Neo-conservatism, legitimacy and the theory of public capital*. Leiden: EJ. Brill.

Wittchen, H. U., & Jacobi, F. (2005). Size and burden of mental disorders in Europe: A critical review and appraisal of 27 studies. *European Neuropsychopharmacology, 15*, 357–376.

Wittgenstein, L. (1961). *Tractatus logico-philosophicus*. London: Routledge and Kegan Paul.

Wolf, P. J., Macedo, S., Ferrero, D. J., & Venegoni, C. (2004). *Educating citizens: International perspectives on civic values and school choice*. Washington, DC: Brookings Institution Press.

Worthen, B. R. (1993). Critical issues that will determine the future of alternative assessment. *Phi Delta Kappa, 74*.

Wringe, C. A. (1981). *Children's rights*. London: Routledge and Kegan Paul.

Wynne, E. (1978). Behind the discipline problem: Youth suicide as a measure of alienation. *Phi Delta Kappa, 59*, 308–315.

Yona, Y. (2005). *What is multiculturalism?: On the politics of differences in Israel* (Ruth Ramot, Ed.). Tel Aviv: Babel. [Hebrew]

Yona, Y. (1991). Cultural pluralism versus cultural integration and their affects on education. *Megamot, 37*(1), 121–138. [Hebrew]

Young, J. (1999). *The exclusive society: Social exclusion, crime and difference in late modernity*. London: Sage.

Youniss, J., Bales, S., Christmas-Best, V., Diversi, M., McLaughlin, M., & Silbereisen, R. (2002). Youth civic engagement in the twenty-first century. *Journal of Research on Adolescence, 12*(1), 121–148.

Zalewski, M. (2000). *Feminism after postmodernism: Theorising through practice*. London: Routledge.

Zaretky, E. (1976). *Capitalism, the family, and personal life*. London: Pluto.

Zeichner, K. M., & Liston, D. P. (1990). Traditions of reform in U.S. teacher education. *Journal of Teacher Education, 41*(2), 3–20.

Zimmerman, B. J. (2002). Becoming a self-regulated learner: An overview. *Theory into Practice, 41*(2), 64–72.

Zimmerman, J. (2002). *Whose America? Culture wars in the public schools.* Cambridge, MA; London: Harvard University Press.

Zuboff, S. (1988). *In the age of the smart machine: The future of work and power.* New York: Basic Books.

Zucker, L. G. (1987). Institutional theories of organizations. *Annual Review of Sociology, 13,* 443–464.

NAME INDEX

SUBJECT INDEX

WITHDRAWAL'

Lightning Source UK Ltd.
Milton Keynes UK
13 August 2010

158403UK00001B/4/P